WORLD POLITICS

Trend and Transformation

SIXTH EDITION

WORLD POLITICS
Trend and Transformation

SIXTH EDITION

Charles W. Kegley, Jr.
University of South Carolina

Eugene R. Wittkopf
Louisiana State University

ST. MARTIN'S PRESS
New York

Sponsoring editor: Beth A. Gillett
Development editor: Bob Nirkind
Manager, publishing services: Emily Berleth
Senior editor, publishing services: Douglas Bell
Production supervisor: Dennis Para
Art director and cover design: Lucy Krikorian
Text design: Joan Greenfield
Project management and graphics: York Production Services
Map illustrations: Maryland CartoGraphics, Inc.
Photo research: Joyce Deyo
Cover illustration: Terry Hoff/Jerry Leff Associates, Inc.

Library of Congress Catalog Card Number: 95-73204

Manufactured in the United States of America.

1   0   9   8   7
f   e   d   c   b

For information, write:
St. Martin's Press, Inc.
175 Fifth Avenue
New York, NY 10010

ISBN: 0-312-13725-7

Published and distributed outside North America by
MACMILLAN PRESS LTD
Houndmills, Basingstoke, Hampshire RG21 6XS and London
Companies and representatives throughout the world

ISBN: 0-333-68835-X

A catalogue record for this book is available from the British Library.

Acknowledgments

Acknowledgments and copyrights appear at the back of the book on pages 561–564, which
constitute an extension of the copyright page.

For my twin brother, John, and his loving wife, Mary

CWK

For Debra and Jonathan

ERW

Summary Table of Contents

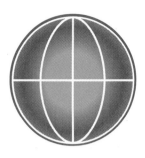

Contents

PART I: TREND AND TRANSFORMATION IN WORLD POLITICS

PART II: THE ACTORS AND THEIR RELATIONS

PART III: THE POLITICS OF GLOBAL WELFARE

PART IV: WORLD CONFLICT AND ITS MANAGEMENT

CHAPTER 12
RESORTING TO FORCE: ARMED CONFLICT BETWEEN AND WITHIN STATES

CHAPTER 13
THE MILITARY QUEST FOR NATIONAL SECURITY: ARMS AND THE CHANGING CHARACTER OF POWER

CHAPTER 15
THE REALIST ROAD TO SECURITY: ALLIANCES,
THE BALANCE OF POWER, AND ARMS CONTROL   442

CHAPTER 16
LIBERAL PATHS TO PEACE: INTERNATIONAL LAW,
ORGANIZATION, INTEGRATION, AND DEMOCRATIZATION   478

PART V: TOWARD THE TWENTY-FIRST CENTURY

CHAPTER 17
THE GLOBAL PREDICAMENT: TEN QUESTIONS
ON THE CUSP OF A NEW CENTURY   **517**

Focus Boxes and Maps

LIST OF MAPS

Preface

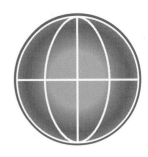

Understanding the rapid changes of twentieth century world politics, especially since World War II, poses an enormous challenge to students, scholars, and policymakers alike. Without the Cold War to frame an inquiry and understanding, there is little agreement about which dimensions of world politics will be most important in the coming century. This uncertainty necessitates the need to critically examine the theoretical underpinnings of our knowledge, asking not only what is new but also how we know what we know about the forces of change and continuity in the world around us. That is our purpose in *World Politics: Trend and Transformation*. By comprehensively covering theory and evidence, we can inform our understanding of relations among global actors, the historical developments and issues that underlie them, and the ways in which trends currently unfolding are shaping the global future.

In this, the sixth edition of *World Politics: Trend and Transformation*, we attempt to keep pace with the dramatic march of events and the evolution of concepts and theories that help us make sense of international relations. We have also made some dramatic changes of our own—among them, a move to a dynamic full-color interior, an all-new photo program, a significantly expanded use of figures and maps, and a more user-friendly design—all in an effort to make our message more accessible to undergraduate students.

• • •

OVERVIEW OF THE SIXTH EDITION

Part I: Trend and Transformation in World Politics

Part I explains the macro, or holistic, view that frames the book's analyses. Chapters 1 and 2 focus on contending analytic perspectives that scholars and policymakers have developed to comprehend the trends and transformations occurring in world politics. These theoretical traditions are drawn upon throughout the book to clarify and enhance an understanding of contemporary world politics.

Part II: The Actors and Their Relations

Part II investigates the principal actors on the world stage. Because states command particular attention, we explore their foreign policy decision-making processes. Great-power rivalries, as played out in three global conflicts of the twentieth century, are emphasized in this section, as is an expanded focus on the Global South and the roots and consequences of global inequalities. We also examine the role that nonstate actors—international organizations, ethnonational groups, religious movements, terrorists, and multinational corporations—play in influencing contemporary world politics, and the ways in which the international environment, in turn, shapes their character.

Part III: The Politics of Global Welfare

Part III analyzes issues related to material welfare. States' position in the world political economy are given special attention. The impact of the globalization of world political economy and the challenge it poses to states' autonomy, how the dynamics of demographic changes now sweeping the world affect international politics, and the challenges posed by pressures on the global environment are also examined.

Part IV: World Conflict and Its Management

Part IV examines issues related to peace and security. Threats caused by recent trends in armed conflicts within and between states, factors spurring preparations for national defense, and the exercise of coercive diplomacy are just some of the issues covered. These are the types of concerns that have traditionally occupied center stage in analyses of world politics. Despite the end of the Cold War, they still command attention in a world rife with civil wars and the proliferation of weapons.

Part V: Toward the Twenty-First Century

We conclude with a discussion of how underlying trajectories in world politics might influence future trends. We discuss how today's world will affect the world of tomorrow and the impact that today's trends will exert on the policy problems and issues that today's students—the policymakers and citizens of tomorrow—will face in the twenty-first century.

• • •

CHANGES IN THE SIXTH EDITION

The global changes that have taken place since the publication of the fifth edition prompted us to revisit and refine every passage in the book. In addition, we sought to expand and improve its theoretical focus and enhance its coverage. The sixth edition both captures and explains major changes in the world and the meaning of emerging trends and transformations. This edition also introduces several new pedagogical devises.

- **Dynamic full-color design.** With the addition of full-color, students can more easily interpret maps, photographs, and illustrations.
- **More maps.** We have expanded the number of maps to twenty-seven, many of which extend across spread pages, so that students can easily distinguish areas being discussed.
- **New illustrations.** Fifty new full-color illustrations appear throughout the sixth edition with instructive captions to further the students' understanding of the text.
- **Completely redesigned tables, charts, and maps.** With the advent of full color, the complete illustrative program has been redesigned for uniformity and clarity.

- **Key terms.** Key terms are now included at the end of each chapter.
- **Comprehensive glossary.** Definitions of key terms are listed in a new end-of-book glossary which enables students easy access to information.

Beyond changes in design, substantial changes in the organization and contents of the book have been made.

- Chapter 1: Our introductory chapter, "Confronting Twenty-First Century World Politics: The Investigative Challenge," has been reorganized to provide a cohesive thematic focus for the book. Questions in this chapter identify issues that are discussed throughout the remainder of the text.
- Chapter 2: "The Theoretical Interpretation of World Politics: Rival Perspectives" has been reorganized to capture recent changes in theoretical interpretations of world politics and the controversies that exist between contending approaches.
- Chapter 4: "Great-Power Politics: Past, Present, and Future" has been revised to summarize not only long-term changes in the changing nature of relationships among the great powers, but also predictions about the likely character of these relations in the twenty-first century.
- Chapters 6 and 7: In response to reviewers, these chapters—which were previously a single chapter—offer an increased coverage of "International Organizations in World Politics: Universal and Regional Actors" (Chapter 6), and "Nonstate Actors in World Politics: Ethnonational Groups, Religious Movements, Terrorists, and Multinational Corporations" (Chapter 7).
- Chapter 8: Our treatment of the world political economy has been reorganized to emphasize three central concepts—liberalism, mercantilism, and hegemony—and how they relate to the intersection of politics and markets in the contemporary world.
- Chapter 9: This is a new chapter that replaces the previous emphasis on the Third World in the world political economy (whose coverage has been incorporated in the revised and updated Chapter 5). "Vanishing Borders: The Globalization of Politics and Markets" now examines the impact on states and the state system arising from the rapid globalization of information, capital, production, and labor in the interdependent world marketplace.
- Chapter 10: "The Demography of World Politics: Patterns, Problems, and Possibilities" expands our previous treatment of demographic issues in new directions. The causes and consequences of the rapid growth of world population to a projected level of 10 billion by the middle of the next century is given detailed treatment.
- Chapter 11: "The Ecology of World Politics: Security and Sustainability on a Small Planet" is also new. This chapter gives in-depth attention to the global challenges to environmental preservation and examines the problems and possibilities of balancing competing demands in a world poorly organized to address transnational issues.
- Chapters 12, 13, and 15: The discussion of armed force and its control has been reorganized. By reordering the sequence of coverage of recent changes in the use of armed force and the response of the international community, these chapters provide better continuity.

- Chapter 14: A new chapter, "Coercive Diplomacy: The Use of Power for Defense, Deterrence, and Bargaining" has been added to the sixth edition. Focusing on both nuclear and conventional deterrence for defense and economic sanctions as instruments of coercion, this chapter brings together previously disparate discussions of how states exercise influence with weapons and by methods other than war.
- Chapter 16: This chapter develops a theme introduced in previous chapters by examining the role that democratic governance plays in promoting peace in the world political system, while addressing recent changes in international law and their ethical implications.

● ● ●

INSTRUCTIONAL PACKAGE

World Politics: Trend and Transformation is accompanied by an Instructor's Manual prepared by Professor Gregory A. Raymond of Boise State University. The manual includes chapter outlines, summaries, learning objectives, teaching suggestions, Internet applications, and suggested readings. The manual contains transparency masters of the major maps that appear in the book. It also includes a test item file containing over five hundred essay and multiple-choice questions—the latter of which are graded as to degree of difficulty. The test bank is available on computer disk for DOS, MAC, and Windows formats as well as in hard copy, and is accompanied by software necessary for test construction.

● ● ●

ACKNOWLEDGMENTS

Many people have contributed to making the sixth edition the most ambitious revision since the book was first published in 1981. In addition to the many people named in previous editions, we wish to acknowledge the special assistance and advice provided by those who have helped to make this, a leading text, even better. We greatly appreciate the constructive and supportive comments and suggestions that were offered by the reviewers of the sixth edition: Vincent Auger, Hamilton College; Glenn Chafetz, University of Memphis; Larry Elowitz, Georgia College; Ernest Morgan, University of Wisconsin, Eau Claire; Choudhury M. Shamim, California State University, Fullerton; Marc V. Simon, Bowling Green State University; and James Troisi, Rochester Institute of Technology.

At St. Martin's Press, our past editor Don Reisman and our new editor Beth Gillett and editorial director Steve Debow are to be thanked for pushing for a new format and style, including the introduction of color and photos. Bob Nirkind, our development editor, and Doug Bell, our senior project editor, exercised professionalism and prodding throughout the timely ordeal that brought this edition into publication. In addition, Dolores Wolfe and the staff at York Production Services contributed significantly to the preparation, polish, and production of the book.

Beyond the St. Martin's staff and their associates, we are pleased to acknowledge the following for their contributions: Elizabeth Allen, Shannon Lindsey Blanton, Leann Brown, Sallie Buice, Dan Caldwell, Roger Coate, Jim Cross, David Danna, Kyle Dillard, Richard Harknett, Margaret Hermann, Fernando Jimenez, Christopher Kautz, John Kinnas, Jeffrey Laurenti, Jeffrey Morton, Christina Payne, Heather Podlich, Gregory Raymond, Joseph Reap, Alpo Rusi, Sten Rynning, Linda Schwartz, Richard Schultz, Harvey Starr, Rodney Tomlinson, Bingxiao Wang, Michael Don Ward, and Franke Wilmer.

Charles W. Kegley, Jr.
Eugene R. Wittkopf

About the Authors

CHARLES W. KEGLEY JR. received his doctorate from Syracuse University. Currently, he is Pearce Professor of International Relations at the University of South Carolina. President of the International Studies Association (1993–1994), Kegley has held appointments at Georgetown University, the University of Texas, Rutgers University, and the People's University of China. He is the editor of *Controversies in International Relations Theory: Realism and the Neoliberal Challenge* (St. Martin's Press, 1995) and *The Long Postwar Peace* (HarperCollins, 1991). With Gregory A. Raymond, Kegley is the coauthor of *A Multipolar Peace? Great-Power Politics in the Twenty-First Century* (St. Martin's Press, 1994) and *When Trust Breaks Down: Alliance Norms and World Politics* (University of South Carolina Press, 1990).

EUGENE R. WITTKOPF received his doctorate from Syracuse University. Currently R. Downs Poindexter Professor of Political Science at Louisiana State University, Wittkopf is a past president of the Florida Political Science Association and of the International Studies Association/South. He has also held appointments at the University of Florida and the University of North Carolina at Chapel Hill. Wittkopf is the author of *Faces of Internationalism: Public Opinion and American Foreign Policy* (Duke University Press, 1990) and the editor of the second editions of *The Future of American Foreign Policy* (St. Martin's Press, 1994) and *The Domestic Sources of American Foreign Policy* (St. Martin's Press, 1994).

Together, Kegley and Wittkopf have coauthored and edited several texts and readers for St. Martin's Press, including *American Foreign Policy: Pattern and Process*, fifth edition (1996); *The Future of American Foreign Policy* (1992); *The Nuclear Reader: Strategy, Weapons, War*, second edition (1989); and *The Domestic Sources of American Foreign Policy* (1988). They are also the coeditors of *The Global Agenda: Issues and Perspectives*, fourth edition (McGraw-Hill, 1995).

WORLD POLITICS

Trend and Transformation

SIXTH EDITION

CHAPTER 1

Confronting Twenty-First-Century World Politics: The Investigative Challenge

OUTLINE

- Continuity, Change, and Cycles in World Politics
- Image and Reality in World Politics
- Organizing Inquiry: Actors, Issues, and Their Interaction
- Toward the Future

Great things are achieved by guessing the direction of one's century.

—Giuseppe Mazzini,
Italian political leader, 1848

Profound and powerful forces are shaking and remaking our world, and the urgent question of our time is whether we can make change our friend and not our enemy.

—Bill Clinton,
U.S. president, 1993

Today, the world stands on the threshold of a new millennium and a new era. Stimulated by the end of the Cold War, the tidal wave of change witnessed in the past decade has been overwhelming. The conflict between the United States and the Soviet Union, which colored virtually every dimension of the political, economic, and social aspects of world politics for nearly fifty years, is over. The Berlin Wall has been dismantled, the Soviet Union has disintegrated, communism has collapsed, Germany is united, and the European Union and NATO have expanded their geographic reach. Moreover, democracy has spread throughout much of the world, and international trade has grown to unprecedented levels. Nonetheless, hopes that the post-Cold War world will be peaceful have been dashed as violent conflict remains rampant in much of the world and especially in the developing countries of the Global South.

How can we best understand the political convulsions in the world that confront us almost daily? How can we anticipate their future significance? We must begin with an appreciation of the interaction of previous ideas and events with current realities. As philosopher George Santayana cautioned, "Those who cannot remember the past are condemned to repeat it." Similarly, British Prime Minister Winston Churchill once remarked that "The farther backward you look, the farther forward you are likely to see."

Thus, to understand the dramatic changes in world politics today and how they will shape the future, we must view them in the context of a long-term perspective that examines how the **international political system**—the patterns of interaction among world political actors—has changed and how its fundamental characteristics have resisted change. What do evolving diplomatic practices suggest about the current state of world politics? Are the dramatic changes that have recently sent shock waves throughout the world symbolic of an earthquake in world affairs, clearing the way for a truly new world order? Or will these dramatic developments ultimately prove temporary, mere spikes on the seismograph of history?

• • •

CONTINUITY, CHANGE, AND CYCLES IN WORLD POLITICS

Every historical period is marked to some extent by change. Now, however, the pace of change seems more rapid and its consequences more profound than ever. To many observers, the cascade of events on the eve of the twenty-first century implies that a revolutionary restructuring of world politics is unfolding. Numerous integrative trends point to that possibility. The countries of the world are drawing closer together in communications, ideas, and trade, as well as in peace and security. Even disintegrative trends point toward restructuring. The end of stability imposed by the **bipolar distribution of power** between the United States and the Soviet Union and their respective allies (a bipolar international system contains two dominant power centers), the proliferation of conventional and unconventional weapons, global environmental deterioration, and the resurgence of nationalism and ethnic conflict all portend a restructuring marked by disorder. The countervailing forces of integration and disintegration point toward a transformation in world politics as extensive and important as the system-disrupting convulsions which swept the world following World Wars I and II.

Differentiating meaningful transformations (true historical watersheds) from ephemeral changes (those that gradually unfold with the passage of time but sometimes fail to last) is difficult. Transformations do not fall neatly into easily defined periods, signaling that one system has truly ended and a new one has begun. Still, major turning points in world politics usually have occurred at the end of major wars, which typically disrupt or destroy preexisting international arrangements. In this century, World Wars I and II stimulated fundamental breaks with the past, as each set in motion major transformations in world politics. The end of the Cold War was a historical breakpoint of no-less-epic significance. As U.S. president George Bush put it in 1992, the changes stimulated by the end of the Cold War were "of biblical proportions," providing countries an opportunity, for the first time since 1945, to rethink the premises underlying their interests, purposes, and priorities.

Despite all in world politics that is radically different, much remains the same. Indeed, "history usually makes a mockery of our hopes and expectations." Thus leaders must "question . . . the ways and areas in which the future is likely to resemble the past" (Jervis 1991–92).

The dismantling of the Berlin Wall in November 1989, helped signal the end of the Cold War. As exuberant citizens chipped away at the last vestiges of a divided nation, Germany moved toward reunification for the first time in over 40 years.

How can we determine when an existing pattern of relationships gives way to a new international system? Political scientist Stanley Hoffmann (1961) argues that we have a new international system when we have a new answer to any one of three questions: (1) *What are the system's basic units?* (e.g., nation-states or transnational religious movements); (2) *What are the predominant foreign policy goals that these units seek with respect to one another?* (e.g., territorial conquest or material gain through trade); and (3) *What can these units do to one another with their military and economic capabilities?*

These criteria might lead us to conclude that today a new system *has* emerged. First, new trade partnerships have been forged in Europe, North America, and the Pacific Rim, and these trading blocs may behave as unitary, or independent, actors as they compete with one another. Moreover, international organizations, such as the World Trade Organization and the European Union, now sometimes flex their political muscles in contests with individual states; and transnational religious movements, like Islamic fundamentalism, challenge the **state system** itself (a system of **nation-states,** autonomous political units whose people perceive themselves unified by a common language, culture, or ethnic identity). At the same time, some nation-states have disintegrated into smaller units. The Soviet Union, a dominant world force for decades, has fragmented into fractious political entities searching for national identity and autonomy. Other national units could disintegrate as well—peacefully, like the former Czechoslovakia, or violently, like the former Yugoslavia.

Second, territorial conquest is no longer the predominant goal of many states' foreign policies. Instead, their emphasis has shifted from traditional military methods of exercising influence to economic means. Meanwhile, ideological contests, like that between the democratic capitalism of the United States and the Marxist-Leninist communism of the Cold War-era Soviet Union, no longer comprise the primary cleavages in international politics.

Third, advances in the proliferation of weapons technology have altered profoundly the damage that states can inflict on one another. Great powers alone no longer control the world's most lethal weapons. Their economic well-being, however, is sometimes dependent on those with an increasing capacity to destroy.

The profound changes in units, goals, and capabilities of recent years have dramatically altered the ranking of states in the pecking orders that define the structure of international politics. Still, the hierarchies themselves endure. The *economic hierarchy that divides the rich from the poor*, the *political hierarchy that separates the rulers from the ruled*, the *resource hierarchy that makes some suppliers and others dependents*, and the *military asymmetries that pit the strong against the weak*—all still shape the relations among states, as they have in the past. Similarly, the perpetuation of international anarchy and insecurity continues to encourage preparations for war and the use of force without international mandate. Thus change and continuity coexist, with both forces simultaneously shaping contemporary world politics.

The interaction of constancy and change makes it difficult to predict whether the twenty-first century will give birth to a wholly new and different international system. What is clear is that this interaction will determine future relations among global actors. This perhaps explains why **cycles** so often appear to characterize world politics: Periodic sequences of events occur that resemble patterns in earlier periods. Thus the impression is frequently conveyed that "the more things change, the more they stay the same." Because the emergent international system shares many characteristics with earlier periods, historically minded observers may experience *déjà vu*—the illusion of having already experienced something actually being experienced for the first time.

The challenge, then, is to observe objectively unfolding global realities in order to describe and explain them accurately, and hence to understand their future impact. This requires that we understand the role that images of reality play in shaping our expectations. It also requires a set of tools for analyzing the forces of constancy and change that affect our world and the world of the future. Thus, the remainder of this chapter will examine briefly the role that images of reality play in understanding world politics, and then will describe the theoretical orientation of the book. Chapter 2 will examine the analytical tools we will use in the remainder of this book to study trends and transformations in world politics.

● ● ●

IMAGE AND REALITY IN WORLD POLITICS

We all carry mental images of world politics—explicit or implicit, conscious or subconscious. But whatever our level of awareness, our images simplify "reality" by exaggerating some features of the real world while ignoring others. Thus we live in a world defined by our expectations and images.

These mental pictures, or perceptions, are inevitably distortions, as they cannot fully capture the complexity and configurations of even physical objects, like the world itself (see Focus 1.1). Thus many of our images of the world's political realities may be built on illusions and misconceptions. Even images that are now accurate can easily become obsolete if our perceptions of world politics fail to recognize changes in the world. Indeed, the world's future will be determined not only by changes in the "objective" facts of world politics but also by the meaning that people ascribe to those facts, the assumptions on which they base their interpretations, and the actions that flow from these assumptions and interpretations—however accurate or inaccurate they might be.

The Nature and Sources of Images

There is nothing harmful about simplifying views of the world. Just as cartographers' projections simplify complex geophysical space so we can better understand the world, each of us inevitably creates a "mental map"—a habitual way of organizing information—to make sense out of a confusing abundance of information. Although mental maps are neither inherently right nor wrong, they are important because we tend to react according to the way the world appears to us rather than the way it is. How we *view* the world (not what it is really like) determines our attitudes, beliefs, and perhaps our behavior. Political leaders, too, are captives of this tendency. As political scientist Richard Ned Lebow (1981) warns, "Policymakers are prone to distort reality in accord with their needs even in situations that appear . . . relatively unambiguous."

Most of us—policymakers included—look for information that reinforces preexisting beliefs about the world, assimilate new data into familiar images, mistakenly equate what we believe with what we know, and deny information

The Cartography of World Politics
Projections of Reality

These four maps depict the distribution of the earth's land surfaces and territory, but each portrays a different image. Each is a model of reality, an abstraction that highlights some features of the world while ignoring others, but all distort reality in one way or another. One distortion they all share is their depiction of the world, which is a sphere, as a flat surface. The difficulty cartographers face can be appreciated by trying to flatten an orange peel.

MAP 1.1

Orthographic Projection

The orthographic projection, centering on the mid-Atlantic, conveys some sense of the curvature of the earth by using rounded edges. The relationships among sizes and shapes are inevitably inaccurate in some places, but the distortions are less than in other representations.

MAP 1.2

Mercator Projection

This mercator projection, popular in sixteenth-century Europe, is a classic Eurocentric view of the world. It placed Europe at the center of the world and exaggerated the continent's importance relative to other land masses. Europe appears larger than South America, which is twice Europe's size, and two-thirds of the map is used to represent the northern half of the world and only one-third the southern half.

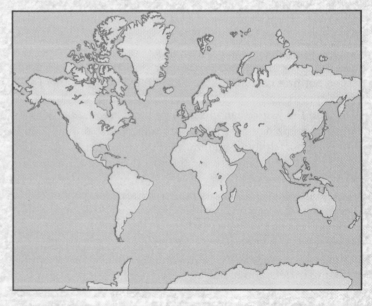

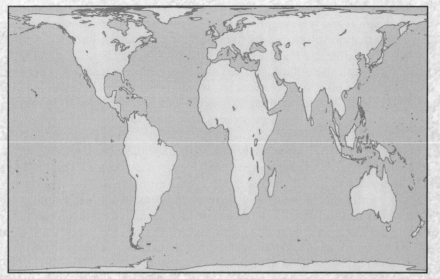

MAP 1.3

Peter's Projection

In the Peter's projection each land mass appears in correct proportion and in its correct position in relation to all others. In contrast with most geographic representations, it draws attention to the less-developed countries of the Global South where more than three-quarters of the world's population today lives.

MAP 1.4

World Time View

This map is a modified south pole projection portraying the world's twenty-four standard time zones. Note that these zones often follow state borders rather than nice, straight latitude lines. Knowledge of time-zone differences is critical in today's economically interdependent world.

SOURCE: IVN Communications, Inc.

that contradicts previous expectations. We process information using **schematic reasoning;** that is, we rely on learned ways of psychologically perceiving new information and we interpret it in light of our memories (Rosenberg 1988). We use information shortcuts both to make political judgments and to help orient our attitudes and beliefs toward specific events and policy issues. A *schema* thus aids in the organization of information and shapes our perceptions of the world.

We organize information about the world, because this helps us to simplify it. Our goal is "to cope with an extraordinarily confusing world by structuring views about specific foreign policies according to [our] more general and abstract beliefs" (Hurwitz and Peffley 1987). Our preexisting values and beliefs encourage us to accept some images as accurate while rejecting from our consciousness others that are incongruent with our prior beliefs (a psychological conflict known as "cognitive dissonance" [see Festinger 1957]). Thus our view of world politics depends not just on what happens in the world but also on how we interpret and internalize those events; our mental maps inevitably help to shape our dispositions toward world affairs.

People's perceptions of and reactions to conflicting or inconsistent information often differ because the act of viewing is not passive. The mind selects, screens, and filters what it perceives. Several factors influence our perceptions of politics:

- Our psychological needs, drives, and dispositions (e.g., trust or mistrust) which are ingrained in our personalities as a result of early childhood experiences.

- Our views of international affairs (e.g., tolerance or fear of cultural diversity) as filtered through the socialization or learning we receive as children from parents, teachers, and peer groups.

- Our images of world history as shaped by the teachers and history books to which we are exposed.

- Opinions about world affairs articulated by our frequent associates, such as close friends.

- Attitudes expressed by policymakers, political pundits, and others whose expertise we respect.

- Positions we occupy and roles we perform (student, parent, bureaucrat, policymaker, diplomat, etc.).

Tolerance of ambiguity and receptivity to new ways of organizing thinking vary among individuals and personality types. Some people are receptive to diversity and therefore better able than others to revise perceptual habits to accommodate new realities. Nevertheless, to some extent, we are all prisoners of the perceptual predispositions that have shaped us and which in turn shape our attitudes, beliefs, and images of world politics.

The Role of Images in World Politics

We must be careful not to assume automatically that what applies to individuals applies to entire countries. Still, leaders' images of historical circumstances often predispose them to behave in particular ways toward others, regardless of "objective" facts. For instance, the loss of 26 million Soviet lives in the "Great Patriotic War" (as the Russians refer to World War II) created an exaggerated fear of foreign invasion, which caused a generation of Soviet policymakers to perceive U.S. defensive moves with considerable suspicion and often alarm. Similarly, the founders of the new United States viewed eighteenth-century European power politics as "dirty," contributing to two seemingly contradictory tendencies later evident in U.S. foreign policy: (1) America's isolationist impulse (its disposition to withdraw from world affairs), and (2) its determination to reform the world in its own image. The former led the country to reject membership in the League of Nations after World War I; the latter gave rise to the U.S. globalist foreign policy after World War II, which committed the country to active involvement nearly everywhere on nearly every issue. Most Americans failed to recognize that others might regard such a far-reaching international policy position as arrogant or threatening; they saw in the country's actions only good intentions. (As President Carter once lamented, "The hardest thing for Americans to understand is that they are not better than other people.")

Because leaders and citizens are prone to ignore or reinterpret information that runs counter to their beliefs and values, mutual misperceptions often fuel discord in world politics, especially when relations between countries are hostile. Distrust and suspicion arise as one conflicting party views the other in the same way that it is viewed by its adversary—that is, as "mirror images" develop. (This clearly happened in Moscow and Washington during the Cold War.) Self-righteousness often leads one party in a conflict to view its own actions as constructive but its adversary's responses as negative and hostile. When this occurs, conflict resolution is extraordinarily difficult, as the Cold War and the recurrent ethnic conflicts since illustrate. Thus fostering peace is not simply a matter of expanding trade and other forms of transnational contact, or even bringing political leaders together in international summits. Rather, it is a matter of changing deeply entrenched beliefs.

Although our mental maps of world politics are resistant to change, change is possible. It sometimes occurs when we experience punishment or discomfort as a result of clinging to false assumptions. (As Benjamin Franklin once observed, "The things that hurt, instruct.") Dramatic events in particular can alter international images, sometimes drastically. The Vietnam War caused many Americans to adjust their previous images about the utility of force in contemporary world politics. The defeat of the Third Reich and revelations of atrocities committed before and during World War II caused the German people to confront their past as they prepared for a democratic future imposed by the victorious allies. The use of atomic bombs against Japan in the waning days of World War II caused many Japanese to confront the horrors of modern warfare and the immorality of weapons of mass destruction. More recently, the unexpected collapse of communist rule in the Soviet Union and Eastern Europe prompted policymakers and political commentators alike to reexamine their assumptions about foreign policy priorities in a new, post-Cold War system. Often such jolting experiences encourage us to create new mental maps, perceptual filters, and criteria through which we may interpret later events and define situations.

As we shape and reshape our images of world politics and its future, we need to think critically about the foundations on which our perceptions rest. Are they accurate? Are they informed? Might they be adjusted to gain greater understanding and empathy? This rethinking is one of the challenges we face in confronting the world politics of the twenty-first century.

As the world watched and read in horror, stories of ethnic hatred, genocidal butchery, mass rape, and forced migration poured out of Bosnia in the early- to mid-1990s. Conjuring up images of the holocaust in Europe during World War II, the situation in Bosnia prompted politicians and citizens throughout the world to ask if or when their country should intervene. It was not until late 1995 that an agreement was reached to send NATO troops to oversee the peace process.

• • •

ORGANIZING INQUIRY: ACTORS, ISSUES, AND THEIR INTERACTION

To predict which forces will dominate the future, we must think in multicausal terms. No trend or trouble stands alone; all interact simultaneously. The future is influenced by many determinants, each connected to the rest in a complex web of linkages. Collectively, these may produce stability by inhibiting the impact of any single disruptive force. If interacting forces converge, however, their combined effects could accelerate the pace of change in world politics, moving it in directions not possible otherwise.

A Macropolitical Perspective

Because world politics is complex and our images of it often discordant, it is not surprising that scholars differ in their approaches to understanding the contemporary world. In this book we adopt a **macropolitical** perspective, which draws attention to: (1) the characteristics, capabilities, and interests of the principal "actors" in world politics (nations, states, and various nonstate participants in international affairs); (2) the principal welfare and security issues that populate the global agenda; and (3) the patterns of cooperation and contention that influence the interactions between and among actors and issues. As we probe these interactions, we will discover why **politics**—the exercise of influence to affect the distribution of particular values, such as power, prestige, or wealth—is the most pervasive and controversial aspect of international affairs.

Our macropolitical perspective directs attention to the interaction of constancy and change on the eve of the new millennium, but it avoids dwelling on any particular events, countries, individuals, or other transitory phenomena whose long-term significance is likely to diminish. Instead, the perspective seeks to identify behaviors that cohere into general global patterns—trends and transformations that measurably affect global living conditions. Thus we explore the nature of world politics from a perspective that places general patterns into a larger, lasting theoretical context, providing the conceptual tools and theories that will enable us to interpret subsequent developments.

The Levels of Analysis

Our macropolitical perspective fits well with a distinction commonly used to understand world politics. Many international relations scholars argue that world politics can be understood best by focusing on one (or more) of three levels. Known as **levels of analysis,** this classification distinguishes: (1) individuals, (2) states or other world political actors, and (3) the international system itself.

The **individual level of analysis** refers to the personal characteristics of humans, including average citizens whose behavior has important political consequences and those responsible for making important decisions on behalf of state and nonstate actors. Here, for example, we may properly locate the impact of individuals' images on their political attitudes, beliefs, and behavior.

The **national level of analysis** consists of the authoritative decision-making units that govern states' foreign policy processes and the attributes of those states (e.g., their type of political system and level of economic and military power), which both shape and constrain leaders' foreign policy choices. The processes by which states make decisions regarding war and peace and the capabilities of states to carry out their decisions, for instance, fall within the national level of analysis.

The **system level of analysis** refers to interactions of states and nonstate global actors whose behaviors ultimately shape the international political system and the levels of conflict and cooperation that characterize world politics. The capacity of rich states to dictate the choices of poor states properly falls within the system level of analysis. So does the capacity (or incapacity) of the United Nations to maintain peace.

Differentiating levels of analysis is important in emphasizing that no single source produces transformations in world politics. Because interrelationships exist across the levels of analysis, trends and transformations in world politics are affected by forces operating at each level and by interactions among them. As a result, our analytical focus on actors, issues, and their interactions will begin (in Chapter 3) with an examination of decision-making processes within states, which remain the principal actors in world politics. We will give some coverage of the individual level of analysis, as we consider the role of leaders as makers and movers of history. But the bulk of the chapter will also address how other forces at the national or domestic level can constrain the impact of individuals on foreign policy decisions and also on world politics generally.

We will then turn our attention to the actors in world politics and examine how their characteristics and capabilities affect their interests and influence in the world. "Great powers" are the focus of attention in Chapter 4, "lesser powers" in Chapter 5; both inquiries properly fall within the national level of analysis. In Chapters 6 and 7 we will extend this level to include nonstate actors—international organizations, multinational corporations, religious and enthnonational movements, and terrorist groups—which challenge the supremacy of states either by transcending or subverting their sovereign control over their destinies.

The next group of chapters properly falls within the international system level of analysis. Here we shift attention to global issues and inquire into how the characteristics, capabilities, and interests of the principal actors in world politics affect interactions and outcomes on the principal welfare and security issues on the global agenda. Welfare issues—economics, demography, and the environment—are the subjects of Chapters 8 through 11; Chapters 12 through 16 examine security issues—war and peace.

● ● ●

TOWARD THE FUTURE

Chapter 17 concludes our inquiry into the trends and transformations comprising contemporary world politics. It draws on the ideas and information presented in earlier chapters in order to address ten questions regarding the global issues that will dominate political discourse during the next decade. We anticipate those questions by posing several here which will inform our inquiry in the chapters that follow.

Pondering the Future: Critical Questions at the Dawn of the New Millennium

1. Are States Obsolete? The territorial state has been the primary actor in world politics for more than three centuries. The post-Cold War resurgence of nationalism throughout the world attests to the continuing quest by national independence movements for statehood, as the principal drive of enthnonational movements is to secure their own national existence within the (legally) impenetrable shell of state sovereignty.

Although in some respects the territorial-state is flourishing, observes French political scientist Pierre Hassner (1968), in others it is dying, as "it can no longer fulfill some of the most important traditional functions." In fact, some have proclaimed "the end" of the state (Guéhenno 1995) and concluded that the very sovereignty of states is eroding in the face of growing challenges from at home and abroad.

> A wide variety of forces has made it increasingly more difficult for any state to wield power over its people and address issues it once considered its sole prerogative. Among these forces are the communications revolution, the rise of transnational corporations, increasing migration, economic integration, and the global nature of economic and environmental problems.
>
> The increasing lack of [state] control, an inability to solve pressing problems, and the fact that few states' boundaries or interests coincide with the nationalities within have exacerbated mistrust of political leaders and institutions in many states. Governments are perceived as not representing the interests of, not delivering security to, and not providing for the well-being of their constituents. As a result, peoples are looking elsewhere for representation of their views and provision of their needs, further eroding the authority of states. (Stanley Foundation 1993, 16)

"While states may not be about to exit from the political stage, and while they may even continue to occupy center stage, they do seem likely to become vulnerable and impotent" (Rosenau 1995). Can the state cope with the challenges it now faces? Auguste Comte, a nineteenth-century French political philosopher, argued that societies create institutions to address problems and meet human needs. When they are no longer able to perform these functions, they disappear. Today, as the managerial capabilities of states (irrespective of form of government) fail to inspire confidence, their future seems increasingly in doubt.

2. Is Interdependence a Cure or a Curse? Global interdependence lies at the heart of the external challenges states now face. As the range of global issues has expanded, interdependence has reduced states' ability to manage. Mutual vulnerabilities reduce states' autonomy by curtailing their control of their own fates.

From one perspective, an awareness of the common destiny of all, alongside the declining ability of many sovereign states to cope with global problems through national means, may energize efforts to put aside interstate competition. Conflict, according to this reasoning, will recede, as few states are able to disentangle themselves from the interdependent ties that bind them together. Consequently, we should welcome the continued tightening of interstate linkages, which strengthen the fragile tapestry of international relations.

From another, more pessimistic perspective, interdependence will not lead to transnational collaboration. Regardless of how compelling the need or how rewarding the benefits may be, contact and mutual dependence will breed enmity, not amity. The absence of a global community persists, as does international anarchy, and nostalgia for the more autonomous state abounds. Intertwined economies will sour relations more often than sweeten them. Under conditions of fierce competition, scarcity, and resurgent nationalism, the temptation may be irresistible to seek isolation from foreign economic dependence by creating barriers to trade and other transactions. The temptation to achieve political and economic benefits by military force or by trade protection will also continue. Thus the tightening web of global interdependence foretells danger, not just opportunity.

3. Is Technological Innovation a Blessing or a Burden? "The dynamics of globalization unleashed by technology," political scientist James N. Rosenau (1995) concludes, "are the dominant catalyst in world affairs." The consequences, however, are not certain. Technological innovations, like interdependence, solve some problems but cause others. As Nobel laureate economist Wassily Leontief warned in 1987, "Technology is now, for better or worse, the principal driving force behind the ongoing rapid economic, social, and political change. Like any irrepressible force, the new technology can bestow on us undreamed of benefits but also inflict irreparable damage." Not only can technological innovations create new ways of preventing or treating disease, they can also enhance the sophistication and destructiveness of weapons of war.

Discoveries in microelectronics, information processing, transportation, energy, agriculture, communications, medicine, and biotechnology profoundly affect our lives and shape our future. They have united the globe into a single international market and common culture, while paradoxically breaking down people's sense of citizenship and community (Barber 1995). "There appears to be a fundamental lag between the current rate of technological change and the rate of adjustment to these changes among decision makers" (Blumenthal 1988). The technological catalyst of change requires proper and constructive management, but is this possible in a world wracked by disintegrative as well as integrative trends?

4. Will Geo-Economics Supersede Geopolitics? Throughout modern history, states have been the dominant political actors in world politics and have com-

As we consider the future, we must ask ourselves whether technological innovation is inevitably the answer to our concerns. Although we are now able to send satellites into space and receive photos from planets we will never visit, we remain unable to eliminate hatred or aggression, or to achieve peace on earth.

peted with one another militarily for position and prominence in the hierarchy of international power. For more than three centuries, world politics has been largely a record of preparing, waging, and recovering from interstate war. Military might was equated with prestige and influence, and military conquest became the means to economic as well as political preeminence.

To some, the next battlefield in world politics will center on economic issues. National destinies will be determined by commercial competition, not military conquest. If issues of **geo-economics** (the distribution of wealth) become more important than conventional issues of **geopolitics** (the distribution of political and military power), will states' foreign policies also change? If wealth is converted into political muscle, nationalistic pride can give rise to competition and self-assertiveness. But economic interdependence and tight commercial relationships can also collapse into trade disputes and political rivalry. Nevertheless, the apparent shift of priorities to the economic dimensions of world politics is certain to shape the distribution of twenty-first-century global power. This shift is also likely to accelerate the porousness of national borders and the homogeneity of commercial products available in an increasingly integrated global marketplace.

5. What Constitutes Human Well-Being in an Ecologically Fragile Planet? The once popular "limits-to-growth" proposition—the belief that the world cannot forever increase its productive capacity—has been replaced by the maxim of sustainability, which emphasizes "the growth of limits." Thus **sustainable development** means learning to live off the earth's interest without encroaching on its capital.

Gross national product (GNP)—the total value of goods and services produced in a nation during a specified period, usually a year—is the common measure of economic well-being throughout the world and "is closely bound up with human welfare. . . . Human welfare has dimensions other than the economic one. But it is rightly held that the economic element is *very* important, and that the stronger the economy the greater the contribution to human welfare" (Daly and Cobb 1989).

14

A state's increasing economic output has different consequences for poor societies than for rich ones. To the inhabitants of most Global South countries, growth in GNP may mean more food, better housing, improved education, and an increased standard of living. However, affluent people in the Global North already enjoy these basic amenities; therefore, additional income usually allows them to satisfy comparatively trivial needs.

The global impact of population growth as well as the continued striving for economic growth are great. Whereas people in poor countries contribute negligibly to production but make few demands on world resources, to feed their high standard of living people in rich countries contribute greatly to depletion of the world's resources and pollution of its spaces. In both cases, continued population growth is detrimental—for poor societies, because it inhibits increases in per-capita income and welfare; for rich societies, because it further burdens the earth's delicate ecological system. Unbridled exploitation and consumption, unhinged from responsibility to others, are ultimately self-destructive. As Soviet President Mikhail Gorbachev warned in 1988, we must halt "humanity's aggression against nature."

These ideas challenge the very foundations of Western civilization. Although sustainable development is a more realistic prospect, even it will be hard to realize. Sustainable economic welfare, like sustainable wealth, requires sensitivity not only to economic growth but also to natural-resource depletion, environmental damage, and the value of leisure and liberty (United Nations Development Programme 1993). But is there an alternative? Can growth in a finite world proceed infinitely? How long can finite energy sources sustain uncontrolled consumption before automobiles sputter to a stop, industries grind to a halt, and lights go out? How many pollutants can the atmosphere absorb before irreparable environmental damage results? And how many people can a delicately balanced ecosystem support?

The Challenge of Understanding

Understanding today's world requires a willingness to confront complexity. A true but complicated idea always has less chance of success than a simple but false one, the French political sociologist Alexis de Tocqueville (1969 [1835]) cautioned more than 160 years ago. The challenge is difficult but the rewards warrant the effort. Humankind's ability to chart a more rewarding future is contingent on its ability to entertain complex ideas, to free itself from the sometimes paralyzing grip of the past, and to develop a questioning attitude about rival perspectives on international realities. On that hopeful yet introspective note, we begin our exploration of world politics at the dawn of a new millennium.

● ● ●

KEY TERMS

international political system
bipolar distribution of power
state system
nation-states
cycles
schematic reasoning
macropolitical
politics

levels of analysis
individual level of analysis
national level of analysis
system level of analysis
geo-economics
geopolitics
sustainable development
gross national product (GNP)

CHAPTER 2

The Theoretical Interpretation of World Politics: Rival Perspectives

It's important that we take a hard, clear look . . . not at some simple world, either of universal goodwill or of universal hostility, but the complex, changing and sometimes dangerous world that really exists.

—JIMMY CARTER,
  U.S. president, 1980

Seek truth through facts.

—MAO ZEDONG, *president,*
  People's Republic of China, 1966

Imagine yourself a newly elected president of the United States. You are scheduled to deliver a State of the Union Address on your views of the current world situation and your foreign policy to deal with it. To prepare your speech, you will face the task of both defining those aspects of international affairs most worthy of attention and explaining the reasons for their priority. This challenge, in turn, will require that you interpret world politics by identifying the concepts and issues which best communicate how the global condition can be understood meaningfully. You must, in short, think *theoretically*. At the same time, you must be careful, because your interpretations will necessarily make assumptions about international realities that your citizens might find questionable. The effort to describe the world convincingly is bound to result in controversy, because reasonable people often see realities differently.

In this chapter we distinguish among the major theoretical perspectives scholars and policymakers use to interpret international relations. Since the perceived "realities" of international affairs which these positions seek to explain influence their content, we will examine how perceived changes in underlying international conditions have shaped various theories. In addition, our review of contending political theories will also identify the intellectual heritage which informs this text.

• • •

UNDERSTANDING WORLD POLITICS:
THE ELUSIVE QUEST FOR THEORY

Social scientists construct different theories to make international events understandable. Over time, these **paradigms,** or models that scholars fashion, are revised to explain new developments in world affairs as new problems cry out for understanding and solutions. Thus, the paths to knowledge that guide the thinking both of scholars and of policymakers in different historical circumstances tell us much about world politics itself.[1]

---

[1]The word "paradigm" is commonly used to describe the dominant way of looking at a particular subject, such as international relations. Derived from the Greek *paradeigma*—meaning an example, a model, or a pattern—the general idea underlying the term "paradigm" is that we often base our thoughts about an area of inquiry on our judgments regarding which of its characteristics are most important, what puzzles need to be solved, and what criteria should govern their investigation.

Paradigms can be used to compare the present to the past and to determine what issues in a changing world are perceived to be most important because, throughout history, frameworks or paradigmatic ways of viewing international conditions have been abandoned when their assertions have failed to mirror the prevailing patterns of international behavior.

Major wars have often brought about significant changes in the theoretical interpretation of world affairs and influenced "what ideas and values will predominate, thereby determining the ethos of succeeding ages" (Gilpin 1981). Three such system-transforming wars have dominated the twentieth century: World War I, World War II, and the Cold War. "Every war . . . has been followed in due course by skeptical reassessments of supposedly sacred assumptions" (Schlesinger 1986) and reshaped policymakers' perceptions of world politics and the policy programs to best preserve world order. Each struggle caused the dominant paradigm to be jettisoned and encouraged the search for new theoretical orientations.

The theoretical perspectives fashioned during this century demonstrate the impact of major wars on the study of world politics. Six of these perspectives will be discussed here: (1) current history, (2) liberal idealism, (3) realism, (4) behavioralism, (5) neorealism, and (6) neoliberalism.[2]

Current History

International relations as a distinct field of intellectual inquiry is largely a twentieth-century phenomenon. Its historical roots lie in **current history,** an approach that focuses on the description of historical events rather than on theoretical explanation.

When the formal study of international relations began at the dawn of the twentieth century, the world abounded with optimism. Many people believed that peace and prosperity had taken root and would persist. The Hague peace conferences in 1899 and 1907 had inspired hope of controlling arms and sparing Europe another series of wars like those between 1848 and 1870. Moreover, numerous individuals—including American industrialist Andrew Carnegie, who gave much of his fortune to the cause of world peace—assumed that as industrialization progressed and the costs and risks of war increased, the chance of protracted war among the great powers would decline dramatically (see also Angell 1910).

---

[2]This inventory is selective. At least six additional schools of thought regarding particular aspects of world politics also deserve attention and will be introduced in chapters where they best help to interpret the topic covered. First, as explained in Chapter 3, decision-making theory accounts for the ways leaders and other actors seek to make policy choices rationally, and the limits to this aspiration. Second, to understand the relationship between national power and international order, hegemonic stability theory, a hybrid of liberal/neorealist theory (Gill 1993b), examines what happens when a clearly predominant state, a "hegemon," exercises leadership and control of the international system by setting and enforcing the rules governing international trade, finance, investment, and other issues, such as environmental regulation (see Gilpin 1981; Levy 1991). Third, long-cycle theory seeks to explain the historical ebb and flow of world politics, global leadership, and systemwide war (Goldstein 1988; Modelski and Thompson 1996). The rise and fall of the great powers and empires is its central concern. Fourth, world-system theory looks at system dynamics from a long-term, structural perspective, emphasizing its economic underpinnings, to explain the Western capitalist societies' rise to dominance and the lack of economic development in many other geographic areas (see Wallerstein 1980). Fifth, dependency theory examines the pattern of dominance and dependence which characterizes the unequal relationship between the world's rich and poor states (Packenham 1992). Finally, advocates of the comparative study of foreign policy seek to probe the similarities and differences in states' international circumstances, national attributes and capabilities, foreign policy decision-making processes, and individual policymakers (see Hermann, Kegley, and Rosenau 1987).

In those tranquil times, students of international relations studied history to glean insight on the events of the day. The study of international relations consisted mainly of commentary about personalities and events, past and present. Rarely did scholars seek to generalize theoretically about the "lessons" of history or about the principles or "laws" that might account for states' characteristic responses to similar stimuli or influences.[3]

The large-scale death and destruction which World War I exacted from 1914 to 1918 destroyed the security that had made current history a comfortable approach to world politics. This catastrophe was a painful lesson which stimulated the search for knowledge to address contemporary policy problems in a theoretical context. However interesting descriptions of past wars might be, they were of dubious use to a world in search of ways to prevent wars of mass destruction. For those purposes, policymakers and scholars needed a **theory**—a statement attempting to account for general phenomena or patterns rather than explaining the unique or individual instances of the general phenomenon of which it is part—which could reliably predict war and instruct leaders on the best policies to prevent it.

Liberal Idealism

World War I initiated a paradigmatic revolution in the study of international relations, in which several perspectives competed for attention. While the approach of current history continued to claim some disciples in the waning days of World War I, after Russia's Bolshevik Revolution, Marxist-Leninist thought became increasingly influential, with its critique of capitalism's creation of inequality, class conflict, and imperialistic war. In the 1930s, with the rise of Adolf Hitler in Germany, national socialism (or fascism) also challenged conventional European thinking about world politics. Nazism, the German variant of national socialism, was particularly provocative. Not only did Nazism glorify the role of the state (as opposed to that of the individual) in political life, it also championed war as an instrument of national policy. Emerging as dominant, however, was a perspective known as **idealism,** which assumed that people were not by nature sinful or wicked but that harmful behavior was the result of structural arrangements motivating individuals to act in their own self-interest.

The Idealist World View. Because idealists draw their philosophy from what has been called the liberal school of thought, they are sometimes referred to as "liberal idealists."[4] After World War I, they became known simply as "idealists," even if they were a diverse group within the larger liberal tradition.

---

[3]Sir Halford Mackinder (1919) and Alfred Thayer Mahan (1890) were exceptions. Both sought to generate theoretical propositions pertaining to the influence of geographic factors on national power and international politics. Their efforts laid the foundations for the study of political geography, which survives today as an important approach to world politics (see Demko and Wood 1994).

[4]Post-World War I idealism, as advocated by such scholars and policymakers as Alfred Zimmern, Norman Angell, James T. Shotwell, and Woodrow Wilson, derived from ancient liberal philosophy (recall the Sermon on the Mount) and has been interpreted variously in different periods. At the core of liberalism is an emphasis on the impact of ideas on behavior, the equality and liberty of the individual, and the need to protect people from excessive state regulation.

Influenced by David Hume and Jean Jacques Rousseau, Immanuel Kant (left) in *Perpetual Peace* (1795) helped to redefine modern liberal theory by advocating global (not national) citizenship, free trade, and a federation of democracies as a means to peace. Richard Cobden (right) primarily foresaw the possibility for peace across borders; in his view, if contact and communication among people could expand through free trade, so too would international friendship and peace, secured by prosperity which would make people interdependent and no longer in need of military forces to pursue rivalries.

Collectively, the post-World War I idealists embraced a world view based on the following beliefs:

1. Human nature is essentially "good" or altruistic, and people are therefore capable of mutual aid and collaboration.[5]

2. The fundamental human concern for others' welfare makes progress possible (i.e., the Enlightenment's faith in the possibility of improving civilization was reaffirmed).

3. Bad human behavior, such as violence, is the product not of flawed people but of evil institutions which encourage people to act selfishly and to harm others.

4. War is not inevitable and its frequency can be reduced by eradicating the institutional arrangements that encourage it.

5. War is an international problem requiring collective or multilateral, rather than national, efforts to control it.

From this comes a conceptualization of the individual as the seat of moral value and virtue and the belief that human beings should be treated as ends rather than means. Liberalism emphasizes ethical principle over the pursuit of power. Liberalism's modern proponents include such thinkers as Immanuel Kant, Thomas Jefferson, James Madison, John Stuart Mill, John Locke, David Hume, Jean Jacques Rosseau, and Adam Smith. For reviews and summaries of the liberal legacy as a perspective on world politics, see Doyle (1995), Howard (1978), and Zacher and Matthew (1995).

[5]The role of human nature in theories of politics is controversial. See Lewontin, Rose, and Kamin (1984), Nelson (1974), and Wilson (1993) for reviews and critical discussions.

6. International society must reorganize itself in order to eliminate the institutions that make war likely, and nations must reform their political systems so that self-determination and democratic governance within states can help pacify relations among states.

While not all idealists subscribed to each of these tenets with equal conviction, they shared a moralistic, optimistic, and universalistic image of international affairs.

The Idealist Reform Program. Although idealists differed significantly in their prescriptions for reforming the international political system (see Herz 1951), they generally fell into one of three groups. The first group advocated creating international institutions to replace the anarchical and war-prone balance-of-power system, characterized by coalitions of independent states formed to wage war or to defend a weaker coalition partner from attack. In place of this competitive unregulated system, idealists sought to create a new one based on **collective security.** This approach dealt with the problem of war by declaring any state's aggression was an aggression against all, who would act in concert to thwart the dominance-seeking aggressor. The League of Nations was the embodiment of collective security, reflecting simultaneously the idealists' emphasis on international institutions as a mechanism for coping with war and social injustice and the possibility of international cooperation for global problem solving.

A second group of idealists emphasized the use of legal processes such as mediation and arbitration to settle disputes and inhibit recourse to armed conflict. This facet of the idealists' policy prescriptions was illustrated by the creation in 1921 of the Permanent Court of International Justice to litigate interstate conflicts and by the ratification of the Kellogg-Briand Pact of 1928, which "outlawed" war as an instrument of national policy.

A third group followed the biblical injunction that nations should beat their swords into plowshares. This orientation was exemplified by efforts during the 1920s, such as those negotiated at the Washington and London naval conferences, to secure arms control and disarmament agreements.

Several corollary ideas gave definition to the idealists' emphasis on encouraging global cooperation through international institutions, law, and disarmament. These included:

- The need to substitute attitudes that stressed the unity of humankind for those that stressed parochial national loyalties to independent sovereign states.
- The use of the power of ideas through education to arouse world public opinion against warfare.
- The promotion of free international trade in place of economic nationalism.
- The replacement of secret diplomacy by a system of "open covenants, openly arrived at."
- The termination of interlocking bilateral alliances and the power balances they sought to achieve.

In seeking a more peaceful world, some idealists saw the principle of **self-determination**—giving nationalities the right through voting to become independent states—as a means to redraw the globe's political geography to make national borders conform to ethnic groupings. Related to this was U.S. president Woodrow Wilson's call for democratic domestic institutions. "Making the world safe for democracy," idealists believed, would also make it secure and free from war. Wilson's celebrated Fourteen Points speech, delivered before Congress in 1918, proposed the creation of the League of Nations and, with it, the pursuit of other idealists' aims. This speech, perhaps better than any other statement, expressed the sentiments of the idealist world view and program.

Although idealism dominated policy rhetoric and academic discussions during the interwar period, little of the idealist reform program was ever attempted, and even less of it was achieved. When the winds of international change again shifted and the Axis Powers pursued world conquest, idealism as a world view receded.

Realism

The drive for world conquest that led to World War II provoked strong criticism of the idealist paradigm. Critics blamed the outbreak of war on what they believed to be the idealists' naive legalistic and moralistic assumptions about the possibility of peace and progress through human aspiration, and alleged that idealists were utopians who neglected the realities of power politics (see Carr 1939). The lessons the critics drew from the interwar period gave shape to a new set of perceptions and beliefs.

Advocates of the new, ascendant paradigm known as **realism,** or alternatively as **realpolitik** as a general philosophy, emerged to frame an intellectual movement whose message reads like the antithesis of idealism.[6] Because it was compelling—and because it remains so today—it deserves careful scrutiny.

The Realist World View. As a political theory, realism can trace its intellectual roots to the ancient Greek historian Thucydides and his account of the Peleponnesian War between Athens and Sparta (431–404 B.C.E.), the writings of Kautilya (minister to the Maurya emperor of India more than two thousand years ago), and especially the political thought of the Italian theorist Niccoló Machiavelli and the English philosopher Thomas Hobbes.

Realism, as applied to twentieth-century world politics, views the state as the most important actor on the world stage since it answers to no higher political authority. Moreover, conflicts of interests among states are assumed to be inevitable. Realism also emphasizes the ways in which the anarchical nature of international politics dictates the choices that foreign policymakers, as rational problem solvers who must calculate their interest in terms of power, must make. (See Chapter 3 for discussion of the "rational" actor.)

Within the realist paradigm, the purpose of statecraft is national survival in a hostile environment. To this end, no means is more important than the acquisition of **power**—the capacity to exercise influence over others, especially by military means. Similarly, no principle is more important than **self-help**—the ultimate dependence of the state on its own resources to promote its interests and protect itself. In this conception, state **sovereignty,** a cornerstone of international law, gives heads of state the freedom—and responsibility—to do whatever is necessary to advance the state's interests and survival.

According to this paradigm, respect for moral principles is a wasteful and dangerous interference in the rational pursuit of national power. To the realist, therefore, questions about the relative virtues of the values within this or that ide-

---

[6]Among the principal prophets of this new world view were E. H. Carr (1939), George F. Kennan (1951, 1954), Hans J. Morgenthau (1948), Reinhold Niebuhr (1947), and Kenneth W. Thompson (1960). For critical reviews of the realist paradigm, see Brown (1994), O. Holsti (1995), Smith (1986), and Vasquez (1993).

In *The Prince* (1532) and *The Leviathan* (1651) Niccoló Machiavelli and Thomas Hobbes, respectively, emphasized a political calculus based on interest, prudence, power, and expediency above all other considerations. This formed the foundation of what became a growing body of modern realist thinking which accepts the drive for power over others as necessary and wise statecraft.

ological system cannot be allowed to interfere with sound policy making. A state's ideological or ethical preferences are neither good nor bad—what matters is whether its self-interest is served. Thus, the game of international politics revolves around the pursuit of power: acquiring it, increasing it, projecting it, and using it to bend others to one's will. At the extreme, realism appears to accept war as normal and rejects morality as it pertains to relations between individuals.

At the risk of oversimplification, realism's message can be summarized in the form of ten assumptions and related propositions:

1. A reading of history teaches that people are by nature narrowly selfish and ethically flawed, and cannot free themselves from this deficiency.

2. Of all of people's evil ways, no sins are more prevalent, inexorable, or dangerous than their instinctive lust for power and their desire to dominate others.

3. The possibility of eradicating the instinct for power is a utopian aspiration.

4. Under such conditions, international politics is—as Thomas Hobbes put it—a struggle for power, "a war of all against all."

5. The primary obligation of every state—the goal to which all other national objectives should be subordinated—is to promote the "national interest," defined as the acquisition of power.

6. The nature of the international system dictates that states acquire sufficient military capabilities to deter attack by potential enemies.

7. Economics is less relevant to national security than is military might; it is important primarily as a means of acquiring national power and prestige.

8. Allies might increase a state's ability to defend itself, but their loyalty and reliability should not be assumed.

23

9. States should never entrust the task of self-protection to international organizations or international law and should resist efforts to regulate international conduct.

10. If all states seek to maximize power, stability will result from maintaining a balance of power, lubricated by fluid alliance systems.

Realism in the Nuclear Age. The dour and pessimistic realist thinking which dominated policy making and academic discourse in the 1940s and 1950s fit the needs of a pessimistic age. World War II, the onset of rivalry between the United States and the Soviet Union, the expansion of the Cold War into a global struggle between East and West, the stockpiling of nuclear weapons, and the periodic crises that threatened to erupt into global violence all confirmed the realists' emphasis on the inevitability of conflict, the poor prospects for cooperation, and the divergence of national interests among incorrigibly selfish, power-seeking states.

The realists' interpretations appeared particularly persuasive, given the prevailing patterns of behavior. States and their incessant competition were accordingly seen as the defining elements of global reality; all other aspects of world politics became secondary. At the same time, the view that a threatening international environment demanded that foreign policy take precedence over domestic problems also appeared cogent. As the historical imperatives of "power politics" required unceasing attention to preserving peace, the logic of *realpolitik* asserted that military security was the essence of world politics.

The Limitations of Realism. However persuasive were the realists' arguments about the essential properties of international politics, their contentions and conclusions were frequently at odds and even contradictory.

> Critics . . . noted a lack of precision and even contradiction in the way classical realists use such concepts as "power," "national interest," and "balance of power." They also see possible contradictions between the central descriptive and prescriptive elements of classical realism. On the one hand, nations and their leaders "think and act in terms of interests defined as power," but, on the other, statesmen are urged to exercise prudence and restraint, as well as to recognize the legitimate national interests of other nations. Obviously, then, power plays a central role in classical realism. But the correlation between the relative power balance and political outcomes is often less than compelling, suggesting the need to enrich analyses with other variables. (O. Holsti 1995, 38)

Thus, once analysis moved beyond the belief that people are wicked and the rhetoric requiring that foreign policy serve the national interest, important questions remained: What policies best serve the national interest? Do alliances encourage peace or instability? Do arms promote national security or provoke costly arms races and war? Are states more prone to act aggressively when they are strong or weak? Are the interests of states better served through competition with one another or through cooperation? If humankind is unchanging, then how do we explain the observable evolution and transformation of the international system? Indeed, how do we explain the growth of collaborative multilateral institutions, economic expansion, and states' observable willingness to abide by ethical principles and agreements rather than ruthlessly to exploit others when the opportunity arises?

Because such questions are empirically verifiable and answering them satisfactorily requires real-world evidence and rigorous analysis, realism began to be questioned. Although it presented a distinctive perspective on international affairs, its paradigm lacked a methodology for resolving competing claims. Realism offered no criteria for determining what data were significant and what rules to follow to interpret relevant information. Even the policy recommendations that purportedly flowed from its logic were often divergent. Realists themselves, for example, were sharply divided as to whether U.S. intervention in Vietnam served American national interests and whether nuclear weapons contributed to international security.

A growing number of critics also pointed out that realism did not account for significant new developments in world politics. For instance, it could not explain the forces behind the new institutions beginning to be constructed in Western Europe in the 1950s and 1960s, where the cooperative pursuit of mutual advantage rather than narrow self-interest appeared to dominate (at least in economic, if not always in military, affairs). Other critics began to worry about realism's disregard both for ethical principles and for the material and social costs that some of its policy prescriptions seemed to impose, such as retarded economic growth resulting from unrestrained military expenditures. Consequently, by the end of the 1960s, realism found itself bombarded by criticism.

Realism's Continuing Relevance. Despite the shortcomings of realism, much of the world continues to think about international politics in its terms. Indeed, realism enjoyed a resurgence in the early 1980s, as the embittered Cold War competition between the United States and the Soviet Union entered a new phase and the role of military power in world politics received renewed emphasis. In addition, the bloody wars in the former Yugoslavia in the 1990s similarly rekindled enthusiasm for *realpolitik*. Finally, realism provides great insight into states' continuing drive for national security through military means.

The continuing relevance of realism also finds expression in its recent "new" reformulation, known as "neorealism" or "structural realism." Like the realist tradition out of which it derived, this variant recognizes the anarchical nature of world politics and the dominance of the nation-state in the global political arena. However, it severs the link that realists postulated between human nature and the behavior of states in world politics. To neorealists, the structure of the system rather than the unceasing lust for power exclusively dictates national leaders' foreign policy choices. Thus neorealism speaks directly to the influence of the structure of world power on the units within it, focusing, for example, on the consequences of one rather than several great-power rivals' domination. We shall return to consider neorealist theory, but first we will briefly address the methodological debate that dissatisfaction with classical realism provoked in the 1960s.

Behavioralism

Realism prepared the way for serious theoretical thinking about global conditions and the empirical linkages among them. Nonetheless, as dissatisfaction with its shortcomings mounted, a counterreaction—cast largely in terms of language and method—gained momentum in the 1960s and early 1970s. Because it was defined largely by its application of scientific methods to international relations, **behavioralism,** as it came to be known, is better described as a methodology than as a theoretical perspective.

Science versus Traditionalism. Behavioralism in international relations was part of a larger movement spanning the social sciences. Often referred to as the "scientific" approach, behavioralism challenged the preexisting modes of studying human behavior, now called "traditionalism," as well as the ways in which traditionalists derived their truth claims. This resulted in an often heated debate between the behavioralists and traditionalists as to the principles and procedures most appropriate for investigating international phenomena. The debate centered on the meaning of theory, the requirements for adequate theory, and the methods best suited to testing theoretical propositions. Indeed, "theorizing about theory" (Singer 1960) rather than theorizing about international relations dominated this debate. The literature of the period attests to the extent to which methodological issues rather than substantive ones commanded the attention of professional analysts (see Knorr, and Rosenau 1969; Knorr and Verba 1961). This perhaps reflected the uncertainty and immaturity of a science in its early stages of development.

A Science of International Politics? A number of shared assumptions and analytic prescriptions were at the core of the behavioral movement. For instance, behavioralism sought generalizations or statements about international regularities that held across time and place. Science, the behavioralists claimed, is primarily a generalizing activity. The purpose of scientific inquiry, therefore, is to discover recurrent patterns of behavior and their causes. From this perspective—a view incidentally consistent with that of many "traditional" realists and liberal idealists—a theory of international relations should be defined as a statement of the relationship between two or more variables, which specifies the conditions under which the relationship(s) hold and explains why the relationship(s) should hold. To uncover such theories, behavioralists leaned toward using comparative cross-national analyses rather than case studies of particular countries at particular times. Behavioralists also stressed the need for data about the characteristics of countries and how they behave toward one another. Hence, the behavioral movement spawned and encouraged the comparative and quantitative study of international relations (see, for example, Rosenau 1980; Singer 1968).

What made behavioralism innovative was not so much its reliance on controlled comparative techniques and quantitative analysis as its attitude toward inquiry. Behavioralists sought greater rigor and precision in analysis. They advocated replacing subjective belief with verifiable knowledge, supplanting impressionism and intuition with testable evidence, and substituting data and reproducible information for mere opinion. In this sense, they embraced liberal idealism's "high regard for modern science" and its "attacks against superstition and authority" (Hall 1993). In place of appeals to the "expert" opinion of authorities, behavioral scientists sought to acquire knowledge cumulatively by suspending judgments about truth until they had sufficient evidence to support them. They aspired to conduct objective or value-free research; they strived to replace ambiguous verbal definitions of concepts with so-called operational ones, built on indicators on which empirical tests could be conducted and whose meaning was easily communicated from one analyst to the next; and they sought to avoid the tendency of previous scholarship to select facts and cases to fit preexisting hunches. Instead, *all* available data, those which contradicted as well as those which supported existing theoretical hypotheses, were to be examined. Knowledge, they argued, would advance best by assuming a cautious, skeptical attitude toward any empirical statement. "Let the data, not the armchair theorist, speak." "Seek evidence, but distrust it." These slogans represented the behavioral posture toward the acquisition of knowledge.

Advocates of behavioralism were understandably enthusiastic about their approach. They came armed with new tools for analyzing international relations, with newly generated data for testing the competing hypotheses of decades of traditional speculation, and sometimes with generous research support from governments and private foundations. An entire generation of scholars was trained to study international relations with powerful new conceptual and methodological tools. In the process, some behavioralists addressed empirical questions at the core of competing ideas about states' social and political organization, including propositions grounded in realism and also Marxist and other ideas about the causes and consequences of the inequalities within and among states.

Postbehavioralism. Gathering verifiable knowledge is a difficult and often tedious task requiring dedication and patience. Early enthusiasm and optimism began to wane as the effort invested failed to produce prompt results. Even within the behavioral movement, voices began to ask embarrassing questions about the approach and its suitability. One of the early proponents of behavioralism, David Easton (1969), asked if the field was not moving into a period of "postbehavioralism," marked by increasing attention to the policy relevance of research.

At the heart of this self-scrutiny was a common set of criticisms: (1) that some devotees of behavioralism had become preoccupied with method to the exclusion of real-world problems; (2) that behavioralists often ignored policymakers' need for data-based knowledge about how to protect their state's security and make the world a better place; and (3) that behavioral methodology, which sought to ground theories in hard data, relied on past patterns of human experience that sometimes failed to apply to the rapidly changing world or the future. Hence the findings might be historically accurate but largely irrelevant to today's or tomorrow's world.

Although some behavioral research spoke directly to the moral issues that differentiated realism and liberal idealism, it was criticized nonetheless for neglecting many ethical questions raised in a world of poverty, hunger, violence, and other forms of malaise. Hence the postbehavioral critique called for a new research agenda that would focus on new issues and reexamine their underlying philosophical implications from a multidisciplinary perspective. However, the advocates of new approaches to international relations rarely recommended discarding scientific methods, despite the harsh criticism of "postmodern deconstructivists" (see Focus 2.1). More commonly they urged the application of such methods to new kinds of questions or to the reconstruction of theories grounded in the realist and liberal traditions (e.g., Wayman and Diehl 1995).

Extending Realism: The Neorealist Structural Approach

Realism remains an important theoretical perspective underlying contemporary analyses of national security affairs. More recently, it has gained popularity in reconstructed form as a general theory of international politics. This reformulated perspective, known as **neorealism,** is a variant of realism that

FOCUS 2.1

Is Understanding International Complexity beyond the Analyst's Capability?
The Postmodern Critique of Contemporary Theoretical Interpretation

The most recent critique of behavioralism, **postmodernism** is an approach to the study of international relations since World War II which emphasizes the study of texts, hidden meanings, and discourse in the writings and speeches of policymakers and analysts who interpret world affairs. It represents what is often described as a "post-positivist" reaction. **Positivism** is a philosophical tradition underlying the scientific method and concerned with positive facts and phenomena, to the exclusion of speculation about ultimate causes or origins. Thus behavioralists and those committed to the scientific method as a way of understanding the social and political world are typically described as positivists. Postmodernists are post-positivistic because they call for a reexamination of the philosophical basis for making truth claims in international relations theory.

As with the earlier debate between traditionalists and behavioralists, postmodernism is part of a broader movement in the humanities, variously known as "critical social theory," "poststructuralism," or "deconstructionism." Those associated postmodern theorists interpret the particular meaning and intentions of particular texts and the cultural context in which they are communicated. Critical theories take the inherently subjective nature of images of world politics and the "social construction of reality" as their point of departure (for examples, see Ashley and Walker 1990, Der Derian 1995, Onuf 1989, Sjolander and Cox 1994, and Walker 1993; for a critique of the postmodern critique, see Rosenau 1992).

Postmodern critical introspection into the foundations of scientific methods of inquiry in general and international relations theory in particular is characterized by questioning whether it is possible to truly understand reality. Postmodernists believe that there is no objective international reality that we can discover—it is inherently intangible, and what we assume to be "true" masks the values on which we base our analyses. The purpose of inquiry, therefore, is to expose the fallacy of those who contend that they understand reality. To this end, postmodernists refuse to study international relations; instead, they study the texts, "subtexts" (hidden meanings), and language in the writings, speeches, and arguments of policymakers and analysts who interpret world affairs. Revealing the distortions and misrepresentations of these "shrewd deceivers" through the deconstruction of words and texts, deconstructionists aim to identify the coexisting "multiple realities" and the fictional basis within the "stories" of modern authorities that assert stable truths. In short, postmodernism is a skeptical attack on conventional approaches to the study of international relations which attempts to show how they create reality rather than convey it through literary constructions and the reader's preconceived assumptions.

emphasizes the anarchic structure of world politics rather than human nature in its explanation of foreign policy behavior. For this reason, neorealism is sometimes referred to as **structural realism** theory because it emphasizes the influence of the global system's structure on the behavior of the units that comprise it (see Keohane 1986a).

A Systems Theory of International Politics. The pioneer of neorealism, Kenneth N. Waltz, in his influential book, *Theory of International Politics* (1979), set out to convert the loose and disjointed body of realist "thought" into a formal "theory" (Waltz 1995). "To systematize political realism into a rigorous, deductive systemic theory of international politics" (Keohane 1986b), neorealism dismisses explanations of international politics developed at the individual and national levels of analysis and argues that explanations at the level of the international system are sufficient to account for the main trends in world politics. As Waltz (1995) expressed his neorealist conceptualization of the determinants of international behavior, "international structure emerges from the interaction of states and then constrains them from taking certain actions while propelling them toward others."

As in realism, in neorealism anarchy and the absence of central institutions above states characterize the structure of the system. States remain the primary actors acting according to the principle of self-help and seeking to ensure their survival. Thus, it is the neorealists' view that states do not differ in the tasks they face, only in their capabilities. Capabilities define the position of states in the system, and the distribution of capabilities defines the structure of the system.

Power also remains a central concept in neorealism. However, the quest for power is no longer considered an end in itself, as in realism; nor does it derive from human nature. Instead, states always pursue power to survive. As Waltz (1979) explains, the "means fall into two categories: internal efforts (moves to increase economic capability, to increase military strength, to develop clever strategies) and external efforts (moves to strengthen and enlarge one's own alliance or to weaken and shrink an opposing one)." Furthermore, because the instinct for survival drives states, neorealism asserts that balances of power automatically form, regardless of whether "some or all states consciously aim to establish and maintain a balance, or whether some or all states aim for universal domination" (Waltz 1979). Once the international system is formed, it "becomes a force that the units may not be able to control; it constrains their behavior and interposes itself between their intentions and the outcomes of their actions" (Ruggie 1983).

Implications of Systemic Constraints. To neorealists, the structure of the system, rather than the characteristics of the units that comprise it, determines outcomes. Although neorealists recognize that states' goals sometimes "fluctuate with the changing currents of domestic politics, are prey to the vagaries of a shifting cast of political leaders, and are influenced by the outcomes of bureaucratic struggles," they contend that such factors as whether governments are democracies or dictatorships tell little about the process whereby states come to pursue the goal of balancing power with power. Instead, "structural constraints explain why the [same] methods are repeatedly used despite differences in the persons and states who use them" (Waltz 1979).

> In its stress on the structure of the international system, that is, the state of anarchy among sovereign states, [neo]realism attaches little or no importance to what is going on inside states—what kind of regimes are in power, what kind of ideologies prevail, what kind of leadership is provided. According to [neo]realists, the foreign policies of all states are basically driven by the same systemic factors—they are like so many billiard balls, obeying the same laws of political geometry and physics. (Harries 1995, 13)

Neorealist theory also helps to explain why the prospects for international cooperation and change often appear so dim and why states are naturally wary of others and strive to compete. The anarchical structure of the system compels states to be sensitive to their *relative position* in the distribution of power.

> When faced with the possibility of cooperating for mutual gain, states that feel insecure must ask how the gain will be divided. They are compelled to ask not "Will both of us gain?" but "Who will gain more?" If an expected gain is to be divided, say, in the ratio of two to one, one state may use its disproportionate gain to implement a policy intended to damage or destroy the other. Even the prospect of large absolute gains for both parties does not elicit their cooperation so long as each fears how the other will use its increased capabilities. (Waltz 1979, 105; see also Snidal 1993)

Impediments to cooperation thus result not from the parties' attitudes toward potential collaborative efforts, but rather from the insecurity that the anarchical system breeds. "The condition of insecurity—at the least, the uncertainty of each about the other's future intentions and actions—works against their cooperation" (Waltz 1979), as does states' fear of dependence on others.

Not everyone, however, agrees that the prospects for international cooperation are so remote. Some liberals acknowledge that although conflict among states has been endemic throughout much of world history, so has international cooperation; they point out that the record suggests that patterns can change and that increased interdependence can lead to even higher levels of cooperation. This expectation lies behind the so-called neoliberal challenge to realism and neorealism which has arisen recently (see Baldwin 1993; Kegley 1995).

Neoliberalism

As the Cold War ended, dissatisfaction with realism and neorealism began to rise. Arguing that it was time for a new, more rigorous idealist alternative to realism, critics pointed to several shortcomings: (1) power-politics perspectives failed to predict the peaceful end of the Cold War and international social change in general; (2) research suggested that the "underlying theory of war and peace [of realism and neorealism was] flawed" (Vasquez 1993) because realists "oversimplified the concept of power and misunderstood the lessons of history" (Kober 1990); and (3) it appeared that realism's approach would "not be an adequate guide for the future of international politics" (Jervis 1992), because the broadened post-Cold War global agenda included many questions and problems "which realist theory could not reach" (Scholte 1993). The problems of AIDS, ecological deterioration, economic underdevelopment, and global warming were among those for which realism was seen deficient.

Asking "Is realism finished?" (Zakaria 1992–93), these critics contended that there was a need to rethink neorealism since they perceived it to be "a research enterprise in crisis" (James 1993). But they went beyond this prescription by advocating that "the recovery of liberalism" (Little 1993) be treated as a theoretical goal in international relations. This view gained a following among policymakers. For example, in accord with Francis Fukuyama's conclusion (1992b) that there were "good reasons for examining aspects of the liberal international legacy once again," U.S. President Bill Clinton in 1995 maintained that "In a world where freedom, not tyranny, is on the march, the cynical calculus of pure power politics simply does not compute. It is ill-suited to the new era." In light of this growing sentiment, in the early 1990s emerged **neoliberalism,** a new approach to world politics which concentrates on the ways that international organizations and other nonstate actors promote international cooperation.[7]

Neoliberalism seeks to build theories of international relations by giving the basic tenets of classical liberalism and post-World War I idealism a fresh examination.[8] Taking heart in the international prohibition, through community con-

---

[7]This analytic departure goes by several labels, and is sometimes alternatively called "neoliberal institutionalism" (Grieco 1995), "neoidealism" (Kegley 1993), or "neo-Wilsonian idealism" (Fukuyama 1992a).

[8]Studies of regional integration—processes whereby sovereign states might be politically unified—began to flourish in the 1950s and 1960s, paving the way for the new liberal idealist theorists which emerged in the 1990s. Because the expansion of trade, communication, information, technology and immigrant labor propelled Europeans to sacrifice portions of their

sensus, of such previously entrenched practices as slavery, piracy, dueling, colonialism, and the slaughter of certain animals, neoliberalism emphasizes the prospects for progress, peace, and prosperity. It departs from neorealism on many assumptions and shifts the interpretation to explore the mechanisms by which such cooperation and change might be fostered (see Focus 2.2). In particular, neoliberalism focuses on the ways in which such influences as democratic governance, public opinion, mass education, free trade, liberal capitalism, international law and organization, arms control and disarmament, collective security and multilateral diplomacy, and ethically inspired statecraft can improve life on our planet. Because they perceive change in global conditions as progressing through cooperative efforts, neoliberal theorists maintain that the ideas and ideals of the liberal legacy today can describe, explain, predict, and prescribe international conduct in ways that they could not during the conflict-ridden Cold War.

Like realism and neorealism, neoliberalism does not represent a cohesive intellectual movement or school of thought (see Zacher and Matthew 1995 for an overview of the divergent stands within neoliberal theorizing). Neoliberals operate from different assumptions, examining different aspects of the processes through which international change and cooperation might be promoted. Some, like neorealists, embrace a structural theory which examines the characteristics of the international system. Others concentrate on the characteristics of the units and subunits that comprise it, such as the types of governments (democracies or dictatorships) and leaders who govern states. Still other neoliberals give primary attention to the influence of international institutions like the United Nations and nonstate actors like multinational corporations. All neoliberals, however, share an interest in probing the conditions under which the convergent and overlapping interests among otherwise sovereign political entities may result in cooperation.

To illuminate these similarities and differences among neoliberals, we will examine two theoretical perspectives which paved the way for neoliberalism's acceptance and are a part of its orientation: complex interdependence and international regimes. For the sake of brevity, we have selected only these two examples from among the many other neoliberal perspectives, such as the feminist critique of conventional theories in general and realism in particular (see Focus 2.3).

Complex Interdependence as a World View. As an explicit analytical perspective, **complex interdependence** arose in the 1970s to challenge the key assumptions of its rival theoretical framework, realism. Questioning the prevailing assumption that states are the only important actors in world politics, it treated other actors, such as multinational corporations and transnational banks, as "important not only because of their activities in pursuit of their own interests, but also because they act as transmission belts, making government policies in various countries more sensitive to one another" (Keohane and Nye 1988). In this sense complex interdependence is a holistic, systemic conception which views world politics as the sum of its many interacting parts in a "global society" (see O. Holsti 1995).

The complex interdependence school also questioned whether national security issues were truly dominant in states' decision-making agendas. Under conditions of states' mutual vulnerability, it seemed that their foreign policy

sovereign independence in order to create a new political community out of previously separate units (see Chapters 6 and 16) and these developments were outside of realism's world view, they called for a theory grounded in the liberal tradition to explain them.

Point-Counterpoint
The Debate between Neoliberalism and Neorealism

According to David Baldwin (1993, 4–8): six focal points characterize the current debate between neoliberalism and neorealism:

- *The Nature and Consequences of Anarchy.* Although no one denies that the international system is anarchical in some sense, there is disagreement as to what this means and why it matters. . . .
- *International Cooperation.* Although both sides agree that international cooperation is possible, they differ as to the ease and likelihood of its occurrence. . . .
- *Relative versus Absolute Gains.* Although it would be misleading to characterize one side as concerned with relative gains and the other as concerned only with absolute gains, neoliberals have stressed the absolute gains [and common interests] from international cooperation, while neorealists have emphasized relative gains [by assuming that actors will ask, "Who will gain more?"].

- *Priority of State Goals.* Neoliberals and neorealists agree that both national security and economic welfare are important, but they differ in relative emphasis on these goals [with neoliberals stressing the latter and neorealists the former].
- *Intentions versus Capabilities.* Contemporary neorealists . . . emphasize capabilities more than intentions [whereas neoliberals emphasize] intentions, interests, and information [instead of] the distribution of capabilities. . . .
- *Institutions and Regimes.* Both neorealists and neoliberals recognize the multitude of international regimes and institutions that have emerged since 1945. They differ, however, with respect to the significance of such arrangements. . . .

Looking at the world, which set of assumptions seems to be the most accurate lens for interpreting contemporary world politics?

---

agendas had become "larger and more diverse," because a broader range of "governments' policies, even those previously considered merely domestic, impinge[d] on one another" (Keohane and Nye 1988).

In addition, this perspective disputed the popular notion that military force is the only means of exercising influence in international politics, particularly among the industrial and democratic societies in Europe and North America. "Intense relationships of mutual influence exist between these countries, but in most of them force is irrelevant or unimportant as an instrument of policy" (Keohane and Nye 1988).

Advocates of the complex-interdependence perspective extended many of these insights to the issues concerning international economic interdependence that arose during the 1970s and, later, to environmental protection. International institutions commanded a central place in many of these analyses, as demonstrated in Robert O. Keohane and Joseph S. Nye's (1977, 1989) *Power and Interdependence,* the classic statement on the complex-interdependence extension of liberalism. A careful reading of the work reveals that this perspective does not altogether reject realism. Rather, the initial concern of its adherents was "the conditions under which the assumptions of realism were sufficient or needed to be supplemented by a more complex model of change" (Nye 1987; see also Keohane 1983). Keohane and Nye sought in particular to account for **international regimes,** or the norms and rules for behavior that are created when cooperation becomes institutionalized and actors expect them to be followed (see Krasner 1982). Complex interdependence eventually became a central component of the neoliberal perspective and has been used widely in analyses of international pol-

32

What's Wrong with International Relations Theory?
The Feminist Critique

Feminist theory, a body of scholarship that emphasizes gender in the study of world politics, arose in the 1960s in response to the pronounced disregard of females in discussions about public and international affairs and the injustice and inequality that this prejudice caused. The mainstream literature on world politics underestimated or ignored the contributions of women, treating differences in men's and women's status, beliefs, and behaviors as unimportant. Gender roles were also ignored, along with the evidence that sexism is a pillar of the war system (Reardon 1985) and that a remedy for this problem might be to give women the prominence and power in policy making that traditionally they have been denied (see Beckman and D'Amico 1994; Peterson and Runyan 1993).

As feminist theory crystallized, it moved away from focusing on a history of discrimination against women and began to direct much of its criticism at realism. In particular, many gender studies alleged that realism, formulated and dominated by males, ignored the human roots of global conditions and promoted an essentially masculine interpretation of international relations that was inattentive to human rights and rife with rationales for aggression.

Derived in part from liberal principles supportive of fair play, justice, and the philosophical acceptance of love over power, feminist theory moved beyond this initial critique of realism's bias to chart an independent theoretical course (Keohane 1989). This perspective has focused on the performance of women as leaders of government and as members of infantry combat units (Grant and Newland 1991), as well as on theoretical explorations of the plight of women in business and in the Global South.

Perhaps the greatest impact of feminist theory in the field of international relations, however, has been its rejection of the realist preoccupation with states' military strategies in favor of developing strategies for world security (see Tickner 1992). In this sense, feminist theory, like neoliberalism generally, is motivated by the quest for discovering the paths to greater international cooperation. In liberating conventional theory from its narrow focus, can feminist theory open a window on the full range of international activity and point the way toward a fuller appreciation of the ways human beings influence the global condition?

---

itics that seek to understand states' willingness to enter into cooperative agreements with one another under conditions of anarchy and fears of dependence and exploitation (Nye 1988).

International Regimes. Although the international system is still characterized by anarchy, its nature is more properly conceptualized as an ordered anarchy, and the system as a whole as an "anarchical society" (Bull 1977), because cooperation, not conflict, is often the observable outcome of relations among states.

Given this reality, the question arises: How can institutionalized procedures and rules for the collective management of global policy problems—international regimes based on coordinated cooperation—be established and preserved? Interest in this question derives from two goals: first, "a desire to understand the extent to which mutually accepted constraints affect states' behaviors" (Zacher 1987), and second, an interest in devising strategies for creating a less disorderly "world order."

Regimes are institutionalized or regularized patterns of cooperation in a given issue-area, as reflected by the rules that make a pattern predictable. As Stephen Krasner (1982) explains, "It is the infusion of behavior with principles and norms that distinguishes regime-governed activity in the international system from more conventional activity, guided exclusively by narrow calculations of interest." Thus, an essential property of a regime is that it constitutes "a sys-

MAP 2.1

**Regimes and the Transnational
Management of Global
Problems: Acid Rain**

Acid rain is a transboundary
pollutant which attacks
countries differently. Because it
knows no national boundaries
and its sources often lie abroad,
a solution to acid rain's
corrosive effects requires
international cooperation. The
rules of international *regimes*
help to enforce such
cooperation.

SOURCE: Adapted from Seager
(1995), 48–49.

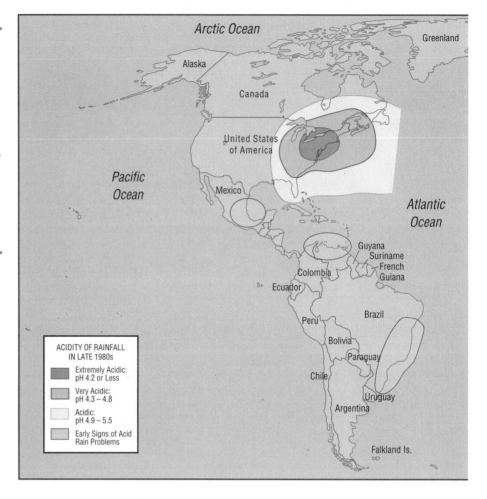

tem of injunctions about international behavior" (Smith 1987). Because the
international-regime perspective directs attention to institutions and to the ways
in which norms influence state behavior, as opposed simply to the pursuit of
national interests, it is perhaps best viewed as an attempt to reconcile the liberal
idealist and realist perspectives on world politics (Haggard and Simmons 1987).

The global monetary and trade rules created during and after World War II
are vivid examples of international regulatory regimes. These rules, as well as
particular sectors within the trade system, have been the focus of considerable
inquiry from the regime perspective. Together the monetary and trade regimes
comprised a *Liberal International Economic Order (LIEO)* which limited government intervention in the world political economy and otherwise facilitated
the free flow of capital and goods across national boundaries. The International Monetary Fund (IMF) and the General Agreement on Tariffs and Trade
(GATT) played important institutional roles in the LIEO and reconfirmed the
importance of international institutions in fostering transnational cooperation
(see Chapter 8 for elaboration).

Most illustrations of the regime perspective appear in the world political
economy arena; until recently relatively few "security regimes" (Jervis 1982) had
emerged in the defense issue-area. Early exceptions were the nuclear nonproliferation regime and the regime that the United States and the Soviet Union
used to manage their crises (see George 1986). With the end of the Cold War,

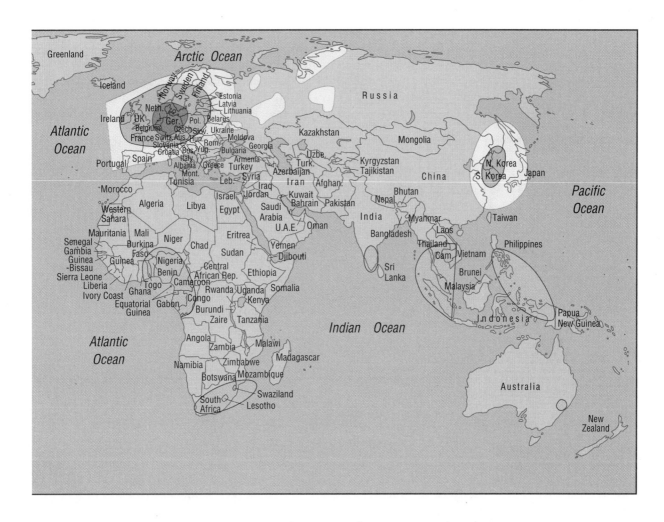

the pressures of interdependence may propel creation of regimes in widening areas of international conduct to facilitate states' control over their common fates (Zacher 1991). This is likely to accelerate efforts to grapple theoretically with the causes and consequences of multilateralism (see Caporaso 1992).

• • •

INTERNATIONAL POLITICS IN A WORLD OF CHANGE

To understand our changing world and to make reasonable prognoses about the future, we must begin by arming ourselves with an array of information and conceptual tools, entertaining rival interpretations of world politics, and questioning the assumptions on which these contending world views rest. Because there are several alternative, and sometimes incompatible, ways of organizing theoretical inquiry about world politics (see Table 2.1), the challenge of capturing the world's political problems cannot be reduced to any one simple yet compelling account. Each paradigmatic effort to do so has ultimately been abandoned as developments in world affairs eroded its continuing relevance. Although every generation has brought a new fad or two to theoretical inquiry, few have been able to provide lasting answers. Although grand theories usually do not look very grand with the passage of time, they often regain their attractiveness when global transformations make them useful once again for interpreting world politics.

Armed with the theories introduced in this chapter, we understand the importance of being sensitive to the diverse dimensions of world affairs, as well as the need for different theories to interpret aspects of international relations. Thus, we can now begin to address difficult questions. To determine which theories will best guide clear thinking, we turn, in Part II, to examine the actors in world politics.

As we proceed, it will be necessary to consider the magnitude of the challenge. The task of interpretation is complicated because the world is itself complex. As one scholar frames the challenge:

> Conceptually speaking, world affairs today can be likened to a disassembled jigsaw puzzle scattered on a table before us. Each piece shows a fragment of a broad picture that as yet remains indiscernible. Some pieces depict resurgent nationalism; others show spreading democracy; some picture genocide; others portray prosperity through trade and investment; some picture nuclear disarmament; others picture nuclear proliferation; some indicate a reinvigorated United Nations; others show the UN still enfeebled and ineffective; some describe cultural globalization; others predict clashing civilizations.
>
> How do these pieces fit together, and what picture do they exhibit when they are appropriately fitted? (Puchala 1994, 17)

TABLE 2.1   **The Quest for Theory: Four Perspectives**

Model	Liberal Idealism	Realism	Behavioralism	Neoliberalism
Core concern	Institutionalizing peace	War and security	Discovering through science "laws" about the causes and consequences of interstate interaction	Fostering interstate cooperation on the globe's shared economic, social, and ecological problems
Major submodel(s)	International law; international organization; democratization	Neorealism; structural realism	Comparative study of foreign policy; quantitative analysis	Complex interdependence and regimes
Outlook on global prospects	Optimistic/progress	Pessimistic/stability	Progress through reason	Expectation of cooperation and creation of a global community
Key units	Institutions transcending states	Independent states	Individuals, states, and the international system	Individuals; "penetrated" states and nonstate transnational actors
Motives of actors	Collaboration; mutual aid; meeting human needs	National interests; zero-sum competition; security; power	Rational choice, as modified by environmental opportunities and constraints	Global interests; justice; peace and prosperity; liberty; morality
Central concepts	Collective security; world order; law; integration; international organization	Structural anarchy; power; national interests; balance of power; polarity	Theory building and hypothesis testing with reproducible evidence and deductive modeling	Transnational relations; law; free markets; interdependence; integration; liberal republican rule; human rights; gender
Prescriptions	Institutional reform	Increase national power; resist reduction of national autonomy	Ground policy advice on verifiable knowledge	Develop regimes and promote democracy and international institutions to coordinate collective responses to diverse global problems

Theories can guide us in fitting the pieces together to form an accurate picture. However, in evaluating the usefulness of any theory to interpret global conditions, the historical review in this chapter suggests that it would be wrong to oversimplify or to assume that a particular theory—however useful at the moment—will remain useful in the future. All theories are maps of possible futures. However, as the American poet Robert Frost observed in 1911, any belief we cling to long enough is likely to be true again someday, because "Most of the change we think we see in life is due to truths being in and out of favor." So in our theoretical exploration of world politics, we must critically assess the accuracy of our impressions, avoiding the temptation to embrace one world view and abandon another without any assurance that their relative worth is permanently fixed.

● ● ●

KEY TERMS

paradigm	sovereignty
current history	behavioralism
theory	neorealism
idealism	postmodernism
collective security	positivism
self-determination	structural realism
realism	neoliberalism
realpolitik	complex interdependence
power	international regimes
self-help	feminist theory

CHAPTER 3

Foreign Policy Decision Making: Coping with International Circumstances

OUTLINE

- The Emergence of the Modern State System
- The International and Internal Determinants of Foreign Policy Behavior
- The Unitary Actor and Rational Decision Making
- The Bureaucratic Politics of Foreign Policy Decision Making
- The Role of Leaders in Foreign Policy Decision Making
- Constraints on Foreign Policy Making in a Transforming World:
  Problems and Prospects

Foreign policy is the system of activities evolved by communities for changing the behavior of other states and for adjusting their own activities to the international environment.

—GEORGE MODELSKI,
Political scientist, 1962

We can no longer afford a [policy-making] process that results in duplication or programs that work at cross purposes. . . . Simply put, if we are not clear about where we want to go and about our options for getting there, we will not fare well in the post-Cold War era.

—*U.S. Department of State,*
Management Task Force, 1993

$\mathbf{I}$n studying world politics we typically use the term **actor** to refer to entities that are its primary performers. These entities include countries (e.g., the United States and Japan), international organizations (the United Nations), multinational corporations (General Motors and Sony), "nongovernmental organizations" (Greenpeace), nonstate nations (the Kurds in Iran and Iraq), and terrorist groups (the Irish Republican Army). The image is that of a stage on which those most capable of capturing the drama of world politics act out the roles assigned to them. The leading actors dominate the center of the stage, and the supporting players are less evident as they move along the periphery.

Although we will discuss each type of actor in later chapters, here we focus on countries, usually called "states." We particularly emphasize the processes states use to make foreign policy decisions designed to cope with challenges from abroad. States demand attention because international law gives them status as the principal repositories of economic and military capabilities in world affairs, and assigns to them alone the legal right to use force.

• • •

THE EMERGENCE OF THE MODERN STATE SYSTEM

As a network of relationships among independent political units, the state system was born with the Peace of Westphalia in 1648, which ended the Thirty Years' War in Europe. Thereafter, European rulers refused to recognize the authority of the Roman Catholic church, replacing the previous system of papal governance with geographically and politically separate states which recognized no authority above them. The newly independent states were all given the same legal rights: territorial inviolability, the freedom to conduct foreign relations and negotiate treaties with other states, and the authority to establish whatever form of government they thought best and to rule their own population. The concept of sovereignty—that no one is above the state—captures these legal rights.

Whatever its advantages and disadvantages, the Westphalian system still colors every dimension of world politics, and provides the terminology used to describe the primary units in international affairs. Although the term "nation-state" is often confusingly used interchangeably with "state" and "nation," technically the three are different. A **state** is a legal entity that enjoys a permanent population, a well-defined territory, and a government capable of exercising sovereignty. A **nation** is a collection of people who, on the basis of ethnic, linguistic, or cultural affinity, perceive themselves to be members of the same group. Thus the term nation-state implies a convergence between territorial states and the psychological identification of people within them which is relatively rare, as there are few independent states comprised of a single nationality.[1]

When we speak generically about **foreign policy** and the decision-making processes that produce it, we mean the goals that officials representing states seek abroad, the values that underlie those goals, and the means or instruments used to pursue them. To begin our inquiry into how states make foreign policy choices, we first consider the environment to which national decision makers respond—the setting for their choices and the circumstances outside national borders that provoke the necessity for choice. Next we look at decision making as a *rational* process before considering two ways of viewing national decision making: the bureaucratic politics and the hero-in-history models. We conclude by examining how states' national attributes influence their foreign policy behavior.

• • •

THE INTERNATIONAL AND INTERNAL DETERMINANTS OF FOREIGN POLICY BEHAVIOR

Geostrategic location, military might, economic prowess, and system of government are all variables that affect foreign policy choice. Still, due to the diversity of states as well as their different locations and positions within the contemporary state system, it is difficult to generalize about the influence of any one factor or combination of factors.

To determine the relative impact of specific factors under different circumstances, we must first distinguish between the international and internal influences on policy choice (note the levels-of-analysis distinction pictured in Figure 3.1).[2] International or "external" influences on foreign policy include all activi-

---

[1]Most states are populated by many nations, and some nations are not states. These "nonstate nations" are ethnic groups, such as Native American tribes in the United States, Sikhs in India, or Basques in Spain, composed of people without sovereign power over the territory on which they live. Some seek national (ethnic) independence and/or merger with another state with which they feel greater solidarity. For this reason the ethnonational movements seeking self-determination and statehood are referred to as the "Fourth World." See Chapter 7 for a discussion of nonstate nations and ethnonational independence movements active throughout the world.

[2]In classifying the determinants not only of states' foreign policies but also of trends in world politics generally, the level-of-analysis concept introduced in Chapter 1 helps to clarify the presentation that will be used to describe the influences on states' decision-making processes. Recall that states and the international system comprise two distinct levels, the "national" level, encompassing domestic characteristics, and the "systemic" or international level, encompassing interstate relations and temporal changes in them. The possibility should not be ignored that these two traditionally discrete realms have become increasingly fused in what has become known as "intermestic politics" to highlight the integration of domestic and foreign policy. As the U.S. Department of State (1993, 79) observes, today "the assertion that 'all foreign policy is ultimately local' is closer to the mark than many in government admit."

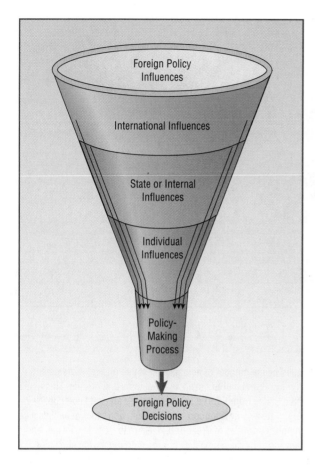

FIGURE 3.1

**The Major Sources of States' Foreign Policy Decisions:
Influences at Three Levels**

The factors that shape the foreign policies of states can be categorized at three basic levels. At the external level are those features of the international system, such as the prevalence of civil wars and the extent of trade interdependence, which condition the kinds of choices which a leader is likely to make. At the state level are internal or domestic influences, such as the state's type of political system or the opinions of its citizens, which impact on the kinds of foreign policy choices which the leader is likely to reach. At the individual level are the characteristics of the leader—his or her personal beliefs, values, and personality—which shape the leader's perceptions and the range of options contemplated. All three levels of influence simultaneously affect decisions, but their relative influence usually depends on the issues and circumstances at the time of decision.

SOURCE: Adapted from Kegley and Wittkopf (1996), 15.

ties occurring beyond a country's borders that structure the choices its officials make. Such factors as the content of international law, the number of military alliances, deterioration of the global environment, and the changing levels of international trade sometimes profoundly affect the choices of decision makers.

Internal or "domestic" influences, on the other hand, are those that exist at the level of the state, not the system. Here attention focuses on variations in **states' attributes,** such as military capabilities, level of economic development, and type of government, that may influence different states' foreign policy behavior. Examples of both types of influences follow.

Geopolitics

One of the most important influences on a state's foreign policy behavior is its location and physical terrain. The presence of natural frontiers, for example, may profoundly guide policymakers' choices (see Map 3.1). Consider the United States, which has prospered because vast oceans separate it from Europe and Asia. This advantage, combined with the absence of militarily powerful neighbors, permitted the United States to develop into an industrial giant and at times to practice safely an isolationist foreign policy without any immediate security threat for over 150 years. Consider also mountainous Switzerland, whose topography and geostrategic position have made the practice of neutrality a compelling foreign policy posture.

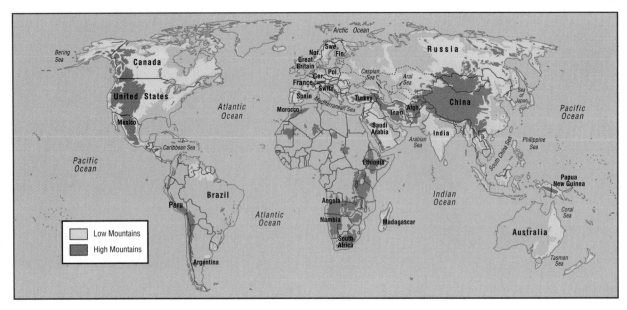

MAP 3.1

Geographic Influences on Foreign Policy

How countries act toward others is shaped by the number of neighboring states on their borders and whether they are protected from invasion by natural barriers such as mountains and oceans. This map suggests how the separation of the United States from Eurasia has encouraged an isolationist policy during many periods in America's history. Note also how topography, location, and other geopolitical factors may have influenced the foreign policy priorities of Great Britain, Germany, China, Finland, and states in South America—hypotheses advanced by the geopolitics approach to international politics.

Similarly, maintaining autonomy from continental politics has been an enduring theme in the foreign policy of Great Britain, an island country whose physical separation from Europe served historically as a buffer separating it from entanglement in major-power disputes on the continent. Preserving this protective shield has been a priority for Britain and helps to explain why the British government in the early 1990s resisted greater integration of its economy into the community of fifteen countries that comprised the European Union (see Chapters 6 and 16).

Most countries are not insular, however; they have many states on their borders, denying them the option of noninvolvement in world affairs. Germany, which sits in the geographic center of Europe, historically has found its domestic political system and foreign policy preferences profoundly affected by its geostrategic position. In this century alone, even before the unification of East and West, Germany had "undergone five radical changes in political personality—from Wilhelm II's empire to the Weimar Republic, from Hitler's *Reich* of the Thousand Years to its two postwar successors, the Federal Republic of Germany . . . and the German Democratic Republic" (Joffe 1985). Significantly, these changes have been tied directly to the geopolitical aspects of war, the five noted above by lethal wars and the sixth—unification—by a Cold War, whose conclusion made possible the peaceful absorption of communist East Germany into West Germany's capitalistic democracy.

In much the same way, extended frontiers with the former Soviet Union shaped the foreign policies of China and Finland. Finland's neutrality in the Cold War contest between the United States and the Soviet Union helped ensure its survival in the face of a powerful and threatening neighbor. China, on the other hand, has long regarded its relationship with the (now defunct) Soviet Union as unequal, and in the late 1960s the two communist giants clashed militarily as the Chinese sought to rectify past injustices. The "unequal treaties" between China and outside powers, which encapsulate these perceived injustices, resulted in part from China's size and location, which made it an easy target for the great powers that had carved it into spheres of influence with relative ease in previous centuries.

Like China, the Latin American countries have found themselves geographically near a much stronger power, the United States, whose capabilities are in part a function of geophysical resource endowments. Latin America has long been the object of studied interest and frequent intervention by the giant to the north. Economic dependence on the United States has given rise to an understandable concern for Yankee **imperialism**—what Egypt's President Nasser defined as "the subjugation of small nations to the interests of the big ones"—which has been a continuing theme in many Latin American states' foreign policies. In this sense the countries of Latin America share a concern with other states that find themselves unable to compete on an equal footing with the world's more advantaged powers.

History is replete with many other examples of geography's influence on states' foreign policy goals, which is why geopolitical theories are useful (see Demko and Wood 1994). The **geopolitics** school of realist thought and political geography generally stresses the influence of geographic factors on state power and international conduct.[3] The underlying principle behind the geopolitical perspective is self-evident: Leaders' perceptions of available foreign policy options are influenced by the geopolitical circumstances that define their states' place on the world stage.

Geopolitics is only one aspect of the external environment that may influence foreign policy. Additional external factors that intertwine to shape states' foreign policy behavior include the characteristics of other states and changes in their relative position in the international hierarchy of power and prestige. In other chapters we will discuss these influences. Here, we comment briefly on three internal attributes of states that influence their foreign policies: military capabilities, economic development, and type of government.

Military Capabilities

The proposition that states' internal capabilities shape their foreign policy priorities is captured by the demonstrable fact that states' preparations for war strongly influence their later use of force (see Levy 1989a; Vasquez 1993). Thus

---

[3]Illustrative of the early geopolitical thinking is Alfred Thayer Mahan's (1890) *The Influence of Sea Power in History,* which maintained that control of the seas shaped national power. Thus states with extensive coastlines and ports purportedly enjoyed a competitive advantage in the race for hegemony or global leadership. Later geopoliticians, such as Sir Halford Mackinder (1919) and Nicholas Spykman (1944), stressed that not only location but topography, size (territory and population), climate, and distance between states are powerful determinants of the foreign policies of individual countries.

Iraqi dictator Saddam Hussein in 1990 used his country's formidable military capabilities to invade Kuwait. He was later repelled by the superior force of nearly 40 states, led by the United States in Operation Desert Storm. The case suggests the lesson that the power to destroy does not necessarily give an aggressor the power to control or get its way.

while all states may seek similar goals, their ability to realize them will vary according to their military capabilities.

Because military capabilities limit a state's range of prudent policy choices, they act as a mediating factor on leaders' national security decisions. For instance, in the 1980s Libyan leader Muammar Qaddafi repeatedly provoked the United States through anti-American and anti-Israeli rhetoric and by supporting various terrorist activities. Qaddafi was able to act according to his personal preferences largely because neither bureaucratic organizations nor a mobilized public existed in Libya to constrain his personal whims and militaristic foreign policy preferences. However, Qaddafi was doubtlessly more highly constrained by the outside world than were the leaders in the more militarily capable countries toward whom his anger was directed. Limited military muscle compared with the United States precluded the kinds of bellicose behaviors he threatened to practice.

Conversely, Saddam Hussein, the Iraqi dictator, made strenuous efforts to build Iraq's military might (partly with the help of U.S. arms sales) and by 1990 had built the fourth-largest army in the world. Thus the invasion of Kuwait became a feasible foreign policy option. In the end, however, even Iraq's impressive military power proved ineffective against a vastly superior coalition of military forces, headed by the United States, which forced Saddam Hussein to capitulate and withdraw from the conquered territory.

Economic Development

The level of economic and industrial development a state enjoys affects the foreign policy goals it can pursue. Generally, the more economically developed a state is, the more likely it is to play an activist role in the world political economy. Rich states have interests that extend far beyond their borders and typically possess the means necessary to pursue and protect them. Not coincidentally, states that enjoy industrial capabilities and extensive involvement in international trade also tend to be militarily powerful—in part because military might is a function of economic capabilities. Historically, only the world's most scientifically sophisticated industrial economies have produced nuclear weapons, which many regard as the ultimate expression of military prowess. In this sense nuclear weapons are the *result* of being powerful, not its cause.

For four decades after World War II, the United States and the Soviet Union stood out as superpowers precisely because they benefited from a combination of vast economic and military capabilities, including extensive arsenals of nuclear weapons and the means to deliver them anywhere. This enabled both states to practice unrestrained globalism; their "imperial reach" and interventionist behavior were seemingly unconstrained by limited wealth or resources. In fact, major powers (rich states) have been involved in foreign conflict more frequently than minor powers (poor states). For this reason gross national product (GNP) is often used in combination with other factors to distinguish great powers from middle-ranked or minor powers, and by itself is an important element of state capability predicting the extensiveness of states' global interests and involvements.

Although economically advanced states are more active globally, this does not mean that their privileged circumstances dictate adventuresome policies. Rich states are often "satisfied" ones, which have much to lose from the onset of revolutionary change or global instability and which usually perceive the status quo as best serving their interests (Wolfers 1962). As a result, they often forge international economic policies to protect and expand their envied position at the pinnacle of the global hierarchy.

Levels of productivity and prosperity also affect the foreign policies of the poor states at the bottom of the hierarchy. Some dependent states respond to their economic weakness by complying subserviently with the wishes of the rich on whom they depend. Others rebel defiantly, sometimes succeeding (despite their disadvantaged bargaining position) in resisting major-power efforts to control their international behavior.

Thus efforts to generalize about the economic foundations of states' international political behavior often prove unrewarding. Although levels of economic development vary widely among states in the international system, they alone do not determine foreign policies. Instead, leaders' *perceptions* of the opportunities and constraints that their states' economic resources provide may be a powerful determining influence on their foreign policy choices.

Type of Government

A third important attribute affecting states' international behavior is their political system. Although neorealism would predict otherwise, type of government demonstrably constrains important choices, including whether the use of force is threatened and whether the threat is carried out (Nincic 1992). Here the important distinction is between **constitutional democracy** (representative government) on one end of the spectrum and **autocratic rule** (authoritarian or totalitarian) on the other.

In neither democratic (sometimes called "open") nor autocratic ("closed") political systems can political leaders long survive without the support of organized domestic political interests (and sometimes the mass citizenry). But in democratic systems those interests are likely to be politically potent, dispersed beyond the government itself, and active in their pressure on the government to make policy choices that benefit them. Public opinion, interest groups, and the mass media are more visibly a part of the policy making process in democratic systems, with the public participating openly in an effort to penetrate and influence the government's policies in ways that closed political systems actively prevent. Similarly, the electoral process in democratic societies more meaningfully frames choices and produces results about who will lead than typically occurs in authoritarian regimes, where the real choices are made by a few elites behind closed doors. In short, in a democracy public opinions and preferences matter and, therefore, differences in who is allowed to participate and how much they exercise their right to participate are critical determinants of foreign policy choice (see Ray 1995; Russett 1993).

Compare, for example, the foreign policy of Saudi Arabia, controlled by a king and royal family, with that of Switzerland, governed by a multiparty democratic process. In the former, foreign policy decisions sometimes have been bold and unexpected, as exemplified by the Saudi royal family's revolutionary policies in summoning U.S. military forces to its territory during the 1991 Persian Gulf War, in contravention of long-standing Arab policies designed to prevent Western encroachments against Muslim lands. In Switzerland, where voting and mass political participation heavily influences decisions about Switzerland's international activities, the policy of neutrality has been pursued without deviation since 1815.

Although public preferences help shape democratic societies' foreign policies, so too does **elitism** (Mills 1956). Often, even in democratic governments, decisions are made by a small ruling elite; this is especially true when international crises erupt. Military-industrial complexes, obtrusively evident in many countries, are examples of elite groups sometimes believed to exercise disproportionate control over defense policy making, in both turbulent and calm times. Elitism's rival model, known as **pluralism,** sees policy making as an upward-flowing process in which competitive domestic groups pressure the government for policies responsive to their interests and needs. Pluralism is a peculiarly democratic phenomenon that is widespread even if its effects are sometimes difficult to pinpoint.

Foreign Policy Performance in Democracies. The proposition that domestic stimuli, and not simply international events, are a source of foreign policy is not novel. In ancient Greece, for instance, the realist historian Thucydides observed that what happened within the Greek city-states often did more to shape their external behavior than what each did to the others. He added that Greek leaders frequently concentrated their efforts on influencing the political climate within their own polities rather than on managing relations with other Greek city-states. Similarly, leaders today sometimes make foreign policy decisions for domestic political purposes—as, for example, when bold or aggressive acts abroad are intended to influence election outcomes at home or to divert public attention from economic woes.[4]

---

[4]Of interest here is the "scapegoat" phenomenon, according to which even democratic leaders provoke war and crises abroad to distract their populations from economic and political problems at home. For an examination of the scapegoat phenomenon and the "diversionary theory of war," see Levy (1989b).

Some see the intrusion of domestic politics into foreign policy making as a disadvantage of democratic political systems which undermines their ability to deal decisively with foreign policy crises or to bargain effectively with less-democratic adversaries and allies. As the French political sociologist Alexis de Tocqueville (1969 [1835]) put it more than a century ago, democracies are "decidedly inferior" to centralized governments in the management of foreign relations because they are prone to "impulse rather than prudence." Democracies, so this reasoning goes, are slow to respond to external dangers but, once they are recognized, tend to overreact to them (see Focus 3.1). "There are two things that a democratic people will always find difficult," de Tocqueville mused, "to start a war and to end it." In contrast, authoritarian regimes can "make decisions more rapidly, ensure domestic compliance with their decisions, and perhaps be more consistent in their foreign policy" (Jensen 1982). But there is a cost: "Authoritarian regimes often are less effective in developing an innovative foreign policy because of subordinates' pervasive fear of raising questions." In short, the concentration of power and the suppression of public opposition can be dangerous as well as advantageous.

The Spread of Democracy and Its Consequences. The impact of regime type on foreign policy is likely to take on added significance in the post-Cold War world, as democracies have sprung up where they have never before existed. Between 1974 and 1980, more than thirty countries converted their governments from dictatorial to democratic rule. This pace accelerated during the 1980s in democratization's "third wave" (Jaggers and Gurr, 1995). By 1992, more than half the world's governments were, for the first time, democratic (see Map 3.2). Although modest reversals have been evident since 1993 and Russia's commitment to democratization was in doubt in 1996, the long-term global trend toward democratization appears to be entrenched (Jaggers and Gurr, 1995).

As the tide of freedom spread, speculation arose as to its long-term impact. Francis Fukuyama (1989), a high-level official in the U.S. State Department, predicted that "we may be witnessing . . . the end of mankind's ideological evolution and the universalization of Western liberal democracy as the final form of government." The contagious expansion of democratic states could end, of course, because many of these fledgling new democracies are fragile, and some are faltering. If they do survive, however, and if new democratic governments take root elsewhere, a transformation of the international system of the twenty-first-century could occur.

Because changes in domestic political regimes often precede changes in foreign policy behavior (see Rosati, Hagan, and Sampson 1994), the recent growth of democracy has provoked neoliberals to predict that a world increasingly dominated by democratic governments will be a more peaceful one. Their reasons for this prophecy vary. Yet most rely on the logic of Immanuel Kant in his 1795 treatise, *Perpetual Peace*. In this pioneering liberal theoretical statement, Kant posited that democracies are inherently less warlike than autocracies because under republican rule leaders are accountable to the public, thus restraining democracies from waging war. Because ordinary citizens would have to supply the soldiers and bear the human and financial costs of imperial policies, he contended, liberal democracies are "natural" forces for peace.

The liberal idealist paradigm (recall Chapter 2) provides theoretical support for this prediction, and empirical evidence buttresses it. Whereas democracies experience as many wars as nondemocratic polities (Small and Singer

Democracies in Foreign Affairs
A U.S. Policymaker's Characterization

A leading American policymaker and realist political scientist, George F. Kennan, advanced the following thesis:

> I sometimes wonder whether a democracy is not uncomfortably similar to one of those prehistoric monsters with a body as long as this room and a brain the size of a pin: He lies there in his comfortable primeval mud and pays little attention to his environment; he is slow to wrath—in fact, you practically have to whack his tail off to make him aware that his interests are being disturbed; but, once he grasps this, he lays about him with such blind determination that he not only destroys his adversary but largely wrecks his native habitat. You wonder whether it would not have been wiser for him to have taken a little more interest in what was going on at an earlier date and to have seen whether he could not have prevented some of these situations from arising instead of proceeding from an undiscriminating indifference to a holy wrath equally undiscriminating. (Kennan 1951, 59)

To be questioned here is the realist thesis that democracies are decidedly inferior to nondemocratic regimes. Does the nature of democratic rule help or hinder those governments' capacities to realize their goals under anarchy?

1976), democracies almost never initiate wars against one another (Doyle 1995; Ray 1995; Russett 1993). In addition, they are prone to mediate their disputes (Dixon 1994; Raymond 1994) and to seek one another as alliance partners (Siverson and Emmons 1991)—a communitarian effect evident since World War II which arguably has contributed to the claim that "we have not had a real war between democracies in over a century and a half" (Rummel 1983, 48). Consequently, if democracy continues to spread, this trend may be critically important to the future preservation of international peace.[5]

These observations about the ways in which states' attributes relate to their foreign policy–making processes highlight the extent to which internal conditions influence the foreign policy choices of even great powers (see Snyder 1991). Contrary to realism's premise, the record shows that the type of government, and more specifically whether leaders are answerable to the public, strongly influences the kinds of goals states pursue abroad. Citizens' freedom clearly constrains their leaders' choices and influences liberal democracies' pattern of inter-

---

[5]However, we must be careful not to assume that the historically tight linkage between democracy and peace will necessarily hold in the future. As Samuel Huntington (1989) warns, "The 'democratic zone of peace' argument is valid as far as it goes, but may not go all that far." Democracies are prone to aggression during times of economic and domestic crisis (Morgan and Campbell 1991), and important exceptions exist to the general rule that democratic regimes are less bellicose (Wright 1942). In addition, the record of democratic states' active participation in colonial wars undermines liberal idealism's expectation that democratic rule is an antidote to imperialism (see Chan 1984). So, too, does democratic states' frequent practice of military intervention short of war (Kegley and Hermann 1996). Indeed, critics note that the longest surviving democracy, the United States, initiated or supported military or paramilitary actions against elected governments in Chile, Grenada, Nicaragua, and Panama, and that Hitler came to power through the ballot, only to wage the most destructive war in history. Consequently we must suspend judgment on the question of whether a world of democracies will necessarily be a more peaceful world.

1955

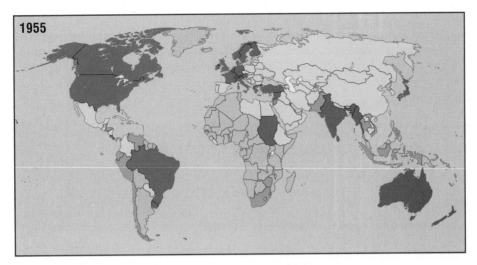

- ■ Democracy
- ▨ Anocracy (Quasi Democracy)
- ▢ Autocracy
- ▦ No Data

1985

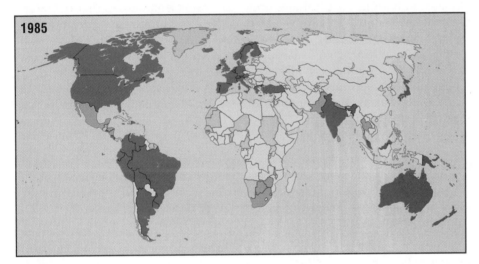

1992

MAP 3.2

The Diffusion of Democracy

Throughout most of modern history, the majority of states were ruled autocratically. As this map shows, since the mid-1950s an increasing number of states have undertaken political reforms leading to transitions away from autocratic and toward democratic rule (with "anocracies" or quasi-democracies wavering between the extremes). Liberal theory maintains that the spread of democracy will produce more peaceful relations between members of the growing community of liberal democracies.

SOURCE: Polity III data set (Jaggers and Gurr 1995). Graphics adapted from John O'Loughlin, Michael Don Ward, and Michael Shin at the University of Colorado.

national interactions. Many developments in world politics examined in later chapters will draw further attention to the internal roots of external behavior.

Having described the international settings to which policymakers respond and the internal factors that influence their decisions, we now turn to examine *how* foreign policy decisions are reached. We begin with the rational model of decision making.

• • •

THE UNITARY ACTOR AND RATIONAL DECISION MAKING

According to the theory of realism, the primary goal of states' foreign policies is to ensure their survival. From this viewpoint, strategic calculations about national security are the primary determinants of policymakers' choices. Domestic politics and the process of policy making itself are of secondary concern.

States as Unitary Actors

Realism, in both its classical and neorealist forms, emphasizes that the international environment determines state action. It assumes that foreign policy making consists primarily of adjusting the state to the pressures of a world system without global governance whose essential properties will not vary. Accordingly, it presumes that all states and the individuals responsible for their foreign policies confront the problem of national survival in similar ways. Thus all decision makers are essentially alike in their approach to foreign policy making:

> If they follow the [decision] rules, we need know nothing more about them. In essence, if the decision maker behaves rationally, the observer, knowing the rules of rationality, can rehearse the decisional process in his own mind, and, if he knows the decision maker's goals, can both predict the decision and understand why that particular decision was made. (Verba 1969, 225)

Because realists believe the goals and corresponding approach of leaders to foreign policy choices are the same, the decision-making processes of each state can be studied as though it were a **unitary actor**—a homogeneous or monolithic unit with few or no important differences within the state unit that affect its choices. One way to picture this assumption is to think of states as billiard balls and the table on which they interact as the state system. The balls (states) continuously clash and collide with one another, and the actions of each are determined by its interactions with the others, not by what occurs inside it. According to this realist view, the leaders who make foreign policy, the types of governments they head, the characteristics of their societies, and the internal economic and political conditions of the states they lead are unimportant.

Policy Making as Rational Choice

The decision-making processes of unitary actors that determine definitions of national interests are typically described as rational. For our purposes, we can define **rationality** or **rational choice** as purposeful, goal-directed behavior exhibited when "the individual responding to an international event . . . uses the best information available and chooses from the universe of possible responses that alternative most likely to maximize his [or her] goals" (Verba 1969). Scholars who study decision making and advise policymakers on ways to improve their policy-making skills describe rationality as a sequence of decision-making activities involving the following intellectual steps:

1. *Problem recognition and definition.* The need to decide begins when policy-makers perceive an external problem with which they must deal and attempt to define objectively its distinguishing characteristics. Objectivity requires full information about the actions, motivations, and capabilities of other actors as well as the character of the international environment and trends within it. The search for information must be exhaustive, and all the facts relevant to the problem must be gathered.

2. *Goal selection.* Next, those responsible for making foreign policy choices must determine what they want to accomplish. This disarmingly simple requirement is often difficult. It requires the identification and ranking of *all* values (such as security, democracy, and economic well-being) in a hierarchy from most to least preferred.

3. *Identification of alternatives.* Rationality also requires the compilation of an exhaustive list of *all* available policy options and an estimate of the costs associated with each alternative course of action.

4. *Choice.* Finally, rationality requires selecting from competing options the single alternative with the best chance of achieving the desired goal(s). For this purpose, policymakers must conduct a rigorous means-ends, cost-benefit analysis guided by an accurate prediction of the probable success of each option.[6]

The requirements of perfect rationality are stringent. Nonetheless, policy-makers often describe their own behavior as resulting from a rational decision-making process designed to reach the "best" decision possible. Moreover, some past foreign policy decisions reveal elements of this idealized process.

The 1962 Cuban missile crisis, for example, illustrates several ways in which the deliberations of the key U.S. policymakers conformed to a rational process (Allison 1971; for a reassessment, see Nathan 1992). Once Washington discovered the presence of Soviet missiles in Cuba, President John F. Kennedy formed a crisis decision-making group and charged it to "set aside all other tasks to make a prompt and intensive survey of the dangers and all possible courses of action." Six options were ultimately identified: Do nothing; exert diplomatic pressure; make a secret approach to the Cuban leader Fidel Castro; invade Cuba; launch a surgical air strike against the missiles; or blockade Cuba. Before the group could choose among these six, it had to prioritize goals. Was removal of the Soviet missiles, retaliation against Castro, or maintaining the balance of power the objective? Or did the missiles pose little

---

[6]The concept of rationality has been defined in different ways. At this point we employ a "procedural" definition of rationality. Later we will contrast it to the "instrumentalist" definition used in rational-choice theory, which is better suited to individuals than to the policy-making process whereby organizations make foreign policy choices and which is often derived from mathematical cost-benefit analyses (see Bueno de Mesquita and Lalman 1992; Levy 1990–91; and Nicholson 1992).

threat to vital U.S. interests? Until the missiles were determined to pose a serious threat to national security, "do nothing" could not be eliminated as an option.

Once the advisers agreed that their goal was removing the missiles, their discussion turned to evaluating the options of a surgical air strike or a blockade. They eventually chose the latter because of its presumed advantages, including the demonstration of firmness it permitted the United States and the flexibility about further choices it allowed both parties.

The decision of President George Bush to send a military force to the Middle East following Iraq's invasion of Kuwait on August 2, 1990, is another example of crisis decision making that conforms in part to the model of rational choice. As in the Cuban case, the "do nothing" option was quickly dismissed by the president and his advisers. Instead, "much of the initial debate among senior government officials on August 2 and 3 focused on diplomatic and economic retaliation against Iraq, and possible covert action to destabilize and topple Saddam Hussein" (Woodward and Atkinson 1990). By August 4, Bush decided to mount a military response. Two days later, after vowing that Iraq's invasion of Kuwait "will not stand," he ordered the dispatch of U.S. troops to pursue three missions: to deter further Iraqi aggression, to defend Saudi Arabia, and to "improve the overall defense capabilities of the Saudi peninsula" (Woodward and Atkinson 1990). Eventually, those defensive missions gave way to an offensive one designed to force Iraq out of Kuwait.

Impediments to Rational Choice

Despite the apparent application of rationality in these crises, rational choice is often more an idealized standard used to evaluate preferences than an accurate description of real-world behavior. Theodore Sorensen—one of President Kennedy's closest advisers and speechwriters, and a participant in the Cuban missile deliberations—has written not only about the steps policymakers in the Kennedy administration followed as they sought to emulate the process of rational choice[7] but also of how actual decision making often departed from it:

> Each step cannot be taken in order. The facts may be in doubt or dispute. Several policies, all good, may conflict. Several means, all bad, may be all that are open. Value judgments may differ. Stated goals may be imprecise. There may be many interpretations of what is right, what is possible, and what is in the national interest. (Sorensen 1963, 19–20)

Despite the virtues rational choice promises, the impediments to its realization are substantial. Some are human, deriving from deficiencies in the intelligence, capability, and psychological needs and aspirations of those who make foreign policy decisions under conditions of uncertainty. Others are organizational, since most decisions require group agreement about the national interest and the wisest course of action to pursue. Reaching agreement is not

---

[7]Sorensen (1963) described an eight-step process for policy making that is consistent with the model we have described: (1) agreeing on the facts; (2) agreeing on the overall policy objective; (3) precisely defining the problems; (4) canvassing all possible solutions; (5) listing the possible consequences that flow from each solution; (6) recommending one option; (7) communicating the option selected; (8) providing for its execution.

easy, however, as reasonable people with different values often disagree about goals, preferences, and the probable results of alternative options. Thus the impediments to sound (rational) policy making are not to be underestimated.

Scrutiny of the actual process of decision making reveals other hindrances. Available information is often insufficient to recognize emergent problems accurately, resulting in decisions made on the basis of incomplete information. In fact, rationality is usually "bounded" (Simon 1982), not "comprehensive," as policymakers must deal with approximations of perfect information. Moreover, the available information is often inaccurate, because the bureaucratic organizations on which political leaders depend for advice screen, sort, and rearrange it.

In addition, determining what goals best serve the national interest is difficult: "Decision making often takes place within an atmosphere marked by value-complexity and uncertainty. The existence of competing values about a single issue forces value trade-offs; uncertainty refers to the absence of complete and well-organized information on which to base a confident policy choice" (Walker 1991).

Furthermore, decision makers' inability to gather and digest large quantities of information rapidly constrains their capacity to make informed choices. Because policymakers work with overloaded agendas and short deadlines, the search for policy options is seldom exhaustive. "There is little time for leaders to reflect," observes former U.S. Secretary of State Henry Kissinger (1979). "They are locked in an endless battle in which the urgent constantly gains on the important. The public life of every political figure is a continual struggle to rescue an element of choice from the pressure of circumstance." In the choice phase, then, decision makers rarely make value-maximizing choices. Instead of selecting the one option or set of options with the best chance of success, they typically end their evaluation as soon as an alternative appears that seems superior to those already considered. Herbert Simon (1957) describes this as "satisficing" behavior. Rather than "optimizing" by seeking the best alternative, decision makers are routinely content to choose the first option that meets minimally acceptable standards. Because they frequently face "unresolvable" choices that preclude satisfaction across competing preferences, often only "admissible" ones appear available (see Levi 1990).

As **prospect theory** tells us, the ability to make decisions is hindered by individuals' psychological problem in abandoning formed opinions and their tendency to overreact in crises. When estimating potential gains and losses, people are inclined to select the option that looks preferable to some past "reference point" rather than a riskier one with better prospects for gains (Levy 1992; also Stein and Pauly 1993). In a phrase, foreign policy makers are more "risk acceptant" with respect to gains than they are "risk averse" with respect to potential losses. Like investors who will take big risks in the hope of making big profits but will hold losing investments too long, policymakers will view the prospects of new policies hopefully but cling to failed policies long after their deficiencies have become apparent. This may account for the propensity of leaders to refuse to terminate a crisis for fear of public criticism (Bostdorff 1993).

The assumption that states are unitary actors partially explains the discrepancy between the theory and practice of rational decision making. States are administered by individuals with varying beliefs, values, preferences, and psychological needs, and such differences generate disagreements about goals and alternatives that are seldom resolved through tidy, orderly, rational processes. These procedures may be described better as **muddling through,** or incremental policy changes through small steps (Lindblom 1979). As one former U.S. policymaker put it, "Rather than through grand decisions or grand alternatives, policy changes seem to come through a series of slight modifications of existing policy, with new policy emerging slowly and haltingly by small and usually tentative steps, a process of trial and error in which policy zigs and zags, reverses itself, and then moves forward" (Hilsman 1967).

Despite the image that policymakers seek to project, the actual practice of foreign policy decision making is an exercise that lends itself to miscalculations, errors, and fiascoes. Policymakers tend "to avoid new interpretations of the environment, to select and act upon traditional goals, to limit the search for alternatives to a small number of moderate ones, and finally to take risks which involve low costs" (Coplin 1971). Thus, although policymakers sometimes can absorb new information quickly under great pressure and take calculated risks through deliberate planning, more often the degree of rationality "bears little relationship to the world in which officials conduct their deliberations" (Rosenau 1980; see Table 3.1.)

Although rational foreign policy making is more an ideal than a reality, we can still assume that policymakers aspire to rational decision-making behavior, which they may occasionally approximate. Indeed, as a working proposition, it is useful to accept rationality as a picture of how the decision process *should* work as well as a description of key elements of how it *does* work:

> Officials have some notion, conscious or unconscious, of a priority of values; . . . they possess some conceptions, elegant or crude, of the means available and their potential effectiveness; they engage in some effort, extensive or brief, to relate means to ends; and . . . therefore, at some point they select some alternative, clear-cut or confused, as the course of action that seems most likely to cope with the immediate situation. (Rosenau 1980, 304–5)

TABLE 3.1 Foreign Policy Decision Making in Theory and Practice	
Ideal Rational Process	**Common Actual Practice**
Accurate, comprehensive information	Distorted, incomplete information
Clear definition of national interests and goals	Personal motivations and organizational interests bias national goals
Exhaustive analysis of all options	Limited number of options considered, none thoroughly analyzed
Selection of optimal course of action most capable of producing desired results	Course of action selected by political bargaining and compromise
Effective statement of decision and its rationale to mobilize domestic support	Confusing and contradictory statements of decision, often framed for media consumption
Careful monitoring of the decision's implementation by foreign affairs bureaucracies	Neglect of the tedious task of managing the decision's implementation by foreign affairs bureaucracies
Instantaneous evaluation of consequences followed by correction of errors	Superficial policy evaluation, uncertain responsibility, poor follow-through, and delayed correction

THE BUREAUCRATIC POLITICS OF FOREIGN POLICY
DECISION MAKING

Picture yourself as a head of state charged with managing your nation's relations with the rest of the world. To make the right choices, you must seek information and advice, and you must see that the actions your decisions generate are carried out properly. Who can aid you in these tasks? Out of necessity, you must turn to those with the expertise you lack.

In today's world, states' extensive political, military, and economic relations require dependence on large-scale organizations. Leaders turn to these organizations for information and advice as they face critical foreign policy choices. Although this is more true of major powers than of small states, even those without large budgets and complex foreign policy bureaucracies make most of their decisions in an organizational context (Korany 1986). The reasons are found in the vital services that organizations perform which enhance the state's capacity to cope with changing global circumstances.

Foreign Policy–Making Organizations

Making and executing a state's foreign policy generally involves many different governmental organizations. In the United States, for instance, the State Department, Defense Department, and Central Intelligence Agency are all key participants in the foreign policy machinery. Other agencies also bear responsibility for specialized aspects of U.S. foreign relations, such as the Treasury, Commerce, and Agriculture departments. Multiple agencies with similar responsibilities also characterize the foreign affairs machinery of most other major powers, whose governments face many of the same foreign policy management problems as the United States.

Bureaucracy, Efficiency, and Rationality

Bureaucratic management of foreign relations is not new. However, with the internationalization of domestic politics in this century, the growth of large-scale organizations to manage foreign relations has spread. Bureaucratic procedures based on the theoretical work of the German social scientist Max Weber are commonplace, primarily because they are perceived to enhance rational decision making and efficient administration.

Bureaucracies increase efficiency and rationality by assigning responsibility for different tasks to different people. They define rules and standard operating procedures that specify how tasks are to be performed; they rely on systems of records to gather and store information; and they divide authority among different organizations to avoid duplication of effort. Bureaucracies also permit the luxury of engaging in forward planning designed to determine long-term needs and the means to attain them. Unlike heads of state, whose roles require attention to the crisis of the moment, bureaucracies are able to consider the future as well as the present.

Even the existence of many organizations may sometimes be a virtue. In seeking foreign policy choices and the alternatives with which to meet them, the presence of several organizations can result in "multiple advocacy" (George 1972), thus improving the chance that all possible policy options will be considered.

The Limits of Bureaucratic Organization. What emerges from our description of bureaucracy is another idealized picture of the policy-making process. Before jumping to the conclusion that bureaucratic decision making is a modern blessing, however, we should emphasize that the foregoing propositions tell us how bureaucratic decision making *should* occur; they do not tell us how it *does* occur. The actual practice and the foreign policy choices that result depict a reality of burdens as well as benefits.

Consider again the 1962 Cuban missile crisis, probably the single most threatening crisis in the post-World War II era. The method that U.S. policy-makers used in orchestrating a response to the surreptitious deployment of offensive Soviet missiles to Cuba is often viewed as having nearly approximated the ideal of rational choice. From another decision-making perspective, however, the missile crisis reveals how decision making by and within organizational contexts sometimes compromises rather than facilitates rational choice.

In his well-known book on the missile crisis, *Essence of Decision* (1971), Harvard political scientist Graham Allison identified two elements in the **bureaucratic politics model** (see also Bendor and Hammond 1992; Caldwell 1977; C. Hermann 1988). One, which he calls "organizational process," reflects the constraints that organizations place on decision makers' choices. The other, "governmental politics," draws attention to the "pulling and hauling" that occurs among the key participants in the decision process.

One way in which large-scale bureaucratic organizations contribute to the policy-making process is by devising **standard operating procedures (SOPs)**—established methods to be followed in the performance of designated tasks—for coping with policy problems when they arise. For example, once the Kennedy administration opted for a naval quarantine of Cuba during the missile crisis to prevent further shipments of Soviet missiles, the Navy could carry out the president's decision according to previously devised procedures. These routines, however, effectively limit the range of viable policy choices from which policymakers can select options. Rather than expanding the number of policy alternatives in a manner consistent with the logic of rational decision making, what organizations are prepared to do shapes what is and is not considered possible. In the Cuban crisis, a surgical air strike designed to destroy the Soviet missiles then under construction was seen as preferable to the blockade, but when the Air Force confessed that it could not guarantee complete success in taking out the missiles, the alternative was dropped. Thus organizational capabilities limited the alternatives from which the Kennedy administration could choose to realize its goal of removing all Soviet missiles from Cuban soil.

Governmental politics, the second element in the bureaucratic politics model, is related to the organizational character of foreign policy making in complex societies. Not surprisingly, the many participants in the deliberations that lead to policy choices often define issues and favor policy alternatives that reflect their organizational affiliations. "Where you stand depends on where you sit" is a favorite aphorism reflecting these bureaucratic imperatives. Consequently, many students of the subject suspect that professional diplomats typically favor diplomatic approaches to policy problems, while military officers routinely favor military solutions.

Because the players in the game of governmental politics are responsible for protecting the nation's security, they are "obliged to fight for what they are convinced is right." The consequence is that "different groups pulling in different directions produce a result, or better a resultant—a mixture of conflict-

During crises that threaten a country's national security, decisions are usually made by the head of state and a small group of advisers from the leader's inner circle, and *not* by large-scale bureaucracies. Pictured here are members of the *ad hoc* decision-making team that President John F. Kennedy assembled to respond to the Cuban missile crisis, which included Attorney General Robert Kennedy, presidential adviser Theodore Sorensen, and Secretary of Defense Robert McNamara.

ing preferences and unequal power of various individuals—distinct from what any person or group intended" (Allison 1971). Rather than being a value-maximizing process, then, policy making is itself intensely political. Thus, one explanation of why states make the choices they do lies not in their behavior vis-à-vis one another but within their own governments. And rather than presupposing the existence of a unitary actor, "it is necessary to identify the games and players, to display the coalitions, bargains, and compromises, and to convey some feel for the confusion" (Allison 1971). From this perspective, the decision to blockade Cuba was as much a product of *who* favored the choice as of any inherent logic that may have commended it. Once Robert Kennedy (the president's brother and the attorney general), Theodore Sorensen (the president's special counsel and "alter ego"), and Secretary of Defense Robert McNamara united behind the blockade, how could the president have chosen otherwise?

"Who favored what" also colored President Bush's decision in 1991 to dispatch troops to Saudi Arabia. Although key Pentagon officials might have been expected to be hawkish, some—specifically Dick Cheney, Secretary of Defense, and Colin Powell, the four-star general who was Chairman of the Joint Chiefs of Staff—only reluctantly supported the military option. Instead, members of the president's White House staff, notably Brent Scowcroft (the president's national security adviser and a retired air force lieutenant general) and the president himself (a World War II navy pilot) were the principal advocates of a military response (Woodward 1991). Scowcroft continued to push a reluctant military as the crisis evolved, until in the fall, the strategic plan changed from defense to offense.

The disastrous Vietnam War, which the professional military regarded as a debacle in part because it lacked public support at home and a clear political objective abroad, helps to explain the Pentagon's nonaggressiveness on the military option. General Powell, who served President Reagan as national security adviser and believed that "There is no legitimate use of military force without a political objective," apparently gave so much political advice during the early days of the crisis over Kuwait that "Cheney firmly suggested that the president would be better served if Powell offered more military advice" (Woodward and Atkinson 1990).

In some sense, what the military could offer constrained the Bush administration in much the same way that it affected Kennedy in the Cuban situation. For many years the Pentagon had been preparing for "low-intensity" conflicts in jungle or forested terrain. Thus, its standard operating procedures were ill suited to the conduct of mechanized warfare in the flat, open, and featureless desert terrain of the Middle East. Those plans did not prepare the United States for the military situation it faced when Iraq invaded Kuwait.

Daunting logistical obstacles confronted the Pentagon as it contemplated a mission in a distant region without U.S. military bases, and the gut response of Powell and others during the early hours of the crisis was despair about the absence of preparations. How, then, to proceed? As in Cuba, the choice was shaped by previous decisions. The United States relied on a plan first devised in the early 1980s. A massive air- and sealift of military personnel and equipment and ground deployment of heavy armor and antitank weapons (Woodward and Atkinson 1990) became the basis for Operation Desert Shield. Once the president had ordered troops to the Persian Gulf region, a process was under way that the professional military could support and execute, and it became their standard for operations.

Attributes of Bureaucratic Behavior. In addition to their influence on the policy choices of political leaders, bureaucratic organizations possess several other characteristics that affect the decision-making environment. One such characteristic derives from the proposition that bureaucratic agencies are parochial and that every administrative unit within a state's foreign policy–making bureaucracy seeks to promote its own purposes and power. Organizational needs (such as large staffs and budgets) come before the state's needs, sometimes encouraging the sacrifice of national interests to bureaucratic interests (not because bureaucrats selfishly put their own interests over the country they serve but, instead, because they often come to see their own interests as the state's). Bureaucracies fight for survival, even when their usefulness has vanished: "Programs that don't concoct some new argument or other for their continuing indispensability also tend to survive. This is because of [an] immutable law of government: even the most anachronistic, abysmal, extravagant and counterproductive government program will do at least one thing that is hard to assault" (Greenfield 1995).

As a corollary, bureaucratic parochialism breeds competition among the agencies charged with foreign policy responsibilities. Far from being neutral or impartial managers, desiring only to carry out orders from the head of state, bureaucratic organizations frequently take policy positions designed to increase their own influence relative to that of other agencies. Characteristically they are driven to enlarge their prerogatives and expand the conception of their mission, seeking to take on other units' responsibilities and to gain the powers that go with those responsibilities. Thus organizations driven by the need to enhance their own importance often determine states' foreign policies.

To protect their own interests, bureaucratic organizations attempt to reduce interference from and penetration by political leaders to whom they report as well as from other agencies within the government. Because knowledge is power, a common device for promoting organizational exclusivity is to hide inner workings and policy activities from others. The "invisible government" operating within the U.S. National Security Council during the Reagan administration illustrates this syndrome. Lieutenant Colonel Oliver North used his authority as a staff member of the council to orchestrate a secret arms-for-hostages deal with the Iranian government, part of what became popularly known as the Iran-*contra* affair.

The natural inclination of professionals who work in large organizations is to adapt their outlook and beliefs to those prevailing where they work. This reinforces the tendency of bureaucracies to act as entities unto themselves. Every bureaucracy develops a shared "mind-set" or dominant way of looking at reality akin to the **groupthink** characteristic of the cohesiveness and solidarity that small groups often develop (Janis 1982). An institutional mind-set discourages creativity, dissent, and independent thinking; it encourages reliance on standard operating procedures and deference to precedent rather than the exploration of new options to meet new challenges.

The Consequences of Bureaucratic Policy Making. A corollary of the notion that bureaucracies are often self-serving and guardians of the status quo is their willingness to defy directives by the political authorities they are supposed to serve. Bureaucratic unresponsiveness and inaction sometimes manifest themselves as lethargy. At other times bureaucratic sabotage is direct and immediate, as vividly illustrated again by the United States' experience in the 1962 Cuban missile crisis. While President Kennedy sought to orchestrate U.S. action and bargaining, his bureaucracy in general, and the navy in particular, were in fact controlling events by doing as they wished.

> [The bureaucracy chose] to obey the orders it liked and ignore or stretch others. Thus, after a tense argument with the navy, Kennedy ordered the blockade line moved closer to Cuba so that the Russians might have more time to draw back. Having lost the argument with the president, the navy simply ignored his order. Unbeknownst to Kennedy, the navy was also at work forcing Soviet submarines to surface long before Kennedy authorized any contact with Soviet ships. And despite the president's order to halt all provocative intelligence, an American U-2 plane entered Soviet airspace at the height of the crisis. When Kennedy began to realize that he was not in full control, he asked his secretary of defense to see if he could find out just what the navy was doing. McNamara then made his first visit to the navy command post in the Pentagon. In a heated exchange, the chief of naval operations suggested that McNamara return to his office and let the navy run the blockade. (Gelb and Halperin 1973, 256)

Bureaucratic stubbornness is a recurrent annoyance to world leaders in dictatorial and democratic political systems alike. The resistance of bureaucracies to change is one of the major problems that reformers in the Soviet Union and the other centralized communist countries of Eastern Europe encountered, impairing their efforts to chart new policy directions and to remain in power. The foreign policy process in China, also a centralized communist regime, operates similarly. It is "subject to the same vicissitudes of subjective perception, organizational conflict, bureaucratic politics, and factional infighting that bedevil other governments, perhaps more so given its size" (Whiting 1985). And in the United States nearly all chief executives have complained at some time about how the bureaucracy ostensibly designed to serve them has undercut their policies (see Focus 3.2). The implementation of foreign policy innovations thus poses a major challenge to most leaders (see Smith and Clarke 1985).

Bureaucratic resistance is not the only inertial force promoting status quo foreign policies and preventing change. The dynamics of governmental politics, which reduce policy choices to the outcome of a political tug of war, also retard the prospects for change. From the perspective of the participants, decision making is a high-stakes political game in which differences are often settled at the least common denominator instead of by rational, cost-benefit calculations. As former U.S. Secretary of State Henry Kissinger described the process:

> Each of the contending factions within the bureaucracy has a maximum incentive to state its case in its most extreme form because the ultimate outcome depends, to a considerable extent, on a bargaining process. The premium placed on advocacy turns decision making into a series of adjustments among special interests—a process more suited to domestic than to foreign policy. This procedure neglects the long-range because the future has no administrative constituency and is, therefore, without representation in the adversary proceedings. Problems tend to be slighted until some agency or department is made responsible for them. . . . The outcome usually depends more on the pressure or the persuasiveness of the contending advocates than on a concept of over-all purpose. (Kissinger 1969, 268)

Thus it is not surprising that bureaucracies throughout the world are frequently the object of criticism by both the political leaders they ostensibly serve and the citizens they so often touch.

● ● ●

THE ROLE OF LEADERS IN FOREIGN POLICY DECISION MAKING

The course of history is determined by the decisions of political elites. Leaders and the kind of leadership they exert shape the way in which foreign policies are made and the consequent behavior of states in world politics. "There is properly no history, only biography" is the way Ralph Waldo Emerson encapsulated the view that individual leaders move history.

Leaders as Makers and Movers of World History

This **hero-in-history model** of policy decision making equates states' action with the preferences and initiatives of the highest governmental officials. We expect leaders to lead, and we assume new leaders will make a difference. We reinforce this image when we routinely attach the names of leaders to policies, as though the leaders were synonymous with the state itself, as well as when we

Bureaucratic Obstacles to Decisive Foreign Policy Making
Accounts by U.S. Leaders

You should go through the experience of trying to get any changes in the thinking, policy, and action of the career diplomats and then you'd know what a real problem was. But the Treasury and the State Department put together are nothing as compared with the Navy. . . . To change anything in the Navy is like punching a feather bed. You punch it with your right and you punch it with your left until you are exhausted, and then you find the damn bed as it was before you started punching.

—Franklin D. Roosevelt

I sit here all day trying to persuade people to do the things they ought to have sense enough to do without me persuading them.

—Harry S Truman

There is nothing more frustrating for a President than to issue an order to a Cabinet officer, and then find that, when the order gets out in the field, it is totally mutilated. I have had that happen to me, and I am sure every other president has had it happen.

—Gerald Ford

You know, one of the hardest things in a government this size is to know that down there, underneath, is the permanent structure that's resisting everything you're doing.

—Ronald Reagan

The federal government is now organized in a way that requires all the decision making to be handled by a centralized authority. But we don't have time to let information wend its way slowly up the hierarchy, through layer after layer of middle managers. . . . For too long, government has been an obstacle to change.

—Al Gore

It would seem that many leaders feel that a major obstacle to carrying out their policies is their own governments' resistance to their initiatives. This is why bureaucracies are often seen as responsible for policy problems, and leaders are seen as handcuffed and unable to lead.

ascribe most successes and failures in foreign affairs to the leaders in charge at the time they occur. The equation of U.S. foreign policy with the Nixon Doctrine in the 1970s and the Reagan Doctrine in the 1980s are examples of this tendency.

Citizens are not alone in thinking that leaders are the decisive determinants of states' foreign policies and, by extension, world history. Leaders themselves seek to create impressions of their own self-importance while attributing extraordinary powers to other leaders. The assumptions they make about the personalities of their counterparts, consciously or unconsciously, in turn influence their own behavior toward them (Wendzel 1980), as political psychologists who study the impact of leader's perceptions and personality on their foreign policy preferences demonstrate (see Kelman 1965).

One of the dilemmas that leader-driven explanations of foreign policy behavior pose is that the movers and shakers of history often pursue decidedly irrational policies. The classic example is Adolph Hitler, whose determination to seek military conquest of the entire European continent proved disastrous for Germany. How do we square this kind of behavior with the logic of realism, which says that survival is the paramount goal of all states and that all leaders engage in rational decision making designed to maximize the benefits to their state and minimize the costs? If the realists are correct, even defects in states' foreign policy processes cannot easily explain such wide divergences between how leaders sometimes decide and what cold cost-benefit calculations would predict.

We can explain this divergence in part by distinguishing between procedural rationality and instrumental rationality (Zagare 1990). **Procedural rationality** is the foundation of the realists' billiard-ball image of world politics. It views all states as acting similarly because all decision makers engage in the same "cool and clearheaded ends-means calculation" (Verba 1969) based on perfect information and a careful weighing of all possible alternative courses of action. **Instrumental rationality,** on the other hand, is a more limited view of rationality, which says simply that individuals have preferences and, when faced with two or more alternatives, they will choose the one that they believe will yield the preferred outcome.

The implications of these seemingly semantic differences are important. They demonstrate that rationality does not "connote superhuman calculating ability, omniscience, or an Olympian view of the world," as is often assumed when the rational-actor model we have described is applied to real-world situations. They also suggest that an individual's actions may be rational even though the process of decision making and its product may appear decidedly irrational (Zagare 1990). Why did Libya's leader, the mercurial Muammar Qaddafi, repeatedly challenge the United States, almost goading President Ronald Reagan into a military strike against the North African desert country in 1986? Because, we can postulate, Qaddafi's actions were consistent with his preferences, regardless of how "irrational" it was for a fourth-rate military power to take on the world's preeminent superpower.

Factors Affecting the Capacity to Lead

Despite the popularity of the hero-in-history model, we must be wary of ascribing too much importance to individual leaders. Their influence is likely to be much subtler than popular impressions would have us believe. Henry Kissinger, himself a highly successful U.S. diplomatic negotiator, once described as "the most powerful individual in the world in the 1970s" (Isaak 1975), in 1985 urged against placing too much reliance on personalities:

> [There is] a profound American temptation to believe that foreign policy is a subdivision of psychiatry and that relations among nations are like relations among people. But the problem [of easing protracted conflicts between states] is not so simple. Tensions . . . must have some objective causes, and unless we can remove these causes, no personal relationship can possibly deal with them. We are [not] doing . . . ourselves a favor by reducing the issues to a contest of personalities.

Most leaders operate under a variety of political, psychological, and circumstantial constraints that limit what they can accomplish and reduce their control over events. In this context, Emmet John Hughes, an adviser to President Dwight D. Eisenhower, concluded that "all of [America's past presidents] from the most venturesome to the most reticent have shared one disconcerting experience: the discovery of the limits and restraints—decreed by law, by history, and by circumstances—that sometimes can blur their clearest designs or dull their sharpest purposes." Abraham Lincoln in 1864 summarized his presidential experience with the conclusion, "I have not controlled events, events have controlled me."

The question at issue is not whether political elites lead or whether they can make a difference. They clearly do both. But leaders are not in complete control, and their influence is severely constrained. Thus personality and personal political preferences do not determine foreign policy directly. The relevant question, then, is not whether leaders' personal characteristics make a difference, but rather under what conditions their characteristics are influential.[8]

The impact of leaders' personal characteristics on their state's foreign policy generally increases when their authority and legitimacy are widely accepted by citizens or, in authoritarian or totalitarian regimes, when leaders are protected from broad public criticism. Moreover, certain kinds of circumstances enhance individuals' potential impact. Among them are new situations that free leaders from conventional approaches to defining the situation; complex situations involving a large number of different factors; and situations without social sanctions, which permit freedom of choice because norms defining the range of permissible options are unclear (DiRenzo 1974).

A leader's **political efficacy** or self-image—that person's belief in his or her own ability to control events politically—will also influence the degree to which personal values and psychological needs govern decision making (DeRivera 1968). Conversely, when a sense of self-importance or efficacy is absent, self-doubt will undermine a leader's capacity to lead and to initiate policy changes. This linkage is not direct, however. The citizenry's desire for strong leadership will affect it as well. For example, when public opinion strongly favors a powerful leader, and when the head of state has an exceptional need for admiration, foreign policy will more likely reflect that leader's inner needs. Thus Kaiser Wilhelm II's narcissistic personality allegedly met the German people's desire for a symbolically powerful leader, and German public preferences in turn influenced the foreign policy that Germany pursued during Wilhelm's reign, ending in the disaster of World War I (Baron and Pletsch 1985).

Other factors undoubtedly influence how much leaders can shape their states' choices, too. For instance, when leaders believe that their own interests and welfare are at stake, they tend to respond in terms of their private needs and psychological drives. Recall the highly personalized policy reactions of the Shah of Iran and Ferdinand Marcos of the Philippines when they felt themselves personally threatened by internal insurrections that led to their regimes' overthrow. When circumstances are stable, however, and when leaders' egos are not entangled with policy outcomes, the impact of their personal characteristics is less apparent.

The amount of information available about a particular situation is also important. Without pertinent information, policy is likely to be based on leaders' personal likes or dislikes. Conversely, "the more information an individual has about international affairs, the less likely is it that his behavior will be based upon nonlogical influences" (Verba 1969).

---

[8]As Margaret G. Hermann has observed, the impact of leaders is modified by at least six factors:

(1) what their world view is, (2) what their political style is like, (3) what motivates them to have the position they do, (4) whether they are interested in and have any training in foreign affairs, (5) what the foreign policy climate was like when the leader was starting out his or her political career, and (6) how the leader was socialized into his or her present position. World view, political style, and motivation tell us something about the leader's personality; the other characteristics give information about the leader's previous experiences and background. (Hermann 1988, 268)

Similarly, the timing of a leader's assumption of power is significant. When an individual first assumes a leadership position, the formal requirements of that role are least likely to restrict what he or she can do. That is especially true during the "honeymoon" period routinely given to new heads of state, during which time they are relatively free of criticism and excessive pressure. Moreover, when a leader assumes office following a dramatic event (a landslide election, for example, or the assassination of a predecessor), he or she can institute policies almost with a free hand, as "constituency criticism is held in abeyance during this time" (Hermann 1976).

A national crisis is an especially potent circumstance that increases a leader's control over foreign policy making. Decision making during crises is typically centralized and handled exclusively by the top leadership. Crucial information is often unavailable, and leaders see themselves as responsible for outcomes. Not surprisingly, therefore, historical figures reputed to have been great leaders (e.g., Napoleon Bonaparte, Winston Churchill, and Franklin D. Roosevelt) customarily arise during periods of extreme tumult. Leaders are heroes capable of determining events. The moment may make the person, rather than the person the moment, in the sense that a crisis can liberate a leader from the constraints that normally would inhibit his or her capacity to control events or engineer foreign policy change.

History abounds with examples of the seminal importance of political leaders who arise in different times and places and under different circumstances to play critical roles in shaping world history. Mikhail Gorbachev dramatically illustrates an individual's capacity to change the course of history. Many experts believe that the Cold War could not have been brought to an end, nor Communist Party rule in Moscow terminated and the Soviet state set on a path toward democracy and free enterprise, had it not been for Gorbachev's vision, courage, and commitment to engineering these revolutionary, system-transforming changes (see Bundy 1990). Ironically, those reforms led to his loss of power when the Soviet Union imploded in 1991.

Limits to the Hero-in-History Model

Having said that the hero-in-history model may be compelling, we must be cautious and remember that leaders are not all-powerful determinants of states' foreign policy behavior. Rather, their personal impact varies with the context, and often the context is more influential than the leader (see Focus 3.3).

Thus, the utility of the hero-in-history model of foreign policy is questionable. The "great person" versus **zeitgeist** (spirit of the times) debate is pertinent here. At the core of this enduring controversy is the question, perhaps unanswerable, of whether the times must be conducive to the emergence of great leaders or whether great people would have become famous leaders whenever and wherever they lived (see Greenstein 1987). At the very least, the hero-in-history model appears much too simple an explanation of how states react to challenges from abroad. Most world leaders follow the rules of the game of international politics, which suggests that how states cope with their external environments is often influenced less strongly by the types of people heading them than by other factors. Put differently, states respond to international circumstances in often similar ways, regardless of the predispositions of their leaders. This may account for the striking uniformities in state practices in a world of diverse leaders, different political systems, and turbulent change. In

Do Leaders Make a Difference?

Some theorists, such as neorealists, embrace the assumption of rationality and assume that any leader will respond to a choice in the same way: The situation structures the reaction to the existing costs and benefits of any choice. But does this assumption square with the facts? What do we know about the impact of people's perceptions and values on the way they view choices? Political psychology tells us that the same option is likely to have different value to different leaders. Does this mean that different leaders would respond differently to similar situations?

Consider the example of Richard Nixon. In 1971, Americans took to the streets outside the White House to protest the immorality of Nixon's bombing policies in Vietnam. His reaction was to shield himself from the voice of the people, without success, as it happened. Nixon complained that "Nobody can know what it means for a president to be sitting in that White House working late at night and to have hundreds of thousands of demonstrators charging through the streets. Not even earplugs could block the noise."

Earlier, on a rainy afternoon in 1962, John F. Kennedy faced a similar citizen protest. Americans had gathered in front of the White House for a Ban the Bomb demonstration. His response was to send out urns of coffee and doughnuts and invite the leaders of the protest to come inside to state their case, believing that a democracy should encourage dissent and debate.

Nixon saw protesters as a threat; Kennedy saw them as an opportunity. This comparison suggests that the type of leader can make a difference in determining the kinds of choices likely to be made in response to similar situations.

this sense, realists' postulates about states' foreign policy goals deriving from the rational calculation of opportunities and constraints and, above all, stressing survival are not without foundation.

• • •

CONSTRAINTS ON FOREIGN POLICY MAKING IN A TRANSFORMING WORLD: PROBLEMS AND PROSPECTS

Can states respond to the demands that external challenges and internal politics simultaneously place on their leaders? For many reasons, that capability is increasingly strained.

Foreign policy choice occurs in an environment of uncertainty and multiple, competing interests. On occasion, it is also made in situations when policymakers are caught by surprise and a quick decision is needed. The stress these conditions produce impairs leaders' cognitive abilities and may cause them—preoccupied with sunk costs, short-run results, and postdecisional rationalization—to react emotionally rather than analytically.

Although a variety of impediments stand in the way of wise foreign policy choice, it is possible to design and manage policy-making machinery to reduce their impact. No design, however, can transform foreign policy making into a neat, orderly system. It is a turbulent political process, which involves complex problems, a chronic lack of information, and a multiplicity of conflicting actors.

The trends and transformations currently unfolding in world politics are the products of countless decisions made daily in diverse places throughout the world. Some decisions are more consequential than others, and some actors making them are more important than others. Throughout history, great powers like the United States have at times stood at the center of the world political stage, possessing the combination of natural resources, military might, and the means to project power worldwide that earned them great-power status. How such major powers have responded to one another has had profound consequences for the entire drama of world politics. To better understand that, we turn our attention next to the dynamics of great-power rivalry on the world stage.

● ● ●

KEY TERMS

actor	rationality, rational choice
state	prospect theory
nation	muddling through
foreign policy	bureaucratic politics model
states' attributes	standard operating
imperialism	procedures (SOPs)
geopolitics	groupthink
constitutional democracy	hero-in-history model
autocratic rule	procedural rationality
elitism	instrumental rationality
pluralism	political efficacy
unitary actor	zeitgeist

CHAPTER 4

Great-Power Politics:
Past, Present, and Future

OUTLINE

In an international system characterized by perhaps five or six major powers . . . order will have to emerge much as it did in past centuries: from a reconciliation and balancing of competing national interests.

—HENRY A. KISSINGER,
Former U.S. Secretary of State, 1994

The old geopolitical order is passing from the scene and a new order is being born. . . . In the next millennium, humanity's fate will be shaped by a new set of winners and losers.

—JACQUES ATTALI,
*President, European Bank for Reconstruction
and Development, 1991*

Although change is characteristic of world politics, one constant stands out: great-power rivalry for position in the hierarchy of states. British historian Arnold J. Toynbee (1954) underscores this fact in his famous cyclical theory of history, explaining: "The most emphatic punctuation in a uniform series of events recurring in one repetitive cycle after another is the outbreak of a great war in which one power that has forged ahead of all its rivals makes so formidable a bid for world domination that it evokes an opposing coalition of all the other powers."

Toynbee's conclusion lies at the center of realism. The starting point for understanding world politics, maintains Hans J. Morgenthau (1985), the leading post-World War II classical realist theorist, is to recognize that "All history shows that nations active in international politics are continuously preparing for, actively involved in, or recovering from organized violence in the form of war."

Cycles of war and peace have dominated twentieth-century world politics. World Wars I and II, which began in Europe and then spread to engulf the entire world, were fought by fire and blood. The Cold War, which pitted the United States against the Soviet Union, was fought by different means but was no less intensive. Each of these three global wars set in motion major transformations in world politics. In this chapter we explore the causes and consequences of these great-power rivalries that led to total war. By examining their origins and impact, we can better anticipate the character of great-power relations in the twenty-first century.

• • •

THE QUEST FOR GREAT-POWER HEGEMONY

Great-power war is not unique to this century. Changes in the balance of power over the past five hundred years have regularly preceded war's outbreak. For this reason, the relationship between the great powers' rise and fall and global instability is a core concern in theories of world politics.

One viewpoint, **long-cycle theory,** seeks to explain why periods of war and peace are associated with shifts in the major states' relative power (see

Levy 1997; Modelski and Thompson 1989, 1996), and why each global war witnesses the emergence of a victorious **hegemon,** a dominant leader capable of dictating "the rules and arrangements by which international relations, political and economic, are conducted" (Goldstein 1988; compare Nye 1988). With its acquisition of unrivaled power, the hegemon reshapes the existing system by creating and enforcing rules to preserve not only world order but also the hegemon's own dominant position.

Hegemony characteristically imposes an extraordinary tax on the world leader, which must bear the costs of maintaining economic and political order and preserving an empire. In time, as the weight of global responsibilities take their toll, new rivals rise to challenge the increasingly vulnerable world leader. Historically, this struggle for power has set the stage for another global war, the demise of one hegemon, and the ascent of another.

Long-cycle theory also draws attention to the fact that "world politics has rarely been reordered without a major war" (Jervis 1991–1992). "Only after such a total breakdown has the international situation been sufficiently fluid to induce leaders and supporting publics of dominant nations to join seriously in the task of reorganizing international society to avoid a repetition of the terrible events just experienced" (Falk 1970). Table 4.1 summarizes, over the past five hundred years, the cyclical rise and fall of great powers, their wars, and their efforts to restore order after these wars.

TABLE 4.1 The Evolution of Great-Power Rivalry for World Leadership since 1495

Preponderant State(s) Seeking Hegemony	Other Powers Resisting Domination	Global War	New Order after Global War
Portugal	Spain, Valois, France, Burgundy, England, Venice	Wars of Italy and the Indian Ocean, 1494–1517	Treaty of Tordesillas, 1517
Spain	The Netherlands, France, England	Spanish-Dutch Wars, 1580–1608	Truce of 1609; Evangelical Union and the Catholic League formed
Holy Roman Empire (Habsburg Spain and Austria-Hungary)	Shifting ad hoc coalitions of mostly Protestant states (Sweden, Holland) and German principalities as well as Catholic France against remnants of papal rule	Thirty Years' War, 1618–1648	Peace of Westphalia, 1648
France (Louis XIV)	The United Provinces, England, the Habsburg Empire, Spain, major German states, Russia	Wars of the Grand Alliance, 1688–1713	Treaty of Utrecht, 1713
France (Napoleon)	Great Britain, Prussia, Austria, Russia	Napoleonic Wars, 1792–1815	Congress of Vienna and Concert of Europe, 1815
Germany, Austria-Hungary, Turkey	Great Britain, France, Russia, United States	World War I, 1914–1918	Treaty of Versailles creating League of Nations, 1919
Germany, Japan, Italy	Great Britain, France, Soviet Union, United States	World War II, 1939–1945	United Nations, 1945; Potsdam, 1945; Bretton Woods, 1944
United States, Soviet Union	Great Britain, France, China, Japan	Cold War, 1945–1991	NATO/Partnerships for Peace, 1995; World Trade Organization, 1995

Long-cycle theory is disarmingly simple, and for this reason it is not without critics. Must great powers rise and fall as if by the law of gravity—what goes up must come down? There is something disturbingly deterministic in a proposition which implies that global destiny is beyond policymakers' control.[1] Still, long-cycle theory provides important insight into a fundamental continuity in world politics and provokes questions about whether this entrenched cycle can be broken. Thus it usefully orients us to a consideration of the three great-power wars of the twentieth century and the lessons they suggest.

• • •

THE FIRST WORLD WAR

World War I tumbled onto the world stage when a Serbian nationalist seeking to free Slavs from Austrian rule assassinated Archduke Ferdinand, heir to the throne of Austria-Hungary, at Sarajevo in June 1914. In the two months that followed, this event sparked a series of moves and countermoves by states and empires distrustful of each other's intentions, shattering the world's peace.

Before the assassination at Sarajevo, two hostile alliances had already formed, pitting Germany, Austria-Hungary, and the Ottoman Empire against France, Britain, and Russia. The strategic choices of the two alliances culminated in the cataclysm that involved the world's most powerful states. By the time the longest European war in a century had ended, nearly ten million people had died, empires had crumbled, new states were born, and the world's geopolitical map was redrawn.

---

[1]Fundamental hypotheses drawn from long-cycle theory are difficult to confirm. Long-cycle theorists disagree on whether economic, military, or domestic factors produce these cycles, as well as about their comparative influence. They also fall short in accounting for differences in different historical epochs for vanishing great powers (see Lundestad 1994).

Major wars are sometimes ignited by seemingly small, singular events. For example World War I (1914–1918), known as the Great War because it involved most of the major world powers and was the largest-ever armed conflict, was sparked by the assassination of Archduke Francis Ferdinand of Austria-Hungary by a Serbian nationalist in Sarajevo in 1914.

How can such a catastrophic war be explained? Although the answers are
numerous, many converge around *structural* explanations. Their theme holds
that World War I was an inadvertent war, not the result of anyone's master plan.
Instead, it was a war bred by uncertainty and circumstances beyond the control
of those involved, but one that none either wanted or expected.

Structuralism. Many historians find a structural interpretation convincing
because on the eve of World War I "the sort of military system that existed in
Europe at the time—a system of interlocking mobilizations and of war plans
that placed a great emphasis on rapid offensive action—directly led to a conflict
that might otherwise have been avoided" (Trachtenberg 1990–1991).

Proponents of structuralism emphasize the great powers' prior rearmament efforts as well as their alliances and counteralliances—The Triple Alliance
of Germany, Austria-Hungary, and Italy, initiated in 1882 and renewed in 1902,
and the *entente cordiale* between Britain and France, forged in 1904—created a
momentum that, along with "the pull of military schedules," dragged European
statesmen toward war (Tuchman 1962) and dictated the great powers' reactions
to the 1914 Austrian succession crisis.

A related element in the structuralist explanation focuses on the nineteenth
century, prior to the outbreak of hostilities, when Britain dominated world politics. An island country isolated by temperament, tradition, and geography
from European affairs, Britain's sea power gave it command of the world's
shipping lanes and control of a vast empire stretching from the Mediterranean
to Southeast Asia. As such, the British Empire was a world leader without rival,
and this dominance helped to deter aggression. However, Germany would
mount a challenge to British power.

Although Germany did not become a unified country until 1871, it prospered
and used its growing wealth to create a formidable army and navy. With strength
came ambition and resentment of British preeminence. As the predominant military and industrial power on the European continent, Germany sought to compete for international position and status. As Kaiser William II proclaimed in
1898, Germany had "great tasks outside the narrow boundaries of old Europe."
With Germany ascendant, the balance of power shifted, as its rising power and
global aspirations altered the European geopolitical landscape.

Germany was not the only newly emergent power at the turn of the century, however. Russia was also expanding and becoming a threat to Germany. The
decline in power of the Austro-Hungarian Empire, Germany's only ally, heightened Germany's fear of Russia—the reason for its strong reaction to Archduke
Ferdinand's assassination. Germany became convinced that a short, localized,
and victorious war was possible, fearing an unfavorable shift in the balance of
power in the event of a long war. Accordingly, while the advantages seemed
clear-cut, Germany gave Austria-Hungary a "blank check" to crush Serbia,
which proved to be a serious miscalculation.

To Germany's imperial rulers, the risk involved in the blank check made
sense from the viewpoint of preserving the Austro-Hungarian Empire. The disintegration of the empire would have left Germany isolated without an ally.
Unfortunately for Germany, its guarantee provoked an unexpected reaction from
France and Russia, as the two powers on Germany's eastern and western bor-

ders joined forces to defend the Slavs. Britain then abandoned its traditional "splendid isolation" and joined France and Russia in opposing Germany. Although the immediate objective was to defend Belgian neutrality, the war later expanded across the ocean when in April 1917 the United States, reacting to German submarine warfare, entered the conflict. For the first time ever, war became truly global in scope.

This chain reaction and the rapidity of escalation that led to World War I fit the interpretation that it was an "inadvertent war." Simply put, European leaders were not in full control of their own fate. Still, historians ask why they miscalculated so badly. Did they simply fail to recognize their primary interest in successfully managing the crisis? If so, was this because their alliances gave them a false sense of assurance, blinding them to danger and dragging them into a conflict that was not a part of anyone's design?

Rational Choice. "Rational choice theory" provides an alternate interpretation of World War I. From this perspective, the war's outbreak was a result of German elites' preference for a war with France and Russia in order to consolidate Germany's position on the continent, confirm its status as a world power, and deflect domestic attention from its internal troubles (Kaiser 1990). "It was the men gathered at the Imperial Palace in Berlin," Volker R. Berghahn (1995) concludes, "who pushed Europe over the brink."

If this interpretation is correct, then World War I is best seen as the consequence of the quest for power which realists believe is an "iron law of history." In this view, Germany's challenge to British dominance was driven by its desire to become a leading state and to prevent it from being surpassed by lesser challengers, who were also growing in strength (Gilpin 1981). From this perspective, World War I can be interpreted as "an attempt by Germany to secure its position before an increasingly powerful Russia had achieved a position of equality with Germany (which the latter expected to happen by 1917)" (Levy 1995).

As these alternative interpretations suggest, the causes of War World I remain in dispute. Controversies about motives and causes—the decisive forces behind historic events—are difficult to resolve. Structural explanations, which emphasize the distribution of power, and rational choice explanations, which direct attention to the calculations and goals of particular leaders, undoubtedly help us to understand the sequences that produced the world's first truly global war. We must, however, also consider additional factors that, in association with these underlying causes, led to the guns of August.

Other Explanations. Some historians see the growth of **nationalism** (especially in southeastern Europe) and long-suppressed ethnic and national hatreds as exerting a strong cultural influence on the inability of European statesmen to avoid war.[2] Domestic unrest inflamed these passions, as did the pressure for war applied by munitions makers who played on nationalistic sentiments

---

[2]As discussed in Chapters 7 and 12, nationalism is widely regarded as a cause of war. It is "a state of mind, permeating the large majority of a people and claiming to permeate all its members," which "recognizes the nation-state as the ideal form of political organization and the nationality as the source of creative cultural energy and of economic well-being" (Kohn 1944).

(Blainey 1988). The reaction of the Austro-Hungarian Empire to the assassination crisis suggests the potency of national passions. Nationalism and ethnic hatred fed Austria-Hungary's diabolic image of the enemy, its hypersensitivity about the preservation of the empire, and its overconfidence in its military capabilities.

Austria-Hungary was not the only player governed by nationalistic passions. The Germans and Russians were also driven by the ethnocentric assumption of their special importance and superiority, which caused them to make serious miscalculations. In particular, Germany's lack of empathy prevented it from understanding "the strength of the Russians' pride, their fear of humiliation if they allowed the Germans and Austrians to destroy their little protégé, Serbia, and the intensity of Russian anger at the tricky, deceptive way the Germans and Austrians went about their aggression" (White 1990).

Still, as powerful as these national passions were, World War I would not likely have unfolded without Anglo-German commercial rivalry, the Franco-Russian alliance, Germany's blank check to Austria-Hungary, and—perhaps most important—the formation of two entangling alliances. "One cannot conceive of the onset of World War I without the presence of the Triple Entente, which existed as an alliance of ideologically dissimilar governments" uniting Britain, France, and Russia (Midlarsky 1988). Consequently, the division of the multipolar balance-of-power system that drew the growing number of great-power contenders into two opposing coalitions—and the absence of a hegemon to maintain order—may have made war inevitable, even though "political leaders in each of the great powers . . . preferred a peaceful settlement" of their differences (Levy 1990–1991).

The Consequences of World War I

World War I was tragic in its human, social, economic, and political costs. It destroyed both life and property and changed the face of Europe (see Map 4.1). In its wake, three empires—the Austro-Hungarian, Russian, and Ottoman (Turkish)—crumbled, and in their place emerged the independent states of Poland, Czechoslovakia, and Yugoslavia. In addition, the countries of Finland, Estonia, Latvia, and Lithuania were born. The war also contributed to the overthrow of the Russian czar in 1917. As we will see later in this chapter, the destruction of the monarchy by the Bolsheviks and the emergence of communism under the leadership of Vladimir I. Lenin produced a change in government and ideology that would have far-reaching consequences.

Despite its costs, the coalition consisting of Britain, France, Russia, and (later) the United States and Italy succeeded in defeating the threat of domination posed by the Central Powers (Germany, Austria-Hungary, Turkey, and their allies). Moreover, the war set the stage for a determined effort to build a new international system that could prevent another war.

> For most Europeans, the Great War had been a source of disillusionment. . . . When it was all over, few remained to be convinced that such a war must never happen again. Among vast populations there was a strong conviction that this time the parties had to plan a peace that could not just terminate a war, but a peace that could change attitudes and build a new type of international order. . . .

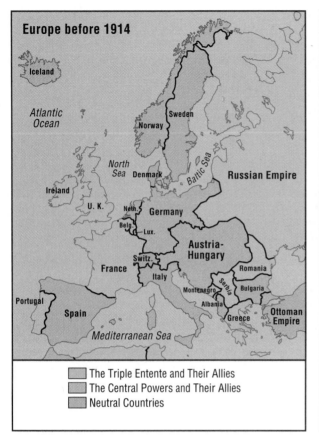

Europe before 1914

Iceland

Atlantic Ocean

North Sea

Norway
Sweden

Denmark

Ireland

U. K.

Neth.
Germany
Belg.
Lux.

France
Switz.

Italy

Portugal

Spain

Russian Empire

Baltic Sea

Austria-Hungary

Romania

Serbia
Montenegro
Bulgaria
Albania
Greece
Ottoman Empire

Mediterranean Sea

The Triple Entente and Their Allies
The Central Powers and Their Allies
Neutral Countries

Europe after 1920

Iceland

Atlantic Ocean

North Sea

Norway
Sweden

Denmark

Ireland

U. K.

Neth.
Germany
Belg.
Lux.
Alsace-Lorraine

France
Switz.

Italy

Portugal

Spain

Finland

Est.
Latv.
Lith.

Soviet Russia

Baltic Sea

Poland

Czech.

Austria
Hungary
Romania

Yugoslavia
Bulgaria
Albania
Greece
Turkey

Mediterranean Sea

Soviet Russia
Russian Losses
Germany in 1919
German Losses
Austria in 1919
Austrian Losses
Bulgaria
Bulgarian Losses
Turkey

M A P   4 . 1

Territorial Changes in Europe following World War I

SOURCE: Maps adapted from *Strategic Atlas Comparative Geopolitics of the World's Powers*, 3rd Edition by Gérard Chaliand and Jean-Pierre Rageau. Copyright © 1993 by Gérard Chaliand and Jean-Pierre Rageau. Reprinted by permission of HarperCollins Perennial, Inc.

For the first time in history, broad publics and the peacemakers shared a conviction that war was a central problem in international relations. Previously, hegemony, the aggressive activities of a particular state, or revolution had been the problem. In 1648, 1713, and 1815, the peacemakers had tried to resolve issues of the past and to construct orders that would preclude their reappearance. But in 1919 expectations ran higher. The sources of war were less important than the war itself. There was a necessity to look more to the future than to the past. The problem was not just to build a peace, but to construct a peaceful international order that would successfully manage all international conflicts of the future. (Holsti 1991, 175–76; 208–9)

World War I evoked revulsion for war and for the doctrine of realism that rationalized great-power rivalry, arm races, secret alliances, and balance-of-power politics. The experience led the policymakers gathered at the Paris peace talks at the Versailles Palace to reevaluate assumptions about the rules of statecraft and to search for other principles for building a new world order. These deliberations led to policies rooted in the idealism of liberal international relations theory.

The two decades following World War I were the high point of liberal idealism. Woodrow Wilson's reform program, expressed in his "Fourteen Points" speech, summarized the idealist call for a diplomacy of "open covenants, openly arrived at"; "making the world safe for democracy" by making leaders accountable to public opinion; creating the first universal international organization (the League of Nations) to mediate disputes and safeguard peace; and the substitution of collective security for interlocking alliances and the balance-of-power system they create.

Liberal idealists also advocated making states accountable to international law; permitting national independence movements to determine their own fate according to "self-determination" (as seen in the creation of Poland, Czechoslovakia, and Yugoslavia); and promoting global prosperity through free trade. Both the Washington Naval Conference, which sought to maintain the arms balance, and the **Kellogg-Briand Pact** (or Pact of Paris) in 1928, which outlawed the traditional right of states to make war, were characteristic of the reforms that the idealist vision inspired. Nevertheless, the idealists' proposals failed to deter the resumption of great-power rivalry. Another system-transforming global war was on the horizon.

● ● ●

THE SECOND WORLD WAR

Although it lost World War I to a coalition of states, Germany did not lose its hopes for global status and influence. On the contrary, they were intensified. Thus conditions were ripe for the second great-power war of the twentieth century, as Germany again pursued an aggressive course.

Global in scope, World War II was a struggle for power cast in the image of realism. It pitted a fascist coalition striving for world supremacy—the Axis trio of Germany, Japan, and Italy—against an unlikely "grand alliance" of four great powers who united despite their incompatible ideologies—communism in the case of the Soviet Union and democratic capitalism in the case of Britain, France, and the United States.

The world's fate hinged on the outcome of this massive effort to meet the Axis threat of world conquest and restore the balance of power. Success was achieved over a six-year ordeal, but at a terrible cost: Each day twenty-three thousand lives were lost, as the war resulted in the death of fifty-three million people worldwide (for an account of the campaigns that finally led to victory, see Weinberg 1994).

The Causes of World War II

Several factors propelled renewal of Germany's hegemonic ambitions. Domestically, German nationalism inflamed latent **irredentism** (forceful recovery of lost territory) and rationalized the expansion of German borders, both to regain provinces ceded to others and to absorb Germans living in Austria, Czechoslovakia, and Poland. The rise of **fascism**—the Nazi regime's ideology championing racism, flag, fatherland, nationalism, and imperialism—animated this renewed imperialistic push. That set of beliefs glorified the "collective will" of the nation and preached the most extreme version of realism, *machtpolitik* (power politics), to justify the forceful expansion of the German state.

German aggression was fueled further by resentment of the punitive terms imposed at the 1919 Paris peace conference by the victor of World War I (France, Great Britain, Italy, Japan, and the United States). Bending to French pressure, the Peace of Paris (the Versailles treaty) insisted on the destruction of Germany's armed forces, the loss of territory (such as Alsace-Lorraine, which Germany absorbed following the Franco-Prussia war of 1870–1871), and the imposition of heavy reparations to compensate the Allies for the damage that German militarism had exacted. In addition, the Austro-Hungarian Empire was splintered into divided political units.

Not only was the Peace of Paris punitive; more significantly and painfully, it prevented Germany's reentry into the international system as a coequal member. (Germany was denied membership in the League of Nations until 1926.) As a result of its exclusion, Germany, propelled by nationalistic sentiments and the rise of fascism, sought to recover its rightful status as a great power by force of arms.

Proximate Causes. Why did the victorious great powers permit German rearmament? A key reason was the failure of the British hope for Anglo-American collaboration to maintain world order, which vanished when the United States, in a fit of anger, repudiated the Versailles peace treaty and retreated to isolationism. As a result, Britain and France each fought for its own advantage in the treatment of Germany. While France wanted to deter Germany's reentry into the international system and prevent its revival, Britain, in contrast, preferred to preserve the new balance of power by encouraging German rearmament and recovery as a counterweight against the chance that France or the Soviet Union might dominate continental Europe. Thus Britain's belief that a revitalized Germany would help preserve the balance of power led it to neglect the threat of growing German power.

Acquiescence to German rearmament and other militaristic maneuvers led to the policy of "appeasement" to pacify potential aggressors with concessions. Adolf Hitler, the German dictator who by the mid-1930s controlled Germany's fate, pledged not to expand German territory by force. He betrayed that promise in March 1938 when he forced Austria into union with Germany (the *Anschluss*). Shortly thereafter he demanded the annexation of the German-populated area of Sudetenland in Czechoslovakia (see Map 4.2). The fears that German expansionism provoked led to the September 1938 Munich Conference attended by Hitler, British Prime Minister Neville Chamberlain, and leaders from France and Italy (Czechoslovakia was not invited). Under the erroneous conviction that appeasement would halt further German expansionism and lead to "peace in our time," Chamberlain and the others agreed to Hitler's demands.

Rather than satisfying Germany, appeasement whetted its appetite and that of the newly formed fascist coalition of Germany, Italy, and Japan, whose goal was to overthrow the international status quo. Disillusioned with Western liberalism and the Paris settlements, and suffering economically from the effects of the Great Depression of the 1930s, Japan embraced militarism. In the might-makes-right climate that Germany's imperialistic quest for national aggrandizement helped to create, Japanese nationalists led their country on the path to imperialism and colonialism. Japan's invasions of Manchuria in 1931 and China proper in 1937 was followed by Italy's absorption of Abyssinia in 1935 and Albania in 1939, and both Germany and Italy intervened in the 1936–1939 Spanish civil war on the side of the fascists, headed by General Francisco Franco, while the Soviet Union supported antifascist forces.

Europe in 1938

Europe in 1945

USSR before the War	France	U.S. Occupation Zones
Soviet Annexations	French Occupation Zones	Other Western States, Allies
Soviet Influence	Great Britain	Neutral States
Soviet Occupation Zones	British Occupation Zones	Iron Curtain (1947)

MAP 4.2

Territorial Changes in Europe following World War II

SOURCES: Based on Europe 1938 from Kegley and Raymond (1994), 118; Europe 1945 from Chaliand and Rageau (1993), 49.

Despite these aggressive actions elsewhere, appeasement of Germany proved to be the catalyst for the century's second global war. After Germany occupied the rest of Czechoslovakia in March 1939, Britain and France belatedly reacted by joining in an alliance to protect the next likely victim, Poland. They also opened negotiations in Moscow in hopes of enticing the Soviet Union to join the alliance, but failed. Then, on August 23, 1939, Hitler, a fascist, and the Soviet dictator Joseph Stalin, a communist, stunned the world with the news that they had signed a nonaggression pact. Now certain that Britain and France would not intervene, Hitler promptly invaded Poland on September 1, 1939. Britain and France, honoring their pledge to defend the Poles, declared war on Germany two days later. World War II had begun.

The war expanded rapidly as Hitler turned his forces to the Balkans, North Africa, and westward. The powerful, mechanized German troops invaded Norway and marched through Denmark, Belgium, Luxembourg, and the Netherlands. They swept around France's defensive barrier, the Maginot Line, and forced the British to evacuate a sizable expeditionary force from the French beaches at Dunkirk. Paris itself fell in June 1940, and in the months that followed, the German air force, the Luftwaffe, pounded Britain in an attempt to

In the 1930s the nationalistic ideologies of National Socialism and Fascism—which regarded the state as supreme, accepted dictatorship, and called for expansion at the expense of neighboring countries—took root in Germany and Italy. Consistent with the realist view that states have an inherent right to expand, dramatic political rallies attended by Italian dictator Benito Mussolini and German Führer Adolf Hitler were staged to glorify the state and military power.

force it into submission as well. Instead of invading Britain, however, the Nazi troops attacked the Soviet Union, Hitler's former ally, in June 1941.

On December 7, 1941, Japan launched a surprise assault on the United States at Pearl Harbor. Almost immediately, Germany also declared war on the United States. The unprovoked Japanese assault and the German challenge pushed U.S. aloofness and isolationism aside, enabling President Franklin Roosevelt to forge a coalition with Britain and the Soviet Union to oppose the fascists.

Underlying Causes. Many historians regard the reemergence of a multipolar power distribution as a key factor in the onset and expansion of World War II. The post–World War I system was placed "at risk when the sovereign states, which were its components, became too numerous and unequal in power and resources, particularly when (as happened after 1919) the great powers were reduced in number and new, lesser states proliferated" (Calvocoressi, Wint, and Pritchard 1989). In 1914, Europe had only twenty-two key states, but by 1921 the number nearly doubled. When combined with resentment over Versailles, the Russian Revolution, and the rise of fascism, the increased number of states and the resurgence of nationalistic revolts and crises made "the interwar years the most violent period in international relations since the Thirty Years' War and the wars of the French Revolution and Napoleon" (Holsti 1991).

The collapse of the international economic system during the 1930s was also a major contributor to the war. Great Britain found itself unequal to the leadership and regulatory roles it had performed in the world political economy before World War I. Although the United States was the logical successor

78

to Britain as world economic leader, its refusal to exercise leadership hastened the war. "The Depression of 1929–1931 was followed in 1933 by a world Monetary and Economic Conference whose failures—engineered by the United States—deepened the gloom, accelerated nationalist protectionism, and promoted revolution" (Calvocoressi, Wint, and Pritchard 1989). In this depressed global environment, heightened by deteriorating economic circumstances at home, Germany and Japan sought solutions through imperialism abroad.

The failure of the League of Nations to mount a collective response to the German, Japanese, and Italian acts of aggression symbolized the weak institutional barriers to war. When Germany withdrew from the League of Nations in 1933, as did Italy in 1937, war clouds gathered which the League was powerless to dispel.

The Soviet Union's invasion of neutral Finland in 1939 provoked public indignation. In a final act of retaliation, the League of Nations expelled the Soviet Union. Nonetheless, characteristically, the burden of defense fell on the shoulders of the victim. Ninety thousand fiercely independent Finns gave their lives in the "Winter War" to defend their country while the rest of the astonished world watched and cheered but did little to help.

Psychological forces also led to World War II. These included "the domination of civilian discourse by military propaganda that primed the world for war," the "great wave of hypernationalism [that] swept over Europe" as "each state taught itself a mythical history while denigrating that of others," and the demise of democratic governance (Van Evera 1990–1991).

In the final analysis, however, the war would not have been possible without Adolph Hitler and his plans to conquer the world by force. Hence "German responsibility for the Second World War is in a class of its own" (Calvocoressi, Wint, and Pritchard 1989). Under the mythical claim of German racial superiority as a "master race" and virulent anti-Semitism and anticommunism, Hitler waged war to create an empire that could resolve the historic competition and precarious coexistence of the great powers in Europe by eliminating Germany's rivals.

The broad vision of the Thousand-Year Reich was . . . of a vastly expanded—and continually expanding—German core, extending deep into Russia, with a number of vassal states and regions, including France, the Low Countries, Scandinavia, central Europe, and the Balkans, that would provide resources and labor for the core. There was to be no civilizing mission in German imperialism. On the contrary, the lesser peoples were to be taught only to do menial labor or, as Hitler once joked, educated sufficiently to read the road signs so they wouldn't get run over by German automobile traffic. The lowest of the low, the Poles and Jews, were to be exterminated. . . .

To Hitler . . . the purpose of policy was to destroy the system and to reconstitute it on racial lines, with a vastly expanded Germany running a distinctly hierarchical and exploitative order. Vestiges of sovereignty might remain, but they would be fig leaves covering a monolithic order. German occupation policies during the war, whereby conquered nations were reduced to satellites, satrapies, and reservoirs of slave labor, were the practical application of Hitler's conception of the new world order. They were not improvised or planned for reasons of military necessity. (Holsti 1991, 224–25)

Having faced ruinous losses in Russia and a massive allied bombing campaign at home, Germany's Thousand-Year Reich lay in ruins by May 1945. By August, Japan was devastated as well, as the U.S. atomic bombing of Hiroshima and Nagasaki destroyed Japan's receding hope of carrying on its war of conquest.

The Allied victory over the Axis redistributed power and reordered borders, resulting in a new geopolitical terrain. The Soviet Union absorbed nearly 600,000 square meters of territory in the west from the Baltic states of Estonia, Latvia, and Lithuania, and from Finland, Czechoslovakia, Poland, and Romania—territorial changes that enabled the Soviet Union to recover what Russia had lost in the 1918 Treaty of Brest-Litovsk after World War I. Poland, a victim of Soviet expansionism, was compensated with land taken from Germany. Germany itself was divided into occupation zones that eventually provided the basis for its partition into East and West Germany. Finally, pro-Soviet regimes assumed power throughout Eastern Europe (see Map 4.2, p. 77). In the Far East, the Soviet Union took the four Kurile Islands—or the "Northern Territories," as Japan calls them—from Japan; and Korea was divided into Soviet and U.S. occupation zones at the thirty-eighth parallel.

The end of World War II also generated uncertainty and mistrust. The agreements governing goals, strategy, and obligations which had guided the collective Allied effort to defeat the common enemy began to erode even as victory neared. Victory only magnified the great powers' growing distrust of one anothers' intentions in an environment of ill-defined borders, altered allegiances, power vacuums, and economic ruin.

The "Big Three" leaders—Winston Churchill, Franklin Roosevelt, and Joseph Stalin—met at Yalta in the Crimea in February 1945 to design a new world order, but the vague compromises they reached concealed the differences percolating below the surface. Following Roosevelt's death in April and Germany's unconditional surrender in May, the Big Three (with the United States now represented by Harry Truman) met again at Potsdam in July 1945. The meeting ended without agreement, and the facade of Allied unity began to fade.

Despite the emergent differences between the United States and the Soviet Union, World War II, like all previous great-power wars, paved the way for a new global system. The Allies' plans for a new postwar structure of peace had begun even as the war raged, and as early as 1943 the Four Power Declaration advanced principles for allied collaboration in "the period following the end of hostilities." The product of the Allies' determination to create a new international organization to manage the postwar international order—the United Nations—was conceived in this and other wartime agreements. Consistent with the expectation that the great powers would cooperate to manage world affairs, China was promised a seat on the United Nations Security Council along with France and the Big Three. The purpose was to guarantee that all of the dominant states would share responsibility for keeping the peace.

In practice, however, the United States and the Soviet Union mattered most. The other major-power victors (especially Great Britain) had exhausted themselves during the war and fell from the apex of the world-power hierarchy. The vanquished, Germany and Japan, also fell from the ranks of the great powers. Germany was partitioned into four occupation zones, which the victorious powers later used as the basis for creating the Federal Republic of Germany (West Germany) and the German Democratic Republic (East Germany). Japan, having been devastated by atomic bombs and then occupied by the United States, was also removed from the game of great-power politics. Thus, as the French political sociologist Alexis de Tocqueville had foreseen in 1835, the Americans and Russians now held in their hands the destinies of half of mankind. In comparison, all other states were dwarfs. In a competition that eventually became known as the Cold War, Washington and Moscow used the fledgling United Nations not to keep the peace, but to pursue their competition with each other. As the most recent great-power war of the twentieth century, the Cold War still casts its shadow over the post-Cold War geostrategic land-scape.

● ● ●

THE COLD WAR

As World War II drew to a close in 1945, it became increasingly clear that a new era of international politics was dawning. Unparalleled in scope and unprece-dented in destructiveness, the second great war of the twentieth century not only had brought about a system dominated by two superstates, the United States and the Soviet Union, whose combined power and resources far sur-passed those of all the rest of the world; it also hastened the disintegration of the great colonial empires assembled by imperialist states in previous cen-turies, thereby emancipating many peoples from foreign rule. The emergent international system, unlike earlier ones, featured a distribution of power con-sisting of many sovereign states outside the European core area which were dominated by the two most powerful. In addition, the advent of nuclear weapons radically changed the role that threats of warfare would play hence-forth in world politics. Out of these circumstances grew the competition between the United States and the Soviet Union for hegemonic leadership.

The Causes of the Cold War

Determining the origins of the twentieth century's third hegemonic battle for domination is difficult because the historical evidence is open to different inter-pretations (see Gaddis 1972; Melanson 1983). Nonetheless, an evaluation of its postulated causes can help us to understand the sources of great-power rival-ries and also to explain why this one, unlike other twentieth-century conflicts, ended without recourse to great-power violence.

A Conflict of Interests. Realism provides one structural explanation of the Cold War's determinants: The preeminent status of the United States and the Soviet Union at the top of the international hierarchy made each naturally suspicious of the other and their rivalry inescapable. These circumstances gave each superpower reasons to fear and to struggle against the other's potential global leadership (Tucker 1990).

But was the competition truly necessary and predetermined? The United States and the Soviet Union each had demonstrated an ability to subordinate its ideological differences and competition for power to larger purposes during World War II (Gaddis 1972, 1983). Neither had sought unilateral advantage relentlessly, while both had expressed their hope that cooperation would con-tinue and had reached agreements toward that purpose. President Roosevelt, for example, advocated preserving accommodation through an informal accord to let each superpower enjoy dominant influence in its own **sphere of influence,** or specified area of the globe. Rules written into the United Nations charter, obligating the United States and Soviet Union to share (through the UN Security Council) responsibility for preserving world peace, further reflected the expectation of continued cooperation.

If cooperation was the superpowers' hope and aspiration when World War II ended, then why did they fail to achieve it? To answer that question, we must go beyond the logic of *realpolitik* and probe other explanations of the origins of the Cold War.

Ideological Incompatibilities. A second interpretation holds that the Cold War was simply an extension of the superpowers' mutual disdain for each other's political system and way of life. As U.S. Secretary of State James F. Byrnes argued at the conclusion of World War II, "there is too much difference in the ideologies of the U.S. and Russia to work out a long-term program of cooperation." To the extent that such assumptions were widely held in both Washington and Moscow, as they undoubtedly were, ideological differences made the Cold War a conflict "not only between two powerful states, but also between two different social systems" (Jervis 1991).

U.S. animosity was stimulated by the 1917 Bolshevik revolution, which brought to power a government that embraced the Marxist critique of capitalistic imperialism. Whether real or imagined, U.S. fears of Marxism stimulated the emergence of anticommunism as a counterideology (Commager 1983; Morgenthau 1983). Accordingly, the United States embarked on a missionary crusade of its own, dedicated to containing and ultimately removing the despised atheistic communist menace from the face of the earth.

American foreign policy was fueled by the fear that communism's appeal to Europeans and the world's less-fortunate countries would make its continued spread likely. This prophecy was popularized in the 1960s as the **domino theory,** the view that one country's fall to communism would cause the fall of its neighbors in a chain reaction like a row of falling dominoes, thus bringing the entire world under communist domination unless checked by U.S. power.

Similarly, Soviet policy was fueled by the belief that capitalism could not coexist with communism in the long run since the two systems were incompatible. Each was destined to struggle with the other. The purpose of Soviet policy, therefore, was to pursue this struggle by pushing the pace of the historical process in which communism eventually would prevail. However, Soviet planners did not believe that this historical outcome would automatically occur. They felt that the capitalist states, led by the United States, sought to encircle the Soviet Union and smother communism in its cradle, and that it was the Soviet obligation to resist. As a result, ideological incompatibility ruled out compromise as an option (see Focus 4.1). Although the adversaries may have viewed "ideology more as a justification for action than as a guide to action," once the interests that they shared disappeared, "ideology did become the chief means which differentiated friend from foe" (Gaddis 1983).

Misperceptions. A third explanation describes the Cold War as rooted in psychological factors, particularly in the superpowers' misperceptions of each other's motives. Their conflicting interests and ideologies were secondary.

Mistrustful actors are prone to see in their own actions only virtue and in those of their adversaries only malice. When such **mirror images** exist (in which

Ideology as a Cause of International Friction
Was the East–West Conflict Irreconcilable?

Many scholars believe that all ideological systems of belief see other ideologies as a threat, and this competition breeds hatred and hostility in international affairs. Noting that many wars were actually struggles between religions (such as Christianity against Islam during the Crusades), they maintain that ideological contests over *ideas*, such as that between communism and capitalism, cause nations and states to fight. A conflict driven by ideology "excludes the idea of coexistence. How can [one] compromise or coexist with evil? It holds out no prospect but opposition with all might, war to the death. It summons the true believer to a *jihad*, a crusade of extermination against the infidel" (Schlesinger 1983). Lenin described the predicament—prophetically, it turned out—this way: "As long as capitalism and socialism exist, we cannot live in peace; in the end, either one or the other will triumph—a funeral dirge will be sung either over the Soviet Republic or over world capitalism."

adversaries see each other in similar terms, as themselves as good and the "other" as evil), hostility is inevitable (Bronfenbrenner 1971). Moreover, when perceptions of an adversary's evil intentions become accepted as dogma, prophecies often become self-fulfilling.[3]

Mirror images and **self-fulfilling prophecies** contributed heavily to the onset of the Cold War. The two countries' leaders imposed on events their definitions of reality and then became captives of those visions. As expectations shaped how leaders interpreted developments, what they saw influenced what they got. George F. Kennan, the American ambassador to the Soviet Union in 1952, noted that misread signals were common to both sides:

> The Marshall Plan, the preparations for the setting up of a West German government, and the first moves toward the establishment of NATO were taken in Moscow as the beginnings of a campaign to deprive the Soviet Union of the fruits of its victory over Germany. The Soviet crackdown on Czechoslovakia (1948) and the mounting of the Berlin blockade, both essentially defensive . . . reactions to these Western moves, were then similarly misread on the Western side. Shortly thereafter there came the crisis of the Korean War, where the Soviet attempt to employ a satellite military force in civil combat to its own advantage, by way of reaction to the American decision to establish a permanent military presence in Japan, was read in Washington as the beginning of the final Soviet push for world conquest; whereas the active American military response, provoked by this move, appeared in Moscow . . . as a threat to the Soviet position in both Manchuria and in eastern Siberia. (Kennan 1976, 683–84)

Thus, in the Cold War's formative stage, U.S. leaders and their allies in the West saw the many crises that erupted as part of a Soviet plan for world domination. The Soviets saw these same crises altogether differently—as tests of

---

[3]Prophecies are sometimes self-fulfilling because the future can be affected by the way it is anticipated. The tendency is illustrated by arms races: Mistakenly anticipating that a rival is preparing for an offensive war, a potential victim then arms in defense, thereby provoking the rival to fulfill the prophecy by arming out of fear.

their resolve and as Western efforts to encircle and destroy their socialist experiment. Both states operated from the same "inherent bad-faith" image of the rival's intentions. In this respect, their images were identical. Mistrust led to misperceptions, which in turn bred conflict.[4]

Additional factors beyond those rooted in divergent interests, ideologies, and images undoubtedly combined to produce this explosive Soviet-American hegemonic rivalry. Scholars have yet to sort out their relative causal influence. However, to grasp more completely the dynamics of this great-power rivalry in particular (and others in general), it is useful to move beyond its causes and examine its character.

The Characteristics of the Cold War

As the Cold War evolved over the next four decades, its character changed in part because of the two rivals' policies and in part because of changing global circumstances. Several conspicuous patterns are observable, however, amidst continual change. The history of the superpowers' Cold War interactions reveals three primary characteristics:

- Periods of intense conflict alternated with periods of relative cooperation; and reciprocal, action-reaction exchanges were also evident (friendly U.S. initiatives toward the Soviet Union were reciprocated in kind).

- Both actors were willing to disregard their respective professed ideologies whenever their perceived national interests rationalized such inconsistencies; for example, each backed allies with political systems antithetical to its own when the necessities of power politics seemed to justify doing so.

- Throughout the Cold War contest, both rivals consistently made avoidance of all-out war their highest priority. Through a gradual learning process involving push and shove, restraint and reward, tough bargaining and calm negotiation, the superpowers created a **security regime,** or rules for the peaceful management of their disputes.

These characteristics become visible when we inspect the evolution of the superpowers' relationship. For this, we divide the Cold War into three chronological phases, shown in Figure 4.1.

Confrontation, 1945–1962. A brief period of wary Soviet-American friendship soon gave way to mutual antagonism when the Cold War began. In this short period of **unipolarity**—one characterized by a single dominant power center in the international system—the United States alone possessed the capacity to devastate its adversaries with the atomic bomb.

Despite this restraining factor, all pretense of collaboration rapidly vanished as the superpowers' vital security interests collided in confrontations in

---

[4]If the Cold War originated in conflicting images and in each superpower's insensitivity to the impact of its actions on the other's fears, it is difficult to assign blame for the deterioration of Soviet–American relations. Both countries were responsible because both were victims of their misperceptions. The Cold War was not simply a U.S. response to communist aggression (the orthodox American view), nor was it simply a product of postwar American assertiveness (the revisionist historians' position; see Schlesinger 1986). Each of the great powers felt threatened, and each had legitimate reasons to regard the other with suspicion. Consequently, we can view the Cold War as a conflict over reciprocal anxieties bred by the way policymakers on both sides interpreted the other's actions.

countries outside their clearly defined respective spheres of influence. At this critical juncture, George F. Kennan, then a diplomat in the American embassy in Moscow, sent to Washington his famous "long telegram" assessing the sources of Soviet conduct. Kennan's conclusions were ominous: "In summary, we have here a political force committed fanatically to the belief that with [the] U.S. there can be no permanent *modus vivendi*, that it is desirable and necessary that the internal harmony of our society be disrupted, our traditional way of life be destroyed, the international authority of our state be broken, if Soviet power is to be secure."

Kennan's ideas were circulated widely in 1947, when the influential journal *Foreign Affairs* published his views in an article signed "X" instead of with his own name. In this article, Kennan argued that Soviet leaders forever would feel insecure about their political ability to maintain power against forces both within Soviet society and in the outside world. Their insecurity would lead to

FIGURE 4.1

U.S.–Soviet Relations during the Cold War, 1948–1991

The evolution of U.S.–Soviet relations during the Cold War displays a series of shifts between periods of conflict and cooperation. As this figure shows, each superpower's behavior toward the other tended to be reciprocal, and, prior to the Cold War's end, confrontation prevailed over cooperation.

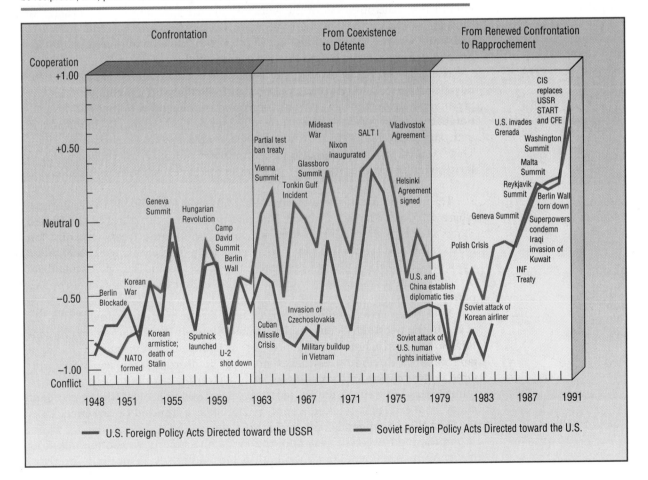

an activist—and perhaps aggressive—Soviet foreign policy. However, the United States had the power to increase the strains under which the Soviet leadership would have to operate, which could lead to a gradual mellowing or final end of Soviet power. Thus, Kennan concluded: "In these circumstances it is clear that the main element of any United States policy toward the Soviet Union must be that of a long-term, patient but firm and vigilant *containment* of Russian expansive tendencies" (Kennan 1947, emphasis added).

Soon thereafter, President Harry S Truman made Kennan's assessment the cornerstone of American postwar policy. Provoked in part by violence in Turkey and Greece, which he and others believed to be communist inspired, Truman declared, "I believe that it must be the policy of the United States to support free peoples who are resisting attempted subjugation by armed minorities or by outside pressures." Eventually known as the **Truman Doctrine,** this statement defined the strategy that the United States would pursue for the next forty years to deter the Soviet Union's perceived hegemonic ambitions, over Kennan's objections (see Focus 4.2). This strategy, called **containment,** sought to prevent the expansion of Soviet influence by encircling the Soviet Union and intimidating it with the threat of a military attack.

A seemingly endless series of new Cold War crises soon followed. They included the Soviet refusal to withdraw troops from Iran in 1946; the communist coup d'état in Czechoslovakia in 1948; the Soviet blockade of West Berlin in June of that year; the communist acquisition of power on the Chinese mainland in 1949; the outbreak of the Korean War in 1950; the Chinese invasion of Tibet in 1950; and the on-again, off-again Taiwan Straits crises that followed. The "war" was no longer merely "cold;" it had become an embittered worldwide quarrel that threatened to escalate into open conflict.

Nonetheless, superpower relations began to improve in the 1950s. After the Soviets broke the U.S. atomic monopoly in 1949, shifts in the balance of power prompted a movement away from confrontation. The risks of massive destruction necessitated restraint and changed the terms of the struggle. In particular, both superpowers began to expend considerable resources recruiting allies. Their success produced a distribution of military power characterized by **bipolarity,** with the United States and its allies at one pole and the Soviet Union and its allies at the other.

The focal point of the superpowers' jockeying for influence was Europe, where the Cold War first erupted. The principal European allies of the United States and the Soviet Union divided into the North Atlantic Treaty Organization (NATO) and the Warsaw Treaty Pact, respectively. These alliances became the cornerstones of the superpowers' external policies, as the European members of each alliance willingly yielded to the leadership of its superpower patrons.

To a lesser extent, alliance formation outside of Europe involved other states in the two titans' contest. The United States in particular sought to contain Soviet (and Chinese) influence on the Eurasian landmass by building a ring of allies, including countries not only in Europe such as Turkey and Greece, but beyond in Iran and South Korea, on the very borders of the communist world. In return, the United States promised to protect these new client states from external attack in a strategy known as **extended deterrence.** Thus the Cold War expanded across the entire globe.

In the rigid two-bloc system of the 1950s, the superpowers often talked as if war were imminent, but they both acted cautiously (especially after the

Was Militant Containment Necessary?

Whether a military containment strategy was appropriate remains controversial. George F. Kennan thought that U.S. leaders misinterpreted his celebrated statement. He explained:

> I . . . went to great lengths to disclaim the view, imputed to me by implication . . . that containment was a matter of stationing military forces around the Soviet borders and preventing any outbreak of Soviet military aggressiveness. I protested . . . against the implication that the Russians were aspiring to invade other areas and that the task of American policy was to prevent them from doing so. "The Russians don't want," I insisted, "to invade anyone. It is not in their tradition. They tried it once in Finland and got their fingers burned. They don't want war of any kind. Above all, they don't want the open responsibility that official invasion brings with it." (Kennan 1967, 361)

As Kennan lamented, "the image of a Stalinist Russia poised and yearning to attack the West, and deterred only by [U.S.] possession of atomic weapons, was largely a creation of the Western imagination." Cautioning against "demonizing the adversary, overestimating enemy strength and overmilitarizing the Western response" (Talbott 1990), Kennan recommended a political rather than a military containment approach. It is worth considering whether, if Kennan's recommendations had been followed, the Cold War would have become so bitter or lasted so long.

Korean War). President Eisenhower and his Secretary of State, John Foster Dulles, pursued a strategy termed "rollback," which promised to move what was called the "Iron Curtain" separating East and West by "liberating" the "captive nations" of Eastern Europe. They pledged to respond to aggression with "massive retaliation," and criticized the allegedly "soft" and "restrained" Truman Doctrine, claiming to reject containment in favor of an ambitious "winning" strategy that would finally end the confrontation with godless communism. However, containment was not replaced by a more assertive strategy. Despite their threatening language, U.S. leaders promised more than they delivered. In 1956, for instance, the United States failed to respond to a call for assistance from Hungarian freedom fighters, who had revolted against Soviet control with armed resistance.

Because the Soviet Union remained strategically inferior to the United States, Nikita Khrushchev (who assumed the top Soviet leadership position following Joseph Stalin's death in 1953) pursued a policy of **peaceful coexistence** with capitalism. (Communist China protested, accusing Khrushchev of "revisionism" and challenging the Soviet claim to leadership of the international communist movement.) Nonetheless, the Soviet Union at times cautiously sought to increase its power in places where opportunities appeared to exist. As a result, the period following Stalin's death saw many Cold War confrontations, with Hungary, Cuba, Egypt, and Berlin becoming the flash points.

Despite the intensity and regularity of U.S.–Soviet confrontations, no threat to peace resulted in open warfare as both superpowers took accommodative steps toward improving relations. For example, the 1955 Geneva summit provided an important forum for the antagonists' meaningful dialogue about world problems, and in 1956 the Soviets dissolved the *Cominform* (the Communist Information Bureau, which coordinated the work of communist parties in other states).

From Coexistence to Détente, 1963–1978. Despite the Geneva conference, a dark shadow loomed over hopes for a superpower rapprochement. As the arms race accelerated, the threats to peace multiplied. In 1962 the surreptitious placement of Soviet missiles in Cuba set the stage for the greatest test of the superpowers' capacity to manage their disputes—the Cuban missile crisis, which became the Cold War's most serious challenge to peace. The superpowers stood eyeball to eyeball. Fortunately, one (the Soviet Union) blinked, and the crisis ended. This "catalytic" learning experience both reduced enthusiasm for waging the Cold War by military means and expanded awareness of the suicidal consequences of a nuclear war.

The growing threat of mutual destruction, in conjunction with the growing parity of American and Soviet military capabilities, made coexistence or nonexistence appear to be the only alternatives. Given this equation, finding ways to coexist became compelling. At The American University commencement exercises in 1963, U.S. President John F. Kennedy explained why tension reduction had become essential and war could not be risked:

> Among the many traits the people of [the United States and the Soviet Union] have in common, none is stronger than our mutual abhorrence of war. Almost unique among the major world powers, we have never been at war with each other. . . .
>
> Today, should total war ever break out again—no matter how—our two countries would become the primary targets. It is an ironical but accurate fact that the two strongest powers are the two in the most danger of devastation. . . . We are both caught up in a vicious and dangerous cycle in which suspicion on one side breeds suspicion on the other and new weapons beget counterweapons.
>
> In short, both the United States and its allies, and the Soviet Union and its allies, have a mutually deep interest in a just and genuine peace and in halting the arms race. . . .
>
> So let us not be blind to our differences, but let us also direct attention to our common interests and to the means by which those differences can be resolved. And if we cannot end now our differences, at least we can help make the world safe for diversity.

Kennedy signaled a shift in how the United States hoped thereafter to bargain with its adversary, and the Soviet Union reciprocally expressed its interest in more cooperative relations. Installation in 1963 of the "hot line," a direct communication system linking the White House and the Kremlin, followed. So did the 1967 Glassboro summit and several negotiated agreements, including the 1963 Partial Test Ban Treaty, the 1967 Outer Space Treaty, and the 1968 Nuclear Nonproliferation Treaty. In addition, the superpowers agreed to accept the permanence of European borders, including tacitly those that divided Germany. Thus, in style and tone the United States and Soviet Union began to depart from past confrontational tactics, laying the foundation for "détente."

Soviet-American relations took a dramatic turn with Richard Nixon's election in 1968. Coached by his national security adviser, Henry A. Kissinger, President Nixon initiated a new approach to Soviet relations that in 1969 he officially labeled **détente.** The Soviets also adopted this term to describe their policies toward the United States.

In Kissinger's words, détente sought to create "a vested interest in cooperation and restraint," "an environment in which competitors can regulate and

As East–West tension waned, cooperation increased during the détente phase of U.S.–Soviet relations in the late 1960s. A considerable part of this departure from past confrontation was due to compromises at the bargaining table. Pictured here, President Richard Nixon, one of the architects of the U.S. "linkage" strategy along with Secretary of State Henry Kissinger is toasting with Soviet Premier Leonid Brezhnev and fellow dignitaries their meeting to discuss approaches to relaxing tensions between the super powers.

restrain their differences and ultimately move from competition to cooperation." To engineer the relaxation of superpower tensions, Nixon and Kissinger pursued a **linkage strategy** to bind the two rivals in a common fate by making peaceful superpower relations dependent on the continuation of mutually rewarding exchanges (such as trade concessions). Furthermore, linkage made cooperation in one policy area contingent on acceptable conduct in other areas.

The shifts in policy produced results, as relations between the Soviets and Americans "normalized." As Figure 4.1 shows, cooperative interaction became more commonplace than hostile relations. Visits, cultural exchanges, trade agreements, and joint technological ventures replaced threats, warnings, and confrontations.

Arms control stood at the center of the dialogue surrounding détente. The **Strategic Arms Limitation Talks (SALT),** initiated in 1969, sought to restrain the threatening, expensive, and spiraling arms race. The talks produced two agreements, the first in 1972 (SALT I) and the second in 1979 (SALT II); however, SALT II was signed but never ratified by the United States, due to opposition in Congress. This failure underscored the substantial differences that still separated the superpowers.

From Renewed Confrontation to Rapprochement, 1979–1991. Despite the careful nurturing of détente, its spirit did not endure. In many respects, the Soviet invasion of Afghanistan in 1979 catalyzed détente's demise. As President Jimmy Carter viewed it, "Soviet aggression in Afghanistan—unless checked—confronts all the world with the most serious strategic challenge since the Cold War began." In retaliation, he advanced the **Carter Doctrine** declaring America's willingness to use military force to protect its interests in the Persian Gulf. In addition, he attempted to organize a worldwide boycott of the 1980 Moscow Olympics and suspended U.S. grain exports to the Soviet Union.

Relations deteriorated dramatically thereafter. President Ronald Reagan and his Soviet counterparts (first Yuri Andropov and then Konstantin Chernenko) delivered a barrage of confrontational rhetoric. Reagan asserted that the Soviet Union "underlies all the unrest that is going on" and described the Soviet Union as "the focus of evil in the modern world." The atmosphere was punctuated by Reagan policy adviser Richard Pipes's bold challenge in 1981 that the Soviets would have to choose between "peacefully changing their Communist system . . . or going to war." Soviet rhetoric was equally unrestrained and alarmist.

As talk of war increased, preparations for it escalated as well. The arms race resumed feverishly, and the contestants put weapons above all other priorities, at the expense of addressing domestic economic problems. The superpowers also extended the confrontation to new territory, such as Central America, and renewed their public diplomacy (propaganda) efforts to extol the virtues of their respective systems throughout the world.

Dangerous events punctuated the renewal of conflict. The Soviets destroyed Korean Airlines flight 007 in 1983; the United States invaded Grenada soon thereafter. Arms control talks then ruptured, the Soviets boycotted the 1984 Olympic Games in Los Angeles, and the **Reagan Doctrine** pledged U.S. support of anticommunist insurgents who sought to overthrow Soviet-supported governments in Afghanistan, Angola, and Nicaragua. In addition, American leaders spoke loosely about the "winability" of a nuclear war through a "prevailing" military strategy that included the threat of a "first use" of nuclear weapons in the event of conventional war. Relations deteriorated as the compound impact of these moves and countermoves took their toll. The new Soviet leader, Mikhail Gorbachev, in 1985 summarized the alarming state of superpower relations by fretting that "The situation is very complex, very tense. I would even go so far as to say it is explosive."

However, the situation did not explode. Instead, prospects for a more constructive phase improved greatly following Gorbachev's view that it was vital the Soviet Union practice what he referred to as "new thinking" in order to achieve a rapprochement or relaxation of tensions. He sought to reconcile the Soviet Union's differences with the capitalist West in order to halt the deterioration of his country's economy and international position. In Gorbachev's words, these goals dictated "the need for a fundamental break with many customary approaches to foreign policy." Shortly thereafter, he embarked on domestic reforms to promote democratization and the transition to a market economy.

Acknowledging that Soviet economic growth had ceased and its global power had eroded, Gorbachev proclaimed his desire to end the Cold War contest. "We realize that we are divided by profound historical, ideological, socioeconomic, and cultural differences," he noted in 1987 during his first visit to the United States. "But the wisdom of politics today lies in not using those differences as a pretext for confrontation, enmity, and the arms race." Soviet spokesperson Georgi Arbatov elaborated, informing the United States that "we are going to do a terrible thing to you—we are going to deprive you of an enemy."

Surprisingly, the Soviets did what they promised: They began to act like an ally instead of an enemy. Building on the momentum created by the **Intermediate-range Nuclear Forces (INF) disarmament agreement,** signed in 1987, the Soviet Union agreed to end its aid and support for Cuba, withdrew from

Afghanistan and Eastern Europe, and announced unilateral reductions in military spending. Gorbachev also agreed to two new disarmament agreements, **Strategic Arms Reduction Talks (START)** for deep cuts in strategic arsenals, and the **Conventional Forces in Europe (CFE)** treaty to reduce the Soviet presence in Europe (see Chapter 15 for a description of these agreements). In addition, the Soviet Union liberalized its emigration policies and permitted greater religious freedom. As these seismic changes shook the world, the Soviet Union then sped its reforms to introduce democracy and a market economy, eagerly seeking (and receiving) economic assistance from the West.

The pace of steps to rapprochement—the establishment of cordial relations—then accelerated, and the "normalization" of Soviet-American relations moved rapidly. The Cold War—which began in Europe and had centered on Europe for forty-five years—ended there in 1991, when the Soviet Union dissolved. All communist governments in the Soviet "bloc" in Eastern Europe, including even hardline Albania, permitted democratic elections in which Communist Party candidates routinely lost. In all instances, capitalist free market principles replaced socialism. To nearly everyone's astonishment, the Soviet Union acquiesced in these revolutionary changes (see Focus 4.3). Without resistance, the Berlin Wall came down, Germany reunited, and the Warsaw Pact dissolved.

The failed conservative coup against Gorbachev in August 1991 put the nail in the coffin of Communist Party control in Moscow, the very heartland of the international communist movement. As communism was repudiated in the Soviet Union, a new age began. Communism was in retreat, and as a result massive changes swept world politics.

The abrupt end of the Cold War suggested something quite different from the lesson of the two World Wars, that great-power rivalries are doomed to end in armed conflict. The Cold War was different; it came to an end peacefully. This suggests that great powers are capable of settling their struggles without bloodshed, and that it is sometimes possible for them to manage their competition and resolve their disputes.

The Consequences of the Cold War

The end of the Cold War has altered the face of world affairs in profound and diverse ways. It held out the promise of international peace but, at the same time, raised the specter of new kinds of global instability. As George Bush lamented in November 1991, "The collapse of communism has thrown open a Pandora's box of ancient ethnic hatreds, resentment, even revenge."

One consequence warrants particular attention: What does Russia's decline (and the rising popularity of Communist Party politician's) bode for the future? Can we expect another fifty years of great-power peace? Or will the transformed balance of power be a prelude to another great-power rivalry, and possibly war?

In the long run, Russia could again emerge as a superpower if it overcomes its long-neglected domestic problems. Lying in the heartland of Eurasia, a bridge between Europe and the Pacific Rim, with China and India to the south, Russia stands militarily tall—although it is ringed by emerging great-power rivals (see Map 4.3). However, the immediate consequence of the Cold War's end is a transformed global hierarchy in which the former Soviet Union is no longer a challenger to U.S. hegemonic leadership. In accepting the devolution of its

Why Did the Cold War End Peacefully?

Opinions differ as to why the Cold War ended without mass destruction. The inferences drawn are important, because they will affect leaders' thinking about how to manage future great-power rivalries.

To some observers, the policies George Kennan recommended in his famous "X" article now appeared prophetic. In his version of nonmilitary containment, Kennan anticipated that this would "promote tendencies which must eventually find their outlet in either the breakup of or the gradual mellowing of Soviet power." Many believe that this was precisely what did happen, albeit more than forty years later!

Neorealists, in contrast, emphasize the contribution of nuclear weapons, the essential parity of military power, rigid bipolarity, and extended deterrence through alliances. In 1991, for example, an adviser to U.S. President Reagan, Richard Perle, articulated the realist view in his contention that "Those who argued for nuclear deterrence and serious military capabilities contributed mightily to the position of strength that eventually led the Soviet leadership to choose a less bellicose, less menacing approach to international politics."

Liberals and neoliberals cite other influences, as in political analyst Ted Galen Carpenter's (1991) observation that "Many of the demonstrators . . . who sought to reject communist rule looked to the American system for inspiration. But the source of that inspiration was America's reputation as a haven for the values of limited government, not Washington's $300-billion-a-year military budget and its network of global military bases."

Although no consensus has materialized about the ways in which these factors individually or in combination put an end to the Cold War, a fundamental question sits at the center of this postmortem speculation. Did *militant* containment force the Soviet Union into submission, or did Soviet leaders succumb to the inherent *political* weaknesses of communism, which caused an internal economic malaise which left them unable to conduct an imperial policy abroad or retain communist control at home? In other words, was the end of Communist Party rule accepted because of the intimidation of U.S. military strength? Or was the outcome produced by other political and economic influences within the Soviet Union, as suggested in 1991 by Georgi Arbatov, Director of the U.S.S.R.'s Institute for the USA and Canada Studies, who argued that the realist theory "that President Reagan's 'tough' policy and intensified arms race . . . persuaded communists to 'give up' is sheer nonsense. Quite to the contrary, this policy made the life for reformers, for all who yearned for democratic changes in their life, much more difficult. . . . The conservatives and reactionaries were given predominant influence. . . . Reagan made it practically impossible to start reforms after Brezhnev's death (Andropov had such plans) and made things more difficult for Gorbachev to cut military expenditures."

Sorting out the contribution of different causes to ending the Cold War will doubtless intrigue historians for decades, just as determining the causes for its onset has done.

---

external empire, the Soviet Union has made the most dramatic peaceful retreat from power in history. The United States now sits alone at the top of the international hierarchy.

• • •

THE FUTURE OF GREAT-POWER POLITICS: A COLD PEACE?

With the end of the Cold War both the United States and the Soviet Union found themselves liberated from a rivalry that had extracted enormous resources and reduced their economic strength relative to other ascending great powers, such as China, Germany, and Japan. In this sense, both "lost" (see Lebow and Stein 1994). Caught breathless, each superpower now faces unfamiliar circumstances. No longer is there "a clear and present danger to delineate the purpose of power, and this basic shift [has] invalidated the framework for much of the thought and action about international affairs in East and West since World War II" (Oberdorfer 1991).

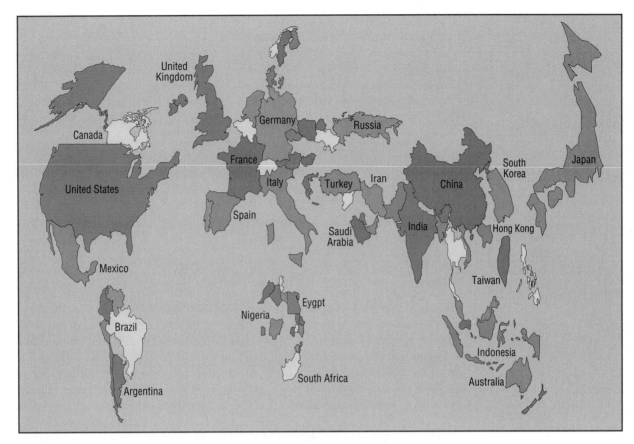

MAP 4.3

Emerging Centers of Power in a New International Hierarchy

Which countries are powerful and which are relatively weak can be estimated by different kinds of indicators. One common approach to predicting the power potential of states (i.e., their ability to project power and exercise influence in the world) is to measure and compare the size of their economies. This map pictures the distribution of power in 1994; the relative size of countries reflects the relative size of their gross domestic product. In this estimate, the United States, Japan, China, Germany are the economic powerhouses, and Russia is a secondary power, ranking below Italy, India, and the United Kingdom, among others.

SOURCE: Map adapted from *Handbook of International Economic Statistics 1995* (1995), 22.

Post-Cold War Scenarios

The peaceful end of the Cold War does not ensure a peaceful future. On the contrary, the insights of long-cycle and realist theories predict pessimistically that prevailing trends in the diffusion of economic power will lead to renewed competition, conflict, and perhaps even warfare among the great powers, and that the range of new problems and potential threats will multiply. As political scientist Robert Jervis explains,

> Cyclical thinking suggests that, freed from the constraints of the Cold War, world politics will return to earlier patterns. Many of the basic generalizations of international politics remain unaltered: It is still anarchic in the sense that there is no international sovereign that can make and enforce

93

laws and agreements. The security dilemma remains as well, with the problems it creates for states who would like to cooperate but whose security requirements do not mesh. Many specific causes of conflict also remain, including desires for greater prestige, economic rivalries, hostile nationalisms, divergent perspectives on and incompatible standards of legitimacy, religious animosities, and territorial ambitions. To put it more generally, both aggression and spirals of insecurity and tension can still disturb the peace. (Jervis 1991–1992, 46)

To realists, great-power rivalry for power and position is likely to resume because the international anarchy that promotes it continues to shape the international conduct of states. Realists also foresee probable instability resulting from the changes unfolding in the international system's structure if U.S. hegemonic preponderance continues to decay. As rivals rise to challenge U.S. leadership, a new structure will emerge.

A Twenty-First-Century Multipolar World

While the distribution of power in the Cold War system was bipolar, the post-Cold War world promises to be very different. Russia's demise produced a new unipolar structure, fleeting though it may be. In early 1991, when it victoriously fought the Persian Gulf War, the United States basked in a "unipolar moment." It was the "one first-rate power [with] no prospect in the immediate future of any power to rival it. . . . [It was] the only country with the military, diplomatic, political and economic assets to be a decisive player in any conflict in whatever part of the world it [chose] to involve itself" (Krauthammer 1991b).

This condition is not likely to last into the next millennium, however. As Figure 4.2 shows, the long-term trajectories of history unmistakably point to the coming of a world in which China, and perhaps other great powers, will rapidly rise to challenge U.S. financial prominence and political clout, even if U.S. military supremacy remains unchallenged in the short run. China, Japan, and others are growing in economic power relative to the United States, and this suggests that the pecking order of the world's countries is likely to look very different by the year 2020 than it does now. We call such a future world **multipolar** in order to contrast it with situations where either one (unipolar) or two (bipolar) countries possess overwhelming power.

The Challenge of Multipolarity. The character of a new multipolar structure may be very different from the stability that characterized the unipolar and bipolar phases of international politics since World War II. In part this is because the emergence of a number of comparatively equal great powers will introduce more complexity and uncertainty about allegiances and alignments. This may also be the case because "international security issues will exhibit themselves in all their variety once again—issues of markets, resources, technology, ethnic animosities, political philosophy, and different conceptions of world order, as well as armies and nuclear weapons" (Carter 1990–1991). The multipolar global agenda will encompass continuing concerns with military security—the focus of realism—alongside mounting concerns about the great powers' economic relations, the topic on which liberal international relations theory concentrates.

Many theorists point out the dangers inherent in multipolar distributions of power. Their warnings are inspired by the historical record, which suggests

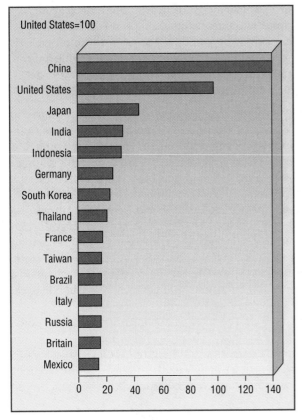

United States=100

China
United States
Japan
India
Indonesia
Germany
South Korea
Thailand
France
Taiwan
Brazil
Italy
Russia
Britain
Mexico

0   20   40   60   80   100   120   140

FIGURE 4.2

Economic Projection of the Fifteen Largest Global Economies by 2020

Using purchasing power parities (PPPs) to account for differences in countries' price levels, the World Bank forecasts the probable size of the largest economies. The projections show that the rank order of the largest economic powerhouses by 2020 will be substantially different from today's. The political and military consequences are not predicted, but long-cycle theory postulates that the economic changes will breed political and even military conflict.

SOURCE: McGranahan (1995), 59.

that if we look to the past to anticipate the future, we have many reasons to fear the reemergence of this kind of system. Today's hopes for great-power cooperation in the wake of the Cold War have many precedents. The end of every previous great-power war was followed by an initial hopeful burst of collaborative institution building to forge a stable new order among the victorious powers. But each of these great-power designs, constructed at the conclusion of a multipolar period's war, ultimately proved temporary. Precedents include the Peace of Westphalia (1648), the Treaty of Utrecht (1713), the Concert of Europe (1815), the League of Nations (1919), and the United Nations (1945). In each case, as the new distribution of power underwent changes in the great powers' relative strength, collaboration gave way to competition. Sooner or later, every previous multipolar system collapsed, as one or more of the major powers expressed dissatisfaction with the existing hierarchy, rejected the rules on which they had agreed to manage their relations, and attempted by force to overturn the status quo. Rivalry has routinely resulted in a hegemonic struggle for supremacy ending in a new catastrophic general war, each more destructive than the preceding one. This invites the sobering conclusion that

> in a world of sovereign states a contest among them over the distribution of power is the normal condition and . . . such contests often lead to war. . . . The reasons for seeking more power are often not merely the search for security or material advantage. Among them are demands for greater prestige, respect, deference, in short, honor. Since such demands involve judgments even more subjective than those about material advantage, they are

95

still harder to satisfy. Other reasons emerge from fear, often unclear and intangible, not always of immediate threats but also of more distant ones, against which reassurance may not be possible. The persistence of such thinking in a wide variety of states and systems over the space of millennia suggests the unwelcome conclusion that war is probably part of the human condition and likely to be with us for some time yet. (Kagan 1995, 569)

Multipolar politics looks especially menacing when we take into account the interplay of military and economic factors in the perceived rankings of the great powers. In a new multipolar environment, without the stark simplicities and the self-evident symmetries of a bipolar system, any effort to maintain partnerships is likely to prove problematic. In such a system, differentiating friend from foe will be more difficult because allies in military security are likely to be rivals in trade relationships. In Lester Thurow's (1992) apt phrase, the United States, Europe, and Japan are likely to go "head to head" on the economic battlefield. In this arena we can expect China and perhaps a reascendant Russia, India, and Indonesia to join the fray. The U.S.–Japan and U.S.–China disputes in the mid-1990s about security issues at the very time they were also arguing about "fair trade" illustrate the tensions that can easily escalate between powers at the pinnacle of the global hierarchy.

The diffusion of wealth predicts the likely intensification of great-power political competition. Throughout history, changes in comparative *economic* advantage have preceded *political* competition. When multipolarity has existed, economic rivals have struggled to protect their wealth and have competed politically for economic position, with military conflict usually following (J. Snyder 1991).

A "new Cold War" could emerge between any pair of great powers, such as the United States and China, if their competition escalates. However, this need not always be the case; cooperation could increase as well. Quite different and inconsistent political types of great-power relations could immerge in the economic and military spheres. The probability of economic rivalry and conflict is generally high, whereas the likelihood of security cooperation for many of these same relationships is also high. For example, the United States, Japan, and China exhibit conflict in their commercial relations but also have shown a capacity to manage their security relations collaboratively. Table 4.2 presents a projection of the kind of cross-cutting bilateral relationships that could develop among the great powers in the next century. It estimates the probability of military cooperation and economic conflict between any pair of the five major powers. The potential for economic conflict is given in the upper right-hand portion of the diagonal and the potential for military cooperation through alliances in the lower left portion.

Awareness of these different possibilities may have been behind U.S. Secretary of State Lawrence Eagleburger's warning in 1989:

> We are . . . returning to a more traditional and complicated time of multipolarity, with a growing number of countries increasingly able to affect the course of events despite the wishes of the superpowers. . . . The issue . . . is how well the United States accomplishes the transition from overwhelming predominance to a position more akin to a 'first among equals' status, and how well America's partners—Japan and Western Europe—adapt to their newfound importance. The change will not be easy for any of the players, as such shifts in power relationships have never been easy.

| TABLE 4.2 | The New Great-Power Chessboard: Economic Rivalry and Military-Alliance Possibilities |

	United States	Japan	Germany	Russia	China
United States	—	H	H	L	H
Japan	H	—	H	M	M
Germany	M	L	—	M	L
Russia	M	L	L	—	H
China	L	L	L	M	—

Note: Lower left matrix classifies the probability of military alignments, whereas upper right matrix pictures the probability of economic conflict, with the symbols H = high, M = medium, and L = low signifying the likely character of the bilateral relationships that may develop in the new millennium.

SOURCE: Adapted from Kegley and Raymond (1994), 197.

Few observers see advantages resulting from the situation that former U.S. Secretary of State Henry A. Kissinger described in 1993: "for diplomatic purposes there are no longer two superpowers, but five or six more or less equal power centers. . . . The United States is militarily the strongest, but the circumstances in which its military power is relevant are diminishing." This, Kissinger summarized, poses a serious challenge because "the United States has very little experience with a world that consists of many powers and which it can neither dominate nor from which it can simply withdraw in isolation."

Yet, we have no way of knowing whether the future will resemble the gloomy past history of multipolar systems. Patterns and practices can change, and it is possible for policymakers to learn from previous mistakes and avoid repeating them.

Responding to Multipolarity's Challenge. What, then, can the great powers do to prevent the resumption of their rivalry? What security policies should they pursue in order to avoid the dangers of shared power and rapid transitions in their position and strength in the great-power hierarchy?

The answers are highly uncertain. As we will discuss in Chapters 13–16, debate about the methods of guaranteeing international security in Washington, Moscow, Berlin, Beijing, and Tokyo today revolves around four basic options. Each is actively under consideration, and each will become more or less practical, prudent, or problematic for each great power depending on the circumstances that materialize in tomorrow's multipolar world.

A *unilateral* conception of a great-power's role represents one possible option. Acting alone is especially attractive for a self-confident great power assured of its independent strength. With sufficient power, a potential hegemon can be self-reliant. Unilateralism can involve isolationism, an attempt to exert hegemonic leadership, or an effort to play the role of a "balancer" who skillfully backs one side or another in a great-power dispute, but only when necessary to maintain a military equilibrium between the disputants.

Cultivation of a *specialized relationship* with another great power, similar to that between Great Britain and the United States in this century, illustrates a second approach some great powers might pursue. The "condominium" partnership between the United States and Russia advocated by former U.S. Deputy Secretary of Defense Fred Charles Iklé (1991–1992) suggests the kind of relationships that could develop. There are several variants of this strategy, including informal understandings, cooperations (sometimes termed **ententes**), and formal alliances concretized by treaties.

A third strategy under consideration is construction of a **concert,** or a cooperative agreement among the great powers to manage the international system jointly and to prevent international disputes from escalating to war (see Rosecrance 1992). The Concert of Europe, at its apex between 1815 and 1822, is the epitome of previous great-power efforts to pursue this path to peace.

Finally, some policymakers recommend that today's great powers unite with the lesser powers in constructing a true system of **collective security.** The principles rationalizing the formation of the League of Nations in 1919 exemplify this *multilateral* approach to peace under conditions of multipolarity.

Whichever combination of approaches predominates in the strategies forged to prevent great-power rivalries from escalating to war in a multipolar future, the ultimate outcome will not depend on the great powers alone. The policy response of other, less-powerful actors is likely to be increasingly important in shaping world politics, and their role must also be examined. We begin in Chapter 5 with a consideration of the history and characteristics of those states at the bottom of the international system's hierarchy, the Global South, and of the foreign policy interests and goals that motivate their behavior.

• • •

KEY TERMS

long-cycle theory
hegemon
nationalism
Kellogg-Briand Pact
irredentism
fascism
machtpolitik
sphere of influence
domino theory
mirror images
self-fulfilling prophecy
security regime
unipolarity
Truman Doctrine
containment
bipolarity
extended deterrence
peaceful coexistence

Cominform
détente
linkage strategy
Strategic Arms Limitation
 Talks (SALT)
Carter Doctrine
Reagan Doctrine
Intermediate-range Nuclear
 Forces (INF) disarmament
 agreement
Strategic Arms Reduction
 Talks (START)
Conventional Forces in
 Europe (CFE) treaty
multipolarity
entente
concert
collective security

CHAPTER 5

The Global South: Roots and Consequences of Global Inequalities

OUTLINE

[The] widening gulf [between rich and poor states] breeds despair and instability. It imperils our world.

—JAMES GUSTAVE SPETH, *Administrator,*
United Nations Development Programme, 1995

What the countries of the South have in common transcend their differences. . . . The primary bond that links the countries and peoples of the South is their desire to escape from poverty and underdevelopment.

—*The South Commission, 1990*

The end of colonialism is one of the most remarkable developments in twentieth-century world politics. As U.S. Secretary of State George Shultz observed in 1983, "Since the Second World War, the world has undergone a vast transformation as more than one hundred new nations have come into being. An international system that had been centered on Europe for centuries, and that regarded all non-European areas as peripheral or as objects of rivalry, has become in an amazingly short span of time a truly global arena of sovereign states."

Despite their legal status as independent entities, sovereignty could not erase the colonial heritage and insecurity growing out of the political, economic, and military vulnerabilities that the former colonies faced. Indeed, the new states born after World War II were thrust into an international system they had no voice in shaping but whose structures and processes they viewed as barriers to overcoming the vast array of problems that beset them at home. Thus the new states—almost uniformly poor—found themselves on the periphery of an international order dominated by the great powers—almost uniformly rich—at the core of the system.

During the Cold War the term **Third World** was used to describe the world's poorer, economically less developed states, which tended to share a common colonial heritage. The concept first emerged to distinguish the growing number of newly emerging states from those identified with either the East or West in the Cold War struggle, but it soon took on largely economic connotations (Berger 1994; Wolf-Phillips 1987). Compared with the industrialized countries—the **First World**—the Third World had failed to grow economically or otherwise advance toward the degree and type of economic development experienced in Western Europe, North America, and Japan. The **Second World**—consisting of the Soviet Union, its allies, and other communist societies—was distinguished by a commitment to planned economic practices rather than reliance on market forces to determine the supply of and demand for goods and services. Today the states comprising the former Second World are commonly described as "economies in transition."

While "Third World" continues to have relevance as a concept referring to the disjuncture in the development experiences of the First World and virtually everyone else, it also carries Cold War baggage that is no longer useful. The term **Global South** is preferable to distinguish the First World—now properly thought of as the **Global North**—from the rest of the world. As always, placement of particular states within these categories is sometimes problematic. Many of the economies in transition are particularly difficult to place, and thus comprise a group somewhere between the North and South. Otherwise, the confluence of particular characteristics along four dimensions distinguish the two: politics, technology, wealth, and demography.

States comprising the Global North are democratic, technologically inventive, wealthy, and aging, as their societies tend toward zero population growth. Some in the Global South share many of these characteristics, but none shares them all. Saudi Arabia is rich but not democratic; China is technologically inventive but not wealthy; India is democratic but burdened with an enormous and growing population; and Singapore is both wealthy and technologically innovative, with a comparatively modest population growth rate, but is not democratic. Beyond this are many nations that are not democratic, technologically innovative, or wealthy, but who are experiencing rapid population growth which places increasing strains on already overtaxed social and ecological systems with too few economic resources and political capabilities to match the challenge. These, the least developed of the less developed countries, are sometimes described today as the "Third World's Third World." Many, but not all, are in Africa south of the Sahara.

The political, technological, economic, and demographic differences between North and South underlie the "North-South conflict." This long-festering dispute between the world's rich and poor nations rests on a striking fact: The Global South is home to more than 80 percent of the world's people but commands less than 20 percent of its wealth, with the reverse true in the Global North. Given these disparities—illustrated in Figure 5.1—the contest between the wealthy North and the poor South historically has stressed economic and related welfare issues, but the conflict, as economist Robert Heilbroner (1991) notes, is "inherently a politics of mutual suspicion and struggle."

In this chapter we examine the roots and consequences of the often stark contrasts that set countries of the Global South apart from others and the foreign policy postures that flow from them. We will find that considerable diversity characterizes the Global South. Still, the common threads uniting these countries make it useful to treat them as a cluster of state actors in world politics quite distinct from the "great powers" at the apex of the global hierarchy. We begin with an examination of colonialism and imperialism, historical experiences that most developing countries have shared and which have shaped in distinctive ways their contemporary world views and their position in the international hierarchy.

• • •

THE RISE AND FALL OF EUROPEAN EMPIRES

The emergence of the Global South as an identifiable entity in world politics is a distinctly contemporary phenomenon. Although most Latin American countries were independent before World War II, not until 1946 did the floodgates of decolonization first open. In the next four decades a profusion of new states joined the international community as sovereign entities, nearly all carved from British, French, Belgian, Spanish, and Portuguese empires. In some cases, the dependent relationships had existed for hundreds of years. More often the areas granted independence had been colonized in the late 1800s, when a wave of new imperialism swept the world. Today, few colonies remain. Although the dozen or so remaining dependent territories may yet become independent members of the world community, most have populations of less than 100,000

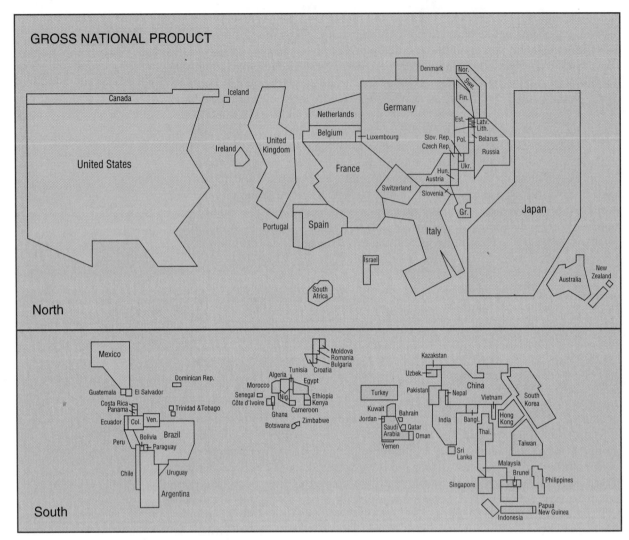

GROSS NATIONAL PRODUCT

North

South

FIGURE 5.1

Differences in the Global North and South

If the countries of the world are redrawn to reflect the size of their economies and populations, the world would appear lopsided indeed: Most of the wealth is in the North, most of the people are in the South.

and many have expressed a preference to retain their current political status. In short, the political process known as **decolonization**—the freeing of colonial peoples from their dependent status—is now complete.

The vestiges of colonialism remain, however, with important consequences for contemporary world politics. The tribal and ethnic conflicts now so prevalent often have colonial roots, as the imperial powers drew borders within and between their domains with little regard to the internal makeup of local populations. Similarly, the immense disparity in income and wealth between many of the world's rich and poor states may lie in the imperial past, when the European powers exploited their overseas territories for their own advantage. Thus, as viewed through the eyes of nationalist leaders in many of the emerging states during the past half-century, the disparity between the rich North and the poor South is seen as the consequence of **neocolonialism** or **neoimperialism**—unequal exchanges that permit the advantaged to exploit the disadvantaged through international economic processes institutionalized by the rich.

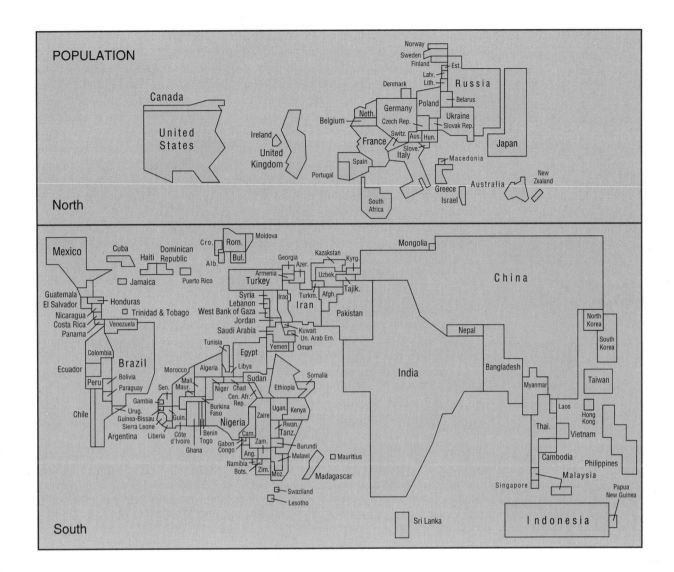

The First Wave of European Imperialism

The first wave of European empire building began during the fifteenth century, as the Dutch, English, French, Portuguese, and Spanish used their military power to achieve commercial advantage overseas. As scientific innovations made the adventures of European explorers possible, merchants followed in their wake, "quickly seizing upon opportunities to increase their business and profits. In turn, Europe's governments perceived the possibilities for increasing their own power and wealth. Thus commercial companies were chartered and financed, with military and naval expeditions frequently sent out after them to ensure political control of overseas territories" (Cohen 1973).

The economic strategy underlying the relationship between colonies and colonizers during this era of "classical imperialism" is known as **mercantilism:** an economic philosophy advocating government regulation of economic life to

103

increase state power and security. European rulers believed that power flowed from the possession of national wealth measured in terms of gold and silver. Developing mining and industry to attain a favorable balance of trade (exporting more than they imported) was one way to accumulate the desired bullion. "Colonies were desirable in this respect because they afforded an opportunity to shut out commercial competition; they guaranteed exclusive access to untapped markets and sources of cheap materials (as well as, in some instances, direct sources of the precious metals themselves). Each state was determined to monopolize as many of these overseas mercantile opportunities as possible" (Cohen 1973). To maximize the power and wealth of the state, states saw the acquisition of territory by conquest as a natural complement to active government management of the economy.

By the end of the eighteenth century the European powers had spread themselves, although thinly, throughout virtually the entire world, but the colonial empires they had built now began to crumble. Britain's thirteen North American colonies declared their independence in 1776, and most of Spain's possessions in South America won their freedom in the early nineteenth century. Nearly a hundred colonial relationships worldwide were terminated in the half-century ending in 1825 (Bergesen and Schoenberg 1980, 236).

As Europe's colonial empires dissolved, the mercantilist philosophy that had sustained classical imperialism also waned. As the Scottish political economist Adam Smith argued in his 1776 treatise, *The Wealth of Nations,* national wealth grew not through the accumulation of precious metals but rather from the capital and goods they could buy. Smith's ideas about the "invisible hand" of the marketplace domestically and internationally exerted an important influence in the development of **classical liberal economic theory.** Following the thinking of Smith and others, belief in a system of free international trade consistent with the precepts of **laissez-faire economics** (minimal governmental interference in the market) became the accepted philosophy governing international economic relations (see also Chapter 8). European powers continued to hold numerous colonies, but the prevailing sentiment was now more anti- than pro-imperial.

The Second Wave of European Imperialism

Beginning in the 1870s and extending until the outbreak of World War I, a second wave of imperialism washed over the world as Europe, joined later by the United States and Japan, colonized new territories at a dramatically rapid rate. The portion of the globe that Europeans controlled was one-third in 1800, two-thirds by 1878, and four-fifths by 1914 (Fieldhouse 1973, 3). As illustrated in Map 5.1, nearly all of Africa was now under the control of only seven European powers: Belgium, Britain, France, Germany, Italy, Portugal, and Spain. In all of the Far East and the Pacific, only China, Japan, and Siam (Thailand) remained outside the direct control of Europe or the United States. China, too, was divided into spheres of influence by foreign powers, and Japan itself practiced imperialism by occupying Korea and Formosa (Taiwan). Elsewhere, the United States expanded across its continent, acquired Puerto Rico from Spain, extended its colonial reach westward to Hawaii and the Philippines, leased the Panama Canal Zone "in perpetuity" from the new state of Panama (an American creation), and exercised considerable political leverage over several Caribbean lands, notably Cuba. The British Empire, built by the preeminent imperial

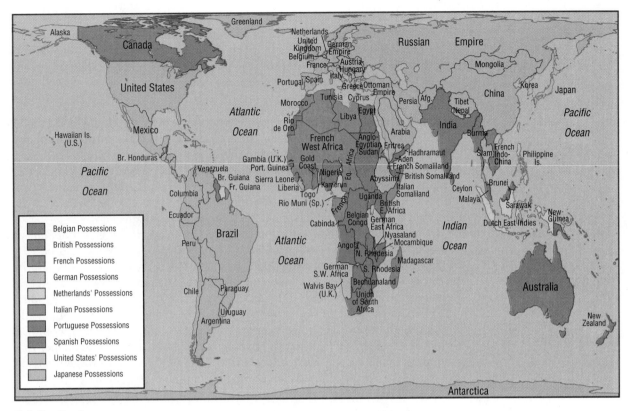

MAP 5.1

Global Imperialism, 1914

Map legend:
- Belgian Possessions
- British Possessions
- French Possessions
- German Possessions
- Netherlands' Possessions
- Italian Possessions
- Portuguese Possessions
- Spanish Possessions
- United States' Possessions
- Japanese Possessions

power of the era, symbolized the imperial wave that in a single generation engulfed the entire world. By 1900 it covered one-fifth of the earth's land area and comprised perhaps one-fourth of its population (Cohen 1973, 30). As British imperialists were proud to proclaim, it was an empire on which the sun never set.

In contrast with classical imperialism, extraordinary competition among the imperial powers marked the "new imperialism" of the late nineteenth century. As the industrial revolution swept across Europe, military might and economic penetration went hand-in-hand as the imperial powers subjugated foreign territories, which became important symbols of national power and prestige. In the process, local inhabitants of the conquered lands were often ruthlessly suppressed.

> The imperial powers typically pursued their various interests overseas in a blatantly aggressive fashion. Bloody, one-sided wars with local inhabitants of contested territories were commonplace; "sporting wars," [Prussian leader Otto von] Bismarck once called them. The powers themselves rarely came into direct military conflict, but competition among them was keen, and they were perpetually involved in various diplomatic crises. In contrast to the preceding years of comparative political calm, the period after 1870 was one of unaccustomed hostility and tension. (Cohen 1973, 30)

105

What explains the new imperialism that engulfed the world little more than a century ago? Having abandoned their earlier acquired empires, why did most of the great powers—and those that aspired to great-power status—engage in the expensive and often vicious competition to control other peoples and territories? The answers are rooted in economics and politics.

Economic Explanations of the New Imperialism. With the industrial revolution capitalism grew emphasizing the free market, private ownership of the means of production, and the accumulation of wealth in the hands of a few. Marxist theorists saw imperialism's aggressive competition as the product of capitalists' need for profitable overseas outlets for their surplus ("finance") capital. Here is where V. I. Lenin made one of his distinctive contributions to the communist thinking later described as "Marxism-Leninism."

In his famous monograph, *Imperialism, The Highest Stage of Capitalism*, published in 1916, Lenin argued that military expansion abroad was produced by the "monopoly stage of capitalism." If this was true, as Lenin theorized, the only way to end imperialism was to abolish capitalism. Classical or liberal economists, on the other hand, regarded the new imperialism not as a product of capitalism as such but rather as "a response to certain maladjustments within the contemporary capitalist system which, given the proper will, could be corrected" (Cohen 1973). What the two perspectives shared was the belief that economics explained the new imperialism: "The fundamental problem was in the presumed material needs of advanced capitalist societies—the need for cheap raw materials to feed their growing industrial complexes, for additional

Ruthless, aggressive, grandiose, and braced by feelings of superiority, Britain's imperial armed forces marched into battle dedicated to seizing land and power for God and country.

markets to consume their rising levels of production, and for investment outlets to absorb their rapidly accumulating capital" (Cohen 1973). Thus, from
both the Marxist and classical (liberal) perspectives, the material needs of capitalist societies explained their imperial drive.

World-system analysts also embrace an economic explanation of the new
imperialism akin to the Marxist explanation. **World-system theory** arose in
part in response to the theories of political development and nation building
prevalent during the 1950s and 1960s and seeks to explain the rise to dominance of the capitalist societies of the Global North and the lack of economic
development elsewhere (Wallerstein 1974a; 1974b; 1980; 1988). World-system
theorists postulate that a single capitalist world economy emerged during what
they commonly described as the "long sixteenth century," which stretched from
1450 to 1640. During this time a world division of labor developed which
demarcated "core" (industrial) political entities from those in the world's (non-
industrial) "periphery." Northwest Europe first emerged as the core. As the
industrial revolution proceeded, the core states exchanged manufactured goods
for agricultural and mineral products produced in the colonial territories at the
periphery. From this perspective, colonization became the principal political
mechanism of imperial control, designed to incorporate external areas into the
capitalist world-economy (Boswell 1989).

Despite the emphasis that world-system theory places on economics, even
its advocates recognize that the new imperialism of the late eighteenth century
differed significantly from the previous colonial period. "The earliest colonies
were usually coastal trading posts for merchants involved in long-distance pre-
ciosity exchange with the contact periphery, such as the spice trade. Following
rivers upstream, these were later superseded by settler colonies involved in the
production of necessities, primarily mining and cash-crop agriculture using
coerced labor." In contrast, after 1870, colonies effectively became occupation
zones in which a small number of European sojourners coerced an indigenous
population into production for the world-economy (Boswell 1989).

Political Explanations of the New Imperialism. Political factors also explain
the new imperialism. J. A. Hobson, a pioneering student of the primacy of politics, argued in his influential 1902 book, *Imperialism*, that the jockeying for
power and prestige between competitive empires had always characterized
state behavior in the European balance-of-power international system. Thus
imperialism through overseas expansion was simply an extension of the competition for dominance that European powers had long pursued among themselves.

By the 1800s Britain emerged from Europe's perpetual conflict as the
world's leading power in politics and economics. From its position as the
world's new rule maker, it became the chief promoter of free international trade
(which, incidentally, promoted disproportionate economic growth in the core
relative to the periphery [McGowan 1981]). By 1870, however, Britain's superiority was on the wane. Germany emerged on the European continent as a powerful industrial nation, as did the United States in the Western Hemisphere.
Understandably, Britain tried to protect its privileged position in the international division of labor in the face of growing competition from the newly
emerging core states. Its efforts to maintain the status quo help to explain the
second wave of imperial expansion—especially in Africa, whose partition
served the imperial powers at the expense of local populations.

As Africa's ignominious fate illustrates, the European powers competed for power not in Europe itself, but in the peripheral areas of the capitalist world system, where competition for political preeminence led to economic domination and exploitation. As in the mercantile system of the past, Europe's colonies were integrated into the world political economy solely for the purpose of serving the interests of the colonial powers. "The political victors controlled investment and trade, regulated currency and production, and manipulated labor, thus establishing structures of economic dependency in their colonies which would endure far longer than their actual political authority" (Spero 1990).

The British-sponsored laissez-faire system of free international trade promoted rapid economic growth in many colonial territories, but economic development elsewhere proceeded even more rapidly. Western Europe, North America, Australia, and New Zealand were able to complete their industrial revolutions during this period and to advance as industrial societies. Thus the gap between the world's rich and poor nations began to take shape.

Colonialism and Self-Determination in the Interwar Period

Political attitudes following World War I turned decidedly anti-imperial. The Versailles peace settlement that ended World War I embraced the principle of national **self-determination,** which U.S. President Woodrow Wilson had advocated in justifying American participation in the war. Self-determination meant that nationalities would have the right to decide which authority would represent and rule them. Wilson and others who shared his liberal-idealist convictions believed that freedom of choice would lead to the creation of nations and governments content with their territorial boundaries and therefore less inclined to make war. In practice, however, the principle was applied almost exclusively to war-torn Europe, where six new states were created from the territory of the former Austro-Hungarian Empire (Austria, Czechoslovakia, Hungary, Poland, Romania, and Yugoslavia). Other territorial adjustments were also made in Europe, but the proposition that self-determination should be extended to Europe's overseas empires enjoyed little serious support.

Still, the colonial territories of the powers defeated in World War I were not simply parceled out among the victorious allies, as had typically happened in the past. Instead, the territories controlled by Germany and the Ottoman Empire were transferred under League of Nations auspices to countries that would govern them as "mandates" pending their eventual self-rule. In the Middle East, France assumed the mandate for Syria, and Britain assumed it for Iraq, Transjordan, and Palestine. In Africa, most of the German colony of Tanganyika went to Britain; the West African colonies of Cameroon and Togoland were divided between Britain and France; and the Union of South Africa gained responsibility for the mandate governing German South-West Africa. In the Pacific area, Australia, New Zealand, and Japan acquired jurisdiction over the former German colonies.

Many of these territorial decisions shaped political conflicts during the next half-century or more. The decisions relating to the Middle East and Africa were especially crucial, as the League of Nations called for the eventual creation of a Jewish national homeland in Palestine and arranged for the transfer of control over South-West Africa (now called Namibia) to what would become the white minority regime of South Africa.

The principle implicit in the League of Nations mandate system gave birth to the idea that "colonies were a trust rather than simply a property to be exploited and treated as if its peoples had no right of their own" (Easton 1964). None of Germany's former colonies or provinces was annexed outright following World War I, for example, setting an important precedent for the negotiations after World War II, when territories of the defeated powers placed under the United Nations trusteeship system were not absorbed by others but were promised eventual self-rule.

The End of Empire

Imperialism threatened the world again in the 1930s and early 1940s, as Germany, Japan, and Italy sought to expand their political control in Europe, Asia, and Africa. With the defeat of the fascist powers, the threat of regional empire building receded and support for self-determination gained momentum. The decolonization process accelerated in 1947, when the British relinquished political control of the Indian subcontinent and India and Pakistan joined the international community as sovereign members. War eventually erupted between the new states as each sought to gain control over disputed territory in Kashmir. It ignited twice more, in 1965 and again in 1971, when East Pakistan broke away from West Pakistan to form the new state of Bangladesh. Violence also broke out in Indochina and Algeria in the 1950s and early 1960s as the French sought to reaffirm political control over colonial territories they had held before World War II. Similarly, bloodshed followed closely on the heels of independence in the Congo (now Zaire) when the Belgians granted their African colony independence in 1960, and it dogged the efforts of Portugal to battle—unsuccessfully—the winds of decolonization that swept over Africa as the 1960s wore on.

Despite these political convulsions, decolonization for the most part was not only extraordinarily rapid but also remarkably peaceful. This may be explained by World War II having sapped the economic and military vitality of many of the colonial powers. World-system analysts contend that a growing appreciation of the costs of empire also eroded support for colonial empires (Strang 1990; 1991). Regardless of the underlying cause, colonialism became less acceptable in a world increasingly dominated by rivalry between East and West. The Cold War competition for political allies and the fear of large-scale warfare militated against efforts to suppress revolutions in overseas empires. Decolonization "triumphed," political scientist Inis Claude (1967) wrote, "largely because the West [gave] priority to the containment of Communism over the perpetuation of colonialism."

The United Nations also played a role in the "collective delegitimization" of colonialism (Claude 1967). With colonialism already in retreat, Global South states took advantage of their growing numbers in the UN General Assembly to secure passage in 1960 of the historic Declaration on the Granting of Independence to Colonial Countries and Peoples. "The General Assembly proclaimed that the subjection of any people to alien domination was a denial of fundamental human rights, contrary to the UN Charter, and an impediment to world peace and that all subject peoples had a right to immediate and complete independence. No country cast a vote against this anticolonial manifesto. . . . It was an ideological triumph" (Riggs and Plano 1994).

As the old order crumbled—and as the leaders in the newly emancipated territories found that political freedom did not translate automatically into political autonomy, economic independence, and domestic well-being—the conflict between the rich nations of the Global North and the emerging states of the Global South took shape. And it continues today: While some see future international struggle as centered on a "clash of civilizations" (Huntington 1993), others argue that "'civilization clash' is not so much over Jesus Christ, Confucius, or the Prophet Muhammad as it is over the unequal distribution of world power, wealth, and influence, and the perceived historical lack of respect accorded to small states and peoples by larger ones" (Fuller 1995).

• • •

THE GLOBAL SOUTH: COMMONALITIES AND DIVERSITY

The Global South is sometimes described today as "zones of turmoil." The phrase draws attention to the multiple differences between the North and South. In contrast with the Global North, where "peace, wealth, and democracy" are widespread, most of the world's people live in "zones of turmoil and development, where poverty, war, tyranny, and anarchy will continue to devastate lives" (Singer and Wildavsky 1993; see also Kennedy 1994). Particularly noteworthy is that the states comprising the Global North are democratic, while many in the Global South are not. Because democracies tend not to fight one another, Northern nations solve their differences peacefully; by contrast, in the Global South, violent conflict remains rife both within and among nations.

Democracy has spread rapidly and widely since the end of the Cold War, becoming the preferred mode of governance throughout much of the Global South (China, Cuba, North Korea, and Vietnam being obvious exceptions). In 1993, for example, elections were held in forty-three countries throughout the world—in some nations for the first time (UNDP 1995, 13). More than half of the countries in Africa are now pursuing democratic reforms, highlighted by the end of *apartheid* and the beginning of majority rule in South Africa. And in eastern Europe and the former Soviet Union the democratic experiment is underway. Still, democracy remains fragile in many places, often lacking the stable institutional arrangements that characterize mature democracy in the Global North. Furthermore, many in the Global South lack well-developed domestic market economies, where individual entrepreneurship and private enterprise determine market forces. While history does not speak conclusively about the ability of democracy to survive in the absence of capitalism, the pattern prevalent in the Global North suggests that democracy may not thrive without the existence or development of market economies.[1] If it cannot, the latest wave of democratization may fall victim to the more difficult task of promoting market economies where none existed previously. In short, the success of the now widespread democratic experiment is not guaranteed.

Differences in technological capabilities also separate North and South. Countries comprising the Global South typically have been unable to evolve an indigenous technology appropriate to their own resources. Instead, they depend critically on powerful multinational corporations (MNCs) spawned in the North to transfer technical know-how from the world's rich to its poor. This

---

[1]It has long been argued that economic development is a "requisite" to democracy (Lipset 1959; also see Dahl 1989). For an empirical study that summarizes previous research and examines this proposition cross-nationally, see Burkhart and Lewis-Beck (1994).

means that research and development expenditures are directed toward solutions to the North's problems, with the consequence that technological advances seldom meet the needs of the South (Singer and Ansari 1988). And as the world moves into the information age, the most striking developments again are taking place in the North, not the South. Map 5.2 provides a sense of the unequal diffusion of information technology by charting the geographic distribution of computer connections to the global Internet. As the map shows, the highest density of connections is in the Global North—North America, western Europe, Japan, and Australia. The lowest is in countries in Africa South of the Sahara, among the poorest countries in the world.

The unequal distribution of the world's wealth and its people, in all of its manifestations, both reflects and explains the poverty of the South. As noted earlier, the four-fifths of humanity who live in the South account for only one-fifth of the world's total economic product. These are the polities commonly called **developing countries,** which the World Bank defines as those whose GNP per capita averaged (in 1993) less than $8,626 annually. (GNP per capita is calculated by dividing a country's total production of goods and services by its population.) The World Bank defines those with a GNP per capita above this level as **developed countries,** which includes principally the twenty-one member states of the Organization of Economic Cooperation and Development

M A P   5 . 2

Uneven Spread: Global Connections to the Internet

The information age promises that people, businesses, and institutions will be able to communicate with one another and transact business with one another almost instantaneously, but the spread of technology is uneven. Information technology is spreading rapidly in the Global North, while much of the Global South lags far behind.

SOURCE: *Time* (1995), 81.

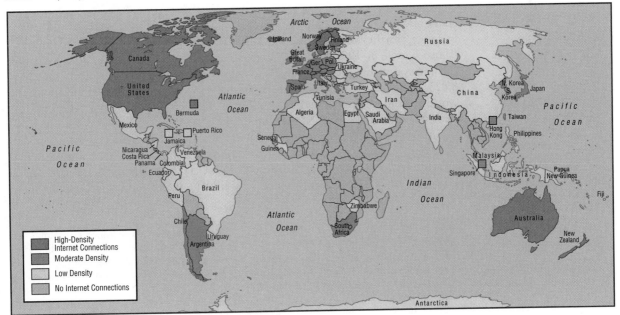

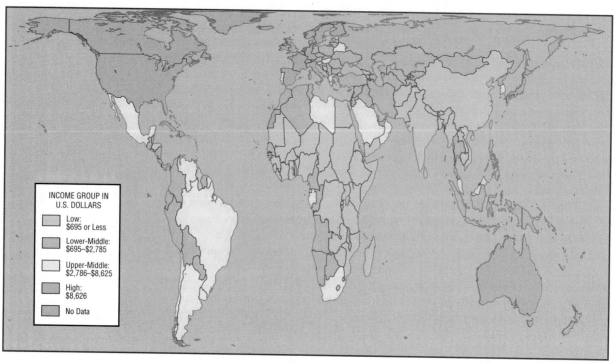

MAP 5.3

Groups of Economies: The Geographic Distribution of GNP per Capita 1993

SOURCE: *World Development Report 1995* (1995), pp. 158–59.

(OECD) otherwise known as the Global North ("zones of peace, wealth, and democracy").[2]

Among the developing countries ("zones of turmoil"), wide variations in economic performance are evident, as we have suggested. The World Bank, for instance, further divides the developing world into "low-income countries" (those which in 1993 had a GNP per capita of $695 or less); "lower-middle-income countries" ($696–2,785); and "upper-middle-income countries" ($2,786–8,625). Map 5.3 GNP per capita. shows the geographic distribution of the world's economies grouped according to their comparative economic performance as measured by GNP per capita.

Although GNP per capita is the most widely used measure of countries' economic performance, we must be cautious about using it as a measure of individuals' economic well-being (see Focus 5.1). Still, the measure is useful as we try to understand countries' widely divergent economic performance and

---

[2]The World Bank's high-income category includes several countries classified as members of the Global South, as they fail to meet the political, technological, or demographic characteristics of the OECD members that generally define the Global North. Among them are four oil exporting countries (Brunei, Kuwait, Qatar, and the United Arab Emirates), three newly industrialized economies (Hong Kong, Singapore, and Taiwan), and Cyprus and Israel. In each, either the United Nations or leaders in the countries themselves regard them as developing countries. Two tiny European countries, Andorra and San Marino, both recently admitted to the United Nations, join the OECD members to define the Global North.

Measuring Living Standards
GNP per Capita versus Purchasing Power Parity

The most widely used international yardstick of national wealth is gross national product (GNP) per capita. Much of this measure's popularity probably stems from its availability. GNP is the total of all goods and services produced by a country's economy in a given year—but that's all it is. The measure does not directly address how the average consumer in a country is faring. GNP per capita is a good indicator, however, for comparing large gaps in national wealth among countries. An African country with only $300 GNP per capita, for example, is obviously worse off than an industrialized country with a far higher value. But the measure's usefulness ends there.

GNP per capita is often mislabeled as "per-capita income," suggesting that it is the average money income for a person in a country. This mislabeling implies that GNP per capita can be used as a type of standard-of-living measure. But it really does not measure living standards in any meaningful way. For example, GNP per capita in the United States in 1993 was $24,750. But per-capita money income was only $15,574—quite a difference. In Japan, 1993 GNP per capita was $31,450. Comparing the GNP of Japan and the United States suggests that the average person in Japan was about 1.3 times better off than the average American—at least according to GNP. Can the average Japanese actually buy 1.3 times more goods and services of the same quantity and quality than the average American?

Economists have worked for years to develop another internationally comparable measure of living standards called "purchasing power parity (PPP)." Although based on a complex econometrics model, simply put, PPP compares the cost of goods in the purchasing power of each country's currency *in that country* to what the same things might cost in the United States.

One major caveat is that the PPP cannot take into account the *quality* of such goods. The quality of a Russian Lada automobile compared with a Nissan Sentra or Ford Taurus is an obvious example. The comparative size of apartments in Europe with those in the United States is another.

While neither GNP nor PPP provides a perfect picture of a country's standard of living, these measures give an interesting snapshot of current economic conditions. What is more, the two measures provide some surprisingly different conclusions. Study the table below to see what we mean.

Comparison of GNP per Capita and Purchasing Power Parity

Country	1993 GNP per Capita	1993 PPP
Switzerland	$36,410	$23,620
Japan	31,450	21,090
United States	24,750	24,750
United Kingdom	17,970	17,750
Greece	7,390	8,360
Mexico	3,750	7,100
Brazil	3,020	5,470
Russia	2,350	5,240
Indonesia	730	3,140
Egypt	660	3,530
China	490	2,120
Nigeria	310	1,480
India	290	1,250
Mozambique	80	380

Note: The U.S. dollar is used as the standard.

SOURCE: Population Reference Bureau, *1995 World Population Data Sheet.*

what it portends for the lives and livelihoods of their people. Furthermore, the geographic variations in the world's material (economic) well-being depicted in Map 5.3 are overlaid by other economic characteristics to create more refined clusters of countries that further define the diversity of the Global South. Five clusters warrant particular attention: the least developed of the developing countries, exporters of oil and other fuels, newly industrialized economies, economies in transition, and emerging markets. In each case, some combination of domestic and international political and economic considerations defines the characteristics peculiar to the groups and why they are of special interest in today's world politics.

More than a half-billion people live in forty-five countries classified by the United Nations as the **least developed of the developing countries (LLDCs).** More than two-thirds are in Africa; most of the rest are in Asia (see Table 5.1).

Poverty is the most striking characteristic of the LLDCs. Indeed, the average annual GNP per person in these countries is only about *one U.S. dollar per year!* Clearly no one could live on such a meager sum if money were the only currency; and in fact much of the economic activity in the LLDCs takes place outside the markets (typically in the agricultural sector) where traditional, western-oriented measures of economic activity occur. To the extent that the LLDCs are involved in the world political economy, their role is largely that of exporters of (nonfuel) primary products, including foodstuffs (e.g., cocoa, coffee, and tea), minerals (e.g., copper), hides, and timber. Still, because the LLDCs consume most of what they produce, theirs is typically a "subsistence economy."

Poverty and its causes manifest themselves in many ways, including high rates of population growth. The rate of population growth in the LLDCs in 1995 exceeded 2.8 percent—far in excess of the average worldwide rate of 1.5 percent. This means that it will take only twenty-five years for the population of the least developed nations to double, compared with two and a half *centuries* for the Global North. But at the same time that LLDCs' population growth is nearly twice the world average, their economic growth rates in the recent past have

TABLE 5.1 The Least Developed of the Less Developed Countries Classified by Geographic Region and Income Group (circa 1995)

Income Group	East and Southern Africa	West Africa	East Asia and Pacific	South Asia	Middle East and North Africa	The Americas

Low income	Burundi
	Comoros
	Ethiopia
	Lesotho
	Madagascar
	Malawi
	Mozambique
	Rwanda
	Somalia
	Sudan
	Tanzania
	Uganda
	Zaire
	Zambia
		Benin
		Burkina Faso
		Central African
		  Republic
		Chad
		Equatorial Guinea
		Gambia
		Guinea
		Guinea-Bissau
		Liberia
		Mali
		Mauritania
		Niger
		São Tomé and
		  Principe
		Sierra Leone
		Togo
			Cambodia
			Laos
			Myanmar
				Afghanistan
				Bangladesh
				Bhutan
				Nepal
					Yemen	Haiti

Lower-middle income	Angola Djibouti	Cape Verde	Solomon Islands Vanuatu Western Samoa	Maldives		

averaged less than one-tenth of 1 percent per year.[3] Growth rates elsewhere almost uniformly have been higher. Thus the rich get richer and the poorest of the poor stay pretty much the same from one decade to the next.

There are other ways in which life for people in the least developed of the developing countries has changed little from that of their ancestors. Life expectancy at birth averages only fifty-one years among the LLDCs (compared with seventy-six years in the Global North (UNDP 1995, 157, 196). Infant mortality rates are among the highest in the world. Less than half of the adult population is able to read and write, and the proportion is even lower among women. And agriculture remains the dominant form of productive activity (although the share of industry in the GNP of the least developed countries has increased in recent years). Similarly, four out of every five people in the LLDCs live in rural areas (UNDP 1995, 167) at the same time that the world is undergoing rapid urbanization. By contemporary standards, then, poverty and an absence of hope for escaping it are the most striking characteristics of the least developed of the developing countries.

Oil-Exporting Countries

The poverty of the LLDCs contrasts starkly with the comparative wealth of the developing-country exporters of oil and other fuels, which includes members of the prominent and sometimes controversial Organization of Petroleum Exporting Countries (OPEC). Although most of the oil exporters fall into the lower-middle or upper-middle income groups, some—notably OPEC members Kuwait, Qatar, and the United Arab Emirates—fall into the high-income group, where their standards of living as measured by GNP per capita rival those of many countries in the Global North (see Table 5.2).

Even the poorest of the poor countries are intertwined in today's interdependent world political economy. However, the importance of export markets to the oil exporters sets them apart from others in the Global South. For them, the opportunities and constraints of global interdependence have special significance, as they shape the ability of governing elites to build a better economic life for their people. In the early 1970s, for example, OPEC was able to drive up the price of oil on global markets, resulting in huge financial gains for its members. As government revenues increased, expenditures on economic development programs (and military weapons) typically followed. But global oil prices peaked in the mid-1980s and then plunged dramatically. Constrained by declining export revenues, government programs designed to enhance domestic economic growth often fell victim. As a result, many oil-exporting countries are not dramatically better off today than they were two decades ago, when OPEC was able to use its "commodity power" to force a fourfold increase in the international price of oil (see, e.g., Zanoyan 1995).

---

[3]Data referred to in this and the previous paragraph are from the Population Reference Bureau (*1995 World Population Data Sheet*), *The World Bank Atlas 1995*, and the U.S. Arms Control and Disarmament Agency (1995). Calculations for the least developed of the developing countries, for which data are incomplete (and represent estimates at best), do not always include the same countries. Thus they should only be regarded as illustrative, not definitive. The population growth rates are rates of natural increase, which measure the excess of births over deaths.

Newly Industrialized Economies

The **newly industrialized economies (NIEs)** are also intimately intertwined in the world political economy, but they have navigated the shoals of global economic interdependence more successfully than OPEC members and other oil exporters. Their success lies in moving beyond the export of primary products—characteristic of both the LLDCs and the oil exporters—to the export of manufactured goods. Today the NIEs are simultaneously among the largest exporters of manufactured goods in the international marketplace and the most prosperous members of the Global South (see Table 5.3).

Four states among the NIEs—the so-called **Asian Tigers:** South Korea, Hong Kong, Singapore, and Taiwan—are particularly notable. Taking advantage of comparatively low wage rates, the governments of the Asian NIEs have aggressively promoted domestic economic strategies designed to promote *export-led* economic growth. Pursuing policies analogous to the imperial powers of a previous era, the governments' neomercantilist practices include protecting so-called "infant industries" from foreign competition and promoting growth of manufacturing industries through various financial incentives. Dramatic increases in economic growth virtually unparalleled elsewhere in the world has followed. With population growth generally in check, the economic performance of the Asian Tigers positions them to join the ranks of the world's wealthiest states in the Global North.

Economies in Transition

As we have noted, the **economies in transition,** all remnants of the former Second World, occupy a place somewhere between the Global North and

---

TABLE 5.2 The Global South's Oil-Exporting Countries Classified by Geographic Region and Income Group (circa 1995)

Income Group	East and Southern Africa	West Africa	East Asia and Pacific	Eastern Europe and Central Asia	Middle East and North Africa	The Americas
Low income		*Nigeria*				
Lower-middle income	Angola	Congo	*Indonesia*	Turkmenistan	*Algeria* *Iran* *Iraq*	Ecuador
Upper-middle income		*Gabon*			Bahrain *Libya* *Oman* *Saudi Arabia*	Trinidad and Tobago *Venezuela*
High income			Brunei		*Kuwait* *Qatar* *United Arab Emirates*	

Note: Members of the Organization of Petroleum Exporting Countries (OPEC) are shown in bold italics.

TABLE 5.3	Newly Industrialized Economies Classified by Geographic Region and Income Group (circa 1995)

Income Group	East Asia and Pacific	The Americas
Upper-middle income	South Korea	Argentina Brazil Mexico
High income	Hong Kong Singapore Taiwan	

South. Placing them is difficult in part because the transition from planned to market economies confounds the task of placing a fair monetary value on the goods and services produced where, previously, governments, not market forces, determined supply and demand. Furthermore, many of these countries developed significant manufacturing capabilities under centralized economic planning which emphasized heavy industry. Although many of these industries are dinosaurs in the emerging information age, the skills and educational bases of the populations that built and operated them position the economies in transition advantageously as they cope with the structural adjustments necessary to compete in a capitalist world economy. Still, in terms of their comparative eco-

Advantaged by the availability of a compliant workforce used to long hours, tedious work, and low pay, newly industrialized economies are able to promote aggressive export marketing strategies that capitalize on low manufacturing costs.

TABLE 5.4 Economies in Transition Classified by Geographic Region and Income Group (circa 1995)

Income Group	Eastern Europe and Central Asia		
Low income	Albania Armenia	Georgia Tajikistan	
Lower-middle income	Azerbaijan Bulgaria Croatia Czech Rep. Kazakhstan Kyrgyz Rep.	Latvia Lithuania Moldova Poland Romania	Russia Slovak Rep. Turkmenistan Ukraine Uzbekistan
Upper-middle income	Belarus Estonia	Hungary Slovenia	

nomic performance, most economies in transition share characteristics with the Global South, as they fall into the low- and lower-middle income categories (see Table 5.4).

Emerging Markets

The triumph of capitalism over socialism has profoundly affected the way the world's governments choose to organize their economics as well as their politics. One theorist has gone so far as to proclaim that the end of the Cold War signals the "end of history"—"the end of mankind's ideological evolution and the universalization of Western liberal democracy as the final form of government" (Fukuyama 1989). If capitalism and free enterprise follow democracy, as many hope, democratic capitalism may someday become the dominant form of political economy (i.e., the intersection of states and markets) throughout the world.

The World Bank and the International Finance Corporation (a World Bank affiliate) have identified twenty-six developing and transitional economies as **emerging markets,** those whose domestic political economies are particularly ripe for foreign investment. As Table 5.5 suggests, neither geography nor current levels of comparative economic performance define the emerging markets. Instead, they are characterized by the potential for exceptionally high investment returns based on economic promise (founded on structural changes not unlike those experienced by the economies in transition, of which some are also regarded as emerging markets) as well as current performance. These economies are experiencing nothing short of economic revolutions stimulated by their own governments and local elites. The value of their currencies is being stabilized, inflation is being brought under control, and businesses once owned by the government are being "privatized" (converted to private ownership). While the emerging markets pose unusual foreign investment risks—as witnessed by recent economic crises in Mexico and Indonesia—the lure of foreign capital to fuel domestic economic change is often as attractive to local political leaders as is the promise of rich rewards to foreign investors. The change in attitudes among the

TABLE 5.5	Emerging Markets Classified by Geographic Region and Income Group (circa 1995)							
Income Group	East and Southern Africa	West Africa	East Asia and Pacific	South Asia	Eastern Europe and Central Asia	Rest of Europe	Middle East and North Africa	The Americas
Low income	Zimbabwe	Nigeria	China	India Pakistan Sri Lanka				
Lower-middle income			Indonesia Philippines Thailand		Poland	Turkey	Jordan	Columbia Peru
Upper-middle income	South Africa		Korea, Rep. Malaysia		Hungary	Greece Portugal		Argentina Brazil Chile Mexico Venezuela
High income			Taiwan					

recipients of foreign investment may not signal the "end of history," but it does represent a dramatic turnaround in thinking about the causes of and cures for underdevelopment once prevalent throughout the Global South.

● ● ●

WHY UNDERDEVELOPMENT?

Our discussion to this point implicitly sees **development** as "the ability of a nation to produce economic wealth, which in turn transforms society from a subsistence- or agricultural-based economy to one where most of society's wealth is derived from the production of manufactured goods and services" (Balaam and Veseth 1996). Urban populations, high literacy rates, well-fed people, and economies driven increasingly by the service sector mark today's developed economies. Why has the Global South lagged so far behind the Global North in its comparative national well-being and the associated correlates of development? And why have the development experiences even within the Global South differed so widely?

Our discussion of the diversity evident in the Global South seemingly leads to the conclusion that underdevelopment is explained by a combination of factors indigenous to developing countries and inherent in their relationships with the Global North—a plight for some, a promise for others. Some theorists attempt to explain the underdevelopment of most developing economies alongside the seeming ability of some to move beyond the experience of most by directing attention primarily toward what happens within Global South states. Other theorists focus on the position of developing countries in the world political economy. We will identify and briefly discuss three variants on these viewpoints, each of which has influenced policy thinking during the past half-century: classical economic development theory, structuralist theories of dominance and dependence, and neoclassical theory.

Classical Economic Development Theory

Classical theories of economic development first emerged in the early post-World War II era and soon became "conventional." Based on the definition of development as increasing increments of per-capita GNP, these Western-oriented theories of "modernization" emphasized the barriers to development posed by the internal characteristics of Global South countries themselves. They then sought to devise ways of overcoming these barriers, often recommending that the wealthy countries supply various "missing components" of development, such as investment capital, through foreign aid or private foreign direct investment (Todaro 1994).

Once sufficient capital was accumulated to promote economic growth, classical (liberal) theorists predicted that its benefits would eventually "trickle down" to other segments of society. In this way, everyone, not simply a privileged few, would enjoy the benefits of rising affluence. Walt W. Rostow, an economic historian and U.S. policymaker, formalized this theory in an influential book entitled *The Stages of Economic Growth* (1960). He predicted that traditional societies entering the development path inevitably would pass through various stages by means of the free market and eventually would become similar to the mass-consumption societies of the capitalist Global North. That prognosis ultimately proved wrong, as did other classical ideas about the route to economic development. Structural theorists who emphasize the role of developing nations in the world political economy purport to explain why the ideas (and ideals) of classical theorists failed.

Structural Theories

Two prongs of structuralism merit attention, as both locate the causes and potential cures of most developing countries' persistent underdevelopment in the patterns of dominance and dependence that characterize their position in the global hierarchy. One is world-system theory, to which we have already alluded; the other is dependency theory and a liberal variant of it called "dualism."

Dependency Theory and Dualism. Dependency theory builds on Lenin's theory of imperialism, but it goes beyond Lenin to account for changes that have occurred since he first wrote his treatise. Its central proposition is that the relationship between the advanced capitalist societies at the core of the world political economy and the developing countries at the periphery is exploitative.[4] Dependency theorists reject Rostow's stages-of-growth thesis, arguing that underdevelopment "is not a stalled stage of linear development, a question of precapitalism, retarded or backward development, but rather a structural position in a hierarchical world division of labor" (Shannon 1989). In short, the underdevelopment of the Global South results from its position in a world political economy dominated by others.

---

[4]For a sampling of some of the extensive dependency theory literature, see Amin (1974); Baran (1968) Emmanuel (1972) Frank (1969) and the special issue of *International Organization* on dependence and dependency in the global system edited by James A. Caporaso (1978). Todaro (1994) reviews the basic tenets of neo-Marxist views of dependency; Smith (1979, 1981) provides insightful critiques of dependency theory; and Caporaso (1980) and Packenham (1992) discuss the theoretical controversies surrounding the perspective.

Political economist Andre Gunder Frank (1969) wrote a classic treatment of underdevelopment in Latin America that led him to conclude that "The now developed countries were never underdeveloped, though they may have been undeveloped." The reason, he argued, was colonialism—the historical expansion of the capitalist system that "effectively and entirely penetrated even the apparently most isolated sectors of the underdeveloped world."

Other theorists—frequently called *dependentistas*—shared Frank's concern about the "enslavement" of the South at the hands of the capitalist North. As Theotonio Dos Santos (1970) argued, "The relation of interdependence between the two or more economies, and between these and world trade, assumes the form of dependence when some countries (the dominant ones) can expand and can be self-sustaining, while others (the dependent ones) can do this only as a reflection of that expansion, which can have either a positive or a negative effect of their immediate development."

Dependent countries are vulnerable to penetration by outside forces. Dependency theorists argue that the overseas branches of giant multinational corporations (MNCs) headquartered in the North are the agents of the penetration and that their role is transferring profits from the penetrated societies to the penetrators. Foreign investment—whether private investments by MNCs or foreign economic and military aid from other governments—also is an instrument of penetration. Technological dependence and "cultural imperialism," perpetrated through ideas alien to the indigenous cultures of Global South societies, are among the consequences. The dependency argument continues by stating that once penetration by advanced capitalist states has occurred, the inherently unequal exchanges that bind the exploiters and the exploited are sustained by elites within the penetrated societies themselves, whose privileged positions in their own societies become tied to the dominant powers.

The argument that a privileged few benefit from dependency while others in their societies suffer is not wholly dissimilar from the familiar concept of **dualism** which even liberal theorists recognize. Dualism refers to the existence of two separate economic and social sectors operating side by side. Dual societies typically have a rural, impoverished, and neglected sector operating alongside an urban, developing, or modernizing sector—but with little interaction between the two. Thus whatever growth occurs in the industrial sector in dual societies "neither initiates a corresponding growth process in the rural sector nor generates sufficient employment to prevent a growing population in the stagnant sectors" (Singer and Ansari 1988). Multinational corporations in many cases contribute to dualism as "they tend to promote the interests of the small number of well-paid modern-sector workers against the interests of the rest by widening wage differentials . . . and to worsen the imbalance between rural and urban economic opportunities by locating primarily in urban areas and contributing to the flow of rural-urban migration" (Todaro 1994).

Like dependency theorists, those who emphasize the dualism evident in the Global South economies reason that it lies in their colonial past, when the imperial powers regarded themselves as the best producers of manufactured goods and their colonies as the best suppliers of basic foodstuffs and raw materials. This relationship produced few "spread effects" in the colonial economies' secondary and tertiary sectors. Eventually, rapid population growth overwhelmed the ability of the colonies' rising incomes to generate continued economic growth (Higgins and Higgins 1979). Dependency theorists nonetheless reject the dualist argument as an explanation of the structure of Global South countries' economic and social systems and their position in the world political economy. Instead of a division into "modern" and "traditional" sectors, they maintain that in fact there is only a "single international capitalist economy," which determines social, economic, and political outcomes throughout the global economy.

World-System Theory. World-system theorists, who also emphasize the structural aspects of the Global South's development dilemma, share dependency theorists' view that the world is divided into a core (the advanced capitalist states) and a periphery (the developing states). However, they take a longer-term perspective on the emergence of disparities between the two and the forces that determine where states are positioned in the global division of labor, treating the actors in world politics in terms of classes much as Karl Marx regarded class as the basic unit of social analysis.

For world-system theorists, a critical issue is how states fit into the international division of labor. "Economic activities in each part of a true world-economy depend on and make possible the activities of the other parts," they argue. "The result is an economic system that includes a number of cultural areas, states, or societies but constitutes a single economy based on a complex division of labor. Each part or area has acquired a specialized role producing goods that it trades to others to obtain what it needs. Thus, the world-economy is tied together by a complex network of global economic exchanges" (Shannon 1989).

The core–periphery concept, again, is particularly important. "Within the world division of labor, core states specialize in the production of the most 'advanced' goods, which involves the use of the most sophisticated technologies and highly mechanized methods of production ('capital-intensive' production). At least until recently, this meant that core states specialized in the production of sophisticated manufactured goods." Within the periphery, on the other hand, economic activities "are relatively less technologically sophisticated and more 'labor intensive'. . . . For most of the modern era, production for export was concentrated on raw materials and agricultural commodities" (Shannon 1989). Historically, those on the periphery also have been militarily inferior to core states and administratively less well organized, which limited their ability to compete with the capitalist states.

World-system theorists cannot easily explain the industrialization now taking place in the periphery. To account for this, they have introduced the *semiperiphery* to accommodate geographic areas or countries, such as the NIEs, that do not fall neatly into either the core or the periphery in the current international division of labor. Dependency theorists also have difficulty explaining these countries' growth. To explain the anomaly, they sometimes use the term "dependent development" to describe the industrialization of peripheral areas in a system otherwise dominated by the Global North. The term suggests the possibility of industrial development, but not outside the confines of a continuing dominance–dependence relationship between North and South.

Neoclassical Development Theory

Structural theory was particularly popular during the 1970s, helping to galvanize leaders throughout the Global South behind the cause of structural reform of the world political economy and the multilateral institutions that help to run it, such as the World Bank and the International Monetary Fund. By the 1980s, however, these same institutions increasingly came to reflect the thinking of neoclassical theorists, who emphasized a diminished government role in the economic life of the Global South.

> The [neoclassical theorists] argue that by permitting competitive free markets to flourish, privatizing state-owned enterprises, promoting free trade and export expansion, welcoming investors from developed countries, and eliminating the plethora of government regulations and price distortions in factor, product and financial markets, both economic efficiency and economic growth will be stimulated. . . . What is needed, therefore, is not a reform of the international economic system or a restructuring of dualistic developing economies or an increase in foreign aid or attempts to control population growth or a more effective central planning system. Rather, it is simply a matter of promoting free markets and laissez-faire economics within the context of permissive governments that allow the "magic of the marketplace" and the "invisible hand" of market prices to guide resource allocation and stimulate economic development. (Todaro 1994, 85–86)

Neoclassical theorists could point to the Asian NIEs as examples of the success associated with free market principles. Although the governments of the Asian Tigers routinely intervene in the marketplace, the success of their export-led path to economic growth has stimulated others to emulate their practices. In addition, the emerging markets are in some sense fulfillments of neoclassical predictions that market economies will thrive where the political atmosphere minimizes government interference in markets, and that individual initiatives are more likely to occur in an atmosphere of political freedom. Studies of the relationship between development and democracy tend to confirm the liberal argument (see, e.g., UNDP 1991; Pourgerami 1991; Moon and Dixon 1985).

The experience of the NIEs and the emerging markets suggests that economic progress and promise are within the grasp of Global South countries (see also Chapter 9). Still, neoclassical theory cannot explain one of the most striking features of the contemporary world political economy: that the gap between the world's rich and poor nations as a whole has not narrowed but instead continues to widen. Consider, for example, that in 1950 the ratio between incomes in the industrializing societies of western Europe and the rest of the world was probably about two to one (Brown 1972, 42). By 1850 the gap had opened to ten to one, and by 1960 to nearly fifteen to one. Since 1950, as the developed nations tripled their per-capita wealth, those at the periphery experienced virtually no change (Durning 1990, 136). James Gustave Speth, head of the United Nations Development Programme (UNDP), noted at the outset of the 1995 UN World Summit for Social Development that the gap between the world's richest 20 percent and its poorest 20 percent had not narrowed over the previous three decades but in fact had *doubled*. Add to this the knowledge that nearly all of the world's population growth in the next century will occur in the Global South and it becomes clear why the gap between the world's rich and poor will continue to widen. Clearly, then, closing the gap between the rich and poor nations is not a realistic goal to which governing elites in most of the

Global South can aspire, but failing to do so is worrisome. As historian Paul Kennedy (1994) has written, "The greatest challenge global society faces today is preventing this faultline [separating the Global North and South] from erupting into a world-shaking crisis."

• • •

WHAT IS DEVELOPMENT?

If the economic chasm separating rich and poor states is unbridgeable—with potentially dire consequences for the future of world politics—does this mean that "development" is an impossible dream for 80 percent of humanity? Or, instead, do we need to broaden our understanding of development to move beyond the classical conception which sees it as little more than increasing increments in per-capita GNP?

The Global South in fact has made dramatic strides toward improving the lot of its inhabitants, thus narrowing the gap in *human* disparity between North and South even as the *economic* gap between them has widened. From this perspective, the Global South "has covered as much distance during [the past thirty years] as the industrial world did in a century. Life expectancy is now seventeen years longer than it was in 1960. Infant mortality has been more than halved. The combined enrollment in primary and secondary school is nearly 1.5 times higher. . . . Even though the South has a per-capita GNP that is a mere 6 percent of the North's, it now has a life expectancy that is 85 percent, and nutritional levels and adult literacy that are 81 percent of those in the North" (UNDP 1995, 15). Evidence like this shows that the human dimension of development is often much brighter than the economic. But the converse may also be true: While the Global North enjoys higher per-capita incomes than the Global South, the adverse side of wealth is also all too evident: high rates of violent crime, alcohol and drug abuse, heart disease, divorce, and HIV infection. Even among the "developed" countries, then, the *human dimension of development* warrants concern.

Basic Human Needs

The human dimension of development first gained attention in the 1970s. Partly in response to the tenets of dependency theory popular among Global South political leaders—which allege that the causes of underdevelopment lie in the patterns of dominance and dependence between rich and poor states—the World Bank and foreign aid donors in the Global North increased their emphasis on the seeming inability of foreign aid recipients to improve the daily lot of their own citizens. Advocates of the "basic human needs" perspective argued that the trickle-down effect projected by conventional theories of economic development failed to materialize because of official corruption and other barriers to growth, caused by Global South countries themselves. Particularly striking was the large number of people determined to be living in "absolute poverty"—without access to safe water or adequate nutrition, sanitation, and health services—which today includes as many as one-fifth of humanity (UNDP 1995, 160–61). Thus, in contrast with structural theories of underdevelopment, the basic human needs perspective placed the blame for the persistence of underdevelopment squarely on the Global South itself.

The basic human needs perspective stimulated a search for new ways to measure development beyond those focusing exclusively on economic indicators. Eventually the United Nations Development Programme (UNDP) devised a **human development index (HDI)** to measure societies' ability to improve the well-being of their own citizens. Its successive *Human Development Reports* have contributed measurably to a debate on the meaning of human development that has been ongoing in national and international forums throughout the 1990s, including, for example, the 1992 UN Conference on Environment and Development, the 1994 UN Conference on Population and Development, and the 1995 World Summit for Social Development.

The concept of human development underlying the index devised by the UNDP (described in Focus 5.2) spreads broadly across contemporary life, embracing not only economics but also the environment, politics, and social welfare in both the developing and developed worlds. The concept is based on the belief that "the real purpose of development should be to enlarge people's choices."

The measurement of human development remains some distance removed from the concept of human development, but its refinement since its introduc-

FOCUS 5.2

Measuring Development
GNP per Capita versus Human Development

Human development is a process of enlarging people's choices. In principle, these choices can be infinite and can change over time. But at all levels of development, the three essential ones are for people to lead a long and healthy life, to acquire knowledge, and to have access to the resources needed for a decent standard of living. If these essential choices are not available, many other opportunities remain inaccessible. . . .

According to the concept of human development, income clearly is only one option that people would like to have—though certainly an important one. But it is not the sum-total of their lives. The purpose of human development is to enlarge all human choices, not just income.

The concept of human development is much broader than the conventional theories of economic development. Economic growth models deal with expanding GNP rather than enhancing the quality of human lives. Human resource development treats human beings primarily as an input in the production process—a means rather than an end. Welfare approaches look at human beings as beneficiaries and not as agents of change in the development process. The basic

human needs approach focuses on providing material goods and services to deprived population groups rather than on enlarging human choices in all fields.

Human development, by contrast, brings together the production and distribution of commodities and the expansion and use of human capabilities . . . It thus focuses on enlarging human choices—and it applies equally to developing and industrial countries. . . .

The HDI has three components: life expectancy at birth; educational attainment, comprising adult literacy . . . and a combined primary, secondary, and tertiary enrollment ratio . . . ; and income.

The HDI value for each country indicates how far that country has to go to attain certain defined goals: an average life span of eighty-five years, access to education for all, and a decent level of income. The closer a country's HDI is to one, the less the remaining distance that country has to travel.

SOURCE: From UNDP (1995), 11–12, 18.

TABLE 5.6 Level of Human Development and Related Economic Attributes (selected countries)

	HDI Rank	HDI Value	Per-Capita GDP Rank	Income Group	Economic Group
High Human Development (HDI value .80 or higher): 63 of 174 countries comprising 30 percent of world population					
Canada	1	.95	8	High	Developed
United States	2	.94	1	High	Developed
Costa Rica	28	.88	60	Lower-middle	Developing
South Korea	31	.88	38	Upper-middle	NIE/EM
Singapore	35	.88	16	High	NIE
United Arab Emirates	45	.86	4	High	Oil exporter
Poland	51	.86	71	Upper-middle	ET/EM
Ukraine	54	.84	68	Lower-middle	ET
Thailand	58	.83	55	Lower-middle	EM
Brazil	63	.80	64	Upper-middle	NIE/EM
Medium Human Development (HDI value .50 to .799): 64 of 174 countries comprising 39 percent of world population					
Turkey	66	.79	65	Lower-middle	EM
Iran	70	.77	62	Lower-middle	Oil exporter
Saudi Arabia	76	.76	33	Upper-middle	Oil exporter
Jordan	80	.76	74	Lower-middle	EM
South Africa	95	.71	80	Upper-middle	EM
Tajikistan	103	.64	129	Low	ET
China	111	.59	123	Upper-middle	Oil exporter
Gabon	114	.58	78	Low	EM
Vanuatu	119	.54	122	Lower-middle	LLDC
Zimbabwe	121	.54	121	Low	Developing
Cape Verde	123	.54	127	Low	LLDC
Low Human Development (HDI value less than .50): 47 of 174 countries comprising 31 percent of world population					
India	134	.44	141	Low	EM
Madagascar	135	.43	165	Low	LLDC
Yemen	137	.42	113	Low	LLDC
Nigeria	141	.41	134	Low	Oil exp/EM
Haiti	148	.36	149	Low	LLDC
Senegal	152	.34	127	Lower-middle	Developing
Djibouti	154	.34	136	Lower-middle	LLDC
Angola	164	.29	161	Lower-middle	Oil exp/LLDC
Niger	174	.21	156	Low	LLDC

Note: The following abbreviations are used: NIE—newly industrialized country; ET—economy in transition; EM—emerging market; LLDC—least developed of the developing countries.

SOURCE: Adapted from UNDP (1995), 18, 20.

tion in the early 1990s continues. Importantly for our purposes as we assess the meaning of "development," the index incorporates income within its calculation (using a strategy that measures its diminishing utility as countries become richer). The reason is simple: "Growth is not the end of development—but . . . the absence of growth often is" (UNDP 1995).

Human Development and Economic Growth. Table 5.6 records the HDI for 30 countries within three HDI categories and their rank among 174 polities (which include some dependent territories, such as Hong Kong, in addition to most sovereign states). The table also includes each country's rank among the 174 in terms of its 1992 per-capita gross domestic product (GDP)[5] (using the concept of purchasing power parity discussed in Focus 5.1) and its position in the income and other economic groups used in Tables 5.1 through 5.5.

A comparison of the countries' human development performance with their per-capita GDP reveals a close correlation between the two. Note, for example, that none of the high-income countries falls within the low human development category; similarly, none in the lowest income category falls within the high human development group. The unmistakable pattern is that the level of human development (and quality of life?) is highest in the Global North, where, on average, economic prosperity is also highest. Conversely, it is generally lower in the Global South, where per-capita economic output is measurably lower.

Still, the evidence shows remarkably wide variations in how people live in different countries, which are not determined exclusively by differences in income levels. Indeed, the evidence demonstrates that *there is no automatic link between income and human development.* "A look at the . . . differences between HDI and real GDP per capita clearly shows that such countries as Costa Rica and Madagascar used their economic growth to enhance the lives of their people. And even though most countries in the Middle East made significant progress in human development over the past thirty years, they still have considerable scope for distributing the benefits of economic growth more equitably" (UNDP 1995).[6] It is also interesting that most of the economies in transition rank higher on the HDI list than on the per-capita GDP list. In short, income alone is a poor indicator of human development.

Inequalities. A pitfall shared by both GNP per capita and HDI is that neither is able to measure inequalities within societies. Just as wealth is distributed very unevenly at the international level, it often is concentrated in the hands of a few elites in the Global South. In Colombia, for example, the share of income enjoyed by the top 20 percent exceeded 55 percent in the early 1990s, while the bottom 20 percent of the population shared only 3.6 percent—a ratio between the richest and poorest quintiles of more than fifteen to one. In Japan, by contrast, the top 20 percent commanded 37.5 percent and the bottom 20 percent nearly 9 percent—or a ratio of about four to one (*World Development Report 1995* 1995, 220–21). Although the quality of the data necessary to make accurate

---

[5]Gross domestic product (GDP) and gross national product (GNP) both measure the production of goods and services within a given time period, differing only in whether residency (GDP) or nationality (GNP) is used to delimit the geographic scope of production. GNP measures production by a nation's citizens or companies, regardless where the production occurs. GDP measures production occurring with the territory of a state, regardless of the national identity of the producers.

[6]Welfare or "redistributive" policies like those designed to meet basic human needs or otherwise enhance human welfare and growth-oriented policies assumed to produce welfare gains through trickle-down effects are often regarded as antiethical, as one can only be attained at the expense of the other. See Moon and Dixon (1992) for empirical evidence that challenges the trickle-down hypothesis while supporting the view that meeting basic human needs promotes long-term economic growth.

Despite the end of apartheid and the election of President Nelson Mandela in 1994, the disparity between black and white income in South Africa is profound. The country's black majority constitutes 41 percent of the nation's unemployment rate, while the white minority—comprising only 13 percent of the population—still owns 75 percent of the land.

calculations of income inequalities varies widely, available evidence suggests that the degree of income inequality is twice as great in the Global South as in the Global North.[7]

Just as per-capita measures of economic production mask income inequalities, the HDI fails to reveal important variations in human development within countries. In Brazil, for example, the HDI value for the Northeastern region of the country is only two-thirds that of the South. Thus "South Brazil would rank alongside Luxembourg (number 27 in the global rankings), while [Northeast] Brazil would rank between Bolivia (113) and Gabon (114)" (UNDP 1995, 22). Or consider South Africa, an emerging market country with an upper-middle income and a medium level of human development: "If white South Africa were a separate country, it would be among the highest-ranking countries in the world. Black South Africa would rank 128 (just after Cameroon). Not just two different communities, but two different worlds" (UNDP 1995, 22). Even in the United States wide disparities exist in the HDIs of white, African-American, and Hispanic populations.

Gender differences in human development are particularly pronounced. In Burundi for example, the literacy rate (in 1990) was 47 percent among adult men but only 20 percent among adult women (UNDP 1995,77). But the differences between men and women extend beyond literacy. Women comprise a much smaller proportion of the nonagricultural work force than men, and their pay for the same work is routinely less. They hold fewer teaching positions at all levels of education and fewer Ph.D.s than men; and their share of adminis-

---

[7]These calculations are based on income inequality ratios between the top and bottom 20 percent of the populations in forty-four Global South countries (not including any of the economies in transition) compared with twenty-one Global North countries as reported in the *Human Development Report 1995* (UNDP 1995, 178–79, 203). The ratios are 12.0:1 in the South and 6.3:1 in the North. Because of wide differences in time periods covered and reporting methodologies by individual countries, these comparisons should be considered only suggestive. For a detailed study of the relationship between inequality and poverty, see Morley (1994).

trative and managerial jobs is minuscule. Much the same holds in politics, where (in 1994) women held only 10 percent of the seats in parliaments world-wide and only 6 percent of national cabinet posts. The reason? "the current institutional, legal, and socioeconomic constraints to [women's] access to opportunities" (UNDP 1995). Furthermore, gender differences continue at the most basic levels of human development: More girls than boys die at a young age; access to adequate health care is more restricted for females than males; and access to education at all levels is more difficult for women than men. Thus it is easy to conclude that women remain victims of abuse and discrimination just about everywhere (MacFarquhar 1994; see also Arat 1995).

Gender inequalities—like the gap between the world's rich and poor, both within and across nations—are pervasive and not easily changed. Still, measurable progress has been achieved in improving the daily lot and future prospects of millions of people during the past several decades. This progress includes women, who—across a range of experiences comprising human development—have closed the gender gap prevalent worldwide but especially throughout the Global South. Indeed, the record of the past several decades presents "an arresting picture of unprecedented human progress and unspeakable human misery, of humanity's advance on several fronts mixed with humanity's retreat on several others, of a breathtaking globalization of prosperity side by side with a depressing globalization of poverty" (UNDP 1994).

What each of us chooses to emphasize in weighing the prospects for human development, even as the economic gap between rich and poor widens, will inevitably be influenced by the perceptual lens through we choose to view "reality." The gap between the world's rich and poor undeniably continues to widen, and millions continue to live in conditions of almost unimaginable deprivation. Nonetheless, measurable progress in human development has occurred and will likely continue (see Focus 5.3). Thus the future of world politics will not only be "a politics of mutual suspicion and struggle" between the Global North and South but also a contest between those who see global regress as inevitable and those who see global progress as possible.

• • •

BEYOND DOMINANCE AND DEPENDENCE?

Vast political, economic, and social differences separate North and South. Together they paint a picture of the Global South "as weak, vulnerable, and insecure—with these traits being the function of both domestic and external factors" (Ayoob 1995).

Coping with insecurity has long dominated the foreign policy goals of Global South states, often bringing them into contention with the Global North and thus helping to frame the long-simmering dispute between rich and poor countries. Ironically, the end of the Cold War magnified the task developing nations face. Just as the threat of war in the Global North receded with the end of Soviet–American rivalry, the great powers' incentives to moderate conflict in the Global South also receded. Violent conflict thus remains a pervasive fact of life throughout much of the Global South, as the **security dilemma**—the perception that the defensive weapons one state acquires pose an offensive threat to a potential adversary—continues to prompt foreign policy behavior throughout much of the developing world.

The end of the Cold War also removed Northern incentives to assist Southern countries with foreign economic and military aid. If Global South countries

A Balance Sheet on Human Development in the Global South

Progress	Deprivation
• Over the past three decades, the population with access to safe water almost doubled, from 36 percent to 70 percent.	• About 17 million people die every year from infectious and parasitic diseases, such as diarrhea, malaria, and tuberculosis.
• Net enrollment at the primary [education] level increased by nearly two-thirds during the past thirty years, from 48 percent in 1960 to 77 percent in 1991.	• About 130 million children at the primary level and more than 275 million at the secondary level are out of school.
• In adult literacy and school enrollment, the gaps between women and men were halved between 1970 and 1990 in developing countries.	• Among the world's 900 million illiterate people, women outnumber men two to one. And girls constitute the majority of the 130 million children without access to primary school.
• Despite rapid population growth, per-capita food production rose by more than 20 percent during the past decade.	• Nearly 800 million people do not get enough food, and about 500 million people are chronically undernourished.
• During the past decade, fertility rates declined by more than one-third.	• Maternal mortality in developing countries, at 350 per 100,000 live births, is about nine times higher than in [developed] countries.
• During the past two decades, the lives of about 3 million children were saved every year through the extension of basic immunization.	• The under-five mortality rate, at one hundred per thousand live births, is still nearly seven times higher than in industrial countries.
• Developing countries' contribution to global emissions is less than one-fourth of that of industrial countries, even though their population is 3.5 times higher.	• About 200 million people are severely affected by desertification; every year, some 20 million hectares of tropical forest are cleared outright or grossly degraded.
• More than two-thirds of the population in developing countries lives under relatively pluralistic and democratic regimes.	• At the end of 1993, there were more than 13 million refugees in the developing world.

SOURCE: Extracted and adapted from UNDP (1995), 16, 33, 34.

want to participate in the world political economy, increasingly they must do so on the North's terms. Thus, as economic interdependence continues apace with the globalization of the world political economy, the economic vulnerabilities of those already insecure will multiply.

Power and wealth have long been the driving forces of world politics. Indeed, realists argue that military power is a function of economic prowess. Among the wealthy countries of the Global North, however, military power is largely irrelevant to an understanding of patterns of international conflict and cooperation, as democratic societies settle their disputes nonviolently. In the Global South, on the other hand, strategies designed to maximize power and wealth continue to animate states' foreign policies. Thus the post-Cold War era is "the tale of two worlds in international politics." In the Global North "economic interdependence, political democracy, and nuclear weapons lessen the security dilemma. . . . The result is a relationship consistent with a liberal model of international politics. Conflicts do not disappear, but they are not resolved militarily." Conversely, in the Global South, "A variety of political systems ranging from democracies to monarchies coexist side by side, and interdependence between peripheral states is subordinate to dependence on core states. Pressures for expansion are still present, stemming from goals of wealth, population, and protection as well as from internal instabilities." As a result, "military force is still a valued means for influencing outcomes and increasing state power," and "power and wealth are still linked" (Goldgeier and McFaul 1992). It is useful, therefore, to examine the foreign policy goals of Global South countries as they strive for power and wealth, particularly in their relationships with the Global North.

In Search of Power

The search for power and the search for wealth are not easily separated, as realists rightly argue, but the states emerging after World War II themselves tended to place the two dimensions on separate tracks. The **nonaligned states** would become those determined to strike a neutral course in the Cold War contest, while the "Third World" referred to a broader group (including, for example, many Latin American states allied with the United States whose independence had been secured in the nineteenth century) which focused more directly on the patterns of dominance and dependence in North–South economic relations. (Few economic ties existed between the Second and Third Worlds.)

Nonalignment. The nonalignment movement began in 1955, when twenty-nine Asian and African countries met in Bandung, Indonesia, to devise a strategy to combat colonialism. Shortly thereafter, leaders of the mostly former colonies met in Belgrade, Yugoslavia, where they created a lasting political coalition, the **Nonaligned Movement (NAM),** whose membership would later grow to more than one hundred countries.

Because the new states could not materially affect the outcome of the Cold War, they tried through nonalignment to maximize their own gains while minimizing their costs. The strategy, as preached with firebrand language at periodic summits, first convened in 1961, stimulated keen efforts by both the United States and the Soviet Union to woo the uncommitted to their own side while preventing their alignment with the other. Nonalignment in effect enabled developing states to play one superpower off against the other in order to gain advantage for themselves. The Cold War competitors—in keeping with the sensitivity each manifested toward the other in a bipolar context perceived as a **zero-sum** contest, where one side's gains were the other's loss—were willing players in the game, often using foreign economic and military aid to win friends and influence allies.

The end of the Cold War dissipated much of the competitive rationale that sustained foreign aid in the past. It also removed whatever facade of strength nonalignment may once have provided the Global South. As a Southern political device, nonalignment is "now lost," having "died" with the Cold War. "More than that, the way the East–West rivalry ended, with the values and systems of the West vindicated and triumphant, undermined the very basis of the nonaligned movement, which had adopted as its foundation a moral neutrality between the two blocs" (Chubin 1993).

Although nonalignment as a political strategy may now be an anachronism, the nonaligned movement and the spirits that animated it live on. As the Nonaligned Movement prepared for its second post-Cold War summit in late 1995, its leaders claimed that the ideals envisaged by its founders more than three decades earlier remained unchanged. "When the Nonaligned Movement began, it was inspired by one motive—that developing countries could take decisions and positions in international politics depending on their own interests and not according to one or other of the superpowers," explained the foreign minister of Colombia, which acted as the host of the eleventh summit of the nonaligned states. "This continues to be valid," he added.

At issue for the nonaligned states today is how to promote their interests in a one-superpower world. The Global South is particularly sensitive to the elitist character of the United Nations Security Council and how profoundly decisions there—where it has virtually no voice but in which the United States is now dominant—can affect its future (Chubin 1993; Korany 1994; see also Jonah 1993). Consequently, serious proposals to make Germany and Japan permanent members of the Security Council (along with Britain, China, France, Russia, and the United States) or in other ways to enlarge it have run aground developing states' insistence that a nonaligned state or one of the larger developing countries (such as Brazil, Indonesia, Mexico, or South Africa) be given a seat among the mighty.

The numerical majority of the Global South has long translated into greater political power within the world organization than any of its members would command individually. Nonalignment further enhanced that clout, as the Soviet Union often sided with the developing states in the General Assembly, particularly on decolonization issues. Now, however, the locus of power within the United Nations is firmly lodged in the U.S.-dominated Security Council, and the United States can veto most matters of substance originating in the General Assembly, where the Global South commands an overwhelming majority. Therefore, developing countries feel threatened by ideas like humanitarian intervention (military intervention to cope with human suffering or to right the wrongs of a government against its own people) and the U.S. posture toward the proliferation of weapons of mass destruction (denying them to others while keeping them for itself). Thus, in a U.S.-dominated world the Global South worries that the new world order may reveal "the reemergence of a more open and explicit form of imperialism, in which national sovereignty is more readily overridden by a hegemonic power pursuing its own self-defined national interest" (Bienefeld 1994).

Zones of Turmoil. States of the Global South have always been acutely sensitive to their autonomy and sovereignty. Thus the UN Security Council's increased concern with intervention in the Global South to protect human rights, promote democracy, ensure nonproliferation, and enhance other arguably legitimate values often is perceived as a threat to the Global South states' independence and integrity. The benefits that Southern states may once have enjoyed as a consequence of Soviet and American efforts to win their allegiance also had their costs. More often than not, developing nations were the battleground on which the superpowers' covert activities, paramilitary operations, and proxy wars were played out. The states of the Global South have borne the burden of more than 90 percent of the conflicts and 90 percent of the casualties of inter- and intrastate violence in the past half-century (Brown, Lenssen, and Kane 1995, 110; see also Chapter 12). The pattern continues in the post-Cold War world.

Nearly fifty violent conflicts of various magnitude have occurred in each year since the end of the Cold War, claiming at least 5 million victims—probably many more (*World Disasters Report 1995* 1995, 111). Virtually every region of the world has experienced the horrors of war in this decade (see Figure 5.2), yet all of the conflicts share an important characteristic: They engulf the world's poorer states and their peoples, not the rich. Furthermore, nearly all of them occurred within states, not among them. Indeed, the 1991 Persian Gulf War was one of the few wars the post-Cold War world has experienced involving clear-cut aggressive behavior by one sovereign state against another. To be sure, the conflicts in Chechnya, Nagorno-Karabakh, Southern Lebanon, and the Balkans all have had important international ramifications, but none of them paralleled Saddam Hussein's invasion of Kuwait. Instead, all reveal the consequences of insecurity born of both internal and external factors that characterize the states—and would-be nation-states—comprising the Global South.

The causes of violent, intranational warfare in the Global South are multifaceted. Still, it is striking that today's great powers—unlike the United States and the Soviet Union of the Cold War—have generally refrained from intervening in these conflicts, choosing instead to let the antagonists themselves determine the outcomes. The conflict in Bosnia-Herzegovena, for example, raged for more than three years before the United States and its NATO allies used military might to force the combatants to the bargaining table. Here, as elsewhere, the end of the superpowers' efforts to maintain a balance of power between them—a characteristic Cold War behavior pattern—helps to explain the reluctance to become involved militarily in what was once a common Cold War bat-

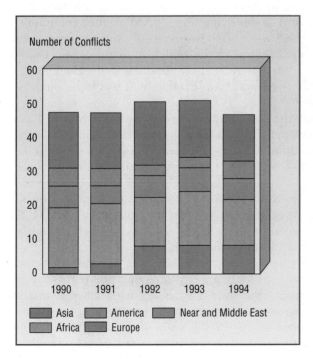

FIGURE 5.2

The Geographic Spread of Intranational Conflict, 1990–1994

Violent conflict remains ubiquitous in the post-Cold War world, as every world region has been plagued by violence in this decade. But it now takes place primarily within states, not between them.

SOURCE: *World Disasters Report 1995* (1995), 112.

tlefield. Without the perceived need to balance power with power in the Global North, the great powers also will not engage in balancing in the South unless vital interests (e.g., access to oil) or particular domestic considerations (placating ethnic interests) demand action (Goldgeier and McFaul 1992).

Arms Acquisitions. Faced with seemingly endless conflict at home or abroad, it is not surprising that political leaders in the Global South would join the rest of the world in its quest to acquire modern weapons of war—including in some cases (China, India, Iraq, North Korea, Pakistan) nuclear weapons. Often this meant that the *burden* of military spending (measured by the ratio of military expenditures to GNP) was highest among those least able to bear it. Thus the societal costs of military spending (which typically exceeded expenditures on health and education) bore little relationship to the level of development. Whether a state was embroiled in a war or threatened by ethnic, religious, or tribal strife at home proved more relevant.

Until recently, few Global South states produced their own modern weapons of war; instead, they imported them. The United States and the Soviet Union were the principal weapons suppliers during the Cold War, often providing arms to would-be friends and allies as outright grants. Beginning in the 1970s, as the United States prepared to reorient its own foreign policy in a post-Vietnam world, the United States began to *sell* arms to others, particularly Middle Eastern oil-exporting countries such as Iran and Saudi Arabia, whose new-found wealth in the aftermath of dramatic oil price increases in the early 1970s enabled them to buy huge quantities of the most sophisticated conventional weapons. The United States willingly sold them in hopes of stabilizing the volatile Middle East region as a bulwark against communist expansionism. It also saw fit to supply Israel with sophisticated weapons to protect it from a possible attack by newly armed Arab states. Elsewhere, the United States sold weapons as part of a program designed to shore up states facing communist threats (sometimes actual, sometimes imagined) without having also to supply American troops (as in Vietnam) to secure the "Free World" against communist encroachment. Predictably, the Soviets often responded by supplying weapons to those targeted by the United States. In the Middle East the Soviet Union became the chief benefactor of the "radical" Arab states committed to the destruction of Israel, notably Syria and Iraq. Eventually it would become the world's leading arms supplier.

The end of the Cold War, the onset of peace processes in the Middle East, and other developments have radically altered the global arms market during the 1990s. Global expenditures on the weapons of war dropped markedly in the wake of the Cold War's demise. With this has come a dramatic change in the relative burden of military spending. Between 1983 and 1993 the burden ratio for the world as a whole dropped from 5.7 percent to 3.3 percent (the lowest since 1960), and from 6.1 percent to 3.1 percent for the developing world (U.S. Arms Control and Disarmament Agency 1995, 24). As military spending declined, so did arms purchased from foreign suppliers.

Even as military spending and arms transfers decline generally, effective demand (the ability to pay) remains high in the Middle East and parts of Asia. The two segments of Figure 5.3 illustrate this, along with other dramatic changes in arms transfers that have taken place in the past decade. Saudi Arabia, the largest importer of arms in the waning years of the Cold War, saw its share of the import market grow from 40 percent in the late 1980s to more than

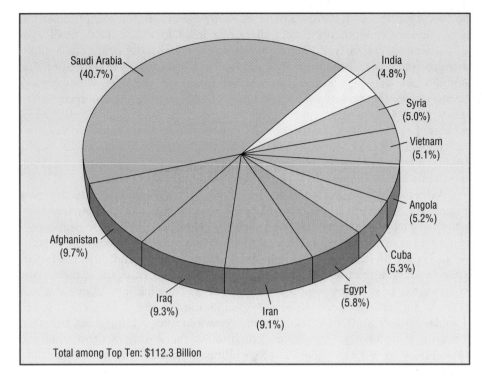

Saudi Arabia
(40.7%)

India
(4.8%)

Syria
(5.0%)

Vietnam
(5.1%)

Angola
(5.2%)

Cuba
(5.3%)

Egypt
(5.8%)

Iran
(9.1%)

Iraq
(9.3%)

Afghanistan
(9.7%)

Total among Top Ten: $112.3 Billion

FIGURE 5.3

**Arms Transfer Agreements to
Top Ten Recipients, 1987–1990**

Perceptions of threat motivate states to acquire arms. Thus the Middle East has been a major recipient of arms transfers since the 1980s. But the patterns have changed with the end of the Cold War and the security challenges of the Gulf War. Saudi Arabia and Kuwait have increased their share of arms purchases, while the demand registered by Afghanistan, Iran, and Iraq has declined.

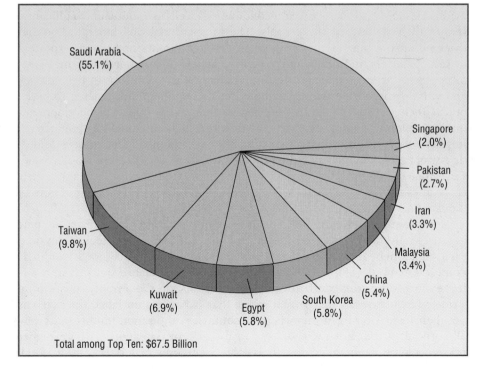

Saudi Arabia
(55.1%)

Singapore
(2.0%)

Pakistan
(2.7%)

Iran
(3.3%)

Malaysia
(3.4%)

China
(5.4%)

South Korea
(5.8%)

Egypt
(5.8%)

Kuwait
(6.9%)

Taiwan
(9.8%)

Total among Top Ten: $67.5 Billion

**Arms Transfer Agreements to
Top Ten Recipients, 1991–1994**

SOURCE: Adapted from Grimmer,
(1995), 58.

135

55 percent in the early 1990s. Kuwait also emerged as a principal purchaser of arms. Both developments reflect their responses to the security challenges posed by the Persian Gulf War. At the same time, Iraq disappeared as a major arms recipient as it faced pressure from the United Nations arms embargo. And Afghanistan, the second-leading arms recipient in the 1987–1990 period, dropped from the top ten after Soviet troops withdrew from the Southwest Asian country and U.S. military support was no longer needed to bolster rebel forces seeking the overthrow of the Marxist regime there. The supply side reflects similar changes, as the United States has replaced the Soviet Union as the world's leading arms supplier—in part because of the resounding capabilities of its military hardware, as demonstrated in the Gulf War (see also Chapter 13).

As before, persistent conflict and perpetuation of the security dilemma explain the Southern urge to arm. Still, the human costs of preparing for war—whether intra- or international, whether for defensive or offensive purposes—remain high. The countries of the Global South had hoped to reap the benefits of the "peace dividend"—the global savings from arms expenditures made possible by the end of the Cold War—to enhance their fortunes and reduce the comparative cost of ensuring their own security. They had hoped in particular that the savings the great powers realized as they shifted their foreign policy agendas away from Cold War confrontation would release large sums for use in bettering the economic and human condition of the world's less fortunate, but their hopes were quickly dashed. Expenditures on the weapons of war have been reduced, but the "dividends" have not been "reinvested" to enhance the economic fortunes of the Global South.

In Search of Wealth

The persistent underdevelopment of (most) developing states explains their drive for greater wealth and a better life for their people, but their place in the configuration of global power, economic as well as political, significantly shapes their pursuit of these goals. The international division of labor that emerged during the colonial era—when developing nations became exporters of raw materials and other agricultural products and importers of manufactured goods—persisted long after imperialism and, according to dependency and world-system theorists, contributed to their underdevelopment. To break out of their dependent status and pursue their own industrial development, many developing countries (particularly those in Latin America) pursued an **import-substitution industrialization** strategy, designed to encourage domestic entrepreneurs to manufacture products traditionally imported from abroad. Governments (often authoritarian) became heavily involved in managing their economies and in some cases themselves became the owners and operators of industry.

Import-substitution industrialization eventually fell from favor, in part because manufacturers often found that they still relied on technology and even component parts imported from the North to produce goods for their domestic markets (Sklair 1991; see also Foley 1995). The recent preference is for **export-led industrialization,** the antithesis of the import-substitution strategy: Its logic rests on the realization that "what had enriched the rich was not their insulation from imports (rich countries do, in fact, import massively all sorts of goods) but their success in manufactured exports, where higher prices could be commanded than for [Global South] raw materials" (Sklair 1991).

As exemplified by the newly industrialized economies, the shift toward export-led growth strategies has transformed many Global South countries from being suppliers of raw materials into manufacturers of products already available in the Global North. Thus a new international division of labor is emerging, as production, capital, labor, and technology are increasingly integrated worldwide and decision making becomes transnational. "The old ideas of national autonomy, economic independence, self-reliance, and self-sufficiency have become obsolete as the national economies become increasingly integrated and the state becomes the agent of the international system" (Dorraj 1995)

Not all Global South economies are positioned to survive in this competitive global environment. Many of the least developed countries continue to remain heavily dependent on raw materials and other primary products for their export earnings. Even the NIEs arguably have not moved beyond the dependent-development stage, as their export goods are in the old, declining industries of the Global North whose technology is easily transferred to the semiperiphery (see Shannon 1989). Nonetheless, the economies of the Global South will not be immune from the rapid globalization of the world political economy now underway.

> As many [Global South] economies abandon the inward-looking national-ist, populist, and socialist policies of the past and embrace outward-looking approaches in their trade and development strategies, they will be further integrated into the world capitalist economy. While some may benefit from such integration and prosper, others may become more vulnerable to crises and fluctuations prevalent in capitalist economic cycles. Impoverished and dependent, . . . much of the [Global South] is ill-equipped to reap the benefits of global interdependence. (Dorraj 1995, 2–3)

How to cope with dominance and dependence thus remains a continuing theme in the developing countries' search for wealth as well as power. Several of their strategies as they relate to the Global North warrant attention.

A New International Economic Order. The emerging nations of the Global South were born into a political-economic order with rules they had no voice in devising. Beginning in the 1950s, they began to pursue alternatives designed to give them a greater role in shaping their own economic futures; most centered on the United Nations where their growing numbers gave them greater influence than they otherwise would have commanded. In the 1960s they formed a coalition of the world's poor, the **Group of 77** (known in diplomatic circles simply as the G-77) and used their voting power to convene a United Nations Conference on Trade and Development (UNCTAD), which later became a permanent organization within the UN family of organizations, often acting as a vigorous voice for the Global South on development issues.

A decade later the G-77 (now numbering more than one hundred countries) again used its numerical majority in the United Nations to push for a **New International Economic Order (NIEO),** which challenged the Liberal International Economic Order (LIEO) championed by the United States and the other capitalist powers since World War II. Motivated by the "commodity power" that oil-exporting nations seemed to have achieved when they forced dramatic increases in world oil prices in the winter of 1973–74, the Global South sought to force the North to abandon the practices that perpetuated dominance and dependence as explained by dependency theory—to which many Southern political leaders subscribed. Structural conflict (Krasner 1985) encapsulated the contest between North and South as the NIEO turned on questions of who would govern the distribution of world wealth and how they would make their choices. Not surprisingly, the Global North rebuffed the South's efforts at reform, and the North–South exchange gradually degenerated into a dialogue of the deaf.

The Global South's determination to replace the existing structures and processes of the world political economy with a New International Economic Order is now little more than a footnote to the history of the continuing contest between the world's rich and poor states (see Rothstein 1988a). Many of the issues raised then still continue to populate the global agenda, as do key philosophical issues about the role of the state in managing international economic transactions. Whereas the philosophy of liberalism on which the LIEO rests is premised on the principle of limited government intervention, "economic nationalists" assign the state a more aggressive role in fostering national economic welfare. "In a world of competing states," political economist Robert Gilpin (1987) notes, "the nationalist considers relative gain to be more important than mutual gain. Thus nations continually try to change the rules or regimes governing international economic relations in order to benefit themselves disproportionately with respect to other economic powers." Clearly that viewpoint continues to apply to many nations in the Global South (as well as to some in the North), even as privatization and a return to market mechanisms rather than state-run enterprises characterizes recent trends domestically. Indeed, the tension between liberalism and mercantilism applies broadly to the issues that now animate the world political economy as we will discover in Chapter 8, where we give detailed attention to these competing viewpoints.

Regional Economic Arrangements. With the failure of reform envisioned in the NIEO, the integration of Global South countries into the process of globalization will occur according to the rules dictated by the North. Are there alternatives? Do regional arrangements enable Global South states to take advantage of growing economic interdependence to achieve their goals of enhanced wealth and a better future for their people?

Efforts to promote regional economic arrangements enjoy a long history, but the evident division of the world political economy into three "trade blocs"—one centered on Europe (with the European Union as its hub), a second centered in the Western Hemisphere (with the United States at the center), and a third in Asia (with Japan as the dominant economy)—has given them new impetus. Consider some of recent developments:

- *In the Americas:* The North American Free Trade Agreement (NAFTA), formalized in 1993, brings Canada, Mexico, and the United States into a single free-trade area whose market size rivals that of the European Union. Plans envision Chile's early addition to NAFTA and the development of a hemisphere-side free trade area (in which tariffs among member countries are eliminated) in the early twenty-first century.

- *Also in the Americas:* The Mercosur agreement, which links Argentina, Brazil, Paraguay, and Uruguay in Latin America's largest trade bloc, hopes to incorporate the Andean Group (Bolivia, Peru, Ecuador, Colombia, and Venezuela) in its free-trade union.

- *In Asia:* The association of Asia-Pacific Economic Cooperation (APEC), an informal forum created in 1989 that now encompasses eighteen nations (including the United States), has committed itself to create a free-trade zone among its members during the next twenty-five years.

- *Also in Asia:* The seven members of the Association of South-East Asian Nations (ASEAN), first established in 1967 by Brunei, Indonesia, Malaysia, the Philippines, Singapore, and Thailand but which now also includes Vietnam, have agreed to set up a free-trade area by 2003.

- *In Africa:* The Southern African Development Community (SADC), formed in 1980 and now encompassing Angola, Botswana, Lesotho, Malawi, Namibia, Mauritius, Mozambique, South Africa, Swaziland, Tanzania, Zambia, and Zimbabwe, has pledged to develop a free-trade area and common currency by the end of the century.

- *In Eastern Europe:* The Central European Free Trade Agreement (CEFTA), created in 1992 by the Czech Republic, Hungary, Poland, and Slovakia, proposes to transform itself into a free-trade zone by early in the next century.

Will the lofty expectations of these regional politico-economic groups be realized? Political will and shared visions are indispensable ingredients explaining the success of regional trade schemes. Economic complementarity is another essential component, as the goal is to stimulate greater trade among the members of the free-trade area, not simply between it and others. If one or more countries in a regional trade regime exports products that each of the others wants, chances of success are greater; if, on the other hand, they all tend to export the same products or to have virtually no trade with one another (typically the case in Africa), failure is more likely.

A related issue is whether regional trade schemes will actually create new trade or simply divert existing trade patterns, arguably in a less-efficient direction. Historical experience with successful experiments (as in the European Union) and unsuccessful experiments (the Latin American Free Trade Association [LAFTA]) suggest that arrangements like NAFTA will succeed, but that others run the risk of trade diversion (as in Latin America) or outright failure (as in sub-Saharan Africa) (World Bank 1995a). In short, prospects for the success of regional trade regimes seem greatest when Global South countries cobble their futures to Northern states—but on terms that the North dictates, of course (see also Shaw 1994). That conclusion hardly augurs well for regional economic arrangements as means to end long-established patterns of dominance and dependence between North and South.

Trade, Aid—or Nothing?

"Trade, not aid" has long been a demand of developing nations as they seek to improve their position in the world political economy. The experience of the NIEs supports the view that access to markets in the developed world will spur economic growth in the Global South. However, market access has become increasingly difficult as domestic politics in the Global North creates pressure to reduce developing countries' ability to export products that compete with Northern industries. Thus trade may be preferred to aid, but it is not a ready alternative.

Aid, too, may no longer be a means that developing nations can rely on in their search for wealth, as changes in the donor countries' domestic climates, propelled by the end of the Cold War, have dramatically reduced their inclination to provide what some foreign aid critics see as "international welfare." Smith Hempstone, U.S. ambassador to Kenya, put it caustically but also clearly: "With the Soviets out of the game, we can no longer be blackmailed into giving money to projects which we know are not beneficial to the countries concerned" (cited in Newark 1995).

"Foreign aid" comes in a variety of forms and is used for a variety of purposes. Some aid consists of outright grants of money, some of loans at concessional rates, and some of shared technical expertise. Although most foreign aid is bilateral—meaning the money flows directly from one country to another—an increasing portion is now channeled through international institutions like the World Bank, and hence is known as "multilateral aid."

The purposes of aid are as varied as its forms. Security objectives typically are pursued through military assistance of one kind or another, but economic aid is also used for these purposes. The United States, for example, "paid" for military base rights in many Third World countries during the Cold War with varying amounts of economic as well as military aid. In addition, it continues to target Israel and Egypt as major recipients of economic assistance because of their critical role in furthering U.S. political and security goals in the Middle East.

While disaster relief and other humanitarian purposes are also met with grants and loans, the economic development of the Global South has been a primary aim of most foreign aid donors since World War II. The assumption that development will support other goals, such as commercial advantage and the growth of free markets and democratic political systems, rationalizes most donors' assistance programs (see Table 5.7). Today, however, these traditional rationales are under widespread attack in many donor countries, particularly in the United States which, until recently (when overtaken by Japan), has provided more bilateral aid and provided more resources to multilateral institutions than any other aid donor.

TABLE 5.7   The Foreign Policy and Economic Goals of Foreign Aid Donors

Time Frame	Primary Objectives	Expected Byproducts	Types of Donors
Long-range	1. Economic development; reduce poverty 2. Eventual self-sufficiency of recipient	1. Political stability 2. Democratization 3. Arab/Muslim solidarity	1. Western 2. Western 3. Arab (OPEC)
Medium-range	1. Maintain diplomatic presence in recipient 2. Symbolize friendships and commitments to, and support for, recipient 3. Maintain access to, and influence over, recipient's domestic and foreign policies	1. Commercial, trade opportunities 2. Enrich bilateral relations	1. All donors 2. All donors 3. Great powers
Immediate	1. Change recipient's current domestic or foreign policies 2. Sustain recipient's regime in power 3. Humanitarian emergency relief	1. Obtain support for donor's foreign policies 2. Protect donor's core objectives 3. Possible future goodwill	1. Great powers 2. Great powers 3. All donors

SOURCE: Adapted from Holsti, 1992, p. 191.

Virtually all states comprising the Global North (plus several Arab countries) provide large sums to developing nations each year. Nonetheless, the volume of aid has largely stagnated since the end of the Cold War (see Figure 5.4)—and this at the very time that the number of aid supplicants has increased as Russia and the other economies in transition, who once provided aid to others, are now on the receiving end. Faced with skeptical, even antagonistic domestic constituents in donor countries, foreign aid is a policy instrument in search of a rationale. Commonly stated goals that would (might?) give foreign aid new life include poverty reduction, human development, environmental protection, reduced military spending, enhanced economic management, development of private enterprise, enhancement of the role of women, and the promotion of democratic governance and human rights (World Bank 1993a). Existing practice in Russia and Ukraine also suggests that disarmament—specifically the dismantlement and storage of chemical and nuclear weapons—may also be facilitated with foreign aid support. In many cases these goals are consistent with neoclassical development theory and a renewed emphasis in the changing world of development assistance on "market fundamentalism" (Newark 1995). In all, however, these goals point toward conditions that recipient countries must meet if they are to receive rich nations' largesse.

Developing nations have long chafed under the conditions or "strings" attached to donors' aid, believing that aid is their right and an obligation of rich countries in recompense for years of unequal exchange perpetrated through colonialism and imperial rule. Consequently, they often view foreign aid as an

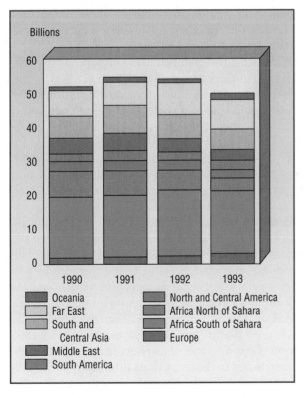

FIGURE 5.4

Regional Distribution of Bilateral and Multilateral Aid, 1990–1993

An increasing amount of foreign aid now goes to African states, generally among the poorest of the developing countries, but the total volume of aid has stagnated, despite an increase in the number of aid supplicants stimulated by the end of the Cold War.

Note: The data include the Central Asian states formerly part of the Soviet Union but exclude Russia, the European states formerly part of the Soviet Union, and the former command economies in Eastern Europe.

SOURCE: Adapted from *Development Cooperation* (1995), H2–H6.

instrument of neocolonialism and neoimperialism and have been especially critical of the "conditionality" imposed by the International Monetary Fund and other multilateral institutions in recent years, allegedly to make them more competitive in the world political economy.

Faced with the reality of stagnant, even diminishing foreign aid dollars, rich and poor states met in Copenhagen in 1995 at the UN Summit for Social Development, determined to find a way to stretch scarce resources. Although the neocolonial/neoimperial charge lurked in the background, the developing countries demonstrated pragmatism in the new foreign aid environment as they quickly supported a proposed "20:20 compact" for human development: Foreign aid donors would be asked to earmark 20 percent of the aid dollars for human development efforts, including meeting basic human needs; and recipient nations in return would be expected to devote 20 percent of their own resources to similar efforts. Thus they recognized that without conditions, foreign aid might cease flowing altogether.

● ● ●

THE GLOBAL SOUTH IN THE NEW MILLENNIUM

As the globalization of the world political economy proceeds apace, commercial opportunities, patterns of immigration and emigration, and the spread of disease will be influenced less and less by national boundaries. Thus the distinction between the Global North and the Global South may also fall by the wayside. Already we have learned that great diversity characterizes the Global South along the very dimensions that differentiate it from the Global North: demography, politics, technology, and wealth. Nonetheless, those comprising the Global South continue to share much in common, making it useful to treat them as a distinct cluster of state actors in world politics.

The relationships between the world's developed and developing countries will doubtlessly continue to change in the waning days of the twentieth century, but exactly how remains uncertain. A turn inward, toward isolationist foreign policies in the Global North, could lead to a posture of "benign neglect" of the South. Conversely, the end of bipolar confrontation characteristic of the Cold War could usher in a new era of North–South cooperation determined to forge solutions to common problems, ranging from commercial to environmental and security concerns (Feinberg and Boylan 1991). Elements of both approaches are already evident, although the ultimate path that the Global North will pursue in the new millennium remains murky.

Meanwhile, it is useful to remember the historical forces underlying the emergence of the Global South (the "Third World") as an analytical as well as a political concept. Those who learned to regard themselves as its members shared important characteristics and experiences. Most were colonized by people of another race, experienced varying degrees of poverty and hunger, and felt powerless in a world system dominated by the affluent countries that once, and perhaps still, controlled them. Considerable change has occurred among the nations newly emergent as the post-World War II decolonization proceeded, but much also remains the same. Thus a former under-secretary general of the United Nations (Jonah 1991) concluded in the immediate aftermath of the Cold War's demise that the concept "Third World" would continue to be used because "fundamentally . . . the Third World is a state of mind."

KEY TERMS

Third World
First World
Second World
Global South
Global North
decolonization
neocolonialism, neoimperialism
mercantilism
classical liberal economic theory
laissez-faire economics
world-system theory
self-determination
developing countries
developed countries
least developed of the developing
   countries (LLDCs)
newly industrialized economies (NIEs)

Asian Tigers
economies in transition
emerging markets
development
dependency theory
dualism
human development index (HDI)
security dilemma
nonaligned states
Nonaligned Movement (NAM)
zero-sum
import-substitution industrialization
export-led industrialization
Group of 77
New International Economic Order
   (NIEO)

CHAPTER 6

International Organizations in World Politics:
Universal and Regional Actors

The nation-state remains the fundamental entity for cooperation in defense, and action should be intergovernmental based on cooperation between nation-states and not dictated by supranational bodies.

—MALCOLM RIFKIND,
British Secretary of Defense, 1995

A broad assortment of new actors is appearing on the world scene. . . . The United Nations must help these new actors find their places within a coherent international community of the future.

—BOUTROS BOUTROS-GHALI,
U.N. Secretary-General, 1996

The 1648 Peace of Westphalia, which ended the Thirty Years' War, also began a trend toward the replacement of the Christian Empire led by the Holy Roman Emperor and the Pope and established the independence of sovereign territorial states. That trend began to reverse direction when European states started to integrate in the 1950s. Symbolically, on February 7, 1992, when the treaty on European Union was signed in Maastricht, the Netherlands, European states moved a step away from the absolute sovereign control of states over their territory, and toward the reassertion of authority by supranational international institutions over states.

The history of world politics for the past three centuries has largely been a chronicle of interactions among nation-states. Today, states remain the dominant form of political organization in the world. Their interests, capabilities, and goals significantly shape world politics. However, the supremacy of the state has been severely challenged. Increasingly, world affairs are being influenced by organizations transcending national boundaries—universal international organizations like the United Nations and regional organizations like the European Union—whose members are states. Diverse in scope and purpose, these actors perform independent roles and exert global influence.

In this chapter we examine the growth and impact of these transnational organizations. Then in Chapter 7 we will examine a variety of other "nonstate actors," such as ethnonational and religious movements and multinational corporations, which are also increasingly active on the world's stage. Our purpose in these chapters is not simply to describe these actors' existence, but more broadly to determine whether their activities undermine the continuing autonomy of the state. Thus we focus throughout on the capacity of national governments to manage global change, as well as the role of international organizations in the transformation of world politics.

There are two principal types of international organizations: **Intergovernmental organizations (IGOs)** are those whose members are nation-states; **nongovernmental organizations (NGOs)** are those whose members are private individuals and groups. Neither type is peculiar to the twentieth century, although both are now more pervasive than ever. The number of each type of organization increased sharply during the latter part of the nineteenth century, as international commerce and communications grew alongside industrializa-

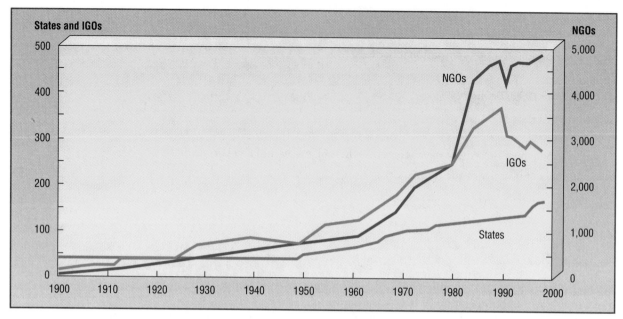

FIGURE 6.1

The Number of States, IGOs, and NGOs since 1900

The number of independent states has increased greatly in the twentieth century, especially since the decolonialism movement began after World War II, but the number of intergovernmental organizations (IGOs) and especially nongovernmental organizations (NGOs) has grown even more rapidly.

SOURCES: States, Polity III data (Jaggers and Gurr 1995); IGOs and NGOs, *Yearbook of International Organizations, 1993/94* (1993), 1699, and moving averages from selected prior volumes.

tion. In 1909, there were 37 IGOs and 176 NGOs. Thereafter, their growth accelerated (see Figure 6.1). By 1960 there were 154 intergovernmental and 1,255 nongovernmental organizations, and by 1993 these numbers had surged to 272 and 4,830, respectively (*Yearbook of International Organizations, 1993/94* 1993, 1699).[1]

This growth has created a complex network of overlapping national memberships in transnational associations. In 1991, for example, the United States participated in more than 2,100 international organizations, over twice the number it participated in only two decades earlier. On a global scale, the national representations of some two hundred countries and territories in 4,917 international organizations numbered more than 118,000 (*Yearbook of International Organizations 1991/92* 1991, vol. 2: 1171–1669). The cooperative

[1]These figures imply that it is easier to identify international organizations than it actually is. In principle, IGOs are defined by their structure and permanence; they meet at relatively regular intervals, have specified procedures for making decisions, have a permanent secretariat or headquarters staff (Jacobson 1984), and "do not have direct access to many of the material resources normally available to states" (Young 1995). If these criteria were relaxed, the number of IGOs would far surpass the nearly three hundred "conventionally defined" organizations just cited, as would the number of NGOs. An additional 1,464 international bodies would qualify for inclusion as IGOs, as would more than 7,929 other nongovernmental entities that share some characteristics with NGOs (see *Yearbook of International Organizations 1993/94* vol. 1 [1993]: 1698).

activities of these "networks of interdependence" (Jacobson 1984) span the entire range of issues confronting international society: trade, defense, disarmament, economic development, agriculture, health, culture, human rights, the arts, illegal drugs, tourism, labor, education, debt, the environment, international crime, humanitarian aid, telecommunications, science, immigration, and refugees, to name just a few.

While more than 95 percent of the international organizations now in operation are nongovernmental, the remaining 5 percent are more important because their members are states. The IGOs that governments create and join will remain preeminent as long as the preeminence of states themselves persists, because IGOs "derive their importance from their character as associations of states" (Jacobson 1984), which give them whatever authority IGOs exercise.

IGOs share in common the fact that they are composed of states. However, they vary widely in their purposes and breadth of membership. One study found that only eighteen qualify as general-purpose organizations, and of these only the United Nations approximated universal membership. The rest, making up more than 97 percent of the total, were limited in their membership and purposes (Jacobson 1984, 48). Table 6.1 illustrates these differences. The variation among the organizations in each category is great, particularly with single-purpose, limited-membership types. The North Atlantic Treaty Organization (NATO), for example, is primarily a military alliance, while others, such as the Organization of American States (OAS), promote both economic development and political reforms.

Still, most IGOs engage in a comparatively narrow range of activities whose purposes are usually economic and social, such as the management of trade, transportation, and other types of functional cooperation. In this sense IGOs are agents as well as reflections of global social and economic interdependence.

Nongovernmental organizations also differ widely. Due to their number and diversity, they are even more difficult than IGOs to characterize and classify. The Union of International Associations, which maintains comprehensive,

TABLE 6.1	A Simple Classification of International Intergovernmental Organizations

Geographic Scope of Membership	Range of Stated Purpose	
	Multiple Purpose	Single Purpose
Global	United Nations World Trade Organization UNESCO	World Health Organization International Labor Organization International Monetary Fund
Interregional, regional, subregional	European Union Organization for Security and Cooperation in Europe Organization of American States Organization of African Unity League of Arab States Association of South East Asian Nations	Nordic Council North Atlantic Treaty Organization International Olive Oil Council International North Pacific Fisheries Commission

up-to-date information about them, categorizes 9 percent of some 4,830 NGOs as universal membership organizations, with most of the remaining 91 percent classified as intercontinental or regionally oriented membership organizations (*Yearbook of International Organizations, 1993/94* [1993], vol. 1: 1698). Functionally, NGOs span virtually every facet of modern political, social, and economic life, ranging from earth sciences to health care, from language, history, culture, and theology to law, ethics, security, and defense.

It is useful to think of NGOs as intersocietal organizations that help promote agreements among states on issues of international public policy. Many NGOs interact formally with the IGOs that operate as servants of the state. For instance, as many as one thousand NGOs actively consult with various agencies of the extensive United Nations system (Boutros-Ghali 1992–1993), and maintain offices scattered in more than a hundred cities throughout the world. The partnership between the two types of entities enables them to work (and lobby) together in pursuit of common policies and programs.

Although widespread geographically, NGOs' impact is greater in the advanced industrial states than in the developing world. "This is so because open political systems, ones in which there is societal pluralism, are more likely to allow their citizens to participate in nongovernmental organizations, and such systems are highly correlated with relatively high levels of economic development" (Jacobson 1984). The composition of their membership therefore also tilts in the direction of the Global North rather than the Global South.

In this chapter, we will discuss some prominent and representative IGOs, including the United Nations, the European Union, and various other regional organizations.

● ● ●

THE UNITED NATIONS

The **United Nations (UN)** is the best-known international organization. Its special characteristics distinguish it from most others; for instance, its membership approximates universality. The end of the Cold War helped realize the goal of universality, as in 1991, Latvia, Lithuania, Estonia, North Korea, and South Korea—long denied a place in the UN—finally gained admission. In addition, the breakup of the Soviet Union also enabled the newly independent former Soviet republics (i.e., the "successor states") to join in 1992. By the end of 1994, with the entry of Palau, the organization's membership climbed to 185 countries and will probably grow further when and if long-standing controversies about the status of potential new members are settled (see Focus 6.1).

In addition to its nearly universal membership, the United Nations is also a multipurpose organization. As Article 1 of the United Nations Charter states, its objectives are to:

- maintain international peace and security;
- develop friendly relations among nations based on respect for the principle of equal rights and self-determination of peoples;
- achieve international cooperation in solving international problems of an economic, social, cultural, or humanitarian character, and in promoting and encouraging respect for human rights and for fundamental freedoms for all;

The Politics of UN Membership
The Case of Taiwan

Almost every country, it seems, wants to be a member of the United Nations (Switzerland being the big exception). However, membership requires support from the powerful existing members of the organization, and the politics governing this process can be complex and conflictual, as illustrated by the case of Taiwan:

It may be a mystery why any country should want to join the United Nations. Paying dues and being shot at in the name of peace would seem to have limited appeal. But joining the club has become part of growing up. Palau became independent just the other day and was immediately welcomed into the UN, once officials discovered where it was. All the more reason to consider the strange case of Taiwan, a poor little rich country eternally condemned to wait in the cold; an outsider wistfully looking in at the club's 185 members busily making important speeches to each other.

Most of these countries would probably be happy enough to allow Taiwan in were it not for opposition by China, which says that Taiwan is not a proper country at all, but a rebel province pretending to be a country. It is an odd notion. Taiwan is clearly a country, and rather a successful one: the world's ninth-largest provider of overseas investment, much of it in China itself, and with foreign reserves about equal to Japan's. It is shaking off its old authoritarianism and, as shown in its latest elections . . . , is turning into a robust democracy.

There's the rub. Taiwan's new freedoms, with the emergence of politicians unafraid to speak their minds, have alarmed China. The Beijing government's long-held vision of a "greater China" incorporating Taiwan, along with Hong Kong and Macau, has become blurred. Back in 1987 China and Taiwan had seemed to be reaching an accommodation, through unofficial talks in third countries. But as democracy has grown in Taiwan, China's attitude has become chillier. Threats to invade the island are being made for the first time since the 1970s.

Taiwan must take some of the blame for its confusing status. Officially, it still calls itself the Republic of China and its rulers claim to be China's only legitimate government. Not surprisingly, this irritates the authorities in Beijing, always sensitive to challenges to their own legitimacy. But Taiwan accepts that it is being academic. It no longer parades the fiction that it rules all China. Instead, it says there are two governments of equal standing, in Taipei and Beijing. It agrees that Taiwan is part of China for fear that declaring formal independence would give the Chinese an excuse to invade. (*The Economist*, December 10, 1994, 16)

Committed to the high ideal of inclusiveness, the United Nations remains a product of the ideological preferences of its dominant members, who often do not embrace the universalist ideal for their own political reasons.

- function as a center for harmonizing the actions of nations in the attainment of these common ends.

These ideals have carried the United Nations into nearly every corner of the complex network of relations among states. Its conference machinery has become permanent; it has provided a mechanism for the management of international conflict; and it has become involved in a broad range of global welfare issues.

Peace and security figured prominently in the thinking of those responsible for creating the United Nations and its predecessor, the League of Nations. Following the onset of each of the world wars, world leaders mounted concerted efforts to cope with future threats to peace. A conviction at the core of liberal idealism—that war is not inevitable but can be eliminated by reforming the anarchical structures that encourage it—inspired both efforts. The first, the League of Nations, sought to prevent a recurrence of the catastrophe of World War I by replacing the balance-of-power system with one based on the princi-

The United Nations was constructed by liberal idealists and realists who believed that global change could be coordinated through universal international institutions. At the San Francisco Conference of the United Nations, between April 25 and June 26, 1946, the United Nations Charter was drafted. More than fifty years later, we might ask whether the design was sufficient to prepare the United Nations to lead in global governance.

ple of *collective security*. According to that principle, aggression by any one state is aggression against all others, who are then obliged to unite in collective action against the aggressor. When the League failed to restrain Germany, Japan, and Italy during the 1930s and global warfare broke out again, the League collapsed.

At the start of World War II the U.S., British and Russian allies began planning for a new international organization—the United Nations—to maintain the peace after the war's end. However, faith in the United Nations' ability to maintain international peace and security quickly eroded. The world organization soon became paralyzed by the unforeseen Cold War conflict between the United States and the Soviet Union.

The five major powers allied during World War II against Germany and Japan (the United States, the Soviet Union, Britain, France, and China) became permanent members of the Security Council and reserved the right to veto its actions. This formula reflected the assumption that the major powers would act together to support the principle of collective security in order to maintain the postwar peace. Consequently, unanimous agreement among the five permanent members was essential, for without it the council would be deadlocked and no action could occur. As it turned out, that agreement infrequently materialized.

False Start: The United Nations during the Cold War

The Security Council rapidly fell victim to the Cold War. Between 1945 and 1955, the Soviet Union, unable to mobilize a majority on its side, exercised its veto power 77 times to prevent action on matters with which it disagreed. In all, it accounted for three-fourths of the 149 vetoes cast in the first three decades of the UN's existence. But obstruction did not come from the Soviet Union alone. During the UN's formative period, the United States did not have to veto Security Council actions it opposed because it possessed a "hidden veto," an ability to persuade a sufficient majority of other council members to vote negatively so as to avoid the stigma of casting the single blocking vote. This ability derived from the composition of the Security Council, on whose nine (later fifteen) members the United States could easily depend to provide a pro-Western majority. When the UN's membership grew and that support was no longer assured, the United States itself became obstructionist, and after 1970 began to veto resolutions with which it disagreed. By the time the Cold War ended in 1991, the United States had exercised its veto power 72 times, twice as often since 1966 as all other permanent council members combined. As a result, the Security Council was often paralyzed, as vetoes severely restricted the UN's ability to undertake collective action. This impotence was aggravated by repeated financial crises since the mid-1960s caused by both superpowers' refusal to pay their mandated fees. Together, the East–West conflict and chronic financial problems during the Cold War destroyed the UN's capacity to operate as its creators had hoped.

The changing composition of the UN's membership also reduced its capacity for concerted action. As its size increased, the organization's membership became less homogeneous. This process increased sharply with the Fifteenth General Assembly in 1960, when seventeen new states joined the United Nations, nearly all of them African. By 1985 well over half of the organization's members came from Africa and Asia, whereas in 1945 less than one-fourth of them came from these two regions, and their domination has increased since (see Figure 6.2). Thereafter the Third World increasingly dominated the United Nations and this dominance gave rise to the North–South dispute. Disagreement and disunity were the byproducts of the UN's larger and increasingly diverse membership, which pursued divergent goals. Consequently, between 1960 and 1990, the United Nations experienced considerable disunity which proved to be a great obstacle to collective UN action.

Fresh Start? The United Nations after the Cold War

The three barriers to the UN's performance—great-power rivalry, insufficient funds, and disunity—were somewhat reduced when the Cold War collapsed. The great powers on the Security Council at last began to behave in the manner that the framers of the United Nations Charter expected them to, by setting aside their differences in order to maintain international peace. How far the United States and the Soviet Union had progressed became strikingly clear in 1990 when they joined forces to organize a collective UN effort to turn back Iraq's aggression in Kuwait. With Russia's repudiation of communism, collaborative crisis-management activities increased exponentially. The former antagonists' new cooperative attitude and renewed efforts to empower the United Nations to preserve world order and promote global prosperity were reflected in their mutual advocacy of "consensus decision making" in the Security Council (i.e., without voting in order to deter the use of vetoes) and their push to revitalize the moribund Military Staff Committee.

Many observers hoped that post-Cold War major-power cooperation would permit an enhanced UN role in world affairs. Bolstered by the Security Council's demonstration of "the capacity to initiate collective measures essential for

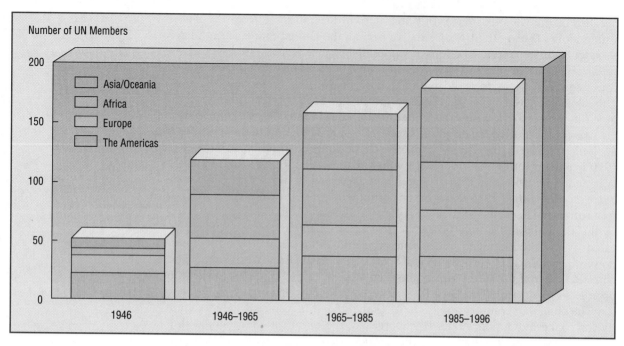

Number of UN Members

- ☐ Asia/Oceania
- ☐ Africa
- ☐ Europe
- ☐ The Americas

1946 1946–1965 1965–1985 1985–1996

FIGURE 6.2

The Changing Membership of the United Nations, 1946–1996

Since the United Nations was created, its members increasingly have included countries from the Global South. This shift has influenced the kinds of interests and issues the organization has confronted, moving the global agenda from the priorities of the great powers in the North to the developing states in the South.

SOURCE: United Nations.

the maintenance of peace in a new world order" (Russett and Sutterlin 1991), as well as the Clinton administration's endorsement of what UN Ambassador Madeleine Albright termed "assertive multilateralism," the prospects for this approach appeared promising. However, as the UN's delayed and weak peace-keeping operations in the Balkans and elsewhere illustrated, huge obstacles remained to the humanitarian goals of preventing genocide and protecting innocent victims from aggression. As Secretary-General Boutros-Ghali lamented in August 1995, "Everywhere we work, we are struggling against the culture of death." Hope for the UN's effectiveness dimmed, its limitations perhaps rooted in the ways it is organized for its ambitious and wide-ranging purposes.

The Organization of the United Nations: System and Structure

The Security Council is one of six principal organs established by the United Nations Charter; the others are the General Assembly, the Economic and Social Council, the Trusteeship Council, the Secretariat, and the International Court of Justice. In the General Assembly—the only organ that represents all the member states—decision making follows the principle of majority rule, with no state given a veto.

Unlike the Security Council, which is empowered by the UN Charter to initiate actions including the use of force, the General Assembly can only make

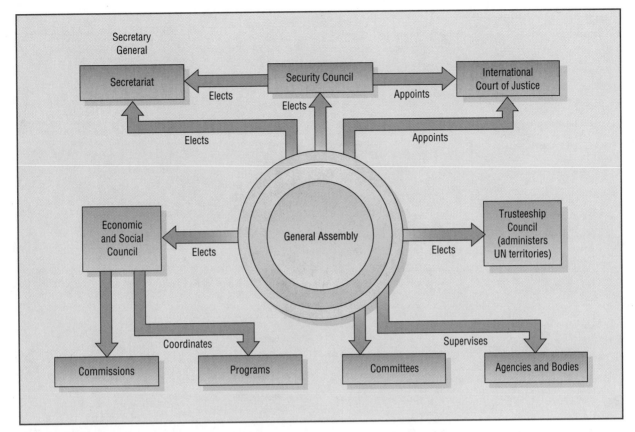

FIGURE 6.3

The Structure of the United Nations

The United Nations comprises six major organs, each of which specializes in particular activities. This figure outlines the major responsibilities of each principal organ and its relationship with the others.

SOURCE: Adapted from Taylor (1990), 49.

recommendations. Unforeseen by the founders of the United Nations, however, this limited mandate enabled the General Assembly to become a partner with the Security Council in managing security. The General Assembly is also now the primary body for addressing social and economic problems, which have grown in number and importance.

In response, the United Nations has evolved into an extraordinarily complex set of political institutions. Thus, today it is not one organization but a decentralized conglomerate of countless committees, bureaus, boards, commissions, centers, institutes, offices, and agencies.[2] If any one occupies a central role in the overall structure of the United Nations, it is the General Assembly (see Figure 6.3).

[2]The United Nations also often relies heavily on the many nongovernmental organizations it helps to fund that are not under its formal authority. This involvement blurs the line between governmental and nongovernmental functions. Examples include the United Nations Children's Fund (UNICEF), the United Nations for Population Fund Activities, and the United Nations University, fulfill their missions in part through nongovernmental entities.

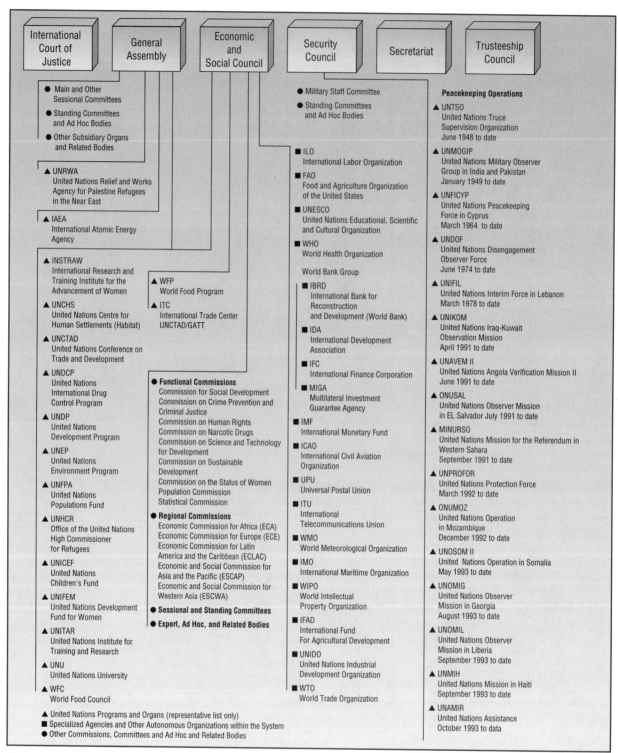

International Court of Justice

General Assembly

- Main and Other Sessional Committees
- Standing Committees and Ad Hoc Bodies
- Other Subsidiary Organs and Related Bodies

▲ UNRWA
United Nations Relief and Works Agency for Palestine Refugees in the Near East

▲ IAEA
International Atomic Energy Agency

▲ INSTRAW
International Research and Training Institute for the Advancement of Women

▲ UNCHS
United Nations Centre for Human Settlements (Habitat)

▲ UNCTAD
United Nations Conference on Trade and Development

▲ UNDCP
United Nations International Drug Control Program

▲ UNDP
United Nations Development Program

▲ UNEP
United Nations Environment Program

▲ UNFPA
United Nations Populations Fund

▲ UNHCR
Office of the United Nations High Commissioner for Refugees

▲ UNICEF
United Nations Children's Fund

▲ UNIFEM
United Nations Development Fund for Women

▲ UNITAR
United Nations Institute for Training and Research

▲ UNU
United Nations University

▲ WFC
World Food Council

Economic and Social Council

▲ WFP
World Food Program

▲ ITC
International Trade Center UNCTAD/GATT

● **Functional Commissions**
Commission for Social Development
Commission on Crime Prevention and Criminal Justice
Commission on Human Rights
Commission on Narcotic Drugs
Commission on Science and Technology for Development
Commission on Sustainable Development
Commission on the Status of Women
Population Commission
Statistical Commission

● **Regional Commissions**
Economic Commission for Africa (ECA)
Economic Commission for Europe (ECE)
Economic Commission for Latin America and the Caribbean (ECLAC)
Economic and Social Commission for Asia and the Pacific (ESCAP)
Economic and Social Commission for Western Asia (ESCWA)

● **Sessional and Standing Committees**

● **Expert, Ad Hoc, and Related Bodies**

▲ United Nations Programs and Organs (representative list only)
■ Specialized Agencies and Other Autonomous Organizations within the System
● Other Commissions, Committees and Ad Hoc and Related Bodies

Security Council

- Military Staff Committee
- Standing Committees and Ad Hoc Bodies

■ ILO
International Labor Organization

■ FAO
Food and Agriculture Organization of the United States

■ UNESCO
United Nations Educational, Scientific and Cultural Organization

■ WHO
World Health Organization

World Bank Group

■ IBRD
International Bank for Reconstruction and Development (World Bank)

■ IDA
International Development Association

■ IFC
International Finance Corporation

■ MIGA
Multilateral Investment Guarantee Agency

■ IMF
International Monetary Fund

■ ICAO
International Civil Aviation Organization

■ UPU
Universal Postal Union

■ ITU
International Telecommunications Union

■ WMO
World Meteorological Organization

■ IMO
International Maritime Organization

■ WIPO
World Intellectual Property Organization

■ IFAD
International Fund For Agricultural Development

■ UNIDO
United Nations Industrial Development Organization

■ WTO
World Trade Organization

Secretariat

Trusteeship Council

Peacekeeping Operations

▲ UNTSO
United Nations Truce Supervision Organization
June 1948 to date

▲ UNMOGIP
United Nations Military Observer Group in India and Pakistan
January 1949 to date

▲ UNFICYP
United Nations Peacekeeping Force in Cyprus
March 1964 to date

▲ UNDOF
United Nations Disengagement Observer Force
June 1974 to date

▲ UNIFIL
United Nations Interim Force in Lebanon
March 1978 to date

▲ UNIKOM
United Nations Iraq-Kuwait Observation Mission
April 1991 to date

▲ UNAVEM II
United Nations Angola Verification Mission II
June 1991 to date

▲ ONUSAL
United Nations Observer Mission in EL Salvador July 1991 to date

▲ MINURSO
United Nations Mission for the Referendum in Western Sahara
September 1991 to date

▲ UNPROFOR
United Nations Protection Force
March 1992 to date

▲ ONUMOZ
United Nations Operation in Mozambique
December 1992 to date

▲ UNOSOM II
United Nations Operation in Somalia
May 1993 to date

▲ UNOMIG
United Nations Observer Mission in Georgia
August 1993 to date

▲ UNOMIL
United Nations Observer Mission in Liberia
September 1993 to date

▲ UNMIH
United Nations Mission in Haiti
September 1993 to date

▲ UNAMIR
United Nations Assistance
October 1993 to data

F I G U R E   6 . 4

The United Nations System

The United Nations is a collection of many affiliated IGOs. This figure shows the system in operation at the start of 1995.

SOURCE: United Nations.

The increase in UN bodies and activities parallels the growth of international interdependence and cross-cutting linkages since World War II, as well as the increasing ways in which states have used the UN to accomplish their own aims. Countries in the Global South, for instance—seizing advantage of their growing numbers under the one-state, one-vote rules of the General Assembly—now guide UN involvement in directions of particular concern to them. Although the United Nations began as a Western-dominated political organization, the developing countries have since become its dominant voice. This balance is reflected in the growing diversity of its affiliated agencies, which address the full array of the world's problems and needs (see Figure 6.4).

The Global South countries' use of the UN forum to further their aims and interests regarding decolonization and economic development contrasted with the U.S. view of the United Nations as a platform to pursue its own Cold War strategies. During the 1970s the United States suffered a series of defeats: In 1971 the General Assembly voted to seat Communist China in the world body. In 1974 the General Assembly extended permanent observer status to the Palestine Liberation Organization against U.S. opposition. In 1975 the General Assembly went on record branding Zionism "a form of racism and racial discrimination." And in 1983 the United States was the target of an overwhelmingly approved resolution deploring the U.S. invasion of Grenada.

However, this era of struggle between the Global South and the United States has shifted with the Cold War's collapse. Although control of UN peacekeeping operations and financial support of UN operations no longer divide the Global North and the Global South in the same way they routinely did when the United States (and the Soviet Union) had a singular military agenda in mind and the developing countries had a quite different social, economic, and environmental one, differences remain. Today the less-developed countries resist domination by the Global North while at the same time they fear the Global North increasingly ignores its needs.

North–South differences over perceived priorities are reflected in the continuing debate over the UN's budget (see Focus 6.2). This debate centers on how members should interpret the organization's Charter, which states that "expenses of the Organization shall be borne by the members as apportioned by the General Assembly."[3]

At issue, of course, is not simply money (which remains, with a 1996 total regular assessment at $2.6 billion, a comparatively paltry sum) but differences in images of what is important and which states should have political influence. Poor states argue that needs should determine expenditure levels rather than the other way around. Major contributors, sensitive to the amounts asked of them and the purposes for the funds, are hesitant to pay for programs they

---

[3]The UN budget consists of three distinct elements: the regular budget (including the expenditures of the fifteen specialized agencies of the United Nations, each of which has its own budgetary procedures), the peacekeeping budget, and the budget for voluntary programs. States contribute to the voluntary programs and some of the peacekeeping activities as they see fit. The regular program and some of the peacekeeping activities are subject to assessments.

The precise mechanism by which assessments are determined is complicated (see Laurenti 1995), but generally assessments are designed to reflect states' capacity to pay. Thus the United States, which has the greatest capacity to pay, contributes 25 percent of the regular UN budget, whereas several dozen poor nations pay the minimum, which is 0.01 percent of the regular budget. The United States is also a prime contributor to UN peacekeeping and voluntary programs.

Budgets and Influence in the United Nations

When the General Assembly apportions expenses, it does so according to majority rule. The problem is that those with the most votes (i.e., the less developed countries) do not have the money, and those that do (i.e., the more developed countries) do not have the votes. These wide disparities appear in the comparison of UN budget assessments and relative voting strength in the General Assembly (based on UN scale of assessments approved in 1995 for the UN's 185 members in 1996 and 1997 [UN Doc. A/49/11]).

This figure shows that the eight largest contributors to the United Nations command only eight votes, although they will pay 70 percent of its costs in 1997. At the other end of the spectrum, the poorest members, who collectively will pay only 30 percent of UN costs, command 177 votes. Thus financial disputes reflect the "tension between the principle of sovereign equality of member states, permitting the more numerous developing countries to wield considerable influence over the kinds of issues on which the UN's attention and resources are focused, and the need to set priorities and manage more effectively the UN's limited monies and manpower, an increasing concern of the developed countries" ("Financing the United Nations," n.d.).

Consequently, we might ask whether this system is fair. Do the UN's financial procedures institutionalize a system of taxation without fair representation? Or do the great powers and wealthy members bear financial responsibilities commensurate with their influence?

Percent of Total Budget	Number of Votes
Small Contributors 177 Countries Pay 30 Percent	
Main Contributors 8 Countries Pay 70 Percent	

= 10 Percent of Budget Assessment

Budgets and Influence: Disparities in UN Budget Assessments and Voting Strength in the General Assembly

oppose.[4] Often, the Global South countries set the agenda in the General Assembly but fail to pay for it or to spend the time lobbying for political support from other important UN groups. In fact, about 90 percent of states from the Global South are also regularly in arrears (Laurenti 1995, 12–15).

Against the background of these cash-flow problems other disputes among the UN's members usually arise, as is demonstrated in the politics within its

[4]In particular, the United States has expressed its dissatisfaction with the United Nations by refusing to pay its debt obligations. Members' accumulated debts totalled almost $2.3 billion at the start of 1996, which threatened to bankrupt the UN; "of that figure, the United States owed more than $1.2 billion" (*International Herald Tribune* 338 [February 8, 1996]: 41). Earlier, the United States found another way to register its dissatisfaction with what it saw as the anti-Western drift of many UN bodies: It ended its membership in them. In the 1970s, for example, the Carter administration withdrew for a time from the International Labor Organization in an attempt to influence the direction of its policies, and during the Reagan administration the United States also withdrew from the 159-member UNESCO (United Nations Educational, Scientific and Cultural Organization) in response to what it regarded as the politicization of the body and its hostility toward Western values (including in particular freedom of communication), thereby depriving UNESCO of one-fourth of its budget.

affiliated agencies. The end of the Cold War and the positive contribution The United Nations made shortly thereafter in repelling Iraqi aggression, in securing the release of American and European hostages in Lebanon, in overseeing elections in Cambodia, and in ending the stalemate over Namibia at the time were reflected in the great powers' growing willingness to assist the UN financially in its expanded peacekeeping responsibilities (see Chapter 16). Since then, however, "peacekeeping fatigue" has set in, and the distance between the UN's political goals and financial support remains troublesome.

The UN's Shifting Purposes and Priorities

The history of the United Nations' first fifty years reflects the fact that both rich countries and developing countries have used the organization to promote their own foreign policy goals, profoundly affecting the UN's overall agenda and performance (see Figure 6.5). In some respects, however, the Global South historically has been more effective than either the United States or the other great powers in using the UN's institutional structures and procedures to advance its interests. For example, the General Assembly's one-state, one-vote rule helped the Global South to focus global attention on the issue of colonialism and to "delegitimize" it as a form of political organization. Likewise, the United Nations Special Fund was a partial response to pressure from the Global South for large amounts of UN economic development aid.

As their numbers in the United Nations increased in the 1960s, Global South states pressed even more vigorously on economic development and other issues of particular concern to them beyond the great-power military competition that preoccupied the superpowers. The developing countries' interests found expression in a host of world conferences and special General Assembly sessions held since the early 1970s (see Focus 6.3). However, because these conferences frequently became forums for heated exchanges between North and South, their contribution to solving—not just bemoaning—global problems was rather limited.

The conference technique represents an approach to global decision making marked with pitfalls. Developing countries prefer broadly based institutional settings in which the one-state, one-vote principle gives them an advantage. In this way institutional procedures promote the Global South's interests. In contrast, the prosperous countries of the North prefer small, functionally specific forums, usually outside the General Assembly, which, they believe, "are more likely to involve those states that have a real stake in the outcome of the deliberations." According to this viewpoint, "large, general-purpose bodies only encourage ill-informed participation by states uninvolved in the issue at hand and thus increase the likelihood of irresponsibly politicizing the agenda" (Gregg 1977). Nonetheless, the conference strategy has become an accepted mechanism for pursuing a North–South dialogue on issues of particular interest to the Global South, whose effect has been "to change attitudes, to stimulate political will, and to raise the level of national and global interest in the subject. . . . The industrialized states, although reluctantly, in general continue the dialogue in their own enlightened self-interest" (Feld and Jordan 1994).

On the eve of the twenty-first century, the United Nations can be expected to attempt to play an active role in *both* the area of peace and security and in that of social and economic enhancement. As we will examine in Chapter 16, however, the prospects for future UN peacekeeping is uncertain, and the capacity for the globe's most powerful IGO to "identify, and focus on, what the United Nations can do best" (Boutros-Ghali 1995) in the latter category of global

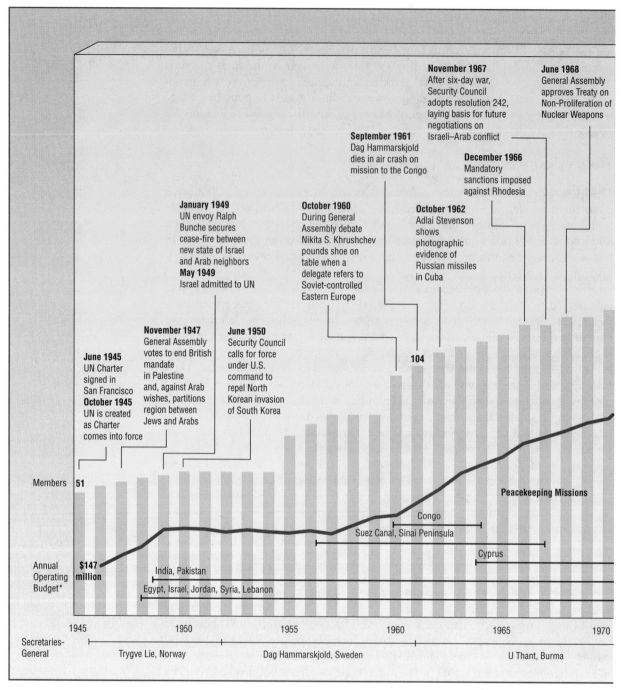

FIGURE 6.5

The UN at Fifty: A Look at Its First Half-Century

As the United Nations has grown from 51 countries in 1945 to nearly 190, its mission, its budget, and criticism of the way it operates have mushroomed, too. At fiftieth-anniversary ceremonies in New York in October 1995, world leaders offered prescriptions for making the UN a more effective force in the post-Cold War era. This figure highlights the major issues and developments in the UN's history between 1945 and 1995.

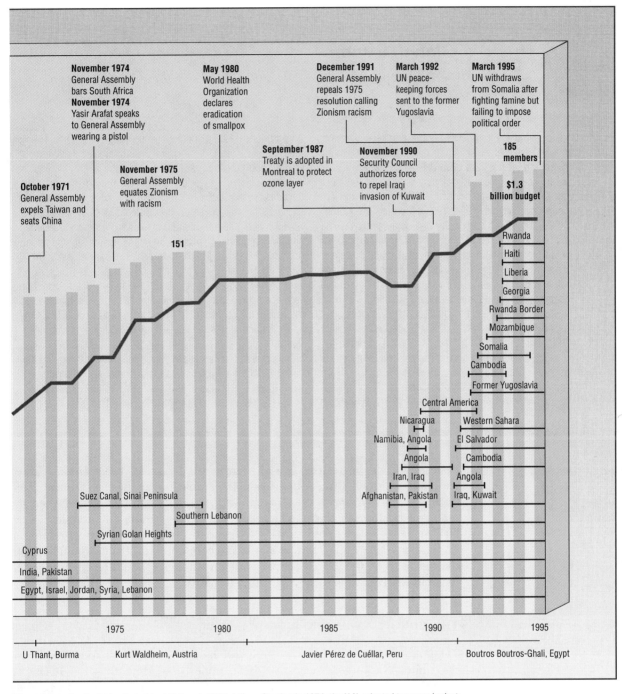

October 1971
General Assembly
expels Taiwan and
seats China

November 1974
General Assembly
bars South Africa
November 1974
Yasir Arafat speaks
to General Assembly
wearing a pistol

November 1975
General Assembly
equates Zionism
with racism

151

May 1980
World Health
Organization
declares
eradication
of smallpox

September 1987
Treaty is adopted in
Montreal to protect
ozone layer

December 1991
General Assembly
repeals 1975
resolution calling
Zionism racism

November 1990
Security Council
authorizes force
to repel Iraqi
invasion of Kuwait

March 1992
UN peace-
keeping forces
sent to the former
Yugoslavia

March 1995
UN withdraws
from Somalia after
fighting famine but
failing to impose
political order

185
members

$1.3
billion budget

Rwanda
Haiti
Liberia
Georgia
Rwanda Border
Mozambique
Somalia
Cambodia
Former Yugoslavia
Central America
Nicaragua
Namibia, Angola
Angola
Iran, Iraq
Afghanistan, Pakistan
Western Sahara
El Salvador
Cambodia
Angola
Iraq, Kuwait

Suez Canal, Sinai Peninsula
Southern Lebanon
Syrian Golan Heights
Cyprus
India, Pakistan
Egypt, Israel, Jordan, Syria, Lebanon

1975   1980   1985   1990   1995

U Thant, Burma   Kurt Waldheim, Austria   Javier Pérez de Cuéllar, Peru   Boutros Boutros-Ghali, Egypt

*Annual operating budget adjusted for inflation, in 1994 dollars. Starting in 1974, the U.N. adopted two-year budget-ing. Data after 1973 are the annual average for the corresponding two-year period.

SOURCE: *The New York Times,* October 22, 1995, 8.

A Global Agenda
The Shifting and Multiple Issues the United Nations Faces

The range of subjects the United Nations addresses speaks to the agenda of issues especially important to the Global South. Included, among others, have been UN-sponsored world conferences that have raised consciousness globally on such issues as the human environment (1972), law of the sea (1973), population (1974, 1984, 1994), food (1974), women (1975, 1980, 1985, and 1995), human settlements (1976), basic human needs (1976), water (1977), desertification (1977), disarmament (1978 and 1982), racism and racial discrimination (1978), technical cooperation among developing countries (1978), agrarian reform and rural development (1979), science and technology for development (1979), new and renewable sources of energy (1981), least developed countries (1981), aging (1982), the peaceful uses of outer space (1982), Palestine (1982), the peaceful uses of nuclear energy (1983), the prevention of crime and the treatment of offenders (1985), drug abuse and illicit trafficking in drugs (1987 and 1992), the protection of children (1990), the environment and economic development (1992), transnational corporations (1992), indigenous peoples (1992 and 1994), internationally organized crime (1994), social development (1995), and housing (1996).

The subjects of world conferences during the past two decades are in effect a list of "the most vital issues of present world conditions," whereas the conferences themselves "represent a beginning in a long and evolving process of keeping within manageable proportions the major problems of humanity" (Bennett 1988). In this the United Nations, spurred on by the Global South, can take some credit. To critics, however, these expensive conferences and debates generate vague, do-good talk but not meaningful solutions; they charge that many countries ignore the principled rhetoric the conference documents propose. Defenders' counter argument is that by exposing the global implications of such problems as crushing world-wide poverty, the United Nations arouses the concern necessary to address the dangers, and that if the UN were given the power it needs for meaningful global governance, members could alleviate these conditions.

issues also will be tested. The challenge will be great, because the United Nations—with only three-fourths as many employees as the U.S. Central Intelligence Agency (*Harper's* 291 [November 1995], 10)—can be no more than the mandates and power that the member states give to it. As one high-level U.N. civil servant, Brian Urquhart (1994), described the UN's political dilemma, "Either the UN is vital to a more stable and equitable world and should be given the means to do the job, or peoples and governments should be encouraged to look elsewhere. But is there really an alternative?"

• • •

THE EUROPEAN UNION

The political tug-of-war between individual states and groups of states within the United Nations is suggestive of an underlying principle—that IGOs are products of the interests of the states that comprise them. This severely inhibits the ability of IGOs to rise above interstate conflicts and to independently pursue their own purposes. In the words of political scientist Inis Claude (1967), "The United Nations has no purposes—and can have none—of its own." This is even truer of other IGOs. Because they cannot act autonomously and lack the legitimacy and capability for independent global governance, perhaps IGOs are better viewed as instruments of states' foreign policies and arenas within which to debate issues than as independent actors.

When states dominate international organizations, as they do the United Nations, the prospects for international cooperation decline because as realist

Small island states such as Thuru Island in the Maldives may appear to be tiny paradises. However, they are exceptionally vulnerable to both natural catastrophes and human threats. If international organizations like the United Nations will not help to protect them, who will?

theorists emphasize, states typically resist any organizational actions that could compromise their interests, there are severe limits on the capacity of international organizations for collective action to engineer global change.

A rival hypothesis—that cooperation among powerful states is possible and that international organizations help produce it—emerges from neoliberal theorizing. This viewpoint is especially pertinent to the **European Union (EU)** (known before 1994 as the European Community [EC]).

The process of European integration began with creation in 1951 of the European Coal and Steel Community (ECSC), the European Atomic Energy Community (Euratom, 1957), and the European Economic Community (EEC, 1957). Since the late 1960s, the three have shared common organizational structures, and, in successive steps, came to be called simply, the European Community. Its membership has grown and its geographical scope broadened as the Union has expanded in a series of waves to encompass (in 1996) fifteen countries: Belgium, France, Germany, Italy, Luxembourg, and the Netherlands (who were the original "Six"); Denmark, Ireland, and the United Kingdom (who joined in 1973); Greece (1981); Portugal and Spain (1986); and Austria, Finland, and Sweden (1995).

Organizational Components and Decision-Making Procedures

The structure of the European Union consists of an Executive Commission, a Council of Ministers, a European Parliament, and a Court of Justice (see Figure 6.6).

The Union's central component, the Council of Ministers, consists of cabinet ministers drawn from the European Union's member states, who participate in the council when the most important decisions are made. In this respect

161

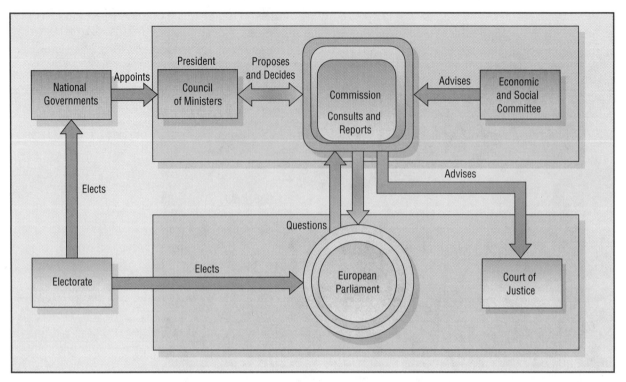

FIGURE 6.6

The Structure of the European Union

The European Union is a complex organization, with different responsibilities performed by various units. This figure charts the principal institutions and the relationships among them that collectively lead to EU decisions and policies.

SOURCE: Adapted from Taylor (1990), 112.

the European Union is an association of states very similar to the United Nations. But the EU is more than this, as evidenced by its other elements and decision-making procedures.

Central among the other components of the European Union is the Commission, which consists of twenty commissioners (two each from Britain, France, Germany, Italy, and Spain, and one each from the remaining member states). A professional staff of more than twenty-five thousand civil-service "Eurocrats," who in principle owe loyalty to the European Union rather than to its national constituents, assists the Commission. The Commission proposes legislation, implements EU policies, and represents the European Union in international trade negotiations. It also manages the EU's budget, which, in contrast with most international organizations, derives part of its revenues from sources not under the control of member states.

The European Parliament is chosen by direct election of the citizenry of the EU's member states. Its more than six hundred delegates debate issues in the same way that national legislative bodies do under popular democracy, but its legislative powers are less pervasive than in a typical domestic parliamentary system. Still, the European Parliament is distinctive, in that most international organizations' legislative bodies represent states (e.g., the UN General Assembly), not individual citizens or transnational political parties.

The Court of Justice is also distinctive in this respect. Comprising fifteen judges, the court interprets EU law for national courts and rules on legal questions raised by the institutions of the EU, by member states, or—in an important deviation from traditional patterns—by individuals. Its decisions are binding, which also distinguishes the European Court of Justice from most other international tribunals.

Figure 6.7 illustrates decision-making processes in the EU. There are two procedures for the adoption of directives and regulations—consultation and cooperation. Which procedure is followed depends on the nature of the proposal, with the principal difference being that the European Parliament plays a greater role in the cooperative than in the consultative process. In both, however, the central role of the Commission is evident, as it has been the driving force behind European integration.

Under the imaginative leadership of Jacques Delors, President of the Commission, the European Community in 1987 adopted the Single European Act, a major amendment to the 1957 Treaty of Rome which created the European Economic Community (popularly known for many years as the European Common Market). The act eliminated members' veto power for most issues to create, in principle, a true European "single" market on January 1, 1993. The goal at the time was a free flow of goods, services, people, and money—a market free of internal borders, similar to the way the United States is free of internal restraints. Although some progress since then has been made toward the ideal, it has been halting and the most ambitious part of the package, a monetary union and a single currency by the end of the century, remains an elusive goal (see Chapter 8).

Supranationalism or Pooled Sovereignty?

How, then, is the European Union best characterized? How are its structures and decision-making procedures best described, as compared to the United Nations and other international organizations?

The EU has the power to make some decisions binding on its national members without being subject to their individual approval. In this sense it is a **supranational entity.** That is, it is not an organization of or among states, but one that goes beyond them to create a new political entity that supersedes the individual countries which comprise it. This description mirrors the visionary hopes of the founders of the various European institutions that make up the EU. They saw on the horizon a "United States of Europe" which would relieve the bitter antagonisms, particularly between France and Germany, that had periodically plunged Europe into destructive wars.

Although the EU incorporates some supranational elements, the term **pooled sovereignty** (Keohane and Hoffmann 1991) better captures its essence, as states remain paramount in its institutional structures and decision-making procedures. Pooled sovereignty encapsulates a central property of the present European Union. No transfer of authority to a central body has occurred. Instead, critical decisions are still made in the Council of Ministers, where states dominate, and most EU decisions still depend on national governments for implementation. Sovereignty is nonetheless shared, in the sense that decision-making responsibility is now spread among governments, and between them and the EU's institutions.

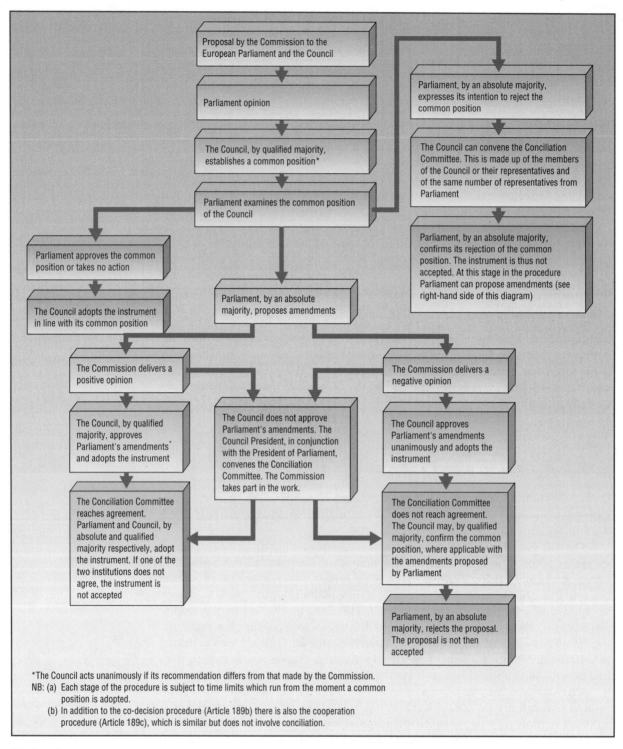

FIGURE 6.7

The Co-Decision Procedure for the European Union

The European Union uses two procedures—a consultation and a cooperation one—for the adoption of regulations. The one chosen depends on the nature of the proposal being considered.

SOURCE: The European Commission Delegation to the United States (1994), 10, 11.

Awareness that EU members decide by majority rule on some issues is critical to an understanding of pooled sovereignty. A major obstacle to effective decision making in the past was that most substantive proposals required unanimous approval. That rule (also used in other international institutions, such as the UN Security Council) enabled member states to protect their national interests as they alone defined them. For instance, France took advantage of this provision to thwart Community action in the late 1960s by simply refusing to send a minister to its meetings. The resulting impasse, called the "empty chair" crisis, spurred the development of new decision-making procedures.

Today, in a radical departure from past practices, and despite recurrent fears that a minority will block the will of the majority, the European Union requires only a qualified voting majority on most internal market decisions.

> Unlike [typical] international organizations, the European [Union] as a whole has gained some share of states' sovereignty: The member states no longer have supremacy over all other authorities within their traditional territory, nor are they independent of outside authorities. Its institutions have some of the authority normally associated with institutions of sovereign governments: On certain issues individual states can no longer veto proposals before the Council [of Ministers]; members of the Commission are independent figures rather than instructed agents. (Keohane and Hoffmann 1991, 13)

The EU's nature is also described by its functions. On the one hand, it is so distinctly different from traditional international organizations that it is virtually in a class by itself. On the other, it is self-evidently not (yet) a rival of the state as the dominant form of political organization, even in Europe. The principle of sovereignty as a defining legal attribute holds that the state alone has dominion over its internal and external affairs. The EU's authority in external affairs is greatest in matters of international trade and related welfare issues, is seriously circumscribed in political affairs, and has yet to develop in military affairs. This was clearest in the EU's weak response since 1991 to the Persian Gulf and Balkans wars and the 1996 dispute between Greece and Turkey over a set of Aegean islands, demonstrating that the collectivity was both unwilling and ill-equipped to act quickly and decisively to protect the region's threatened economic and security interests. Its unresponsiveness during the Gulf crisis led Belgium's Foreign Minister Mark Eyskens to conclude that Europe "is an economic giant, a political dwarf, and a military worm."

Europe: An Economic Giant

The historical development of the European Union attests to the preeminence of military security in the minds of those who sought to forge a new Europe out of the ashes of World War II. Still, the EU has scored its most dramatic successes on the economic front. Today the European Union collectively represents a combined gross national product of more than $6 trillion and a combined population of 375 million, making it the largest, richest single consumer market in the world. The EU's total gross domestic product and its population exceed those of the members of the recently created North American Free Trade Agreement, its closest economic rival.

As previously noted, the expanded European Union builds on previous precedents. In 1991 the seven members of the **European Free Trade Associa-**

tion (EFTA), (created in 1960 as a counterpoint to the European Economic Community) concluded a treaty with the EU to create the world's largest trading area. The agreement anticipated a single European "common market," embracing nineteen countries and more than 385 million people. Although the treaty did not allow the EFTA countries (Austria, Finland, Iceland, Liechtenstein, Norway, Sweden, and Switzerland) power in setting EU trade policies, it set the stage for their participation in the benefits of the single market, eliminating barriers to the movement of money, products, and workers within the EU. In addition, the treaty eased the way for individual EFTA members to join the EU as full partners, which Austria, Finland, and Sweden did in January 1995.

Further expansion of the European Union's membership and geographical boundaries can be anticipated. Under consideration is bringing a Muslim nation, Turkey, into largely Christian Europe (providing that Turkey can improve its human rights record and deepen its commitment to democracy, a precondition to EU membership). In addition, the EU has opened talks on eventually expanding east to include six former communist states (Poland, the Czech Republic, Slovakia, Romania, Bulgaria, and Hungary), providing they can meet the democratic and economic requirements for inclusion. As Map 6.1 suggests, the expansion of the European Union has transformed the geopolitical landscape of the continent.

Beyond these continuing discussions, still other countries have positioned themselves as candidates for potential EU membership. For example, Cyprus, Malta, and Switzerland have from time to time expressed interest in joining, and Russia and other former members of the Soviet Union have voiced an interest in membership in the EU as well. In addition, the Baltic states (Estonia, Latvia, and Lithuania) and Albania signed accords in June 1995, which will enable them to fully join the European Union when their laws and markets converge with those of the EU. Thus a dramatically larger European Union may be in place by the turn of the century, especially if the intergovernmental conference scheduled for 1996 to reform the EU's institutions so they can accommodate the East Europeans' accession proves successful.[5]

However, the disintegrative forces of nationalism could prevent progress toward an enlarged European Union. Future prospects became much less optimistic than they were in early 1993, when unanimous approval of the Maastricht Treaty was widely anticipated. Continuing resistance to the spirit and timetable of the accord has since dispelled much of this optimism for achieving a true common market soon. Instead, the search has turned to finding a compromise agreement acceptable to all the members, whose enthusiasm has been reduced by a mid-1990s recession and by the continuing differences between its more industrialized northern members and those in southern Europe.

The reforms associated with the slogan "Europe 1992" promised to move the EU from a **customs union,** in which customs duties are eliminated, and

---

[5]The EU is also linked to a large number of developing countries in Africa, Caribbean, and Pacific (ACP) through the Lomé Convention, first signed in 1975 and renewed at periodic intervals since, most recently in 1989 for a ten-year period. The Lomé Convention provides the ACP countries tariff-free access to the EU single market without the necessity of reciprocal concessions for EU exports to their economies. It also sets up a commodity price stabilization scheme and provides a framework for the allocation of EU foreign aid to these countries. In addition to the ACP countries, the EU has agreements with several other countries throughout the Global South and has signed a cooperative agreement with ASEAN (the Association of South East Asian Nations) covering trade, economic, and development issues.

MAP 6.1

Members of the European Union, 1996

The European Union has grown from six to fifteen members by January 1995. Norway, bucking a regional trend, voted in 1994 to stay out of the world's largest trade and political bloc. Candidates for potential future admission include (among others) Turkey, Poland, the Czech Republic, Slovakia, Romania, Bulgaria and Hungary, but questions remain if and when the EU's boundaries will expand to encompass as many as 22 countries.

from the free movement of workers, which the former EC also enjoyed, to a genuine **common market,** in which the frontiers between member states are completely abolished. A genuine common market would require the removal of countless inhibitions long apparent in Europe, including restraints on the free movement of goods. It also would require the harmonization of product standards (e.g., uniform socket sizes for electrical appliances), variations in rules governing taxation and capital movements, regulations on transport standards (e.g., rules governing truckers' driving hours, rest periods, and driving teams), and the like. Such inhibitions safeguard national interests and autonomy. By inference, their elimination would dispel ancient nationalistic rivalries and promote the further pooling of sovereignty between the EU's national members and the union's institutions. In this context the commitment to majority rule in the Council of Ministers, rather than the previous practice of consensus decision making, takes on added meaning. Majority rule, reaffirmed in the Single European Act, restricts the ability of individual member states to veto key decisions with which they disagree.

Yet, as noted, nationalistic resistance has not declined. More than a few skeptics predict that the EU's ambitious plans will ultimately fail. Although national governments successfully implemented scores of directives issued by the Commission in social, environmental, economic, and monetary policy, the hope that these steps could lead to the eventual political union of Europe has not been fulfilled.

Europe: A Political Dwarf and a Military Worm?

Members of the European Union have sought since 1970 to coordinate their efforts in hopes of devising a common position on foreign policy issues. This collective spirit, known as **European Political Cooperation (EPC)**, emerged at the Paris Summits of 1972 and 1974 to establish regular meetings between EU foreign ministers. Nonetheless, states often went their own way, and members' foreign policies failed to speak with a single voice.

Complex issues and barriers confront Europe's efforts to forge what is now known as EU's "common foreign and security policy" (CFSP). As a doctrine, the objectives are:

- To safeguard the common values, fundamental interests, and independence of the Union.
- To strengthen the security of the Union and its Member States in all ways.
- To preserve world peace and strengthen international security, in accordance with the principles of the United Nations Charter as well as the principles and objectives of the Conference on Security and Cooperation in Europe (CSCE), which were laid down in the Helsinki Final Act of 1975 and the Paris Charter of 1990.
- To promote international cooperation.
- To develop and consolidate democracy and the rule of law, and respect for human rights and fundamental freedoms.

To fulfill these objectives, the EU must redefine and refine its foreign policy mission and identity, as well as reach consensus about its relationship with the other European security organizations with which most of the EU's members are also affiliated. Of these, the North Atlantic Treaty Organization (NATO) is the most important.

Without a Soviet security threat and the Cold War to consolidate the diverse members, the very existence of NATO became a subject of debate. Yet, members of NATO have reaffirmed their commitment to the alliance. In 1993 they agreed, under U.S. future threat (at a time of great uncertainty in Russia). This was welcomed by Poland, Hungary, and the Czech Republic, which sought entry to NATO. Januscz Onyskiewicz, the Polish defense minister, summarized the aspiration in 1992 by noting, "NATO is seen by central European countries as a pillar of stability which can cast a shadow of stability on the East." Pleading for NATO's eastern expansion, Russian leaders have also repeatedly requested that Russia be placed on a fast track to join the Atlantic alliance (whose primary historical purpose ironically was to deter a massive Soviet invasion of Western Europe).

In response to the changing European geostrategic landscape, the NATO defense ministers endorsed a U.S. plan at the October 1993 summit in Travemuende, Germany. Known as the **Partnership for Peace,** this plan proposed that NATO offer limited military "partnerships" to virtually any European country interested, including Russia and the former Warsaw Pact states. U.S. Secretary of Defense Les Aspin described the partnership proposal as a first step toward possible—though not automatic—NATO membership for the old Soviet-bloc states. While the NATO defense ministers accepted this position, they stopped short of offering full membership to NATO's former East bloc. The new partners will participate in NATO peacekeeping missions and crisis-management operations, but the plan does not guarantee the security of their borders—a privilege enjoyed by NATO's existing members. This decision to restructure NATO thus redirects its goals in a fundamental way and shifts East–West security relationships in a new direction. However, the ultimate consequences of the Partnership for Peace for European security are uncertain. Initiated at a time when NATO is redefining its role on a continent in political transition, the new plan raises fears among its opponents that it could disrupt and disintegrate the alliance itself. And the hapless way in which the whole EU and NATO slept when southern Europe was splintering in the former Yugoslavia, until the United States became engaged, suggesting the difficulties these institutions continue to have developing a common policy on emergent security threats.

The nine-country European military pact known as the **Western European Union (WEU)** is another symbol of the EU's proclaimed resolve to act in unity on defense problems. The WEU, which in 1994 made nine former Warsaw Pact countries associate partners, could eventually emerge as the military arm of the European Union and reduce European dependence on U.S. military might and leadership. While NATO exists, there is little urgency to develop closer military cooperation among EU members, which find themselves involved in a variety of overlapping organizations whose very complexity interferes with coordinated European security policies (see Figure 6.8).

Closer cooperation on foreign and national security policy is a prerequisite to the "United States of Europe" which the European Union's visionary founders once sought. National differences continue to make a unified EU foreign and defense policy an elusive goal, and even the form of a potential European government for a common European citizenship remains a divisive, unresolved issue. Still, a single Europe remains a compelling idea for many Europeans. Consolidation could be in Europe's future. But so could disintegration and the resurrection of intra-European discord and even war (see Mearsheimer 1990).

• • •

OTHER REGIONAL ORGANIZATIONS

Since Europe's 1950s initiatives toward economic and political integration, a dozen or so regional economic schemes have been created in various other parts of the world, notably among states in the Global South. Most seek to stimulate regional economic growth. The major regional organizations in the Global South include:

- The Latin American Integration Association (LAIA), also known as *Asociación Latinoamericana de Integración* (ALADI), established in 1981 to promote freer regional trade. Its members are Argentina, Bolivia, Brazil, Chile, Colombia, Ecuador, Mexico, Paraguay, Peru, Uruguay, and Venezuela.

- The Association of South East Asian Nations (ASEAN), established in 1967 to promote regional economic, social, and cultural cooperation. Its mem-

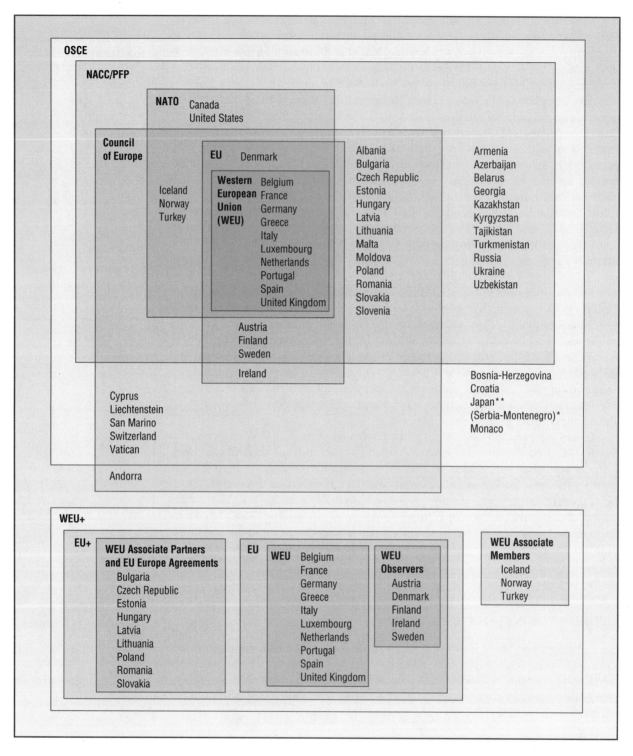

FIGURE 6.8

The Criss-Crossing Memberships of Europe's Primary International Institutions

Europe has built a series of organizations, and the over-lapping structure has made collective decision making difficult.

*Suspended from activities **Observer status. SOURCE: *Nato Review* 43 (November 1995), 30.

bers are Brunei, Indonesia, Malaysia, the Philippines, Singapore, and Thailand, with Papua having observer status. ASEAN met in August 1995 to discuss the possibility of closer ties and an eventual merger between a planned free trade zone among the ten countries in Southeast Asia and a similar zone that already exists between Australia and New Zealand. The purpose of this plan is to operate as a counterweight outside the orbit of Japan, China, the United States, and the other great powers.

- The Caribbean Community and Common Market (CARICOM), established in 1973 to promote economic development and integration. Its members are Antigua, the Bahamas, Barbados, Belize, Dominica, Grenada, Guyana, Jamaica, Montserrat, St. Kitts and Nevis, St. Lucia, St. Vincent and the Grenadines, and Trinidad and Tobago.

- The Council of Arab Economic Unity (CAEU), established in 1964 from a 1957 accord to promote economic integration among Arab nations. Its members are Egypt, Iraq, Jordan, Kuwait, Libya, Mauritania, Palestine, Somalia, Sudan, Syria, United Arab Emirates, and Yemen.

- The Economic Community of West African States (ECOWAS), established in 1975 to promote regional economic cooperation. Its members include Benin, Burkina, Cape Verde, Cote d'Ivoire, Equatorial Guinea, the Gambia, Ghana, Guinea, Guinea-Bissau, Liberia, Mali, Mauritania, Niger, Nigeria, Senegal, Sierra Leone, and Togo.

- The Southern African Development Community (SADC), established in 1992 to promote regional economic development and integration. Its members are Angola, Botswana, Lesotho, Malawi, Mozambique, Namibia, Swaziland, Tanzania, Zambia, and Zimbabwe.

- The South Asian Association for Regional Cooperation (SAARC), established in 1985 to promote economic, social, and cultural cooperation. Its members are Bangladesh, Bhutan, India, Maldives, Nepal, Pakistan, and Sri Lanka.

- The Asia-Pacific Economic Cooperation (APEC) forum, created in 1989 as a gathering of twelve nations without a defined goal. APEC has grown to eighteen countries (including the United States) that collectively account for 38 percent of the world's population and 52 percent of world gross domestic product (Biers and Forman 1994, A6). At its November 1994 meeting in Jakarta, APEC set for itself the explicit goal of free trade—the removal of barriers to the sale of goods across borders.

It is hazardous to generalize about organizations as widely divergent in membership and sometimes in purpose as this list suggests (for comparisons with other regional IGOs, see U.S. CIA, 1994, 439–68). None has achieved anything approaching the same level of economic integration and supranational institution building as accomplished in Western Europe. The particular reasons underlying the modest success of the attempts vary, of course (see Chapter 16), but they share a common denominator: national political leaders' reluctance to make choices that would undermine their governments' sovereignty. Still, these attempts at regional cooperation demonstrate states' belief that they are unable to resolve individually the problems that confront them collectively.

In this sense, the state seems ill suited for both managing transnational policy problems and serving as an agent of organized cooperative efforts to do so. The effect of collective problem-solving institutions on world politics is therefore problematic. This viewpoint is reinforced by another transnational manifestation of the transformation of world politics—the growth and growing activity of nonstate actors such as ethnonational movements and multinational corporations. In considering the actors in world affairs, we need to put these types of units into the picture. In Chapter 7 we turn our attention to their behavior.

• • •

KEY TERMS

intergovernmental organizations (IGOs)
nongovernmental organizations (NGOs)
United Nations (UN)
European Union (EU)
supranational entities
pooled sovereignty

European Free Trade Association (EFTA)
customs union
common market
European Political Cooperation (EPC)
Partnership for Peace
Western European Union (WEU)

Nonstate Actors in World Politics: Ethnonational Groups, Religious Movements, Terrorists, and Multinational Corporations

OUTLINE

- Ethnonational Groups
- Religious Movements
- International Terrorists
- Multinational Corporations
- Nonstate Actors and the Transformation of World Politics

The protection of the nation against destruction from without and disruption from within is the overriding concern of all citizens. . . . Nothing can be tolerated that might threaten the coherence of the nation.

—HANS J. MORGENTHAU,
  Realist scholar, 1967

Twin forces [offer a push-pull challenge to states because] economic and technological forces all over the globe are compelling the world toward integration while ethnic and religious tensions tear nations apart.

—BILL CLINTON,
  U.S. president, 1993

The idea that the state has full and exclusive control over its destiny is increasingly questionable. Borders are porous, and states are vulnerable both to external pressures and to challenges from people *within* their boundaries.

Today, these **nonstate actors** are numerous, increasingly active, and self-assertive. Nonstate actors include ethnic minorities within states seeking independence (such as the Tamils in Sri Lanka and Basques in Spain) as well as internationally active ethnic groups in two or more countries (e.g., the Kurds in Iran, Iraq, and Turkey) who challenge the state's authority. They also include religious institutions (e.g., the Orthodox Christian Church) and multinational corporations (e.g., Exxon and IBM) whose purposes may collide with states' national interests. The diversity among these groups is striking, even though all are dedicated primarily to their own parochial interests rather than those of any particular country.

In this chapter we will bring into perspective nonstate entities as actors in world politics, a category that includes many types of actors:

> The term "nonstate entity" covers an enormously broad range of groups. On the most basic level, nonstate entities are associations of individuals and/or groups that are not established by agreements among states. This broad definition includes such disparate entities as transnational corporations and the business associations they establish to promote their interests, professional associations, ethnic groups, major religious organizations, terrorist groups, and social movements. (Riddell-Dixon 1995, 289)

To simplify our task, we will concentrate attention on the most visible and controversial nonstate actors: ethnonational groups, religious movements, terrorists, and multinational corporations.[1] In examining these entities, we consider

---

[1]This is not meant to overlook the active and constructive role performed by literally thousands of "nongovernmental organizations" (NGOs) (see Chapter 6). These are also private international actors whose members are not states but instead people drawn from the populations of two or more states, and these NGOs of concerned global citizens and grassroot groups tackle many global problems (such as environmental deterioration and human rights abuses). They have made a powerful contribution. For example, NGOs such as Amnesty International, the Red Cross, the World Wildlife Federation, and the Union of Concerned Scientists work with both states and intergovernmental organizations (IGOs), and their efforts have led to the successful creation of *regimes* to regulate many transnational problems. While these NGOs' story is rich (and complex), we will cover in this chapter only the major NGOs whose impact arouses debate worldwide.

whether world politics is undergoing a transformation as new types of political units compete for influence with the territorial state, which has been dominant for the past three centuries. If in the future that dominance disappears, the state-centric structure of the international system will disappear with it.

• • •

ETHNONATIONAL GROUPS

On the surface, the images of the all-powerful state and of governments as sovereign and autonomous rulers of united nations are not very satisfactory. These images exaggerate the extent to which the state resembles a unitary actor, as realists often ask us to picture it. In truth, the unitary-actor conception is very misleading, because states are highly penetrated and few are tightly unified and capable of acting as a single unit with a common purpose.

Many political scientists see a pressing "need to deal with the consequences of the declining ability of various governments to govern," and to confront the fact that one of the main forces contributing to "the erosion of effective government and of public confidence in government is the seeming insolvable nature of ethnic and religious differences that make political and social peace in more and more states a problematic exercise" (Shultz and Olson 1994). One must also, it has been suggested, face the possibility that "the omnipotent nation-state of this century is a historical anomaly" which "may be sickly and pale" because "nationalism is on the rise" (Mead 1995).

Nationalism, Nationality, and Ethnicity

Although the state unquestionably remains the most powerful actor in world affairs, nationalism and nationality are potent cultural factors influencing how states perform. Many people pledge their primary allegiance not to the state and government that rules them, but rather to their **ethnonational group** which shares a common civilization, language, cultural tradition, and ties of kinship. They view themselves as members of their nationality first and of their state only secondarily.[2]

Acknowledgment of the importance of **ethnic nationalism** (people's loyalty to and identification with ethnonational groups) in world affairs reduces the relevance of the unitary state. Many states are divided, multiethnic societies: "Of the world's 190 countries, 120 [in 1994 had] politically significant minorities" (Gurr 1995, 213). These divisions and the lack of unity within states makes thinking of international relations as exclusively interactions between unified states dubious. Relations between **ethnic groups** are also vitally important, as contact is customarily widespread between groups who define their identity by their common ancestry.

---

[2]This definition follows the interpretation of E. K. Francis (1976), which presupposes that "cultural affinities manifest in shared linguistic, religious, racial, or other markers . . . enable one community to distinguish itself from others" (Riggs 1994). As Okwudiba Nnoli (1993) elaborates, ethnicity is "a phenomenon associated with contact between cultural-linguistic communal groups . . . characterized by cultural prejudice and social discrimination. Underlying these characteristics are the feelings of pride in the in-group, and the exclusiveness of its members. It is a phenomenon linked . . . to forms of affiliation and identification built around ties of real or putative kinship."

The Fourth World. The pervasiveness of ethnic nations alongside states is so commonplace that many feel the voice of the people behind the ethnonationalist movements they lead must be given its due (Wilmer 1993). Their shout is loud, and aroused nationalists are now fighting back across the globe in rebellion against the injustice, misery, and prejudice they perceive the state to have perpetrated against them. This segment of global society is conventionally referred to as the **Fourth World** to heighten awareness of many "native" or "tribal" **indigenous peoples** within most countries, the poverty and deprivation that confronts them, the state's occupation of the land from which they originate, and the methods these movements are pursuing.

Fourth World activities and liberation movements are present in many countries throughout the globe. Every nationality, it appears, craves a state of its own. In part, this quest is inspired by and is a reaction to the evidence that between 1900 and 1987 about 130 million indigenous people were slaughtered by state-sponsored **genocide** in their own countries (Rummel 1994). In other areas, conflicts below the threshold of overt armed violence between the state and its ethnonational groups are heated and appear to be growing. As Table 7.1 shows, these "Fourth World Wars," active hostilities between indigenous nations and the state, are spread throughout every region of the globe.

Ethnonational Challengers to the State. The many ethnonational challengers to the state defy characterization because they are too diverse, with the distinctions between indigenous peoples and ethnic minorities hard to draw. While this makes counting their numbers difficult, a rough estimate can be provided by observing linguistic similarity. In this respect, the number of ethnolin-

Many subnational groups of nations and indigenous peoples reside on the territory of existing states, which govern them. To protect their human rights and national identity, Fourth World groups have organized meetings such as the World Conference of Indigenous Peoples in Rio de Janeiro, Brazil, in May 1992.

TABLE 7.1	States and Indigenous Nations at War

States	Indigenous Nations
Nicaragua and Honduras	Miskito, Sumo, and Rama
El Salvador	Pipil
Guatemala and Mexico	Mayan, Zapotec, and Mixe
Indonesia	Timorese, Papuans, and Moluccans
Philippines	Kalinga, Bontoc, Morazan, and Sabah
India	Naga, Sikhs, Misoram, and Kachins
Sri Lanka	Tamil
Brazil	Yananomu
Malaysia	Sarawak and Sabah
Lebanon	Maronites, Palestinians
South Africa	Ovimbundu, Harrah (Namibia), and Bantu
Syria, Iraq, Iran, Turkey, and Russia	Kurds
Spain	Basques
Italy	Corsicans and Sardinians
Israel	Palestinians
Iran and Pakistan	Baluchis
Turkey	Armenians
Afghanistan and Pakistan	Pathans
Afghanistan and Russia	Pathans, Tadziks, and Turkmen
Burma and Thailand	Karens
Ethiopia	Eritrea, Tigre, Somalis, Hara, and Wollo
Morocco and Mauritania	POLISARIO, a political movement

SOURCE: Ryser (1985), 307.

guistic divisions that separate cultures is huge. "Measured by spoken languages, the single best indicator of a distinct culture, all the world's people belong to six thousand cultures; four to five thousand of these are indigenous ones. Of the [nearly six] billion humans on the planet, some 190 to 625 million are indigenous people" (Durning 1993, 81).

Still, this indicator may be somewhat misleading, since the belief systems and backgrounds that animate the people in ethnonational movements are varied and often overlapping. Beyond language, these movements are based on numerous combinations of cultural, racial, and religious orientations. Thus it is extremely difficult to classify and count the abundant variety of national movements or "nonstate nations" (Bertelsen 1977) struggling for independence and statehood against the governments that dominate them.

One characteristic of ethnonational movements is very clear, however: Most transcend the existing borders that separate the 190 sovereign states recognized as independent under the rules of international law, and are spread not only within these boundaries but across them. World or transnational cultures recognize no international borders (see Map 7.1). One scenario is that the future will be darkened by violent clashes between "world civilizations" or transnational cultures, every bit as destabilizing and destructive as the East–West ideological clash of the Cold War. According to this proposition, the main source of international conflict "will not be primarily ideological or eco-

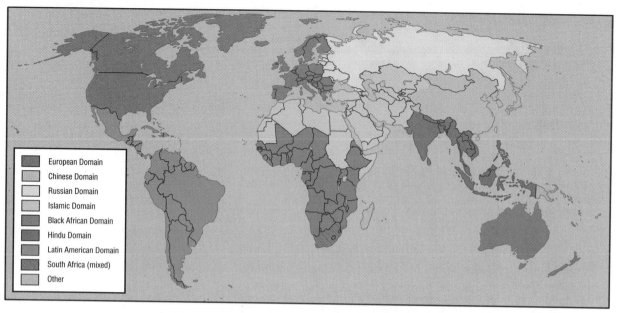

MAP 7.1

The World's Great Cultural Domains

SOURCE: Adapted from Chaliand and Rageau, (1992), p. 37.

nomic," but rather cultural, between "nations and groups of different civilizations" (Huntington 1993).[3]

National Disintegration and Global Instability

Mobilized ethnonational movements threaten the preservation of existing states. If disintegration results, so will the earth's territorial boundaries as drawn by cartographers of the future. When people identify with the culture of their nationality more intensely than they do with their country, we can expect many separatist revolts by peoples struggling for self-determination. This can sometimes occur through the peaceful separation of formerly united states, as almost happened in November 1995 when a slim majority of Quebec's voters upheld Canadian unity and which *did* occur in Czechoslovakia on December 31, 1992, when that country split peacefully, through the so-called "velvet divorce," into the independent Czech and Slovak republics. More frequently, aroused nationalism is likely to lead to violent efforts to separate nationalities into independent countries. The bloody ethnic warfare that racked the former Yugoslavia beginning in 1991 is symptomatic of this consequence, which tragically included the use by both the Bosnian Serbs and Croats of atrocities and **ethnic cleansing**—a program of terror, destruction, and murder to force out the rival nationality. The tribal warfare in Burundi, Somalia and Rwanda also epitomize the horror that results when ancient hatreds spill into warfare.

---

[3]According to political scientist Samuel Huntington (1993), who first popularized the thesis of a coming "clash of civilizations," there are seven or eight major civilizations (Western, Confucian, Japanese, Islamic, Hindu, Slavic-Orthodox, Latin American, and possibly African), as well as minor ones such as the Afro-Caribbean.

Tragically, hate and hostility have traditionally led to terrorism and genocide against out-groups, often victimized for being a minority. Racial and ethnic prejudice have commonly led to inter-communal warfare, such as the U.S. government's policy of expulsion and extermination of Native Americans, Fascist Germany's annihilation of six million Jews, and Japan's death marches and slavery of those it conquered in the early victories of World War II. More recently, in 1994 ethnic conflict escalated to genocide in Rwanda, where as many as one million Tutsis died in relentless bloodletting. This photo depicts the results of one such bloodbath.

These divisions of states into segregated fragments along ethnic and cultural lines are different from the *political* partitions that resulted in the division of Korea, Vietnam, Germany, and China into separate states. States, in short, are inherently fragile because nearly all are weak coalitions of multiple nationalities that can easily splinter (Chatterjee 1993). Consider, for example, the share of indigenous populations of the following countries: Bolivia, 70 percent; Peru, 40 percent; Mexico, 12 percent; the Philippines, 9 percent; Canada, 4 percent (Durning 1993, 83). Cultural diversity is also captured by the number of distinct languages spoken in "megadiversity" countries, of which Indonesia's 670, Nigeria's 410, India's 380, Australia's 250, and Brazil's 210 are exceptional examples (Durning 1993, 86). To speak of these states as "united" is a great exaggeration.

Ethnonational multiculturalism is a potential long-term threat to the state's survival, because the aspiration of ethnonational groups to a national homeland can only be fulfilled through the fragmentation of the territorial integrity of existing states. The success of these separatist movements may result in the balkanization of the world.

The long-term conflict between the Palestine Liberation Organization (PLO) and the state of Israel illustrates the potential for two kinds of processes to produce new states. For four decades the Palestinian nation sought by every means available, including terrorism and war, to create a state from the territories that Israel claimed and controlled. That search destroyed life but failed to create independence. Then, through dialogue and negotiation, another process was pursued, which produced a comprehensive peace accord in September 1993. Israel and Jordan agreed to permit the Palestinians to form a government and create a new state in the West Bank territory which was returned to them by Israel. The accord symbolizes the possibility for nationalities to become independent states through discussion and compromise rather than force. This conceivably could serve as a model for other ethnonational inde-

179

pendence movements, providing that the peace process continues in the wake of the assassination of Israeli Prime Minister Yitzhak Rabin by a Jewish extremist in November 1995.

Another possibility is that racism and intolerance could spawn a new era of tribal warfare. In this grim scenario, the lack of the Cold War stalemate to hold such ethnonational conflicts in check will render states powerless to suppress ancient rivalries and animosities. The ethnic wars in 1993 between Armenians and Azerbaijanis, which pulled Russia, Turkey, and Iran perilously close to combat, and the separatist revolt in Georgia to create an independent state of Abkazia, could foreshadow future transnational ethnic turmoil in many other places. Russia appears particularly vulnerable to ethnonational revolts in the nine republics where Russians comprise less than 50 percent of the population.

Although **interethnic competition** is a phenomenon that dates to biblical times, it is a plague of the post–World War II era. Some of the most explosive flashpoints in the world are the products of disputes between groups in multi-ethnic and culturally heterogenous countries, such as Afghanistan, Belgium, Canada, Nigeria, Russia, Somalia, Spain, Sri Lanka, and the United Kingdom, to name a few. Ethnopolitical cleavages have produced a surge of serious conflicts since 1945. According to *The Minorities at Risk Project* (Gurr 1994), almost 300 of these struggles have occurred between 1945 and 1994, and the trend has accelerated since the 1960s (see Figure 7.1). As this inventory reports, "all but five of the twenty-three wars fought in 1994 [were] based on communal rivalries and ethnic challenges to states. About three-quarters of the world's refugees, estimated at nearly 27 million people, [were] in flight from or [were] displaced by these ethnic conflicts. Eight of the United Nations' thirteen peace-keeping operations [were] aimed at separating the protagonists in ethnopolitical conflicts" (Gurr 1994, 350).

The inherent **ethnocentrism** underlying ethnonationalism—the belief that one's nationality is special and superior and that others are secondary and inferior—breeds ethnic conflict. Nationalists find it easy to condone marginalizing and oppressing "outside" nationalities, while ethnocentric peoples are prone to reject conciliation and compromise with other nationalities. This barrier to cooperation, and its conflict-generating consequences, was highly evident between 1993 and 1995 in the crumbling peace talks and escalating warfare in the Balkans, as negotiations among the Serbs, Croats, and Bosnians produced no concessions until NATO used force to propel the combatants to the bargaining table.

If ethnonationalist values spread and intensify throughout the globe, violence is likely to do the same. As a result, the forces of disunion and disintegration could overwhelm the power of the state, which previously has bound diverse nationalities into a common purpose. To the extent that conflict within and between ethnically disunited and divided states becomes the primary axis on which twenty-first-century world politics revolves, the power and independence of the state can be expected to decline exponentially in a new era of global instability (Barber 1995). The perils should not be underestimated. As Russian Foreign Minister Andrei V. Kozyrev warned the United Nations in September 1993, the threat of ethnic violence today is "no less serious than the threat of nuclear war was yesterday." The existence of three to five thousand active national separatist movements in the world (Nietschmann 1991) punctuates the potential peril, as does the evidence that between 1945 and 1995 one-third of all armed conflicts were internal resistance or secession revolts (K. Holsti 1995, 321; see also Chapter 12).

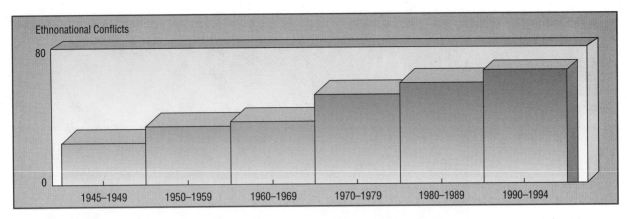

FIGURE 7.1

Ethnonational Groups Involved in Serious Conflicts, 1945–1994

Since World War II, nearly three hundred disputes between ethnic groups erupted. The frequency of these cultural conflicts has steadily risen, reaching epidemic proportions since the Cold War ended. Ethnic conflicts are now a primary cause of mass violence in the world.

SOURCE: Minorities at Risk Project (Gurr 1994), 350.

● ● ●

RELIGIOUS MOVEMENTS

In theory, religion would seem a natural worldwide force for international unity and harmony. Yet in the name of religion, millions have died. The Crusades, between the eleventh and fourteenth centuries, left millions of Christians and Muslims dead, while the religious conflicts during the Thirty Years' War (1618–1648) between Christian Catholics and Protestants took the lives of nearly one-fourth of all Europeans.

A large proportion of the world's nearly six billion people is estimated to be members of religious movements (i.e., politically active organizations based on strong religious convictions). At the most abstract level, a religion is a system of thought shared by a group which gives its members an object of devotion and a code of behavior by which they can ethically judge their actions. Whereas this definition points to commonalities across the great diversity of organized religions in the world, it nonetheless fails to capture that diversity. The world's principal religions vary greatly in the theological doctrines or beliefs they embrace. They also differ widely in the size of their following, in the geographical locations where they are most prevalent (see Map 7.2), and in the extent to which they engage in political efforts to influence international affairs.

These differences make it risky to generalize about the impact of religious movements on world affairs. Those who study religious movements comparatively note that a system of belief provides religious followers with their main source of identity, and that this identification with and devotion to their religion springs from the natural tendency to perceive the values of their own religion as superior to other belief systems. Thus, most religious movements

181

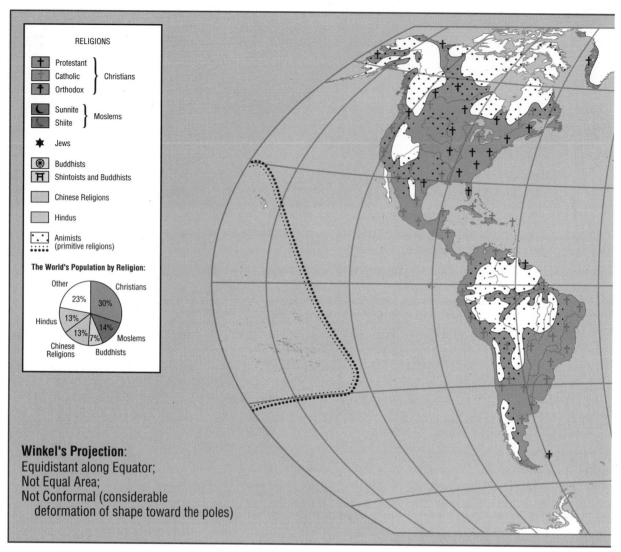

RELIGIONS

Protestant
Catholic } Christians
Orthodox

Sunnite } Moslems
Shiite

Jews

Buddhists

Shintoists and Buddhists

Chinese Religions

Hindus

Animists
(primitive religions)

The World's Population by Religion:

Other
23%

Christians
30%

Hindus
13%

Chinese
Religions
13%

7%

14%
Moslems

Buddhists

Winkel's Projection:
Equidistant along Equator;
Not Equal Area;
Not Conformal (considerable
    deformation of shape toward the poles)

MAP 7.2

**The Geographic Concentration of
the World's Principal Religions**

SOURCE: Adapted from *International Herald Tribune World Atlas.* Copyright, 1994 Lieber Kartor AB and Maps International AB, Stockholm.

believe that they should be universal—that is, accepted by everyone throughout the world. To confirm their faith in their movement's natural superiority, many religions actively proselytize to convert nonbelievers to their faith, engaging in evangelical crusades to win followers of other religions over to their beliefs. This is usually performed by persuasion, through missionary activities to win over hearts and minds of infidels and nonbelievers. But at times the conversion has been by the sword, tarnishing the reputations of some international religious movements (see Focus 7.1).

In evaluating the impact of religious movements on international affairs, it is important to distinguish carefully the high ideals of their doctrines from the activities of the people in these religious bodies. The two realms are not the same, and each can be judged fairly only against the standards they set for themselves. To condemn what large-scale organizations sometimes do when they abuse the principles of the religions they administer does not mean that

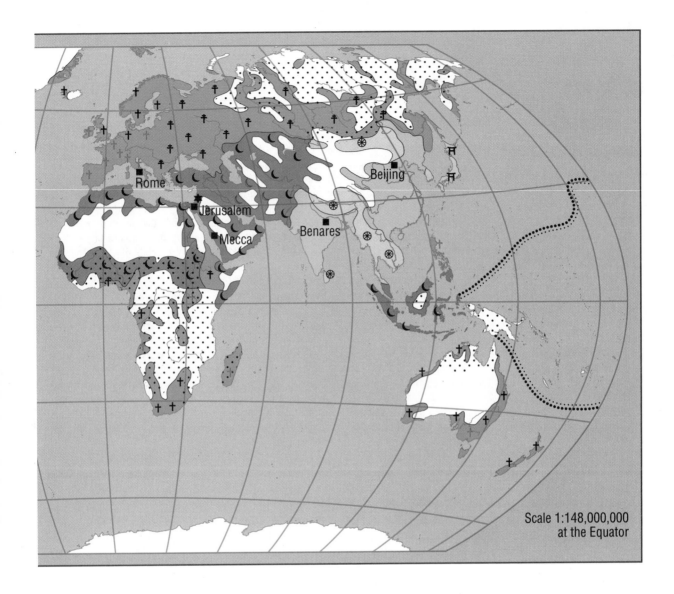

Scale 1:148,000,000
at the Equator

the principles themselves are deserving of condemnation. Moreover, although many students of international relations draw a causal linkage between the activities of religious movements and the outbreak of political conflict and violence (Juergensmeyer 1993), this does not apply to all religions.[4] More accurately, these movements are sources of international tension when they are radical—heavily involved in political action on a global scale and fanatically dedicated to the promotion of their cause. The leaders of *extreme militant religious movements* are convinced that those who do not share their convictions

---

[4]Consider the Hindu ideology of tolerance of different religions, which teaches that there are many paths to truth, and accepts pluralism among diverse populations. Similarly, Buddhism preaches pacifism, as did early Christianity, which prohibited Christians from serving in the armies of the Roman Empire (later, by the fourth century, only Christians were permitted to serve, as church and state became allies).

Religious Movements

Forces for Transnational Peace and Harmony, or Catalysts to Holy Wars?

High ideals inspire the believers of nearly all the world's major religious movements. Indeed, many of the principles they espouse are very similar: reverence for the sanctity of life, acceptance of all people as creations of the deity as equal (regardless of race or color), and the need for self-sacrifice and compassion. These are noble ideals. They speak to universals across time and place—to enduring values in changing times. Moreover, they recognize no boundaries for their eternal validity—no north, no south, no east or west—but only true virtue whenever found, and the relevance of moral precepts (e.g., the prohibition of killing and the value of working for the betterment of humankind) throughout the entire world.

If all the world's great religious movements—approximately 1.8 billion Christians, 972 million Muslims, 733 million Hindus, 315 million Buddhists, and 18 million Jews—espouse universalistic ideals that accept all people's rights, why are some of those same religions often seen as sources of international conflict—even hatred and war? Sociologists of religion answer that it is because these same universalistic religions are managed by organizations that often adopt a particularistic outlook (see Juergensmeyer 1993). They see the world through an ideological lens that views outsiders as a threat and a rival, whose very command of loyalty and allegiance represents a challenge to their own claim of universality. In a word, religious movements often practice intolerance—disrespect for diversity and the right of people to freely embrace another religion's beliefs. The next logical step is for fanatics to paint these imagined enemies as evil, unworthy of mercy, and to justify violence against them.

This inclination of extremist religious movements to evoke prejudice and aggression leads some realist theorists of international politics to conclude that such movements are more a menace than a pacific influence. Observing that most wars have been fought in the name of religion, these realist critics ask the world to acknowledge the viciousness and mean-spiritedness of followers who betray their religion's humanistic and global values by championing a style of religious thought that denies that morality is about nourishing life, not destroying it.

must be punished, and that compromise with them is not acceptable. Richard Shultz and William Olson explain:

> While not all radical religious movements involved in politics are alike, they share certain similar characteristics:
>
> 1. Militant religious political movements tend to view existing government authority as corrupt and illegitimate because it is secular and not sufficiently rigorous in upholding religious authority or religiously sanctioned social and moral values.
>
> 2. They attack the inability of government to address the domestic ills of the society in which the movement exists. In many cases the religious movement substitutes itself for the government at the local level and is involved in education, health, and other social welfare programs. . . .
>
> 3. They subscribe to a particular set of behavior and opinions that they believe political authority must reflect, promote, and protect in all governmental and social activities. This generally means that government and all of its domestic and foreign activities must be in the hands of believers or subject to their close oversight.

4. They are universalists; unlike ethnic movements, they tend to see their views as part of the inheritance of everyone who is a believer. This tends to give them a transstate motivation, a factor that then translates their views on legitimacy of political authority into a larger context for action. In some cases, this means that international boundaries are not recognized as barriers to the propagation of the faith, even if this means the resort to violence.

5. They are exclusionists; they relegate all conflicting opinions on appropriate political and social order to the margins, if they do not exclude them altogether. This means second-class citizenship for any nonbeliever in any society where such a view predominates.

6. Finally, they are militant, willing to use coercion to achieve the only true end. (Shultz and Olson 1994, 9–10)

Although militant religious movements are not the only nonstate actors whose ideologies and activities may contribute to violence, many experts believe that they tend to stimulate five types of international activities. The first is **irredentism**—the attempt by a dominant religion or ethnic group to reclaim territory once possessed but later lost in an adjacent region from a foreign state

Religion, politics, and violence are often not seen as contributing to one another. But in many countries, religious bodies are supported by the armies of the state, while the state supports the transnational activities of religious movements abroad. In South America, for instance, the Catholic Church's "liberation theology" has led some members to work hand in hand with the governments the church supports, as well as to join forces with revolutionary groups in the so-called "Marxist-Catholic alliance" to bring about reforms in the repressive governments it opposes.

that now controls it. Force is often rationalized for this purpose. The second is **secession** or **separative revolts**—the attempt by a religious (or ethnic) minority to break away from an internationally recognized state. Here, again, force is sometimes used, often with arms and aid supplied by third parties that support the secessionist goals. When these separationist revolts succeed, states disintegrate into two or more new political units. The third type of international activity that militant religions tend to incite is **migration**—the departure of religious minorities from their countries of origin to escape persecution. Whether expelled or moving by choice, the result—a fourth consequence of militant religion—is the same: The emigrants create **diasporas** or communities which live abroad in host countries but maintain sentimental, economic, and political ties with their homelands. And finally, as we shall see, a fifth effect of militant religions is **international terrorism** in the form of support for radical coreligionists abroad who are fighting for their religious convictions. Here, again, violence is frequently the product.

If we critically inspect the compound consequences of the activities of militant religious movements, we come away with the impression that as a force on the world stage religious movements not only bring people together but also divide them. Religious movements often challenge state authority, and religious-driven separatism can break countries apart. The possible result, some predict, is that over time "the world may fracture into five hundred states from the current two hundred (UNDP 1994). Others put the ultimate number lower but talk of a new kind of state—something akin to a corporate holding company—with the central government little more than a shell and power residing in the regions" (Davis 1994).

Against this prophecy, we must contemplate another dimension of the sometimes-close connection between religions and states: Many states actively support particular religions while repressing minority religions (see Map 7.3, pp. 188–189). It is important to recognize just how closely states and religions are allied in many countries, with each reinforcing the power of the other. And this observation, in turn, leads us to consider how terrorist groups sometimes influence the relationships between states and militant religions.

● ● ●

INTERNATIONAL TERRORISTS

Terrorist groups are another kind of nonstate actor on the world stage, whose activities exacerbate international tensions and undermine the state's authority and power (see also Focus 7.2). Like ethnonational movements and religious groups, terrorist groups are difficult to identify because their motives, tactics, and membership differ widely. However, there are similarities as well. **Terrorists** are commonly defined as groups seeking through the threat or use of violence to further their political objectives, usually in opposition to state governments.

Terrorism was known in ancient times, as seen in the assassination of tyrants in ancient Greece and Rome, and by the Zealots of Palestine and the Hashashin of medieval Islam. In the nineteenth century, terrorism became associated with the anarchist bombings and with murders and destruction of property by nationalist groups such as the Armenians and Turks. Today terrorism flourishes as a tactic growing out of this history. The religious, ethnic, or political movements and minorities now practicing terrorism seek through violence to obtain the advantages of the majority, and to extract revenge and

Where the Creed Is Greed

The Threat of the Global Network of Organized Crime

In November 1994 the United Nations sponsored a conference in Naples, Italy, to confront a growing menace: the emergence of international organized crime (IOC). Attended by more than eight hundred delegates from 136 countries and thirty international organizations, the conference alerted the international community to the growth of what UN Secretary-General Boutros Boutros-Ghali termed an "empire of criminals," whose criminal activities range from slavery to trafficking in weapons, human organs, toxic wastes, illegal drugs, and nuclear materials.

International organized crime represents a new kind of nonstate actor—new in the sense, according to Claire Sterling (1994) in *Thieves' World*, that criminal organizations which were once local (such as the Italian-Sicilian Mafias, the Japanese *Yakuza*, the Chinese *Triads*, and the Colombian cocaine cartels) are now internationally linked in a global network that cooperates to exploit the institutional weaknesses of a decentralized state system. According to Sterling's evidence, a "planetwide criminal consortium" has been established that is without precedent, running by its own rules, outside the law, to victimize the international community. The motive is not to promote ideological beliefs or religious creeds, but pure profit: the search for easy money, by any means necessary. This code of conduct accepts violence as a honorable necessity. As Sterling sees it, "the Mafia and its confederates are the ultimate terrorists of our times."

The absence of an animating ideology beyond wealth does not mean that international organized crime groups and ethnic and terrorist groups are disconnected, however:

> Just as criminal organizations search out opportunities in the midst of ethnic conflict, ethnonational movements likewise find advantages in their associations with organized crime or in developing their own criminal capabilities.
>
> Ethnonational minority groups pursuing either separation from or political realignment within an existing state require

resources. Through arrangements with organized crime, these movements can gain access to arms, information, and the means to help finance their operations. There is ample evidence that this is happening in Peru, Turkey, Lebanon, the Balkans, and elsewhere. An illustrative example of these types of interconnections is found in the links in heroin trafficking from Southwest Asia. Here Afghan groups, usually Pathans, have links to Pakistani, Iranian, or Indian groups who help in production and transiting. These groups, in turn, have links to Kurdish or Palestinian groups that help move heroin through Iran, Lebanon, or Turkey to Europe. In return, the various resistance movements in Turkey, Iran, and Afghanistan receive capital with which to fund their operations. They are convenient relationships.

Criminal organizations likewise find advantages in these ties. The presence of violent ethnic conflict and government turmoil provides opportunities and incentives for criminal activities. In situations where government and law enforcement [are] ineffective, criminal organizations thrive. In Pakistan, for example, government authority is excluded from tribal areas, and it is precisely in these areas where organized drug production and smuggling are most evident. Burma shows a similar pattern. In Peru, Colombian drug traffickers work with the *Sendero Luminoso* [terrorists] to impair government enforcement efforts, not only against drug smuggling, but also against the very presence of government itself.

IOCs benefit from other by-products of ethnic conflict and state dissolution. One such by-product is the population migration these conflicts generate. European countries harboring large refugee populations have identified a spectrum of organized criminal activities taking place within these communities, and the immigrant groups themselves are frequently the victims of these criminal ventures. Ethnic diaspora communities abroad serve as operational bases and safe havens for criminal organizations. (Shultz and Olson 1994, 28–29)

vengeance against those states and majority populations that the terrorist groups perceive as oppressors. Terrorist groups seek political freedom, privilege, and property—values they think persecution has denied them.

Whereas religious fanaticism is responsible for approximately 20 percent of international terrorist incidents (James 1995, 6), the primary goals of most terrorist groups are independence and statehood. Terrorists are often the "international homeless," whose main objective is to obtain for themselves a

MAP 7.3

Caesar and God: State Support for Particular Religions in a Pluralistic World Community

Many states support particular organized religions and repress or merely tolerate others. This map displays the distribution of states' attitudes toward religion and shows the extent to which many countries try to encourage a religious belief, while that religion also sustains the state.

SOURCE: Adapted from Kidron and Siegel (1995), 110–11.

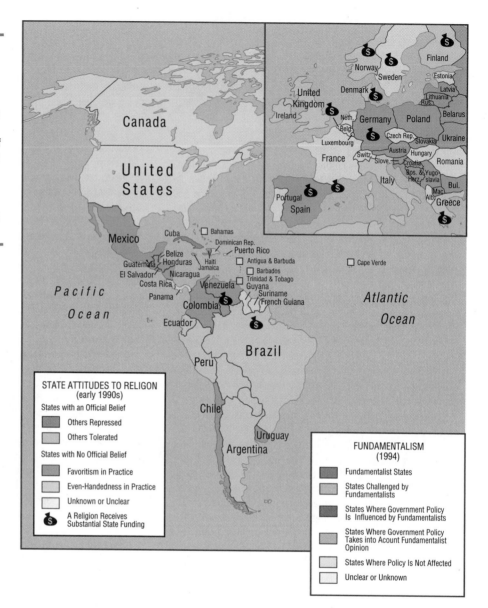

STATE ATTITUDES TO RELIGON
(early 1990s)

States with an Official Belief

- Others Repressed
- Others Tolerated

States with No Official Belief

- Favoritism in Practice
- Even-Handedness in Practice
- Unknown or Unclear
- A Religion Receives Substantial State Funding

FUNDAMENTALISM
(1994)

- Fundamentalist States
- States Challenged by Fundamentalists
- States Where Government Policy Is Influenced by Fundamentalists
- States Where Government Policy Takes into Account Fundamentalist Opinion
- States Where Policy Is Not Affected
- Unclear or Unknown

territory and state they can control without external interference. But it would be a mistake to lump together all terrorist movements; although they share violent tactics often crossing national borders, terrorist movements are more diverse than they are similar (see Focus 7.3).

When viewing the activities of contemporary terrorist groups, one can safely conclude that most of these nonstate actors challenge existing states and their sovereignty. However, **state terrorism** must also be included in any objective assessment, for some of the most ruthless acts of violent terrorism have been practiced by states' governments against those opposed to them. Historical examples of state terrorism include the "reign of terror" by the French revolutionary government in 1793 against the counterrevolutionary opposition, the violence practiced by Russian Bolsheviks after 1917 against their opponents (especially by the repressive regime of Joseph Stalin), and the actions of the

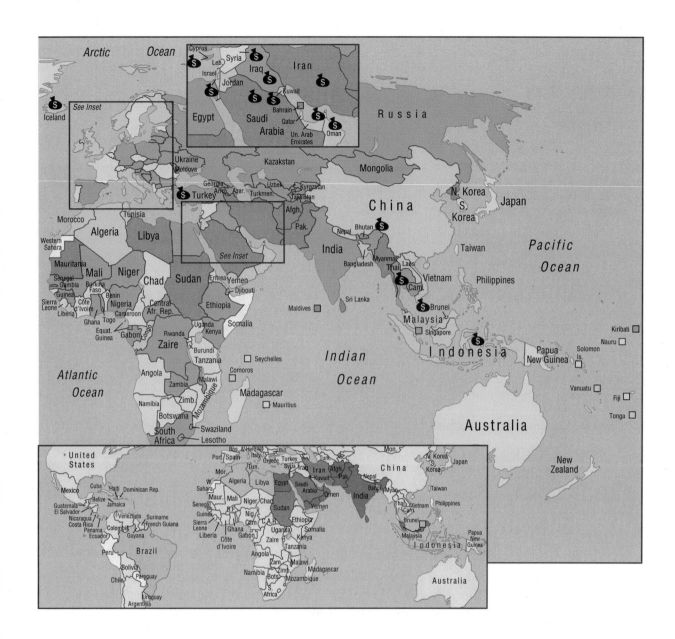

genocidal Nazi regime of Adolph Hitler in Germany which killed millions in the 1930s and 1940s. The state, in short, can and has fought back against opposition to its sovereign authority with terrorist tactics sometimes more militant and destructive than those used by insurgents and revolutionaries. We should therefore not underestimate states' capacity and willingness to combat by force challengers to their sovereignty and perceived national interests.

• • •

MULTINATIONAL CORPORATIONS

Multinational corporations (MNCs)—business enterprises organized in one society with activities in another growing out of direct investment abroad—are a

189

Some Active Terrorist Groups

The following descriptions of modern terrorist movements are provided by the U.S. Department of State's Office of the Coordinator for Counterterrorism (1994), 41–67. Although not exhaustive, they convey the degree to which terrorist groups seek a combination of religious, ethnic, and political goals which generally aim to challenge the authority of existing states.

Group	Description
• Abu Nidal Organization (ANO)	• Led by Sabri al-Banna, the ANO was headquartered in Iraq (1974–1983), Syria (1983–1987), and now Libya, and operates internationally to coordinate the activities of various other Muslim terrorist groups.
• Armed Islamic Group	• An extremist group that seeks to overthrow the secular Algerian government and replace it with an Islamic state.
• Basque Fatherland and Liberty (ETA)	• Founded in 1959, the group once committed to Marxism seeks to create an independent homeland in Spain's Basque region.
• HAMAS (Islamic Resistance Movement)	• Emerging in 1987 from the Palestinian branch of the Muslim Brotherhood, HAMAS pursues—often by violent means—the goal of an Islamic Palestinian state in place of Israel.
• Hizballah (Party of God)	• Radical Shia religious group seeking to establish an Iranian-style Islamic Republic in Lebanon.
• Kach and Kahane Chai	• Stated goal is to restore the biblical state of Israel and to halt the peace process in Palestine. A right-wing Jewish extremist who was a member of Eyal (an offshoot of the radical Kach movement) assassinated Israeli Prime Minister Yitzhak Rabin in November 1995 to stop his plans for Israel: withdrawal from parts of the West Bank.
• The Party of Democratic Kampuchea (Khmer Rouge)	• Communist insurgency hoping to destabilize the Cambodian government. Under Pol Pot's leadership, a campaign of genocide killed more than one million people during its four years in power in the late 1970s.
• Provisional Irish Republican Army (PIRA)	• Radical group formed in 1969 as the secret armed wing of Sinn Fein, the legal political movement seeking to remove British forces from Northern Ireland and unify Ireland.
• *Sendero Luminoso* (Shining Path)	• Guerrilla insurgency formed in the late 1960s by a former university professor whose stated goals are ridding Peru of foreign influences, destroying existing Peruvian institutions, and replacing them with a peasant revolutionary regime.

fourth type of nonstate actor. Since World War II, MNCs have grown dramatically in scope and potential influence alongside the expansion of the world political economy. As a result, they have provoked considerable discussion and much animosity.

The numbers and immense size of MNCs add to the controversy surrounding their role and impact. By the mid-1990s more than 38,500 MNCs worldwide with more than 250,000 foreign affiliates generated $5.2 trillion in global sales, outpacing worldwide exports of goods and services (*World Investment Report 1995* [1995, 3–4]). MNCs also employed more than 73 million people, roughly 10 percent of all paid employees outside of agriculture and nearly 20 percent of the employees in the Global North (*World Investment Report 1994* 1994, xxiii). Each MNC job also typically generates additional jobs. The Nike footwear company, for example, employs about 9,000 people on its core staff but another 75,000 through subcontracting. Conservatively, then, MNCs can be expected to generate one additional job for each job in the corporation, bringing the number of jobs associated with MNCs to at least 150 million.

The MNCs' expansion has been facilitated by transnational banks (TNBs), which themselves have become major forces in the world political economy. In 1995 the combined assets of the world's twenty largest banks exceeded $8.4 trillion (see Table 7.2). Reflecting other global economic trends, three-fourths of the world's top TNBs were headquartered in Japan.

As MNCs have grown in scope and power, concern has understandably been raised about whether they undermine the ability of seemingly sovereign states to control their own economies and therefore their own fates. Is it possible that MNCs are shaking the very foundations of the present international

TABLE 7.2 The World's Top Twenty Banks, 1995 (ranked by assets)

Transnational Bank	Billions of Dollars
Sanwa Bank Ltd., Japan	$588.3
Dai-Ichi Kangyo Bank Ltd., Japan	587.8
Fuji Bank Ltd., Japan	577.1
Sumitomo Bank Ltd., Japan	571.9
Sakura Bank Ltd., Japan	565.4
Mitsubishi Bank Ltd., Japan	553.5
Norinchukin Bank, Japan	500.4
Industrial Bank of Japan	437.8
Mitsubishi Trust and Banking Corp., Japan	394.0
Long-Term Credit Bank of Japan, Japan	375.5
Deutsche Bank A.G., Germany	367.8
Sumitomo Trust and Banking Ltd., Japan	355.9
Tokai Bank Ltd., Japan	351.6
Mitsui Trust and Banking Ltd., Japan	331.2
Credit Agricole Mutuel, France	328.0
Credit Lyonnaise, France	327.8
Asahi Bank Ltd., Japan	317.5
HSBC Holdings Plc., Britain	314.4
Daiwa Bank Ltd., Japan	304.7
Chase Manhattan Corp., United States	297.0

SOURCE: Malkin (1995), 1.

Multinational Corporations in World Politics
A Balance Sheet of Claims and Criticisms

MNCs have been praised and condemned alternatively, depending on how their performance is viewed. The record is mixed and can be evaluated differently in terms of different criteria. Below is a "balance sheet" summarizing the major arguments, pro and con.

Positive	Negative
• Increase the volume of world trade.	• Give rise to oligopolistic conglomerations that reduce competition and free enterprise.
• Assist the aggregation of investment capital that can fund development.	• Raise capital in host countries (thereby depriving local industries of investment capital) but export profits to home countries.
• Finance loans and service international debt.	• Breed debtors and make the poor dependent on those providing loans.
• Lobby for free trade and the removal of barriers to trade, such as tariffs.	• Limit the availability of commodities by monopolizing their production and controlling their distribution in the world marketplace.
• Underwrite research and development that allows technological innovation.	• Export technology ill suited to underdeveloped economies.
• Introduce and dispense advanced technology to less-developed countries.	• Inhibit the growth of infant industries and local technological expertise in less-developed countries while making Global South countries dependent on Global North technology.
• Reduce the costs of goods by encouraging their production according to the principle of comparative advantage.	• Conspire to create cartels that contribute to inflation.
• Generate employment.	• Curtail employment by driving labor competition from the market.
• Encourage the training of workers.	• Limit workers' wages.
• Produce new goods and expand opportunities for their purchase through the internationalization of production.	• Limit the supply of raw materials available on international markets.
• Disseminate marketing expertise and mass-advertising methods worldwide.	• Erode traditional cultures and national differences, leaving in their place a homogenized world culture dominated by consumer-oriented values.
• Promote national revenue and economic growth; facilitate modernization of the less-developed countries.	• Widen the gap between the rich and poor countries.
• Generate income and wealth.	• Increase the wealth of local elites at the expense of the poor.
• Advocate peaceful relations between and among states in order to preserve an orderly environment conducive to trade and profits.	• Support and rationalize repressive regimes in the name of stability and order.
• Break down national barriers and accelerate the globalization of the international economy and culture and the rules that govern international commerce.	• Challenge national sovereignty and jeopardize the autonomy of independent states.

system? Or is this question perhaps based on exaggerated estimates of the MNCs' influence and therefore unwarranted?

The benefits and costs attributed to MNCs as they emerged to a position of prominence since World War II have been many and complex (see Focus 7.4). Here we examine four major issues: their global reach and economic power, their impact on host and home countries, their involvement in politics, and their long-run impact on world politics.

MNCs' Global Reach and Economic Power

The modern MNC characteristically maintains an elaborate overseas network of affiliates to coordinate manufacturing and marketing globally. The creation of the European Economic Community (EEC) in 1957 stimulated this form of business organization and the internationalization of production that it fostered. Because the original six EEC members hoped to create a common external tariff wall around their common market, it made economic sense for U.S. firms to build production facilities in Europe. In this way they could remain competitive by selling their wares as domestic rather than foreign products, with their additional tariff costs.[5] Ultimately, "the primary drive behind the overseas expansion of today's giant corporations is maximization of corporate growth and the suppression of foreign as well as domestic competition" (Gilpin 1975).

Since the stimulus given them by the EEC, the world's giant producing, trading, and servicing corporations have become the agents of the globalization of production. Table 7.3 illustrates their economic and perhaps political importance in world politics, ranking firms by annual sales and states by gross domestic product (GDP). The profile shows that 37 percent of the world's top one hundred economic entities are multinational corporations. Among the top fifty entries, multinationals account for only nine, but in the next fifty, they account for twenty-eight. Their financial clout thus rivals or exceeds that of many countries; indeed, "sales of the ten largest corporations exceed the combined GNP of the one hundred smallest countries" (*World Watch* 9 [January/ February 1996], 37).

Although the growth of multinational firms is a global phenomenon, the Global North is home to about ninety percent of MNC parent corporations. Historically the United States has been the home country for most multinationals, but Germany now heads the list, followed by Japan. Together the three countries account for nearly forty percent of all parent corporations headquartered in the Global North (*World Investment Report 1995* 1995, 8). They also account for a large share of both the stock and flow of foreign direct investment.

Foreign direct investment (FDI)—formally defined as "ownership of assets in one country by residents of another for purposes of controlling the use of those assets" (Graham and Krugman 1995)—measures the investment activ-

---

[5]The reasons for direct investments overseas are more complex than this simplified explanation suggests. According to *product-cycle theory*, for instance, overseas expansion is essentially a defensive maneuver designed to forestall foreign competitors and thus maintain the global competitiveness of domestically based industries. This theory views MNCs as having an edge in the initial stages of developing and producing a new product and then having to go abroad to protect export markets from the foreign competitors that naturally arise as the relevant technology becomes more widespread or imitated. In the final phase of the product cycle, "production has become sufficiently routinized so that the comparative advantage shifts to relatively low-skilled, low-wage, and labor-intensive economies. This is now the case, for example, in textiles, electronic components, and footwear" (Gilpin 1975; see also Vernon 1971).

TABLE 7.3 Countries and Corporations: A Ranking by Size of Economy and Sales, 1994

Rank	Country/Corporation	GNP/Sales ($ billions)	Rank	Country/Corporation	GNP/Sales ($ billions)
1	United States	6,737.0	51	MOBIL (U.S.)	56.6
2	Japan	4,321.0	52	Pakistan	55.6
3	Germany	2,075.0	53	NISSAN MOTOR (Japan)	53.8
4	France	1,355.0	54	SAMSUNG (South Korea)	51.3
5	Italy	1,101.0	55	PHILIP MORRIS (U.S.)	50.6
6	Britain	1,069.0	56	IRI (Italy)	50.5
7	China	630.2	57	SIEMENS (Germany)	50.4
8	Canada	569.9	58	Chile	50.1
9	Brazil	536.3	59	Ireland	48.3
10	Spain	525.3	60	New Zealand	46.6
11	Russia	392.5	61	VOLKSWAGEN (Germany)	46.3
12	Mexico	368.7	62	Algeria	46.1
13	South Korea	366.5	63	Burma	45.0*
14	Netherlands	338.1	64	Peru	44.1
15	Australia	320.7	65	CHRYSLER (U.S.)	43.6
16	India	278.7	66	TOSHIBA (Japan)	42.9
17	Argentina	275.7	67	UNILEVER (Br./Neth.)	41.8
18	Switzerland	265.0	68	Syria	41.5*
19	Belgium	231.1	69	Egypt	41.0
20	Taiwan	220.7*	70	Hungary	39.0
21	Sweden	206.4	71	NESTLÉ (Switzerland)	38.9
22	Austria	197.5	72	ELF AQUITAINE (France)	37.0
23	Indonesia	167.6	73	United Arab Emirates	36.9*
24	Turkey	149.0	74	HONDA MOTOR (Japan)	35.8
25	Denmark	145.4	75	ENI (Italy)	34.8
26	Iran	138.2*	76	FIAT (Italy)	34.7
27	GENERAL MOTORS (U.S.)	133.6	77	SONY (Japan)	34.6
28	Thailand	129.9	78	TEXACO (U.S.)	34.4
29	Saudi Arabia	126.6	79	NEC (Japan)	33.2
30	South Africa	125.2	80	Czech Republic	33.1
31	Norway	114.3	81	DU PONT (U.S.)	32.6
32	FORD MOTOR (U.S.)	108.5	82	CHEVRON (U.S.)	32.1
33	EXXON (U.S.)	97.8	83	PHILIPS ELECTRONICS (Neth.)	31.7
34	Finland	95.8	84	Kuwait	31.4
35	ROYAL DUTCH/SHELL (Br./Neth.)	95.1	85	Libya	31.1*
36	Poland	94.6	86	DAEWOO (South Korea)	30.9
37	Portugal	92.1	87	PROCTOR & GAMBLE (U.S.)	30.4
38	TOYOTA (Japan)	85.3	88	Morocco	30.3
39	Ukraine	80.9	89	Nigeria	30.0
40	Greece	80.1	90	RENAULT (France)	30.0
41	Israel	78.1	91	FUJITSU (Japan)	29.1
42	Malaysia	68.7	92	MITSUBISHI ELECTRIC (Japan)	28.8
43	HITACHI (Japan)	68.6	93	ABB ASEA BROWN BOVERI (Switz.)	28.3
44	Singapore	65.8	94	Romania	27.9
45	Philippines	63.3	95	HOECHST (Germany)	27.8
46	IBM (U.S.)	62.7	96	ALCATEL ALSTHOM (France)	26.6
47	GENERAL ELECTRIC (U.S.)	60.8	97	Belarus	21.9
48	DAIMLER-BENZ (Germany)	59.1	98	Uzbekistan	21.1
49	Venezuela	59.0	99	Kazakhstan	18.9
50	Colombia	58.9	100	Luxembourg	16.0

SOURCES: *World Bank Atlas 1996* 1995, 18 19, with missing data entries (identified by an asterisk [*]) for 1994 based on 1993 figures provided by the U.S. Arms Control and Disarmament Agency (1995), 37; MNCs annual sales, *Fortune* (July 25, 1995), 143.

MNC investments, as revealed, for example, in the value of factories and equipment built up over a period of time. The "flow" of FDI reveals the current investment activities of MNCs. Thus FDI stocks reveal the current structure of global production and the primary locus of economic activity, while FDI flows provide insight into their changing patterns.

Foreign investment stock today is heavily concentrated in the Global North, which is the source of most investment capital (outflows) and its favored target (inflows). In particular, the Japan-European Union-North America triad dominates global investments (see Figure 7.2). This pattern replaces an earlier "bipolar" investment configuration, when the United States and a handful of European countries (acting independently of one another) dominated the investment world. By the end of the 1980s, however, Europe began increasingly to act as a unified entity, and Japan actually surpassed the United States as a major source of foreign investment, with much of it directed at the United States itself.

The current tripolar investment pattern emerged from the corporate preferences of each partner to consolidate its own market hold and to gain a foothold in the other two regions. As revealed in Figure 7.2, the United States and the European Union preferred to invest in each other rather than Japan, and Japan preferred the United States to Europe. The result is a serious imbalance between Japan and the other two partners, with the outward flow of stocks from Japan much greater than the inward flow. This imbalance parallels Japan's trade imbalance with other countries, notably the United States (see Chapter 8). Out of such imbalances, tougher competition among the three economic blocs, as well as political struggle, can be expected (Thurow 1992).

As the market strategies of major corporations in the United States, Europe, and Japan pursued control of their existing markets and expansion in new regional markets, they also adopted strategies that sought "to build up regionally integrated core networks of affiliates, clustered around their home country" (Centre on Transnational Corporations 1991). Figure 7.3, which depicts the automobile operations of Toyota Motor Company in four ASEAN countries, illustrates the kind of regionalized network in one industry that this strategy has produced in many others.

As a result of this clustering strategy, foreign direct investment is now heavily regional. Each of the principal host countries in eastern Europe and the Global South receives the bulk of its funds from a single member of the investment triad, typically the one geographically closest to it. The effect is to reinforce—perhaps to cause—the growing regionalization of the world political economy across a range of dimensions, not only in investment but also in production and trade (see also Chapter 8).

Although the Global North is both home and host to most FDI stock, the Global South's share of FDI flows increased during the 1970s—only to see it plummet during the debt crisis of the early 1980s. Flows to the South have increased somewhat in the 1990s, with the emerging economies an increasingly favored target. We will return to this point in Chapter 9.

The Impact of MNCs on Home and Host Nations

In addition to its global reach and economic power, MNCs' domestic impact on both home and host countries is a matter of widespread concern. MNCs allegedly exercise their power at great cost to their home or parent countries.

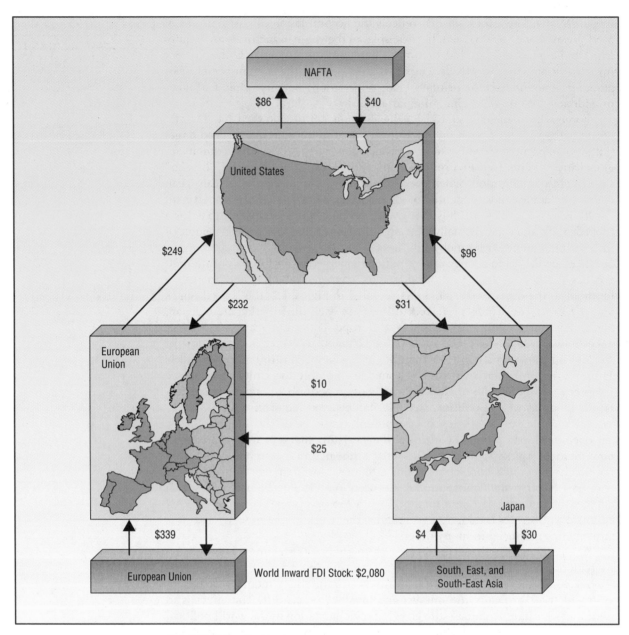

FIGURE 7.2

A Tripolar Foreign Investment World: Investment Flows Among and Within the Japanese, European Union, and U.S. Clusters, 1993 (billions of dollars)

The investment strategies of MNCs have led to the regionalization of foreign direct investment, with imbalances evident in the flows between the United States, European Union, and Japan. The United States, in turn, is closely tied to its NAFTA partners and Japan to other Asian states, while the European Union invests primarily within its own borders.

SOURCE: *World Investment Report 1995* (1995), 11.

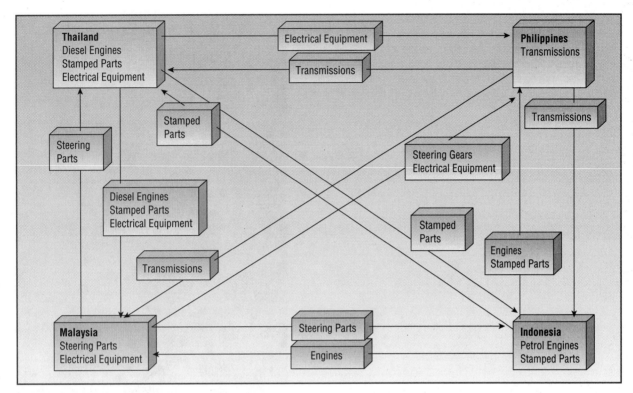

FIGURE 7.3

Automobile Operations of Toyota in Four ASEAN Countries

A recent trend has been multinational corporations' practice of producing their products in different countries. Such production patterns make it difficult to identify the national origin of the manufactured goods sold in the international marketplace and monitoring of exports almost impossible. This figure captures this pattern by tracing the four states in the Association of South East Asian countries where Toyota manufactures its automobile parts.

SOURCE: Centre on Transnational Corporations (1991), 62.

Charges against them include shifting productive facilities abroad to avoid labor unions' demands for higher wages. According to this view, because capital is more mobile than labor, the practice of exporting production from industrially advanced countries to industrially backward countries—where labor is cheap and unions weak or nonexistent—causes structural unemployment in the advanced countries. Others contend, however, that MNCs help reduce balance-of-payments deficits, create new employment opportunities, and promote competition in both domestic and foreign markets.

If home countries have incurred both costs and benefits, have host countries shared similar experiences? "As privileged organizations," David E. Apter and Louis W. Goodman (1976) note, MNCs "hold a unique position among growth-inducing institutions able to affect the direction of development." This implies that MNCs may promote development as much as they impede it. It is nonetheless true that countries in the Global South historically have viewed multinationals with considerable and often emotionally charged suspicion.

197

Many nationalists blame multinational corporations for the problems they perceive to affect their country's economy and social conditions. Foreign firms often face a backlash. In 1995, Hindu nationalists in India—the world's largest democracy—protested economic reforms that would open the country's borders to liberal trade and investment. These and other opponents pledged to drive some of the world's best-known brands out of the Indian market.

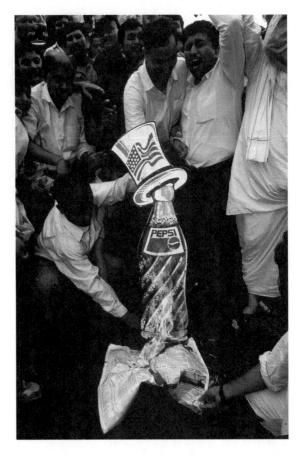

Although this viewpoint has changed noticeably in recent years (developing countries now compete with one another to attract foreign direct investment), MNCs are more important to the developing countries' overall GNP and to their most-advanced economic sectors than they are to the developed states' economies.

Politics and Multinational Corporations

Another area of apprehension regarding MNCs' role as nonstate actors is their involvement in the domestic political affairs of local or host countries. In some instances this concern has extended to MNCs' involvement in the domestic politics of their home countries, where they actively lobby their governments for policies that will enhance the profitability of their business activities abroad. In turn, both host and home governments have sometimes used MNCs as instruments in their foreign policy strategies.

Perhaps the most notorious instance of an MNC's intervention in the politics of a host state occurred in Chile in the early 1970s. There, International Telephone and Telegraph (ITT) tried to protect its interests in the profitable Chiltelco telephone company by seeking to prevent the election of Marxist-oriented Salvador Allende as president and later by seeking his overthrow. ITT's efforts to undermine Allende included giving monetary support to his political opponents and, once Allende was elected, pressuring the U.S. government to disrupt the Chilean economy. Eventually Allende was overthrown by a military dictatorship.

At times MNCs' practices have been embarrassing to home countries—as when the West German government found that a German firm had sold mustard gas manufacturing equipment to Libya. On other occasions they seemed to defy the home country—as when the French subsidiary of Dresser Industries of Dallas, Texas, exported energy technology to the Soviet Union in defiance of a U.S. government effort to thwart it.

In addition, MNCs often lobby their home governments for policies that back their disputes with host governments, although they are not always successful in these endeavors. The U.S. stipulation, made in the early 1970s, that foreign aid would be cut to any country that nationalized U.S. overseas investments without just compensation is representative of the tendency for home-state governments to support their own MNCs' overseas activities.

More broadly, MNCs have assisted in promoting the emergence of free trade. In this sense, they have been active participants in the process by which governments have reached agreements on rules liberalizing economic transactions in the global marketplace.

However, at another level, MNCs headquartered in one country have sometimes worked at cross-purposes with the parent government by serving the wishes of the host government. During the 1973–1974 oil crisis, for example, the governments of the Organization of Petroleum Exporting Countries (OPEC) received assistance from the multinational oil companies to achieve OPEC's goal of using oil as a political weapon against the West. As the corporations reaped huge profits, their home countries suffered greatly.

The political role of the MNC in home and host countries remains vague. Perhaps the conclusion that best characterizes its impact is one that pictures the MNC as "a stimulant to the further extension of state power in the economic realm" (Gilpin 1985).

> Only the state can defend corporate interests in international negotiations over trade, investment, and market access. Agreements over such things as airline routes, the opening of banking establishments, and the right to sell insurance are not decided by corporate actors who gather around a table; they are determined by diplomats and bureaucrats. Corporations must turn to governments when they have interests to protect or advance. (Kapstein 1991–1992, 56)

Still, the blurring of the boundaries between internal and external affairs adds potency to the political role that MNCs unavoidably play as actors at the intersection of foreign and domestic policy.

MNCs Impact

Because multinationals often make decisions over which national political leaders have little control, a fourth significant issue regarding MNCs is whether their influence will lead to the erosion of the international system's major structural foundation—the principle that the state alone is sovereign.

The question of control is especially pertinent to countries in the Global South, although it is not limited to them. As one senior U.S. foreign policy official declared at the time of the Dresser Industries controversy, "Basically we're in an impossible situation. You don't want to get rid of the advantages of this international economic system, but if you try to exercise control for foreign policy reasons, you cut across sovereign frontiers."

Bemoaning the suspicion that multinationals "steal" U.S. technology and fail to "generate or retain wealth and quality jobs within [U.S.] borders," the U.S. Office of Technology Assessment in 1993 called for new rules to "balance interests . . . between nations and firms" (Dentzer 1993). However, the MNCs' complex patterns of ownership and licensing arrangements make the problem unmanageable, because it is often difficult to equate the MNCs' interests with particular national jurisdictions (Reich 1990). General Electric, for example, one of the most "American" of all U.S. MNCs, has granted licenses for the production of energy-related equipment to Nuovo Pignone of Italy, Mitsubishi and Hitachi of Japan, Mannessmann and AEG Telefunken of West Germany, John Brown Engineering of Great Britain, and Thomassen Holland of the Netherlands (U.S. Congress, Office of Technology Assessment 1981). Controlling such a complex pattern of interrelationships, joint ventures, and shared ownership for any particular national purpose is nearly impossible. "The internationalization of the economy—which the U.S. spearheaded—has rendered obsolete old ideas of economic warfare," Richard J. Barnet, coauthor of *Global Reach* (Barnet and Müller 1974), observed in 1982. "You can't find targets any more, and if you aim at a target you often find it's yourself."

The multinationals' potential long-run influence is depicted in *Global Dreams: Imperial Corporations and the New World Order:*

> The emerging global order is spearheaded by a few hundred corporate giants, many of them bigger than most sovereign nations. Ford's economy is larger than Saudi Arabia's and Norway's. Philip Morris's annual sales exceed New Zealand's gross domestic product. The multinational corporation of twenty years ago carried on separate operations in many different countries and tailored its operations to local conditions. In the 1990s large business enterprises, even some smaller ones, have the technological means and strategic vision to burst old limits—of time, space, national boundaries, language, custom, and ideology. By acquiring earth-spanning technologies, by developing products that can be produced anywhere and sold everywhere, by spreading credit around the world, and by connecting global channels of communication that can penetrate any village or neighborhood, these institutions we normally think of as economic rather than political, private rather than public, are becoming the world empires of the twenty-first century. The architects and managers of these space-age business enterprises understand that the balance of power in world politics has shifted in recent years from territorially bound governments to companies that can roam the world. As the hopes and pretensions of government shrink almost everywhere, these imperial corporations are occupying public space and exerting a more profound influence over the lives of ever larger numbers of people. (Barnet and Cavanagh 1994, 14)

Whether the corporate visionaries who manage the MNCs will help to create a more prosperous, peaceful, and just world—as free-trade liberal theorists hope and others, whose interests are threatened by a new world political economy, fear—is debatable. "For some, the global corporation holds the promise of lifting [humankind] out of poverty and bringing the good life to everyone. For others, these corporations have become a law unto themselves; they are miniempires which exploit all for the benefit of a few" (Gilpin 1975).

The existence of multinational corporations "has become a fact of life. They are now permanent—and influential—players in the international arena" (Spero 1990). Their challenge to the existing international system of states should not be taken lightly. The U.N. Commission on Transnational Corporations forcefully poses the issue:

> A growing number of international norms has produced a body of international soft law on transnational corporations; it is, however, limited in scope and does not adequately match the globalization of business activity. In an era of globalization, it is increasingly difficult to distinguish between national and international issues of governance. The capacity of governments to manage their economies and achieve national objectives in areas ranging from fiscal policy to environmental control is being strained by the growing importance of transnational corporations in the international economy. Many issues related to corporate responsibility cannot be resolved satisfactorily in the context of a single national legal regime. . . . The effective and stable governance of international economic relations requires not only the unleashing of market forces and private enterprise, but also effective international instruments to deal with the broad range of issues related to the globalization of business activity—problems that are beyond the capacity of national regimes of governance. (Commission on Transnational Corporations 1991, 33)

• • •

NONSTATE ACTORS AND THE TRANSFORMATION OF WORLD POLITICS

Because ethnonational movements, religious groups, and international terrorists—alongside international organizations and multinational corporations—challenge the state's authority, they also challenge the very pillars on which the contemporary state system is built. An adequate conceptualization of contemporary world politics must acknowledge the influence of nonstate actors, because, as political theorist Richard Falk argues, it is misleading "to view the world as consisting of territorial units each exerting supreme authority within its borders, but not elsewhere." Falk explains:

> Even if a few states can still defend their territory against an invading army, not even the most powerful can protect its people and cities against a devastating surprise attack by guided missiles, and none can control the flow of images and ideas that shape human tastes and values. The globalized "presence" of Madonna, McDonald's and Mickey Mouse make a mockery of sovereignty as exclusive territorial control. A few governments do their best to insulate their populations from such influences, but their efforts are growing less effective and run counter to democratizing demands that are growing more difficult to resist. . . . Interdependence and the interpenetration of domestic and international politics, the mobility and globalization of capital and information, and the rising influence of transnational social movements and organizations are among the factors that make it anachronistic to analyze politics as if territorial supremacy

continued to be a generalized condition or a useful fiction. In particular, sovereignty, with its stress on the inside/outside distinction as between domestic and international society, seems more misleading than illuminating under current conditions. (Falk 1993, 853)

This by no means indicates that the state is dead, however. States retain a (near) monopoly on the use of coercive force in the international system, and they continue to shape the transnational interactions of nonstate actors. The state still molds the activities of nonstate actors more than its behavior is molded by them. It "may be anachronistic, but we have yet to develop an alternative form of societal organization that is able to provide its members with both wealth and power" (Kapstein 1991–1992). Therefore, it would be premature to abandon the focus on the state in international politics, just as it would be inadequate to regard the state as the only relevant actor or the sole determinant of the globe's fate.

● ● ●

KEY TERMS

nonstate actors
ethnonational groups
ethnic nationalism
ethnic groups
Fourth World
indigenous peoples
genocide
ethnic cleansing
interethnic competition
ethnocentrism

irredentism
secession or separative revolts
migration
diasporas
international terrorism
terrorists
state terrorism
multinational corporations (MNCs)
foreign direct investment (FDI)

States and Markets: Monetary and Trade Relations in an Interdependent World Political Economy

OUTLINE

- Liberalism, Mercantilism, and Hegemony
- Liberalism, Mercantilism, and Hegemony in the International Monetary System
- Liberalism and Mercantilism in Practice: Free Trade and Protectionism
- Liberalism, Mercantilism, and Hegemony in the International Trade System
- The Turbulent 1990s: Triumph or Trouble?

An effective multilateral trading system becomes more important for the United States every day. During the Cold War America could throw its weight around, but its relative strength is declining. . . . As our ability to call the shots dwindles, rules that everyone agrees on become more vital.

—JEFFREY E. GARTEN,
U.S. Under Secretary of Commerce for International Trade, 1995

Governments should interfere in the conduct of trade as little as possible. Once bureaucrats become involved in managing trade flows, the potential for misguided decisions rises greatly.

—PETER SUTHERLAND,
Director-General, General Agreement on Tariffs and Trade, 1995

In 1944 forty-four states allied in war against the Axis powers met in the New Hampshire resort community of Bretton Woods. Their purpose was to devise rules and new institutions to govern international monetary and trade relations after the war. As the world's preeminent economic and military power, the United States played the leading role at Bretton Woods. Its proposals were shaped by its perception of the causes of the 1930s' economic catastrophe and its beliefs about the role the U.S. dollar and economy should play in the postwar world. The United States sought monetary stability, free trade, and open markets—all central tenets of what would become the "Bretton Woods system," based on the premises of economic liberalism.

Britain also played an important role at the conference. Led by John Maynard Keynes—whose theories about the role of the state in managing inflation, unemployment, and growth influenced a generation of economic thinking throughout the capitalist world—the British delegation won support for the principle of strong state action in states facing economic problems. That perspective conforms less closely with liberalism than with the principles of mercantilism, which assign a greater role to states than to markets in governing economic interactions.

Despite these differences, the rules established at Bretton Woods reflected a remarkable level of agreement. They would govern international economic relations for a quarter-century following World War II, sustained by the three political bases on which Bretton Woods rested (Spero 1990). First, power was concentrated in the rich countries of Western Europe and North America, restricting the number of states whose agreement was necessary to make the system operate effectively. Neither Japan nor the Global South posed an effective challenge to Western dominance. The participation of the then-communist states of Eastern Europe and the Soviet Union in the global marketplace was limited as well. Second, these states preferred an open international economic system combined with a commitment to limited government intervention if necessary, a shared interest which facilitated the system's operation. The onset of the Cold War helped cement Western unity on economic issues. Faced with a common external enemy, the Western industrial countries perceived economic cooperation as necessary not only for prosperity but also for security. That perception promoted a willingness to share economic burdens. Third, Bretton Woods rested on the United States' sole leadership and others' acceptance of that role. Again, the Cold War was important in encouraging the United States to assume the burdens of leadership and getting others to follow.

The political bases of the Bretton Woods system crumbled in the early 1970s, as symbolized by the end of the system of fixed currency exchange rates at its core. As a result, the term no longer usefully captures the structures and processes of international economic relations. Still, liberalism—a preference for market mechanisms over government intervention—remains the principle around which international economic relations are organized. In fact, the commitment to liberalism in politics and economics is even more pronounced with the end of the Cold War, as democracy and the urge to privatize and otherwise reduce government involvement in markets have spread worldwide. Thus it is useful to characterize the structure of the international economic system as a **Liberal International Economic Order (LIEO)**—one based on such free market principles as openness and nondiscrimination.

Still, the practice of liberalism (if not always the theory) is under attack from many quarters, including its chief proponents. When the president of the United States calls the king of Saudi Arabia to secure a multibillion-dollar sale of U.S.-built passenger jets—as Bill Clinton did—free trade is victimized. When the European Union risks failure of a seven-year multilateral effort to reduce trade barriers rather than abandon a system of expensive agricultural subsidies that protects inefficient domestic producers from foreign competition—as did occur—mercantilism reigns supreme. States and markets, it seems, coexist in tension with one another.

The term **political economy** highlights the intersection of politics (states) and economics (markets) in world politics. The two are intimately intertwined—although their goals sometimes differ—as the search for power and wealth has animated international politics since the birth of the state system more than three centuries ago. Its relevance today is captured in the extensive interdependent relationships between states and markets which knit national and global welfare into a single tapestry.

The growing volume of international trade is the most visible indication of international interdependence. World exports now exceed $4.2 trillion annually, accounting for roughly 14 percent of world economic output. Dramatic increases in world trade since World War II have fueled the unprecedented growth in global welfare since then; indeed, one could not have occurred without the other. Thus the Liberal International Economic Order put into place a half-century ago has been remarkably successful.

States nonetheless worry that interdependence may compromise their sovereignty and security. The reason is clear: **interdependence** is a condition of mutual sensitivity and mutual vulnerability (Keohane and Nye 1989; see also Cooper 1968). By "sensitivity" we mean that changes in one society are readily transmitted to another through their mutual interactions (e.g., inflation). Governments have little immediate impact on these transnational reverberations. By "vulnerability," more nearly a power or political relationship, we mean that changes in the rules and policies of one state affect another (e.g., trade embargoes). Here government action is central. States often seek to maximize their gains through international involvement while minimizing their sensitivity and vulnerability to others. Their behavior flows naturally from a desire to increase the domestic benefits of international economic transactions and to lessen their adverse consequences.

In this chapter we focus on the critical role of the United States in shaping and maintaining the Liberal International Economic Order crafted at Bretton Woods. We also examine how changes in its power and prominence have affected (and been affected by) changes in the world political economy since World War II. We begin by exploring the contest between liberalism and mercantilism as alternative political-economy philosophies underlying the different strategies states pursue in their quest for power and wealth. We next investigate hegemonic stability theory, which blends elements of liberalism and mercantilism, and then use it to examine the U.S. role in managing international monetary and trade relations. In Chapter 9 we will expand the themes developed here as we shift attention from monetary and trade interdependence to a broader range of phenomena underlying the globalization of the world political economy.

• • •

LIBERALISM, MERCANTILISM, AND HEGEMONY

The contest between mercantilism and liberalism—between states and markets—explains differences in how states cope with the world political economy. The differences are critical internationally, as they help us to understand why international cooperation in pursuit of goals all states seem to want is often so elusive.

State power is also a part of the equation. Those at the pinnacle of the world's political-economic hierarchy—appropriately labeled "hegemons"—are able to exert disproportionate influence over others by shaping the rules governing the world political economy. Britain was the hegemonic power in the late nineteenth century; since World War II the United States has assumed that role. Buttressed by supportive economic structures and a liberal ideology at home, both used their military superiority and economic advantage to create international economic structures in which market forces played a powerful role and enjoyed more legitimacy than state intervention and control (Gilpin 1987; Krasner 1976). Ironically, however, a liberal order based on the economic strength of a preponderant power contains the seeds of its own destruction, thus encouraging the hegemon to abandon liberalism and embrace mercantilism.

Economic Liberalism

Liberalism and mercantilism have been described by political economist Robert Gilpin (1987) as competing "ideologies" based on "fundamentally different . . . conceptions of the relationships among society, state, and market," adding that "it may not be an exaggeration to say that every controversy in . . . international political economy is ultimately reducible to differing conceptions of these relationships."[1]

Liberalism as a *political* theory builds on the presumption of humankind's natural inclination to cooperate and directs attention to individual liberty

---

[1] Gilpin and others include Marxism as a third competing ideology. We confine our attention here to liberalism and mercantilism. We treat contemporary versions of Marxism elsewhere, under the rubric of structural theories. Such theories are particularly important in understanding patterns of dominance and dependence between rich and poor nations, as we saw in Chapter 5.

under the law. Consequently, it is closely related to the world view of liberal idealists described in Chapter 2. Liberal *economic* theory also emphasizes the cooperative side of human nature, premised on the assumption that individuals act in rational, unemotional ways. While economic liberals do realize that individuals act out of self-interest, they believe that the public interest is still served through the mutually beneficial exchanges among individuals from which all benefit.

Adam Smith (an eighteenth-century political economist who helped define the precepts of classical liberalism as well as modern-day economics) used the metaphor of the "invisible hand" of the market to describe how the public interest is served by the pursuit of private gain. Smith believed that humans' natural proclivity is to "truck, barter, and exchange." Hence the importance of the marketplace, which produces collective as well as private gain. David Ricardo, an early nineteenth-century British political economist, added an important corollary to this thinking as applied to the international economy. Ricardo demonstrated conclusively that when all states specialize in the production of those goods in which they enjoy a **comparative advantage** and trade them for goods in which others enjoy an advantage, a net gain in welfare for both partners in the form of higher living standards will result. The principle of comparative advantage would become a touchstone for explaining the advantages of free trade and the wisdom of liberal (open) international economic systems (see Focus 8.1). Benjamin Franklin summarized the liberal premise more than two centuries ago: "No nation was ever ruined by trade."

Liberals like Smith, Ricardo, and Franklin believed that markets work best when free of government interference. They reasoned that economic processes governing the production, distribution, and consumption of goods and services operate according to certain natural laws. They saw politics—the exercise of power—as unavoidable (if unpalatable), recognizing that states do have some functions to perform in society—providing for the national defense, for example. Generally, however, they feared the potential abuse of state power and saw no need for its heavy hand in the marketplace. (Today people subscribing to these views are described as conservatives, not liberals. Hence it is important to note that the tenets described here are those of *classical* liberalism, not its modern variants, which tend to call for greater state involvement in markets and society, not less.) The hallmark of liberal economic theory, then, is its commitment "to free markets and minimal state intervention. . . . Liberals believe economics is progressive and politics is regressive. Thus they conceive of progress as divorced from politics and based on the evolution of the market" (Gilpin 1987).

Transferred to the international level, these ideas mean that trade and other forms of economic relations "are a source of peaceful relations among nations because the mutual benefits of trade and expanding interdependence among national economies will tend to foster cooperative relations. . . . A liberal international economy will have a moderating influence on international politics as it creates bonds of mutual interests and a commitment to the status quo" (Gilpin 1987).

There is a fly in the liberal ointment, however. Although liberal economic theory promises that the "invisible hand" will maximize efficiency so that everyone will gain, it does not promise that everyone will gain equally. Instead, "everyone will gain in accordance with his or her contribution to the whole, but . . . not everyone will gain equally because individual productivities differ.

Comparative Advantage and the Gains from Trade

Start with two countries, such as Japan and the United States. Each produces cameras and computers. Assume that the hypothetical figures below show output per hour for workers in each country.

	Worker Productivity	
	Japan	**United States**
Units of camera output per hour	9	4
Units of computer output per hour	3	2

Clearly Japan has an absolute advantage in both products, as Japanese workers are more productive in turning out cameras and computers than the American workers. Does this mean the two countries cannot benefit by trading with one another? If trade does occur, should each country continue to allocate its resources as in the past? The answer to both questions is no.

Each country should specialize in that item in which it has the greatest comparative cost advantage or least comparative cost disadvantage, and trade with others. Because Japan is three times more productive in cameras than computers, it should direct more of its resources into the photographic industry. One cost of doing so is lost computer output, but Japan can turn out three additional camera units for every computer unit given up. The United States, on the other hand, can obtain only two computer units.

Like their Japanese counterparts, American workers are also more productive in making cameras than computers. Still, U.S. resources should be directed to computers because the United States is at a smaller disadvantage compared with Japan in this area. If the United States specializes in computers and Japan in cameras and they trade with one another, each will benefit. The following scenario shows why.

Begin with 100 workers in each industry before specialization:

Japanese Output

Cameras: 900

Computers: 300

United States' Output

Cameras: 400

Computers: 200

Shift 10 Japanese workers from computer to camera production; Shift 20 American workers from camera production to computers:

Japanese Output

Cameras: 990

Computers: 270

United States' Output

Cameras: 320

Computers: 240

Trade 80 Japanese cameras to the United States; Trade 30 American computers to Japan:

Japanese Benefits from Trade

Cameras: 910

Computers: 300

United States' Benefits from Trade

Cameras: 400

Computers: 210

By shifting Japanese resources into the production of cameras and U.S. resources into computers, the same total inputs will cause camera and computer output to rise 10 units each. The reason is because resources are now being used more efficiently. Benefits to both countries can be realized when each trades some of its additional output for the other's. Japan ends up with more cameras than before specialization and trade and with the same quantity of computers, while the United States finds itself with more computers and the same number of cameras. More output in both countries means higher living standards.

The message derived from the logic of comparative advantage is clear. If all countries were to concentrate on those products they can produce most efficiently, the world's output and income would increase, and everyone's standard of living would rise.

Under free exchange, society as a whole will be more wealthy, but individuals will be rewarded in terms of their marginal productivity and relative contribution to the overall social product" (Gilpin 1987). This applies at the international level as well: The gains from international trade may be distributed quite unequally, even if the principle of comparative advantage governs. Liberal economic theory ignores these differences, as it is concerned with *absolute* rather than *relative* gains. Other theorists, however, are more concerned with how the benefits of trade and other economic exchanges are distributed than with their total benefits.

Mercantilism

Mercantilism enjoys a long history in the story of states' quest for power and wealth. Its theoretical underpinnings prompted Adam Smith to write his famous critique in *The Wealth of Nations*, and its practice prompted rebellious American colonists to dump British tea into the Boston harbor in 1773.

Mercantilism advocates government regulation of economic life to increase state power and security, as we learned in Chapter 5. It emerged in Europe as the leading political-economy philosophy after the decline of feudalism and helped to stimulate the first wave of Europe's imperialist expansion, which began in the fifteenth century. Accumulating gold and silver was seen as the route to state power and wealth—and overseas colonies were a path to that end.

While states no longer try to stockpile precious metals, many continue to intervene in the marketplace. In the contemporary context, then, **neomercantilism** refers to "a trade policy whereby a state seeks to maintain a balance-of-trade surplus and to promote domestic production and employment by reducing imports, stimulating home production, and promoting exports" (Walters and Blake 1992). Its advocates are sometimes called "economic nationalists." For them, economic resources are the source of state power. The core belief is that "economic activities are and should be subordinate to the goal of state building and the interests of the state. All nationalists ascribe to the primacy of the state, of national security, and of military power in the functioning of the international system" (Gilpin 1987).

As an ideology of political economy, mercantilism shares much in common with political realism: Realists and mercantilists both see the state as the principal world actor; both view the international system as anarchical; and both dwell on humans' aggressive, confrontational proclivities. "Economic nationalists . . . stress the role of power in the rise of a market and the conflictual nature of international economic relations; they argue that economic interdependence must have a political foundation and that it creates yet another arena of interstate conflict, increases national vulnerability, and constitutes a mechanism that one society can employ to dominate another" (Gilpin 1987).

While liberals emphasize the benefits of cooperation and mutual exchanges, mercantilists worry that the gains realized by one side of the bargain will come at the expense of the other. For them, "relative gains" are more important than "absolute gains," even if this means some loss of welfare (e.g., reduced income) in the short run. An American economic nationalist, for instance, would complain about a trade agreement that promised the United States a 5 percent growth in income and the Japanese 6 percent. Although the bargain would assure an increase in U.S. living standards, its position compared with Japan's would erode. Indeed, projected over the long-run, such seemingly small differences would eventually lead to Japan's replacement of the United States as the world's largest economy—an outcome clearly unacceptable to American economic nationalists. Calculations like these explain why achieving mutual gains through international cooperation is so difficult.

An American Economic Nationalist Speaks Out

Since America's tariff walls have been torn down, to propitiate the insatiable gods of "free trade," vast swatches of our industry—radios, TVs, VCRs, steel, autos, textiles, shipping, mining, cameras, robotics—have been sacrificed. America's Rust Belt testifies to the triumph of free trade ideology over national interests.

—Patrick J. Buchanan, *The Arizona Republic*, October 21, 1993

What is good for General Motors is no longer good for America if General Motors is shutting down plants in Michigan and Ohio and opening them up outside Mexico City.

All four presidents on Mount Rushmore were economic nationalists. All four believed that it was the duty of the national government to produce policies that led to economic independence, the industrial supremacy of the American nation, and the highest standard of living in the world for American workers.

—Patrick J. Buchanan, *International Herald Tribune*, February 1, 1996

The theory of realism explains that states often shun cooperation because of the anarchical character of the international system which creates fear. States fear one another and therefore are wary of one another's motives. Moreover, because the international system is a self-help system, states alone are responsible for their survival and well-being. As a result, fear and uncertainty encourage each state to spend "a portion of its effort, not forwarding its own good, but in providing the means of protecting itself against others" (Waltz 1979).

The insecurity that breeds competition rather than cooperation is especially evident in national security affairs. It also applies to international economic relations in the eyes of those who see states' power and wealth as inextricably linked. "Even if nation-states do not fear for their physical survival, they worry that a decrease in their power capabilities relative to those of other nation-states will compromise their political autonomy, expose them to the influence attempts of others, or lessen their ability to prevail in political disputes with allies and adversaries" (Mastanduno 1991). Thus states are "defensively positional actors"—they seek not only to promote their domestic well-being but also to defend their rank (position) in comparison with others (see Grieco 1995).

The "relative gains issue" tells us why international cooperation under anarchical conditions is so difficult. More broadly, liberalism and mercantilism as competing ideologies of political economy help us to understand why liberal (open) international economies are preferred by some and reviled by others (see Focus 8.2). It is not surprising, then, that policymakers from different countries often pursue widely dissimilar policies in their international economic relations. Some see free trade to be in their interest; others devise policies to protect their economies from foreign imports. Some see the marketplace as the means to the greatest good for the greatest number; others seek to tilt the playing field to their own advantage. Hegemonic stability theory helps us to reconcile these competing policies and their underlying world views.

Hegemonic stability theory blends elements of liberalism and mercantilism. It argues that the preponderance of military and economic power in the hands of a single state—a hegemon—promotes stability in an international economic system based on the principles of liberalism. Thus it differs from the theory of realism, otherwise closely associated with mercantilism, in that realism sees the balancing of power among competing actors as the route to system stability (see Chapter 15). The two share the proposition that *state power* is the key to understanding how order emerges from an anarchial international system. Hegemonic stability theory in particular "assumes that a liberal economic system cannot be self-sustaining but must be maintained over the long term through the actions of the dominant economy" (Gilpin 1987).

Hegemony is the ability to "dictate, or a least dominate, the rules and arrangements by which international relations, political and economic, are conducted" (Goldstein 1988; cf. Nye 1990). In the world political economy it refers to a preponderance of material resources that give it control over raw materials, capital, and markets, and a competitive advantage in the production of highly valued goods (Keohane 1984).

From its vantage point as a preponderant power, a hegemon is able to promote rules for the system as a whole which protect its own interests. Hegemons like the United States (and Britain before it), whose domestic economies are based on capitalist principles, prefer liberal (open) international economic systems, because their comparatively greater control of technology, capital, and raw materials gives them more opportunities to profit from a system free of mercantilist restraints. Their economies typically serve as "engines of growth" for others in the "liberal train."

But hegemons also have special responsibilities. They must coordinate states' macroeconomic policies, manage the international monetary system that enables one state's money to be exchanged for others', make sure that countries facing balance-of-payments deficits (imbalances in their financial inflows and outflows) will find the credits necessary to finance their deficits, and serve as lenders of last resort during financial crises. If the most powerful states cannot do these things, they are likely to move toward more closed (protected or regulated) domestic economies, which may undermine the open international system otherwise advantageous to them (Block 1977). This makes tariffs, monetary regulations, and other mercantilist policies which prevent competitive market forces from determining economic transactions more widespread and undermines the liberal economic order. In short, hegemonic states not only have the greatest capacity to influence the system; they also have the greatest responsibility for its effective operation.

Costs and Benefits of Hegemony. As a hegemon exercises its responsibilities, it confers what are known as public or **collective goods.** These are benefits everyone shares and from which no one can be excluded selectively. National security is a collective good that governments try to provide for all of their citizens, regardless of the resources that individuals contribute through taxation. In world politics, "international security, monetary stability and an open international economy, with relatively free and predictable ability to move goods, services and capital are all seen as desirable [collective] goods. . . . More generally, international economic order is to be preferred to disorder" (Gill and Law 1988).

Those who enjoy the benefits of collective goods but pay little or nothing for them are **free riders.** A hegemon typically tolerates free riders, partly because the benefits that the hegemon provides encourage other states to accept its dictates. Thus both gain, much as liberalism sees the benefits of cooperation as a "positive-sum" outcome—meaning that both sides in a bargain stand to gain from their relationship. If the costs of leadership begin to multiply, however, the hegemon will become less tolerant of others' free-riding. In such a situation the benefits of cooperation increasingly will be seen as one-sided or zero-sum. In a zero-sum situation the benefits one partner realizes come at the expense of the other. In short, one side's gain is the other's loss.

Charles Kindleberger (1973), an international economist, first theorized about the order and stability that a preponderant power provides. In his effort to explain the Great Depression of the 1930s, Kindleberger concluded that "the international economic and monetary system needs leadership, a country which is prepared, consciously or unconsciously, . . . to set standards of conduct for other countries; and to seek to get others to follow them, to take on an undue share of the burdens of the system, and in particular to take on its support in adversity." Britain played this role from the Congress of Vienna in 1815 until the outbreak of World War I in 1914; and the United States assumed the British mantle in the decades immediately following World War II, as we have noted. In the interwar years, however, Britain was unable to play its previous leadership role, and the United States, although capable of leadership, was unwilling to exercise it. The void, Kindleberger concluded, was a principal cause of the "width and depth" of the Great Depression which engulfed the world in the 1930s.

In the breach caused by Britain's inability to provide the leadership needed to promote world order and stability and the United States' disinclination to assume this role in the years prior to World War II, the world was plunged into the Great Depression. As international trade dried up in its wake, harbor activity in port cities slowed to a crawl, and longshoremen—such as those pictured here—found themselves without work.

The Causes of Hegemonic Decline. Although hegemonic powers benefit from the liberal economic systems that their power promotes, the very success of liberalism eventually erodes the bases on which it rests.

> Economic competition and the price mechanism drive the market economy toward ever higher levels of productive efficiency, economic growth, and the integration of national markets. In time, the market produces profound shifts in the location of economic activities and affects the international redistribution of economic and industrial power. The unleashing of market forces transforms the political framework itself, undermines the hegemonic power, and creates a new political environment to which the world must eventually adjust. With the inevitable shift in the international distribution of economic and military power from the core to rising nations in the periphery and elsewhere, the capacity of the hegemon to maintain the system decreases. Capitalism and the market system thus tend to destroy the political foundations on which they must ultimately rest. (Gilpin 1987, 77–78)

The ability of leading economies to adapt to the changing circumstances they themselves promote is critical to maintenance of their dominant position. Britain was unable to adapt, and fell from its top-ranked position. Is the United States destined to suffer the same fate? Although it is an emotionally charged issue in the United States, the signs of hegemonic decline are not easily dismissed.

- In 1947, the United States accounted for nearly 50 percent of the combined gross world product. By 1960, its share had slipped to 28 percent, by 1970 to 25 percent, and by 1980 to 23 percent. Since then the proportion has ranged between 22 and 26 percent.

- Since the late 1970s, average annual GNP growth rates in Europe, China, Japan, and the Newly Industrialized Economies have typically outstripped the United States.

- The U.S. share of world industrial output of both "sunset industries," such as steel and automobiles, and "sunrise industries," such as microelectronics and computers, has declined.

- During the 1970s and the 1980s, labor productivity grew more rapidly in Europe and Asia than in the United States.

- The U.S. share of world financial reserves has declined abruptly as the United States moved from being a principal creditor nation to the world's largest debtor.

- U.S. dependence on foreign energy sources, first evident in the early 1970s, has continued unabated into the 1990s.

Thus in all the areas essential to hegemony—control over raw materials, capital, and markets, and competitive advantages in production—U.S. preponderance has waned.

Some analysts argue that the causes of U.S. decline are rooted in its military commitments accumulated during the Cold War. Historian Paul Kennedy (1987) argued that "imperial overstretch" is the cause of America's fall from prominence, as "The United States now runs the risk that the sum total of [its] global interests and obligations is nowadays far larger than the country's power to defend them all simultaneously." The theory rests on what Kennedy calls a truism, namely "that a power that wants to remain number one for generation after generation requires not just military capability, not just national will, but also a flourishing and efficient economic base, strong finances and a healthy social fabric, for it is upon such foundations that the country's military strength rests in the long term" (Kennedy 1992; see also Dietrich 1992).

Critics of the popular "declinist" thesis that Kennedy and others advanced in the 1980s were quick to seize on what they saw as the unfair parallels between the American and earlier British experiences as well as continuing U.S. dynamism (see, e.g., Nau 1990; Nye 1990). Still, the inability of the U.S. political economy to perform equally with its economic rivals was not easily dismissed, leading policymakers and critics from both sides of the American political spectrum to begin to examine the relationship between the nation's poor domestic economic performance (e.g., its low domestic savings rate, poor educational performance, stagnant productivity, declining work habits, and rising demands for welfare-state entitlements) and its inability to compete more effectively with its economic rivals (see, e.g., Krauthammer 1991b; Luttwak 1993; Nunn and Domenici 1992).

"Competitiveness" became a key concept in the Clinton administration's approach to political-economy issues as it determined to reverse the course of U.S. relations with economic competitors. "Aggressive unilateralism" often described the administration's approach to trade issues. Clinton himself intervened with Saudi Arabia to win an aircraft contract for Boeing Corporation, for example, and his administration redirected money budgeted to the defense department to particular private-sector industries, hoping to augment their ability to compete with foreign producers of defense-sensitive products. These and other controversial policies and practices were motivated by the view that competition from America's trade partners, of the sort hegemonic stability theory predicts, diminished the American living standards, thus rationalizing a retreat from liberalism and the embrace of mercantilism.

Like "declinism," the competitiveness debate evokes strong emotional responses that range well beyond economics. It includes not only concern about educational achievement and worker productivity (the amount of output produced per worker per hour), but also bitter controversies about the impact of immigrant labor—both legal and illegal—on wage rates among less-skilled U.S. workers (see also Chapter 9).

Economist Paul Krugman became an especially vocal critic of the argument that real income growth in the United States lagged because of many U.S. firms' inability to sell in world markets. Krugman supports his argument with evidence that a decline in domestic productivity explains almost all of the decline in American living standards between 1973 and 1990. The same is true in Europe and Japan: "In each case, the growth rate of living standards essentially equals the growth rate of domestic productivity—not productivity relative to competitors, but simply domestic productivity. Even though world trade is larger than ever before, national living standards are overwhelmingly determined by domestic factors rather than by some competition for world markets" (Krugman 1994; see also Drucker 1994). "The moral," Krugman continues, "is clear":

As a practical, empirical matter the major nations of the world are not to any significant degree in economic competition with each other. Of course, there is always a rivalry for status and power—countries that grow faster will see their political rank rise. So it is always interesting to *compare* countries. But asserting that Japanese growth diminishes U.S. status is very different from saying that it reduces the U.S. standard of living—and it is the latter that the rhetoric of competitiveness asserts. (Krugman 1994, 35)[2]

Beyond economics at home and abroad, the end of the Cold War has altered appreciably U.S. willingness to assume the burdens of maintaining the liberal international economic order it once championed. An undisputed hegemonic power typically can afford to be less concerned about its relative power position than others. It is therefore less likely to attempt to maximize its share of the global market than are aspiring hegemons or other economic powers undergoing a decline in their relative power position. As a hegemon's dominance erodes, however, its behavior on trade and other issues can be expected to change. The United States once tolerated—indeed, encouraged—other states to practice mercantile policies as it sought to cement Western solidarity in the fight against communism. Today it is "less inclined, in economic disputes with its allies, to subordinate its national economic interests to the pursuit of political harmony or solidarity within the alliance" (Mastanduno 1991). Why? Because it is no longer immune from the relative gains problem. Instead, the United States, like others, increasingly acts in a defensively positional manner—just like any "ordinary country."

The Consequences of Hegemonic Decline. What happens when a hegemon's preponderant power declines? Domestically we would expect it to turn inward, as the forces of economic nationalism gain politically at the expense of liberalism. Internationally, hegemonic stability theory predicts that disorder will result. In extreme instances, global war may follow; for example, the hegemonic decline of Britain and the absence of U.S. leadership may have precipitated the two world wars of the twentieth century (see Gilpin 1981).

Orderliness and stability marked the world political economy from the end of World War II until the early 1970s—a period of unchallenged U.S. hegemony. Since then, however, as American dominance has waned, the world political economy has been wracked by periodic crises and instability. Still, the system has not collapsed, as it did in the years between World Wars I and II. Is this because the processes of hegemonic decline have yet to play themselves out? Or, as some would argue, is the decline of American power a myth? Or is it because the institutions and rules put into place to govern the liberal order during the period of American hegemony have now taken on a life of their own? The last view is the most convincing one among liberal theorists, who believe that the rise of international regimes explains the persistence of order and stability even as American hegemony wanes.

International regimes reflect states' tendency to devise rules for cooperation even under international anarchy. Although most of the international regimes (rules and institutions) that today govern the world political economy were created during the era of U.S. dominance, they have continued to flourish. "By providing more information, establishing mechanisms for monitoring, and generating shared expectations institutions can create an environment in

---

[2]For a critique of Krugman's arguments and a rejoinder, see especially the essays by Clyde V. Prestowitz, Jr., Lester C. Thurow, Stephen S. Cohen, and Krugman in the July/August 1994 issue of *Foreign Affairs*. Also see Burton (1994) and Preeg (1994).

which interstate cooperation is possible even without a single dominant leader" (Krasner 1993; see also Keohane 1984). Thus international regimes may explain why the magnitude and extent of disruptions predicted by the relative decline of U.S. power have not (yet?) materialized.[3]

Liberalism, mercantilism, and hegemony are three concepts that animate state behavior in today's world political economy. They are especially powerful in explaining the changing role of the United States in managing the international monetary and trade systems since World War II, to which we now turn.

• • •

LIBERALISM, MERCANTILISM, AND HEGEMONY IN THE INTERNATIONAL MONETARY SYSTEM

Devising mechanisms to determine the value of nations' currencies in relation to one another was among the tasks that the World War II Allies faced when they met at Bretton Woods. The negotiating parties agreed that the postwar monetary system should be based on fixed exchange rates and assigned governments primary responsibility for enforcing its rules. In addition, they anticipated that the International Monetary Fund (IMF), created at Bretton Woods, would serve as a formal mechanism to help states deal with such matters as maintaining equilibrium in their balance of payments and stability in their exchange rates with one another. The International Bank for Reconstruction and Development, now commonly known as the World Bank, was also created to aid recovery from the war. Today its primary function is promoting economic development in the Global South. The IMF also has assumed new functions, including that of "lender of last resort" when its member states face financial crises. Its help comes with "conditions," however, which often require painful domestic adjustments designed to move those receiving assistance toward liberal economies oriented toward export markets.

Today the IMF and World Bank are important, if controversial, players in the global monetary and financial systems. In the period immediately after World War II, however, they commanded too little authority and too few resources to cope with the enormous devastation of the war. The United States stepped into the breach.

Hegemony Unchallenged

The U.S. dollar became the key to the role that the United States—now the world's hegemonic power—assumed as manager of the international monetary system. Backed by a vigorous and healthy economy, a fixed relationship between gold and the dollar (set at $35 per ounce of gold), and a government commitment to exchange gold for dollars at any time (known as "dollar convertibility"), the dollar became "as good as gold." In fact, others preferred dollars to gold for use in managing their balance-of-payments and savings accounts. Dollars earned interest, which gold did not; they did not incur storage and insurance costs; and they were needed to buy imports necessary for survival and postwar reconstruction. Thus the postwar economic system was

---

[3]The contribution that international institutions make to order and stability under conditions of anarchy is a hotly debated issue among realists and liberals. For a sampling of contending interpretations, see Keohane (1984), Mearsheimer (1994–1995), Keohane and Martin (1995), Ruggie (1995), and the essays in Baldwin (1993) and Kegley (1995).

A Primer on Exchange-Rate Systems

Without a world government, there is no common international currency for carrying on financial transactions and settling international accounts. If states want to trade or engage in other financial transactions with one another, a mechanism must be devised to determine their monies' value in relation to one another. The international monetary system establishes that framework. Its goal is stability in the value of national currencies combined with the flexibility necessary to adjust relative values when circumstances require it.

Currency rates of exchange express the value of one currency, such as the German mark, in relation to another, like the U.S. dollar. There are three types of systems: fixed, floating, and managed.

- A *fixed exchange-rate system* is one in which a government sets the value of its currency at a fixed rate in relation to others' money. The gold standard of the late nineteenth century is an example. National currency values were defined in terms of gold, whose coinage was used as money. The "invisible hand" of the gold market adjusted their relative values, righting imbalances in their balance of payments—at least in theory. In practice, Britain bore a disproportionate share of the burden of ensuring a stable monetary system.

  The Bretton Woods system also was designed as a fixed-exchange-rate system. The United States set the value of its currency at $35 per ounce of gold, and other nations priced their currencies in relation to the dollar,

maintaining value within narrowly defined boundaries. Theoretically, devaluations were permitted if necessary to maintain equilibriums in states' trade and payments and stability in the system as a whole. In practice, Bretton Woods depended critically on the hegemonic power of the United States.

- A system of *floating exchange rates* replaced Bretton Woods in the early 1970s. The link between the dollar and gold was cut. Market forces, rather than government actions, were expected to adjust the relative value of states' currencies to reflect the underlying strengths and weaknesses of their economies. Theoretically, they would more or less automatically adjust imbalances in their trade and payments with one another. In practice, state intervention again proved necessary to ensure monetary stability and flexibility. Without a hegemonic power to perform these tasks, policy coordination among the world's principal economic powers is required, but this, too, has proven elusive.

- The European Union is committed to a *managed exchange-rate system* in anticipation of creating a single European currency by the end of the century. The European Monetary System (EMS) links the currencies of several EU members whose governments pledge to stabilize currency values through government intervention if necessary. In practice, the system has proven highly unstable, as governments lack the necessary will to operate it effectively.

not simply a modified gold standard system; it was a dollar-based system. Dollars became a major component of the international reserves used by national monetary authorities in other countries. They also became a major component of the "working balances" used by private banks, corporations, and individuals for international trade and capital transactions.

In addition to these functions, the dollar became a "parallel currency": It was universally accepted as the "currency against which every other country sold or redeemed its own national currency in the exchange markets" (Triffin 1978–1979). To maintain the value of their currencies, central banks (the chief monetary units) in other countries either bought or sold their own currencies, using the dollar to raise or depress their value. Such intervention was often necessary because states had committed themselves at Bretton Woods to keep fluctuations in their exchange rates within very narrow limits. Thus the Bretton Woods monetary regime was based on **fixed exchange rates,** which ultimately required a measure of government intervention for its preservation (see Focus 8.3).

A central problem of the immediate postwar years was how to get U.S. dollars into the hands of those who needed them most. One vehicle was the Marshall Plan, which provided Western European states with billions of dollars in aid to buy the U.S. goods necessary for rebuilding their war-torn economies. The United States also encouraged deficits in its own balance of payments as a way of providing **international liquidity** (reserve assets used to settle international accounts) in the form of dollars.

In addition to providing liquidity, the United States assumed a disproportionate share of the burden of rejuvenating Western Europe and Japan. It supported European and Japanese trade competitiveness, permitted certain forms of protectionism (such as Japanese restrictions on importing U.S. products), and condoned discrimination against the dollar (as in the European Payments Union, which promoted trade within Europe at the expense of trade with the United States). The United States willingly incurred these costs of leadership because the economic growth they were expected to stimulate in Europe and Japan would eventually provide widening markets for U.S. exports. The perceived political benefits of strengthening the Western world against the threat of communism helped to rationalize acceptance of the costs and the free-riding by others which they entailed.

"The system worked well. Europe and Japan recovered and then expanded. The U.S. economy prospered partly because of the dollar outflow, which led to the purchase of U.S. goods and services" (Spero 1990; see also Eichengreen and Kenen 1994). Furthermore, the role of the dollar as the world's top currency aided the United States' ability to pursue an unrestrained globalist foreign policy. Indeed, U.S. foreign economic and military aid programs were made possible by acceptance of the dollar. Business interests could also readily expand abroad because U.S. foreign investments were often considered desirable, and American tourists could spend their dollars with few restrictions. In effect, the United States operated as the world's banker—a hegemon's perquisite. Other countries had to balance their financial inflows and outflows; in contrast, the United States could operate internationally without the constraints of limited finances. In addition, the dominance of the United States meant that its internal economic circumstances affected other nations in significant ways. Through the ubiquitous dollar, the United States thus came to exert considerable influence on political and economic affairs throughout the world.

Yet there were costs: The enormous number of dollars held by others made the U.S. economy vulnerable to financial shocks abroad. Although American policymakers sought to insulate the economy from these shocks, like the British before them, the nation's leadership role made their task more difficult. The dollar could not be devalued without hurting U.S. allies, for example, nor could inflationary or deflationary policies be practiced without impairing others. Although other countries could use these tools (see Focus 8.4), the U.S. leadership role in the world political economy proscribed their use by the United States.

By the late 1950s, concern began to mount about the long-term viability of an international monetary system based on the dollar. Analysts worried that such a system would be unable to provide the international liquidity necessary to ensure continued economic growth. They also feared that the number of foreign-held dollars eventually would overwhelm the United States' ability to convert them into gold, undermining others' confidence in the soundness of the dollar and the U.S. economy (Triffin 1978–1979).

A Primer on Trade and Payments Balances

Trade is the most important international economic transaction for many states. A deficit in the **balance of trade** results from an imbalance between imports and exports, that is, when a state buys more abroad than it sells. The *merchandise* balance measures only the value of goods bought and sold abroad. Trade in services, which has grown rapidly in recent years, must be added to get a complete picture of the balance between imports and exports.

The **balance of payments** is a more inclusive summary statement of a state's financial transactions with the rest of the world. In addition to imports and exports, the balance of payments includes such items as foreign aid transfers and the income of citizens employed abroad who send their paychecks home. The *current account* measures trade in goods and services plus investment income and payments (e.g., money from and to multinational corporations) and government transactions. The *capital account* measures foreign

nationals' investment of resources abroad and in the home country. The balance of payments is the sum of the balance of trade and the current and capital accounts.

A *balance-of-payments surplus* occurs when more money flows into a country than out of it; a *balance-of-payments deficit* is the reverse. A deficit requires some kind of corrective action. Policies that modify either the level of imports or the value of one's currency relative to others' are possible options, but neither is without costs.

Broadly speaking, there are three (painful) methods a country can use to correct a payments deficit (Isaak 1995). It can embark on deflationary policies at home by raising interest rates or adopting austere budgets. It can restrict the outflow of money by imposing higher tariffs, import quotas, or other mechanisms designed to limit outflow of capital. Or it can increase its international liquidity by borrowing in capital markets or liquidating its foreign exchange reserves.

Hegemony under Stress

As early as 1960 it was clear that the dollar's top currency status, sustained by U.S. hegemony, was on the wane. Several reasons explain its declining position.

First, if the problem in the immediate postwar years was too few dollars, by the 1960s it was too many dollars. The costs of extensive U.S. military activities, foreign economic and military aid, and massive private investments produced increasing balance-of-payments deficits. Although encouraged earlier, the deficits by this time were out of control. Furthermore, U.S. gold holdings fell precipitously in relation to the growing number of foreign-held dollars. Given these circumstances, the possibility of a U.S. devaluation of the dollar made others less confident in it and less willing to hold dollars as reserve currency. France, under the leadership of Charles de Gaulle, went so far as to insist on exchanging dollars for gold (although arguably for reasons related as much to French nationalism as the viability of the U.S. economy).

Second, the increasing monetary and financial interdependence of the Global North's industrial economies led to massive transnational movements of capital. An increasingly complex relationship between the economic policies engineered in one country and their effects on another resulted, as the Global North moved beyond sensitivity interdependence toward vulnerability. This in turn spawned a variety of comparatively formal groupings of the central bankers and finance ministers from the leading economic powers who devised

219

various *ad hoc* solutions (such as currency swaps) to deal with their common problems. They also decided to create Special Drawing Rights (SDRs) in the IMF, a form of reserve assets popularly known as "paper gold," designed to facilitate the growth of international liquidity by means other than increasing the outflow of dollars from the United States.

Third, although the United States was the chief advocate and supporter of the various management techniques devised during the 1960s, none proved sufficient to counter the "dollar crises" which surfaced in the late 1960s and early 1970s. In part this is because Bretton Woods theory and practice never quite matched. Although the Bretton Woods rules permitted states to devalue their currencies, devaluations "proved to be traumatic politically and economically. . . . [They] were taken as indications of weakness and economic failure by states and, thus, were resisted" (Walters and Blake 1992; see also Eichengreen and Kenen 1994). Thus the Bretton Woods regime never operated quite as it was intended.

Fourth, changes in the world political economy undermined the dollar-based Bretton Woods system. By the 1960s Europe and Japan had completely recovered from World War II, as symbolized by their currencies' return to convertibility. Recovery meant that U.S. monetary dominance and the dollar's privileged position were increasingly unacceptable politically; the return to convertibility meant that alternatives to the dollar (such as the German mark and Japanese yen) as media of savings and exchange were now available. The United States nonetheless continued to exercise a disproportionate influence over these others states, even while it was unreceptive to their criticisms of its foreign economic and national security policies, as with the war in Vietnam.

From its position as the dominant power, the United States came to see its own economic health and that of the world political economy as one and the same. In the case of the monetary regime in particular, U.S. leaders treasured the dollar's top currency status and interpreted attacks on it as attacks on international economic stability (see Walters and Blake 1992). That view mirrored the interests and prerogatives of a hegemon, but it did not reflect the reality of a world political economy in transition.

> The exercise of American political and military power on a global basis [had] been designed to gain foreign acceptance of an international monetary order that [institutionalized] an open world economy, giving maximum opportunities to American businessmen. It would be absurd for the United States to abandon its global ambitions simply to live within the rules of an international monetary order that was shaped for the purpose of achieving these ambitions. . . . The fundamental contradiction was that the United States had created an international monetary order that worked only when American political and economic dominance in the capitalist world was absolute. That absolute dominance disappeared as a result of the reconstruction of Western Europe and Japan, on the one hand, and the accumulated domestic costs of the global extension of U.S. power, on the other. With the fading of the absolute dominance, the international monetary order began to crumble. (Block 1977, 163)

Although the United States sought to stave off challenges to its leadership role, its own deteriorating economic situation made that increasingly difficult.

Mounting inflation—caused in part by the unwillingness of the Johnson administration to raise taxes to pay either for the Vietnam War or the Great Society—was particularly troublesome. As long as the value of others' currencies relative to the dollar remained fixed, the rising cost of U.S.-produced goods reduced their relative competitiveness overseas. In 1971, for the first time in the twentieth century, the United States actually suffered a modest (by today's standards) trade deficit of $2 billion, which worsened the next year. Predictably, demands by industrial, labor, and agricultural interests for protectionist trade measures designed to insulate them from foreign economic competition grew.

American policymakers laid partial blame for the U.S. trade deficit at the doorstep of its major trading partners. Japan and West Germany in particular were criticized for maintaining undervalued currencies (yen and marks that did not accurately reflect the cost of goods in those countries). This made their goods attractive internationally (and to American consumers), which in turn enabled them to generate balance-of-trade surpluses by selling more overseas than they bought. Simultaneously, the U.S. position in the global marketplace was deteriorating, as its share of international trade declined and Europe's and Japan's increased.

Faced with these circumstances—symbols of a preponderant power under stress—the United States sought aggressively to shore up its sagging position in the world political economy. In August 1971 President Richard M. Nixon abruptly announced that the United States would no longer exchange dollars for gold. He also imposed a surcharge on imports into the United States as part of a strategy designed to force a realignment of others' currency exchange rates. These startling and unexpected decisions—coming as a shock to the other Western industrial nations, which had not been consulted—marked the end of the Bretton Woods system.

The strident actions of the United States in 1971 were in part a reaction to its growing interdependence with the rest of the world and its realization that it could no longer unilaterally regulate international monetary affairs. In this sense they were predictable responses of an "ordinary country" to the growing challenges it now faced in the world political economy. For the political economy as a whole, however, it also was now clear that the political bases on which the Bretton Woods system had been built lay in ruins. American leadership was no longer accepted willingly by others or exercised willingly by the United States. Power was more widely dispersed among states, and the shared interests that once bound them together had dissipated.

With the price of gold no longer fixed and dollar convertibility no longer guaranteed, the Bretton Woods system gave way to a system of **floating exchange rates**. Market forces rather than government intervention were now expected to determine currency values. The theory underlying the system is that a country experiencing adverse economic conditions will see the value of its currency decline in the marketplace in response to the choices of traders, bankers, and business people. This will make its exports cheaper and its imports more expensive, which in turn will pull the value of its currency back toward equilibrium—all without the need for central bankers to support their currencies. In this way it was hoped that the politically humiliating devaluations of the past could be avoided. Policymakers did not foresee that the new system would introduce an unparalleled degree of uncertainty and unpredictability into international monetary affairs (see Focus 8.5).

Why Do Exchange Rates Fluctuate?

Money works in several ways and serves different purposes. First, it must be acceptable, so that people earning it can use it to buy goods and services from others. Second, it must serve as a store of value, so that people will be willing to keep some of their wealth in the form of money. Third, it must be a standard of deferred payment, so that people will be willing to lend money knowing that when the money is repaid in the future, it will still have purchasing power.

Inflation occurs when the government creates too much money in relation to the goods and services produced in an economy. As money becomes more plentiful and thus less acceptable, it cannot serve effectively as a store of value or a medium of exchange to satisfy debts. Governments work to ensure that their currencies do the jobs intended for them. This means, among other things, that they try to maintain an inflation-free environment.

In the international monetary system, movements in a state's exchange rate occur in part when changes occur in assessments of the underlying economic strength of a country or the ability of its government to maintain the value of its money. A deficit in a country's balance of payments, for example, would likely cause a decline in the value of its currency relative to others. This happens when the supply of the currency is greater than the demand for it. Similarly, when those engaged in international economic transactions change their expectations about a currency's future value, they might reschedule their lending and borrowing. Fluctuations in the exchange rate could follow.

Speculators—those who buy and sell money in an effort to make it—may also affect the international stability of a country's currency. Speculators make money by guessing the future. If, for instance, they believe that the Japanese yen will be worth more in three months than it is now, they can buy yen today and sell them for a profit three months later. Conversely, if they believe that the dollar will be worth less in nine-

ty days, they can sell yen today for a certain number of dollars and then buy back the same yen in ninety days for fewer dollars, making a profit.

Speculators base their decisions on a number of factors. One is their reading of the health of the currency in which they are speculating. If they believe the U S. dollar is weak because the U.S. economy itself is weak, they may conclude that policymakers will permit the dollar to depreciate. A closely related consideration is whether a government is perceived as having the political will to devise policies that will ensure the value of its money, particularly against inflationary pressures. If speculators think it does not, they would again be wise to sell dollars today and buy them back tomorrow at the (anticipated) lower price. In the process, speculators may create self-fulfilling prophecies: They may "prove" that the dollar needs to depreciate in value simply because of the volume of seemingly unwanted dollars offered for sale. The globalization of finance now also encourages managers of investment portfolios to move funds from one currency to another in order to realize gains from differences in nations' interest rates— including their anticipation of how interest rates might change.

In the same way that governments try to protect the value of their currencies at home, they try to protect them internationally by intervening in currency markets. Their willingness to do so is important to importers and exporters, who depend on orderliness and predictability in the value of the currencies they deal in to carry on their transnational exchanges. Governments intervene when countries' central banks buy or sell currencies to change the value of their own currencies in relation to others. Unlike speculators, however, they are pledged not to manipulate exchange rates so as to gain unfair advantage. Whether they can affect their currencies' values in the face of large transnational movements of capital is, however, increasingly problematic.

Hegemony in Decline

According to the theory of hegemonic stability, international economic stability is a collective good that preponderant powers provide. As their power wanes (as arguably the *relative* power of the United States has in the post-Bretton Woods era, most noticeably in the 1970s) economic instability should follow. It did: Two "oil shocks" induced by the Organization and Petroleum Exporting Nations (OPEC) and the subsequent debt crisis that many Global South coun-

SHORT STERLING | L.GILT | BUND | T.BD | BTP | E.MARK | E.SW | E.LA | FTSE
JUN   SEP   SEP   MAR   SEP
9208 9210 9195 9155 9145 9140 9110 9100 9723 9812 9105 10520 9350 9165 9199 9322 8710 25550 HIGH
9165 9175 9140 9125 9109 9103 9105 9100 9711 9716 9069 10507 9270 9142 9183 9305 8640 24940 LOW
3227 1680 1771   305   199   824   570   5   75 23301 24863   78 3991 19380 7570 3206   379   7549 EST. V
91810 91770 91420 91150 91100 90900 90800   9098 10512B 93150 91600   9318B 86850254600 BID
A.9182A 9180A 9144A 9125A 9115A 9100A 9095A 9100A 9099 10515A   9161A   9320A 8695A25470A OFFER
9181   317   9145 9125 9115 9110 9105 9100 9723 9731 9099 10520 9315 9161 9195 9319 8690 25460 TRADE
8 ↑ 16A ↑ 5A ↓ 9B ↓ 10B ↓ 10B ↓ 10B ↓ 5B   ↑ 15 ↑ 15 ↑ 26A ↑ 1A ↓ 5B ↑ 10A ↑ 7 ↑   9A ↑ 17A ↑635A CHANG
                        SEPT 92 T/BOND EDSP 107.06 L/GILT EDSP 97.17   MESS

More than $1 trillion in currency trades take place each day, as currency speculators and investment managers find economic opportunity in differences in interest rates and economic performance in different countries.

tries and others faced created new apprehension and concern about the viability of the existing international economic order. Where hegemony once reigned, various groups of industrial states now evolved a series of quasi-official negotiating forums to cope with monetary and other economic stresses.

The OPEC Decade and Its Aftermath. The first oil shock came in 1973–1974, shortly after the 1973 Yom Kippur War in the Middle East, when the price of oil increased fourfold. The second occurred in 1979–1980 in the wake of the revolution in Iran and resulted in an even more dramatic jump in the world price of oil. As the world's largest oil consumer (then and now), the impact of the twin oil shocks on the United States was especially pronounced—all the more so as each coincided with a decline in domestic energy production and a rise in consumption. As dollars flowed abroad to purchase energy resources (a record $40 billion in 1977 and $74 billion in 1980), U.S. foreign indebtedness, also known as "dollar overhang," grew enormously and became "undoubtedly the biggest factor in triggering the worst global inflation in history" (Triffin 1978–1979). Others now worried about the dollar's value—which augmented its marked decline on foreign exchange markets in the late 1970s and early 1980s, as illustrated in Figure 8.1.

Global economic recession followed each oil shock. Ironically, however, inflation persisted. "Stagflation"—a termed coined to describe a stagnant economy accompanied by rising unemployment and high inflation—entered the lexicon of policy discourse. World inflation already was on the rise prior to the first oil shock (and may have prompted OPEC's action), but rising oil prices

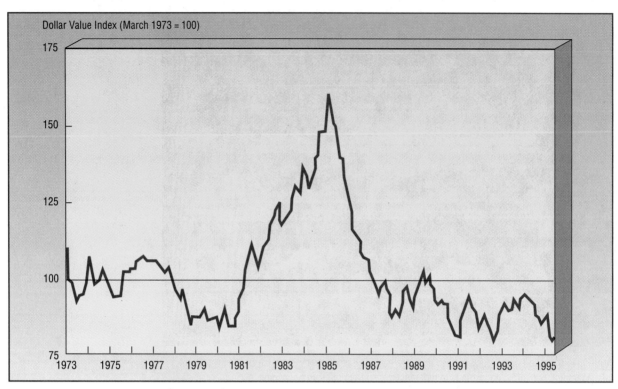

Dollar Value Index (March 1973 = 100)

FIGURE 8.1

In the post-Bretton Woods monetary system of floating exchange rates, the value of the dollar has fluctuated widely, causing uncertainty in the monetary system and disorder in the trading system. Since the mid-1980s the Group of Seven has sought to manage the monetary system by coordinating their domestic economics policies, but their efforts generally have failed.

Note: The index is the weighted-average value of the U.S. dollar against the currencies of ten other major industrialized nations.

SOURCE: 1973–1979: Federal Reserve System (1981), 441; 1980–1994: *Federal Reserve Bulletin*, various issues.

encouraged further inflationary pressures. Normally deflation would accompany reduced economic activity. In the absence of energy alternatives, however, the criticality of oil to the sophisticated industrial economies of the Global North inhibited such an adjustment.

The changing fortunes of the dollar in the early post-Bretton Woods monetary system reflected in part the way the leading industrial powers chose to cope with the two oil-induced recessions. In response to the first, they relied on fiscal and monetary adjustments to stimulate economic recovery and to avoid politically unacceptable unemployment levels. In response to the second—the longest and most severe economic downturn since the Great Depression of the 1930s—they shifted their efforts to controlling inflation through strict monetarist policies (i.e., policies designed to reduce the money supply in the economy). Large fiscal deficits and sharply higher interest rates followed, both particularly apparent in the United States. The other industrial states also experienced higher levels of unemployment than they previously had been willing to tolerate.

None could escape the impact of these developments, including the Global South. Many developing countries borrowed extensively from abroad to pay for the increased cost of energy in order to prevent reductions in domestic economic activity. Borrowing was possible because of the billions of "petrodollars" that flowed to the oil-producing states and that private banks and various multilateral institutions helped to recycle. In the process, however, the debt burden of many states assumed ominous proportions, particularly as interest rates climbed after the second oil shock. The threat of massive defaults by countries unable to service their debts pushed the international monetary regime to the brink of crisis in the early 1980s and again at mid-decade. The crisis atmosphere receded later, but the debt problem persisted.

High interest rates in the United States compared with other countries contributed not only to the debt burden of the Global South but also to the changing fortunes of the U.S. dollar, as increased demand for dollars drove up the exchange rate. Renewed U.S. economic growth, a sharp reduction in inflation, and the perception of the United States as a safe haven for financial investments in an otherwise politically unstable world also helped to restore faith in the dollar. Foreign investors therefore rushed to acquire the dollars necessary to take advantage of profitable investment opportunities in the United States, driving the value of the dollar to new heights (see Figure 8.1). This situation contrasted sharply with the 1970s, when the huge foreign indebtedness of the United States (the "dollar overhang") was the principal fear.

For the United States, the appreciation of the dollar was a mixed blessing. On one hand, it reduced the cost of imported oil; on the other, it increased the cost of U.S. exports to foreign buyers, reducing the competitiveness of American products in overseas markets. This meant the loss of tens of thousands of jobs in industries that produced for export. It also resulted in a series of record trade deficits ($122 billion in 1985, $145 billion in 1986, and $160 billion in 1987) as imports from abroad became relatively cheaper and hence more attractive to American consumers (see Figure 8.2).

The budget deficit of the U.S. government also climbed to record levels at this time, topping $200 billion each year. To deal with the deficit, the United States began to borrow both at home and abroad at a record rate, rapidly eroding the country's international investment position. As the debt climbed and interest payments on it compounded, the United States became a debtor nation for the first time in more than a half-century. Indeed, in only five years it had moved from being the world's biggest creditor nation to its largest debtor. By the early 1990s interest payments on the national debt (the accumulation of past deficits) alone surpassed the government's *combined* expenditures on agriculture, education, the environment, foreign aid, law enforcement, and transportation (Fry, Taylor, and Wood 1994, 257). Faced with rising debts, American policymakers found themselves constrained in dealing with other economic problems. Meanwhile, the American people faced the prospect of diminished living standards, as future generations became increasingly encumbered by the mounting debt legacy.

In a normally functioning market, the combination of a strong dollar and severe trade imbalance would set in motion self-corrective processes which would return the dollar to its equilibrium value. Growing U.S. imports, for

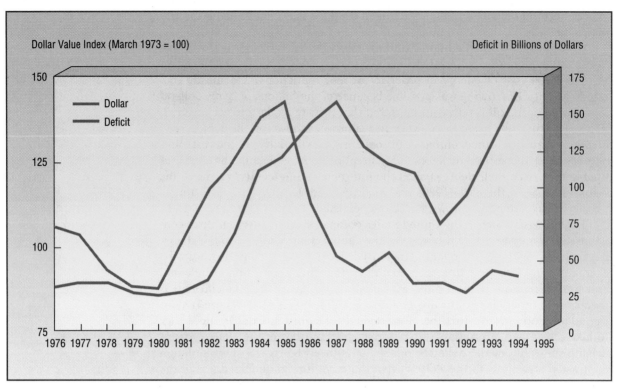

Dollar Value Index (March 1973 = 100)   Deficit in Billions of Dollars

FIGURE 8 . 2

The Dollar and the U.S. Trade Deficit, 1976–1995

As the dollar soared in the mid-1980s, American firms that produced for export were pummeled as their goods were no longer competitive in overseas markets. Meanwhile, U.S. imports grew dramatically, causing a huge deficit in U.S. merchandise trade with the rest of the world. The dollar fell sharply in the latter half of the 1980s, causing a reduction in the deficit but not its elimination. In the 1990s the trade deficit again rose sharply, even as the dollar remained low.

Note: Exchange rates are average monthly rates for the corresponding year.

SOURCE: Dollar exchange rates for 1973–1979 from Federal Reserve System (1981), 441; for 1980–1994 from *Federal Reserve Bulletin*, various issues. Merchandise trade deficit from *Economic Report of the President* (1994), 386.

example—although beneficial to America's trade partners in generating jobs and thus stimulating their return to economic growth—should create upward pressure on the value of others' currencies. Conversely, a drop in U.S. exports should ease the demand for dollars, thereby reducing the dollar's value in exchange markets. These mechanisms did not work as they should have because of the persistently high U.S. interest rates, sustained in part by the high military spending to meet Cold War commitments during the continuing East–West rivalry.

The United States' changing economic fortunes at home and abroad seemed to be a clear sign of its declining hegemony. In this atmosphere historian Paul Kennedy published *The Rise and Fall of the Great Powers (1987)*, a tome with more than a thousand footnotes which nonetheless became a national best seller. Policymakers would take umbrage at Kennedy's gloomy predictions—including George Bush, who during his 1988 acceptance speech for the Republican presidential nomination proudly declared that "America is not a declining nation—it is a rising nation." Yet fears of waning U.S. power clearly struck a responsive cord (and raw nerve?) in many quarters in the United States and abroad.

Toward Pluralistic Policy Coordination. In October 1987, stock prices throughout the world plummeted overnight, resulting in billions of dollars in lost equity (the difference between the market value of investments and debts owed on them). This shocking event revealed the extensive sensitivity interdependence that now marked the world political economy. It also underscored how critical the U.S. economy was to the health of others' economies and how much the value of the dollar internationally depended on the underlying strength of the U.S. economy.

Historically, the United States' commitment to liberal principles made it loath to intervene in the foreign exchange market. By 1985, however, the erosion of U.S. trade competitiveness in overseas markets due to the overvalued dollar had become unpalatable domestically. The United States now abandoned its posture of "passive unilateralism" toward the dollar, encouraging instead a greater degree of "pluralistic cooperation" as it sought more vigorously than before to coordinate macroeconomic policy among the other major industrial powers (Bergsten 1988). In response, the Group of Five (or G-5—composed of the United States, Britain, France, Japan, and West Germany) met secretly in the Plaza Hotel in New York and decided on a coordinated effort to bring down the overvalued dollar. The landmark agreement proved important not only because it signaled an end to the United States' benign neglect toward the vulnerabilities of interdependence, but also because it committed the major economic powers to greater collective coordination of their economic policies through management of exchange rates internationally and interest rates domestically.

Japan now also became a full partner in international monetary management, a move that led to formalization of the **Group of Seven** (the **G-7,** consisting of the G-5 plus Canada and Italy), which holds an annual economic summit (now also addressing political issues) accompanied by considerable pomp and fanfare. For a time the G-7 was arguably "one of the most influential institutions of the twentieth century, bringing into a common forum the leading states of the industrial world and their most powerful personalities" (Smyser 1993), but it has not proven to be an effective alternative to the United States as an instrument of macroeconomic policy coordination.

The dollar did depreciate following the Plaza meeting. However, when it became clear that the agreement made there failed to realize all of its intended goals, the G-5 met again, at the Louvre in Paris, to again discuss monetary management strategies. This time they effectively moved toward exchange-rate "target zones" and pledged to coordinate domestic monetary and fiscal policies to maintain them. In the aftermath of the Louvre meeting, Japan moved away from its export-led economy strategy toward one designed to simulate domestic demand. The United States—which by now was running large trade deficits with Japan—placed particular importance on Japan's strategic shift. Otherwise the meeting was a disappointment, as the goal of achieving macroeconomic policy coordination among the world's leading capitalist states remained episodic (Williamson and Henning 1994).

The Plaza and Louvre agreements nonetheless represented a fundamental shift in the philosophy of exchange-rate management away from the laissez-faire liberalism of the immediate post-Bretton Woods years. This encouraged critics of the floating exchange-rate system to urge even further government intervention in exchange markets (Eichengreen and Kenen 1994). Indeed, disappointment with the Louvre meeting combined with the stock market crash led critics to suggest that the domestic obstacles to G-7 economic cooperation would be overcome only during times of severe crisis or when the entire economic system appeared threatened (Gill 1993a). Thus the liberalism promised in the early 1970s when the United States "closed the gold window" was now giving way to the sentiments that underpinned Bretton Woods, namely, limited government intervention according to agreed-on rules to make the system work.

When Ronald Reagan became president in 1981, he announced that his administration would no longer intervene in foreign exchange markets, but he abandoned that pledge with the Plaza accord. The Bush administration, which came into office in 1989, reverted to the previous U.S. posture of passive unilateralism toward monetary issues—despite chronic U.S. trade and budget debts which in the late 1980s helped to precipitate a long decline in the value of dollar compared with its mid-decade lofty heights (see Figure 8.1).

While the Bush administration practiced passive unilateralism toward the dollar, Germany's central bank, the Bundesbank, maintained high interest rates in an aggressive effort to contain inflationary pressures generated by the cost of unifying the former East and West Germanies. Mimicking the effects on the dollar during Reagan's first term, the mark's value soared, as investors now chose to hold marks rather than dollars, further weakening a dollar already suffering from the effects of recession in the United States. The dollar was dealt another blow when George Bush proclaimed at the 1992 Republican nominating convention that the budget agreement he had worked out with Congress in 1990 to cope with the federal budget deficit was a mistake he would not repeat. Renewed fear about further growth in the already deficit-plagued U.S. economy caused the dollar to plunge even further. Almost simultaneously a currency crisis in Europe, stimulated again by German monetary policy, threatened the European Community's regional monetary system.

As in previous monetary crises, existing mechanisms of macroeconomic policy coordination proved ineffective in coping with the challenges of the early 1990s. That included the G-7, whose leaders have proven unable "to make hard economic choices at home. Each government's emphasis on dealing with seemingly intractable domestic problems . . . constrains joint efforts to stimulate global economic growth or to manage monetary and trade relations, preventing G-7 governments from pursuing disciplined and synchronized fiscal and monetary policies" (Ikenberry 1993; see also Smyser 1993; Whyman 1995).

Bill Clinton went to Washington determined to be the "economic president." He quickly realized, however, that the mounting debt caused by past budget deficits made it virtually impossible for his administration to use fiscal policy to fine-tune the economy. This heightened the importance of monetary policy. Because interest rates and the value of the dollar are often closely linked (lower rates should weaken the dollar and higher rates strengthen it), the importance of macroeconomic policy coordination also heightened.

Although verbally committed to a greater degree of multilateral policy making than the Bush administration, the Clinton administration continued its predecessors' passive policy toward the sagging dollar—this time as a mechanism of righting the trade imbalance between the United States and Japan. However, the U.S. trade deficit not only persisted but actually began to grow again, despite several years in which the dollar was comparatively weak. Eventually the Clinton administration reversed course as it led a series of efforts coordinated with the G-7 and others to prop up the dollar (but to little apparent effect).

The deterioration of the dollar against the mark and yen was particularly troublesome to America's principal trading partners in Europe and Asia. From the Japanese viewpoint, *endaka*—the strong yen crisis—was propelled by the imbalance of Japan's financial transactions with the rest of the world, leading to increased demand for the yen and hence its higher price (Berry 1994). This in turn contributed to a prolonged period of Japanese economic doldrums that contrasted sharply with the "bubble" years of the 1980s.

That neither market forces nor the mercantile behavior of the United States and its economic partners could reverse the course of the dollar compared with the yen is not easily explained. Increasingly, it seems, the volume of world trade and the activities of currency speculators, who use sophisticated electronic means to carry out their transnational exchanges, now also significantly affect national currency values. Over $1.1 trillion in currency trading occurs each day. This means that "each week [currency markets] shift wealth equal to the GDP of the United States. Every five hours, they are trading the equivalent of this year's [1995] U.S. defense budget" (Walker 1995, 53). International sales of stocks and bonds have mushroomed to unprecedented proportions as well. These developments in the globalization of markets severely circumscribe the ability of states—individually or collectively—to affect the value of their currencies in exchange markets. Indeed, Alan Greenspan—chair of the Federal Reserve system, responsible for U.S. monetary policy—has noted that the United States' ability to prop up the dollar by buying it in foreign exchange markets "is extraordinarily limited and probably in a realistic sense nonexistent." The globalization of finance and the removal of barriers to transnational capital flows also have, in Greenspan's words, exposed "national economies to shocks from new and unexpected sources, with little if any lag."

The European Monetary System: A Return to Bretton Woods?

Proposals for reforming the international monetary are widespread. Some see reversion to the classical gold standard as preferable to the current system of floating exchange rates. Others would opt for something like the Bretton Woods system of fixed but adjustable rates. What these and other proposals share in common is a continuing desire for stability and flexibility (see, e.g., Goldstein 1995; Minton-Beddoes 1995; Williamson and Henning 1994), which the current system of floating exchange rates nominally under the management of the world's leading economies acting in concert has failed to achieve. As one analyst put it, "even after a concentrated period of reflection, prompted in part by the fiftieth anniversary of the Bretton Woods conference, there is little agreement on what to do about the exchange rate system. All appraisals conclude that the performance of the world economy could be improved if policy discipline were strengthened and if the frequency and size of exchange rate misalignments could be reduced. But there is little consensus on how to bring that about" (Goldstein 1995).

The European Monetary System (EMS), launched in 1979 by the European Community, blends elements of the Bretton Woods system of fixed exchange rates and the post-Bretton Woods system of floating rates. Short-term fluctuations are guided by the marketplace, but the EMS requires that political consultations precede realignments of European currencies. Hence it is a "managed" system.

For a time the EMS seemed to have been successful in creating a "zone of predictability" (Spero 1990) among Europe's currencies as a precursor to a single European currency and a European central bank. Despite its lofty goals, however, the EMS has been less successful than its advocates once hoped. Changes in European currency rates have been infrequent for many of the same domestic political and economic reasons that currency revaluations under Bretton Woods proved traumatic (Eichengreen and Kenen 1994). In particular, an attempt begun in 1987 to operate within the EMS a fixed exchange-rate system (known as the Exchange Rate Mechanism, or ERM) failed during monetary crises in 1992 and 1993, causing the British to withdraw from the managed system. Although specific effects of the 1992–1993 crises on Britain and others varied, the general message is that fixed exchange rates are difficult to sustain in the face of widely variant domestic economic conditions and political pressures (Williamson and Henning 1994).

The European Union's determination to create a Europe-wide central bank and currency based on a system of managed exchange rates may eventually succeed. (The Maastricht Treaty lays out criteria for a single currency system that govern nations' debt, budget deficits, interest rates, and exchange rates.) Nonetheless, it is an unlikely precursor of a new international monetary system (see Thygesen 1994). On the contrary, the regionalization of the European monetary system reinforces other trends in the world political economy that portend divisive conflict that potentially will engulf security as well as economic issues.

As the preponderant power in the world political economy, the United States has championed liberalism on a global scale. Increasingly, however, it, too, has promoted regionalism as its capacity to shape the rules and institutions governing the world political economy has waned. The shift is especially evident in the recent U.S. posture toward trade issues and conforms to the behavior expected of a hegemonic power in decline.

• • •

LIBERALISM AND MERCANTILISM IN PRACTICE: FREE TRADE AND PROTECTIONISM

The exponential growth of world trade in the second half of the twentieth century has contributed measurably to an unprecedented rise in global economic prosperity. In the last two decades alone merchandise exports have grown from 11 percent to 18 percent of gross world product, and trade in services has grown by more than 22 percent since 1980 (World Bank 1995a, 1). The latest effort to reduce barriers to free trade, known as the Uruguay Round of multilateral trade negotiations, is expected to accelerate these trends. The World Bank projects that world merchandise trade will "grow at more than 6 percent a year, faster than at any time since the 1960s. Trade in services will increase even faster, especially as advances in information and telecommunication technology expand trade in long-distance services (data entry, accountancy, engineering design, software development)" (World Bank 1995a, 5). Thus "trade integration"—the difference between growth rates in trade and gross national (or gross world) product—will bind national economies ever more tightly in interdependent relationships.

These projections assume that the process of liberalizing the world political economy will continue. This, however, remains problematic as the forces of neomercantilism also remain vibrant. Indeed, hegemonic stability theory would lead us to expect that, as U.S. leadership declines, *closure* of the liberal trade regime will inevitably follow as economic nationalists in the United States and elsewhere resort to neomercantilist practices to advance their own interests at others' expense. Thus, whereas liberalism predicts that trade interdependence is the road to a more peaceful world, mercantilists see conflict over states' increasing resort to *trade protectionism* as likely if the decline of American hegemony in the international trade regime continues (see Borrus et al. 1992).

The **Uruguay Round** was the eighth in a series of multilateral trade negotiations since World War II (known as "rounds") conducted under the sponsorship of the **General Agreement on Tariffs and Trade (GATT).** Created in the late 1940s, GATT became the principal international organization designed to promote and protect free trade in the postwar Liberal International Economic Order. Free trade rests on the **most-favored-nation (MFN) principle,** which says that the tariff preferences granted to one state must be granted to all others exporting the same product (tariffs being taxes on goods imported into a country). When states became members of GATT and its successor, the World Trade Organization (WTO), they agreed to apply the MFN principle toward others.

Most-favored-nation treatment is the basic principle on which the WTO/GATT rest. Two other principles are also fundamental: *reciprocity* and *nondiscrimination*. Although parties to the GATT treaty and its successor pledge MFN treatment of one another, actual reductions in tariffs must be negotiated. Reciprocity requires countries to reduce their own tariffs in return for reciprocal reductions by others. Negotiating mutual (reciprocal) reductions in import barriers was the purpose of the GATT trade talks held since World War II.

Nondiscrimination means that goods produced at home and abroad are to be treated the same. "Once foreign goods cross the border into another GATT country, they are to be treated as domestic goods in terms of equal rights of competition. . . . Foreign goods from other GATT members are not to be subject to discriminatory measures, such as higher taxes, compared to those produced domestically" (Isaak 1995).

Free trade is attractive only if everyone can benefit. The principle of comparative advantage central to liberal economic theory is thus a central tenet of free trade, as specialization and trade permit trading states to enjoy a higher standard of living than they otherwise would (recall Focus 8.1). Still, states sometimes seek to enhance their domestic well-being by means that, according to liberalism, undermine their relations with their trade partners, reducing the benefits free trade otherwise promises to both. "Protectionism" is the generic term used to describe a number of policies that "protect" domestic producers from foreign competition.

Beggar-thy-neighbor policies are protectionist practices that seek to enhance domestic welfare by promoting trade surpluses that can be realized only at other countries' expense. They reflect a government's efforts to reduce unemployment through currency devaluations, tariffs, quotas, export subsidies, and other strategies that adversely affect its trade partners. These behaviors encapsulate today's beggar-thy-neighbor strategies which we now call "neomercantilism," contemporary expressions of classical mercantilism that helped propel classical imperialism and the unequal exchanges between exporters and importers it encouraged (see Chapter 5).

Quotas are instruments of neomercantilism. Governments impose quotas to protect domestic producers, regardless of their efficiency relative to foreign producers. **Import quotas** are unilateral policy instruments that usually specify the quantity of a particular product that can be imported from abroad. In the late 1950s, for example, the United States established import quotas on oil, arguing that they were necessary to protect U.S. national security. Hence the government, rather than the marketplace, determined the amount and source of imports.

Export quotas result from negotiated agreements between producers and consumers and seek to restrict the flow of products (e.g., shoes or sugar) from the former to the latter. An **orderly market arrangement (OMA)** is a formal agreement in which a country agrees to limit the export of products that might impair workers in the importing country, often under specific rules designed to monitor and manage trade flows (Boonekamp 1987). The Multi-Fiber Arrangement (MFA) is an example. The MFA is an elaborate OMA which restricts exports of textiles and apparel. It originated in the early 1960s, when the United States formalized earlier informal voluntary export restrictions (VERs) negotiated with Japan and Hong Kong to protect domestic producers from cheap cotton imports. The quota system was later extended to other importing and exporting countries and then, in the 1970s, to other fibers, when it became the MFA. Developing-country textile and apparel exporters chafe under the system, which they see as denying them access to markets in the Global North in clear violation of the MFN and nondiscrimination principles (see Cohen 1983). The elaborate quota system became a matter for heated negotiation during the Uruguay Round, where agreement was finally reached to phase it out over a ten-year period.

Import and export quotas are two examples of trade restrictions known as **nontariff barriers (NTBs).** NTBs have become ubiquitous with the rise of the welfare state. Their effects—sometimes inadvertent and sometimes intentional—often restrain trade. As complex societies strive to protect the welfare of their citizens through numerous and often complex government regulations regarding health and safety, foreign-produced goods frequently cannot compete. NTBs are now a more important form of trade protectionism than tariffs. Prior to the conclusion of the Uruguay Round, for example, the World Bank estimated that more than 40 percent of Global North imports were subject to nontariff trade barriers (*World Development Report 1991* 1991, 104–5; see also Low 1993). Tariffs, on the other hand, are now comparatively unimportant—particularly on industrial goods—as tariff levels have been progressively lowered over the past half-century and will continue to decline under the Uruguay Round agreements (see Figure 8.3).

Among developing countries, whose domestic industrialization goals may be hindered by the absence of protection from the Global North's more efficient firms, the **infant industry** argument is often used to justify mercantilist trade

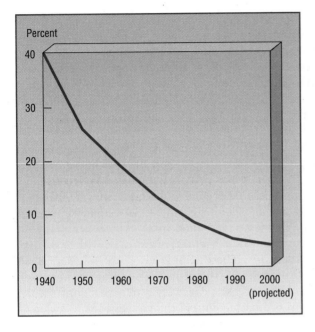

FIGURE 8.3

The Decline of Tariffs in the Industrialized Countries, 1940 Projected to 2000

Tariffs have declined dramatically since the peak period of economic nationalism in the 1930s. With average tariff levels among industrialized countries projected to decline to only 5 percent by 2000 (compared with 40 percent in 1940), tariffs have become a comparatively unimportant restraint on international trade.

SOURCE: Office of the U.S. Trade Representative and the Center for International Economics, as aggregated by *Time*, December 27, 1993, 16.

policies. According to this argument, tariffs or other forms of protection are necessary to nurture young industries until they eventually mature and lower production costs to compete effectively in the global marketplace. Import-substitution industrialization policies, once popular in Latin American and elsewhere, often depended on protection of infant industries (see Chapter 5).

In the Global North, *creating* comparative advantages now motivates the use of **strategic trade policy** as a means of ensuring that a country's industries will remain competitive in the rapidly changing, high-tech environment of the future. Strategic trade is a form of industrial policy that targets government subsidies toward particular industries so as to gain a competitive edge over foreign producers. Ironically, this particular neomercantilist strategy flows naturally from the principle of comparative advantage at the heart of liberal thinking.

Classical theory attributes the basis for trade to underlying differences among states. Some, for example, are better suited to the production of agricultural products, such as coffee, because they have vast tracts of fertile land. Others are better suited to the production of labor-intensive goods, such as shirts and shoes, because they have an abundance of cheap labor. Increasingly, however, economists recognize that comparative advantages take on a life of their own.

> Much international trade . . . reflects national advantages that are created by historical circumstance, and that then persist or grow because of other advantages to large scale either in development or production. For example, the development effort required to launch a new passenger jet aircraft is so large that the world market will support only one or two profitable firms. Once the United States had a head start in producing aircraft, its position as the world's leading exporter became self-reinforcing. So if you want to explain why the U.S. exports aircraft, you should not look for underlying aspects of the U.S. economy; you should study the historical circumstances that gave the United States a head start in the industry. (Krugman 1990, 109)

The policy consequences of such thinking are clear: If contemporary patterns of international trade reflect historical circumstances, states may reasonably conclude that it is beneficial to create advantages that will contribute to the long-run strength of their economies. Curiously, then, the logic of comparative advantage can itself be used to justify government interference in the free market. Although the returns on strategic trade practices are often marginal (Krugman 1990), the fact that some embrace them encourages others to do likewise.

The simultaneous pursuit of liberalism and mercantilism in today's world political economy shows states' determination to reap the benefits of interdependence while minimizing its costs. It also reveals the tension between states and markets, between the promise that everyone will benefit and the fear that the benefits will benefit some and disadvantage others. As we learned earlier, the absence of world government encourages states to be more concerned with how they fare in relation to others—their *relative gains*—than with how they fare individually—their *absolute gains*. These simple yet powerful ideas shed light on the reasons why the United States, the principle advocate of free trade in the post-World War II era, has increasingly engaged in protectionist trade practices, looking more like an "ordinary country" than a hegemonic power.

• • •

LIBERALISM, MERCANTILISM, AND HEGEMONY IN THE INTERNATIONAL TRADE SYSTEM

The importance of the United States to the international trade system derives from the size of its economy and the value of its production sold abroad. With its gross domestic product approaching $7 trillion, the United States is the largest economy in the world—more than two-and-half times larger than Japan, the second largest economy. As a result, it provides an enormous market for the rest of the world. In 1994, for example, the United States imported nearly $660 billion in merchandise from other countries. It also exported $503 billion in U.S.-produced goods, making it (with Germany) one of the world's two leading exporting countries.

But these numbers also show that U.S. exposure to the international trading system is substantial, as trade turnover (exports plus imports) in 1994 exceeded 17 percent of its GDP. As its exposure increases, making it more like other states in this regard, its sensitivity and vulnerability at the hands of others also grow. Even while the United States remains the world's preeminent economic power, then, it has wearied of others' free-riding and is now more prone to engage in neomercantilist practices itself.

Hegemony, Regime Creation, and Regime Transformation

Today the United States accounts for a little more than one-fifth of gross world product; in 1947 it accounted for nearly half. Thus the importance of the United States to the world political economy was even more pronounced in the period immediately following World War II than today. As the world's new hegemonic power, the United States became the preeminent voice in trade as well as monetary affairs.

The liberal trading system the United States promoted in the waning days of World War II, like its posture toward the monetary system, drew on the lessons policymakers learned from the 1930s. The zero-sum, beggar-thy-neighbor policies associated with the intensely competitive economic nationalism of the interwar period were widely believed to have been a major cause of the economic catastrophe of the 1930s, which hastened global warfare. To avoid its repetition, removing barriers to trade became a priority and led to the recurrent rounds of trade negotiations and to the decline in tariff rates worldwide, illustrated in Figure 8.3. As U.S. tariff rates were also reduced, the large U.S. market was opened to foreign producers, stimulating growth in others' economies.

At the time of the Bretton Woods negotiations, the United States envisioned a new International Trade Organization (ITO) which would seek lower restrictions on trade and set rules of commerce. The ITO would thus perform the role in trade policy that the IMF was designed to perform in international monetary management. The organization was stillborn, however. The proposed trading scheme, popularly known as the "Havana Charter," failed to win the approval of the U.S. Congress: "Protectionists opposed the arrangement for being too liberal, and liberals were against it for being too protectionist. . . . Without U.S. support the ITO was dead" (Isaak 1995). And without the ITO, GATT became the cornerstone of the liberalized trade regime the United States sought.

GATT was never intended to be a formal institution with enforcement powers. Instead, a premium was placed on negotiations and reaching a consensus to settle disputes among parties to the agreement, which first and foremost was a commercial treaty. As the trading system changed and disputes multiplied, though, GATT—under pressure from the United States—increasingly became involved in dispute settlement following increasingly legalistic procedures (Bayard and Elliott 1994). Dissatisfaction with GATT's role in resolving disputes and in devising new rules for a rapidly transforming trading system eventually led to a new trade organization, one with "teeth." Again with strong U.S. backing, the Uruguay Round created a **World Trade Organization (WTO)** whose purpose is to monitor the implementation of trade agreements and settle disputes among trading partners. Thus the WTO extends the GATT structure in a manner consistent with what once was envisioned for the failed ITO, as there is now "an explicit treaty-charter agreement establishing an international organization for trade, which can take its place beside the other Bretton Woods organizations" (Jackson 1994).

Hegemonic Power in a Changing Regime

The United States was the principal catalyst to the GATT negotiating rounds designed to liberalize the trading system. As it also opened its own market to others, it tolerated their free riding. We noted earlier, for example, that the United States knowingly acquiesced in Japan's protectionist trade practices and Europe's discrimination against the dollar. Restoring European and Japanese economic vitality was an important U.S. foreign policy goal, however. Furthermore, the long-term economic benefits of their revitalization promised to outweigh the short-term costs. Thus the United States not only permitted but actually encouraged others' relative gains. Evidence supports the wisdom of this strategy: As the average duty levied on U.S. imports declined by more than half between the late 1940s and the early 1960s, world exports nearly tripled.

The high point in the momentum toward a liberal trade regime in industrial products occurred with the mid-1960s Kennedy Round of negotiations, but they did not deal with agriculture. Although trade in agriculture fell beyond the purview of GATT as originally conceived (because the United States wanted it that way) it now became increasingly important. The European Economic Community's (EEC) Common Agricultural Policy (CAP)—which has been described as an "egregiously mercantilist" program (Babai 1993)—posed the immediate challenge. By maintaining politically acceptable but artificially high prices for farm products produced within the EEC, CAP curtailed American agricultural exports to Europe, now a major U.S. trade partner. Disagreements on this issue began to raise doubts among U.S. policymakers about the wisdom of promoting expansionist economic policies from which others benefited. Even today issues about trade in agriculture remain contentious and unresolved.

As Europe (and later Japan) challenged U.S. economic prowess, not only in agriculture but also in other economic sectors, a rising tide of protectionist forces bombarded Congress with trade-restriction demands designed to insulate the United States from foreign economic competition. In turn, the liberal trade regime was now threatened by many of the same forces that undermined the Bretton Woods monetary system of fixed exchange rates—and whose collapse also inhibited progress on a growing number of contentious trade issues.

Hegemony under Stress

To cope with growing protectionist sentiments in the United States, the Nixon administration sought a new grant of authority from Congress to negotiate lower tariff barriers with other nations. (Under the U.S. Constitution, Congress bears primary responsibility for trade policy. Since passage of the Reciprocal Trade Agreements Act of 1934, however, it has delegated to the president authority over the day-to-day management of trade policy, including negotiations with other nations.) This laid the basis for the Tokyo Round of multilateral trade negotiations, concluded in 1979 after nearly six years of bargaining.

The Tokyo Round began in a radically different environment from that of the previous GATT sessions. The value of world trade had grown exponentially, the level of economic interdependence among the world's leading industrial countries had reached levels unprecedented since before World War II, tariffs no longer posed the principal barriers to trade, and the United States no longer enjoyed the prerogatives of an unchallenged hegemon. In this new setting, addressing the new protectionism—nontariff barriers to trade—and reducing barriers to free trade in agricultural products took on greater urgency.

The Tokyo Round did produce a series of standards-of-conduct ("codes") directed at the increasingly troublesome NTBs. It also granted an exception to the principle of reciprocity when it approved of a Generalized System of Preferences (GSP) which granted developing countries preferential access to markets in the Global North. (At U.S. insistence it also adopted a "graduation clause," which stated that as developing countries reached higher levels of development, they would have to compete on a more equal footing with Northern states.) Still, the developing countries, many not members of GATT, generally shunned the accords because of their belief that the Tokyo negotiations did not address the North's protectionist sentiments which deprived them of market access. Furthermore, the Tokyo Round did not clearly reaffirm the principles underlying GATT and the liberal trade regime (Krasner 1979). Nor did it deal effectively with agricultural issues and with the growing incidence of neomercantilist and strategic trade practices that were of special concern to the United States. In fact, GATT's rules and procedures were increasingly irrelevant to the changes taking place in the trade regime, which meant they were often ignored (Graham 1979; see also Bayard and Elliott 1994; Destler 1995).

By the end of the Tokyo Round, it was clear that the promise and practice of free trade diverged widely. Spectacular increases in Japan's exports and overall economic performance during the 1960s and 1970s—soon to be followed by other Asian countries—posed especially formidable challenges not only to the United States but also to the premises of liberalism.

> Any large country rising so rapidly was bound to cause problems for the world trading system. . . . But there were other problems in absorbing Japan as one of the preeminent players in the world trading system. As the first non-Western nation to achieve industrial success, Japan was culturally different. This traditionally closed and close-knit society had maintained substantial formal barriers to imports throughout the 1960s. The pace at which these barriers were dismantled always lagged behind that which Japanese export success would have allowed. . . . Moreover, in contrast to the aggressive business behavior of Japanese firms, the standard style of the Tokyo government in trade diplomacy was not to take the initiative but to await foreign pressure for trade liberalization and to open up markets, bit by bit, in response to this pressure. (Destler 1995, 52)

In short, Japan—and the Asian Tigers and others that imitated its neomercantilist behavior—posed a mighty challenge to the liberal precepts undergirding the Liberal International Economic Order and the shared interests and values that once bound together North America and Western Europe. Europe, in fact, itself now posed a threat to the GATT principle of nondiscrimination, "the core notion that each national government would grant equal treatment to the products of all others adhering to the GATT system." By definition, the EC was "an enormous exception," as "its members agreed to grant one another more favorable (i.e., duty-free) market access than they granted to outsiders" (Destler 1995).

U.S. determination to reverse its burgeoning trade deficit explains why the Reagan administration abandoned its strategy of passive unilateralism toward monetary issues and the value of the dollar in the mid-1980s. The administration also now embraced the concept of *fair trade* as an alternative to free trade, asserting that "the playing field is tilted" against American producers by the mercantilist practices of other governments. The posture parried critics in Congress and the private sector who "came to believe that the process of reciprocal liberalization under the GATT was increasingly biased against the United States." Because "other countries relied more heavily on nontariff barriers and other industrial policies than did the United States, the result of the GATT negotiations' focus on tariffs had been to leave the U.S. market relatively more open." In response, "these critics of U.S. trade policy began to emphasize reciprocity in *levels* of protection—or comparable market access—rather than just reciprocal *changes* in the level of protection. . . . As the focus shifted from the process of liberalization to the actual outcome, . . . threats of market closure, rather than offers of further market opening, became more prominent as a negotiating tool" (Bayard and Elliott 1994). Threats of market closure are consistent with the predictions of hegemonic stability theory: As the costs of leadership begin to outweigh its benefits, contentment with absolute gains from trade give way to concerns about the relative gains of others.

The U.S. Responses to Its Hegemonic Decline

Over the next decade the United States launched a multipronged strategy to right what it saw as the wrongs of the liberal trade regime it had once championed. It fought for a new round of multilateral trade negotiations with a specific mandate to address issues of growing concern to the United States; it pursued unilateral strategies that smacked of the same mercantilist principles it deplored in others; and it moved to create regional structures to balance the European Union and the potential rise of other competitors.

The Multilateral Front. In the early 1980s the United States proposed to its G-7 partners that a new round of trade negotiations focus attention on issues of growing concern to the United States but outside the existing GATT framework. The proposal was "unrealistically ambitious" at the time (Bayard and Elliott 1994), but it eventually became part of the framework for the Uruguay Round of negotiations, which began in 1986. The new issues included barriers to trade in services (insurance, for example), intellectual property rights (such as copyrights on computer software, music, and movies), and investments (stocks and bonds). Agriculture also remained a paramount issue to the United States, as the economic well-being of American agriculture depends more heavily on exports than do other sectors of the economy.

Because world trade in agriculture evolved outside of the main GATT framework, it was not subject to the same liberalizing influences as industrial products (Spero 1990; Low 1993). Agricultural trade is especially controversial because it is deeply enmeshed in the domestic politics of producing states, like the United States and some members of the European Union, for which the global market is an outlet for surplus production. At the core of differences on agricultural trade are the enormous government subsidies that some leading producers pay farmers to keep them competitive internationally.

During the Uruguay Round, the United States aggressively proposed to phase out all agricultural subsidies and farm trade protection programs within a decade. Its proposal gained some support but faced stiff opposition from the EC (particularly France), which viewed it as unrealistic (Low 1993). Sharp differences on the issue led to an impasse in the Uruguay Round negotiations, causing the original 1990 target date for conclusion of the talks to be missed. (In the process, GATT earned a cynical reputation as the "General Agreement to Talk and Talk.") Three years later, when the negotiations finally ended, the United States could claim a measure of success on agricultural issues, as the EC and others agreed to new (but limited) rules on export subsidies, domestic subsidies, and market access.

Global South states figured prominently in several Uruguay Round issues, particularly agriculture and textiles. Trade-related intellectual property rights (TRIPs), one of the new issues confronted at Uruguay, was another. The United States (and other Northern nations) wanted protection of copyrights, patents, trademarks, microprocessor designs, and trade secrets, as well as prohibitions on unfair competition. Developing nations vigorously resisted these efforts along with the concept of "standardized intellectual property norms and regulations throughout the world" (Low 1993).[4] Thus little significant headway was

---

[4]Developing nations had earlier opposed inclusion of counterfeiting on the GATT agenda. The practice—which involves such things as Rolex watches, Apple computers, and photoreproduced college textbooks—is widespread in much of the developing world. The United States has been especially critical of China, arguing that it engages in widespread piracy of computer software, musical compact disks, and video laser disks. Such practices are alleged to have cost American companies as much as $1 billion a year (*New York Times*, July 24, 1994, 8).

made on TRIPs. U.S. initiatives regarding trade-related investment measures (TRIMs) and services (such as banking and insurance) and its efforts to abolish European restrictions on non-European (read American) movies and television programs also met widespread resistance during the negotiations.

However, the United States was successful in its efforts to modernize GATT, symbolized by the new World Trade Organization (WTO), which extends GATT's coverage to products, sectors, and conditions of trade not previously covered adequately. It also enhances previous dispute-settlement procedures by making the findings of its arbitration panels binding on the domestic laws of participating nations (GATT's findings were not binding). And it now deals with the problem of free-riding by being available only to states that belong to GATT, subscribe to all of the Uruguay Round agreements, and make market access commitments. Under the GATT system, free-riding was possible when states (usually small ones) were able to benefit from trade liberalization without having to make contributions of their own. Finally, the WTO embodies certain "legislative powers" which may remove the need for prolonged negotiations that result in large "packages" embracing multiple concessions, as in previous multilateral negotiating sessions. Now it may be possible simply to amend existing rules one at a time (Rabkin 1994; see also Jackson 1994).

Proponents of the WTO saw it as a useful element in states' efforts to keep the instrumentalities of the liberal trade regime consonant with state practices in the increasingly complex world political economy. It was not without detractors, however. Environmentalists in the United States, for example, worried that the WTO would erode their ability to protect hard-won domestic victories against the charge that environmental protection laws restrict free trade. GATT's controversial rulings that a U.S. ban on the import of tuna caught by methods that also ensnare dolphins is illegal—popularly known as the "GATTzilla versus Flipper" debate—symbolized their apprehensiveness. Environmentalists charged that WTO controls in a wide range of areas with environmental implications will be expanded and nontariff trade barriers designed *purposely* to protect the environment (including dolphins) disallowed. (We will examine the controversy surrounding the environmental consequences of free trade in Chapter 11.)

Despite disagreements and disappointments, in late 1993—and in nothing less than a crisis atmosphere—the GATT negotiators struck a bargain. Their product was the most comprehensive trade deal in history, covering everything from paper clips to jet aircraft, from potato chips to computer chips (see Schott 1994). The very bulk of the document symbolized its breadth: "The Final Act signed in Marrakesh, Morocco, on 15 April, 1994 weighed 385 pounds and included over twenty-two thousand pages" (Jackson 1994, 131).

Fear of failure and its consequence for the trade regime and individual nations' economic and political stability were undoubtedly important incentives to the accord. The anticipated consequences of continuing to lower free trade barriers also figured prominently. Analysts predicted that the Uruguay Round would stimulate expansion of global output by billions of dollars in the decade ending in 2003. The agreement was no less important for the United States. U.S. Trade Representative Mickey Kantor predicted that the pact would generate two million jobs for American workers over the next decade. President Clinton claimed that the agreement would "cement our position of leadership in the new global economy." In the end, then, the Uruguay Round had struck a blow for liberalism—and perhaps hegemony.

The Unilateral Front. Even as the United States sought resolution of outstanding trade issues through the multilateral GATT mechanism, it pursued a strategy of "aggressive unilateralism" designed to right what it saw as particular wrongs. The origins of aggressive unilateralism are lodged in the Trade Act of 1974, which laid the basis for the Tokyo Round of trade negotiations. The law included a section called "301," permitting the United States to retaliate against states perceived to engage in unfair trade practices. The 1988 Omnibus Trade Act upgraded that provision to "Super 301," which now *required* the president to identify countries believed to engage in unfair trade practices. Those countries either had to negotiate remedies or face U.S. retaliation.

Although the Super 301 provisions of the law authorizing the U.S. government to investigate and retaliate against specific foreign trade barriers believed to be unfair were "almost unanimously viewed abroad as a clear violation of the GATT" (Walters and Blake 1992), the provisions reflected particular U.S. resentment of the trade policies of Japan and the four Asian NIEs. It also extended beyond them. Between 1975 and 1994 the United States initiated nearly one hundred 301 complaints, with the European Union (23 percent) and Japan (13 percent) the most frequent targets. U.S. efforts to liberalize trade in relation to its partners were successful in about half the cases (Bayard and Elliott 1994, 58–65).

China is among the recent targets of U.S. pique. Its trade imbalance with the United States has grown sharply in recent years, and its trade practices in areas such as intellectual property rights (e.g., pirated copies of computer software and music CDs) have drawn sharp U.S. rebukes and trade sanctions. China had hoped to be among the charter members of the new World Trade Organization when it opened shop in January 1995, but its hopes were dashed when it failed to meet the liberal standards on intellectual property rights and other market-opening standards required by the United States and other WTO members. The United States, in fact, had by this time begun to pursue what many analysts saw as a new "containment" policy designed to pressure China on a range of issues—ranging from copyright and human rights violations to the proliferation of nuclear know-how and the sale of arms to "rogue" states. Still, China is a force to be reckoned with: Its economy is one of the fastest growing in the world and could become the largest in the world in the first quarter of the twenty-first century; its presence in the trade system is also growing, making it a major trading partner of both the United States and Japan and a principal competitor of other countries that export labor-intensive manufactured products (see Dadush and He 1995).

Japan has long been viewed as the preeminent neomercantilist power and is thus also the target of America's own mercantilist ire. "Japan is unique among developed nations in maintaining closed markets," observed Mickey Kantor, the Clinton administration's U.S. Trade Representative. Such attitudes are based on the belief that Japan's persistent balance-of-trade and payments surpluses result from an intimate government-business alliance which tilts the playing field in its favor. The continuing trade imbalance between Japan and the United States—which runs into the tens of billions of dollars each year—reinforces the belief that Japan's trade policies are inherently detrimental to the United States and its commercial interests (see Fallows 1994; for a contrasting view, see Emmott 1994; also Bergsten and Noland 1993).

The Japanese regard foreign products as inferior to those produced domestically. This makes it difficult for those who export to Japan to compete with local firms, even if their products are of equal or superior quality. The Japanese perpetuate this restraint on trade by marketing retail goods with little flags that show the country of origin and by placing imported goods in separate sections of stores.

There is little doubt that Japan's protectionist trade policies inhibit penetration of its market by American firms. Japanese business practices—including, for example, cross-share holding patterns known as *keiretsu* which result in informal corporate bargains—also make foreign penetration difficult, regardless of government policies. American consumers, however, continue to show a marked preference for Japanese products which is not reciprocated on the other side of the Pacific basin, where cultural traditions reinforce the view that foreign products are ill-suited to the Japanese consumer. American producers sometimes feed this perception, for example in U.S. auto makers' refusal until recently to build cars with the steering wheel on the right to conform to the Japanese driving practice.

American exports to Japan have increased considerably in recent years, in part a product of continuing negotiations between the two countries. These included the Structural Impediments Initiative (SII), launched in 1989 shortly after Japan was named as one of three countries engaging in unfair trade practices under Super 301 (Brazil and India were the others). Although the Bush administration chose not to retaliate against Japan, the Clinton administration pursued a more aggressive path following the breakdown of the latest series of Japanese-American trade negotiations known as the "framework" talks.

The framework negotiations followed an agreement reached at the 1993 Tokyo G-7 summit. The United States insisted during the negotiations on using certain quantitative indicators to monitor whether Japan was actually opening its markets in various sectors, including autos, telecommunications, insurance, and medical equipment. (The shift in U.S. strategy reflected growing concern about the *outcomes* of reciprocity, not simply the process.) Japan eventually agreed that quantitative measures could be used to measure progress in opening Japanese markets in some sectors. However, it refused to guarantee the United States any specific market shares, thus side-stepping the contentious issue of "numerical targets." Furthermore, no agreement was reached on automobiles and auto parts. To keep pressure on the Japanese in these markets, the United States promptly set in motion the process that could lead to sanctions and then threatened to impose a tariff increase of 100 percent on luxury automobiles imported into the United States.

The U.S. threat was averted at the eleventh hour when the two sides made an agreement in which both could claim "victory." Still, the principles about states and markets that divide the United States and Japan (and others) remain. A former U.S. trade negotiator explains a common viewpoint among many Americans: "The underlying issue is whether or not cartelistic Japanese business practices are compatible with the principles of free trade. This concern extends far beyond Japan. With Japanese bureaucrats assiduously spreading the gospel of Japanese-style economics to developing economies, and with many countries expressing interest in cloning the Japanese system, the issue on the table [in the auto case] was really the rules of trade in the twenty-first century. Which will govern: mercantilism or free trade?" (Prestowitz 1995).

The Regional Front. In addition to multilateralism and aggressive unilateralism, a preference for building regional arrangements has marked the United States' response to its changing role and position in the changed and changing world political economy. These include the Caribbean Basin Initiative, a program of tariff reductions and tax incentives designed to promote industry and trade in Central America and the Caribbean, launched in 1984; free-trade agreements with Israel and Canada concluded in 1987 and 1989, respectively; and the **North American Free Trade Agreement (NAFTA),** signed by Canada, Mexico, and the United States in 1993.

NAFTA's purpose was to intertwine Mexico and Canada with the United States as a prelude to a wider Western Hemispheric economic partnership, in part to balance the European challenge. Since the 1950s, European leaders have tried methodically to build a more united Europe, beginning especially in the economic sphere as they sought to build a European-wide common market. In the mid-1980s they boldly committed themselves to create a single market by 1992 and followed this with a new Treaty of Union, signed at the Dutch city of Maastricht, which anticipated the development of a single European currency and closer cooperation on foreign political and military affairs.

The latter goal was dashed by the crisis in the former Yugoslavia, which tested the EC's political resolve (see Brenner 1993). The former was postponed, perhaps quashed, by the European monetary crises of 1992 and 1993, which saw the EC's semifixed exchange rate system fail. The European Union nonetheless continues its relentless push toward a continentwide economic union. Its latest moves included the admission of Austria, Finland, and Sweden, expanding the EU to a community of fifteen, and the conclusion of important

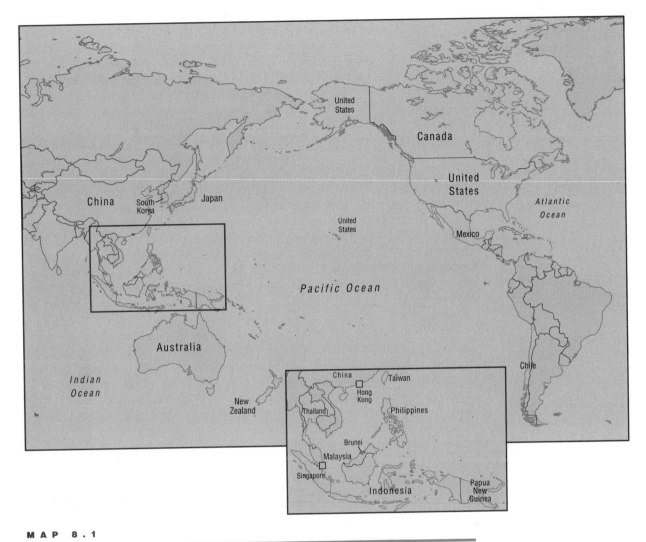

MAP 8.1

Members of Asia-Pacific Economic Cooperation (APEC)

agreements with Russia and several eastern European states which anticipate their eventual inclusion in a European-centered regional economy.[5]

At present there are no visible signs that Japan wishes to build the same kinds of economic structures in the Pacific that Europe and the United States are pursuing. Indeed, Japan's imperial past continues to ignite passionate

[5]Russia has signed a trade agreement with the EU but is less likely to become a full partner in the economic union than other eastern European states. Russia had hoped to join the elite G-7 club as it undertook market reforms designed to replace the planned economy of its socialist past, but this has not happened. Instead, it runs the risk of becoming a "permanently developing country" (Winiecki 1989), as it depends on outside foreign aid to assist in the transition to democracy and economic liberalism while mafia groups on the inside subvert the government's efforts (Handelman 1994; but cf. Åslund 1994). Meanwhile, the Organization of Economic Cooperation Development (OECD), a group roughly synonymous with the Global North, agreed in late 1995 to admit the Czech Republic to the organization, the first time it has accepted an eastern European country as a member.

resentment and fear throughout much of Asia. The United States, meanwhile, has begun to court those nations. Shortly after the Clinton administration's NAFTA victory—urged in part on the grounds that it would enhance U.S. competitiveness with Asia as well as Europe—Clinton hosted the Asia-Pacific Economic Cooperation (APEC) summit, where he preached the virtues of free trade and urged creation of a Pacific free-trade zone (see Map 8.1). The implication is that the United States also wished to portray itself as a Pacific power in the global competition for regional economic power (see Bergsten 1994a). Annual follow-up summits sharpened that image, as the United States helped to stimulate an ambitious commitment to create an Asia-Pacific free-trade scheme by the year 2020. Already the Asian nations have sensed the difficulties they must confront—including the growing antagonism between the United States and China on security as well as economic issues—if they are to realize their goals. Should they be successful, however, APEC would become the largest free-trade area in the world. Meanwhile, the United States and the thirty-three Western Hemispheric states, meeting at the Summit of the Americas in Miami in late 1994, also agreed to begin building a free-trade zone in that region, committing themselves to having a treaty in place and its implementation begun by 2005.

Although NAFTA and related regional initiatives were thought to be consistent with GATT's rules, analysts worried that they violated the principle of nondiscrimination underlying the liberal trade system, taking it one more step toward closure. In particular, many reasoned that U.S. actions contributed to the further development of a regional political economy centered on Asia, Europe, and North America which many analysts have long anticipated, and some have feared.[6] Already more than one-third of world trade takes place within three major world regions (see Figure 8.4). Thus the United Nations concluded in its 1991 world economic survey (United Nations 1991) that "Today the question is not whether these blocs will be formed, but rather how encompassing they will be and how to ensure that they will not harm the [global] trading system."

The ultimate impact of the trend toward regionalization of the world political economy, both nationally and globally, remains uncertain (Kahler 1995). Some analysts, pointing to the dispute-settlement provisions of NAFTA and its side agreements on the environment and other matters, see that agreement as the precursor of future efforts to negotiate settlements on issues that likely will plague the world political economy in the years ahead (see, e.g., Brecher 1993; Hormats 1994).

Others are concerned with the possible impact on security relationships of the transforming economic relationships into regional centers. One line of reasoning—which builds on the logic of strategic trade theory—suggests that "bitter economic rivalry" is a likely outcome of a triangular world political economy because of fear that "there can be *enduring* national winners and losers from trade competition" (Borrus et al. 1992). The result would be mercantile rivalry among the world's principal trading blocs, in which "fear of one another" may be the only force binding them together (Borrus et al. 1992; see also E. Peterson 1994).

---

[6]For a sampling, see Bergsten (1992a, 1992b); Borrus et al. (1992); Hormats (1994); Mead (1990); E. Peterson (1994); and Sandholtz et al. (1992).

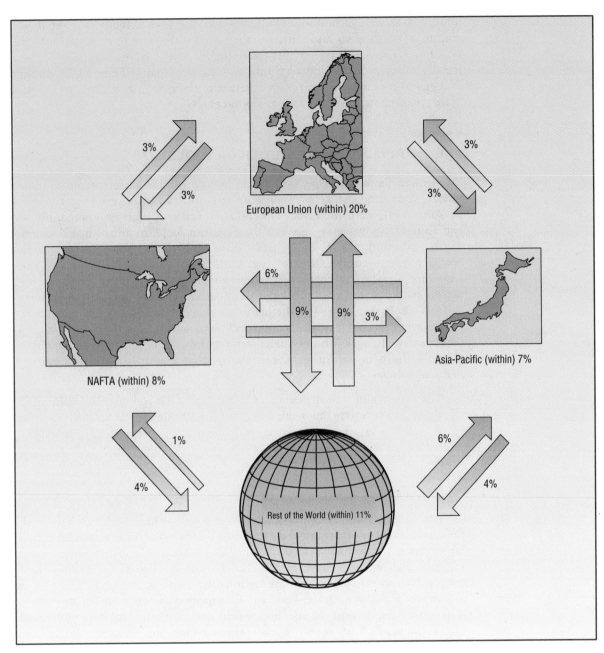

FIGURE 8.4

Share of World Exports within and between Trading Areas, 1994

SOURCE: Adapted from *Direction of Trade Statistics Yearbook 1995* (1995), World, Regional, and Country pages.

Finally, those outside the regional trading blocs have reason to be concerned as well. "For the developing countries, the prospect of a world divided into separate regional centers is disconcerting. It leaves too many countries out of the system altogether, and even those it encompasses are left relatively weaker as their bargaining power is divided. So, even though developing countries in the past have regarded the GATT as a 'rich man's club,' today they see it as a guardian for the clear and fair rules they need if they are to enter the international arena successfully" (Philips and Tucker 1991). Beyond GATT, and now the WTO, however, developing countries have also spanned a growing number of regional economic cooperation schemes of their own, as we saw in Chapter 5. But their chances of success are not great.

● ● ●

THE TURBULENT 1990s: TRIUMPH OR TROUBLE?

The United States, Europe, and Japan advocate quite different philosophies toward states and markets. Japan embraces mercantilism (even as it talks of liberalization), the United States liberalism (even as it practices mercantilism), and Europe sits midway between the two (but looks more inward than outward). Increasingly, economic nationalism "will propel the preeminent economic powers—and the rest of the world with them—into an era of 'real-economik', in which parochial economic interests drive governments to pursue marginal advantage in an international system marked by growing interdependencies" (E. Peterson 1994). Whether a collision of these competing capitalisms can be averted is problematic, as the decline of American economic power and other recent changes "do not augur well for the level of cooperation necessary to avoid the neomercantilist confrontation that could flow from competing national policies."

> The overarching security concerns generated by the common threat from the erstwhile Soviet Union are a thing of the past, and immediate economic concerns now overshadow residual security ties. It is a time of fundamental redefinition of security, policy, and economic relations—but the process of redefinition is proceeding in the absence of the international leadership and corresponding institutions necessary to meet the challenges of escalating economic rivalry. (E. Peterson 1994, 69–70)

A number of other important developments also characterize today's world political economy. The three centers of capitalism may be the principal actors, but others now also play significant roles. Saudi Arabia is a critical factor in the international energy market; the Newly Industrialized Economies have assumed a central role in the international trading system; and China, India, and other "big emerging markets" can be expected to command greater attention in the years ahead. In addition, world commerce has become globalized; global financial flows outstrip trade transactions; and "market forces now largely determine economic outcomes almost everywhere, even in the former command economies of the communist world and in previously closed economies elsewhere (such as India and Mexico)" (Bergsten 1994b).

For some the spread of market forces (i.e., liberalism) precludes the need for new institutions to cope with the changed and changing world political economy. For others the dramatic changes that have taken place during the past decade "suggest a compelling need to reassess the adequacy of the international economic order" (Bergsten 1994b). Their task is made more daunting, however, by the absence of a consensus about what the world political economy should look like, as the contest between liberalism and mercantilism (to which we can add the conflict between rich and poor nations) makes clear. Furthermore, the globalization of commerce and finance increasingly seems to shape, rather than be shaped by, states' policies—thus challenging the sovereign prerogatives of states themselves.

The architecture of a Liberal International Economic Order constructed at Bretton Woods a half-century ago depended not only on a consensus about the appropriate shape of the world political economy but also on U.S. leadership to make it happen. The United States is still the dominant state in the world political economy and continues to perform many hegemonic functions: It tries to manage the international monetary system, maintains a comparatively open market for others' goods, seeks to maintain the flow of capital to would-be borrowers facing financial stress, and works to coordinate economic policies among the world's leading economies. But its willingness to absorb the costs of leadership has waned, and its ability to affect global economic outcomes in preferred directions is simply not what it once was. Both the United States and the world must adjust to the decline of American hegemony.

The shape of the future thus remains uncertain. If liberals are correct, the process of rapid globalization already on the horizon will multiply sensitivity interdependence and, with that, the prospects for economic prosperity and political harmony. If mercantilists are right, however, an emerging era of geo-economics will increase states' vulnerability, increasing the likelihood of political conflict and states' efforts to dominate others.

● ● ●

KEY TERMS

Liberal International Economic Order
   (LIEO)
political economy
interdependence
comparative advantage
neomercantilism
hegemonic stability theory
hegemony
collective goods
free riders
fixed exchange rates
international liquidity
balance of trade
balance of payments
floating exchange rates

Group of Seven (G-7)
Uruguay Round
General Agreement on Tariffs and Trade
   (GATT)
most-favored-nation (MFN) principle
beggar-thy-neighbor policies
import quotas
export quotas
orderly market arrangement (OMA)
nontariff barriers (NTBs)
infant industry
strategic trade policy
World Trade Organization (WTO)
North American Free Trade Agreement
   (NAFTA)

CHAPTER 9

Vanishing Borders:
The Globalization of Politics
and Markets

OUTLINE

- A Global Village?
- The Globalization of Finance
- The Globalization of Trade, Production, and Labor
- The State and Globalization: System Stress or Transformation?

McDonald's in Moscow and Coke in China will do more to create a global culture than military colonization ever could.

—BENJAMIN R. BARBER, *Whitman Professor of
Political Science, Rutgers University, 1992*

Globalization is creating a world that is increasingly interconnected, in which national boundaries are less important, and it is generating both possibilities and problems.

—BOUTROS BOUTROS-GHALI,
UN Secretary-General, 1996

Global trends at the dawn of the new millennium are moving in divergent directions. Stock prices throughout the world surge as institutional investors convert millions of dollars from cash to equity investments. In Chechnya another family member falls victim to ethnopolitical conflict. The value of the dollar drops sharply as the head of the Federal Reserve System shifts U.S. interest-rate policy, causing skittish currency traders to sell billions of dollars and buy yen and marks. The Irish Republican Army resumes its terrorist attacks in London, hoping to force a settlement of the longstanding dispute over Northern Ireland. University students in Istanbul chat with their friends on cellular phones as they sip raki in a local bar. Clad in Levi jeans and Calvin Klein designer shirts, their counterparts in Bangkok rock to the sound of Hootie and the Blowfish.

Integration and disintegration, nationalism and globalism are simultaneous but divergent trends that underlie the transformation of contemporary world politics. They portend very different futures, however. In one scenario, sovereignty is at bay as the globalization of markets and culture transcends the boundaries of the contemporary geopolitical world and erodes the meaning of national identity. In the other, nations and states sometimes compete with one another, although their goals are essentially the same: to attain or retain the trappings of independence from and control over the homogenizing forces now sweeping the world.

Globalization may be defined as "the intensification of economic, political, social, and cultural relations across borders" (Holm and Sørensen 1995b). A critical characteristic of these cross-border interactions is that they "are not originated by national governments." Indeed, governments increasingly are challenged by transforming trends in which borders are becoming transparent (Lopez, Smith, and Pagnucco 1995).

The economic side of globalization dominates the headlines of financial pages and computer trade journals. It is found in "that loose combination of free-trade agreements, the Internet, and the integration of financial markets that is erasing borders and uniting the world into a single, lucrative, but brutally competitive, marketplace" (T. Friedman 1996). The causes and consequences of globalization extend beyond economics, though. Globalization stems from "the onrush of economic and ecological forces that demand integration and uniformity and that mesmerize the world with fast music, fast computers, and fast food—with MTV, Macintosh, and McDonald's, pressing nations into one commercially homogenous global network: one McWorld tied together by technology, ecology, communications, and commerce" (Barber 1992). Globalization implies nothing less than a redistribution of global economic power "which will increasingly translate into a redistribution of political power" (Schwab and Smadja 1996).

In this and the next two chapters we examine the elements of the rapid globalization now engulfing the world and explore their implications for a world political system based on the primacy of the state. Markets stand center stage in the globalization process and thus demand our attention in this chapter. In Chapters 10 and 11 we broaden our net to encompass the demographic and ecopolitical dimensions of a globalizing world. In all three chapters we ask repeatedly how the forces of integration and disintegration affect the well-being of the states and people of the Global North and South as well as the prospects for cooperation and conflict. We begin here with several snapshots of a world of vanishing borders.

• • •

A GLOBAL VILLAGE?

Cellular phones are rapidly sweeping the world, enabling many among the estimated 50 percent of the world population who have never made a phone call to communicate instantly with others ("Wireless Phones Ring Off the Hook" 1995, 7). The rapid growth in the popularity of cellular phones is one element of a larger revolution in telecommunications that is shrinking our world. "The death of distance as a determinant of the cost of communications will probably be the single most important economic force shaping society in the first half of the next century," writes *The Economist* (September 30, 1995, 5–6). "It will alter, in ways that are only dimly imaginable, decisions about where people live and

The revolution in telecommunications has contributed to the death of distance, as virtually instantaneous communications are possible nearly everywhere. Here, in a remote and desolate region of northern Kenya, a Samburu warrior makes a call on his cellular telephone.

work; concepts of national borders; patterns of international trade. Its effects will be as pervasive as those of the discovery of electricity."

Rapid and unrestrained communication is a hallmark of the "global village," an image embraced by many futurologists to portray a world in which vanishing borders will lead to a more peaceful world. Do cellular phones and other means of transnational communication portend an emergent global village? Will life in the village be an improvement over what we now know? Or is the vision of a global village free of conflict and intent only on improving villagers' welfare mere mythology?

The PC and the Internet

Computers are the most visible symbols of globalization. They also are its most potent agents. No area of the world and no arena of politics, economics, society, and culture is immune from the pervasive impact of computer technology. Even victims of enthnopolitical conflict and natural disasters in the remotest corners of the world are connected to others by the laptop computers that relief workers from the International Federation of Red Cross and Red Crescent Societies bring with them.

More than 150 million computers are in use today; more than 90 percent are personal computers (PCs), which have replaced the mainframes of yesteryear. Their number is growing by as many as 18 to 20 million annually (Lopez, Smith, and Pagnucco 1995, 35). Miniaturization has propelled their rapid spread. Microprocessors in today's PCs are incredibly small and growing more powerful at an exponential rate. "Computers owe their growth and impact to a phenomenon dubbed Moore's Law (after Gordon Moore, the founder of Intel), which says that computing power and capacity double every eighteen months. This exponential growth has led to the digital revolution, and it has only just begun" (*The Economist*, July 1, 1995, 4).

The freedom people enjoy with personal computers and their ability to tap into emerging technologies without government intervention is most apparent on the Internet. Individuals routinely "surf" the "Net" without constraints, creating a global, electronic web of people, ideas, and interactions—a **cyberspace**—unencumbered by the borders of a geopolitical world (see Focus 9.1). Governments are not bystanders in the emerging technology of the future, however. Under pressure from the German government, one on-line service company, Compuserve—concerned about the use of the Internet to transmit offensive sexual and neo-Nazi materials—temporarily cut access to more than two hundred sex-related Internet newgroups (arguing it was unable to stop transmissions on a selective basis). The United States also has taken new steps toward regulating the rapidly expanding telecommunications industry. A law passed in early 1996 to promote competition contained a provision requiring television manufacturers to incorporate technology into their sets that will enable parents (or others) to block reception of particular stations or programs.

Because the United States spawned the Internet, is home to more PCs than any other country, and is at the forefront of the telecommunications revolution, its influence on the emerging technology of the future is substantial. In fact, some see America's information capabilities as the basis for continued U.S. influence in culture, politics, and military affairs well into the next century (Nye and Owens 1996).

The Internet
Cyberspace Pros and Cons

The Internet was developed in the late 1960s at the initiative of the U.S. Department of Defense. Its intent was to enable scientists and engineers working on military contracts to share computers, resources, and ideas—the latter through "e-mail," a way of sending messages electronically. Designed to survive a nuclear war, information was transmitted in small "packages" through different routes, making it difficult to eavesdrop on the data and messages sent.

The popularity of the Internet spread slowly throughout the academic world, which by the mid-1980s was its principal user. Two innovations then revolutionized the ease with which the Internet could be used, propelling its popularity beyond academe. One was the invention by Swiss software engineer Tim Berners-Lee of the World Wide Web and "hypertext" to link documents with one another. The other was a software program known as Mosaic (written primarily by Marc Andreesen, an undergraduate student at the University of Illinois), which provides user-friendly access to the "Web" and the "Net."

In 1994 commercial companies surpassed universities as the leading users of the Internet. Today it is the functional equivalent of the "information superhighway" telecommunications specialists have long anticipated and promised.

As the use of the Internet has grown—fueled by the growth of personal computers in homes and businesses—concerns about its uses and abuses surfaced, and questions about whether and how governments might exert control over the "Net" inevitably have followed. Here are contrasting viewpoints about the culture and concerns cyberspace poses.

THE ETHOS OF INDEPENDENCE AND INDIVIDUALITY

The [Internet] classic user takes a libertarian stance, is suspicious of government, disdainful of politicians, and actively hostile towards those who would screw up his paradise with indiscriminate advertising, stupid questions, and "newbie" (naive newcomer) behavior. . . .

Fundamental to the Internet credo are the protection of free speech and the right of every group to be heard. . . .

Enthusiasts see the Internet as a sort of digital Utopia, not because everything on it is admirable, but because it is there at all. The Internet defies centralized authority; its mantra is "do your own thing."

—*The Economist* 336 (July 1, 1995): 14

THE INTERNET ELITE

Theoretically, anyone can post information, but the reality is that the main content of the Internet . . . is controlled by governments, corporations, and academic institutions. . . . The ease with which it is possible to alter information—or merely to shade the truth by selectively culling out unfavorable information—is a real concern. . . . Who will be the custodians of the world's information?

. . . Although the Internet supposedly is available to anyone with a modem and the will to use it, the profile of users is skewed by race, gender, income, and age. . . . Access may be unlimited in theory, but it is restricted by the cost of technology and the steep learning curve for computer neophytes. . . . If electronic communication is the future, what will become of the vast majority of people who can only stand by and watch the worldwide exchange of electrons?

. . . There are disturbing social implications of a future in which human communication increasingly takes place through electronic media. . . . Work will be done at home and transmitted by modem; shopping will be done over the World Wide Web and paid for by debits to our electronic bank accounts. Even entertainment will take place through the computer screen.

. . . No one is examining the question of whether a world split between an elite minority of information-empowered people interacting electronically and a majority mired in information poverty is in anyone's best interests. Do we really want to choose between a "successful" but soulless electronic existence and disenfranchisement?

—H. W., "The Internet Elite," *Bulletin of the Atomic Scientists* 51 (July/August 1995): 44–45

Although computer technology and the Internet are agents of a rapidly globalizing world, wide differences exist in different countries' ability to shape (and be shaped by) a computer-driven technocratic world. As we saw in Chapter 5 (Map 5.2), the spread of the Internet is confined almost exclusively to the Global North and some of the emerging markets, notably those in Asia.

Thus the revolution in computer technology adds to the promise that the process of globalization will be uneven—benefiting some, disadvantaging others.

The Media: Markets or Monopoly?

Ours is often described as the "information age," but a remarkably large portion of the information we receive is controlled by a remarkably small number of media sources. Ownership of the world's media sources increasingly is concentrated in the hands of a few giant national and multinational corporations. In the early 1980s they numbered about fifty; by the early 1990s that had been reduced to twenty. Although thousands of other sources of information about politics, society, and culture are available, their influence is comparatively negligible. In the United States, for example, despite more than twenty-five thousand media outlets, only "twenty-three corporations control most of the business in daily newspapers, magazines, television, books, and motion pictures (Bagdikian 1992, 4). As corporate America merges its media sources into ever larger but fewer numbers (as witnessed, for example, by the entertainment-giant Disney Corporation's buyout of media-giant ABC television), fewer and fewer corporate executives control what Americans hear and see about the world around them. Critics worry that the American people have become a "captive audience," subject to only limited information from limited sources. Nonetheless, the promise of profits and the ability to exercise influence over "news, information, public ideas, popular culture, and political attitudes" spur the corporate giants and their investors onward (Bagdikian 1992).

While the media's impact on the diffusion of Western culture is unassailable, its impact on public affairs is more difficult to trace. Scholars generally agree that the media have the capacity to *set the agenda* of public discourse about political affairs. In the process, they also often shape the discourse itself. Particular power is attributed to CNN (Cable News Network), the twenty-four-hour television news channel beamed around the world. Its global broadcasts of squalor and violence in Somalia, for example, were often viewed as a catalyst to the humanitarian intervention there. Similar scenes of bloodshed in Sarajevo may have contributed to the determination of the United States and its NATO allies to take a proactive role in bringing the disputants in Bosnia to the bargaining table. One critic has described the impact of CNN and the media this way:

> In foreign policy circles these days one often hears that the advent of instantaneous and global technology has given the news media far greater influence in international relations than ever before, robbing diplomacy of its rightful place at the helm in the process. Observers of international affairs call it the CNN curve. . . . It suggests that when CNN floods the airwaves with news of a foreign crisis, it evokes an emotional outcry from the public to "do something." Under the spell of the CNN curve, goes this refrain, policymakers have no choice but to redirect their attention to the crisis at hand or risk unpopularity, whether or not such revision is merited by policy considerations. (Neuman 1995–1996, 109)

Control of television and other media sources by the United States and a small number of European countries became the focus of hot dispute with the Global South during the 1980s. Dissatisfied with the media coverage it receives from news agencies in the Global North and resentful of Northern domination of other forms of communication, Southern countries demanded a New World Information and Communication Order (NWICO). Global South leaders sought to right the imbalance of the information flows from North to South that painted what they perceived to be an unfavorable image of the South. This image, they believed, fostered Northern values, such as consumerism, designed to perpetuate the South's dependence on the North (see, e.g., Mowlana 1983). As the North–South conflict brewed, the United States withdrew from the United Nations Educational, Scientific, and Cultural Organization (UNESCO), in part due its role in promoting the new communications order.

The NWICO has since been removed from the agenda of public (official) discourse, but the issues remain very much alive in nongovernmental organizations and central to the globalization challenge. Noting, for example, that Hollywood is able to beam the Academy Awards around the world to over a billion people, and that American evangelist Billy Graham preached via electronic links to a similar number in over 185 countries in early 1995, one analyst worries about the implications of concentrating so much media power in so few hands. The new global information infrastructure is "especially disturbing because dominance in 'global' products implies not just the ability to ship products around the world, but dominance in cultural exports. This dominance provides the potential to displace indigenous culture with a tide of largely Western, largely consumerist, global conformity. Perhaps globalization is just a nice word that multinational corporations use to hide their efforts to infect the entire world with the cultural virus of commercialism" (Mowlana 1995).

The counterpoint to the "McWorld" of consumerism promoted by a monopolistic media is "Jihad"—one driven by "parochial hatreds," not "universalizing markets" (Barber 1992). Sobering in this context is that the Ayatollah Khomeini, author of the revival of Islamic fundamentalism that swept the shah of Iran from power in 1979, "combined his access to networks of mosques and bazaars with that of electronic communication and cassette tapes" to carry on a successful long-distance bid to create an Iranian theocracy (Mowlana 1995).

Global Health or Global Infection?

Humankind and the threat of disease have always coexisted uneasily. For example, in Kikwit, Zaire, the deadly Ebola virus—after having lain dormant for twenty years—broke out and ravaged its victims with massive hemorrhaging and inevitable death. Globalization not only heightens awareness of health risks but actually multiplies them. Truck drivers in India are primary vehicles for the AIDS (acquired immune deficiency syndrome) epidemic in that country and elsewhere in Asia. Rapid urbanization in much of the world also contributes to the rapid spread of diseases. Growing numbers of refugees forced into unsanitary camps face ravages from cholera and other diseases that can prove as deadly as the violent ethnic conflict they flee. Excessive population growth forces people to move into habitats where unknown microorganisms and killer viruses await them. Growing millions of airline travelers share cabinsealed environments filled with the carriers of potentially fatal diseases (Pirages 1995; also see Garrett 1994; Horton 1995; Morse 1995; Preston 1994).

Many also view narcotic use as a disease. The illicit use of drugs is nonetheless widespread and hugely profitable. Fueled by major production and distribution complexes in the Andes and Southwest and Southeast Asia, the narcotics industry is believed to generate profits of $200–300 billion annually. As profits grow, the power of traffickers expands as well, leading to other worrisome developments. Among them are "the [widening] impact of the illicit drug trade on illegal economic structures and processes in major producing or transit countries; the increasing political corruption in such countries; the growing intrusion of narcocriminal enterprises into the realm of the state and the law . . . ; the successes of narcotics businesses in innovation, avoiding detection, and increasing operating efficiency; and . . . the growing transnational cooperation among criminal empires that deal in drugs and other black-market items" (Lee 1995).

Whether existing institutions of global governance are able to cope with the challenge of globalization is a hotly contested issue. Meanwhile, the capacity of the state to cope with the forces of rapid change is also being tested. As we turn our attention to the globalization of finance, trade, production, and labor, we will find further evidence that "globalization is uneven. It unites but it also divides, creating winners here and losers there." And in an anarchical international political system, "there is no global civil society that can be called on to support global governance" (Sørensen 1995). Like politics and markets, then, politics and the process of globalization are intimately intertwined, as "even the most powerful states cannot escape the imperatives of the global economy" (Sandel 1996). Meanwhile, realization of a global village remains elusive.

● ● ●

THE GLOBALIZATION OF FINANCE

Global finance encompasses "all types of cross-border portfolio-type transactions—borrowing and lending, trading of currencies or other financial claims, and the provision of commercial banking or other financial services. It also includes capital flows associated with foreign direct investment—transactions involving significant control of producing enterprises" (B. Cohen 1996). The **globalization of finance** refers to the increasing transnationalization of financial markets. Its central characteristic (as distinct from "internationalization") is that the emerging system of financial arrangements is not centered on a single state (Balaam and Veseth 1996). Thus globalization "implies the growth of a single unified market where 'overseas' constitutes a geographic distinction, not an economic or regulatory differentiation" (Sobel 1994). While telecommunications specialists talk about the "death of distance," financial specialists talk about the "end of geography," which "refers to a state of economic development where geographic location no longer matters in finance" (O'Brien 1992).

Evidence of financial globalization abounds. Although trade has grown dramatically since World War II, the volume of cross-border capital flows has increased even more. Financial flows now exceed trade in merchandise by twenty to forty times, and the gap continues to widen (Cerny 1994, 324). Further evidence is found in foreign exchange markets, where currency traders—often exchanging more than $1 trillion daily—make profits on the basis of minute shifts in the value of states' currencies.

Securities markets reveal the globalization of finance as well. Foreign investors' activities in U.S. stock markets during the 1980s increased by more than $300 billion. They also set new records in Japan, growing from 4.6 billion yen in 1980 to more than 54 billion in 1987. Between 1980 and 1990 the market value of shares (known as "capitalization") on world stock markets increased from \$2.5 to \$8.2 trillion. "New York's capitalization doubled, London's more than tripled, and Tokyo's increased tenfold" (Sobel 1994, 50–51). In addition, new financial instruments have emerged, leading to new markets in which they are bought and sold. "Derivatives" are one example. These are complex financial instruments that combine speculation in "options" and "futures" designed to hedge against volatility in financial markets, but they require no actual buying of the underlying securities (stocks and bonds). Derivatives now account for trillions of dollars in cross-border transactions and "are rapidly becoming one of the most globalized financial markets" (Cerny 1994, 331, 334).

As these data suggest, markets are being transformed profoundly by the rapid acceleration of financial globalization. We may not yet have experienced the end of geography, but clearly financial globalization "has put governments distinctly on the defensive, eroding much of the authority of the contemporary sovereign state" (Cohen 1996). What explains these changes? And what are their consequences?

Causes and Consequences

Analysts generally agree that at least three developments which cut across politics and economics and the three levels of analysis described in Chapter 1 account for the globalization of finance (Balaam and Veseth 1996; B. Cohen 1996; Cerny 1993). First, the oil crisis of 1973–1974 and the OPEC decade which followed unleashed a rapid increase in global financial flows. As we will see when we examine the debt crisis of the 1980s, the OPEC decade stimulated new patterns of global investments and new tools of financial management.

Second, beginning in the 1970s and accelerating in the 1980s, basic changes began to take place in the philosophy governing the regulation of national financial markets and capital movements. Washington and London ("Reaganism" and "Thatcherism") played key roles in deregulating markets, choosing to emphasize the principles of classic economic liberalism which say that markets operate best when free of government interference. Analysts differ, however, on whether domestic or international considerations stimulated the removal of national barriers to global finance. Some see deregulation as the response to domestic political pressures (Sobel 1994; Haggard and Maxfield 1996), but the change in thinking is more commonly attributed to international causes. As private-market actors became more sophisticated in evading national markets where regulations impeded their access, states responded by lowering their regulatory standards. This stimulated others to do the same as the competitive pressures on states to attract foreign capital multiplied.

Third, technological innovations spurred the globalization of finance. As one analyst has written, "To a great extent the end-of-geography story is a technology story, the story of the computerization of finance" (O'Brien 1992). Another argues that "the development and impact of technology [do] not involve merely the machinery of . . . financial transactions—the electronic equivalent of nuts and bolts—but also the culture of production, competition, and innovation in the financial sector and, indeed, in all of the other sectors of economy and society, which are inextricably intertwined with finance" (Cerny 1994). Still, global finance is different from many other markets in that no physical goods need actually be exchanged in the transaction. Instead, numbers are changed on a computer screen, forming concluding agreements in an instant.

What are the consequences of the globalization of finance? Many economists see the increased mobility of capital as proof that markets become more efficient as they are widened. From their perspective, the exploding volume of international financial transactions is the explanation of still other changes. Among them are the trends toward deregulation and liberalization of markets throughout the world and the convergence of monetary and fiscal policies, particularly among states in the Global North. This is known as the **capital mobility hypothesis,** which says that capital mobility is itself a critical explanation of political and economic changes. The political and social consequences of those changes, however—particularly for workers whose jobs are lost in the globalization of production that global finance fuels—are not always positive (see Kurzer 1993).

The mobility of capital has also changed the global political context. Because financial markets are no longer centered in a single state, the financial system is not subject to regulation by anyone in particular. Instead, it has taken on a life of its own, constraining states' policy choices in the economic arena much as realists argue that the distribution of power constrains their choices in the political-military arena. In other words, at the level of the international system, "the degree of international capital mobility systematically constrains state behavior by rewarding some actors and punishing others" (Andrews 1994; see also Webb 1991). Not only is the *actual* volume of financial flows at issue but also the *potential* for flows to occur, which is a function of states' willingness to lower barriers to capital mobility (Andrews 1994).

Structuralists do not argue that systemic constraints *determine* state behavior, only that they *influence* behavior. Still, if capital mobility is a structural characteristic of the international system in the same way as neorealists argue that the distribution of power is (Waltz 1979), then it provides new insight into the political economy of international politics. This argument reverses our understanding of hegemony, for example. It is not the decline of American hegemony that caused the changes in monetary and trade relations we examined in Chapter 8, according to this viewpoint. Instead, structural change caused the decline of hegemony.

The globalization of finance has changed the political context in another way—by undermining the capacity of states to determine their own future. As states made policy choices that lowered barriers to financial flows, they became agents of globalization. Once set in motion, the globalization process has become self-reinforcing. "The costs of resisting capital mobility, either in isolation [unilaterally] or in combination [with other countries] have dramatically escalated, with the result that states have by and large chosen to accommodate the phenomenon. This decision, taken both individually and collectively, serves to reinforce the market trends that originally induced it" (Andrews 1994).

The "imperatives of international competitiveness" explain the costs and benefits that now encourage states effectively to undermine their ability to determine their own fates. States compete not only for shares of the global markets, but also for the benefits that flow from a world in which markets have become increasingly interconnected. By encouraging the globalization of finance, the power of private markets in the overall structure of the world political economy has grown, "thereby increasingly undermining state power itself and institutionalizing that of the global marketplace. . . . Indeed, states, having set up the conditions in which more open international financial markets were established in the 1970s and 1980s, are now having difficulty controlling their own creations" (Cerny 1994).

Although the globalization of finance has challenged the ability of states to regulate financial markets, states have assumed new functions in global finance: fostering coordination and cooperation to manage the global character of their national economies (Balaam and Veseth 1996; see also Frieden 1991). These functions are illustrated in the role the United States played in resolving the debt crisis that plagued the Global South during much of the 1980s.

The Global South Debt Crisis

OPEC's success in driving up world oil prices in the early 1970s contributed to the belief among Global South countries that commodity power would enable them to "force" the Global North into replacing the existing world economic order with one more compatible with their interests and objectives. Ironically, however, the two oil shocks of the 1970s created an environment in which many Global South countries thought it was wise to borrow heavily from abroad, while they simultaneously eroded the economic bases on which repayment of those loans depended. The accumulation of debt presents no problem "so long as the finances gained are used productively, the world economy is growing, and creditor economies are open to exports of debtors. Under such conditions the borrowers will be able to repay their loans once the investments begin to produce goods" (Grieve 1993). However, none of these conditions held true during the OPEC decade. Instead, this was a time when concern for sovereign (state-owed) debt "dominated—some would say 'consumed'—international economic discussions" in the 1980s, which effectively became the "debt decade" (Nowzad 1990).

The specific event that triggered the debt crisis was the threat in August 1982 that Mexico would default on its loans. Other countries with the largest debts, including Poland, Argentina, and Brazil, also required special treatment to keep them from going into default when they announced they were unable to pay their creditors (that is, service their debts). Their plight was caused by heavy private and public borrowing during the 1970s which saw private loans and investments and public loans at (nonconcessional) market rates become more important than public foreign aid for all but the poorest of the poor countries (Burki 1983).

The first oil shock sparked the "privatization" of Global South capital flows. Dollars flowed from oil consumers in the Global North to oil producers in the Middle East and elsewhere. The latter, unable to invest all of their newfound wealth at home, "recycled" their "petrodollars" by making investments in the industrial nations who were themselves the largest consumers of oil. In the process, the funds available to private banks for lending to others increased substantially.

Many of the non-oil-exporting developing states became the willing consumers of the private banks' investment funds. The fourfold rise in oil prices induced by the OPEC cartel hit them particularly hard. To pay for the sharply increased cost of oil along with their other imports, many chose to borrow from abroad to sustain their economic growth and pay for needed imports. Private banks were willing lenders, as they believed "sovereign risk"—the risk that governments might default—was virtually nonexistent. In addition, the returns on their investments in the Global South were higher than in the industrial world.

For several reasons, however, the debtor nations found repayment of their loans increasingly difficult. Rising interest rates were the most important factor. Some debtors made poor investment decisions as well, while others were victimized by "capital flight," sometimes perpetrated by corrupt officials. Many also suffered from the drop in commodity prices associated with the worldwide recession in the early 1980s, which often meant that the money needed to pay off their loans simply failed to materialize. "Sovereign risk" suddenly became an ominous reality.

The International Monetary Fund assumed a leadership role in securing debt relief for many Global South countries. Although this kept them from defaulting on their loans, it did so at the cost of imposing strict conditions for domestic economic reform on individual debtors. The IMF also typically urged those it helped to increase their exports—meaning it sought an "export-led adjustment" to the debt problem. As we saw in Chapter 5, export-led industrialization, which emulates the economic success of the Asian Tigers, is now a widely preferred strategy for promoting the economic development of developing countries.

The IMF austerity program could claim success from a strictly financial viewpoint (see Amuzegar 1987), but its domestic burdens and political costs proved too overwhelming. Analysts blamed the conditions set by the IMF for the overthrow of the Sudanese government of President Jaafar Nimeri in 1985, for example. Debt and related financial issues also inflamed domestic political conflict in many of the other most heavily indebted countries, including Argentina, Brazil, Chile, Mexico, and Nigeria. All of this encouraged political leaders in the debtor nations to adopt a more defiant posture toward the predicament they faced (see the essays in Riley 1993).

The United States had been a principal supporter of the IMF program but otherwise adopted an arms-length posture toward the debt crisis due to the Reagan administration's ideological antipathy toward intervention in the marketplace (Grieve 1993). In 1985, however, the United States reversed its position. Not only were debtor countries facing domestic turmoil, but the debt crisis also had taken a toll on U.S. industries that produced for export. Secretary of the Treasury James A. Baker developed a plan that sought new loans from private banks and coupled those with renewed efforts to stimulate Global South economic growth via domestic economic reforms in debtor nations. The plan failed when it proved incapable of delivering the promised new resources. Brazil then announced it would suspend interest payments on its $108 billion debt, American banks began to write off some of their loans, and riots in Venezuela over its government's austerity measures killed an estimated three hundred people in 1989. These developments set the stage for a new approach to the nagging debt problem. Again, the United States played the leading role.

Announced in early 1989, the Brady initiative, named after the new secretary of the treasury, focused on debt relief rather than debt restructuring. For the first time concern about the deteriorating situation in the debtor countries and its foreign policy implications became more important then private banks' well-being (Sachs 1989). Slowly the problems of the debtor countries receded from the headlines, spurred in part by the Brady initiative. Also responsible were lower interest rates and renewed economic growth, which by the early 1990s had sharply reduced many debtors' debt service ratio (debt as a percent of exports). Large numbers of states in the Global South continued to suffer from a crushing debt burden and the discipline that structural adjustment, often imposed from the outside, required (see Gardner 1995). No longer was the entire global financial system seriously threatened, however (see, e.g., Cline 1995; Mitchell 1993).

The trauma and hostility caused by the debt crisis that first exploded in August 1982 is difficult to exaggerate. "It called into question the soundness of the international financial and banking system. It was accused of stunting economic growth in the developing countries. It was blamed for social and political instability, specifically for endangering nascent democratic tendencies in certain countries. It mobilized religious, environmental, and other interest groups that usually remain outside the financial fray. It led to calls for repudiation, solidarity, the formation of debt cartels, and the exploitation of financial obligations to obtain concessions in unrelated areas" (Nowzad 1990). Indeed, few issues with origins in the turbulent 1970s better underscored the *mutual sensitivity* and *mutual vulnerability* that interdependence implies.

From the point of view of states' roles in global finance, U.S. intervention made resolution of the debt crisis possible. It paved the way for the realization that debt reduction and cancellation was in the collective interest of everyone, including private banks who risked losing all of their investments if they did not cooperate (see *World Economic and Social Survey 1995* 1995).

The United States was thrust into a similar role in 1995, again in a situation involving Mexico. The Mexican government had pursued domestic economic policies that made it unable to pay its short-term debts. This eroded investors' confidence in Mexican securities, causing them to disinvest quickly. Faced with a balance-of-payments crisis, the Mexican government—in a clear demonstration of states' vulnerability to financial globalization—was forced to devalue the Mexican peso sharply. The United States now led a rescue plan involving the IMF and other states in the Global North to ensure that the Mexican crisis would not cause damaging waves throughout the world political economy (and in the other emerging economies in particular), imperiling private investors as well as states' political and economic interests. The action was unpopular in the United States, though. It suggested the need for more routinized multilateral mechanisms for policy coordination and cooperation to cope with potential future crises as global finance becomes increasingly interlocked though massive cross-border transactions beyond the immediate reach of state regulation.

● ● ●

THE GLOBALIZATION OF TRADE, PRODUCTION, AND LABOR

Growing international trade has propelled widespread advances in global welfare during the past half-century. Its expansion in this decade has been particularly rapid. Even during the early 1990s, when the world experienced a recession in economic growth, world trade growth barely slowed (see Figure 9.1). The recovery of economic growth has since boosted trade growth to new highs, which many expects believe will continue into the next century.

The gains from trade are uneven, however, as we learned in Chapter 8. As a result, domestic protectionist measures designed to cushion or curtail the unfavorable effects of the rapid globalization of trade abound. The Global North often instigates these measures, usually targeting the rapidly growing economies the Global South—particularly in Asia. For the Newly Industrialized

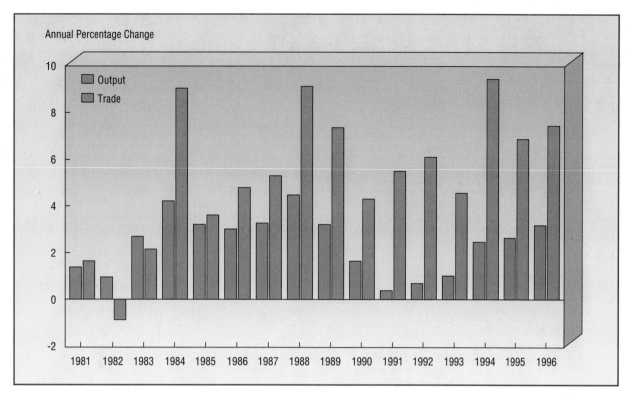

Annual Percentage Change

- Output
- Trade

FIGURE 9.1

Growth of World Output and Trade, 1981–1996

Since the early 1980s, the growth of world trade consistently has outpaced the growth of world economic output. As a result, states' domestic welfare has become more tightly intertwined as states have become more closely integrated into the globalizing world political economy.

SOURCE: *World Economic and Social Survey 1995* (1995), 35.

Economies (NIEs) and emerging markets, though, the globalization of trade has become the preferred route to economic advancement (see also Chapter 5).

Trade Integration: Winners and Losers

Trade integration is the difference between growth rates in trade and gross domestic (or gross world) product. As trade integration grows, so does interdependence. As the data in Figure 9.1 show, the 1990s have witnessed not only growth in trade integration but also a spectacular increase in the *speed* of integration, as growth in trade has consistently outpaced growth in production. The speed of integration has been sharply higher in the Global South than in the North, reflecting the Global South's increasing contribution to trade growth—a trend expected to continue (see Figure 9.2). This also means that the Global South is becoming increasingly important to the economic well-being of the Global North. Still, wide—and predictable—differences exist within the South and the economies in transition. Eastern Europe, Central Asia, and East Asia have experienced the most rapid integration into the world political economy. North Africa, sub-Saharan Africa, and the Middle East lag far behind (World Bank 1995a).

261

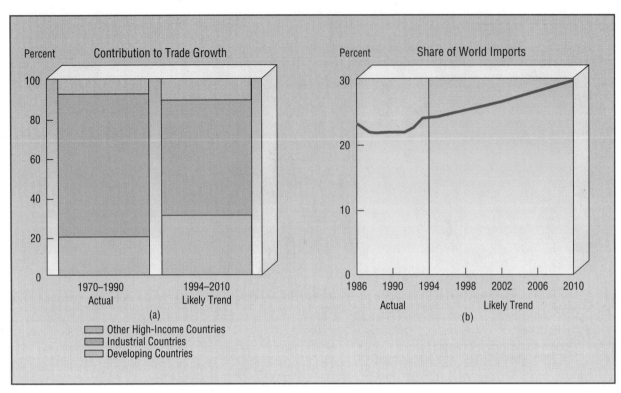

FIGURE 9.2

The Global South in World Trade, Past and Projected

In recent years, international trade has grown more rapidly than the production of goods and services. The Global South's contribution to world trade growth and its rising share of world imports reveal its growing importance to the world political economy.

SOURCE: World Bank (1995a), 58.

The differences among these groups reflect their historical experiences and the different strategies of development that we examined in Chapter 5. They also reflect changes in technology and consumer demands in a globalizing world political economy.

Winners: New Products. Not only is technology the driving force behind the globalization of finance, it is also reshaping patterns of international trade. High-technology electronic goods (i.e., data-processing equipment, telecommunications equipment, and semiconductors and microprocessors) make up an increasing proportion of trade in manufactured goods. The changes are quite dramatic: World exports of the new products increased more than fourfold between 1980 and 1993, and the annual growth rate in their value more than doubled that of manufactured products generally.[1]

The Global North is the major supplier of high-technology goods, accounting for nearly 75 percent of new-product exports in 1993. The United States

---

[1]Our discussion of the production and trade in new products, including the data not otherwise specifically cited, draws on the chapter "International Trade in 'New' Manufactured Products," pp. 171–78 in the United Nations' *World Economic and Social Survey 1995* (1995).

Globalization is sped by the rapid expansion of computer technology. Intel is the world's largest manufacturer of computer chips, tiny microprocessors fifty thousand times faster than the first computers and whose speed grows exponentially with each new innovation. Here, a worker inspects computer chips as they come off the assembly line.

and Japan lead the pack, followed by western Europe. But these patterns are changing rapidly, creating winners not only in products but also among producers.

As we have noted, the Global South's share of world trade, both now and projected into the future, is growing. Its share of manufactured-product exports is growing as well, having increased by 10 percent (to 22 percent) between 1980 and 1993. But its share of total exports of the new products has grown even more—from less than 12 percent in 1980 to more than 28 percent in 1993. This is the area where Asia surpasses all others. Table 9.1 shows the percentage share of new products in the manufactured exports of selected countries and economic groups. The six Asian countries listed account for

TABLE 9.1 **Share of New Products in Manufactured Exports, Selected Countries, 1980–1993 (percentages)**

	1980	1985	1990	1993
Global South	14	13	18	23
Asian NIEs	16	18	28	32
Hong Kong	13	14	17	19
South Korea	11	13	24	24
Singapore	33	36	51	56
Taiwan	16	16	23	25
Other Asian countries				
Malaysia	46	53	52	54
Thailand	1	2	24	25
Global North	8	11	11	13
United States	11	17	17	17
Japan	15	22	24	25

SOURCE: Adapted from *World Economic and Social Survey 1995* (1995), 74.

nearly two-thirds of all developing country exports of the new products. New products comprise nearly one-third of their total output of manufactured goods—twice the level of the United States.

The emergence of Asia as a primary supplier of high-tech manufactured-product exports has resulted from a relocation of production centers during the past two decades. "The pattern of this shift has been as follows: from Japan and the United States to the NIEs and from the Asian NIEs and Japan to Malaysia and Thailand" (*World Economic and Social Survey 1995* 1995). Changes in trade patterns have followed shifts in production. Trade among the Asian NIEs and Malaysia and Thailand and between the NIEs and Japan has literally exploded. As a result, the destination of Asian exports has shifted significantly toward Asia itself and away from the United States.

The determination of the four Asia Tigers and now the new "cubs" (Malaysia and Thailand) to pursue an export-led path to development—including a determination to specialize in high-technology electronic products—has contributed to their success in the production of the new manufactured products. Another important factor is the growing worldwide specialization in the manufacture of these products stemming from "outsourcing" the production of less-technologically sophisticated components to countries where wages are lower. As this happens, other investments and technology follow, with the final products being exported back to many of the same the countries where the investments originated. The Asian NIEs and emerging markets "have been integrated into this process with rapid technological upgrading of exports" (*World Economic and Social Survey 1995* 1995). In short, they have been winners. At the same time, however, many workers in the Global North believe they have been victimized as investment capital and production centers have shifted, an issue to which we will return.

Trade in services also promises to make new winners. Because the United States enjoys comparative advantages in this area, it has been a strong advocate of bringing services under the liberalizing rules of the World Trade Organization, as we saw in Chapter 8. Trade in services already has expanded more than threefold since 1980, with the Global North reaping most of the benefits. Interestingly, however, the Global South has increased its share of this growing trade even more rapidly (see Table 9.2). The spread of information technology and the comparatively lower wage costs in developing economies are among the reasons (see Focus 9.2). In the case of services, then, it appears that—at least for the time being—North and South are both reaping the profits of the globalization of trade.

TABLE 9.2 World Trade in Services, 1980–1993	1980	1985	1990	1993
Trade in commercial services ($ billions)	358	380	791	934
Global North	283	299	648	752
Global South	75	81	143	182
Share of services in total trade (percent)	17	18	20	22
Global North	19	19	23	23
Global South	13	15	18	19

SOURCE: Adapted from World Bank (1995a), 47.

FOCUS 9.2 *Servicing Long Distance*

As the American Airlines jet comes to a stop at the airport in Bridgetown, Barbados, the passengers look forward to vacationing on the sunny island. But for the Caribbean Data Services (CDS), a sister company of American Airlines, the work in processing hundreds of thousands of tickets and boarding passes is about to begin. CDS was established by AMR Corp., parent of American Airlines, in 1983 to cut costs in its data entry operations. With 1,100 employees in 1993, CDS has become the largest private employer in Barbados.

Speed in processing tickets and boarding passes is crucial to the success of CDS, because the faster it can verify the travel to credit card companies and other airlines, the faster the airline collects the cash. CDS employees are paid $3.25 an hour, higher than the average rate in Barbados, but about half the rate paid for similar work in the United States. In 1993 CDS processed about 190 million documents, up from 38 million a decade ago. In recent years CDS has begun accepting work from other companies, including data entry for credit card applications and medical claim forms. Most computers and terminals used by CDS employees are hooked to the computers of its clients. This link allows for same-day turnaround, an important criterion for clients. Some other U.S. airlines have similar off-shore data entry arrangements.

SOURCE: World Bank (1995a), 52.

Losers: Commodities. The "new" international division of labor is reflected in the role of the Asian NIEs in the rapidly expanding trade in new, high-tech products. The "old" division of labor, born of the colonial era, also describes the structure of international trade. Many countries in the Global South continue to depend heavily on export earnings from raw materials and agricultural products, such as oil, copper, cocoa, and coffee. Many Northern nations also export large quantities of minerals and agricultural products. The United States and Canada, for example, were long described as the "breadbasket of the world." However, their dependence on primary products is comparatively small. Not so for the oil-producing countries in the Middle East (whose fortunes we address in Chapter 11) or the producers of non-oil primary products throughout the Global South. For them, developments in the global commodities marketplace are critically important. For the most part, though, commodity trends over the past several decades have been harmful to their development objectives.

As we saw in Chapter 5, the pattern of trade that developed during the colonial and imperial periods of the past made developing economies the principal source of primary-product exports to the colonial powers. They, in turn, made sure their colonies were the principal buyers of their manufactured goods. That pattern persisted even after the states that now comprise the Global South gained their sovereignty. The rapidly developing economies of Asia have managed to break out of this pattern, but many others—particularly in Africa—have not. Thus they continue to be subject to the vagaries of the world market for commodities.

Much evidence supports the argument that the price of commodities since World War II has been erratic in the short-term and downward turning in the long run (see Figure 9.3). Both trends take a heavy toll on primary-product producers.

The **terms of trade** describes the price difference between what commodity producers receive for their exports and what they must pay for their

265

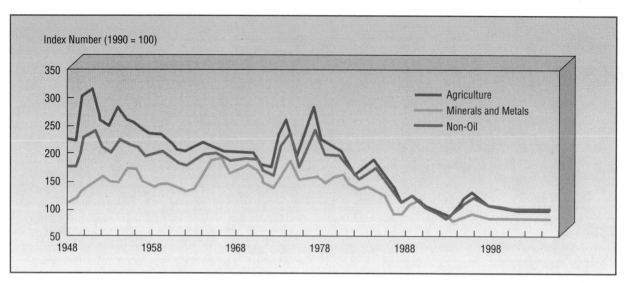

Index Number (1990 = 100)

— Agriculture
— Minerals and Metals
— Non-Oil

FIGURE 9.3

Non-Oil Commodity Prices, 1948 Projected to 2004

Commodities, sometimes called primary products—such as iron ore, copper, bananas, and groundnuts—are a major source of export earnings for many countries, particularly in the Global South. The price of these commodities is erratic in the short run and has experienced a long-term decline. The effect is often devastating on countries without an alternative means of earning income from abroad with which to buy the manufactured goods necessary for their own economic well being.

Note: Data are deflated by the manufactures unit value index.

SOURCE: World Bank (1995a), 19.

imports. Global South countries have long believed that the terms of trade are rigged against them. Buoyed by the logic of dependency theorists (see Chapter 5), the argument is that a combination of two factors perpetuates the adverse term of trade. These factors are: (1) domestic politics in the rich countries, which result in high pay for labor due to the influence of unions and other factors, and (2) the structure of the world political economy, which makes the South dependent on Northern technological innovations to transform primary products efficiently into finished goods.

These ideas led the developing states to place commodity-price stabilization at the top of their agenda for a New International Economic Order (NIEO), which they advanced in the 1970s and early 1980s. The European Community by then had already devised a program (know as STABEX), whose purpose was to stabilize the export earnings of African and Caribbean nations joined to the community. Drawing in part on this experience, the Global South sought an Integrated Programme for Commodities which would establish a common fund supported by producing and consuming nations and administered by an international agency, whose goal would be to ensure stable and remunerative prices for commodity exports. Eventually a watered-down version of their original goals was approved, but it has not played an effective role in stabilizing commodity markets.

Many factors explain the inability of cooperative efforts to stabilize the price of commodities. Among them are the conflicting objectives of producers, who want high prices, and consumers, who want low prices. Beyond this, the uneven distribution of resources makes it difficult to strike a bargain among commodity producers themselves. Canada and Australia, for example, are principal exporters of many widely used primary products, but they do not necessarily share the same interests as others (e.g., Jamaica and Russia) who export those same products.

More importantly from the viewpoint of the globalization of trade, the industrial economies of the Global North increasingly have become uncoupled from the primary-product economies of the Global South (Drucker 1994). Consider the following: "The seminal product of the 1920s was the automobile, which was 60 percent energy and raw materials and 40 percent skills and knowledge; the seminal product of the 1990s is the computer chip, which is 2 percent energy and raw materials and 98 percent ideas, skills, and knowledge" (Marshall 1995). As the information age spreads beyond the North to those in South that are technologically innovative, primary-product producers will be the losers. Large numbers of them, as we have noted, are in Africa south of the Sahara (see Map 9.1, pp. 268–269).

The Multinational Corporation and the Globalization of Production

In the early 1990s Ford Motor Company launched a program called Ford 2000. Its purpose is to transform the world's second-largest industrial firm into its first truly international corporation. Management control will no longer be centered in Dearborn, Michigan, but rather dispersed throughout the world. Already Ford's chairman Alex Trotman—himself from Scotland—proudly proclaims that "there's not an American in charge of any of our national companies in Europe." Ford anticipates changes in its product line as well. Unlike most multinational corporations today, which manufacture and sell products tailored for particular regional markets (such as the Toyota corporation), Ford intends to develop manufacturing capabilities that reduce duplication in different national settings. This also will permit greater standardization and move it along the path toward a "world car" (see Focus 9.3, p. 270). Reduced costs and greater efficiency are the goals.

Ford's plans to develop a truly international corporation is arguably the "highest stage" of corporate development. According to Harvard University's Christopher Bartlett, multinational corporations evolved through four stages. The initial period was one of corporate colonialism, when European MNCs directed their investments toward the nation's colonies. This was followed, after World War II, by the nationalistic period, in which U.S. companies dominated the manufacture of goods and sold them in foreign markets. Today, as noted, most multinationals are in a regional phase, manufacturing and selling products tailored for particular regional markets. From a management point of view, MNCs' overseas operations are "appendages" of a centralized hub (Frown and Swoboda 1994). Ford's plans to move into the fourth stage of MNC development would disperse the hub, much as production facilities themselves are now spread worldwide.

As the multinational corporation has evolved, it has been the primary agent of the globalization of production, propelling as well the extraordinary growth in trade and capital mobility witnessed during the past half-century. As we saw in Chapter 7, today there are more than 38,500 multinational parent companies. The

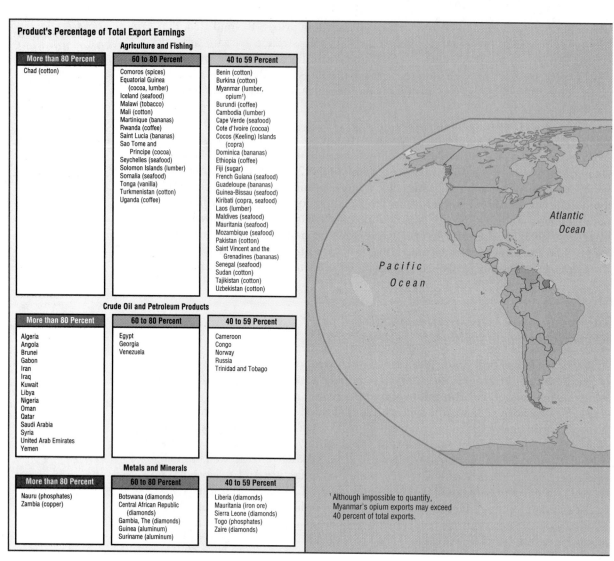

Product's Percentage of Total Export Earnings

Agriculture and Fishing

More than 80 Percent	60 to 80 Percent	40 to 59 Percent

Chad (cotton)	Comoros (spices)
	Equatorial Guinea
	  (cocoa, lumber)
	Iceland (seafood)
	Malawi (tobacco)
	Mali (cotton)
	Martinique (bananas)
	Rwanda (coffee)
	Saint Lucia (bananas)
	Sao Tome and
	  Principe (cocoa)
	Seychelles (seafood)
	Solomon Islands (lumber)
	Somalia (seafood)
	Tonga (vanilla)
	Turkmenistan (cotton)
	Uganda (coffee)
		Benin (cotton)
		Burkina (cotton)
		Myanmar (lumber,
		  opium[1])
		Burundi (coffee)
		Cambodia (lumber)
		Cape Verde (seafood)
		Cote d'Ivoire (cocoa)
		Cocos (Keeling) Islands
		  (copra)
		Dominica (bananas)
		Ethiopia (coffee)
		Fiji (sugar)
		French Guiana (seafood)
		Guadeloupe (bananas)
		Guinea-Bissau (seafood)
		Kiribati (copra, seafood)
		Laos (lumber)
		Maldives (seafood)
		Mauritania (seafood)
		Mozambique (seafood)
		Pakistan (cotton)
		Saint Vincent and the
		  Grenadines (bananas)
		Senegal (seafood)
		Sudan (cotton)
		Tajikistan (cotton)
		Uzbekistan (cotton)

Crude Oil and Petroleum Products

More than 80 Percent	60 to 80 Percent	40 to 59 Percent
Algeria Angola Brunei Gabon Iran Iraq Kuwait Libya Nigeria Oman Qatar Saudi Arabia Syria United Arab Emirates Yemen	Egypt Georgia Venezuela	Cameroon Congo Norway Russia Trinidad and Tobago

Metals and Minerals

More than 80 Percent	60 to 80 Percent	40 to 59 Percent
Nauru (phosphates) Zambia (copper)	Botswana (diamonds) Central African Republic (diamonds) Gambia, The (diamonds) Guinea (aluminum) Suriname (aluminum)	Liberia (diamonds) Mauritania (iron ore) Sierra Leone (diamonds) Togo (phosphates) Zaire (diamonds)

Pacific Ocean

Atlantic Ocean

[1] Although impossible to quantify, Myanmar's opium exports may exceed 40 percent of total exports.

MAP 9.1

The Vulnerable: Commodity–Dependent Economies

Note: The countries highlighted depend on a single commodity for 40 percent or more of their export earnings.

SOURCE: *Handbook of International Economic Statistics 1995* (1995), 130–31.

outward flow of foreign direct investment (FDI) stock attributable to their more than 250,000 foreign affiliates stood at an estimated \$2.4 trillion at the end of 1994 (*World Investment Report 1995*, 9).[2] Most of these stocks are located in the Global North, which is also the primary source and target of the outward flow of FDI.

[2]FDI differs from portfolio investments, such as stock ownership, in that it involves the ownership of physical facilities, such as plant and equipment. FDI also implies "a lasting involvement in the management of enterprises in the recipient economy. . . . In contrast, portfolio equity investment flows are typically more speculative in nature and respond quickly to changing perceptions of risk and reward. As a result, portfolio equity investment is more unstable than FDI" (*World Investment Report 1995* 1995). The latter explains Mexico's most recent balance-of-payments crisis (see also Cline 1995).

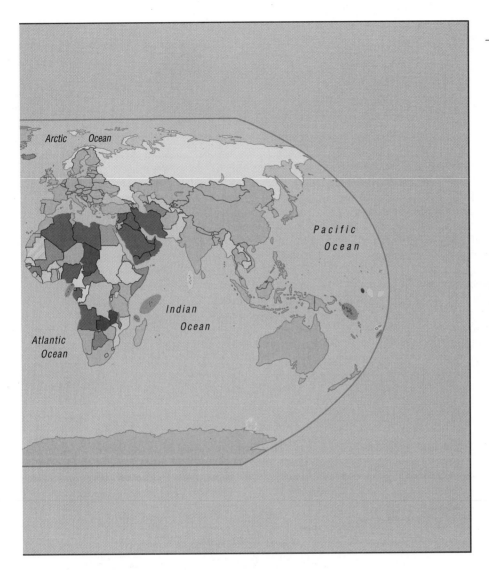

Table 9.3 summarizes these patterns, showing the value of FDI coming into (inflows) and out of (outflows) developed and developing countries in recent years.

The reason for the concentration of FDI in the North is clear: Profits are MNCs' primary motivations, and their investment returns are likely to be greatest in the Global North, where a combination of affluence and political stability reduces investment risks. Still, the Global South is the host of considerable FDI. Although the amounts fluctuate on a yearly basis, the 1990s generally have seen a return to the patterns of the early 1980s, when a growing number of developing countries were viewed as targets of opportunity. Today, those opportunities are in Asia. Ten countries in the Global South accounted for nearly 80 percent of the $74.4 billion invested there in 1993 (*World Investment Report 1995* 1995, 12). Seven of the ten (in order) are in Asia: China, Singapore, Malaysia, Indonesia, Thailand, Hong Kong, and Taiwan. (Argentina, Mexico, and Colombia are the remaining three.)

The impact of foreign direct investment extends beyond money. With it comes technology, managerial expertise, and employment opportunities. Champions of MNCs view these as contributions to the development of less

Ford's Concept of a World Car

Henry Ford's Model T [introduced in 1908] was a "world car," designed for sale in all markets. Components were produced in Detroit, then shipped for assembly to save transportation costs and import duties. The final product was identical everywhere. Western European tastes and driving conditions differed from those of North Americans, however, so Ford soon found it necessary to design a smaller Model Y for production and sale in that market. Eventually, Ford designed distinct models for each western European country in which the firm had production facilities. Vehicles assembled in Germany or Belgium shared no parts with those assembled in the United Kingdom.

Years later, in the 1970s, the Ford Motor Company took advantage of the removal of barriers to intra-western European trade to assemble a single model—the Fiesta—at plants in the United Kingdom, Spain, and Belgium. Ford was able to benefit from economies of scale by shipping many of the standardized components from a single factory. All carburetors, for example, were produced in Ireland, all transmissions in France, all spark-plugs and radiators in the United Kingdom. Building on this western European experience, Ford

attempted to revive the world car concept with the 1981 Escort. In the end, the attempt was unsuccessful, for the only thing the European and American versions of the Escort had in common was a name and two insignificant parts.

In 1993, Ford launched another world car (the Mondeo), this time with more success. It was necessary to lengthen the body of the North American version, named the Ford Contour or Mercury Mystique, but the cars do share a common chassis and all mechanical parts. More world cars are planned, including a 1999 Escort. The aim is to assemble virtually the same car in different markets. Common parts will be purchased from the lowest cost global suppliers, then shipped for assembly in each of the main markets. In addition, savings on development costs are envisaged if more vehicles of a common design are produced. It remains to be seen whether this return to the mass production model of Henry Ford's Model T will prove successful against the totally different global strategy of Japanese automakers.

SOURCE: *World Economic and Social Survey 1995* (1995), 250.

TABLE 9.3   Inflows and Outflows of Foreign Direct Investment, 1983–1994

	Billions of Dollars				Percentages			
	1983–1988 Annual Average	1990	1992	1994	1983–1988 Annual Average	1990	1992	1994
Global North								
Inflows	73	176	111	135	78	83	69	62
Outflows	88	226	171	189	95	93	90	85
Global South								
Inflows	20	35	55	84	22	17	31	38
Outflows	5	17	19	33	5	7	10	15

SOURCE: Adapted from *World Investment Report 1995* (1995), 391, 397.

developed economies. Not surprisingly, nations in the Global South often actively seek MNC investment capital and the other perquisites that flow from it. MNCs are especially important to those who seek to emulate the economic success of the Newly Industrializing Economies, which depend on an ability to sustain growth in exports. Foreign capital is critical in this process.

The developing countries once shunned foreign investments, fearing their adverse economic and political consequences. But no longer. Even Vietnam, once a bitter enemy of the United States, now welcomes American investment dollars.

Foreign investment is not without costs, however (see, e.g., Broad and Cavanagh 1988). With it comes political influence, for example, which sometimes skews the political process in questionable directions. Critics of MNCs also worry that the presumed economic benefits of FDI gloss over their adverse economic consequences. "They see these giant corporations not as needed agents of economic change but more as vehicles of antidevelopment. Multinationals, they argue, reinforce dualistic economic structures and exacerbate domestic inequalities with wrong products and inappropriate technology" (Todaro 1994). (See Focus 9.4.)

Critics contend that MNCs exact a cost not only on the Global South but also on the Global North (recall Focus 7.4). They note that while corporate executives often have a "broad vision and understanding of global issues," they have little appreciation of, or concern for, "the long-term social or political consequences of what their companies make or what they do" (Barnet and Cavanagh 1994; see also Barnet and Müller 1974). These allegedly include a host of maladies, including environmental degradation, a maldistribution of global resources, and social disintegration. Beyond this, critics worry that MNCs are beyond the control of national political leaders.

> The formidable power and mobility of global corporations are undermining the effectiveness of national governments to carry out essential policies on behalf of their people. Leaders of nation-states are losing much of the control over their own territory they once had. More and more, they must conform to the demands of the outside world because the outsiders are already inside the gates. Business enterprises that routinely operate across borders are linking far-flung pieces of territory into a new world economy that bypasses all sorts of established political arrangements and conventions. (Barnet and Cavanagh 1994, 19)

Even the United States—home to thousands of MNCs and a principal source of foreign direct investment funds—is not immune to these processes.

FOCUS 9.4 *Inappropriate Products in a Homogenizing World*

In the 1970s, babies in Third World nations were dying when they might have been thriving. The apparent culprit: ersatz mother's milk made from power. The Nestlé Company, a Swiss-based multinational, had identified Third World mothers as a high-growth marketing opportunity. Nestlé baby formula was aggressively pushed as the "modern" way to feed infants.

In the developed world, baby formula works fine. It may not be as good as mother's milk, but it's reasonably close. As long as the bottles and rubber nipples for the formula are properly sterilized, the mixing water reasonably pure, and the mixing proportions right, babies do well on it.

But in Third World villages in the 1970s, pure water was the exception, not the rule, and the need for sterilization was hard to explain and seldom practiced. Beyond that, the formula was cheap by First World standards, but expensive by Third World reckonings. That makes it fatally tempting to stretch the powder by diluting it too much, thus degrading the nutritional value.

Health care professionals and missionaries working in the Third World were outraged, and they communicated their sadness and anger to Nestlé. which did nothing, and to governments, which didn't seem to care. Nestlé had threatened no nation's security, broken no laws.

But nutritionists and activists in the industrialized world did care, and condemnation of Nestlé's marketing practices became widespread. As word got out, the cause was taken up by nearly 100 private organizations in 65 states. A transnational economic boycott of Nestlé products was launched, coordinated by a U.S.-based transnational citizen coalition, the Infant Formula Action Committee (INFACT).

Whether the boycott had much economic effect on Nestlé's bottom line is hard to pin down. But it became a public relations nightmare for a company that liked to be known for its warm and cuddly hot chocolate and its candy-counter Crunch bars. The INFACT-led transnational campaign ultimately forced Nestlé to abandon its Third World marketing practices, and it also led to the passage in 1981 of a world Health Organization code of conduct governing the marketing and sale of infant formula.

SOURCE: Lopez, Smith, and Pagnucco (1995), 33.

"Although still the largest national economy and by far the world's greatest military power, [it] is increasingly subject to the vicissitudes of a world no nation can dominate" (Barnet and Cavanagh 1994). Meanwhile, some corporate visionaries extol multinational corporations' transnational virtues. "There are no longer any national flag carriers," in the words of Kenichi Ohmae, a Japanese management consultant. "Corporations must serve their customers, not governments."

Labor's Place in the Globalization Process

In his manifesto on the evils of capitalism, Karl Marx urged the workers of the world to unite, throwing off the bondages imposed by the oppressive owners of capital. The assumption was that workers everywhere shared a common purpose and vision. But that is no longer true. As the liberalization of markets throughout the world and their rapid integration globally proceed, labor markets will be profoundly affected. Competition—not solidarity—has intensified. Because the spread of globalization is uneven, some will be winners, others losers.

As recently as the 1970s a third of the world's workers were insulated from the rest of the world through centralized economic planning, as in the former Eastern bloc, and through restrictive trade barriers and the regulation of capital markets elsewhere. "Today, three giant population blocs—China, the republics of the former Soviet Union, and India—with nearly half the world's labor force among them, are entering the global market, and many other countries from Mexico to Indonesia have already established deep linkages. By the year 2000 fewer than 10 percent of the world's workers are likely to be cut off from the economic mainstream" (*World Development Report 1995* 1995, 50).

Accommodating the influx of new workers will be difficult. Already "the world is experiencing the worst employment crisis since the 1930s," according to a former secretary of the U.S. Department of Labor. "Almost one-third of the Earth's 2.8 billion workers are either jobless or underemployed, and many of those who are employed work for every low wages with little prospect for advancement" (Marshall 1995). Europe suffers chronic unemployment, with as much as 12 percent of the labor force idled. Unemployment rates are lower in the United States, but the real wages of most U.S. workers have fallen over the past two decades. Mass unemployment characterizes conditions in many of the economies in transition, while in much of the Global South employment growth has slowed and wage rates have fallen. The costs of the deteriorating employment picture are high.

> High levels of joblessness result not only in an enormous waste of resources but also in human suffering and hopelessness, rising inequality within and between countries, and a host of ills. The conditions threaten social cohesion and undermine democratic institutions—or make them much more difficult to establish. And growing global interdependence causes such problems in one country to affect others negatively as well. (Marshall 1995, 50)

Multinational corporations have been a primary vehicle of growing global interdependence. As we have seen, this often has been made possible by moving manufacturing sites and technical know-how to developing countries, where labor is cheap. Of the 8 million jobs created by MNCs between 1985 and 1992, 5 million were in the Global South. In countries as diverse as Argentina, Barbados, Botswana, Indonesia, Malaysia, Mauritius, Mexico, the Philippines, Singapore, and Sri Lanka, multinationals account for one-fifth of the manufacturing-sector employment (*World Development Report 1995* 1995, 62). Thus workers have benefited from new job opportunities. In a world of highly mobile capital, however, this also makes them vulnerable. "Many developing countries fear that increased competition for funds by other developing countries will lead to a rise in footloose investments, prone to leave at the slightest shock. . . . This problem is especially acute in low-skill industries such as garments and footwear, where firm-specific knowledge is slight and exit costs are low" (*World Development Report 1995* 1995).

Such fears, born of experience, are all too real in the Global North. Workers there fear losing their jobs due to cheap imports made possible by lower-cost production in the Global South or because the companies they work for will relocate abroad. The irony is that economic growth has been rekindled since the recession of the early 1990s. For many, however, this has been a time of "jobless growth." And even if they keep their jobs, employees often blame cheap foreign labor for their own lack of pay hikes, resulting in stagnating living standards.

Wage rates differ widely throughout the world (see Figure 9.4). It is difficult to assess the impact of wage rates in different countries on one another, because labor trends are affected not only by trade but also by technological developments, trends in labor productivity, and migration. However, economic theory does predict that, as a result of international trade, the wage rates in poor countries will be pulled up somewhat. Meanwhile wage rates in rich countries will come down, at least for unskilled workers. "The logic behind this is that trade affects the relative rewards of factors of production by changing the relative price of goods. Opening up to trade increases the price of labor-intensive goods in poor, labor-rich countries, which, as a consequence, shift their resources to the production of labor-intensive goods. This, in turn, raises demand for labor in poor countries, and hence raises relative wages. As relative prices of goods converge in rich and poor countries, so do wages" (Diwan and Revenga 1995). In short, as a consequence of trade, wage rates should tend toward convergence. For some, this means a gain in welfare; for others, it means lost income.

Empirical studies of wage rates in different countries support these expectations (for summaries, see Diwan and Revenga 1995; World Bank 1995a; *World Development Report 1995* 1995). They also show that increased competi-

FIGURE 9.4

Same Work, Different Pay

A construction worker in Seoul makes four times as much as a construction worker in Jakarta; an engineer in Frankfurt makes nearly sixty times as much as a female textile worker in Kenya. In general, skilled workers in the most prosperous nations of the Global North earn sixty times more than the poorest agricultural workers in sub-Saharan Africa.

*Thousand dollars per year, converted at purchasing power parity exchange rates.
SOURCE: Diwan and Revenga (1995), 8.

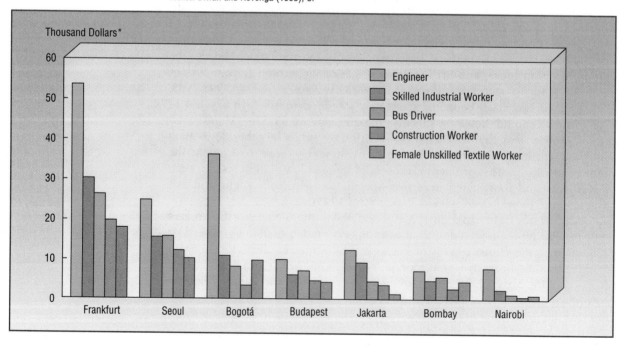

tion from producers in developing countries are responsible in part for growing wage inequality in Australia, Canada, and the United States, as well as for the persistence of high levels of unemployment in Europe. Where analysts disagree is in their determination of what part trade competition plays in these problems. "Most analyses conclude that trade with developing countries can explain only 10 to 30 percent of the industrial countries' labor market difficulties, but some studies come up with more extreme results—on both sides of the argument" (Diwan and Revenga 1995).

People and policymakers act on their *perceptions* of reality rather than on *objective* reality. In this case—regardless of what economists conclude—the belief that cheap foreign labor depresses living standards is cause for rejecting liberalism and embracing neomercantilism. From here it is but a short step toward assailing the multiple prongs propelling the intensification of interdependence which accompanies globalization. Commenting on the European Union's move away from "community preference" (i.e., the absence of tariffs and other barriers within the Union and a single tariff toward nonmembers), in favor of free international trade, a prominent European businessman predicted:

> If we were to return to the ideas of our founding fathers and reimpose community preference, overnight all the enterprises which have moved their production to low-cost countries would have to return. They could no longer competitively import products manufactured outside Europe. Factories would be built, Europeans would be employed, the economy would prosper, and social stability would return. What is more, international corporations wishing to sell their products within Europe would also have to build, employ, and participate in the European economy. From being a community which, at the moment, reeks of death, it would all of a sudden become one of the most exciting places in which to invest and participate. And European corporations would go out to invest and contribute to the prosperity of regions through the world. The same is true for North America. (Goldsmith 1994, 51–52)

With protectionist sentiments widespread in the Global North, countries in the Global South worry that their own hopes for economic advancement cannot be realized unless and until the Global North relaxes its multitude of restrictive trade barriers. Interestingly, however, concern for the impact of low wage rates is no longer confined to the Global North. Faced with the prospect of huge numbers of low-wage Chinese workers entering the work force, some Global South nations now also feel threatened. This is leading them, too, to embrace protectionist trade practices (Diwan and Revenga 1995). Thus the challenge of globalization promises to shape the global political agenda well into the next century.

• • •

THE STATE AND GLOBALIZATION:
SYSTEM STRESS OR TRANSFORMATION?

Rapid globalization, fueled in large measure by the revolution in microelectronics, is a process unlikely to be forestalled. Analysts differ on whether globalization is desirable or despicable, however, depending in part on the scenarios about the future world order that globalization will help create and the political perspectives that inform their world views (Rosenau 1990; see also the essays in Holm and Sørensen 1995c). Some focus on the benefits of globalization for economic well-being; others focus on its unevenness and the prospects for marginalizing large numbers of peoples and states. Some focus on the challenge globalization poses to an international system founded on the state; others are more sanguine about the state's resilience and the prospects for global governance to cope with the challenge of globalization.

Globalization, as the term itself suggests, has been a worldwide phenomenon, but it has been uneven. The intensification of interdependence has been most pronounced among the nations of the Global North and the emerging economies of East Asia, which have reaped its economic benefits. But because it is uneven, globalization also threatens to widen the gulf between the world's rich and poor countries. This is true even within the Global South, which already stands at some distance from the high-consumption societies of the North.

> If the borderless world rewards entrepreneurs, designers, brokers, patent owners, lawyers, and dealers in high-value services, then East Asia's commitment to education, science, and technology can only increase its lead over other developing economies. By contrast, their relative lack of capital, high technology, scientists, and skilled workers, and export-oriented industry makes it difficult for poorer countries to partake in the communications and financial revolution. . . . Some grimmer forecasts suggest the developing world may become more marginalized, partly because of the dematerialization of labor, raw materials, and foodstuffs, partly because the advanced economies may concentrate upon greater knowledge-based commerce among themselves. . . .
>
> As we move into the next century the developed economies appear to have all the trump cards in their hands—capital, technology, control of communications, surplus foodstuffs, powerful multinational companies—and, if anything, their advantages are *growing* because technology is eroding the value of labor and materials, the chief assets of developing countries. (Kennedy 1993, 223–25)

But is technology also eroding the ability of even the rich states to control their economic and political fortunes? Certainly a world of vanishing borders challenges the territorial state, but "the world economy does not operate somewhere offshore, but instead functions within the political framework provided by nation-states" (Kapstein 1994; see also Holm and Sørensen 1995a). State power thus retains its relevance in shaping outcomes even in a world political economy undergoing rapid change (see Krasner 1991; but cf. Cerny 1995). International regimes like those that evolved to promote global governance in monetary and trade affairs may also prove effective as management strategies for coping with the globalization challenge. A key issue is whether states can find a focal point, a norm, around which cooperation could coalesce (Cohen 1996). Liberal theorists in both politics and economics, who focus on the mutual gains stemming from international cooperation, are optimistic about the possibilities. Political realists and neomercantilists, who are concerned more with relative gains than absolute gains, are more pessimistic.

There is another worrisome side to globalization: its impact on the global environment. We began this chapter by asking whether globalization is the route to a global village—one free of conflict and intent only on improving villagers' welfare—or whether this is mere mythology. *Global pillage* is an alternative scenario flowing from globalization. It sees the costs of rapidly accelerating consumption promoted by free trade and the ethos of consumerism as unsustainable. Will that force—the possibility of destroying the planet's very life-support systems—ultimately bind humanity? We probe answers to that question in the next two chapters.

• • •

KEY TERMS

globalization
cyberspace
globalization of finance

capital mobility hypothesis
trade integration
terms of trade

CHAPTER 10

The Demography of World Politics: Patterns, Problems, and Possibilities

We are entering a bifurcated world. Part of the globe is inhabited by Hegel's
. . . Last Man, healthy, well fed, and pampered by technology. The other, larger,
part is inhabited by Hobbes's First Man, condemned to a life that is "poor,
nasty, brutish, and short."

—Robert D. Kaplan,
political journalist, 1994

Fundamental demographic, economic and sociocultural differences between
countries of immigration and countries of emigration are the underlying cause
of this near-universal phenomenon. . . . Immigration policy is linked to
international policy by virtue of its causes.

—Charles Pasqua,
French Minister of State, 1994

How many people can the earth support? The planet's **carrying capacity**—
its ability to support human and other life forms—is not infinite. However,
human ingenuity and rapidly advancing technology have continuously
stretched the boundaries.[1] As a result, the earth doubtless will accommodate
the growth projected for today's nearly 6 billion inhabitants into the next century. But at what cost—to human freedom, human welfare, and the natural
environment necessary to sustain humankind?

The **tragedy of the commons** is a metaphor that highlights the potential
impact of human behavior on the planet's resources and its delicately balanced
ecological systems. First articulated in 1833 by English political economist
William Foster Lloyd and later extended to contemporary problems by human
ecologist Garrett Hardin, the metaphor refers to nineteenth-century English
villages, where the green was common property on which all villagers could
graze their cattle. Freedom of access to the commons was a cherished village
value, and sharing the common grazing area worked well as long as the number of cattle did not exceed the land's carrying capacity. Should that happen,
the pasture would be ruined and the number of cattle the common property
could sustain would be drastically reduced.

Which path would the village herders take—preserving the village green or
ruining it? In the absence of restraints on human freedom—and assuming the
villagers were driven by the profit motive—herders had a maximum incentive
to increase their herds as much as possible. Although the village green eventually would be destroyed if they all behaved this way, in the short run the addition of one more animal would produce a personal gain whose costs would be
borne by everyone. Self-interest thus encouraged all herders to increase their
herds indiscriminately and discouraged self-sacrifice for the general welfare. In
the end, however, the collective impact of their individual efforts to maximize
private gain led to more cattle on the village green than it could sustain, with
the inevitable result: destruction of the common property. "Ruin is the destina-

---

[1]See J. Cohen (1995), especially Appendix 3, for an interesting summary of efforts dating to
the 1600s to estimate how many people the earth can support.

tion toward which all men rush," Hardin (1968) concluded, "each pursuing his own best interest in a society that believes in the freedom of the commons."

The tragedy of the commons provides insight into numerous environmental issues (see Soroos 1995), ranging from excessive fishing of the oceans by a few at the expense of others to transboundary pollution caused when industries spew toxic industrial wastes into the atmosphere. More broadly, the metaphor is a kind of shorthand for situations in which "people so impinge on each other in pursuing their own interests that collectively they might be better off if they could be restrained, but no one gains individually by self-restraint." Thus the commons are a part of a broader set of situations "in which some of the costs or damages of what people do occur beyond their purview, and they either don't know or don't care about them" (Schelling 1978).

The freedom to procreate is a major "unregulated" freedom of choice. "The most important aspect of necessity that we must now recognize," Hardin (1968) wrote, "is the necessity of abandoning the commons in breeding. Freedom to breed will bring ruin to all. . . . The only way we can preserve and nurture other and more precious freedoms is by relinquishing the freedom to breed, and that very soon. . . . Only so, can we put an end to this aspect of the tragedy of the commons."

Not everyone will agree with the ethical implications of Hardin's arguments (see also Hardin 1993). Indeed, few decisions are more intensely personal or more intimately tied to the social and cultural fabric of a society than those about marriage and the family. Furthermore, just as the ultimate carrying capacity of the global ecosystem has proved elastic, the impact of unregulated population growth on social well-being and environmental quality remains unclear. Nonetheless, the balance of both theory and evidence points to a world in which unrestrained population growth will result in lost economic opportunities, environmental degradation, domestic strife, and incentives—perhaps imperatives—for governmental restraints on individual choice. A world interdependent ecopolitically as well as economically, is certain to share the consequences.

Our purpose in this chapter and the next is to explore how changes in demography, the environment, and resources influence world politics. Here we focus on demographic variables—how global trends in births, deaths, migration, and their correlates shape today's world and tomorrow's future. This sets the stage for Chapter 11, where we examine the relationship between environmental and resource trends and the widely shared goals of security and development.

• • •

GLOBAL DEMOGRAPHIC PATTERNS AND TRENDS

The dramatic growth in world population in the twentieth century is historically unprecedented. It took two million years before world population reached 1 billion in 1804; 2 billion was reached in 1927. Since then, additional billions have been added even more rapidly: 3 billion was reached by 1960, 4 billion in 1974, and 5 billion in 1987 (see Figure 10.1). The sixth billion will be added before the end of this century (United Nations 1995, 97). How is this possible? Because world population grows by nearly ten thousand *each hour of every day.* In fact, more people will be added to the world's population in the last fifth of the twentieth century than at any other time in history. If present trends continue uninterrupted, world population will grow to 7.5 billion in 2015, stand at

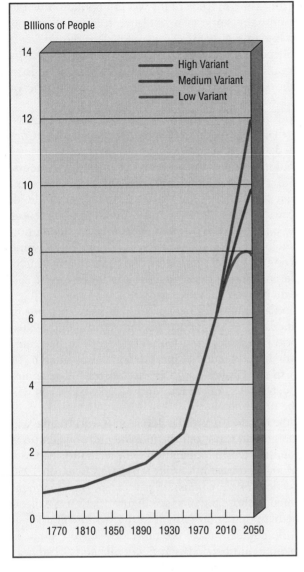

Billions of People

High Variant
Medium Variant
Low Variant

FIGURE 10.1

World Population Growth, 1750 to 1995 and Projected to 2150

World population in the twentieth century has grown from fewer than 2 billion people to nearly 6 billion, with each billion added in less time than the previous billion. Between 2 and 4 billion more will be added between now and the fifth decade of the twenty-first century. Changes in world fertility rates will determine the exact number.

SOURCE: Adapted from United Nations (1995), 101, 226–27, 234–35, 242–43.

9.8 billion in 2050, and reach 10 billion only a few years later—about the time most of today's college students in the Global North will be drawing on their retirement benefits. Indeed, most of those reading this book will have witnessed the largest population surge ever to have occurred in a single generation—theirs.

As difficult as it may be to imagine a world with half again as many people as today, 10 billion is less than what was once projected for the middle of the next century. The latest projection—what the United Nations calls its "medium variant" (the middle line among the three population projections in Figure 10.1)—depends on the assumption that the world fertility rate will continue to decline, as it has for more than a decade, and eventually settle at a point where couples only replace themselves. Without that, population growth could be much more rapid in the first half of the next century, reaching 11.9 billion in the year 2050 (the top line in Figure 10.1), nearly five times the 1950 population (United Nations 1995, 98). In either case, world population will continue to grow throughout the twenty-first century and into the twenty-second. On the other hand, should world fertility slow more rapidly, world population would also grow more slowly and eventually settle at a level much lower than now seems most likely (the bottom line in Figure 10.1).

The rapid growth of world population after reaching 2 billion in 1927 is described by a simple mathematical principle articulated in 1798 by the Reverend Thomas Malthus: Unchecked, population increases in a geometric or exponential ratio (e.g., 1 to 2, 2 to 4, 4 to 8, etc.), whereas subsistence increases in only an arithmetic ratio (1 to 2, 2 to 3, 3 to 4). When population increases at such an accelerating rate, the compound effect can be staggering. Consider, for example, how money deposited in a savings account grows as it earns interest not only on the original investment but also on the interest payments. If each of our ancestors had put a mere ten dollars in the bank for us two hundred years ago, and it accrued a steady 6% annual interest, today we would all be millionaires! Population grows in the same way: It is a function of increases in the original number of people plus those accruing from past population growth. Thus a population growing at a 1 percent rate will double in sixty-nine years, while a population growing at a 2 percent rate will double in only thirty-five years. (The impact of different growth rates on doubling times can be calculated by dividing sixty-nine by the percentage of growth.)

Worldwide, the rate of population growth peaked at just over 2 percent in the late 1960s and then declined to just under 1.6 percent by the mid-1990s. Hence the projection that world population in 2050 will be far less than once thought. Not all countries will share equally in the phenomenon, though. In fact, rapid population growth in the Global South is the most striking demographic development in the post-World War II era, and its consequences will continue to be felt well into the future.

During the next fifty years the developed and the developing worlds alike will experience declining population growth rates, but the incremental contributions of the Global South to expanding world population will actually increase. "Whereas 79 percent of the annual increase in world population between 1950 and 1955 originated in the less developed regions, 95 percent of the increment between 1990 and 1995 originated in those regions [see Figure 10.2]. It is expected that by 2045–2050 all of the net population growth in the world will arise in the less developed regions, as the populations of the more developed regions is expected to be declining in absolute numbers" (*World Economic and Social Survey 1995* 1995, 147). Ours has become, and will remain, a demographically divided world. We can better understand the inevitability of this prediction, and how demographic developments will affect world politics, if we go beyond the simple arithmetic of population growth to explore its dynamics.

• • •

POPULATION DYNAMICS: THE CAUSES OF GLOBAL POPULATION TRENDS

In Austria, the population growth rate in 1995 was 0.1 percent. This is an annual rate similar to that of other Global North countries, where births and deaths have nearly stabilized and population growth is thus near zero. In Kenya, on the other hand, the growth rate in 1995 stood at 3.3 percent, which is typical of other Global South countries (*1995 World Population Data Sheet*). The differences between Austria and Kenya illustrate the larger pattern of demographic differences between North and South. They also illustrate why today's popula-

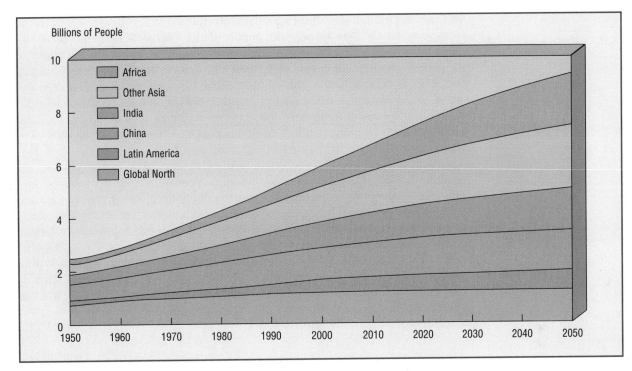

Billions of People

FIGURE 10.2

The Demographic Divide, 1950–2050

Nearly all of the world's population growth in the next half-century will occur in the Global South, with Africa growing most rapidly. By the middle of the twenty-first century, the absolute number of people in the Global North is expected to be declining.

Note: Projections are based on United Nations medium variant estimates shown in Figure 10.1.

SOURCE: Adapted from United Nations (1995), 213–14, 588, 674.

tion surge is confined to the developing countries, where sharply lower death rates since World War II have resulted from advances in medical science, agricultural productivity, and public sanitation. The paradox—illustrated in Figure 10.2—is that population growth is occurring in precisely those countries least able to support a burgeoning number of people. High fertility rates in much of the Global South combined with the sheer number of children that will be born explain why today's realities will lead to ever-wider differences between North and South in the new millennium.

Fertility Rates

The world **fertility rate** (the average number of children born to a woman in her lifetime) is estimated to have been 3.1 in 1995. In the developed world the rate stood at 1.6, which is below **replacement-level fertility** (2.1 children per women, or roughly one couple replacing themselves with two children). In the developing world, however, it stood at 3.5 (and even higher—at 4.0—if China, which has restrictive population policies, is excluded) (*1995 World Population Data Sheet*). These numbers are sharply lower than in the 1960s and 1970s, thus helping to slow the rate of world population growth to its present level.

283

Still, world population cannot stabilize until the world fertility rate falls to the replacement level. Yet throughout much of the Global South, the preferred family size remains far in excess not only of the replacement level but also of the present world fertility rate of 3.1 percent. Among the world's largest states, for example, China is the only Global South country that has achieved the replacement plateau, while four-fifths of the remaining ones continue to experience fertility rates higher than the present world rate (see Table 10.1). The numbers are especially startling in Africa south of the Sahara (e.g., Nigeria), where the region's fertility rate in 1995 stood at 6.2.

The developing countries' high fertility rates derive from a variety of sources. Besides the pleasures that children provide, cultural traditions and religious norms often encourage the bearing of children, ascribing prestige and social status to women based on the number of children they bear and typically placing special value on male offspring. Politics also exerts a force, as many governments deliberately encourage women to have large families, "arguing that this adds to the country's military strength. 'Bear a child,' posters in Iraq proclaimed, 'and you pierce an arrow in the enemy's eye.' Countries such as Iraq and Libya offer many incentives for larger families, as do the Gulf states and Saudi Arabia, anxious to fill their oil-rich lands with native-born rather than foreign workers" (Kennedy 1993).

TABLE 10.1 Population, Fertility, Growth Rates, and Doubling Times for the World's Twenty Largest Countries, 1995

Country	Population (millions)	Fertility Rate	Natural Increase (percent)	Doubling Time (years)
Germany	81.7	1.3	−0.1	*
Russia	147.5	1.4	−0.6	*
Japan	125.2	1.5	0.3	277
France	58.1	1.7	0.3	578
United Kingdom	58.6	1.8	0.2	385
China	1,218.8	1.9	1.1	62
United States	263.2	2.0	0.7	105
Thailand	60.2	2.2	1.4	48
Turkey	61.4	2.7	1.6	44
Indonesia	198.4	2.8	1.6	43
Brazil	157.8	2.9	1.7	41
Mexico	93.7	3.1	2.2	34
India	930.6	3.4	1.9	36
Vietnam	75.0	3.7	2.3	30
Philippines	68.4	4.1	2.1	33
Bangladesh	119.2	4.3	2.4	29
Iran	61.3	5.0	2.9	24
Pakistan	129.7	5.6	2.9	24
Nigeria	101.2	6.3	3.1	22
Egypt	61.9	6.4	3.4	21

*At present rates of growth, the population will never double.

Note: Natural increase (popularly called the growth rate) is the difference between the birth rate and the death rate, converted to a percentage. The rate of natural increase does not consider the impact of migration on population growth or decline.

SOURCE: *1995 World Population Data Sheet* (Washington, D.C.: Population Reference Bureau, 1995).

Economics is perhaps the most potent force, with many children adding to a family's labor force today and providing future security for parents who live in societies that have no public programs for the elderly. When the infant mortality rate is high, the incentives to have many offspring are even greater: The larger the number of children born, the greater the chance that some will survive. Infant and child (under-five) mortality rates have declined dramatically in the past three decades (*The State of the World's Children 1995* 1995, 55), but improvements have been slowest where poverty and population growth are most pervasive. In Sub-Saharan Africa, for instance, one out of every ten children born will die before reaching the age of one, and in South Asia one out of eight will die before age five (*The State of the World's Children 1995* 1995, 84).

HIV/AIDS

Although infant and child mortality rates remain discouragingly high in much of the developing world, at least the direction is downward. Not so with the spread of the human immunodeficiency virus (HIV), which causes AIDS (acquired immune deficiency syndrome). Are world death rates thus destined to rise in the future, reversing the upward trend in world population?

Since the onset of the AIDS pandemic in the late 1970s, the World Health Organization conservatively estimates that 18 million adults have been infected with the deadly virus and expects at least 40 million to be infected by the end of the decade (*The State of the World Population 1995* 1995, 51). Others put the current number of those already HIV-infected at 26 million and estimate that perhaps as many as 110 million will be infected by the year 2000 (Mann and Tarantola 1995, 46, 87). Africa will remain the epicenter of the pandemic, as in the past (see Figure 10.3), but the virus is now spreading rapidly in South and Southeast Asia where 2.5 million people were believed to be HIV-infected in 1994—1 million more than in 1993 (*World Health Report 1995* 1995, 29). By the end of this century, AIDS is expected to be Thailand's leading cause of death, with life expectancy plunging to only forty years a decade later (Shenon 1996, 8).

The spread of AIDS is difficult to predict because many cases go undiagnosed or unreported, particularly in the Global South. Furthermore, the virus that causes AIDS is hard to detect because of its long incubation period. The length of time between an HIV infection and the onset of AIDS averages about ten years. Consequently, even if HIV infections could be immediately halted, the AIDS pandemic would continue to spread.

> Infected people often end up spreading the virus for several years before realizing they have it themselves. In Asia, this pattern has been especially devastating. Many Asian countries have thriving sex industries, and young adults often have multiple sex partners. In addition, rapid economic transformations in much of Asia have created huge populations of internal migrants, whose unstable lives make them particularly vulnerable to infection. (Brown, Lenssen, and Kane 1995, 98).

As the cumulative impact of HIV infections grows, the societal impact of AIDS spreads (Mann and Tarantola 1995). Already AIDS adds heavy burdens to overtaxed health-care systems in many poorer countries. In some African cities, for example, over half of those hospitalized are HIV-infected (*The State of the World Population 1995* 1995, 51). In addition, AIDS' impact on social structures

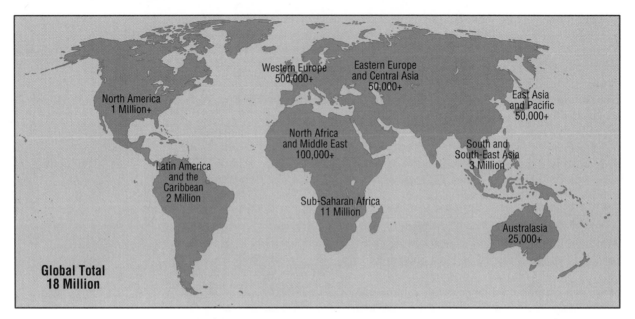

FIGURE 10.3

AIDS' Global Spread: Estimates of Total Adult HIV Infections, 1994

Africa is the epicenter of the AIDS pandemic, but no region of the world is unaffected. Its most rapid spread today is in Asia, home to two-thirds of the world's people. The absolute number of Asia's AIDS victims is almost certain to surpass Africa's.

SOURCE: *The State of the World Population 1995* (1995), 51.

and economic performance is more devastating than its victims' number suggests, as its spread mostly affects young and middle-aged people. Thus income-generation, family caregiving, and food production in countries where agricultural remains heavily labor-intensive will all be affected. Increased mortality among younger age groups also follows; in many African countries life expectancy will be cut by more than twenty-five years by 2010 (Brown, Lenssen, and Kane 1995, 98).[2]

As AIDS spreads, it will affect demographic patterns profoundly in at least some cities and regions, where its ravages may cause negative population growth rates. Still, it will seldom have a significant effect on national population growth, even in countries where HIV infections are highest, as they also have high current population growth rates and the momentum propelled by high growth rates in the past (United Nations 1995). AIDS will take a toll, but it will not alter the world's relentless march toward 10 billion people.

Population Momentum

The surge in the Global South's population in this century is easily explained: It resulted from a combination of high birth rates and rapidly falling death rates. But to understand the population surge projected for the next century—when birth rates throughout the world will decline—we have to understand the force

---

[2]For a detailed examination of the demographic impact of AIDS on the sixteen countries in which it is most prevalent, see United Nations (1995), especially Chapter 4.

of **population momentum,** the continued growth of population for decades into the future because of the large numbers of people now entering their child-bearing years. Like the inertia of a descending airliner when it first touches down on the runway, population growth simply cannot be halted even with an immediate, full application of the brakes. Instead, many years of high fertility mean that more women will be entering their reproductive years than in the past. Not until the size of the generation giving birth to children is no larger than the generation among which deaths are occurring will the population "air-plane" come to a halt.

The population pyramids for Western Europe and Sub-Saharan Africa depicted in Figure 10.4 illustrate the force of population momentum. Africa's age and sex profile is one of rapid population growth, as each new age group (cohort) contains more people than the one before it. Thus, even if individual African couples choose to have fewer children than their parents, Africa's pop-ulation will continue to grow because there are now more men and women of childbearing age than ever before. In contrast, Europe's population profile is one of slow growth, as recent cohorts have been smaller than preceding ones.

FIGURE 10.4

Patterns of Population Change: Population Pyramids for Europe and Sub-Saharan Africa, 1995

Sub-Saharan Africa illustrates population momentum at work. Because of the larger number of people entering their childbearing years, Africa's population will continue to grow even if individual couples have fewer children than their parents. Europe, on the other hand, is reaching a replacement-level population, as the number of people in the most recent cohorts is no larger than their predecessors.

SOURCE: Adapted from United Nations (1994a), 25, 73.

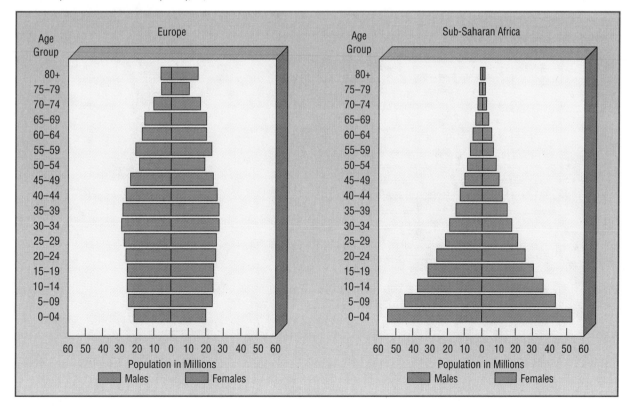

Europe in fact has moved beyond replacement-level fertility to become a "declining" population, described by low birth rates and a growing number of people who survive middle age. A product of an extended period of low birth rates, low death rates, and increased longevity, Europe's age structure is best described as that of a "mature" or "old" society.

As the Global North generally, like Europe, ages, much of the Global South continues to mirror the Sub-Saharan African profile. Because each cohort is typically larger than the one before it, the number of young men and women entering their reproductive years will also grow. Figure 10.5 projects into the future the consequences of the Global South's now proportionately larger fertile age groups and shows why the demographic momentum already in place will produce quite different population profiles in the developed and the developing worlds.

The momentum set in motion by prior population growth explains why world population will continue to grow for many decades into the future. If replacement-level fertility is reached worldwide around the year 2050, it would still not lead to a steady-state population for at least a century. By this time world

FIGURE 10.5

Population Pyramids for the Global North and South, 1995 and 2050

As the population of the Global South ages, those comprising today's large cohorts will contribute to future population growth, as will the even larger number of childbearing children they leave behind. Increased longevity will also add to the Global North's population momentum, but the magnitudes will be comparatively inconsequential because the number in each age group has not expanded in recent years.

SOURCE: Adapted from United Nations (1994a), 25, 73.

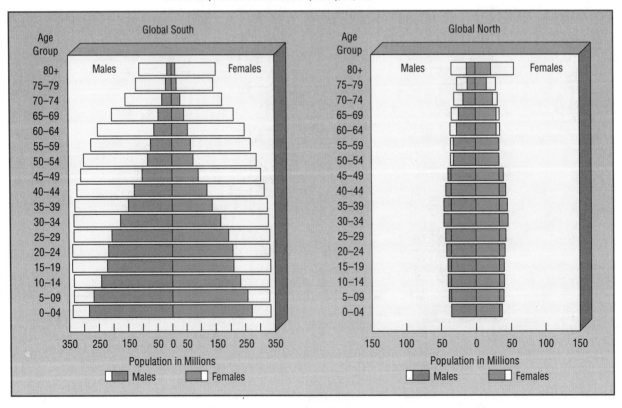

population will have grown to more than 11 billion people. If replacement-level fertility is not reached by this time, or if fertility rates stabilize somewhat above the replacement level, the world's ultimate population will be even larger. The reverse is also true, meaning that a world population well below 11 billion is possible if somehow fertility rates stabilize below 2.1, slowing the impact of population momentum more rapidly (see Figure 10.1). The obvious question, then, is how to reduce current fertility levels to the replacement level—or less. The demographic transition, which describes population changes over time nearly everywhere in the world, suggests some answers.

The Demographic Transition Paradigm

The **demographic transition** describes the change that Europe and later North America experienced between 1750 and 1930, when a condition of high birth rates combined with high death rates was replaced by low birth rates and low death rates. The transition started when death rates began to fall— presumably due to economic growth, rising living standards, and improved disease control. Although the potential for substantial population growth was high, birth rates soon began to decline as well. During this phase of the demographic transition, population growth slowed. In fact, growth rates rarely exceeded 1.5 percent per year (U.S. Department of State 1978, 52).

The demographic transition is now underway virtually everywhere in the world (Lutz 1994). The experience of the Global South, however, differs from that of Europe and North America. Death rates declined precipitously following World War II rather than mirroring the slow, long-term declines of the Global North, largely as a result of more effective "death-control" measures introduced by the outside world. A population explosion inevitably followed, as illustrated by the experience of the Indian Ocean island of Mauritius (see Figure 10.6).

There are two ways to explain the changes in birth and death rates that occur with the demographic transition. One argument says that the decline in death rates itself stimulates a decline in birth rates. This implies that societies eventually reach an "equilibrium" in their mortality and fertility rates.

> When death rates fall because of advances in medicine and better living conditions, the equilibrium is disturbed. The population grows unless birth rates adjust to the new mortality conditions and also decline. The fact that it may take many years after mortality falls for fertility to fall is explained as a perception lag—that is, the time it takes couples to realize that more of their children will live to adulthood, and therefore, to feel secure that they can have fewer births and still achieve their desired number of surviving children. (Lutz 1994, 8)

A second explanation of the demographic transition holds that "modernization" produces declines in both mortality and fertility. According to this argument, birth rates decline because economic growth alters people's preferred family size. In traditional societies children are economic bonuses; as modernization proceeds, they become economic burdens, inhibiting social mobility and capital accumulation. The move from large to small families, with the associated decline in fertility, is therefore usually exhibited when modernization takes place. Eventually birth and death rates both reach very low levels. With fertility rates near the replacement level, low population growth (or none at all) follows.

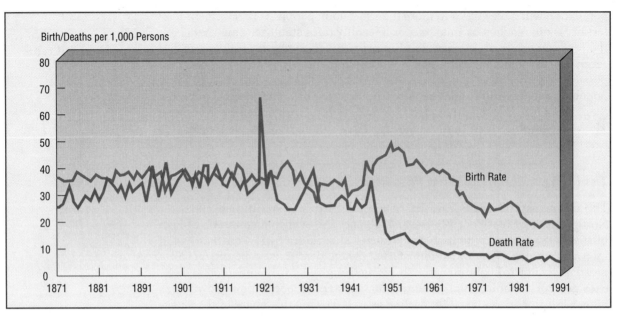

FIGURE 10.6

The Demographic Transition: Birth and Death Rates in Mauritius, 1871–1991

Death rates on the Indian Ocean island of Mauritius declined abruptly after World War II following the eradication of malaria and the introduction of modern medical technology. Rapid population growth followed, as birth rates remained high. The fertility transition occurred much later, when the average number of children born to each woman declined from six to less than three, slowing Mauritius's growth rate.

SOURCE: Lutz (1994), 9.

The "equilibrium" and "modernization" explanations of demographic transitions are not mutually exclusive. They may in fact be at work simultaneously in much of the Global South, where declines in death and birth rates have often occurred in tandem (Lutz 1994). Mauritius is again instructive: The halving of its fertility rate in a single decade occurred "on a strictly voluntary basis—the result of high levels of literacy and education for women—together with successful family-planning programs" (Lutz 1994). Both arguments, then, contain the seeds of population policies that may help push the world fertility rate farther along the path toward the replacement level.

The demographic transition paradigm, in both its equilibrium and modernization variants, assumes that replacement is the endpoint at which fertility levels will ultimately rest. The high and low population projections in Figure 10.1 suggest the consequences of stabilization either above or below replacement—and some current evidence supports both possibilities.

The demographic transition embraces four phases: (1) high birth rate, high death rate; (2) high birth rate, falling death rate; (3) declining birth rate, relatively low death rate; (4) low birth rate, low death rate. Yet in such widely different places as Costa Rica in Central American, Tunisia in North Africa, and Sri Lanka in South Asia, some countries are seemingly stuck somewhere between the second and third stages of the transition: Death rates have fallen to very low levels, but fertility rates seem to have stabilized well above the replacement level. Does the reason lie in social attitudes toward family size remaining unchanged by modernization, unlike Europe and North America? Or, unlike Mauritius, is it caused by inadequate education and family-planning programs? In both cases, women's role in society may be critical, a point to which we will return.

A second puzzle that conventional theories of demographic transitions do not comprehend is the possibility of a fifth phase: declining birth rates even in the face of low death rates. Western Europe's fertility rate has not stabilized at the replacement level, as the demographic transition paradigm predicts, but instead has fallen steadily over the past two decades and now stands at 1.5 (*1995 World Population Data Sheet*). As a result, a secular decline of the continent's population is now in motion, which eventually will lead to a Europe with markedly fewer people than today. A "birthless Germany," for example, faces the prospect of having 15 million fewer people by the year 2030—and a simultaneous dramatic increase in the number of people over sixty (Walker 1995b, 13; see also Heilig, Büttner, and Lutz 1990). Declining fertility rates in western Europe are not easily explained, but they do lead to intense policy disputes, as many believe the region is committing "demographic suicide."

Eastern Europe and Russia have also experienced sharp fertility-rate declines since the end of the Cold War, but here they have been accompanied by rising mortality as well—especially among males (*World Economic and Social Survey 1995* 1995). Russia faces nothing short of a population "implosion." The fertility rate, which averaged just over the replacement level a few years ago, has fallen to only 1.4 (see Table 10.1), and life expectancy among adult men has plummeted to only sixty years—even less in some areas. "The reasons [for these dramatic changes] are varied. An epidemic of alcohol abuse is at least partly to blame, as is severe environmental pollution. And part of the grim picture can be attributed to new birth and death statistics that for the first time in decades actually reflect the bleak reality of life [in Russia]" (Specter 1994).

Now free to leave, many in eastern Europe and the former Soviet Union have opted to migrate elsewhere—often to western Europe, adding another critical variable to the demography of world politics.

Migration

Fertility, mortality, and *migration* are the three basic demographic variables that determine all population changes. Migration figures less importantly in long-range population projections, but its immediate political importance was demonstrated dramatically in the massive migration of Germans from East to West in 1989, in what became a precursor to the fall of the Berlin Wall. Whether migration from one side of the "Iron Curtain" to the other precipitated its final collapse may never be known for sure. However, the dissatisfaction with their political and economic fate that so many thousands demonstrated could not be ignored by the political leaders in the former socialist states.

Transnational migration now affects countries throughout Europe, the Middle East, North America, and elsewhere. Britain and France, for example, continue to receive large numbers of immigrants from their former colonies, while Israel has absorbed a flood of migrants, particularly from Russia. The Middle Eastern oil producers also have received large numbers of migrants in recent years. And the United States, historically a refuge from religious and political persecution and a vision of economic opportunity, continues to provide a home for millions from throughout the world. The 1980s in fact witnessed the largest immigration into the United States since early in the twentieth century. But there was an important difference: In the early part of the century nearly all of the immigrants came from Europe; in the 1980s 80 percent came from Asia and Latin America, stimulated in part by the end of the Vietnam War and political turmoil and civil strife in Cuba, El Salvador, Guatemala, Haiti, and Nicaragua.

• • •

THE GLOBALIZATION OF POPULATION DYNAMICS AND TRENDS

Immigration is now the principal cause of U.S. population growth. There, as in other host countries, the influx of immigrants largely originating in the Global South promises to transform its society. Thus the consequences of a burgeoning world population cannot be confined to the Global South, although most effects are now felt there and will continue to be felt most strongly there. In an interdependent and rapidly globalizing world, the economic, environmental, political, and social consequences of a world population that promises to grow by more than half in the next half-century will be widely shared.

The Causes and Consequences of Migration

Migrants are of two types: refugees and those in search of economic opportunity. **Refugees** are individuals who—because of a well-founded fear of being persecuted on the basis of race, religion, nationality, membership in a particular social group, or political opinions—live outside the country of their origin or nationality and are unable to return to it. According to the United Nations High Commissioner for Refugees, their numbers have swelled from 3 million in the 1970s to a record high of 27 million in 1995.

The number of *legal migrants* is more difficult to determine but is believed to be in excess of 100 million, while the number of *illegal immigrants* is probably around 10 million (Kane 1995a, 9; see also *The State of the World Population 1993* 1993). Thus "about 125 million people live outside the countries where they were born—it is as if the entire population of Japan had packed up and left" (Kane, 1995a). In addition to these people are nearly 30 million "displaced persons"—those involuntarily uprooted from their homes but still living in their own countries.

In Search of Freedom. Refugees and displaced persons alike are often the victims of war. The Persian Gulf War, for example, created a refugee population of 5 million (United Nations 1994a, 111). The war in Afghanistan caused a peak flight of 6.3 million people, and civil conflict and genocide in Rwanda left more than 2 million still classified as refugees in late 1994 (Kane 1995a, 22–24). The persecution, ethnic cleansing, and armed conflict that accompanied the breakup of the former Yugoslavia uprooted nearly 3 million victims, moving Europe to the list of continents with large numbers of refugees for the first time since World War II—a specter that many who remember the horrors of that war hoped would never reappear (see also *World Refugee Survey 1995*, 1995).

War—particularly communal rivalries and ethnic conflicts, which account for a large proportion of the world's refugees and displaced people (Gurr

1994)—may be the force that propels some to make the difficult decision to flee their own homelands. If we understood the causes of war (a topic we explore in detail in Chapter 12) we could better understand the underlying roots of what many now see as a global migration crisis (see, e.g., Weiner 1995).

Human rights abuses must figure prominently in any assessment of why millions of people make the difficult decision to leave. "Refugees know that they cannot expect, at home, the protection of the police, access to a fair trial, redress of grievances through the courts, prosecution of those who violate their rights, or public assistance in the face of disaster. . . . Forcing people to flee is a violation of the human right to remain peacefully in one's home. The direct denial of other basic rights, including the rights of civilians not to be targeted in military actions, often provides the immediate impetus for flight" (Newland 1994).

Demographic variables and their correlates are a closely related logic that applies to migrants in search of economic opportunity as well as refugees.

> In virtually every instance of conflict or poverty today, factors like unmanageable population growth, unsustainable development, even disease and illiteracy have fermented over time in a volatile cocktail of insecurity. It is this combination of factors that ultimately brings people to the sometimes hopeful, but often desperate, hour of departure. . . .
>
> It is significant that countries with stable populations and high levels of education and public health demonstrate a resilience against war and overt persecution and rarely experience refugee and migrant outflows. Many countries ravaged by high infant mortality, low literacy, eroding farmland, and hunger, on the other hand, are highly susceptible to the despots, the politically motivated bigotry, and the extremist politics that eventually force people out, and in fact they have recently seen people leave at record rates. (Kane, 1995a, 6, 10; see also Homer-Dixon 1994; Kaplan 1994)

In search of safety and freedom, more than 200,000 refugees flooded into Tanzania after civil war erupted in Rwanda in April 1994. Sparked by the death of the country's president in a suspicious plane crash, ethnic conflicts between the Hutu majority and Tutsi minority led to genocide as well as mass migration before the year was out.

In Search of Opportunity. Legal migrants—particularly young people in the Global South without productive employment—are among those leaving at record rates. Germany and the United States are favored host (receiving) states, but nearly all of the states in western Europe and now Japan have experienced a rising tide of migrants in recent years (see UNDP 1994, 104–9). Migration also occurs within the Global South. In fact, the bulk of today's migrants in search of opportunity move from one developing country to another (Weiner 1995). But everywhere the pattern is the same: People leave poorer states in search of higher-paying jobs in richer states.

Migrants traveling to faraway lands often take jobs shunned by local inhabitants. Typically this means they earn less than the native people but more than they would earn in their homelands, even when performing the same tasks. Host countries sometimes welcome migrants (as Europe did during the 1970s' "guest worker" era) not only because they accept low wages for undesirable jobs, but also because in many places the host pays little if anything for migrants' health, education, and welfare needs. On the other hand, the home (sending) countries sometimes encourage people to emigrate as a way of reducing unemployment or dealing with other problems (as in the case of Cuban emigration to the United States). Often, however, many of those who leave their home states are the best educated and most talented, causing a serious "brain drain" rarely if ever reversed.

Migrants typically send considerable portions of their income to their families at home. "By the end of the eighties, remittances [money sent home] amounted to more than $65 billion a year according to a World Bank study, second only to crude oil in their value to the world's economy, and larger than all official development assistance. Almost half of this money went to developing countries" (Kane 1995a, 34). Interestingly, the Persian Gulf War caused some 2.5 million immigrant workers (and their dependents) to flee Iran, Iraq, and Kuwait, causing a hardship on other governments (principally Egypt, Jordan, and Yemen) when remittances from their nationals working abroad dried up and the workers required repatriation (United Nations 1994b, 107).

Backlash: Migrants under Nationalist Fire. Although receiving countries can benefit from migration (see, e.g., Passel and Fix 1994), the influx of foreigners has become a matter of growing controversy everywhere.

> In many countries, citizens have become fearful that they are now being invaded not by armies and tanks but by migrants who speak other languages, worship other gods, belong to other cultures, and, they fear, will take their jobs, occupy their land, live off the welfare system, and threaten their way of life, their environment, and even their polity. . . . Virtually every country in western Europe now has a right-wing antiforeign political party or movement. . . .
>
> The sense of crisis is not confined to advanced industrial societies. . . . In portions of Pakistan, India, Bangladesh, Thailand, Mauritania, Senegal, Congo, Nigeria, and Libya, local citizens or their governments have turned against foreigners. (Weiner 1995, 2–3)

With xenophobia (fear of foreigners) on the rise, many among the growing number of refugees seeking asylum are finding the doors to safe havens closing. Security concerns stimulated by terrorist fears are sometimes at work—as in the United States, where many believe the New York World Trade Center bombing would not have occurred had immigration controls been tighter. More often, asylum seekers in the United States and elsewhere "are seen as migrants looking for better economic conditions rather than as refugees with a well-founded fear of being persecuted" (United Nations 1994b). Those seeking political refuge in the United States also have suffered "guilt by association," as a wave of illegal immigrants has contributed to the rising tide of anti-immigrant sentiments in a nation born of immigrants (see Clad 1994; Passel and Fix 1994). Thus thousands of refugees from Haiti and Cuba, who earlier would have found safe haven in the United States, have been repatriated to their homelands or otherwise denied a chance to apply for asylum in the United States.

The end of the Cold War contributed to the increasingly restrictive practices. Once the United States willingly accepted those seeking to escape communist rule as a way of scoring points in the Cold War contest, but no longer (see Kirschten 1994). Pakistan also has shut its door to the surge of refugees from the long, bloody civil war between pro- and anti-Marxist forces in Afghanistan, and many Southeast Asian states have become less hospitable to Vietnamese asylum seekers, forcing many to return to a homeland they once rejected. Meanwhile, Germany has altered its constitution to make granting asylum more restrictive; and the United States has begun to reduce the annual number of new arrivals and to assail the family-based criteria long used to open America's doors to others.

A combination of *push* and *pull* factors has propelled migration to the forefront of the globalization of population dynamics. Human rights violations, environmental degradation, international war, and intranational ethnopolitical conflict—all in some sense related to the Global South's rapidly expanding population—*push* millions beyond their homelands. They also are *pulled* abroad by the promise of political freedom and economic opportunity elsewhere, particularly in the Global North. Indeed, "the growing demand for immigration to the North from the South is related to the 'shrinking' of the world (through revolutions in communication and transport), reduction in economic obstacles to labor movements (despite the increase in political barriers), and the growing reach and absorptive power of international capitalism (even as economic politics in the North has turned more inward-looking and nationalistic)" (Sen 1994). Population growth may encourage outward migration, but "to try to explain the increase in immigration pressure by the growth rate of total population in the [Global South] is to close one's eyes to the deep changes that have occurred—and are occurring—in the world in which we live, and the rapid internationalization of its cultures and economies that accompanies those changes." Nonetheless, to many Northern societies, immigration has become *the population problem*, and shutting the door is increasingly viewed as a solution.

Migration is the primary dimension through which the globalization of population dynamics occurs, but it also will be felt in other ways, including national security considerations, social and economic stresses on development, food production and distribution, and environmental degradation.

The Demography of National Security

Rapid population growth in the Global South promises to make the countries of the developed world a declining fraction of world population, portending potentially troublesome security concerns.

The southern European states of Spain, Portugal, France, Italy, and Greece, whose combined populations, it is estimated, will increase by a mere 4.5 million between 1990 and 2025, lie close to North African countries—Morocco, Algeria, Tunisia, Libya, Egypt—whose populations are expected to grow by 107 million in the same period. The population of the United States is expected to rise by 29 percent by 2025, while its southern neighbors, Mexico and Guatemala, may grow by 63 percent and 135 percent, respectively. (Connelly and Kennedy 1994, 76)

Meanwhile, Canada, a member of the elite Group of Seven—the world's preeminent economic powers—before long will have a population smaller than Ghana, Nepal, and Saudi Arabia (*1995 World Population Data Sheet*).

Realists argue that a country's population size is an important source of political power. The shrinking of the world's larger and more economically prosperous states may thus be a concern, especially as low fertility rates and aging populations in the Global North make it difficult to maintain large armies. In contrast, the abundant youth in developing societies will provide ample supplies of soldiers.

Ironically, the result of economic progress in the Global South over the next several decades may also result in an accelerated shift of economic and political balances of power toward those experiencing rapid population growth. For some, in fact, power is already perceived to be shifting toward those most prone to reject the North's values and challenge its interests. This is particularly so when demographic changes are coupled with rapid economic growth in the Newly Industrialized Economies and elsewhere in the Global South. "Simple arithmetic demonstrates Western folly," a deputy secretary in Singapore's Foreign Ministry has written. "The West has 800 million people; the rest make up almost 4.7 billion. . . . No Western society would accept a situation where 15 percent of its population legislated for the remaining 85 percent" (cited in Connelly and Kennedy 1994).

Varying fertility rates among various ethnic populations will also have internal and international consequences. In Israel, for example, the Jewish population may one day become the minority, as fertility rates among Arabs and Palestinians within Israel's borders outstrip those of Israeli Jews. Similar trends are evident in South Africa, where the white population is already outnumbered and is expected by the year 2020 to comprise only about 10 percent of the total population, compared with the one-fifth it accounted for in the early 1950s (Eberstadt 1991).

The role of demographic changes within societies in stimulating domestic strife and external political conflict is difficult to determine but imprudent to ignore. Lebanon—wracked by violent civil conflict and foreign military intervention for nearly fifteen years beginning in the mid-1970s—is a case in point. There competing Muslim religious sects enjoyed more rapid population growth than the Christian population, upsetting a delicately balanced, if rigid, political structure which proved incapable of adjusting the sectarian tensions. This led not only to death and destruction but also to the exodus of more than one-third of the Lebanese population (Kane 1995a). In South Africa, on the other hand, the black-majority government has an opportunity to prove that flexible policies pursued by democratic political systems may accommodate political demands deeply rooted in ethnic and demographic differences. Time will tell.

AIDS poses a wholly different security issue. Beyond its social and economic costs, foreign and defense policy analysts worry about the political and military implications of the spreading disease. In parts of Thailand one-fifth of twenty-one-year-old military recruits are now infected—and this in a country where AIDS was virtually unknown in 1987 (*World Health Report 1995* 1995, 29). Understandably, then, defense experts fear a gradual weakening of national defense readiness as HIV/AIDS spreads among military personnel. Ensuring the safety of blood supplies for the military, especially in countries with inadequate medical equipment, is a related concern. More broadly, the U.S. State Department has expressed concern about the long-term political stability of countries where the incidence of AIDS is high. It warns that some political leaders may fall because of the disease's impact, leading to power struggles, and that ministerial-level bureaucrats may themselves become HIV-infected (Hamilton 1994).

The Demography of Development, Food Security, and Environmental Preservation

The impact of population growth on economic development, food security, and environmental quality has long been in dispute—and remains so. Two broadly defined groups of analysts approach these issues quite differently. Taking their name and orientation from Thomas Malthus and his classic *Essay on the Principle of Population* (1798), **neo-Malthusians** believe that world population is pushing against the earth's resources, straining its ability to meet the needs of this generation and the next. Neo-Malthusians—many of whom are human ecologists sometimes called "growth pessimists"—routinely point to a host of uncomfortable facts about the present global condition: "Since Malthus wrote, the human population has grown by a factor of six, and total human energy use by a factor of one hundred or so. . . . The forest cover of the earth has been cut by a third and the area of undisturbed wetlands by half. The composition of the atmosphere has been altered by human-generated pollution. Hundreds of millions of people have starved to death; thousands of species have gone extinct" (Meadows 1993).

In contrast with the pessimism of neo-Malthusians, **cornucopians**—many of whom are economists and otherwise known as "growth optimists"—emphasize quite different global trends:

- Global life expectance more than doubled this century from thirty to sixty-four years, while global infant mortality fell from 170 infant deaths per 1,000 births in 1950 to just 60 in 1990. Rapid population growth has occurred not because human beings suddenly started breeding like rabbits but because they finally stopped dropping like flies.

- Despite a tripling of the world's population in this century, global health and productivity have exploded. Today human beings eat better, produce more, and consume more than ever. . . .

- "Overpopulation" is a problem that has been misidentified and misdefined. The term has no scientific definition or clear meaning. The problems typically associated with overpopulation (hungry families, squalid and overcrowded living conditions) are more properly understood as issues of poverty. . . .

- Although some blame dwindling natural resources for the reversals and catastrophes that have recently befallen heavily populated low-income countries, such episodes are directly traceable to the policies or practices of presiding governments. (Eberstadt 1995, 8)[3]

Compelling as the neo-Malthusian and cornucopian perspectives may be, the range of opinion and conviction separating them is less clear than the labels themselves suggest (Meadows 1993). Furthermore, determining which perspective is "right" is difficult, as history does not provide a clear answer. We saw in Chapter 5, for example, that the absolute gap in income between North and South continues but the gap in human development between rich and poor countries has narrowed. Moreover, the relative economic position of many countries within the Global South has improved with time, as their gross economic products have grown more rapidly than their populations, but the total number of people living in absolute poverty continues to grow. Even in Sub-Saharan Africa—which in the last decade has experienced sharp declines in economic growth coupled with the world's most rapid population growth—it is too facile to attribute the former to the latter. Instead, a host of economic and political factors provide a more complete explanation of African ills. These include "the subversion of democracy and the rise of combative military rulers, often encouraged by the cold war (with Africa providing client states—from Somalia and Ethiopia to Angola and Zaire—for the superpowers, particularly from the 1960s onward)." More generally, "Sub-Saharan Africa lags behind other developing regions in economic security, in health care, in life expectancy, in basic education, and in political and economic stability. It should be no great surprise that it lags behind in family planning as well. To dissociate the task of population control from the politics and economics of Africa would be a great mistake and would seriously mislead public policy" (Sen 1994).

What applies in Africa applies elsewhere: Population alone is not the cause of current ills; instead, it is an accomplice that aggravates other problems, including ill-advised government policies, political instability, unsustainable resource consumption, and inadequate technology. We can better appreciate these interactions by examining how the globalization of demographic trends and population dynamics affects economic development, food security, and environmental preservation.

The Demography of Development. Dependent children (those younger than fifteen) in the Global South typically make up about 35 percent of the total population (compared with 20 percent in the developed world) (United Nations 1995, 460, 462). This means there are fewer than two working-age adults for each child under fifteen in developing countries compared with more than three in the Global North. Such a large proportion of dependent children burdens public services, particularly the educational system. It also encourages the immediate consumption of economic resources rather than their reinvestment in social infrastructure to promote future economic growth.

---

[3]Classic neo-Malthusian statements include Paul Ehrlich's (1968) *The Population Bomb*, William and Paul Paddock's *Famine—1975!* (1967), the Club of Rome's *The Limits to Growth* (Meadows et al. 1974), and the 1980 U.S. government's *The Global 2000 Report to the President*, issued by the Carter administration. Important cornucopian rejoinders include Julian L. Simon's *The Ultimate Resource* (1981) and Simon and Herman Kahn's *The Resourceful Earth: A Response to Global 2000* (1984). Examples of the continuing debate between neo-Malthusians and cornucopians include Abernethy (1994); Brown and Kane (1994); Brown et al. (1995, 1996); J. Cohen (1995); Connelly and Kennedy (1994); Gore (1993); Hardin (1993); Kennedy (1993); and the essays in Bailey (1995).

As the children mature, the demands for new jobs, housing, and other human needs multiply. However, the resources to meet them are typically scarce and inadequate. On a global scale, as many as 1.3 billion people will be added to the work force in the Global South between 1995 and 2020 (*The State of the World Population 1994* 1994, 2). In places like Mexico this means that 1 million new jobs must be created every year to absorb the wave of young people entering the labor market. Failure to do so worries political leaders not only in Mexico but also elsewhere, notably the United States. As one Mexican leader warned, "The consequences of not creating [at least] 15 million jobs in the next fifteen years are unthinkable. The youths who do not find them will have only three options: the United States, the streets, and revolution" (cited in Moffett 1994; see also Marshall 1995).

The search for employment propels internal as well as international migration, contributing to the rapid urbanization occurring throughout the world, but especially in the Global South. By the turn of the century half of the world's 6 billion people will live in cities, three-fourths of them in the developing countries. "Another billion—or the equivalent of about sixty more cities the size of New York—will be added by the year 2025. New York itself, the [world's largest] city in 1950, may not even make the list by 2025, as it is overtaken by swelling [Global South] capitals like Jakarta and Manila" (Moffett 1994, 30).

New York, London, and Shanghai were the only cities with populations of 10 million or more in 1950. By the mid-1990s the number had grown to fifteen—eleven of them in the Global South—with even larger "megacities" and "supercities" on the horizon. Lagos, Nigeria, an "urban agglomeration" (in UN parlance) of 9.7 million in 1994, will increase to more than 24 million by 2015; São Paulo, Brazil, with 16 million will grow to 21 million; and Bombay, India, will increase its rank from the world's sixth largest urban agglomeration to the second (behind Tokyo) as it nearly doubles in size to 27.4 million between 1994 and 2015 (United Nations Population Division wall chart *Urban Agglomerations 1994*). Increasingly, the fate of these and other exploding cities in the Global South will determine the fate of nations and whole regions (Linden 1996).

The growth of urban areas in itself is not necessarily bad, but the speed of today's urbanization often is, as it overwhelms the capacity of local governments to keep pace with the multiple demands that accompany urban growth. "It took London 130 years to climb from 1 to 8 million residents. Mexico City covered the same distance in just thirty years, between 1940 and 1970. Sixteen years later the city's population had doubled to 16 million" (Moffett 1994, 31). Thus in Mexico City and elsewhere, rapid urbanization taxes severely the capacity for effective governance. Millions of urban dwellers live in crowded, cramped hovels in sprawling shantytowns and squatter settlements amid mounting garbage dumps, without adequate water or sanitation, without access to adequate health care or education and other social services, but in the constant shadow of pervasive crime and violence. And the environmental and health hazards multiply. Cars, for example, are proliferating more rapidly than people in many cities in the Global South and promise to add dramatically to the pollution of urban areas worldwide. So crushing are the burdens of urban life in many developing countries that one analyst described it as "a close approximation of hell on earth" (Cairncross 1994).

The untoward consequences of urbanization are not confined to city dwellers. Urbanization increases pressures on local agricultural systems as well, because there are fewer hands in the countryside to feed the growing

Rapid development in previously underdeveloped countries has led to untold problems. In the Philippines, for instance, a steady rise in population has forced a migration from the countryside to cities. There citizens have become resigned to menial jobs such as sifting trash at the Smokey Mountain dump, which overlooks the capital city of Manila.

number of mouths in the city. Furthermore, food prices in urban areas are often purposely depressed by governing elites. This has the dual effect of diminishing farmers' incentives to produce while also encouraging them to abandon their lands in search of a better future in the city. Pressures to import food follow. By 2030 only ten Global South countries (India, Bangladesh, Indonesia, Iran, Pakistan, Egypt, Ethiopia and Eritrea, Nigeria, Brazil, and Mexico) are expected to require some 190 million tons of imported grains—an amount equal to nearly all of world grain exports in 1994 (Brown 1995, 115). All ten have rapidly growing urban agglomerations which in many cases will be three or four times as large in 2030 as now.

As fertility rates in the Global South decline, the number of children under fifteen will also steadily decline. If the experience of Europe, North America, and especially Japan is a guide, this should lead to economic gains (Woods 1989). Ironically, however, the demographic life cycle also portends that the countries now most burdened by a rapid population growth among young people also will be those with an increasing number of older dependents, as today's youth grow to maturity and old age fifty years hence. During the next half-century, the population pyramid for developing regions shown in Figure 10.5 will begin to turn upside down due to declining birth rates and increased longevity. This will tip the "dependency ratio"—those no longer economically productive and thus dependent on others in the work force—away from younger people toward the elderly. Urbanization will further increase the social burdens of the world's growing number of elderly people by breaking down the extended families that in traditional societies provide social security for older people. The experience of the Global North demonstrates that there is a distinct disadvantage to this long-term demographic change, as demands for social services, particularly expensive health care, will multiply, burdening the Global South in yet another way (see Focus 10.1).

The "Graying" of Nations

Every month, the present world total of 360 million persons aged 65 and over increases by 800,000. Three decades from now, the world's elderly are projected to number 850 million. This unprecedented growth of the older population has already changed the social and political landscape in industrialized nations, and will increasingly bear upon policies and programmes throughout the developing world. Although issues of health care policy and reform vary enormously among and within continents, most national decisions in the health arena are already—or soon will be—affected by the momentum of population aging.

. . . A majority of today's growth in the numbers of elderly is occurring in the developing countries. The speed of aging is likewise more rapid there than in the industrialized world; while it took 115 years for the proportion of elderly to rise from 7% to 14% in France, the same change in China will occur in fewer than 30 years. The high fertility rates that prevailed in most developing countries from 1950 until at least the early 1970s ensure that the ranks of the elderly will continue to swell during the next four decades.

Related to the demographic transition is the epidemiological transition. This concept refers to a long-term change in major causes of death, from infectious and acute diseases on the one hand to chronic and degenerative diseases on the other. We know that the average individual's risk of becoming disabled rises with age. As entire populations age, the societal prevalence of disability is also likely to increase. And as we live to higher and higher ages, the debate is brewing: does longer life translate into healthier life, or are individuals spending a greater portion of their later years with disabilities, mental disorders, and disease?

. . . Because the oldest consume disproportionate amounts of health care and long-term services, provision of those services will become more costly. Many health systems today are being economically squeezed by the competing desires to keep pace with a growing elderly population and to expand basic coverage to all segments of society. Countries throughout the world are looking beyond their borders for clues about restructuring their health systems, avoiding primary reliance on institutional care, and promoting family care and home care for their aging populations.

SOURCE: Kinsella (1994), 6.

The aging population in the Global North is especially striking in Japan, where the demographic transition began later than elsewhere but was completed more rapidly. While Sweden today is the "oldest" nation, with nearly one-fifth of its citizens sixty-five or older (Kinsella 1994, 6), Japan is the most rapidly aging, with the highest life expectancy in the world. Elderly persons are expected to comprise one-fourth of Japan's population by 2025 (Martin 1989, 7). Already most Japanese workers are over forty.

As Japan continues to age, it will confront troublesome questions about its ability to continue the vigorous economic productivity and high domestic savings rates that have stimulated the projection of its economic power abroad. The Japanese term "child shock" dramatizes the growing crisis forecast by the decline in workers and growth in pensioners. The Japanese government and private-sector groups have joined forces to promote pronatalist attitudes among the Japanese people to raise fertility rates. However, unlike similar efforts undertaken during the 1930s (when war between Japan and the United States loomed on the horizon), the response to these contemporary efforts to stimulate birth rates has been unenthusiastic.

Providing for the increasing number of dependent elderly people relative to the number of productive workers is also a political concern elsewhere in the

Global North. In western Europe the wisdom of pursuing pronatalist policies to reverse the projected decline in its overall population has been intensely debated. Much of the dialogue has turned on questions of individual versus collective welfare. Advocates of pronatalist measures are concerned with the "continued vitality of national populations that do not replace themselves: No children, no future, is the key phrase" (van de Kaa 1987). National pride, concern for the country's place among the world powers, and the prominence of European culture in a world where non-European countries grow much faster also propel pronatalists.

Opponents of pronatalist measures, on the other hand, "dismiss as exaggerated the specter of Europe as a decrepit society of ruminating octogenarians." They "attach no special value to their own cultures" and oppose stimulating population growth in a world where overpopulation is already a serious problem. They believe that "economic resources rather than military resources or population size determine a country's international standing" and that "economic integration is a much more effective way to maintain Europe's international position than stimulating the birth rate." Finally, they question whether it makes sense to stimulate births when Europe already suffers from chronic high unemployment. "With modern technology eliminating jobs, workers are encouraged to work shorter hours, part-time, or retire early, and immigration is halted," the argument continues, "so why should we have more people?" (van de Kaa 1987).

The Demography of Global Food Security. The gloomiest of Thomas Malthus's predictions made two centuries ago is that the world's population will eventually outstrip its capacity to produce enough food to sustain its growing numbers. Malthus based his prognosis on what he regarded as the simple mathematical fact that population grows exponentially while agricultural output grows only arithmetically. He did not foresee that agricultural output would also grow at an increasing rate due to technological innovations.

Increases in the world's food output have been especially remarkable since World War II, far outstripping the largest-ever expansion of world population. The greatest gains occurred as a result of the increased productivity of farmers in the Global North. However, the South also scored impressive results by expanding the acreage devoted to agriculture and, later, by introducing new high-yield strains of wheat and rice—what we now call the "Green Revolution." By the 1980s Indonesia, once a massive importer of food, had largely been removed from the import market; and India, once regarded as a permanent candidate for the international dole, had actually become a modest grain exporter.

Continued growth in world food production is uncertain, yet it is necessary if output is to keep pace with an expanding world population and improved living standards. A former secretary of the U.S. Department of Agriculture describes the challenge in dramatic terms: "In the next two to four generations, world agriculture will be called on to produce as much food as has been produced in the entire 12,000-year history of agriculture" (Freeman 1990, 16). Cornucopians—who point with pride to the continued growth of food production since the 1980s (see Figure 10.7)—confidently predict the challenge will be met, believing that technology will continue to improve agricultural productivity.

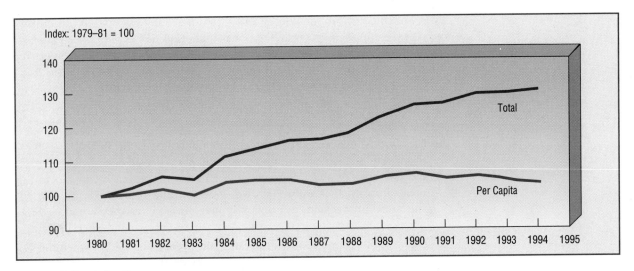

Index: 1979–81 = 100

FIGURE 10.7

Total and Per-Capita Food Production, 1980–1994

World food production has grown by nearly 30 percent since the early 1980s, but per-capita production has remained stagnant. The difference between the trends is largely explained by what is eaten up by population growth.

SOURCES: Adapted from *FAO Yearbook: Production 1990* (1991), 39–40, 49–50; *FAO Yearbook: Production 1994* (1995), 39, 49.

Cornucopians argue that continued advances can be expected as current resources are used more efficiently and high-yield farming practices continue to spread. A case in point is that China's and Vietnam's shedding of the communist agricultural regimen in favor of market-based systems has enabled both to score dramatic per-capita food production gains—ranging from 30 percent to more than 50 percent since the early 1980s—even in the face of rapidly rising populations (*FAO Yearbook: Production 1994* 1995, 49–50). Growth optimists also believe biotechnology contains the seeds of dramatic new breakthroughs now only dimly perceived; already it has produced impressive yields with promise not only for food production but also preservation of the environment and biodiversity. Among them are:

- Rice plants that resist the tungaro virus and thus will produce another 7 million tons of rice per year.

- Wheat plants with the strongest resistance yet to the pervasive rust diseases, one of the worst pests that attack wheat crops all over the world. . . .

- A genetically engineered copy of the natural pork growth hormone that produces hogs with half as much body fat, which means more healthful pork, and raised with one-fourth less feed grain. Think of pork growth hormone as the equivalent of producing millions of extra tons of feed corn from laboratory bacteria instead of ploughed-down wildlife habitat.

- Cloned and tissue-cultured Georgia yellow pine, planted in Brazil, which can produce sixteen times as much pulpwood per hectare per year as a Swedish natural forest. Each acre of the high-yielding trees can protect fifteen wild acres from being logged. . . . (Avery 1995, 67–68)

303

Neo-Malthusians are decidedly less sanguine. They worry that agricultural and other biological systems like ocean fisheries will be unable to sustain rising demand, jeopardizing realization of the goal of global **food security** (continued access by all people to enough food for an active, healthy life.[4] They point to several disturbing trends to illustrate their concern.

- Although food production has increased steadily, per-capita production has generally stagnated (see Figure 10.7).

- The world's fish catch peaked at 100 million tons in 1989—a level believed to be near the maximum sustainable yield of ocean fisheries—and has since grown little, with most increased output attributed to aquaculture (fish farming) (Brown, Lenssen, and Kane 1995, 32–33). The world's rangelands are under similar pressure, as they are grazed beyond their capacity to regenerate themselves (Brown and Kane 1994).

- The world's carryover stocks of grain ("the amount in the bin when the new harvest begins"), which in effect provide the world with a food-security buffer during lean years, has dropped to levels not seen since the 1970s, when grain prices doubled in the face of a global food crisis (Brown et al. 1996, 8).

Neo-Malthusians point to other developments that suggest a less-than-rosy future, including the impact of rising affluence on global food supplies and the resources required to provide them. As wealth increases, people move up the "food ladder," shifting their preferences from beans and rice to steak and chicken, asparagus and apricots. The culinary preferences of more-affluent people also translate into proportionately higher demands on agricultural lands and water resources. Still, ascending the food ladder is the shape of things to come.

China's meat consumption is currently rising by 3 million tons (and 10 percent) per year. Chinese meat consumption has traditionally been very low, but rising per-capita incomes are putting more meat within the reach of many more consumers. Indians do not eat much meat because of their predominant Hindu religion, but the demand for dairy products is rising by 2 million tons per year. Indonesia is Islamic, so its residents do not eat pork, and it has no extensive grazing lands for beef, but poultry consumption is rising at double-digit rates. All told, Asia's diet upgrading is the biggest surge in farm resource demand the world has ever seen. . . . And each ton of added protein demand will require three to five added tons of grain and oilseed production to provide feed to produce the additional animal protein. (Avery 1995, 51–52)

Thus, even as world population growth begins to level off, pressures on world food systems will continue their forward momentum.

Can the world's food-producing systems sustain the growing demand stimulated by population growth and rising affluence? Lester Brown, a prominent

---

[4]Food insecurity, on the other hand, is "the lack of access to sufficient food," and can be either chronic or transitory. "Chronic food insecurity is a continuously inadequate diet resulting from the lack of resources to produce or acquire food. Transitory food insecurity, on the other hand, is a temporary decline in a household's access to enough food. It results from instability in food production and prices, or in household incomes. The worst form of transitory food insecurity is famine" (Reutlinger, 1985).

neo-Malthusian and his associates at the Worldwatch Institute, warn that the earth's carrying capacity is limited and that its limits are rapidly approaching (see, e.g., Brown et al. 1996; Postel 1994). They argue that diminishing returns from fertilizer applications combined with soil erosion, growing water scarcity, and other environmental stresses already undermine the ability of national agricultural systems to provide for a growing world population.

China—which accounts for more than one-fifth of humanity—is especially worrisome. Drawing on the experience of Japan, South Korea, and Taiwan, Brown (1995) argues that the transformation of China from an agricultural to an industrial society will cause its food consumption to quickly outrace production. Increasingly, then, China will have to turn to the world marketplace to feed its billion-plus residents. Evidence is seen in China's food imports from the United States, which tripled in 1995, contributing to record U.S. agricultural exports in excess of $50 million. American farmers doubtless profited, but in a tightly integrated world market based on free-trade logic, prices everywhere can be expected to rise sharply as demand exceeds supply. Who feeds China may thus determine who goes hungry.

Africa's experience already seems to vindicate neo-Malthusians' pessimism. The continent's food production increased by less than 2 percent annually during the 1970s, but its population grew by nearly 3 percent. Starvation and death became daily occurrences in broad stretches of the Sahel, ranging from Ethiopia in the east to Mauritania in the west. The situation was repeated a decade later when, in Ethiopia in particular, the world witnessed the tragic specter of tens of thousands suffering and dying from malnutrition and famine at a time of unprecedented food surpluses worldwide.

As population growth has moved in concert with environmental degradation, sub-Saharan Africa has experienced the tragedy of the commons in all of its most remorseless manifestations. Civil strife, ethnic bloodletting, and war have characterized post-colonial Africa, as conflicts affecting tens of millions of people have ravaged one-third or more of the countries in the region since the 1970s. In some cases, as in Ethiopia, Somalia, and the Sudan, food was actively used as a political weapon. The UN/U.S. humanitarian intervention in Somalia in 1992–1994 sought to curb these practices, but with limited success. Thus the words of Shun Chetty of the UN High Commission for Refugees retain their tragic pertinence: "He who controls roads controls food. He who controls food controls the people."

Growth optimists reject the Malthusian analogy as applied to Africa, particularly the prophecy that excessive population growth causes food deficits. War is not the *consequence* but the *cause* of famine, malnutrition, and starvation, cornucopians argue. "Famines come about when political systems fail to encourage agriculture and distribution successfully. And those political failures have a pattern: They occur in centralized, authoritarian systems. Free-market economics do not produce famines" (Avery 1995; see also Eberstadt 1995; Paarlberg 1994; Sen 1994). Asia's recent experience also seems to vindicate cornucopian logic. The continent's per-capita food production has outstripped all other world regions since the early 1980s, with China and Vietnam leading the pack as each moved toward market-based agricultural systems—and this despite dramatic population increases.

Still, millions go hungry each day. The World Resources Institute (1994, 108) estimates that at the beginning of the 1990s nearly 800 million people in Africa, Asia, Latin American, and the Middle East—representing 20 percent of humanity—suffered chronic undernutrition. Neo-Malthusians urge that, on moral grounds alone, population growth must be stemmed so that those who now suffer most can be relieved. In practice, however, the issue is not a lack of food but its maldistribution. According to the microeconomic principle known as Engel's law, poorer families typically spend a much higher percentage of their budget on food than do higher-income groups. Yet the ability to acquire more food depends on having the income necessary to buy it. "Most people who stop eating do so not because there is insufficient food grown in the world but because they no longer grow it themselves and do not have the money to buy it" (Barnet 1980). From this perspective, poverty—not overpopulation—is the cause of the food deficits so many countries and people experience. But what causes poverty? And what are its cures? Neo-Malthusians and cornucopians both speak to the ills, and both offer prescriptions for dealing with the disease. But who is right?

The Demography of Environmental Preservation. Neo-Malthusians stress environmental degradation in assessing the adverse consequences of population growth. Excessive consumption in the Global North also falls under their indictment. Unless both are curbed, they argue, "ecological overshoot"—exceeding the earth's carrying capacity—will surely follow.

Once again, growth optimists do not accept the pessimists' arguments or conclusions. Still, a kind of global consensus has converged around the wisdom of **sustainable development,** a concept which says that the present generation's needs must be met without compromising the ability of future generations to meet theirs. The concept will figure prominently in our analysis in Chapter 11, where we examine in greater detail how global environmental and resource trends affect world politics. Here we only anticipate that discussion by emphasizing that the links between population growth and environmental stress—like connections between population growth and economic development generally—are not easily unraveled. Population growth doubtless has adverse environmental consequences, but the relationship is not straightforward.

> Many other factors—government policies, the legal system, access to capital and technology, the efficiency of industrial production, inequity in the distribution of land and resources, poverty in the South, and conspicuous consumption in the North—may work separately or together to buffer or increase humankind's impact on the environment. The potential for reducing the effect of population growth depends largely on altering factors such as these that compound the environmental impact of human activity. (World Resources Institute 1994, 27–28)

Thus the environmental toll of population growth and rising affluence seemingly binds humanity in a common fate. Still, as the tragedy of the commons suggests, not everyone will share the costs equally. Herein lies what many describe as the "planetary predicament," as the costs of environmental stress affect the Global North and South quite differently.

Soil erosion, desertification, and deforestation are worldwide phenomena, but they are often most acute where population growth and poverty are most evident (see Postel 1994). The search for fuelwood is a major source of deforestation and a primary occupation in developing countries. Deforestation and soil erosion also occur when growing populations without access to farmland push cultivation into hillsides and tropical forests ill-suited to farming. In the Sahel area of Africa, growing populations of livestock as well as humans hastened the destruction of productive land, producing a desert which led to famine—a graphic illustration of the tragedy of the commons. Excessive population growth led to one of the most densely populated countries in the world. The practice of partitioning farmland among male heirs into ever-smaller parcels created pressure to expand productive land contributing to the vicious ethnic violence and genocide which erupted in 1993 (Kane 1995a).

Where population growth rates remain high a kind of "ecological transition" occurs, which is "almost the reverse of the demographic transition in that its end result is disastrous." "In the first stage, expanding human demands are well within the sustainable yield of the biological support system. In the second, they are in excess of the sustainable yield but still expanding as the biological resource itself is being consumed. And in the final stage, human consumption is forcibly reduced as the biological system collapses" (Brown et al. 1987).

Tragically, an ecological transition applies to much of the developing world. More than one-fourth of the land area of sub-Saharan Africa is "moderately to very severely desertified," and vast areas have "permanently" lost their agricultural potential (World Resources Institute 1990, 91). And the problem extends beyond Africa: Recent estimates put the amount of land affected by desertification at 1.2 billion hectacres—an area equivalent to the size of India and China combined. "That's about 17 percent of the planet's total land area, and the process appears to be accelerating" ("Environmental Intelligence" 1994, 7).

Logic suggests that excessive population growth produces excessive environmental stress. In fact, the consumption patterns associated with affluence are even more debilitating. "A typical resident of the industrialized . . . world uses fifteen times as much paper, ten times as much steel, and twelve times as much fuel as a [Global South] world resident" (Durning 1991, 161).

A consuming society is also a throwaway society. "The Japanese use 30 million 'disposable' single-roll cameras each year, and the British dump 2.5 billion diapers. Americans toss away 180 million razors annually, enough paper and plastic plates and cups to feed the world a picnic six times a year, and enough aluminum cans to make six thousand DC-10 airplanes" (Durning 1991, 161). Each American threw away an average of 1,460 pounds of garbage in 1988, and the amount is expected to grow to nearly 1,800 pounds per person by 2010 (Young 1991, 44). As the mountains of garbage grow, disposing of it has become increasingly difficult.

As noted, we will examine the environmental consequences of rising affluence and population growth in greater detail in Chapter 11. Still, as we anticipate that analysis, the evidence presented here is reason to pause for reflection: If people and wealth both cause environmental stress, what will the twenty-first century bring, as both population growth and rising affluence are already on the horizon?

• • •

POPULATION POLICIES: OPTIMISTS, PESSIMISTS, AND THE INTERNATIONAL RESPONSE

More than two decades have passed since the world community convened its first World Population Conference to address the world's growing population, then already concentrated in the Global South. Meeting in Bucharest in 1974, many delegates from the Global South concluded from Europe's and North America's demographic transitions that declining fertility rates flowed more or less automatically from economic growth. Thus they understandably prescribed policies that focused on economic development and not on the causes of population growth in their own societies. They called on the Global North for assistance in their economic development, reasoning that the population problem would then take care of itself. The slogan "development is the best contraceptive" reflected the prevailing view. Many in the Global North, on the other hand, advocated a more direct attack on what they saw as "the population problem"—namely, excessive population growth which erodes economic opportunities and imperils other values.

A decade later a second World Population Conference was held in Mexico City. By then a new consensus had converged around the critical importance of family planning. Curiously, the United States, previously a major advocate of this viewpoint, departed from this emerging global consensus. Reflecting the conservative political sentiments prevalent in Washington at the time, the U.S. delegation asserted that free market principles should take precedence over government intervention in economic and population matters. It also vigorously opposed abortion as an approach to family planning. China became the object of special ire, prompted by a television exposé of its family-planning practices, which included "human rights abuses . . . [ranging] from mandatory sterilization and abortion to forced insertions of IUDs, all committed in the name of slowing the country's runaway population growth" (Moffett 1994). The United States now withheld support for multilateral as well as bilateral efforts to assist family-planning programs in developing countries, which had the effect of slowing their spread throughout the Global South (Moffett 1994).

Although the views of the United States in 1984 clearly represented a minority perspective, they reflected growing dissatisfaction with earlier neo-Malthusian analyses of the global ecopolitical implications of population growth. Instead, the U.S. position in Mexico City reflected that of cornucopians, who argue that human ingenuity has developed resource-saving (or -substituting) innovations in response to shortages created by population growth, so that population growth is a stimulus, not a deterrent, to economic advancement.

The United States reversed its course following Bill Clinton's election in 1992. Restrictions that denied U.S. funds to some family-planning organizations because of abortion-related activities were lifted almost immediately. Bilateral and multilateral aid designed to support population activities soon began to flow more liberally. The Clinton administration also embraced the premise—effectively denied during the 1980s—that population pressures aggravate social, economic, and environmental problems and may cause political instability. Robert D. Kaplan's (1994) shockingly pessimistic account of "the coming anarchy" in West Africa, stimulated by overpopulation and environmental degradation, not only captured the attention of Washington policymakers but also encapsulated their convictions.

The debate between optimists and pessimists continues unabated. By 1994, however, when the United Nations convened its third decennial world population conference in Cairo, it had moved in new directions. As suggested by the conference title, "International Conference on Population and Development (ICPD)," population and development were now placed on the same track. Thus the ICPD moved beyond population numbers and demographic targets, embracing instead the view that population stabilization can be achieved only in the larger context of human development and sustainable economic growth. The conference paid particular attention to the critical role of women in both population control and the development process.

The Status of Women

The road to Cairo was marked by signposts that increasingly depicted the right of women to control their own bodies and reproductive fate as a basic human right, recognizable under international law (see Focus 10.2). It was also marked by incontrovertible evidence that women's status in society, and especially their education, have an important influence on preferences toward family size.

> Having an education usually means that women delay marriage, seek wage-paying jobs, learn about and have more favorable attitudes toward family planning, and have better communication with their husbands when they marry. Educated women have fewer infant deaths; high infant mortality is associated with high fertility. Similarly, when women have wage-paying jobs, they tend to have fewer children (and conversely, women with fewer children find it easier to work). (Population Reference Bureau 1981, 5; see also Robey, Rutstein, and Morris 1993)

Nevertheless, women throughout the world continue to be disadvantaged relative to men across a broad spectrum of educational statistics, such as literacy rates, school and college enrollments, and targeted educational resources. Women also enjoy less access to advanced study and training in professional fields, such as science, engineering, law, and business. In addition, within occupational groups, they are almost always in less-prestigious jobs, they face formidable barriers against involvement in politics, and everywhere they receive less pay than men. Although these and other gender differences have narrowed in recent years, in most countries the complex social, cultural, economic, and political forces that underlie gender inequalities remain firmly rooted.

Addressing women's rights is difficult because the issues touch deeply entrenched as well as widely divergent religious and cultural beliefs. In many Islamic countries, for example, women must hide their faces with veils in public, and women and men are often completely separated in social and religious activities. These traditions are difficult to understand in many western countries. On the other hand, western conceptions of feminism and women's rights, typically focused on social, political, and economic equality of the sexes, are foreign to women elsewhere, where the issues are personal and the goals pragmatic: "access to capital, the right of inheritance, basic education for girls, a voice in the political establishment and medical systems that let them make choices, especially in reproductive health" (Crossette 1995).

Despite the pitfalls and minefields, the ICPD Programme of Action—endorsed by 180 countries—addressed issues of gender equality and "empowerment" as well as women's reproductive rights. This was a historic step toward global recognition of the critical role that women play in both development and population stabilization (see Ashford 1995; Sen 1995; *The State of the World Population 1995* 1995). Noting that "in all parts of the world, women are facing threats to their lives, health, and well-being as a result of being overburdened with work and of their lack of power and influence," the principles embraced by the conference also called for "the elimination of all kinds of violence against women."

Human Rights and Women's Rights
A Quarter-Century of Progress

Over the past twenty-five years, women's civil rights and reproductive rights have made notable incursions into the international legal and human rights agendas. . . .

1968, United Nations International Conference on Human Rights (Teheran)

The United Nations explicitly addresses the issue of "human reproduction." The Teheran Declaration states: "Parents have a basic human right to decide freely and responsibly on the number and spacing of their children and a right to adequate education and information in this respect. "

1974, World Population Conference (Bucharest)

From "parents," the focus shifts to "couples and individuals," who have a right to the "means" as well as the information and education needed to decide on the number and spacing of their children. The notion of responsibility is also introduced: "The responsibility of couples and individuals in the exercise of this right takes into account the needs of their living and future children, and their responsibilities towards the community."

1975, International Women's Year Conference (Mexico City)

Launching the UN Decade for Women, the conference emphasizes reproductive choice, bodily integrity, and reproductive autonomy: "The human body, whether that of woman or man, is inviolable, and respect for it is a fundamental element of human dignity and freedom."

1979, Convention on the Elimination of All Forms of Discrimination against Women (the Women's Convention)

An unambiguous goal of the convention is equality between women and men in their right and ability to control reproduction. The convention's thirty articles address educational, economic, social, cultural, civic, and political discrimination. Article 12 refers to women's reproductive rights and calls on countries that have ratified the convention to "take all appropriate measures to eliminate discrimination against women in

the field of health care in order to ensure, on a basis of equality of men and women, access to health care services, including those related to family planning." Article 16 urges the elimination of "discrimination against women in all matters relating to marriage and family relations."

1984, World Population Conference (Mexico City)

Conference recommendations emphasize the responsibilities of governments and individuals alike: "The experience of the past ten years suggests that governments can do more to assist people in making their reproductive decisions in a responsible way." Making family planning more available is viewed "as a matter of urgency."

1992, United Nations Conference on Environment and Development (Rio)

Agenda 21, the draft of the meeting's official document, includes discussion of family planning and highlights quality, calling for "women-centered, women-managed, safe and accessible, responsible planning of family size and services."

1993, United Nations World Conference on Human Rights (Vienna)

The Vienna Declaration includes nine paragraphs on "The Equal Status and Human Rights of Women," and, for the first time, violence against women is recognized as a human-rights abuse.

1994, International Conference on Population and Development (Cairo)

ICPD Programme of Action "reaffirms the basic human right of all couples and individuals to decide freely and responsibly the number and spacing of their children and to have the information, education, and means to do so."

SOURCES: *The State of the World Population 1994* (1994), 19; *The State of the World Population 1995* (1994), 2.

In 1995, in Beijing, the United Nations convened its fourth World Conference on Women, the largest-ever gathering of women. Many of the issues regarding women's rights, along with the contentions provoked by differing religious and cultural traditions (including some thought to have been resolved in Cairo), surfaced again during the conference. Nonetheless, its very occurrence continued to focus attention on gender issues and the concept of "gender empowerment" (see Focus 10.3)—the conviction that "only when the potential of all human beings is fully realized can we talk of true human development" (UNDP 1995).

A World Population Plan of Action

Surprisingly, the Cairo debates paid little attention to many issues which by then had become common fare in global population forums—perhaps because the contentious issue of abortion rights commanded center stage during the conference (Chen, Fitzgerald, and Bates 1995). Among the standards were issues of environmental quality, resource conservation, demographic sources of political instability and ethnic conflict, urbanization, and structural inequalities between the Global North and South. Many did figure into the goals articulated in the ICPD Programme of Action. Nonetheless, others now also emerged prominently among the key objectives around which a global consensus was achieved:

- Establishing a long-term goal of stabilizing population growth levels consistent with sustainable development;
- Establishing an international partnership for sustainable development which recognizes the responsibility of the North to address wasteful resource use in conjunction with the South's addressing high rates of population growth;
- Developing a comprehensive approach for national efforts and international assistance programs that includes:
  —addressing the unmet need and demand for family planning and reproductive health services;

In August 1995, women representing the different cultures of the world held the "peace torch" during the opening ceremony for the Nongovernmental Organization Forum on Women at the Olympic Stadium in Beijing. The forum was a companion to the United Nations Fourth World Conference on Women, which met in Beijing from September 4–15.

Woman Power
How Nations Rank

The United Nations Development Programme has devised a "Gender Empowerment Index" that assesses gender equality on a scale from 0 to 1. The closer to 1, the greater women's equality with men. The index is based on power over resources (i.e., earned income measured in per-capita income in purchasing power parity [PPP] dollars); access to professional opportunities and participation in economic decision making (measured by shares of managerial, professional, technical, and administrative jobs); and access to political opportunities (measured by shares of parliamentary seats). Below are the top ten and bottom ten countries, as ranked by the *gender empowerment measure (GEM)*.

Top Ten	GEM	Bottom Ten	GEM
1. Sweden	.76	107. Zaire	.20
2. Norway	.75	108. Nigeria	.20
3. Finland	.72	109. Solomon Islands	.20
4. Denmark	.68	110. Togo	.18
5. Canada	.66	111. Mauritania	.16
6. New Zealand	.64	112. Côte d'Ivoire	.16
7. Netherlands	.63	113. Comoros	.16
8. United States	.62	114. Pakistan	.15
9. Austria	.61	115. Djibouti	.13
10. Italy	.59	116. Afghanistan	.11

SOURCE: Adapted from UNDP (1995), 82, 84–85.

—strategies for preventing HIV/AIDS infection;

—child survival and women's health needs;

—the need to advance the rights and economic, political, and social roles of women;

—improving the education of girls and women; and

—increasing male responsibility in family planning and childrearing.

- Mobilizing institutional capability and financial resources necessary to implement the above goals. (U.S. Department of State *Dispatch* 5, Supplement no. 8 [September 1994], 9)

The Programme of Action also set out specific goals to be achieved by 2015 which deal with access to primary school education, family-planning services, reproductive health, infant and under-five mortality, maternal mortality, and life expectancy.

The proposals contained in the Programme of Action are only recommendations and thus not binding on governments. Indeed, few could be expected to act on all of them, particularly given the enormous resources their realization demands. By the end of this century the expenditures on family planning alone are expected to balloon to $10 billion, nearly double the amount spent in the early 1990s. Even greater sums would be required to meet the goals of increased access to primary education and to health care (including that required by the growing number of HIV/AIDS patients). Global South countries cannot be expected to meet these demands by themselves, and others— meaning governments in the Global North—will be asked to supplement their resources. However, domestic political support for foreign aid among donor countries has virtually disappeared.

Mounting a sustained effort to stem the growth of world population thus remains a formidable challenge. But the goal itself is no longer in dispute—a rather remarkable achievement given the comparatively short time in which the "population problem" has been on the global agenda and the disparate interests and values that motivate states' behavior on the issues it encompasses. As the neo-Malthusian Lester Brown (1994) observes, "The delegates [to the Cairo conference] rejected the idea that human numbers could be allowed to continue growing until they reached 10 to 14 billion as projected, and opted instead for an ambitious Plan of Action to stabilize population at a much lower level. Perhaps the boldest initiative ever undertaken by the United Nations, the Plan reflects a justifiable sense of urgency, and an awareness that growing human demands are already exceeding some of the earth's natural limits."

●　●　●

A PRESCRIPTION FOR OPTIMISM OR PESSIMISM?

Neo-Malthusians and cornucopians paint quite different visions of our future. Might both be right? Rapidly expanding populations stress environmental systems, exacerbate poverty, and encourage reproduction to hedge against the future. Economic development, on the other hand, discourages large families, stimulating reduced birthrates and hence declining population growth rates. So, too, do government family-planning policies. Where we choose to focus attention—dictated by our perceptual lens—will in turn frame our policy prescriptions (see Meadows 1993).

The world's polities have made great strides in recent decades in recognizing the complex causes and consequences of rapid population growth. Whether they have the will and shared vision to cope with the problems and expand the possibilities remains to be seen. Meanwhile, an interdependent and rapidly globalizing world promises that none will be immune to the population trends and dynamics that now engulf the world. As a prominent American foreign policy analyst (Steinbruner 1995) recently concluded, "Both the scale and composition of [the] population surge [facing the world during the next half-century] will have consequences powerful enough not just to affect, but perhaps even to dominate, conceptions of international security."

●　●　●

KEY TERMS

carrying capacity
tragedy of the commons
fertility rate
replacement-level fertility
population momentum
demographic transition

refugees
neo-Malthusians
cornucopians
food security
sustainable development

CHAPTER 11

The Ecology of World Politics: Security and Sustainability on a Small Planet

If the last 150 years had been marked by the kind of climate instability we are now seeing, the world would never have been able to support its present population of five billion people.

—James McCarthy,
Harvard University climatologist, 1995

Once the number of fish that could be sold at market was primarily limited by the number of boats that could be built and manned; now it is limited by the number of fish in the sea.

—Herman E. Daly,
World Bank environmental economist, 1993

When American astronauts first orbited the earth in their Apollo spacecraft, they remarked to millions of listeners about the "blue planet" they saw through their small windows and how the clouds and continents flowed into one another without regard to the political boundaries that humans far below their distant view had imposed on a pristine planet. Those images are still often repeated. However, the improvement in space technology has also enabled us to see from afar uncomfortable images—of atmospheric poisons that encircle the globe; of violent winter and summer storms pounding islands and continents with relentless fury; of massive holes in the ozone shield which protects humans from dangerous ultraviolet rays; of vanishing forests and widening deserts; of diminishing supplies of oil, coal, and other nonrenewable resources on which humankind depends for its welfare. The same technology also enables military commanders to target their opponents in warfare, in order to defend national borders.

Warfare clearly can be laid at the doorstep of humankind. Are the environmental patterns seen from space also of our doing? Is the growth in world population during this century and projected for the next responsible for recurrent and irrefutable images of a global environment under stress? Or are the consumption patterns of the world's wealthy the primary culprits? There is no consensus on these issues, as we learned in Chapter 10. Not surprisingly, then, there is no consensus on how states ought to respond to a world undergoing rapid environmental change any more than on how they should deal with profound demographic, economic, and political transformations.

In this chapter we explore global environmental challenges and responses to them, broadly described in the concept of **ecopolitics**—the intersection of ecology and politics. Ecology deals with the impact of human activity on the environment. Politics, as we have seen, is concerned with the exercise of power. Ecopolitics, then, centers on how political actors influence perceptions of, and responses to, their environments.

Peoples and states today face a range of environmental and resource challenges that is broad indeed. We will confine ourselves to a limited yet representative menu—one that includes issues related to nonrenewable resources, common properties, and renewable resources—as we seek to understand how ecology and politics interact to shape our future. We will find, not surprisingly, that politics is a powerful force that permeates all dimensions of environmental and resource issues, ranging from the evaluation of scientific evidence to prescriptions for dealing with that evidence. Faced with these realities, we examine alternative strategies states have adopted for coping with environmental stress in an anarchical international system and ask how environmental issues intersect with other values that states prize, notably security and economic and social well-being.

• • •

ENVIRONMENTAL SECURITY AND SUSTAINABLE DEVELOPMENT: AN OVERVIEW

"Security" means freedom from fear. It also means freedom from risk and danger. During the Cold War fear of nuclear holocaust haunted much of the world. Security was equated with "national security," which typically connoted freedom from the fear, risk, and danger posed by the threat of war. This required the development of national strategies for coping with the struggle for power central to realist thinking. Today many analysts urge a broader conception of what constitutes security at both the national and global levels.

One view suggests that threats to national security should encompass actions or events that "degrade the quality of life for the inhabitants of a state . . . or narrow the range of policy choices available to the government of a state or . . . private, nongovernmental entities (persons, groups, corporations) within the state" (Ullman 1983). This is the politics of scarcity. The viewpoint says that future international conflict likely will be caused by resource scarcities—restricted access to food, oil, and water, for example, rather than overt military challenges. Compelling as the viewpoint may be, the politics of scarcity remains a state-centric ecopolitical perspective (Dabelko and Dabelko 1995).

"Environmental security" is an alternative viewpoint that seeks to push our thinking beyond borders. Focusing on the transboundary character of challenges to preserving the global environment, it argues that "threats to global life systems such as global warming, ozone depletion, and the loss of tropical forests and marine habitats are just as important to the future of humankind as the threat of nuclear catastrophe" (Porter and Brown 1996) (see Focus 11.1). Environmental degradation challenges states by undercutting economic well-being and the quality of life all of them presumably seek for their citizens. Still, this viewpoint is less akin to the perspective of realists than to that of liberal idealists, who look not to the state but to international organizations and nongovernmental actors as vehicles of interstate cooperation to cope with environmental challenges (Mathews 1989; Zacher and Matthew 1995). Because these efforts to redefine security beyond its state-centric moorings challenge fundamental realist conceptions of world politics, the enterprise is understandably controversial.[1]

Global environmental issues also pose another controversy, one that engages the competing perspectives of cornucopians and neo-Malthusians. Cornucopians believe that if the principles of economic liberalism are followed, the marketplace will right ecological imbalances that threaten humankind. For them, prices are the key adjustment mechanism, helping to produce the great-

---

[1]Compelling arguments on both sides of the controversy can be found in Deudney (1995), Homer-Dixon (1991, 1994), Homer-Dixon, Boutwell, and Rathjens (1993), M. Levy (1995), Myers (1989, 1993), and Renner (1989). For an overview of the competing viewpoints, see Dabelko and Dabelko (1995).

National Security and Environmental Security
Competing or Complementary?

The traditional concept of national security that evolved during the cold war viewed security as a function of the successful pursuit of interstate power competition. . . . Environmental security represents a significant departure from this approach to national security. It addresses two distinct issues: the environmental factors behind potentially violent conflicts, and the impact of global environmental degradation on the well-being of societies and economies. The idea that environmental degradation is a security issue when it is a cause of violent conflict appears to be consistent with the traditional definition of national security. However, . . . [the] focus on threats that do not involve an enemy state or political entity disturbs many theorists and practitioners of national security, for whom the only issues that should be viewed as "security" issues are those that revolve around conflict itself. . . .

The case for environmental security rests primarily on evidence that there has been serious degradation of natural resources (freshwater, soils, forests, fishery resources, and biological diversity) and vital life-support systems (the ozone layer, climate system, oceans, and atmosphere) as a result of the recent acceleration of global economic activities. These global physical changes could have far-reaching effects in the long run. . . .

Each of these environmental threats to global well-being is subject to significant empirical and scientific uncertainty. . . . The uncertainties . . . are comparable, however, to those associated with most military threats that national security establishments prepare for. Military planning is based on "worst-case" contingencies that are considered relatively unlikely to occur, yet military preparations for such contingencies are justified as a necessary insurance policy or "hedge" against uncertainty. . . .

The relationship between scarce natural resources and international conflict is not a new issue. But unlike traditional national security thinking about such conflict, which focuses on nonrenewable resources like minerals and petroleum, the environmental security approach addresses renewable resources—those that need not be depleted if managed sustainably.

SOURCE: Porter (1995), 218–20.

est good for the greatest number. Neo-Malthusians, on the other hand, share more in common with liberal internationalists and mercantilists. For them, markets' failure to account for the cost of excessive exploitation of both renewable and nonrenewable resources requires intervention by nonmarket forces. More fundamentally, it requires revision of the "dominant social paradigm," which says "first, that the free market will always maximize social welfare, and second, that there is not only an infinite supply of natural resources but also of 'sinks' for disposing the wastes from exploiting those resources. . . . Humans will not deplete any resource, according to this world view, as long as technology is given free rein and prices are allowed to fluctuate enough to stimulate the search for substitutes, so absolute scarcity can be postponed to the indefinite future" (Porter and Brown 1996).

The dominant social paradigm—a view shared by cornucopians—is under serious attack by environmentalists and other activists in many national political settings. It is also under attack internationally. "Sustainability" is now perceived as an alternative to unlimited growth, a concept which enjoys widespread support among governments and a broad range of international nongovernmental organizations particularly active in shaping the global environmental agenda (Princen and Finger 1994). Its heritage is traceable to *Our Common Future*, the 1987 report of the World Commission on Environment and Development, popularly known as the Brundtland Commission after the Norwegian prime minister who chaired it. The commission concluded that the world cannot sustain the growth required to meet the needs and aspirations of the world's projected population unless it adopts radically different approaches to basic issues of economic expansion, equity, resource management, energy efficiency, and the like. Rejecting the "limits of growth" maxim popular among neo-Malthusians during the 1970s, it emphasized instead "the growth of limits." The commission defined a "sustainable society" as one that "meets the needs of the present without compromising the ability of future generations to meet their own needs."

The Brundtland Commission report is an important landmark in the rapid emergence of environmental issues as global concerns. The process began in earnest in 1972, when the UN General Assembly convened the first United Nations Conference on the Human Environment in Stockholm. Conferences have since been held on a wide range of environmental topics, with scores of environmental treaties negotiated and new international agencies put into place to promote cooperation and monitor environmental developments (see Haas, Keohane, and Levy 1993). Together they attest to the challenges to the dominant social paradigm.

A second milestone in the development of global environmental consciousness was the **Earth Summit,** which took place in Rio de Janeiro, Brazil, in 1992—the twentieth anniversary of the Stockholm conference on the environment. Formally known as the United Nations Conference on Environment and Development (UNCED), the meeting brought together more than 150 states, fourteen hundred nongovernmental organizations, and some eight thousand journalists. A program of action agreed on at Rio, *Agenda 21*, embodies a political commitment to a broad range of environmental and development goals. Prior to the Earth Summit, the environment and development had been treated separately—and often regarded as in conflict with each other, as development frequently imperils and degrades the environment (see Focus 11.2). Now the concept of *sustainability* galvanized a simultaneous treatment of environmental and development issues. Recognition of the interrelatedness of global welfare issues continued at the 1994 Cairo International Conference on Population and Development (ICED), where population and development were also now placed on the same track.

Because sustainability means living off the earth's interest without encroaching on its capital, it draws attention to meeting the current needs of this generation without depriving future generations of the resources necessary for their own survival. Literally hundreds of books and articles have asked in one way or another how this ambitious goal can be achieved. A common thread throughout them is that sustainability cannot be realized without dramatic changes in the social, economic, and political fabric of the world as we now know it (see Helman 1995). Is that possible? Are individuals willing to sacrifice personal welfare for the common good? Will they sacrifice now to enrich their heirs? The tragedy of the commons metaphor, which we described in Chapter 10, provides little basis for optimism, whether applied to individuals or states. Add to this the anarchical structure of international system—which, as we learned in Chapter 8, discourages states from cooperating with one another out of fear that some will gain more than others—and it becomes clear that while environmental issues and challenges often transcend national

The Making of an Ecological Disaster
The Aral Sea

The Aral Sea [in Central Asia] is dying. Because of the huge diversions of water that have taken place during the past thirty years, particularly for irrigation, the volume of the sea has been reduced by two-thirds. The sea's surface has been sharply diminished, the water in the sea and in surrounding aquifers has become increasingly saline, and the water supplies and health of almost fifty million people in the Aral Sea basin are threatened. Vast areas of salty flatlands have been exposed as the sea has receded, and salt from these areas is being blown across the plains onto neighboring cropland and pastures, causing ecological damage. The frost-free period in the delta of the Amu Dacrya River, which feeds the Aral Sea, has fallen to less than 180 days—below the minimum required for growing cotton, the region's main cash crop. The changes in the sea have effectively killed a substantial fishing industry, and the variety of fauna in the region has declined drastically. If current trends continue unchecked, the sea would eventually shrink to a saline lake one-sixth its 1960 size.

This ecological disaster is the consequence of excessive abstraction of water for irrigation purposes from the Amu Dacrya and Syr Dacrya rivers, which feed the Aral Sea. Total river runoff into the sea fell from an average fifty-five cubic kilometers a year in the 1950s to zero in the early 1980s. The irrigation schemes have been a mixed blessing for the populations of the Central Asian republics—Kazakhstan, Kyrghyzstan, Tajikistan, Turkmenistan, and Uzbekistan—which they serve. The diversion of water has provided livelihoods for the region's farmers, but at considerable environmental cost. Soils have been poisoned with salt, overwatering has turned pastureland into bogs, water supplies have become polluted by pesticide and fertilizer residues, and the deteriorating quality of drinking water and sanitation is taking a heavy toll on human health. While it is easy to see how the problem of the Aral Sea might have been avoided, solutions are difficult. . . .

. . . The Central Asian republics (except for Kazakhstan) are poor: their incomes are 65 percent of the average in the former Soviet Union. . . . The regional population of thirty-five million is growing rapidly, at 2.7 percent a year, and infant mortality is high. The states have become dependent on a specialized but unsustainable pattern of agriculture. Irrigated production of cotton, grapes, fruit, and vegetables accounts for the bulk of export earnings. Any rapid reduction in the use of irrigation water will reduce living standards still further unless these economies receive assistance to help them diversify away from irrigated agriculture. Meanwhile, salinization and dust storms erode the existing land under irrigation. This is one of the starkest examples of the need to combine development with sound environmental policy.

SOURCE: *World Development Report 1992* (1992), 38.

boundaries, they remain hostage to a political structure ill-suited to the effective treatment of global security and welfare issues (see also Ophuls and Boyan 1992).

To better understand the multiple tensions that global environmental issues pose in an anarchical world and how competing perceptions of security and markets shape responses to them, we turn our attention to three interrelated clusters of issues on the global ecopolitical agenda: oil and energy, climate change and ozone depletion, and biodiversity and deforestation. The first involves conflict over a scarce nonrenewable resource in the tradition of commonplace definitions of national security. The other two broaden the net to encompass what many analysts regard as threats to environmental security. We use the latter two clusters to illustrate the problems and pitfalls that state and nonstate actors face as they seek sustainable development of common properties and renewable resources. Following this we will examine the controversy surrounding the impact of international trade on sustainable development.

Deforestation and inappropriate farming techniques often lead to degradation of soils, causing excessive erosion and desertification, as shown in the left-hand picture. Appropriate farming techniques, such as Indonesia's traditional methods of terracing farmlands illustrated on the right, can limit the damage, even in a densely populated and growing society.

• • •

THE ECOPOLITICS OF ENERGY

In April 1990, the average price for a barrel of internationally traded crude oil was less than fifteen dollars. Five months later—stimulated by Iraq's invasion of the tiny oil sheikdom of Kuwait—it was more than forty dollars. For the third time in less than two decades, the world suffered an "oil shock" as the price paid for the most widely used commercial energy source skyrocketed.

Iraq's aggression catapulted the foremost military power in the Arab world into control of one-fifth of the OPEC's oil production and more than one-fourth of its proven reserves of crude oil. The world community launched a dual response: economic sanctions against Iraq in an effort to force its withdrawal from Kuwait followed by an unprecedented UN Security Council decision to authorize the use of "all necessary means" to force Iraq from Kuwait. Seven weeks later, on January 16, 1991, the Persian Gulf War began when a coalition of UN forces launched the most intensive aerial bombardment ever. By February, coalition forces had easily routed Iraqi troops in a one-hundred-hour ground campaign. With Iraq's surrender, the United Nations again used economic sanctions to prod Iraq's compliance with the terms of the truce. Meanwhile, the price of oil reverted to its prewar levels.

Oil and National Security

The Persian Gulf War underscored the importance of oil to the economic security of states dependent on foreign energy supplies and hence to perceptions of their national security. Foreign example, U.S. President George Bush—under whose leadership Iraq's aggression was foiled—never openly admitted that oil was a principal factor propelling his decision to oppose Iraq's Saddam Hussein, but he did acknowledge that short-sighted energy policies had made the United States unduly dependent on Middle Eastern oil to fuel its industrial economy.

"We had moved in the wrong direction," he said. "Now we must act to correct that trend."

Oil also figured prominently in Iraq's own security calculations and hence to its decision to invade Kuwait. Iraq's eight-year war with Iran, which ended in 1988, caused severe domestic economic dislocations and a mounting foreign debt burden. Lower oil prices, caused in part by increased production by other OPEC members, made it more difficult for Iraq to meet its obligations. "In theory, Iraq might have managed the economic pressures by trimming its costly military program, by tightening its belt, and by intimidating its brethren in [OPEC] to curtail their production in order to push prices higher. . . . Saddam, however, saw a quicker fix for the economic ills of his country—sharply higher oil prices and the vast wealth of Kuwait, including its $100 billion in foreign assets" (Quandt 1991).

Political as well as economic factors motivated Saddam Hussein, including an aspiration to dominate the Arab world. Thus control over Kuwaiti oil was a means to an end as well as an end in itself. Nonetheless, the Middle East was once more plunged into open warfare, causing alarm throughout the world. In the end, nearly forty countries contributed to the UN-authorized military response to Iraq's aggression.

The Persian Gulf War culminated two decades of Middle Eastern turmoil in which access to its valued energy resources often figured prominently. That concern remains. Indeed, it is not an exaggeration to suggest that prospects for global prosperity and peace depend on the preservation of order in the volatile Middle East, whose oil is especially critical to the economic fortunes of the Global North. Ensuring access to the region's oil is thus a national security priority for the developed countries. At issue is the ability to protect the region's vast oil fields from terrorist or other attacks, to avert a repetition of the internal political disruptions that have often plagued the region, and to secure the sea lanes of communication along which oil is shipped.

Global Patterns of Energy Consumption

The criticality of oil to the Global North generally and the United States in particular is evident from the disproportionate share of world energy resources they consume. Europe uses more than twice as much energy per capita as the Global South, while Canada and the United States use more than six times as much (*BP Statistical Review of World Energy* 1995, 36). The differences parallel the gap between the world's rich and poor countries, apparent on so many other dimensions of contemporary world politics.

Because energy consumption is critical to the production of goods and services, it is closely correlated with changes in economic activity. From the 1930s to the 1980s, the world's demand for energy increased at almost the same rate as did the aggregate world gross domestic product, reflecting the industrial countries' substitution of energy for labor to facilitate production and transportation. Energy efficiencies typically differed widely among the industrial countries. The United States in particular, whose energy policies depressed the price of energy below its true cost, became not only the most profligate energy consumer but also the most inefficient. Japan and Europe continue to use energy more efficiently today than does the United States. The pattern is evident elsewhere, where other states with similar economic profiles also exhibit widely different energy-use patterns. On the whole, however, the world (including the United States) has made great strides since the oil crises of the 1970s and early 1980s in the efficiency with which it uses nonrenewable energy resources.

Despite increased efficiency, demand for oil continues its upward spiral, spurred in large measure by the Global South, which sees energy as the key to its economic development and higher standards of living (see Figure 11.1). The inescapable if uncomfortable fact is that rising affluence and growing populations in the Global South will propel rising demand for energy from fossil fuels even if per-capita levels of consumption remain unchanged. Urbanization will also play a role, with a greater use of motor vehicles accounting for much of the increase in the demand for oil. The demand for energy exerted by economic growth in Asia will be especially strong. Oil consumption in the region surpassed that of western Europe in 1994 and will surpass North American consumption within a decade (*World Economic and Social Survey 1995* 1995).

As demand for oil and other commercial energy grows in the Global South, the environmental consequences may prove, in the words of the World Resources Institute (1994), "dire at both local and global levels." This concern underlies the indisputable fact that the world's dependence on fossil fuel energy resources is a critical cause of many environmental stresses now facing the world. How did we get into this situation?

Oil Becomes King

Little more than a century ago, fuelwood was the principal energy source. As the mechanical revolution altered the nature of transportation, work, and leisure, coal began to replace fuelwood. Early in the twentieth century, coal became the dominant source of energy throughout the world. New technologi-

FIGURE 11.1

World Oil Demand, 1994 and 2010

World demand for oil is expected to surge by one-third between 1994 and 2010, growing from sixty-eight million barrels per day to ninety-one million barrels. Most of the growth in demand will come from the Global South, which soon will consume more than two-fifths of world oil supplies.

SOURCE: *World Economic and Social Survey 1995* (1995), 168.

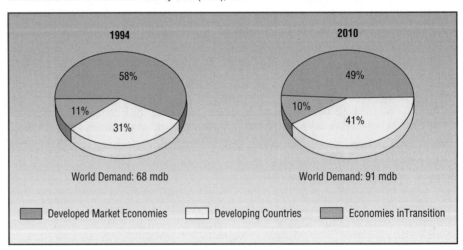

cal developments, particularly the internal combustion engine, then spurred the shift away from coal to oil and, somewhat less so, natural gas. The United States, well endowed with petroleum resources, led the development of oil-based technologies, above all in the automotive and petrochemical industries. Oil now rapidly outpaced coal as the main energy source, and dependence on oil began its rapid rise.

In 1950, when world population stood at roughly 2.5 billion people, world energy consumption was 2.5 billion tons of coal-equivalent energy. Although population increased rapidly during the next quarter-century, energy use increased almost twice as fast, stimulating rapid economic growth (Brown 1979). Rapidly rising production made oil the world's principal source of commercial energy. Everywhere the reasons for the shift to oil were the same: It was cleaner and less expensive than coal. From the end of the Korean War until the early 1970s, world oil prices actually declined compared with the prices of other commodities.

Despite growing dependence on oil, the long-term stability of world oil prices is striking. As Figure 11.2 shows, World War I was followed by a notable spike in the price of oil. Otherwise its price remained stable during this centu-

F I G U R E   1 1 . 2

Crude Oil Prices since 1861

World oil prices have remained comparatively steady during this century, thus reducing the cost of oil relative to other commodities. The two oil shocks of the 1970s and 1980s caused a sharp upturn in oil prices, but they have since receded.

SOURCE: *BP Statistical Review of World Energy* (1995), 12.

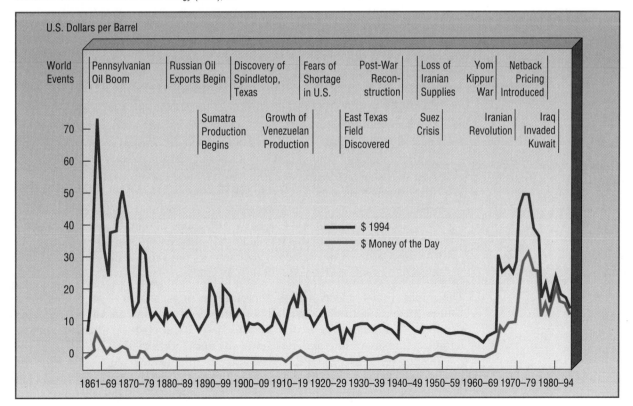

ry. As the price of other commodities as well as manufactured goods rose, oil became relatively cheaper. It therefore made good economic sense to use it in large quantities.

A small group of multinational corporations (known as the "majors") were the chief actors in propelling the worldwide shift from coal to oil. Their operations encompassed every aspect of the business, from exploration to the retail sales of products at their gas stations. Their search for, production of, and marketing of low-cost oil were largely unhindered. Concessions from countries in the oil-rich Middle East and elsewhere were easy to get. The communist states were virtually the only oil-producing countries that barred them. The oil companies were thus able to maintain the price of oil at a level profitable for themselves, even though it declined relative to other commodities. An abundant supply of oil at low prices facilitated the recovery of western Europe and Japan from World War II and encouraged consumers to use energy-intensive technologies, such as the private automobile. An enormous growth in the worldwide demand for and consumption of energy followed.

The continuing search for and exploitation of new oil deposits were needed to sustain the high growth rates in demand. The incentives for developing petroleum reserves outside the Middle East waned, however, as the real cost of oil failed to keep pace with increases in the cost of other commodities, goods, and services. And incentives for developing technologies for alternative energy sources, such as coal, were virtually nonexistent. Eventually this contributed to the rise of OPEC as an important actor in the energy market, as alternatives to the resources it controlled could not easily be replaced. For nearly a decade—until the global price of oil plunged sharply in the mid-1980s—the oil cartel was a pivotal actor not only in energy markets but in the world political economy generally.

Energy Security: An Elusive Goal?

Oil will play the principal role in the global energy picture well into the next century and perhaps beyond. This raises questions about OPEC's potential future role as a price setter and production leader. The historical record leads us to be cautious in predicting the cartel's future role, but signs point toward its continuing importance:

> More than three-quarters of the present proved world oil reserves are in OPEC countries and about two-thirds are located in five Middle East countries: the Islamic Republic of Iran, Iraq, Kuwait, Saudi Arabia, and the United Arab Emirates. . . . At current production levels, the reserve-to-production ratio, an index unusually used to approximate the life expectancy of resources, stands at 84 years for OPEC and at only 18 years for the non-OPEC countries. In the Middle East, the reserve-to-production ratio is 97 years. In the United States, by contrast, the ratio is only 9.5 years. (*World Economic and Social Survey 1995* (1995), 161)

The implication is clear: The major oil-importing countries, particularly the United States, "will remain acutely sensitive to developments in oil-exporting countries" but especially in the Middle East, "where modernization and Islamic revivalism are in conflict" (Stanislaw and Yergin 1993).

Despite sensitivity to OPEC's past and potential future role, it is noteworthy that world oil prices remained comparatively low following the Persian Gulf War despite the embargo of Iraqi oil and the reduction in exports from the former Soviet Union caused by the collapse of much of its productive capability. Those price trends may persist. Based on technological developments that have reduced the cost of finding new oil deposits, the United Nations concludes that "there is considerable reason for optimism that adequate supplies of oil will be forthcoming at current prices (albeit adjusted for inflation)" (*World Economic and Social Survey 1995* 1995). While this may be good news for individual consumers and the world political economy in the short run, it does little to pave the way toward a post-petroleum energy system. In addition, it does not address the threats to national security that states perceive because of the unequal distribution of proven and prospective oil reserves, a critical energy security issue. The security challenge arises not simply from supply and price disruptions like those caused by the first oil shock in 1973–74, but also from balance-of-payments and debt concerns caused by dependence on foreign energy sources. It is noteworthy that many of the most indebted countries in the Global South are also those most heavily dependent on imported energy.

Oil derived from unconventional sources (such as tar sands and shale) and renewable forms of energy (such as solar, tidal, and wind power; geothermal energy; and bioconversion) are among the alternatives to oil that may someday become viable technologically and economically. Their development would reduce dependence on oil from the volatile Middle East and reduce perceptions of national insecurity growing out of the politics of scarcity. However, the comparatively low price of oil—and its projected stability—discourage their development. Meanwhile, coal, natural gas, hydropower, and nuclear power are the principal alternatives to oil. Each, however, faces economic and political uncertainties and poses its own environmental risks.

Coal. Coal is the chief fossil-fuel alternative to oil. Based on the current ratio of reserves to production, oil will last only until about the year 2040, but coal will last for more than two centuries (see Figure 11.3). Coal now accounts for 27 percent of the world's primary energy use, compared with 40 percent for oil and 23 percent for natural gas (*BP Statistical Review of World Energy* 1995, 34).

Although trade in coal increased sharply during the 1980s, most is consumed where it is produced, making it less susceptible to supply disruptions than oil. China, the United States, and the former Soviet Union account for nearly 60 percent of world coal reserves and are its largest consumers. China tops the list of both producers and consumers, as it seeks to fuel its rapid economic expansion almost entirely with coal. Remarkably, coal now accounts for three-fourths of the country's total commercial energy supply (*BP Statistical Review of World Energy* 1995, 34).

Although the use of coal increased sharply in the aftermath of the first oil shock, the social costs—known as **externalities**—associated with its widespread use are substantial. Coal is a major pollutant of the atmosphere, for example. As we will find later, it contributes heavily to the acidification of precipitation and to the release of carbon that contributes to global warming. As a result of environmental concerns and tighter regulations, coal is an unattractive alternative to oil worldwide. Nonetheless, in particular countries, such as China, it is a major energy source, sparking the ire of those who must bear the consequences.

Natural Gas. Natural gas is cleaner and more convenient to use than either oil or coal (see Flavin 1992). Based on the current ratio of reserves to production, natural gas supplies will last for more than sixty years. Unlike coal, however,

FIGURE 11.3

Ratio of Fossil-Fuel Reserves to Production, 1994

At current levels of production, world coal reserves will last much longer than those for oil or natural gas. Based on current patterns, oil will last until about 2040, but the continuing discovery of new reserves can be expected to outpace the world's steady increases in production and consumption.

SOURCE: *BP Statistical Review of World Energy* (1995), 36.

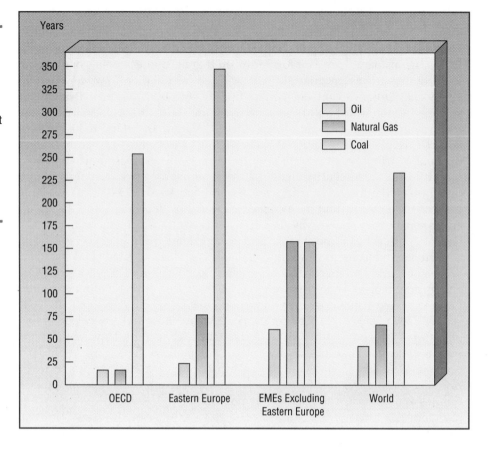

natural gas is distributed very unevenly on a regional basis, which means that its continued development will depend on export trade.

The two largest natural gas markets are the United States and Russia. In 1994 the two countries consumed, respectively, 29 percent and 18 percent of production. Russia is also a major producer of gas and possesses the largest reserves, with 34 percent of the world's proved reserves in 1994. The United States, on the other hand, has less than 4 percent of the world reserves (*BP Statistical Review of World Energy* 1995, 18). Historically the United States has met virtually all of its need for gas from domestic sources. It seems likely, though, that it will have to look increasingly to imports to sustain its high demand. As with oil, the Middle East is a likely source, as it holds nearly one-third of the world's proved reserves but consumes only 6 percent of world production.

Getting gas from the wellhead to consumers is a primary problem. Pipelines are the preferred method of transport, but they are massive and expensive engineering projects which also pose environmental dangers and thus encounter resistance. Liquefied natural gas is an alternative—perhaps the only one for transshipment from the Middle East to North America or to the growing European and Japanese markets—but experts disagree about its safety. That concern, combined with cost considerations and sensitivity to dependence on OPEC sources, has limited the development of liquefied natural gas. Still, because natural gas produces considerably less carbon emissions than either coal or oil, its attractiveness will grow, providing incentives to increase its use throughout the world.

Hydropower. Hydropower accounts for only 2.5 percent of world energy use. Europe is the primary consumer of electricity generated by hydropower, followed by North America, Asia, and Central and South America (*BP Statistical Review of World Energy* 1995, 34). Hydropower has distinct advantages over fossil fuels in that it does not pollute the atmosphere. However, water availability, land-management issues, and financial considerations limit its attractiveness as an alternative to fossil fuels. In China, for instance, the controversial Three Gorges Dam project on the Yangtze River may create more problems than it solves:

> The construction of the dam will flood twenty towns and eleven thousand hectares of farmland, threaten several endangered species such as the Siberian white crane and White Flag dolphin, and uproot some 1.4 million people. . . . Most of these locals will end up on much higher ground, with colder, poorer soils. . . . The Chinese Academy of Sciences acknowledged that five times as much new land would be necessary to equal crop yields in the fertile valley fields that will soon be below the dam's reservoir. (Sachs 1996, 140)

Nuclear Energy. In 1994 nuclear power accounted for just over 7 percent of global energy use, with the United States the single largest consumer followed by France, Japan, and Russia. France uses it most intensively, deriving 40 percent of its total energy use (in 1994) from nuclear power (*BP Statistical Review of World Energy* 1995, 34).

Among known technologies, nuclear energy once was seen as the leading alternative to fossil-fuel dependence but that is no longer the case. Technical and financial problems have forced some countries to reduce or abandon their programs, and in others the political climate has turned markedly against nuclear power, with safety a principal point of contention. Two well-publicized nuclear accidents—one in the United States at the Three Mile Island nuclear power plant in Pennsylvania in 1979 and one at Chernobyl in Ukraine in 1986—dramatized the risks and seemed to vindicate the skeptics who had warned of the dangers posed by nuclear energy.

Catastrophe was averted at Three Mile Island, but even without the threatened meltdown of the reactor core, the accident released the largest-ever level of radioactive contamination by the U.S. commercial nuclear industry. At Chernobyl, however, catastrophe did strike. Thousands are believed to have been killed; hundreds of thousands were forced to evacuate their homes; and the radioactive fallout—"the equivalent of ten Hiroshima bombs"—"left a swath of agricultural land the size of Holland permanently poisoned." (Dobbs 1991, 10). Radioactive fallout spread beyond the Ukraine as well, engulfing much of Europe in the effects of the Chernobyl explosion. The evidence of the human and environmental costs of Chernobyl continues to mount even today, as the number of those ravaged by the catastrophe and its long-term consequences multiplies. Nine years after the disaster, a study commissioned by the European Union estimated that "Chernobyl will be the longest, most high-tech and expensive environmental cleanup the world has attempted—costing billions of dollars and taking perhaps one hundred years to complete" (Rupert 1995).

Concerns about the risks of nuclear power extend beyond the safety of nuclear energy as a means of generating electricity. How and where to dispose of highly radioactive nuclear wastes, for example, is a contentious and unresolved issue virtually everywhere. No safe procedure for handling radioactive nuclear waste—some of which remains dangerous for hundreds of thousands of years—has yet been devised. In the meantime, large quantities have accumulated, posing a substantial threat to environmental safety. The end of the Cold War has compounded the issue, as the dismantling of both nuclear weapons and the facilities that produced them requires means of disposal (see, e.g., Erikson 1994). The cry of local communities is often "not in my back yard" (NIMBY is the popular acronym). The issue is no less contentious internationally, as disposal of nuclear and other toxic wastes figures prominently on the global ecopolitical agenda as a divisive issue between the Global North (which prefers to dump wastes outside its own territory) and the Global South (which would prefer not to be the dump—but often is).

A related fear is that countries that do not now possess nuclear know-how might acquire it, thus gaining the means to develop nuclear weapons. While proliferation is essentially a national security issue, it is linked technologically to nuclear power production for peaceful purposes. Nuclear-generating facilities produce weapons-grade material, specifically highly enriched uranium and plutonium. Neither of these materials, which can be used to create a nuclear weapon, is used commercially as fuel in the current generation of nuclear power reactors. Still, the fear persists that eventually weapons-grade material will place within reach the construction of tens of thousands of nuclear bombs. It was this concern that prompted the United States (with the help of South Korea and Japan) to give North Korea—a long-time political-military adversary—nuclear reactors less susceptible to nuclear weapons production than the path North Korea was following in its own indigenous nuclear program.

This brief exploration of the "energy problematique" demonstrates the centrality of the politics of scarcity in contemporary world politics. Similar concerns animate behavior in other areas involving scarce resources, such as water, where conflict among states is a central issue (see, e.g., Gleick 1993; Postel 1993). Traditional conceptions of national security thus continue to color how states frame and respond to the choices they face in an anarchical yet environmentally interdependent world. Are renewable and common property resources any different?

• • •

THE ECOPOLITICS OF THE ATMOSPHERE

The scores of government negotiators and nongovernmental representatives who converged on Rio de Janeiro in 1992 came in the wake of the hottest decade on record. For years scientists had warned that **global warming**—the gradual rise in world temperature—would cause dramatic changes in world climatological patterns, stimulating widespread changes in the world's political and economic systems and relationships. Perhaps because they had been burned by the heat of the 1980s, negotiators agreed at Rio to a Framework Convention on Climate Change whose purpose is to address the human causes of climate change by reducing emissions of carbon dioxide and other "greenhouse" gases.

Climate Change

Many scientists believe that the gradual rise in the earth's temperature, especially evident since the onset of the industrial revolution, is caused by an increase in human-made gases released into the atmosphere, altering its insulating effects. The atmosphere permits radiation from the sun to penetrate to the earth, but gas molecules form the equivalent of a greenhouse roof by trapping heat remitted from earth that would otherwise escape into outer space. Carbon dioxide (CO_2) accounts for the bulk of **greenhouse gases,** with methane (natural gas), nitrous oxide, ozone, and chlorofluorocarbons (CFCs) comprising much of the rest. As the amount of these gases released into the atmosphere has grown, the global temperature has also risen.[2] Today it is between 0.3 and 0.6 degrees Celsius higher than it was in 1880 (Brown, Lenssen, and Kane 1995, 64).

Critics of the thesis that human activity causes global warming believe that the rise in global temperature is part of the cyclical pattern of temperature changes the world has experienced for tens of thousands of years. That view is increasingly discredited, however. Since 1988, hundreds of scientists from around the world have been organized under the sponsorship of several United Nations agencies to study global climate change. The team, known as the **Intergovernmental Panel on Climate Change (IPCC),** in 1995 stated conclusively for the first time its belief that global climate trends are "unlikely to be entirely due to natural causes." Instead, "the balance of evidence . . . suggests a discernible human influence on global climate." The language is guarded, but its implications are clear. Without significant efforts to reduce the emission of greenhouses gases, the IPCC concluded, global temperatures could rise by as much as 6 degrees Fahrenheit by the year 2100, a dramatic increase equivalent to that which ended the last ice age. Even at the lower end of its estimates (1.4 degrees Fahrenheit), the rise would be faster "than any experienced since human civilization began" (Flavin 1996).

According to the IPCC, the world has already entered a period of climatic instability likely to cause "widespread economic, social, and environmental dislocation over the next century." The effects of continued temperature rises could be both dramatic and devastating:

- Sea levels could rise up to three feet, mostly because of melting glaciers and the expansion of water as it warms up. That could submerge vast areas of low-lying coastal land, including major river deltas; most of the beaches on the U.S. Atlantic Coast; parts of China; and the island nations of the Maldives, the Seychelles, and the Cook and Marshall islands. More than one hundred million people could be displaced.

- Winters could get warmer . . . and warm-weather hot spells like the one that killed five hundred people in Chicago [in the summer of 1995] could become more frequent and more severe.

- Rainfall could increase overall—but the increase wouldn't be uniform across the globe. Thus areas that are already prone to flooding might flood more often and more severely; and since water evaporates more easily in a warmer world, drought-prone regions and deserts could become even drier. Hurricanes, which draw their energy from warm oceans, could become even stronger as those oceans heat up.

---

[2]Although carbon dioxide is the principal greenhouse gas, concentrations of methane in the atmosphere are growing more rapidly. Methane emissions arise from livestock populations, rice cultivation, and the production and transportation of natural gas. Interestingly, the largest concentrations of methane are not in the atmosphere but locked in ice, permafrost, and coastal marine sediments. This raises the possibility that a warming atmosphere will cause more methane to be released into the atmosphere, which would then reinforce the process because of methane's strong warming potential (World Bank 1995b).

• Temperature and rainfall patterns would shift in unpredictable ways. That might not pose a problem for agriculture, since farmers could change their crops and irrigate. Natural ecosystems that have to adapt on their own, however, could be devastated. (*Time*, October 2, 1995, 55)

Climate-Change Culprits. Carbon dioxide emissions are the principal culprits in global warming. They have grown spectacularly as a result of burning fossil fuels for energy and manufacturing cement. The industrial states generally are the principal sources of global carbon emissions, but the United States emits more CO_2 into the atmosphere than anyone. "Thanks to its large buildings, one hundred million cars, and relatively inefficient industries, the United States has per-capita carbon dioxide emissions nearly twice as high as those in western Europe, and five times the world average" (Flavin and Tunali 1995, 15). Elsewhere, China is a major and growing source of concern (see Figure 11.4).

Coal emits more atmospheric pollutants than other fossil fuels, and in China—the world's largest producer and consumer of coal—coal is king. Three-fourths of China's energy for its fast-growing economy comes from coal. China

FIGURE 11.4

Carbon Emissions from Burning Fossil Fuels, 1950–1994

Carbon dioxide (CO_2) is the major contributor to global warming, and the burning of fossil fuels is the primary source of carbon emissions. Carbon emissions by eastern Europe and the former Soviet Union have dropped sharply since the end of the Cold War, but they are growing rapidly in China. The United States remains the largest contributor of greenhouse gases.

SOURCE: World Watch database diskette 1996.

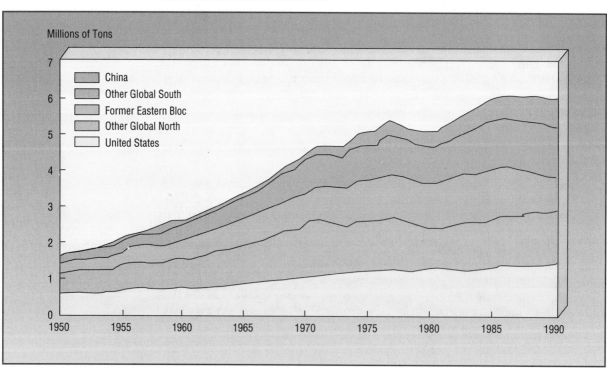

in turn accounts for 10 percent of all greenhouse gas emissions, making it the fastest growing major contributor to global warming.

Coal is a major source of atmospheric sulfur and nitrogen oxides as well. These pollutants return to earth, typically after traveling long distances, in the form of **acid rain,** which adds to the acidification of lakes, the corrosion of materials and structures, and the impairment of ecosystems. Acid rain is a serious problem in much of China. Because the oxides that cause it are also transboundary pollutants, China's domestic energy policies have become a major irritant in its relations with its neighbors, particularly South Korea and Japan (see Map 2.1 in Chapter 2). Nonetheless, China plans to increase the amount of coal it burns by nearly nine hundred million tons a year by 2010 (Tefft 1995, 8; see also World Resources Institute 1994). And other Asian states are following in its path, including populous India which, like China, has sizable coal deposits. Already China and India account for 14 percent of global greenhouse gas emissions. In addition, their combined share of carbon dioxide emissions is expected to grow to one-fourth in the next fifteen years (Tefft 1995, 8).

The Science and Politics of Climate Change. Global climate change contains the elements of a classic tragedy of the commons: It was intended by none yet is seemingly beyond the control of all who must bear its costs. Four strategies are available for avoiding the ruin common properties face when excessively exploited for private gain:

1. *Voluntary restraints*, which come about "through education about the ecological consequences of irresponsible actions and by bringing social pressures to bear on members of the community who have not moderated their actions" (Soroos 1995).

2. *Regulations* that restrict the use of common properties, including penalties for violators.

3. *Partitioning* of the common property so that those who profit from the common property also pay the costs of excessive exploitation.

4. *Common ownership* of the property, which limits access to those with a share in ownership and who in turn share in the profits. "Under such an arrangement, the community as a whole would not only receive all the profits but also absorb all the costs of [excessive exploitation]" (Soroos 1995).

Each of these strategies for averting a commons tragedy has counterparts in states' efforts to cope with environmental challenges they collectively face. In the case of climate change, however—arguably the most threatening of all (Flavin 1996)—global efforts remain confined to voluntary restraints. Because education and social pressures are particularly important here, the role of the IPCC in determining that the world has already entered a period of climatic instability due to rising temperatures takes on added significance. As one prominent environmentalist observed, "The IPCC's influence stems from its unique design. It combines in a single institution independent scientists acting on their professional knowledge with policymakers acting on behalf of governments. Science is separated and protected from political tinkering and at the same time thrust under policymakers' noses. Without realizing what they were doing, governments created in the IPCC an institution that forces them to confront a phenomenon many—if not most—would prefer to ignore" (Mathews 1996). Still, the politics of climate change has proven to be a formidable barrier to achieving even minimal levels of voluntary restraints on the emission of greenhouse gases.

The Framework Convention on Climate Change agreed to at the Earth Summit in 1992 set an ambitious goal: stabilizing the overall concentration in the atmosphere of greenhouse gases as well as reducing their emission worldwide.

> But the convention is only a framework, and imposes minimal obligations on its signatories. Parties are obliged only to develop inventories of greenhouse gas emissions, prepare "national programs" for mitigating and adapting to climate change, and "take climate into consideration" when formulating other government policies. . . . The convention calls on industrial countries to take the lead in limiting emissions, and suggests—but does not require—that they return emissions to the 1990 level or below in the year 2000. (Flavin and Tunali 1995, 12)

In 1995 government negotiators met in Berlin in the first Conference of Parties under the Framework Convention on Climate Change. Despite the expectations generated at Rio three years earlier, little progress had been made in realizing the voluntary restraints agreed to earlier. European states previously at the forefront of efforts to reduce carbon emissions now waffled, and the United States interpreted the treaty's provisions to mean that carbon emissions could actually *increase* if they were offset by reductions in other emissions. Thus "the gradual shift from 'binding limits' to vague 'national targets' and 'goals' . . . turned this portion of the treaty into a sham" (Flavin and Tunali 1995). Furthermore, most nations in the Global South had not adopted any targets at all, despite rapid increases in their own greenhouse gas emissions.

The political power of domestic energy producers and their lobbyists helps explain states' reluctance to move forward on issues of climate change (see Flavin 1996; Gelbspan 1995), despite the mounting evidence pointing toward its human causes and untoward consequences.[3] These domestic interests (typically multinational corporations) enjoy strong allies internationally among the oil-producing states of the Global South. Hard hit by declining oil revenues since the peak of the OPEC decade (see Chapter 8), oil-producing countries vigorously oppose efforts to impose restrictions on carbon emissions, fearing this will further erode demand for the lifeblood of their own economies.

Their interests are not shared by a cluster of nearly three dozen small island states in the Caribbean, Indian Ocean, and South Pacific, however. These states fear that gradually rising ocean levels will flood their lands, literally causing them to vanish. For them, reductions in Global North emission levels far below the 1990 levels agreed to at Rio are imperative. Already, though, reductions to those levels by the year 2000 are beyond reach—as, it seems, are the even more-ambitious goals the imperiled islands see as necessary for their survival.

The small island states eventually may be overwhelmed by the dispute between the Global North and South as to how to deal with a problem colored by widely discrepant perceptions and political interests. The South sees the North—correctly—as the primary culprit in previous greenhouse emissions, while the North sees the South—also correctly—as the primary source of rising

---

[3]As climate negotiators were preparing to meet in Berlin, "a forty-eight by twenty-two-mile chunk of the Larsen Ice Shelf in the Antarctic broke off . . . , exposing rocks that had been buried for twenty thousand years and prompting Rodolfo del Valle of the Argentine Antarctic Institute to tell the Associated Press, 'Last November we predicted the [ice shelf] would crack in ten years, but it has happened in barely two months'" (Gelbspan 1995, 32).

emissions, thus negating any benefits that might be realized by altering its own behavior today. Rising levels of coal burning by China and India alone could undermine any efforts taken today to deal with long-term problems.

The Framework Convention anticipates that technology transfers from rich to poor countries eventually may become a vehicle for coping with the rise of damaging Southern emissions. "Under a concept known in the treaty as 'joint implementation,' it is assumed that one day richer countries will be able to meet part of their treaty obligations by investing in emission reductions in developing countries. The idea is that replacing the inefficient energy systems of developing countries offers cost-effective opportunities for reducing carbon emissions" (Flavin and Tunali 1995). Although some progress has been made along these lines, not all developed countries are keen about the approach, which they see as a costly investment in technology transfers that may be beyond reach. Nor are all developing countries happy with the idea, which they see as a way to permit the rich states to avoid making sacrifices of their own, instead putting pressure on others to make adjustments through "cheap off-sets." Thus friction generated by the North–South fault line may itself contribute to a warming world.

The negotiators at Berlin did break some new ground. They reached a new mandate which "instructs governments to negotiate a treaty protocol 'to elaborate policies and measures, as well as to set quantified limitation and reduction objectives within specified time-frames such as 2005, 2010, and 2020.' Likely to be called the Kyoto Protocol, this agreement is to be signed at the third conference of the parties in Japan in 1997" (Flavin 1996).

Ozone Protection

States' efforts to cope with depletion of the atmosphere's protective ozone layer share similarities with the story of climate change. In this case, however, an international regime has emerged and has been progressively strengthened as scientific evidence pointing toward the environmental damage caused by human activity continues to mount.

Ozone is a pollutant in the lower atmosphere, but in the upper atmosphere it provides the earth with a critical layer of protection against the sun's harmful ultraviolet radiation. Scientists have discovered a marked depletion of the ozone layer—most notably an "ozone hole" over Antarctica which grows at times to be larger than the continental United States—and they have conclusively linked the thinning of the layer to chlorofluorocarbons, a related family of compounds known as halons, hydrochlorofluorocarbons (HCFCs), methyl bromide, and other chemicals. Depletion of the ozone layer exposes humans to increased health hazards of various sorts, particularly skin cancer, and threatens other forms of marine and terrestrial life. The release of many ozone-depleting gases also adds measurably to the accumulation of greenhouse gases that threaten dramatic climate change through global warming.

Scientists began to link halons and CFCs to ozone depletion in the early 1970s. Even before their hypotheses were conclusively confirmed, the United Nations Environment Programme (a UN agency created in the aftermath of the 1972 Stockholm conference) sought some form of regulatory action. The scientific uncertainty surrounding the issue eased the sense of urgency some felt, and differences between the interests of the chemical industry in the United States (where bans were placed on some CFCs, such as aerosol propellants) and

Europe (where they were not) slowed efforts to devise controls. Nevertheless, in 1985 the Vienna Convention on Protection of the Ozone Layer, whose purpose was to control ozone-modifying substances, was concluded. This landmark decision "represented the first international effort to deal formally with an environmental danger before it erupted" (Benedick 1991).

Two years later an even more significant agreement was reached, the Montreal Protocol on Substances That Deplete the Ozone Layer, signed by twenty-three states and the Commission of the European Community. The signatories agreed to reduce their CFC emissions to one-half of their 1986 levels by the turn of the century. The agreement was widely heralded, as its parties accounted for more than 80 percent of global CFC emissions. Even further cuts were proposed later, with an agreement eventually reached calling for the phaseout of CFC production in the Global North by 1996 and in the Global South around 2010. Subsequent agreements called for the phaseout of HCFCs. Originally developed because they were believed to be ozone-friendly alternatives to CFCs and a bridge to further scientific breakthroughs, HCFCs will be phased out completely by 2030 under current agreements (although many European states would prefer to speed up the timetable). Agreement was also reached in late 1995 to completely eliminate by 2010 production of methyl bromide, an ozone-depleting chemical widely used as an all-purpose pesticide.

The rapid move since 1985 to restrict the use of ozone-depleting chemicals contradicts the behavior the tragedy of the commons metaphor would lead us to expect. Rather than exploiting a common property (the atmosphere), states have successfully put their long-term collective interests in environmental protection ahead of short-term individual interests in protecting investments and jobs in the chemical industry (Benedick 1991).

As remarkable as this achievement is, implementation of the ozone regime still faces challenges. Notably, in spite of reductions in CFCs over the past decade, the ozone hole over the Antarctica has continued to expand. Nature eventually will mend the atmospheric damage done by prior ozone-depleting chemical emissions, but it will take decades. Meanwhile, under the current international regime, depletion of the protective ozone shield is expected to accelerate before it begins to regenerate itself (Gurney 1996). An increase in sulfur particles due to volcanic eruptions (like Mount Pinatubo in the Philippines in 1991) and the burning of fossil fuels is a contributing factor. The use of HCFCs as transition chemicals may also be debilitating. Although these compounds do not last as long as CFCs (whose ozone-depleting chemical reactions can last a century or more), they do most of their damage in ten to twenty years—precisely the time frame in which the ozone shield is already at greatest risk (Gurney 1996)—and they contribute markedly to global warming. Some states, however, notably the United States, are unwilling to shorten the time frame for elimination of HCFCs so as to permit the industries that have heavily invested in alternatives to CFCs to recover their investments (Porter and Brown 1996).

A second issue turns on the differing interests of developed and developing countries. Global production of CFCs has declined sharply in this decade as the largest producers (and consumers) prepared for their complete phase-out. This, for the most part, has now been achieved. Production in the Global South, on the other hand, is surging. Demand is growing for refrigerators, air conditioners, and other products using CFCs. Current CFC production in the Global South is still comparatively low. However, as it increases between now and

2010, it will offset the gains realized by stopping production in the North. Developed countries agreed to provide aid to the developing countries to help them adopt CFC alternatives, but thus far they have failed to provide all of the resources promised. Without this support, many in the Global South may not be able to keep their end of the global bargain (see Miller 1995). Meanwhile, a significant illegal trade in both virgin and recycled CFCs has emerged, threatening to further undermine the positive effects of the ozone regime (Porter and Brown 1996).

Despite these challenges to the ozone regime, it stands as a significant achievement in international environmental cooperation. Can it serve as a model for breakthroughs on other issues, notably climate change? The success of the ozone initiative is widely attributed to the growing body of scientific evidence supporting the theory combined with what some see as the absence of a significant requirement for social and economic change (Miller 1995). Other environmental issues do not share these characteristics. Climate change, for example, is an issue of infinitely greater magnitude involving far greater costs and benefits (Sebenius 1991). Contention about the scientific certainty of the evidence on global warming further muddies efforts to avert the tragedy of the commons. Similar issues affect the prospects for new initiatives to protect forests and the earth's biological heritage.

• • •

THE ECOPOLITICS OF FORESTS AND BIODIVERSITY

The world's forests play a critical role in the earth's complex ecological systems as well as in humankind's relationship with the environment and its well-being. Forests are intimately tied to preserving the earth's biodiversity and to protecting the atmosphere and land resources. For these reasons they have been the object of global attention. Some norms have emerged to guide global behavior in the preservation of biodiversity, as we will see, but forests themselves have proved largely impenetrable to such efforts.

Forests

Are the world's forests at risk of destruction through commercial exploitation or at the hands of local populations? Information is inconclusive, but estimates based on trends during the 1980s point toward moderate to considerable **deforestation**[4] in the United States and throughout much of the Global South. Destruction of tropical rain forests in such places as Brazil, Indonesia, and Malaysia is a matter of special concern, as much of the world's genetic heritage is found there (see Map 11.1). Whether this is a matter of *international* concern is, however, a contentious issue. If commercial logging to sell lumber and other wood products in the global marketplace is not a major cause of deforestation, but the expansion of agriculture to meet local agricultural and other needs is, as some argue (Sedjo 1995), why is this a matter for the global community?

The United States went to the Earth Summit hoping to secure an "easy" victory on a statement of principles for global forest conservation—the main

---

[4]Deforestation may be defined as "the permanent depletion of the ground cover of trees to less than 10 percent" (World Resources Institute 1994).

MAP 11.1

Forests and Rain Forests

Deforestation is a global phenomenon, but the rate of deforestation is much higher in the Global South than in the North. Tropical forests in Central and South America, in Africa, and in Southeast Asia have disappeared at an alarming rate.

SOURCE: Seager (1995), 72–73.

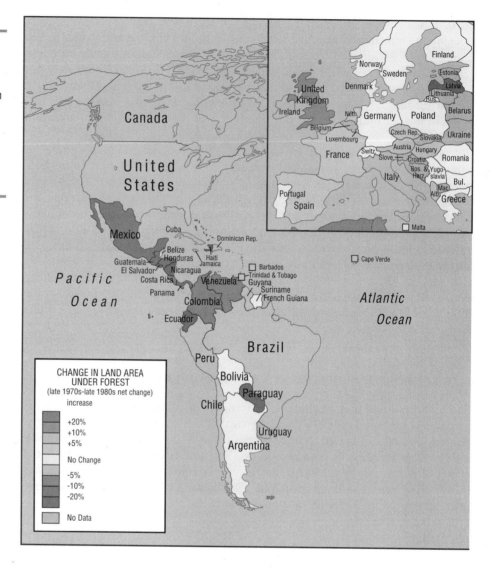

U.S. initiative at UNCED—but quickly ran into opposition. It directed attention to the principle of "global responsibility"; Canada championed "sovereign discretion." Together the two countries "tried to link the principle of the sovereignty of countries over their own forests with the principles of national responsibility and global concern for forests" (Porter and Brown 1996). The Global South objected vigorously.

Led by Malaysia—a principal exporter of tropical wood products—the South feared that the U.S.–Canadian stand was an effort to establish the legal principle that the world's forests are a common property resource, comprising the "common heritage of mankind." What Malaysia (and others in the Global South) feared is that accepting that principle as applied to forests would give the Global North "some right to interfere in the management of the tropical forest countries' resources." In the end the Earth Summit dropped "both the idea of international guidelines for forest management and any reference to trade in 'sustainably managed' forest products" (Porter and Brown 1996). The situation is largely unchanged. The International Tropical Timber Organization

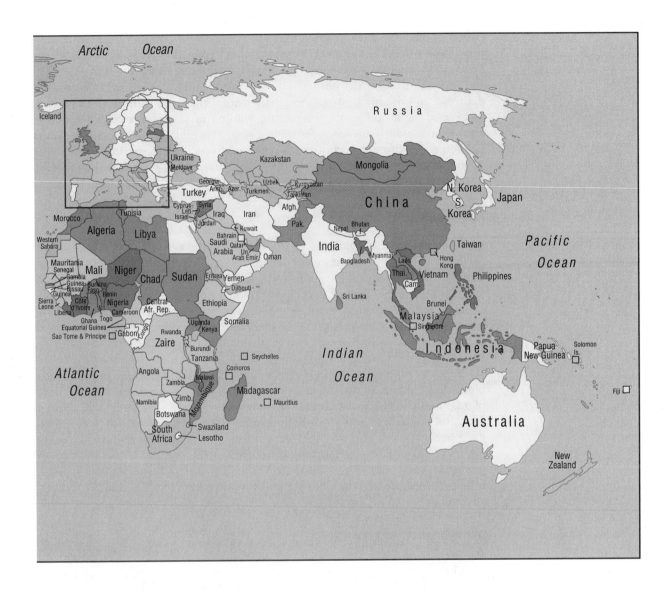

(ITTO) remains the principal international forum for addressing transnational issues (notably trade) in timber products, but it is dominated largely by the timber interests themselves (Porter and Brown 1996).

Meanwhile, population growth in the Global South and demands for increased well-being contribute to higher rates of deforestation in these countries. This sometimes results in desertification, which renders the land useless both for production and as habitat for wildlife. Based on previous trends, it has been estimated that an area about the size of one-fourth to one-half of an American football field is deforested each time another person is added to world population. This means that the addition of another billion people will require between 1.2 million to 2.5 million square kilometers of additional land for food production and other uses (J. Cohen 1995, 338). This contrasts sharply with the situation in the Global North, where reforestation is a common practice (Sedjo 1995; see also McKibben 1995).

The clearing and burning of tropical rain forests to make room for farms and ranches is especially troublesome from the viewpoint of climate change.

Green plants routinely remove carbon dioxide from the atmosphere during photosynthesis. The natural processes that remove greenhouse gases are destroyed when forests are cut down, and, as the forests decay or are burned, the amount of CO_2 discharged into the atmosphere increases. This makes deforestation doubly destructive. Furthermore, the cattle raised on the newly deforested land add to the staggering volume of methane released into the atmosphere, which also contributes to global warming. Nonetheless, the World Resources Institute reports that the rate of tropical deforestation during the 1980s was so rapid that "an area three times the size of France was converted to other uses" (Knickerbocker 1994, 7).

Biodiversity

Biodiversity, or biological diversity, is an umbrella term that refers to the earth's variety of life. Technically it encompasses three basic levels of organization in living systems: genetic diversity, species diversity, and ecosystem diversity. As a practical matter, public attention until recently has been focused almost exclusively on preserving species diversity. Efforts to protect endangered species from extinction and conservation programs designed to protect old-growth forests, tall-grass prairies, wetlands, coastal habitats, coral reefs, and similar areas are illustrative.

Forests, especially tropical forests, are especially important to preserving biodiversity because they are home to countless species of animals and plants, many of them still unknown. Scientists believe that the global habitat contains between 8 and 10 million species. Of these, only about 1.5 million have been named, and most of them are in the temperate regions of North America, Europe, Russia and Australia (Edwards 1995, 215). Destruction of tropical forests, where two-thirds to three-fourths of all species are believed to live, thus threatens the destruction of much of the world's biological diversity and genetic heritage.

Destruction of the world's forests contributes to climate change through global warming and threatens the earth's biodiversity and genetic heritage. Lumbering for commercial purposes exacts a toll on forests, but deforestation due to the expansion of agriculture to meet the needs of a growing population may be a more critical threat.

Some experts worry that, due mainly to human activities, "the world is on the verge of an episode of major species extinction, rivaling five other documented periods over the past half-billion years during which a significant portion of global fauna and flora were wiped out," each time requiring "ten million years or more for the number of species to return to the level of diversity existing prior to the event." Others doubt the imminence of a massive die-out, pointing out that only a small fraction of the earth's species have actually disappeared over the past several centuries (World Resources Institute 1994, 147). Indeed, cornucopians argue that species extinction may not be bad news, as new species may evolve that will prove even more beneficial to humanity (Simon and Wildavsky 1984).

These differing viewpoints, combined with the uneven distribution of known and unknown species among habitats within ecosystems, lie at the foundation of biodiversity as a contentious global issue. Threats to biodiversity have implications for all species. Therefore the issue resembles threats to other common property resources—notably the atmosphere, where climate change and ozone depletion are at issue. However, biodiversity's distributional characteristics make it different from other issues. In particular, because the earth's biological heritage is concentrated in the tropics, the Global South has a special interest in this issue domain.[5] It also has a growing concern about protecting its interest in the face of recent developments. "Traditionally, the genetic character of the many species of plants and animals have been considered a part of the common heritage of humankind, but increasingly they have become the objects of an enclosure movement that is seeking to enclose, privatize, and reduce the building blocks of life to marketable products" (Miller 1995).

Toward Enclosure: The Stakes. Multinational corporations in the Global North are major players in the "enclosure" movement (the claiming of common properties by states or private interests). In India, for example, products from the neem tree "for centuries . . . have been used locally for medicine, contraception, toiletries, timber, fuel, and insecticide. Its chemical properties have never been patented in India, but since 1985 U.S. and Japanese firms have taken out more than a dozen U.S. patents for a variety of neem compounds" (Miller 1995). Ironically, local Indian populations must now compete with MNCs for products long readily available to them, often at sharply higher prices.

Pharmaceutical companies also have laid claim to resources in the Global South. They actively explore plants, microbes, and other living organisms in tropical forests for possible use in prescription drugs. "This is a lucrative field; about 25 percent of the prescription drugs used in the United States have active ingredients extracted or derived from plants" (Miller 1995, 110). An example of a particularly successful project was Eli Lilly's development of drugs from the rosy periwinkle found in Madagascar's rain forest to treat childhood leukemia. Sales of the drugs amounted to about $100 million annually—although Madagascar received nothing for the use of its biological resource. Averting repetition of Madagascar's experience is a central concern among developing countries.

---

[5]Habitat loss, as in the tropics, is especially contentious. As the World Bank notes, habitat loss is the primary threat to terrestrial biodiversity and is "driven largely by human population pressure and demands for material goods. . . . The main causes of habitat loss in land-based ecosystems are conversion for agriculture and settlement, logging and the establishment of tree plantations, and pollution" (World Bank 1995b).

The rapid growth of biotechnology has added incentives for preserving the earth's biological diversity so as to maintain a wide gene pool from which to develop new medical and agricultural products. At the same time, however, genetic engineering in the industrialized world to develop hybrid seeds for new plants threatens the loss of biodiversity. The uneven distribution of biological resources is related to these developments, as farmers and scientists increasingly must look to the Global South for primitive germ plasm (the genetic material containing hereditary information).

> They assume that, as with the high seas, this primitive germ plasm is the common property of humankind. These genetic resources are used to produce genetically altered seeds for the international market. Since these are now patented and are private property, they can then be sold back to [Global South] consumers. The genetically altered seeds often need expensive additives such as chemical fertilizers and pesticides, which are often environmentally as well as financially costly. The picture for [Global South] agriculture deteriorates further when developing-country farmers focus on hybrid varieties to the detriment of, and at the risk of causing the disappearance of, the old varieties. (Miller 1995, 112)

These examples of the issues underlying the global concern for preserving the earth's biological heritage easily could be expanded to encompass a wider and more diverse terrain. Nonetheless, the message would remain generally the same: Preserving biodiversity requires cooperation across a complex array of ecological, economic, and social and cultural fronts. It is at the intersection of these contributing factors that states and nonstate actors must search for the sustainable use of the earth's biological heritage (Edwards 1995). Only tentative steps have been taken in this direction.

Toward Preservation: The International Response. Biodiversity has been a focus of global attention since the 1972 Stockholm conference. Between then and the 1992 Earth Summit, several conferences were held and agreements reached on a number of issues, including many of special concern to developing countries (see Miller 1995). In addition, bilateral agreements were reached along the way that set important precedents for possible alternative arrangements for dealing with the competing interests at stake. Among the most innovative was an agreement between Costa Rica and Merck Corporation, the world's largest pharmaceutical firm. The company agreed to pay for access to Costa Rica's rich tropical forests for drug-related research and to compensate Costa Rica with royalty payments for any products resulting from this research.

What set the Earth Summit apart from previous biodiversity efforts at the international level was the special treatment now given the issue. For instance, a separate Convention of Biodiversity set forth a comprehensive framework for preservation of biodiversity. The road to the convention was rocky, however, as the Global North and South repeatedly clashed. Especially contentious was a proposal to use a recently created **Global Environment Facility (GEF)** within the World Bank (a joint enterprise with the U.N. Environment [UNEP] and Development [UNDP] Programmes) as the instrument for resource transfers from North to South to meet the objectives spelled out in the biodiversity convention as well as in other Earth Summit documents. This controversy was largely due to the developing countries' belief that the World Bank heavily favored the interests of the Global North, which is its principal source of funds.

Eventually more than 150 states signed the Earth Summit's biodiversity convention (the United States being the notable exception), more than agreed to other documents approved at the meeting. As with the Convention on Climate Change, the Convention on Biodiversity is a legally binding document which entered into full force in late 1993. It spells out guidelines for sharing the profits of biotechnology between the Global North and South. It also commits governments to devise national strategies for conserving species and habitats, protecting endangered species, expanding protected areas and repairing damaged ones, and promoting public awareness of the need to protect the earth's heritage.

Still, as in the framework convention on climate change, much remains to be done. Scientific uncertainty about how (or even whether) species can be saved abounds. Balancing the interests of those who seek access to genetic materials with those of others with a stake in sharing in the profits of biotechnology must still be resolved. And agreements on mechanisms to finance the obligations contained in the treaty and creating an institutional mechanism to oversee its implementation must still be reached. As one environmental specialist astutely observes, "governments of most nations . . . recognize the need for rules to preserve those aspects of the global environment that are beyond the jurisdiction of any state." However, they "often balk at agreeing to specific regulations and complying with them" (Soroos 1995). Nonetheless, the convention breaks important ground in addressing simultaneously issues of *conservation* and *equity*, values that are often in competition with one another as global actors seek to avert environmental tragedies (Soroos 1995).

● ● ●

TRADE, THE ENVIRONMENT, AND SUSTAINABLE DEVELOPMENT

We began this chapter by posing the question of whether national security and environmental security are compatible concepts and objectives. A similar contrast may be drawn between free trade and sustainability. Do these concepts and the values they imply complement one another, or are they in conflict? The question is especially pertinent in a rapidly globalizing world in which trade, as we have seen in previous chapters, is often the webwork linking politics, economics, societies, and cultures throughout the world in complex interdependencies.

Liberal economic theory is clear about the benefits that free trade promises. If all states specialize in the production of goods in which they enjoy comparative advantages and trade them with others who enjoy similar advantages in other products, all will prosper. Following this logic, liberal economists conclude that free trade can benefit the environment because of the rising prosperity that free trade generates. "Growth enables governments to tax and to raise resources for a variety of objectives, including the abatement of pollution and the general protection of the environment. Without such revenues, little can be achieved, no matter how pure one's motives may be" (Bhagwati 1993).

Environmentalists question liberal economists' logic, especially because they see economic growth and environmental protection as incompatible goals. One well-known economist steeped in (but critical of) classical theory summarizes the dilemma: "Free traders seek to maximize profits and production without regard for considerations that represent hidden social and environmental costs. They argue that when growth has made people wealthy enough, they will have the funds to clean up the damage done by growth. Conversely, environmentalists and some economists . . . suspect that growth is increasing environmental costs faster than benefits from production—thereby making us poorer, not richer" (Daly 1993).[6]

The concept of sustainable development seeks to bridge these differences, but they remain unresolved. In part this is because the assumptions underlying the principle of comparative advantage no longer hold. As articulated by classical economic theorists like David Ricardo, the gains from trade promised by classical trade theory assume that capital is immobile, and thus that no country invests beyond its borders. Clearly that is no longer true, as we saw in Chapter 9. This means that "comparative advantage becomes irrelevant because capital will flow to countries with an absolute [not comparative] advantage. Countries without such advantage will experience pressure on wage rates, working conditions, environmental regulations, and anything else perceived to hinder competitiveness" (Costanza et al. 1995). Translated, that means environmental protection and preservation can be expected to fall by the wayside as other concerns receive priority.

Beyond the issue of the gains from and costs of trade, environmentalists and liberal economists differ in their assessments of the wisdom of using trade to promote environmental standards (see Focus 11.3). Liberal economists see such efforts as market distortions, while environmentalists view them as useful instruments for correcting market failures, such as markets' inability to incorporate the externalities of environmental exploitation (e.g., atmospheric pollution by chemical companies). Some countries, however, particularly in the Global South, view the use of trade mechanisms to protect the environment as yet another way in which the rich states block entry into lucrative Northern markets, thus keeping the South permanently disadvantaged (Durbin 1995).

The case of tuna imports into the United States, to which we briefly alluded in Chapter 8 (the "GATTzilla versus Flipper" debate), illustrates the sometimes competing demands of trade liberalization and environmental protectionism. Concerned about the unnecessary death inflicted on dolphins by tuna fishers, environmental groups pressured the United States to insert a provision in the Marine Mammal Protection Act (MMPA) regulating the fishing practices of foreign fleets so as to minimize the death of dolphins in the Pacific Ocean. The law banned the import of tuna caught by merchants who also ensnared dolphins as they netted schools of tuna swimming beneath the marine mammals. Mexico responded by filing a challenge with GATT that claimed "how they caught tuna was nobody else's business" (Phillips 1993). The GATT dispute panel ruled in Mexico's favor, effectively lifting the embargo on "dolphin-unsafe" tuna. In doing so, it also seemed to rule that trade agreements designed

---

[6]The World Bank has begun to experiment with a new measure of the "wealth of nations" that counts not only the production of goods and services, as the GNP now does, but that also incorporates how states manage their natural resources and how much they invest in human resources (see World Bank 1995b). For "genuine saving" to occur, according to this innovative procedure, a state must "consume" less than it "produces." According to this new measure of wealth, Australia and Canada are the top-ranked countries in the world, largely because of their vast store of natural resources. Luxembourg, Switzerland, Japan, Sweden, Iceland, Qatar, the United Arab Emirates, Denmark, Norway, and the United States follow (in that order). The methodology also reveals the net "dissaving" throughout much of Africa, which is reflected in a variety of more specific information we have examined in this and previous chapters (see World Bank press release, September 17, 1995).

Free Trade and Sustainable Development
An Oxymoron?

The links between trade and the environment raise three main questions.

1. What are the environmental effects of trade liberalization?

The fear that these effects are generally negative has led to calls for amending trade policies to take explicit account of environmental goals. Recent controversies have concerned the negative effects of the . . . North American Free Trade Agreement [NAFTA] on air and water quality in Mexico and the southwestern United States, of liberalized cassava exports to the [EEU] on soil erosion in Thailand, and of exchange rate depreciation on deforestation in Ghana. But using trade restrictions to address environmental problems is inefficient and usually ineffective. Liberalized trade fosters greater efficiency and higher productivity and may actually reduce pollution by encouraging the growth of less-polluting industries and the adoption and diffusion of cleaner technologies.

In these and other examples, the primary cause of environmental problems is not liberalized trade but failure of markets to price the environment appropriately. . . . Indeed, modifying trade policies to deal with environmental problems may worsen degradation. Thus, restricting the export of logs, as in Indonesia, raises returns to the domestic wood-processing industry and may contribute to inefficient and high-cost production that could worsen deforestation. Usually, more direct instruments than trade policies are available for combating deforestation, soil erosion, or industrial pollution. . . .

2. Should trade policies be used to influence environmental standards in other countries?

The arguments noted above apply here as well and are strengthened by another consideration: Some variation in environmental standards across regions and countries is justified by differences in priorities and in capacities to assimilate pollutants or cope with resource degradation. When countries (typically, the bigger and richer ones) use trade policy to impose their environmental standards, the effect is to protect domestic producers from foreign competition. Applying the same standards to domestic production and imports may be justified when, as with cars or pesticides, consumption leads to environmental damage. But even there, environmental concerns do not warrant uniformity across countries.

Evidence shows that developing countries do not compete for foreign investment in "dirty" industries by lowering their environmental standards. . . . Rather, anecdotal data . . . suggest the opposite: Because it is cheaper for multinational corporations to use the same technologies as they do in industrial countries, these firms can be potent sources of environmental improvement.

3. Should trade policies be used to enforce or implement international environmental agreements?

Trade measures to implement environmental agreements include the Montreal Protocol, which phases out ozone-depleting chemicals; the Basel Convention for controlling the transboundary movement and the disposal of hazardous wastes; and the Convention on International Trade in Endangered Species (CITES), which supports the embargo on ivory trade. The use of trade instruments could be justified in some of these cases. For instance, restricting trade in hazardous and toxic wastes . . . is appropriate if the capacities of many countries to monitor and dispose of these wastes are in doubt. But in most countries, the scale of such trade is small in comparison with the volume of hazardous wastes being generated domestically. Therefore, the concern should be to minimize the production of these wastes and to devise ways of ensuring their safe disposal. A total ban on all trade in hazardous and toxic wastes would be counterproductive because it would prevent the development of collective arrangements for treatment and disposal, even where individual countries, as in western Europe, can specialize in safe and low-cost disposal.

The ban on trade in ivory to protect the African elephant also involves difficult tradeoffs. Available evidence shows that ivory prices have fallen and poaching has declined since the ban became effective. But countries such as Botswana, South Africa, and Zimbabwe have argued that the ivory ban, by raising prices in the long run, will simply make poaching more lucrative. . . . These countries also claim that the ban discriminates against their efforts to manage their elephant herds sustainably by using revenue from hunting and tourism to enrich local people and finance law enforcement.

SOURCE: *World Development Report 1992* (1992), 67.

to liberalize trade can, in the words of U.S. Representative Henry Waxman, "undermine domestic laws designed to protect human health and the environment." The industrialized countries worry that efforts like these, designed to "harmonize" standards in different countries, do more than reduce trade barriers; they also "weaken laws and restrict their options to strengthen environmental regulations if there is a subsequent trade impact" (Durbin 1995).

GATT's tuna–dolphin ruling marked a victory for governments in the Global South who regard environmental laws as restrictive trade barriers designed to shut them out from Northern markets. Even for them, however, the sovereignty issue is troublesome. Is it not possible that industrial countries will use trade agreements to force their environmental standards on countries outside their jurisdictions? (The NAFTA agreement binding Canada, Mexico, and the United States in a free-trade area was finalized only after Mexico agreed to a series of side agreements designed to tighten Mexican environmental laws.) "Unless there is a transboundary or 'spillover' environmental effect, many Southern governments see little reason why industrialized countries should apply environmental standards to foreign countries and their industries. In cases where there is such an effect, developing countries prefer a multilateral approach to addressing the problem—one that provides technical and financial assistance" (Durbin 1995).

The tuna–dolphin controversy illustrates the trade-offs that sometimes must be made between goals which, in principle, seem designed for the same end—namely increasing human well-being. However, a less-benign interpretation of the issue views it as an illustration of the incompatibility of free trade and environmental protection. From this viewpoint, trade encourages states to live beyond their means. It "magnifies the ecological effects of production by expanding the market for commodities beyond national boundaries. . . . It allows nations that have depleted their resource bases or passed strict laws protecting them to reach past their borders for desired products, effectively shifting the environmental impacts of consumption to someone else's backyard" (French 1994).

What happens when everyone does the same thing? The tragedy of the commons metaphor suggests a bleak future. Is ruin the destination toward which humankind rushes?

• • •

TOWARD SUSTAINABILITY

Sustainable development promises a much brighter future. Although the goal remains distant and elusive, the concept's embrace by governments and nonstate actors throughout the world promises continued sensitivity to the impact of human activity on the environment and invites environmentally sensitive responses to the challenges posed. Differences between the rich countries of the Global North and the rapidly growing states in the Global South will continue to spark controversy. Contention will be especially pronounced on issues involving the transfer of resources and technology—as called for to deal with climate change, ozone depletion, biodiversity, and a host of other specific problem areas. This contention will arise in part from differing perceptions as to who is responsible for what but also because of budgetary constraints in the North.

There is little doubt that the Global South, faced with rapidly growing populations and rising affluence, poses increasingly serious environmental challenges. Nonetheless, the trend is already "toward better environmental policies, increased investment in environmental infrastructure and technology, and the pursuit generally of economic development alternatives that minimize environmental impacts" (Helman 1995).

The Global North poses serious environmental challenges as well, as its consumption levels far exceed those of other states. Interestingly, though, as the industrialized countries move into the information age and their economies shift away from "dirty" manufacturing to much cleaner service-oriented activities, the adverse environmental consequences of their economic activities will diminish. Or at least they will decline locally. Trade with other states, however, will ensure continuing pressures on global resources and the environmental burdens they pose.

Economist Herman E. Daly has long argued that the key to solving the dilemma posed by the stress that economic growth places on the environment lies in replacing our current ideas about markets with the concept of a steady-state economy (see, e.g., Daly 1973; Daly 1993; Daly and Cobb 1989). "A steady-state economy is one whose throughput [the speed at which resources are consumed] remains constant at a level that neither depletes the environment beyond its regenerative capacity nor pollutes it beyond its absorptive capacity" (Daly 1993). This is development (qualitative improvements) without growth (quantitative increases in the use or consumption of materials), Daly's definition of sustainable development. "An economy that is steady in scale may still continue to develop a greater capacity to satisfy human wants by increasing the efficiency of its resource use, by improving social institutions, and by clarifying its ethical priorities—but not by increasing resource throughput." Is the world ready for such a revolution in thinking? Even if it is, can the revolution be achieved?

● ● ●

KEY TERMS

ecopolitics

Earth Summit

externalities

global warming

greenhouse gases

Intergovernmental Panel on Climate
  Change (IPCC)

acid rain

deforestation

biodiversity

Global Environment Facility (GEF)

CHAPTER 12

Resorting to Force: Armed Conflict between and within States

OUTLINE

■ Armed Conflicts in the World: Continuities and Change

■ The Causes of Armed Conflict: Rival Theories

■ Armed Conflicts within States

■ Terrorism

■ The Human Tragedy of Violent Conflict

Only the dead have seen the end of conflict.

—George Bush,
U.S. president, 1992

Mankind must put an end to war or war will put an end to mankind.

—John F. Kennedy,
U.S. president, 1961

Daily, the media report human activity in which force is used to settle disputes. Since 1945 not a single day has gone by without war, and the end of the Cold War has not reduced its frequency. For example, in 1994 more than thirty major armed conflicts were fought in twenty-seven locations throughout the world, in such places as Afghanistan, Algeria, Bosnia, Chechnya, Liberia, Rwanda, and Somalia (Sollenberg and Wallensteen 1995, 21). Given its widespread occurrence, it is little wonder so many people equate world politics with violence.

In *On War*, Prussian strategist Karl von Clausewitz advanced his famous dictum that war is merely an extension of diplomacy by other means—"a form of communication between countries," albeit an extreme form. This insight underscores the realist belief that war is an instrument for states to use to resolve their disputes. War, however, is the deadliest instrument of conflict resolution, its onset indicating that persuasion and negotiations have failed.

In international relations, **conflict** regularly occurs when actors interact and disputes over incompatible interests arise. In and of itself, conflict is not necessarily threatening and may be seen as inevitable.[1] However, its costs *do* become threatening when the partners turn to arms to settle their perceived irreconcilable differences.

In this chapter, we explore the challenge that armed conflicts pose in world affairs, examining the character, causes, and magnitude of international violence, as well as changes in it over time. We will investigate three primary ways that armed force is most often used: *wars* between states, *civil wars* within states, and *terrorism*. In the next chapters we will consider the ways in which states and other global actors respond to this challenge and the major approaches they have taken to manage armed conflict.

● ● ●

ARMED CONFLICTS IN THE WORLD: CONTINUITIES AND CHANGE

Our understanding of the amount of armed conflict occurring globally depends in part on the definitions scholars use to establish types and thresholds. If we follow the criteria used by such behavioral or scientific studies as the Correlates of War (COW) project at the University of Michigan (Small and Singer 1982)

---

[1]*War* and *conflict* are different. Conflict occurs when two parties perceive differences between them and seek to resolve those differences to their own satisfaction. Some conflict is inevitable when people interact; therefore we should not regard it as abnormal. Nor should we regard conflict as necessarily destructive, since it can promote social solidarity, creative thinking, learning, and communication—all factors critical to the resolution of disputes (Coser 1956).

and the Peace and Conflict Research project at Uppsala University in Sweden (Wallensteen and Sollenberg 1995), we focus on *major* armed conflicts (with more than one thousand battle deaths). Here we find ample reason why UN Secretary-General Boutros Boutros-Ghali described the international system in 1995 as a "culture of death." Since 1945, we note no less than the initiation of more than 130 wars.

> Counting only those killed directly in the fighting, over 23 million people have perished. Including some of those who died as a result of war-related famine or illness, some 40 million have perished. By one analysis, the number of war deaths during the post-1945 period has been more than twice that in the nineteenth century and seven times that in the eighteenth century. (Kane 1995a, 18–19)

These grim statistics can be put into perspective by observing the trends evident since 1945. As Figure 12.1 shows, the number of ongoing armed conflicts worldwide that claimed one thousand or more lives peaked in 1994 at thirty-four, with nearly three times as many erupting as occurred during the 1950s (when they averaged eleven each year) and twice as many as took place during the 1960s (when they averaged fifteen each year). Counter to this trend, however, the number of the deadliest armed conflicts underway claiming more than one hundred thousand lives has been relatively stable, averaging 8.5 each year in the 1960s, 7.3 in the 1970s, and 10.1 in the 1980s. In the 1990s, the number has declined from 11 in 1991 to 7 in 1994.

Of particular interest are trends in wars *between* established states (such as the Gulf War that followed Iraq's 1990 attack on Kuwait and the Gulf War that followed). Armed conflicts that cross borders and result in one thousand or more battle fatalities have been far less frequent between 1945 and 1994 than all types of armed conflicts in general. According to the Worldwatch Institute, exactly 100 such interstate wars were underway annually during this period, with, on average, 2.5 occurring each year in the 1950s, 2.6 in the 1960s, 2.9 in the 1970s, and 3.1 in the 1980s. In addition, a single war was underway between states in each year between 1990 and 1994 (Worldwatch database diskette 1995). This tells us that although the post-World War II period has not been peaceful, most armed conflicts have been civil wars *within* states instead of wars *between* two recognized countries. While we will look separately at internal wars, we will first look more closely at the characteristics and causes of armed conflicts between states.

The Changing Character of Armed Conflict between States

Over the course of history, armed conflicts have changed in response to innovations in military technology. In the twentieth century, this impact has been especially rapid and influential. Indeed, the increasing destructiveness of modern weaponry has transformed contemporary warfare in three major ways. First, although the duration of interstate wars steadily increased between 1816 and World War II, wars have been shorter since 1945. Presumably, the capacity to inflict massive destruction has brought many armed conflicts between countries to an end sooner than often was the case before that capacity existed.

Second, the average number of countries involved in major wars has fallen sharply since World War II (K. Holsti 1995). This is observable both in the types and number of countries that participate in armed conflicts.

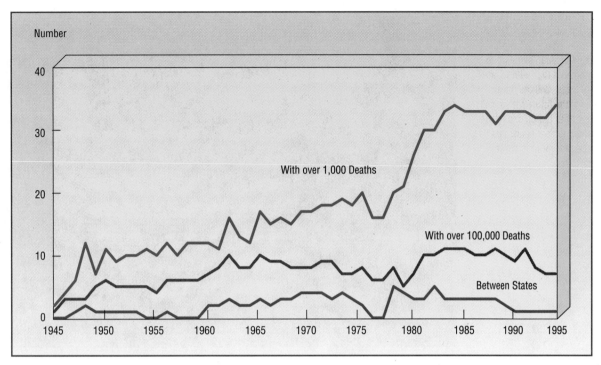

Number

40

30

With over 1,000 Deaths

20

With over 100,000 Deaths

10

Between States

0

1945 1950 1955 1960 1965 1970 1975 1980 1985 1990 1995

FIGURE   12.1

Armed Conflicts throughout the World, 1945–1994

Since 1945, armed conflict has been constant throughout the globe. Between 1960 and 1994, nearly thirty wars claiming more than one thousand lives were active each year, with over nine wars killing more than one hundred thousand people also under way each year in the same period. In addition, the number of wars in progress between countries (not counting foreign interventions into civil wars or wars for independence from colonial rule), on an average, was 2.7 annually. These frequencies suggest that armed conflicts have been common since World War II. However, their attributes and locations have shifted as the international system has evolved.

SOURCES: Worldwatch estimate based on Kane, (1995a), 20, and (1995b), 110–112.

Third, armed conflicts have become increasingly concentrated geographically and now usually involve less developed countries. Since 1945, more than 90 percent of wars have been in the Global South (Kane 1995b, 110). In fact, large-scale armed conflicts involving many participants have become less frequent, reversing the historic pattern that characterized the previous century, when war between the great powers was more common, included more participants, and often took a large toll in human lives. This last change raises questions as to why wars between the great powers have ceased.

Nuclear Weapons and the Obsolescence of Great-Power War?

Paradoxically, during the past half-century the world's most powerful countries have been the most constrained in their use of military strength against one another. Some people believe that the creation of nuclear weapons has produced this outcome. For example, British Prime Minister Winston Churchill

Iraqi dictator Saddam Hussein in 1991 financed a plan to rapidly develop a nuclear weapons arsenal, planning to use it against the United States and its allies. Will this be an omen for the future? If so, will nuclear wars put an end to the so-called nuclear peace that has prevailed for more than fifty years?

articulated this thesis in 1953 when he confessed that on occasion he had "the odd thought that the annihilating character of [nuclear weapons] may bring an utterly unforeseeable security to mankind. . . . It may be that when the advance of destructive weapons enables everyone to kill anybody else no one will want to kill anyone at all." Whatever its causes, peace among the great powers has prevailed since 1945, with a "zone of peace" emerging among them alongside a "zone of turmoil" in the rest of the world (Singer and Wildavsky 1993).

In early 1992, U.S. President George Bush observed at the United Nations that "today the threat of global nuclear war is more distant than ever before." As Melvin Laird, U.S. Secretary of Defense in the Nixon administration, observed, "Nuclear weapons . . . are useless for military purposes." This does not assure us, however, that the threat of wars of mass destruction has disappeared. Increasing numbers of countries in the globe's large "zone of turmoil" stockpile weapons of mass destruction, both overtly and covertly (see Chapter 13). Although warfare is not necessarily the intended purpose and military strategies today often emphasize its prevention, there is no guarantee that **deterrence** (dissuasion by means of military threat) will succeed forever. Although the self-defeating nature of nuclear arsenals may have reduced their usefulness, and nuclear states want not so much to win as to avoid loss, there is no guarantee that a radical regime that acquires nuclear weapons will not use them against its adversaries.

More pessimistically, it is worth contemplating whether the world has escaped nuclear devastation by sheer luck—"less a consequence of intelligent policy than a fortunate concatenation of conditions" (Singer 1991). The laws of probability, some experts reason, decree that the longer nuclear arsenals exist, the more likely a nuclear exchange is to occur. The question is thus not *if*, but *when*, as deterrence is inherently unstable and the odds for nuclear holocaust through a fatal error (whether of judgment, miscalculation, or accident) are high. The limits to rationality under conditions of crisis heighten the potential dangers, as do the unreliable decision-making procedures of large-scale organizations and the probability of "close call" accidents (Sagan 1993).

These apocalyptic thoughts suggest that the widespread belief that nuclear weapons have preserved peace—a ***pax atomica***—may be a fanciful myth (see Vasquez 1991). Also questionable is the corollary proposition that as "the fear of escalating nuclear power reaches further down, [it will inhibit] also the use of lesser force for lesser ends and goals" (Majeed 1991). If the trends in armed conflicts since 1945 tell us anything, it is that recourse to force is likely to continue, even if the proportion of armed conflicts between states declines relative to internal armed conflicts within states. Destruction and death remain rampant. People, it seems, remain willing to kill through organized violence, especially recently in the Global South (Kane 1995b 110).

What ends motivate human beings to continue to resort to force, given the unspeakable casualties? The question provokes a more fundamental set of related questions about the causes of aggression generally. Accordingly, it is useful to review contending theories about the sources from which armed conflicts arise.

• • •

THE CAUSES OF ARMED CONFLICT:
RIVAL THEORIES

Throughout history efforts have been made to explain why states resort to force. Inventories of war's origins invariably conclude that they are incomplete (see Blainey 1988; Howard 1983; Vasquez 1993; Waltz 1954), in part because most agree that war is rooted in multiple sources at various "levels of analysis." For our purposes here, we will divide the most plausible causes into three major levels or categories: individuals, states, and the international system.

The First Level of Analysis: Human Nature and Aggression

In a sense, all wars between states originate from the decisions of national leaders, whose choices ultimately determine whether armed conflict will occur. We must therefore consider the relationship of war to individuals and their choices, and for this, questions about human nature are central.

The repeated outbreak of war has led some, such as psychologist Sigmund Freud (1968), to conclude that aggression stems from humans' genetic programming and psychological makeup. Identifying *Homo sapiens* as the deadliest species, ethologists (those who study animal behavior in order to understand human behavior) such as Konrad Lorenz (1963) similarly argue that humankind is one of the few species practicing **intraspecific aggression** (routine killing of its own kind). Most other species practice **interspecific aggression** (killing only other species, except in the most unusual circumstances—cannibalism in certain tropical fishes being one exception).

Many question these theories on both empirical and logical grounds. If aggression is an inevitable impulse deriving from human nature, then should not all humans exhibit this genetically determined behavior? This, of course, is not the case as many individuals are consistently nonaggressive. In addition, genetics does not explain why individuals may be belligerent at only some times.

Many social scientists thus conclude that war is a learned trait, part of humankind's cultural heritage rather than its biological nature.[2] The 1986 *Seville Statement*, endorsed by more than a dozen professional scholarly associations, maintains that "it is scientifically incorrect" to say that "we have inherited a tendency to make war from our animal ancestors," "that war or any other violent behavior is genetically programmed into our human nature," "that humans have a 'violent brain,'" or "that war is caused by 'instinct' or any single motivation" (see Somit 1990). Political scientist Ted Robert Gurr (1970) expresses the thesis, supported by behavioral research that "The capacity, but not the need, for violence appears to be biologically entrenched in humans." Aggression is a propensity acquired early in life as a result of **socialization** and, therefore, is a learned rather than biologically determined behavior.

Individuals' willingness to sacrifice their lives in war out of a sense of duty to their leaders and country is one of history's puzzles. "The fog of war" is what the Russian author Leo Tolstoy and others have called the fact that people will give their lives in struggles, large and small, whose importance and purpose are sometimes not understood. Clearly, this self-sacrifice stems from learned beliefs that some convictions—such as loyalty to the nation-state—are worth dying for. "It has been widely observed that soldiers fight—and noncombatants assent to war—not out of aggressiveness but obedience" (Caspary 1993). This, however, does not make human nature a cause of war, even if such learned habits of obedience are grounds for participation in the aggression authorized by others, and even if public jingoism encourages leaders to start wars.

Many scholars using behavioral methods to study international relations question the belief that entire nationalities are predisposed to war—that **national character** predetermines national aggression. National character—the shared attributes and values of members of a nationality—can express itself in different ways and can also change. Sweden and Switzerland have managed conflict without recourse to war since 1809 and 1815, respectively, whereas formerly they were aggressive. And until its invasion by China in 1949, Tibet had negotiated its foreign disputes peacefully for eight hundred consecutive years. This suggests that violence is not an inborn characteristic of particular people which predestines periodic outbreaks of aggression. Many nation-states have escaped the tragedy of war; in fact, since 1500 more than one in five have never experienced war (Sivard 1991, 20). This variation across different states over five centuries suggests that war is not endemic and unavoidable: "A vision of a ubiquitous struggle for power or of a determining systemic structure explains recurrence without accounting for non-recurrence or the great deviations from an average pattern of recurrence"(Holsti 1991).

---

[2]Many realists assume that the drive for power is innate and cannot be eliminated. They therefore accept the conclusion suggested by Charles Darwin's theories of evolution and natural selection: Life entails a struggle of the fittest for survival, and natural selection eliminates the traits that interfere with successful competition. Social Darwinism's interpretation of the biological influences on human behavior can be countered by examining why people cooperate and act morally. As James Q. Wilson (1993) argues, Darwinian theory overlooks the fact that "the moral sense must have adaptive value; if it did not, natural selection would have worked against people who had such useless traits as sympathy, self-control, or a desire for fairness in favor of those with the opposite tendencies." The controversy over the nature-nurture question regarding the biological basis of aggression has not been resolved (see Caspary 1993; Nelson 1974; and Somit 1990).

Nobel Prize-winner Ralph Bunche, an African-American U.S. policymaker, argued before the United Nations that "there are no warlike people—just warlike leaders." Similarly, St. Thomas More declared in the sixteenth century that "the common folk do not go to war of their own accord, but are driven to it by the madness of kings." But explaining the role of leaders in making war is not quite that simple, as leaders usually make foreign policies within groups. The social-psychological and bureaucratic setting for decision making and the global environment may exert "an influence independent of the actions and beliefs of individual policymakers. . . . War seems less like something decision makers choose than something that somehow happens to them," even as it happens "through them," through the choices they make (Beer 1981).

The decision for war is better explained, then, not by individual leaders' aggressiveness or by aggressive national character, but by the many political pressures that influence the government leaders who "ultimately decide the great questions of war and peace" (Holsti 1991). Therefore, it is relevant to ask, what domestic factors encourage policymakers to choose war?

The Second Level of Analysis: States' Internal Characteristics and War Involvement

Conventional wisdom holds that variations in states' government, size, ideology, geographical location, population dynamics, ethnic homogeneity, wealth, economic performance, military capabilities, and level of educational attainment influence whether they will engage in war. Drawing on the possibility suggested by Russian political theorist Peter Kropotkin in 1884 that "the word *state* is identical with the word *war*" and the evidence that war has contributed to the rise of the state (Porter 1994), we need to examine some theories addressing the internal characteristics of states that influence leaders' choices regarding the use of force.[3]

Duration of Independence. New states are more likely to initiate wars than are mature states (Wright 1942). Newly independent countries typically go through a period of internal political upheaval, which often serves as a catalyst to external aggression. As the recent national rivalries within and conflicts between the newly independent nations of the former Soviet Union indicate, drives to settle long-standing internal grievances and territorial disputes by force often follow the acquisition of independence. Between 1945 and 1992, all but one of the sixty civil wars were fought in emergent nations, and nearly one-fourth of them became internationalized as the internal bloodletting expanded across borders (Singer 1991, 59, 79). Because the national upheavals and revolutions that produce new states are most common in the newly formed countries of the Global South, it is not surprising that these states "are much more likely to be involved in international conflict" (Gurr 1994).

---

[3]Implicit in this approach is the assumption (embraced by "the comparative study of foreign policy" perspective relied on to discuss foreign policy decision making in Chapter 3) that the differences in the types or classes of states will determine whether they will engage in war. To argue that the prospects for war are influenced most heavily by national attributes and the types of leaders making decisions for states is to challenge the neorealist premise that international circumstances are the most powerful determinants of warfare.

The Feminist Critique of Realism
Cultural Numbing and Violence

Advocates of the cultural origins of war argue that most people in most societies live an everyday experience of disengagement, or "numbness," which disinclines them to oppose their leaders decisions' to wage war. The modern state thus organizes its society to accept war and "builds a culture that affirms death" and accepts senseless carnage (Caspary 1993). In contrast, critics operating from the perspective of feminist theories of international relations argue that the foundation of war worldwide, alongside cultural numbing, is rooted in the masculinist ethos of realism, which prepares people to accept war and to respect the warrior as a hero (see especially Enloe 1993 and Tickner 1992). Gender roles, they assert, supported by realist values contribute to the prevalence of militarism and warfare:

> According to feminist critics, international relations theory as it has evolved incorporates "masculinist" prejudices at each of its three levels of analysis: man, the state, and war. Realists are "androcentric" in arguing that the propensity for conflict is

universal in human nature ("man"); that the logic and the morality of sovereign states are not identical to those of individuals ("the state"); and that the world is an anarchy in which sovereign states must be prepared to rely on self-help, including organized violence ("war"). Feminist theorists would stress the nurturing and cooperative aspects—the conventionally feminine aspects—of human nature; they would expose the artificiality of notions of sovereignty, and their connection with patriarchy and militarism; and they would replace the narrow realist emphasis on security, especially military security, with a redefinition of security as universal social justice. (Lind 1993, 37)

We need to take seriously the potentially powerful cultural origins of armed conflict. Does history support the theory that the prevailing dominant cultural systems in the world, rooted in realism, glorify the state and aggression and, as a consequence, make violence more probable?

Cultural Determinants and the Decay of Moral Constraints. The international behavior of modern countries is influenced strongly by the cultural and ethical traditions of their peoples. In the state system governed by the rules championed by realism, moral constraints on the use of force do not command wide acceptance. Instead, most governments have encouraged their populations to accept whatever decisions their leaders deem necessary for national security, including warfare against adversaries (see Focus 12.1).

To those theorists who embrace the cultural interpretation, the penchant for warfare does not evolve in a vacuum but is produced by the ways in which national societies shape their populations' beliefs and norms. Many governments, through the educational programs they fund in schools and other institutions, indoctrinate values in their political culture that condone the practice of war. Ironically, in a world of diverse national cultures, the messages of obedience and of duty to make sacrifices to the state are common. States disseminate the belief that their right to make war should not be questioned and that the ethical principles of religious and secular philosophies prohibiting violence should be disregarded. Consequently, critics stress the existence of powerful institutions that prepare individuals to subconsciously accept warfare as necessary and legitimate.

National Poverty. A country's level of economic development also affects the probability of its involvement in war. Historically, the most warlike states have

Director Jean Renoir created his cinematic masterpiece, *La Grande Illusion*, to illustrate what he regarded as the irrational absurdity of war, waged by short-sighted people oblivious to the immoral consequences of their aggressive decisions on behalf of the state. Shown here are Pierre Fresnay, Jean Gabin, and Eric von Stroheim plotting war strategy. Did Renoir wish us to ask whether people are blinded by the militaristic values they have been taught by their governments to accept?

been poor, and this pattern persists, as the locale of warfare has shifted since 1945 to the developing countries at the periphery. As U.S. Secretary of Defense Robert S. McNamara explained in 1966, "there is no question but that there is evidence of a relationship between violence and economic backwardness."

Before we conclude that poverty always breeds war, however, we must note that the *most* impoverished countries have been the least prone to start wars with their neighbors. The poorest countries cannot vent their frustrations aggressively because they lack the military or economic resources to do so. Thus the poorest states, like the wealthiest, cannot afford to wage war, but for quite different reasons. The former lack the means; the latter hold weapons too destructive to use.

This pattern does not mean that the poorest countries will always remain peaceful. If the past is a guide to the future, then the impoverished countries that develop economically will be those most likely to acquire arms and engage in future wars. In particular, many studies suggest that states are likely to initiate wars *after* sustained periods of economic growth—that is, during periods of rising prosperity, when they can most afford them (Cashman 1993). This signals danger if countries in the Global South develop rapidly and the new resources development generates are directed toward armament rather than investments in sustained development.

Militarization. The age-old question of whether the acquisition of military power leads to war or peace has assumed renewed emphasis in the post-Cold War era. As Chapter 13 will explain, "the race for the most advanced military technology began in the highly industrialized countries, and for awhile it was confined there. It is now rapidly spreading to the [Global South] largely with assistance both in equipment and technological aid from . . . the developed countries" (Sivard 1991). As a result, the issue is whether this dispersion of weapons also increases the probability of war.

As countries in the Global South accumulate the economic resources to equip their military establishments, many experts believe that war will become more frequent before it becomes less so. This prediction stems from the evidence that fundamental changes in military capability are an important determinant of the onset of war (Vasquez 1993), especially as reflected in the historical pattern in Europe.

During its transition to the peak of development, Europe was the location of the world's most frequent and deadly wars. The major European states armed themselves heavily and were engaged in warfare about 65 percent of the time in the sixteenth and seventeenth centuries (Wright 1942). Between 1816 and 1945, three-fifths of all international wars took place in Europe, with one erupting on average every other year (Singer 1991, 58). Not coincidentally, this happened when the developing states of Europe were most energetically arming in competition with one another. Perhaps as a consequence, the great powers—those with the largest armed forces—were the most involved in, and most often initiated, war (Cashman 1993). Since 1945, however, with the exception of war among the now-independent units of the former Yugoslavia (and clashes among the republics of the former Soviet Union), interstate war has not occurred in Europe. As the European countries have moved up the ladder of development, they have moved away from war with one another (internal turmoil is another matter).

In contrast, the developing countries now resemble Europe prior to 1945. If the Global South follows the European pattern, the immediate future may well witness the specter of a peaceful, developed world surrounded by a violent, less-developed world.

Economic System. Does the character of states' economic systems influence the frequency of warfare? The question has provoked controversy for centuries. Particularly since Marxism took root in Russia following the Bolshevik revolution in 1917, communist theoreticians claimed that capitalism *was* the primary cause of war—that capitalists practice imperialism and colonialism. According to this theory, capitalism produces surplus capital. The need to export it stimulates wars to capture and protect foreign markets. Thus **laissez-faire capitalism**—economies based on the philosophical principle of free markets with little governmental regulation of the marketplace—rationalized militarism and imperialism for economic gain. Citing the demonstrable frequency with which wealthy capitalist societies engaged in aggression, Marxists believed that the only way to end international war was to end capitalism.

Contrary to Marxist theory is liberal theory's conviction that free market systems promote peace, not war. Defenders of capitalism have long believed that free market countries that practice free trade abroad are more pacific. The reasons are multiple, but they center on the premise that commercial enterprises are natural lobbyists for world peace because their profits depend on it. War interferes with trade, blocks profit, destroys property, causes inflation, consumes scarce resources, and encourages big government and counterproductive regulation of business activity. By extension, this reasoning continues, as government regulation of internal markets declines, prosperity will increase and fewer wars will occur (see also Chapter 8).

The evidence for these rival theories is, not surprisingly, mixed. Conclusions depend in part on perceptions regarding economic influences on international behavior, in part because alternative perspectives focus on different dimensions of the linkage. This controversy was at the heart of the ideological debate between East and West during the Cold War, when the relative virtues and vices of two radically different economic systems (socialism and capitalism) were uppermost in people's minds. At the time, communists cited the previous record of wars initiated by capitalistic countries (e.g., Germany, Japan, and the United States in Vietnam) to lend credence to the Marxist interpretation, while ignoring the pacificity of other capitalist states such as Switzerland.

Marxist theory also did not explain communist states' embarrassingly frequent use of force. The Soviet Union invaded Finland in 1939 and Afghanistan in 1979; North Korea attacked South Korea in 1950; Communist China attacked Tibet in 1959; Vietnam invaded Cambodia in 1975; and Cuba intervened militarily in Africa in the 1980s. Moreover, communist states repeatedly clashed with one another during the Cold War (e.g., China and the Soviet Union in 1969, China and Vietnam in 1979 and 1987, the Soviet Union and Hungary in 1956, and the Soviet Union and Czechoslovakia in 1968). Communist or socialist systems participated in roughly 25 percent of all interstate wars between 1945 and 1967, even though only about 15 percent of all countries had socialist economies (Cashman 1993, 133). Thus the thesis that socialist or communist states are inherently nonaggressive failed empirically.

Communism's failure to produce economic prosperity also hastened its rejection in eastern Europe and in the very heartland of the communist experiment, the Soviet Union. With capitalism's triumph over communism, a phase of history appeared to have ended (Fukuyama 1992b). By 1996 only Cuba and North Korea still fully endorsed communist *economic* principles; although communism could yet prove resurgent, at the time all other former advocates appeared committed to free market economies.

The end of the Cold War does not end the historic debate about the link between economics and war, however. The issue of economic influences on international behavior remains, and this basic theoretical question is even likely to command increasing interest, especially given the "shift in the relevance and usefulness of different power resources, with military power declining and economic power increasing in importance" (Huntington 1991a; see also Chapters 8 and 9).

Type of Government. The neoliberal perspective on international politics predicts that democracy, as well as free enterprise, will inhibit the frequency with which governments resort to force to settle their disputes. The belief that democratic policy-making institutions will produce peace follows the liberal conviction of eighteenth-century philosopher Immanuel Kant in *Perpetual Peace* (1795). As a result, Kant predicted that relationships between democracies would be entirely pacific and that as democratic freedom spread worldwide, international relations would become peaceful. Kant felt that public opinion restrains rulers of democratic states from waging war because the mass public would have to supply the soldiers and bear the human and financial costs, and in democracies the rights of the people to be heard and to express their opposition to armed conflict are protected.

History has been kind to Kant's views—the bedrock of the liberal and neoliberal challenges to the realist and neorealist theoretical traditions which discount the importance of government type as a determinant of peace. Scholars now take the consequences of democratization seriously, having discovered that "Although preventive war has been the preferred response of declining authoritarian leaders, no democracy has ever initiated such a war" against another democratic state (Schweller 1992). Simply put, conflicting democracies have regularly dealt with mutual disagreements by accommodation rather than war (Dixon 1994; Doyle 1995; Lake 1992; Russett 1993),[4] chiefly because democracies' political culture embraces norms against aggression as a method of conflict resolution, and institutional procedures reinforce this constraint on leaders' policy choice. Moreover, in democratic states constitutions restrict leaders' freedom; political participation and civil liberties such as free speech and a free press encourage opposition and criticism; and leaders' fear of electoral punishment deters them from undertaking unpopular wars.

Faith in democratization as an antidote to armed conflict has grown in the past several decades in association with the diffusion of democratic governance. As we described in Chapter 3, recently there has been a resurgence of democracy, and this form of governance has grown throughout the world (see Figure 12.2). Between 1974 and 1991, roughly one-third of the countries on the planet converted their political systems to democratic rule.

The wave of democratization since the 1970s has provoked speculation that western liberal democracy will become universal, "the final form of government" (Fukuyama 1992b). As the growth of democracy spreads to the Global South, there is hope that the transition to democratic rule will usher in a new era of peaceful world politics. Indeed, this liberal doctrine has been embedded in the foreign policy of the United States and the other members of the Group of Seven (G-7) (i.e., Britain, Canada, France, Germany, Italy, and Japan) which have defined the promotion of democracy elsewhere as one of their central purposes and strategies for preventing future wars. In President Clinton's 1994 State of the Union Address, for example, he cited the absence of war between democracies as a justification for promoting democratization around the globe (see also Chapter 16).

Although the experience of Western Europe since World War II has helped shape this policy initiative by suggesting that democratic states will not engage in war with one another, we must still be cautious of quick assumptions that democracy is an altogether reliable barrier to war.

> It was, after all, the democratization of conflict in the nineteenth century that restored a ferocity to warfare unknown since the seventeenth century; the bloodiest war in American history remains the one fought between two (by today's standards flawed) democracies—the Civil War. Concentration camps appeared during another conflict between two limited democracies, the Boer War. World War I was launched by two regimes—Wilhelmine Germany and Austria-Hungary—that had greater representation and more equitable legal systems than those of many important states today. And even when modern liberal democracies go to war they do not necessarily moderate the scope of the violence they apply; indeed, sensitivity to their own casualties sometimes leads to profligate uses of firepower or violent

---

[4]This does not mean that democracies never experience war. "It appears that democracies fight as often as do other types of states" (Morgan and Schwebach 1992; also Small and Singer 1976; Wright 1942), because they have been engaged often in "defensive" or preventive wars against dictatorships. But "the democratic peace proposition" (Ray 1995) does hold: Democracies seldom, if ever, fight one another.

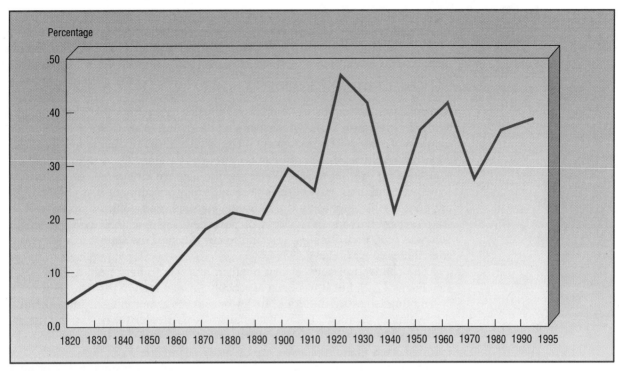

Percentage

FIGURE 12.2

The Percentage of the World's Governments that Are Democratic, 1820–1993

Throughout most of modern history, states have been ruled by monarchies, despots, dictators, and autocrats. But beginning in the twentieth century, democratization has spread sporadically in a series of waves—with an increasing percentage of the world now ruled by democratic institutions that support civil liberties and empower voters to restrict leaders' freedom to initiate wars. This has inspired hope among neoliberals that the spread of democracy will reduce the frequency of armed conflict, as Immanuel Kant predicted in 1795 when the age of democracy was first beginning, and as James Madison, Thomas Jefferson, Woodrow Wilson, and other liberal U.S. theorists also believed.

SOURCE: Hermann, Kegley, and Raymond (1996), based on the Polity III data (Jaggers and Gurr 1995).

> efforts to end wars quickly. Shaky democracies fight each other all the time. . . . We must remind ourselves just how peculiar the wealthy and secure democracies of the West are, how painful their evolution to stability and the horror of war with each other has been. Perhaps other countries will find short-cuts to those conditions, but it would be foolish to assume they will. (E. Cohen 1995, 39)

Thus it would be premature and overly optimistic to assume that the growth of democracy will automatically produce a more peaceful world.

Yet another concern is the frequency with which democratic states have intervened militarily, not only in authoritarian states but in other democratic states as well, in order to force democratic reform. Waging wars to spread democracy, as Woodrow Wilson did when he sent U.S. Marines into Mexico "to teach them to elect good governments," will not make for a more peaceful world. And the democratic peace could collapse because "countries do not become mature democracies overnight. More typically, they go through a rocky transitional period, where democratic control over foreign policy is partial, where mass politics mixes in a volatile way with authoritarian elite politics, and where democratization suffers reversals. In this transitional phase of democratization, countries become more aggressive and war-prone, not less, and they do fight wars with democratic states" (Mansfield and Snyder 1995).

Nationalism. Nationalism—love of and loyalty to a nation—is widely believed to be the cauldron from which wars often spring (Van Evera 1994; see also Chapters 4 and 7). "The tendency of the vast majority of people to center their supreme loyalties on the nation-state," political scientist Jack S. Levy explains, is a powerful catalyst to war. When people "acquire an intense commitment to the power and prosperity of the state [and] this commitment is strengthened by national myths emphasizing the moral, physical, and political strength of the state and by individuals' feelings of powerlessness and their consequent tendency to seek their identity and fulfillment through the state, . . . nationalism contributes to war" (Levy 1989a).

The connection between nationalism and war suffers from a long history (see Focus 12.2), but it has been especially pronounced in the twentieth century. The English essayist Aldous Huxley once termed nationalism "the religion of the twentieth century." Today, nationalism is particularly virulent and intense, and arguably, with racism, "the most powerful movements in our world today, cutting across many social systems" (Gardels 1991).

Most armed conflicts today are fed by nationalist sentiments that promote "war fever . . . accompanied by overt hostility and contempt toward a caricatured image of the enemy," out of which sadistic violence and genocide have historically emanated (Caspary 1993). This entrenched linkage leads some to argue that "Nationalism has often generated aggression abroad [and] has given us some three dozen costly wars in the Middle East since 1945" (Yoder 1991). And the danger could escalate. Nationalism's threat to world order led former Soviet President Mikhail Gorbachev to warn in May 1992 that "the demons of nationalism are coming alive again, and they are putting the stability of the international system to the test. Even the United States itself is not immune from the dangerous nationalism."

This discussion of the characteristics of states that influence their proclivity for war does not exhaust the subject. Many other potential causes internal to the state exist. But however important domestic influences might be as a source of war, many believe that the nature of the international system is even more critical.

The Third Level of Analysis: Cycles of War and Peace in the International System

Classical realism emphasizes that the roots of armed conflicts rest with human nature. In contrast, neorealism sees war springing from the decentralized character of the international system, which requires sovereign states to rely on self-help for their security.

International anarchy may promote war's outbreak, but it fails to provide a complete explanation of its occurrence. To capture war's many structural determinants, we must consider how and why systems change. This requires us to explore the impact of the distribution of military capabilities, balances (and

Nationalism and War

Karl Deutsch, a German-born political scientist who taught for many years at Harvard University, described nationalism and its connection to armed conflict with these moving words:

> *Nationalism* is an attitude of mind, a pattern of attention and desires. It arises in response to a condition of society and to a particular stage in its development. It is a predisposition to pay far more attention to messages about one's own people, or to messages from its members, than to messages from or about any other people. At the same time, it is a desire to have one's own people get any and all values that are available. The extreme nationalist wants his people to have all the power, all the wealth, and all the well-being for which there is any competition. He wants his people to command all the respect and deference from others; he tends to claim all rectitude and virtue for it, as well as all enlightenment and skill; and he gives it a monopoly of his affection. In short, he totally identifies himself with his nation. Though he may be willing to sacrifice himself for it, his nationalism is a form of egotism written large. . . .
>
> Even if most people are not extreme nationalists, nationalism has altered the world in many ways. Nationalism has not only increased the number of countries on the face of the earth, it has helped to diminish the number of its inhabitants. All major wars in the twentieth century have been fought in its name. . . .
>
> Nationalism is in potential conflict with all philosophies or religions—such as Christianity—which teach universal standards of truth and of right and wrong, regardless of nation, race, or tribe. Early in the nineteenth century a gallant American naval officer, Stephen Decatur, proposed the toast, "Our country! In her intercourse with foreign nations, may she be always in the right, but our country, right or wrong." Nearly 150 years later the United States Third Army, marching into Germany following the collapse of the Nazi regime, liberated the huge concentration camp at Buchenwald. Over the main entrance to that place of torture and death, the Nazi elite guard had thoughtfully written, "My Country, Right or Wrong." (Deutsch 1974, 124–125)

In confronting the impact of nationalism on armed conflict, we need to recognize its dual character: It is a force that (1) binds nations and nationalities together in common bonds, and (2) divides nation against nation, nationality against nationality, and is used to justify armed conflicts against other nations.

---

imbalances) of power, the number of alliances and international organizations, and the rules of international law. At issue is how these factors—the system's characteristics and institutions—combine to influence changes in war's frequency. We will examine many of these factors in Chapters 15 and 16. Here we focus on cycles of war and peace at the international level and the structural determinants of armed conflict.

Does Violence Breed Violence? The adage "violence breeds violence" reflects the notion that the seeds of future wars are found in past wars. From this perspective World War II was an outgrowth of World War I, and the successive wars in the Middle East were seemingly little more than one war, with each battle stimulated by its predecessor. Because the frequency of past wars *is* correlated with the incidence of wars in later periods, war appears contagious and its future outbreak inevitable. If so, then something within the dynamics of world politics—its anarchical nature, its weak legal system, its uneven distribution of power, inevitable destabilizing changes in the principal actors' relative power, or some combination of structural attributes—makes the state system a war system.

361

Those believing in war's inevitability often cite the historical fact that war has been so repetitive. We cannot, however, safely infer that past wars have *caused* later wars. The fact that a war precedes a later one does not mean that it caused the one that followed.

Nor does war's recurrence throughout history necessarily mean we will always have it. War is not a universal institution (see Etzioni 1968; Kluckhohn 1944; Mead 1968; Sumner 1968); as we have seen, some societies have never known it, and others have been immune to it for prolonged periods. Moreover, since 1945 the outbreak of armed conflicts between states has declined, despite the large increase in the number of independent countries. This indicates that armed conflict is not necessarily inevitable and that historical forces do not control people's freedom of choice or experiences.

Power Transitions. This notwithstanding, when changes have occurred in the major states' military capabilities, war has often resulted. Although not inevitable, war has been likely whenever competitive states' power ratios (the differentials between their capabilities) have narrowed. Dubbed the **power transition theory,** this structural explanation holds that

> an even distribution of political, economic, and military capabilities between contending groups of states is likely to increase the probability of war; peace is preserved best when there is an imbalance of national capabilities between disadvantaged and advantaged nations; the aggressor will come from a small group of dissatisfied strong countries; and it is the weaker, rather than the stronger, power that is most likely to be the aggressor. (Organski and Kugler 1980, 19)

During the transition from developing to developed status, emergent challengers can achieve through force the recognition that their newly-formed muscles allow them. Conversely, established powers ruled by risk-acceptant leaders often are willing to employ force to put the brakes on their relative decline. Thus, when advancing and retreating states seek to cope with the changes in their relative power, war between the rising challenger(s) and the declining power[s] has become especially likely. For example, the rapid changes in the power and status that produced the division of Europe among seven powers largely equal in military strength are often (along with the alliances they nurtured) interpreted as the tinderbox from which World War I ignited.

As explained in Chapter 15, rapid shifts in the global distribution of military power have often preceded outbursts of aggression, especially when the new distribution nears approximate parity (i.e., equality) and thereby tempts the rivals to wage war against their challengers. According to the power transition theory, periods in which rivals' military capabilities are nearly balanced create "the necessary conditions for global war, while gross inequality assures peace or, in the worst case, an asymmetric, limited war" (Kugler 1993). Moreover, transitions in states' relative capabilities potentially can lead the weaker party to start a war in order either to overtake its rival or to protect itself from domination. Presumably, the uncertainty created by a rough equilibrium prompts the challenger's (usually unsuccessful) effort to wage war against a stronger opponent. Equally persistent is the power transition theory's observation that advantages have shifted from the attacker to the defender: "In earlier centuries the aggressor seemed to have a 50–50 chance of winning the war, but this no longer holds. The chances of the starter being victorious are shrinking. In the 1980s only 18 percent of the starters were winners" (Sivard 1991, 20).[5]

Cyclical Theories. If war is recurrent but not necessarily inevitable, are there other international factors besides power transitions that might also potently explain changes over time in its outbreak? The absence of a clear trend in its frequency since the late fifteenth century, and its periodic outbreak after intermittent stretches of peace, suggest that world history seesaws between *long cycles* of war and peace. This provides a third structural explanation of war's onset.

The more recent formal analysis of such cycles is known as *long cycle theory*. As noted in Chapter 4, its advocates argue that cycles of world leadership and global war have existed over the past five centuries, with a "general war" erupting approximately once every century, although at irregular intervals (Modelski 1987b; Modelski and Thompson 1996; Thompson 1988). Long cycle theory seeks to explain how an all-powerful invisible hand built into the system's dynamics causes such peaks and valleys. Although this theory embraces many contending explanations (see Goldstein 1988), they converge on the proposition that some combination of systemic properties (economic, military, and political) produce the frequency with which major wars have erupted periodically throughout modern history.

The long-cycle perspective is based on the fact that a great power has risen to a hegemonic position about every one hundred years. Using as a measure of dominance the possession of disproportionate sea power, we observe regularly appearing intervals of hegemony (see Figure 12.3). While Portugal and the Netherlands rose at the beginning of the sixteenth and seventeenth centuries, respectively, and Britain climbed to dominance at the beginning of both the eighteenth and nineteenth centuries, the United States became a world leader at the end of World War II. During their reigns, these hegemonic powers monopolized military power and trade and determined the system's rules. Yet no hegemonic power has retained its top-dog position for more than three or four decades. In each cycle, overcommitments, the costs of empire, and ultimately the appearance of rivals led to the delegitimation of the hegemon's authority and to the deconcentration of power globally. As challengers to the hegemon's rule grew in strength, a "global war" has erupted after a long period of peace in each century since 1400. At the conclusion of each previous general war, a new world leader emerged dominant (Modelski 1978, 1987b), and the cyclical process began anew.

Such deterministic theories have intuitive appeal. It seems plausible, for instance, that just as long-term downswings and recoveries in business cycles profoundly affect subsequent behaviors and conditions, wars will produce aftereffects that may last for generations. The idea that a country at war will become exhausted and lose its enthusiasm for another war, but only for a time, is known as the **war weariness hypothesis** (Blainey 1988). Italian historian Luigi da Porto expresses one version: "Peace brings riches; riches bring pride; pride brings anger; anger brings war; war brings poverty; poverty brings humanity;

[5]As in the past (e.g., Japan's attack and subjugation of China in 1931 and 1937), there are more notable recent exceptions: "Since 1945, six out of twenty wars have secured decisive advantage for the initiator (the Vietnam, Six Day, Bangladesh, Yom Kippur/Ramadan, Falklands, and Persian Gulf wars)" (Ziegler 1995).

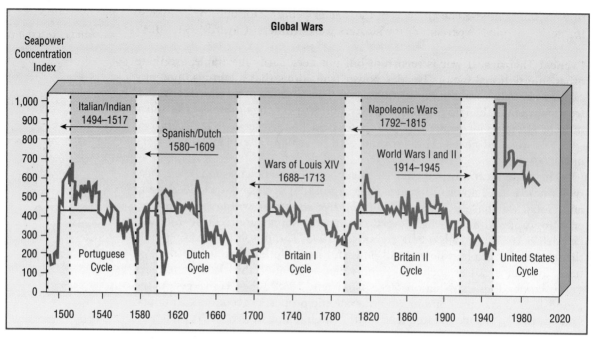

FIGURE 12.3

The Long Cycle of Global Leadership and Global War, 1494–2000

Over the past five hundred years, five great powers have risen to control the international system by dominating it. However, none of these powerful states (except Britain) has managed to reign for long. The past pattern shows that within a generation, the leader's grip on top-dog status has slipped, and in time new rivals have risen to challenge their leadership. About every one hundred years, a global war has erupted to settle the contest. The troubling question is whether this long cycle of war can be broken in the future or whether humankind will again experience a global war to determine which great power will lead.

SOURCE: Adapted from Modelski (1987a), 6.

humanity brings peace; peace, as I have said, brings riches, and so the world's affairs go round." Because it takes time to move through these stages, alternating periods of enthusiasm for war and weariness of war appear to be influenced by learning, forgetting, and aging.

Empirical tests of cyclical theories produce conflicting results. Quincy Wright (1942) suggested that if cycles exist, intervals between major outbreaks of war last about fifty years. In contrast, Lewis F. Richardson (1960a) and Pitirim Sorokin (1937) estimated that cycles extend over two hundred years from peak to peak (although both were somewhat skeptical and cautioned against attaching too much causal importance to their findings).

The validity of cyclical interpretations depends in part on the methods used to measure war's frequency and magnitude. For example, the Correlates of War research project traced cycles in the frequency and character of war between states, breaking the state system since 1815 into six historical periods, with 1848, 1881, 1914, 1945, and 1989 marking the significant turning points scholars conventionally identify in contemporary history. Table 12.1 summarizes the data for the outbreak of interstate wars exceeding one thousand battle deaths, facilitating comparisons across these six successive periods. Measured in this restricted way, the data show that 185 interstate wars erupted between 1816 and 1994, but that the frequency was fairly stable over time until the last period (1989–1994), when these kinds of wars between states greatly declined. Furthermore, if we take the expanding number of countries in the system into account, the frequency of the outbreak of wars since 1816 "actually declines from four per state per decade prior to World War II to two per state per decade since [and even less since the Berlin Wall was dismantled in 1989]. And if we control not for the number of states but the number of *pairs*, the decline appears even more dramatic" (Singer 1991, 57).

This evidence fails to establish the existence of a cycle in war's onset since 1815 (Singer 1981). Moreover, because "no cyclical patterns are apparent when we examine the military experiences of the individual nations which participated in several wars" (Small and Singer 1972), it is doubtful that the international system automatically produces recurrent cycles in wars between sovereign states.

Thus, when we adjust for the increasing number of independent states, the post-World War II and post-Cold War eras appear comparatively more peaceful than do the periods that preceded them. Or do they? A somewhat different picture emerges when attention focuses on the number of wars *under way*, rather than on the number of wars that start. (This measure takes into account the fact that many wars continue, or last, over two or more years.) Interstate war has been in progress almost continuously since the Congress of Vienna in 1815. Although there were eighty-four years between 1816 and 1994 in which no interstate wars began, there were only twenty in which none was in progress (Small and Singer 1982, 149; Singer 1991, 60–75; Wallensteen and Sollenberg 1995, 345–46). The so-called outbreak of peace in the post-Cold War is not mythical, however, as only four large-scale wars were under way between states in the 1989–1994 period (Wallensteen and Sollenberg 1995, 345). Thus, the available evidence "suggests not so much that discrete wars come and go with some regularity, but that, with *some* level of such violence almost always present, there may be certain periodic fluctuations in the amount of that violence" (Small and Singer 1982).

From several theoretical standpoints, therefore, we must question claims that warfare in the twenty-first century—whether long and destructive or short

TABLE 12.1 Frequency with Which 185 Wars between States Have Begun over Six Historical Periods, 1816–1994

Period	Key System Characteristic	Number of Initiated Wars	System Size (average number of states)
1816–1848	Concert of Europe	33	28
1849–1881	Wars of European unification	43	39
1882–1914	Resurgent imperialism	38	40
1915–1944	The Great Depression	24	59
1945–1988	The Cold War	43	117
1989–1994	Post-Cold War multipolarity	4	174

SOURCES: Data for 1816–1988 provided courtesy of the Correlates of War project under the direction of J. David Singer and Melvin Small. Data for 1989–1994 are for wars that "concerned 'classical' interstate conflict, where two internationally recognized countries were waging an armed battle," based on Wallensteen and Sollenberg (1995, 345) and Jaggers and Gurr (1995) for the number of independent states.

and less costly—is structurally predetermined. The historical record provides a basis for assuming that the war system may be disappearing, and that peace between countries is possible. Both long periods of peace and long periods of warfare have existed in the past, and either could follow in the approaching new millennium. But the most recent trends show promise that classical war between states is ceasing to dominate world affairs.

If the disappearance of war is possible over the long run, armed conflict and violence may persist *inside* established states. We now turn from our exploration of the multiple causes of armed conflicts between states to examine armed conflicts within states.

• • •

ARMED CONFLICTS WITHIN STATES

Civil wars—wars within states—have erupted far more frequently than have wars between states. It is these armed struggles that most often capture news headlines worldwide. *The New York Times Magazine* (May 7, 1995), for example, featured a story concluding that "for just about the first time since 1815, no great powers are at one another's throats [but] civil wars and snarling savageries continue on both sides of the Equator." There is a basis in fact for this assertion. Between 1989 and 1994, "the most common conflicts . . . have been internal conflicts over government (civil wars) or over territory (state formation conflicts)." In this period, ninety-nine civil wars erupted, each of which took at least one thousand battle-related deaths each year. Only four of these conflicts were between states; all the rest were civil wars (Wallensteen and Sollenberg 1995, 345).

Civil wars resulting in at least one thousand civilian and military deaths per year erupted 162 times between 1816 and 1992 (Small and Singer 1982; Singer 1991, 66–75; Wallensteen and Axell 1993, 333). Their outbreak has been somewhat irregular. Although at least one civil war was begun in "only" eighty-four (less than half) of these years, over time civil war has become increasingly frequent (see Table 12.2). Of the civil wars since 1816, 60 percent began after 1945, with the frequency steadily climbing each decade in this period.[6]

The number of civil wars under way provides a different picture of its worldwide spread. Between 1816 and 1994, civil wars have been in progress internationally 83 percent of the time (Small and Singer 1982, 251–67; Singer 1991, 66–75; Wallensteen and Sollenberg, 1995, 345). Domestic and not international war is the most frequent form of conflict today. During the five-year period from 1989 to 1993, a total of ninety conflicts were active in at least one year in sixty-one locations around the world, and none of these were "truly international" (Gleditsch 1995, 586). In June 1994, *all* of the thirty-six wars then being fought were civil wars, twenty-one of which had begun more than a decade earlier (*Harper's* 289 [July 1994]: 11).

A notable characteristic of civil wars is their severity. The number of lives lost in civil violence has remained high since the Napoleonic Wars ended in

---

[6]As another inventory documents, "more than two-thirds of all armed conflict in the world since 1945 has taken the form of civil wars," as 129 internal wars broke out between 1945 and 1995 (K. Holsti 1995, 320–321; see also Licklider 1995). However, this development is in part a product of the increase in the number of independent states in the international system, which makes the incidence of civil war statistically more probable.

TABLE 12.2 The Frequency and Severity of 162 Civil Wars, 1816–1992

Period	Number of Civil Wars Begun	System Size (average number of states)	Battle Deaths	Number (percent) of Civil Wars Internationalized through Large-Scale Military Intervention
1816–1848	12	28	93,200	3 (25%)
1849–1881	20	39	2,891,600	1 (5%)
1882–1914	18	40	388,000	3 (17%)
1915–1945	14	59	1,631,460	4 (29%)
1946–1988	60	117	6,222,020	14 (23%)
1989–1992	38	172	Not available	4 (11%)
Totals	162		11,226,280+	29

SOURCE: Data for 1816–1988 provided courtesy of the Correlates of War project under the direction of J. David Singer and Melvin Small. Data for 1989–1992 are based on Wallensteen and Axell (1993).

1815, and casualty rates show an alarming growth, especially since World War II. One symptom is that ten of the fifteen most destructive civil wars between 1816 and 1980 occurred in the twentieth century; of those ten, seven occurred since World War II (Small and Singer 1982, 241). This characteristic is also suggested by Ted Robert Gurr (1970, 3), who found that "ten of the world's thirteen most deadly conflicts [between 1815 and 1965] have been civil wars and rebellions." Although data "are insufficient to estimate the total number of deaths due to [internal] armed conflicts" between 1989 and 1992, "it was undoubtedly more than seventy thousand in 1992 alone" (Wallensteen and Axell 1993, 332), as in that year "war deaths were the highest in seventeen years, extending a pattern of growing violence and human suffering in local wars" (Sivard 1993). As another estimate confirms, the average numbers of deaths that resulted from fifty internal rebellions in 1993–1994 was eighty thousand (Gurr 1994, 352).

The Causes of Civil War

Civil wars stem from a wide range of ideological, demographic, religious, ethnic, economic, social-structural, and political conditions. Civil war and revolution simultaneously have been defended as instruments of justice and condemned as the immoral acceptance of violent change. They contain ingredients of both. Those who engineered the American, Russian, and Chinese revolutions claimed that violence was necessary to realize social change, political freedom, and independence; the powers from whom they sought liberation berated the immorality of their methods.

Internal Rebellion and Secessionist Revolts. Among the sources of civil war, internal violence is a reaction to frustration and **relative deprivation**—people's perception that they are unfairly deprived of the wealth and status that they deserve in comparison with advantaged others (Gurr 1970). When people's expectations of what they deserve rise more rapidly than their material rewards, the probability of conflict grows. That, of course, applies to most of the countries in the Global South today, where the distribution of wealth and opportunities is highly unequal. Note in this context that the seeds of civil strife are often sown by national independence movements. "More than two thirds of all the armed combat in the world between 1945 and 1995 were manifestations of the state-creation enterprise (K. Holsti 1995, 22). The growth of new states in Europe and Asia in the aftermath of the Cold War and the breakup of the Soviet Union has sped increases in local wars. Unrest and discontent—long held in check at the point of a bayonet—have now been released, and secession revolts have escalated, partially as a result (Gurr 1995).

Nationalism and "Neonationalism." Nationalism today is widely regarded as an especially potent cause of war within states because of the arguments about nationalism noted earlier (see also Chapter 7). However, the conditions prevailing today lead many to believe that nationalism will incite "wars of states against nations, wars of succession, and major armed uprisings to oust governments" (K. Holsti 1995) at unprecedented levels. The potential magnitude of nationalism-inspired revolutionary war is great:

> More than 95 percent of the world's . . . states are multinational, that is, composed of many nations, some unconsenting. These . . . states assert sovereignty over the world's three thousand to five thousand nations and peoples. . . . State governments [are pitted] against guerrilla insurgencies and indigenous nations. Most of these wars are over territory, resources, and identity, not ideology. They are hidden from most people's views because the fighting is against peoples and countries that are not even on the map. (Nietschmann 1991, 172–73)

If nationalism is a powerful influence on internal wars, what is termed **neonationalism** adds a new ingredient to this traditional cause. Neonationalism and the localized conflicts it spawns differ from the nationalism previously seen in the Global South.

> Earlier stages of Third World nationalism tended to revolve around the national liberation experience, the zeal engendered by the throwing off of colonial ties. . . . Neonationalism is the product of more recent decades, going beyond classical nationalism and [including] separatist subnationalism; that is, the expression of communal/ethnic aspirations of groups within the nation-state that are unhappy with their lot: Shiites in Iraq, Sikhs in India, Unighur Turks in Chinese Turkestan. It involves strong new drives toward separatism: the Moros in the Philippines, Georgians in the [former] Soviet Union, Catholics in Northern Ireland, Hungarians in Romania, Biafra in Nigeria, even Quebec in Canada. (Fuller 1991–1992, 14–15)

This kind of destabilizing "hypernationalism" is malign because the neonationalist doctrines are used "to justify or motivate large-scale violence [or] the conquest or subjugation of other nationalities" (Snyder 1993). The civil strife that erupted in the Balkans, Somalia, Sudan and Rwanda in the mid-1990s was symptomatic of the new wave of fractional conflicts which neonationalism has ignited.

Ethnonational Conflict. Since World War II, civil wars provoked by ancient ethnic and racial hatreds have been commonplace in multiethnic states. Between

1945 and 1981, 258 cases of ethnic warfare were observable, 40 percent of which involved high levels of violence (Carment 1993, 141). More recently, this armed conflict has reached epidemic proportions. Ted Robert Gurr (1994, 351–52) estimated that 26,759,000 refugees were fleeing the fifty major ethnonational conflicts that were occurring in 1993–1994, each of which was responsible for an average eighty thousand deaths. Most of the victims are innocent children. Between 1983 and 1993, some 10 million children have died from civil strife (Kane 1995a, 20).

As U.S. President Bill Clinton observed in his June 7, 1994, speech before the French National Assembly, militant ethnic nationalism was "on the rise, transforming the healthy pride of nations, tribes, religious and ethnic groups into cancerous prejudice, eating away at states and leaving their people addicted to the political painkillers of violence and demagoguery." Chan Heng Chee, Singapore's former ambassador to the United Nations, in 1993 described the opinion shared by most experts when she observed that "with the end of the Cold War . . . the new problems haunting us will be instability arising from ethnic and religious turmoil. . . . The fault line will . . . to a large extent coincide with racial and ethnic divisions." The danger, warns Irish author Conor Cruise O'Brien (1993b), resides in the fact that ethnonationalism "is something for which people are prepared to kill and die in large numbers, as Serbs, Croats, and Bosnian Muslims [did in the former Yugoslavia], and as, at an even more primordial level, warlike Somalian clansmen are doing." Thus, much of the internal revolts and ethnic warfare currently sweeping the world is less inspired by political motives and economic aims than it is by deeply rooted ethnic animosities. Ethnonational clashes differ greatly from the anticolonial secessionist and separatist movements of the past.

Children often have been the major victims of civil strife. This photo, which received the World Press Award in 1985, depicts children caught in the ethnonational and religious civil war in Beirut, the capital of Lebanon—a country whose population is about two-thirds Muslim and one-fourth Christian, with each faction divided into different sects.

The Economic Sources of Internal Rebellions. The destabilization caused by rapid growth also helps to account for the ubiquity of internal war (see Olson 1971). In contrast with what intuition might suggest, civil violence often erupts in countries in which conditions are improving, not deteriorating. "Economic modernization," former U.S. Secretary of State Henry Kissinger suggested, "leads to political instability rather than political stability." When modernization generates rising expectations which governments are unable to satisfy, civil war often follows. This is the essence of *relative deprivation* as a cause of internal violence, as people who feel themselves to have been denied resources they deserve are often inclined to use force in acts of rebellion (Gurr 1970).

The International Dimensions of Civil War

It is tempting to think of civil war as stemming exclusively from conditions within countries. However, external factors often influence internal rebellions. "Every war has two faces. It is a conflict both between and within political systems; a conflict that is both external and internal. [It is undeniable that] internal wars affect the international system [and that] the international system affects internal wars" (Modelski 1964).

We can distinguish several phases that have influenced the linkage between changes in the international system and the incidence of civil war. First, the effects of imperialism, industrialization, nationalism, and ideology provoked the comparatively high levels of civil war between 1848 and 1870. Second, the breakup of the European colonial empires contributed to the frequent incidence of civil war between the end of World War II and the 1960s. And today, in the post-Cold War era, the discipline imposed by Cold War bipolarity has disappeared, resulting in many states no longer living with the fear that turmoil within their borders will precipitate military intervention by the great powers.

Because the great powers have global interests, historically they have been prone to intervene militarily in civil wars to support friendly governments and to overthrow unfriendly ones. When they did, wars within states became internationalized. But today it is often difficult to determine where an internal war ends and an international one begins. In an interdependent, increasingly borderless world, the difference between involvement and intervention is difficult to distinguish. The two types of armed conflict are closely linked. As Table 12.2 reveals, since 1816 nearly one in five civil wars has become an interstate war through intervention by an external power. More than three-fifths of these large-scale military interventions have occurred since 1945. During the Cold War, many entanglements of the United States (e.g., Lebanon, the Dominican Republic, Korea, Vietnam, Grenada, and Panama) and the Soviet Union (e.g., Hungary, Ethiopia and Afghanistan) were responses to internal instability. Even today, the Global South remains the site of most violent conflicts and military and humanitarian interventions in the world.

Many analysts believe that domestic conflicts become internationalized because leaders who experience internal opposition are inclined to provoke an international crisis in the hope that their citizens will become less rebellious if their attention is diverted to the threat of external aggression. This proposition has come to be known as the **diversionary theory of war** (see Focus 12.3).

The diversionary theory of war is based on the expectation that external war will result in increased domestic support for political leaders. "To put it cynically, one could say that nothing helps a leader like a good war. It gives him

The Diversionary Theory of War
Is There a Connection between Civil Strife and External Aggression?

If leaders assume that national unity will rise when an external threat exists, they may seek to manage domestic unrest by initiating foreign adventures. Indeed, many political advisers counsel this as a solution. For instance, the realist theorist Niccoló Machiavelli in 1513 advised leaders to undertake foreign wars whenever turmoil within their state became too great. Hermann Goering, Adolph Hitler's adviser, also advocated the same idea in Nazi Germany, contending: "Voice or no voice, the people can always be brought to do the bidding of the leaders. That is easy. All you have to do is tell them they are being attacked and denounce the pacifists for lack of patriotism." Similarly, John Foster Dulles (1939), who later became U.S. Secretary of State, recommended "The easiest and quickest cure of internal dissension is to portray danger from abroad."

Whether leaders actually start wars to offset domestic conflict is an empirical question. Many studies have examined the proposition, but few confirm it (see Morgan and Bickers 1992). It seems reasonable to assume that "war with the outside is sometimes the last chance for a state ridden with inner antagonisms to overcome these antagonisms" (Simmel 1956), and that "statesmen may be driven to a policy of foreign conflict—if not open war—in order to defend themselves against the onslaught of domestic enemies" (Haas and Whiting 1956). Yet we cannot demonstrate that leaders undertake these diversionary actions for this purpose. "The linkage depends," political scientist Jack Levy (1989b) concludes, "on the kinds of internal conditions that commonly lead to hostile external actions for diversionary purposes." For example, "democratic states are particularly likely to use force externally during an election year, especially when the election occurs at a time of economic stagnation" (Ostrom and Job 1986). This linkage does not always hold, however. In most cases "where civil unrest preceded external conflict, war was not usually initiated by the strife-torn state. Instead, most wars were initiated by outside powers, with the internally troubled state in the role of the victim" (Cashman 1993).

his only chance of being a tyrant and being loved for it at the same time. He can introduce the most ruthless forms of control and send thousands of his followers to their deaths and still be hailed as a great protector. Nothing ties tighter the in-group bonds than an out-group threat" (Morris 1969).

The argument is logical. However, the relationship between civil and international conflict is, in practice, more complex. In general, the available evidence urges that we question the diversionary theory of war. Perhaps the most compelling reason for some doubt is that "when domestic conflict becomes extremely intense it would seem more reasonable to argue that there is a greater likelihood that a state will retreat from its foreign engagements in order to handle the situation at home" (Zinnes and Wilkenfeld 1971).

• • •

TERRORISM

Terrorism poses another alarming kind of violence in the contemporary world. The instruments of terror are varied and the motivations of terrorists diverse, but "experts agree that terrorism is the use or threat of violence, a method of combat or a strategy to achieve certain goals, that its aim is to induce a state of fear in the victim, that it is ruthless and does not conform to humanitarian norms, and that publicity is an essential factor in terrorist strategy" (Laqueur 1986).

371

Some terrorist activities, such as the 1995 bombing of the U.S. federal government building in Oklahoma City, begin and end in a single country. Many, however, cross national borders. Thus terrorism today has a uniquely transnational character that afflicts many countries. In 1990 terrorists targeted the citizens and property of seventy-three countries, while in 1995 (see Map 12.1) 440 separate terrorist attacks targeted 51 countries (U.S. Department of State 1991, 37; 1996, 1).

Although terrorism has always been with us, it emerged as a significant international problem in the 1960s (Kidder 1990) and grew to epidemic proportions in the 1970s and 1980s. Figure 12.4 shows the changing incidence of terrorism in today's world, the general trend suggesting an increasing level of transnational terrorist activity since 1968, followed by a decline since 1987. International terrorist attacks declined during 1994 to 322, the lowest point in twenty-three years. This was roughly 50 percent fewer than the 665 incidents recorded in 1987, the peak year in international terrorist activity (U.S. Depart-

MAP 12.1

International Terrorist Incidents, 1995

Terrorist acts have occurred in many countries, with some states frequently experiencing this kind of violence in their territorial borders. This map indicates the location and extent of 440 acts of international terrorism in 1995.

SOURCE: U.S. Department of State (1996), 77.

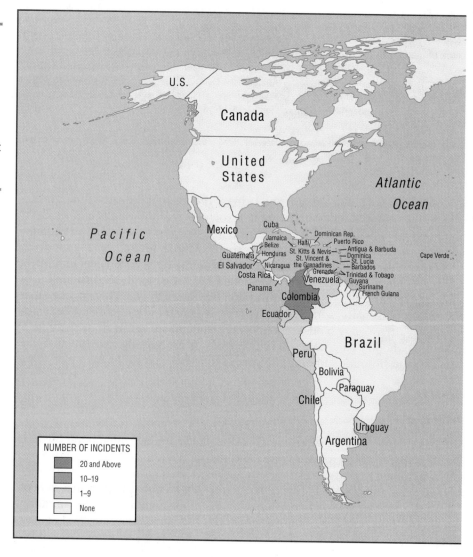

ment of State, 1996, 71). However, in 1995 incidents again climbed to 440 throughout the world.

Terrorism is a tactic of the powerless against the powerful. Thus it is not surprising that political or social minorities and ethnic movements sometimes engage in acts of terrorism (see Chapter 7). Those seeking independence and sovereign statehood, like the Basques in Spain, typify the aspirations that animate terrorist activity. Religion also sometimes rationalizes the terrorist activities of extremist movements, such as the efforts of the Sikh groups who wish to carve out an independent Sikh state called Khalistan ("Land of the Pure") from Indian territory, and of the Islamic extremist group HAMAS to destabilize Israel and sabotage a negotiated peace between Israel and its Arab neighbors. In 1994 attacks by secular terrorist groups declined, while terrorist activities by radical Islamic groups increased (U.S. Department of State 1995), and in November 1995 right-wing Jewish fanatics in the Kach religious terrorist group assassinated Israeli Prime Minister Yitzhak Rabin to derail the peace process in Palestine.

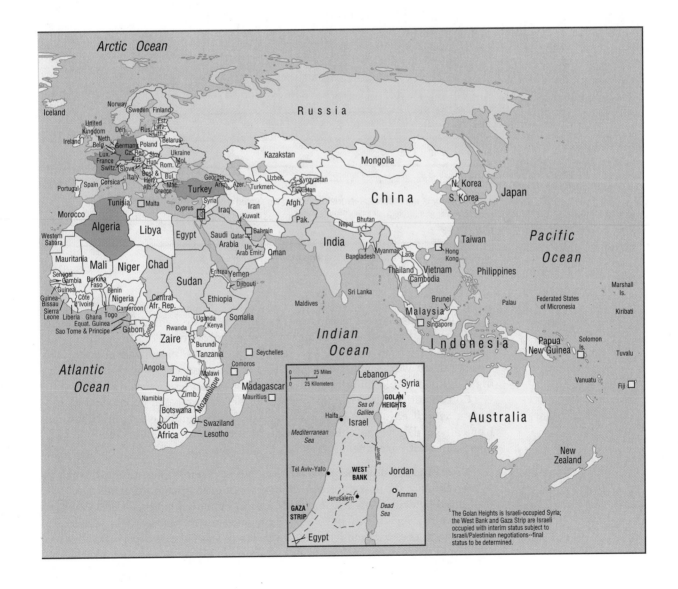

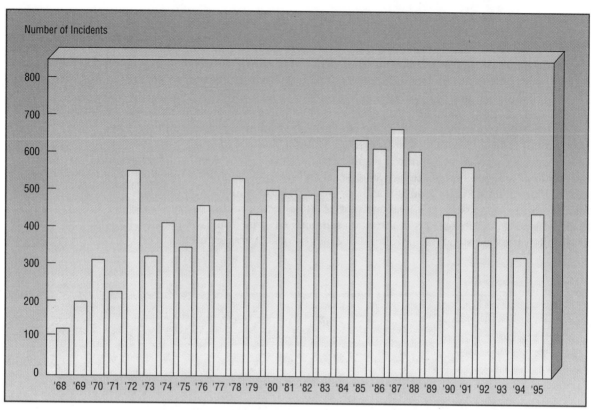

Number of Incidents

FIGURE 12.4

International Terrorist Incidents, 1968–1995

The frequency of international terrorist activity has changed over time since 1968, and the rate each year has ranged between 174 in 1968 and 665 in 1987. These activities appear entrenched but vary over time.

SOURCE: Office of the Coordinator for Counterterrorism, U.S. Department of State.

In the industrialized world, terrorism often occurs where discrepancies in income are severe and where minority groups feel deprived of the political freedoms and privileges enjoyed by the majority. In the urbanized areas of the industrialized world, guerrilla warfare—normally associated with rural uprisings—is not a viable route to self-assertion, but terrorist tactics are.

Consideration of terrorists' motives often obscures the perception of terrorism as a disease: One person's terrorist may be another person's liberator. Ironically, both governments and countergovernment movements claim to seek liberty, and both are labeled terrorists by their opponents.

Those who are described as terrorists, and who reject that title for themselves, make the uncomfortable point that national armed forces, fully supported by democratic opinion, have in fact employed violence and terror on a far vaster scale than what liberation movements have as yet been able to attain. The "freedom fighters" see themselves as fighting a just war. Why should they not be entitled to kill, burn, and destroy as national armies, navies, and air forces do; and why should the label "terrorist" be applied to them and not to the national militaries? (O'Brien 1977, 56–57)

The difference between nationalistic "freedom fighters," whose major complaint is that they lack a country, and governments claiming to protect freedom, often lies in the eye of the beholder. This problem makes the definition of a terrorist group less obvious and more controversial, as what most distinguishes terrorist groups from liberation movements is the outcome.

Although many terrorist groups today undeniably are seeking sovereignty, a broader definition of terrorism would acknowledge that many governments undertake terrorist acts, sometimes against their own people and sometimes by supporting terrorism against other established sovereign states (see Crenshaw 1990). In fact, some states underwrite the activities of terrorist movements that advocate philosophies the state sponsors embrace (or challenge the security of rival states). States often have financed, trained, equipped, and provided sanctuary for terrorists whose activities serve their foreign policy goals (see Chapter 7). The practice of this *state terrorism* is among the charges that the United States leveled in the 1980s against the Soviet Union, Syria, Iraq, and Libya, among others.[7] Similarly, others accused the United States of sponsoring terrorist activities in Vietnam, Chile, El Salvador, Nicaragua, and elsewhere (Schlagheck 1990).

Although many terrorist sanctuaries have disappeared with the end of the Cold War,

> it is unlikely that international terrorism is a passing and transitory phenomenon. The trend toward the weakening of central authority in governments, the rise in ethnic and subnational sentiments, and the increasing fractionalization of the global political process point toward its growth as a form of political protest and persuasion. Classic balance-of-power diplomacy is of little utility in dealing with it, for violent acts of small groups of people, or individuals, are difficult for governments to control. International terrorism is likely to continue and to expand because in the minds of many of its perpetrators it has proven to be "successful." (Pierre 1984, 85)

Indeed, the dangers of terrorism have not waned. Libyan leader Col. Muammar Qaddafi warned in July 1993, "Whatever takes place in America—and you will see a lot more terrorism there—is a function of perceived injustices in other parts of the world. . . . Acts of terrorism in America will be the answer, and they will be more and more violent and spectacular for television purposes around the world." The terrorist threat thus thrives, as shown by the wave of suicide bombing in the Middle East that provoked world leaders to attend a "summit of the peacemakers" conference in March 1996. "The use of terror is more widespread and more effective than is generally recognized" (*The Economist* 338 [March 2, 1996]), and the threat is likely to escalate if terrorists use nuclear, biological or chemical weapons for political blackmail.

---

[7]The attack by Libyan embassy personnel on anti-Qaddafi demonstrators in London in April 1984 is an example of terrorist actions conducted by representatives of a state government. Those who retaliate against terrorist attacks become, in the eyes of the target, terrorist attackers. Thus the U.S. air strike against Libya in April 1986 provoked the charge that the United States itself practiced terrorism. In contrast, in 1995 the United States identified Cuba, Iran, Iraq, Libya, North Korea, Sudan, and Syria as the primary state sponsors of international terrorism (U.S. Department of State 1996).

• • •

THE HUMAN TRAGEDY OF VIOLENT CONFLICT

War exacts a terrible toll on human life, commemorated publicly by black flags of mourning fluttering from the homes of the war dead and memorials at grave sites. Monuments honor the courage of the soldiers who gave their lives in their countries' wars. At the beginning of this century approximately 90 percent of war casualties were military; today about 90 percent of the world's war victims are innocent civilians (UNDP 1994, 47). UNICEF reported, in *The State of the World's Children 1992*, that more than 1.5 million children were killed in wars during the 1980s, and more than 4 million were "physically disabled—limbs amputated, brains damaged, eyesight and hearing lost—through bombing, land-mines, firearms, torture. Five million children are in refugee camps because of war: A further 12 million have lost their homes."

The tragic human consequences of violence are also revealed daily by the efforts of individuals and families seeking to escape its scourge. These are the victims of armed conflict who can be observed fleeing from one country in hopes of finding refuge, and perhaps a better life, in another country. The refugee asylum problem has now assumed global dimensions, as we saw in Chapter 10. Of the twenty largest source countries of refugees in the world in 1995, nineteen were embroiled in internal armed conflict. Religious preference, ethnic origin, and the expression of political dissent are some of the factors that motivate refugees, but armed conflict—along with poverty, persecution, and the pain of hunger and starvation—remains a paramount cause.

The ravages of war are not confined to its human victims, however. Some of its costs are economic, leaving the survivors to pay for the debts and damages. Other costs are ecological, as illustrated by the 1991 Persian Gulf War; although blackened skies have now cleared, the environmental damage may take decades to undo.

Could it be that a world so ingenious in perpetrating violence also will learn that war and violence are too costly, too destructive to continue? If so, can it discover viable paths to peace? In the chapters to follow, we will examine some of the solutions that policymakers and concerned citizens have proposed.

• • •

KEY TERMS

conflict
deterrence
pax atomica
intraspecific aggression
interspecific aggression
socialization
national character
laissez-faire capitalism

power transition theory
war weariness hypothesis
civil war
relative deprivation
neonationalism
diversionary theory of war
terrorism

The Military Quest for National Security: Arms and the Changing Character of Power

OUTLINE

It is an unfortunate fact that we can only secure peace by preparing for war.

—JOHN F. KENNEDY,
   U.S. presidential candidate, 1960

I went into the British Army believing that if you want peace you must prepare for war. I now believe that if you prepare thoroughly for war you will get it.

—SIR JOHN FREDERICK MAURICE,
   British military officer, 1883

The frequency and destructiveness of armed conflicts explain why states are preoccupied with threats to their security and why preparing for defense is so nearly a universal preoccupation. Because the anarchical international system requires that states rely on themselves for protection, **national security**—a country's psychological freedom from fear of foreign attack—is a paramount priority. As a result, policymakers typically assign national security the most prominent place on their foreign policy agendas.

In this chapter we examine why states often respond to perceived threats by arming. We begin by first considering the place of power in world politics. We then evaluate states' practices designed to diminish threats to their security, exploring in particular the great powers' security strategies in the context of general trends in military spending (and their socioeconomic consequences), the arms trade, and weapons technology. This coverage will enable us to introduce for later chapters the dilemmas that armament acquisitions create, how states use weapons for coercive diplomacy, and which paths to peace realists and liberals advocate for escaping the danger of war.

• • •

POWER IN INTERNATIONAL POLITICS

What is this abstraction called *power*, the quest for which realists depict as states' primary motive? Although definitions abound, power remains an ambiguous concept (see Baldwin 1989; Claude 1962; Rothgeb 1993). Nonetheless, because most leaders are schooled in *realpolitik*, they conventionally operate from the traditional assumption that *power* gives states the ability to promote and protect national interests, to win in bargaining situations, and to shape the rules governing the international system. They are inclined to view power as a *political* phenomenon revolving around the capacity of one actor to persuade another to do what it otherwise would not. Thus, we will evaluate first this definition, which sees power as *politics*—the exercise of influence to control and dominate others.

When we view power as the means to control, it is reasonable to ask who is stronger and who is weaker as well as which party will get its way and who will be forced to make concessions? These considerations invite the more fundamental question: What enables states to achieve their goals?

To determine the comparative power of states, analysts usually rank them according to the capabilities or resources presumed necessary to achieve influence over others. For such purposes, multiple factors (most significantly, military and economic capability) measure countries' relative **power potential.** If we could compare each state's total capabilities, according to this logic, we could then rank them by their ability to draw on these resources to exercise influence. Such a ranking would reveal the international system's hierarchy of power, differentiating the strong from the weak, the great from the marginal.

Of all the components of state power, military capability is usually thought to be the most important. Realists regard it as the central element in states' power potential. "Throughout history, the decisive factor in the fates of nations has usually been the number, efficiency and dispositions of fighting forces," they argue. "National influence bears a direct relationship to gross national strength; without that, the most exquisite statesmanship is likely to be of limited use" (German 1960). Because realists assume that the ability to coerce is more important than the ability to reward or to purchase, they believe that military capability is a more important source of power than economic capability. By contrast, other strategic thinkers argue that in the next century, economic competition will be more critical to national strength than military competition. Accordingly, they insist, the economic foundations of national security should receive primary emphasis.

Figure 13.1 presents two parallel rankings of the world's twenty most powerful states as seen from the vantage point of their military spending and the size of their armed forces. Both rankings conform to what most people would likely regard as the world's most "powerful" states.

Power potential also derives from other factors than military expenditures and the number of soldiers. These include the size of a state's economy, its population and territorial size, geographic position, raw materials, degree of dependence on foreign sources of materials, technological capacity, national character, ideology, efficiency of governmental decision making, industrial productivity, volume of trade, savings and investment, educational level, and national morale and internal solidarity.

There is, however, no consensus on how best to weigh these factors. There is also no consensus as to what their relative importance should be in making country comparisons, or what conditions affect the contribution that each makes in the equation that converts capabilities into influence. Although most analysts agree that states are not equal in their ability to influence others, few agree on how to rank their power potential. Consider what divergent pictures of the global hierarchy emerge when the relative capabilities of the great powers are ranked in other categories that realists also define as important (see Table 13.1). Clearly, strength is relative. The leading countries in some dimensions of power potential are not leaders in others, as power comes in many forms, and the global spread of technology has made it increasingly difficult to distinguish powerful and weak states.

Inferring Power from Capabilities

Part of the difficulty of defining the elements of power is that their potential impact depends on the circumstances in a bargaining situation between actors

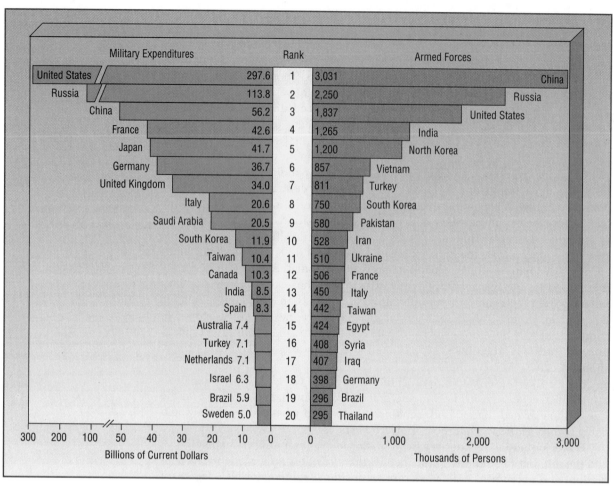

Military Expenditures		Rank	Armed Forces	
United States	297.6	1	3,031	China
Russia	113.8	2	2,250	Russia
China	56.2	3	1,837	United States
France	42.6	4	1,265	India
Japan	41.7	5	1,200	North Korea
Germany	36.7	6	857	Vietnam
United Kingdom	34.0	7	811	Turkey
Italy	20.6	8	750	South Korea
Saudi Arabia	20.5	9	580	Pakistan
South Korea	11.9	10	528	Iran
Taiwan	10.4	11	510	Ukraine
Canada	10.3	12	506	France
India	8.5	13	450	Italy
Spain	8.3	14	442	Taiwan
Australia	7.4	15	424	Egypt
Turkey	7.1	16	408	Syria
Netherlands	7.1	17	407	Iraq
Israel	6.3	18	398	Germany
Brazil	5.9	19	296	Brazil
Sweden	5.0	20	295	Thailand

300 200 100 50 40 30 20 10 0   0   1,000   2,000   3,000

Billions of Current Dollars   Thousands of Persons

FIGURE 13.1

Leading Military Powers, 1993

The end of the Cold War produced significant shifts in the rank of countries' military expenditures and armed forces. In 1995, Russia cut its military spending about 44 percent from the Soviet level in 1991. By contrast, the United States reduced its military spending by about 4.4 percent between 1988 and 1995, but in 1993 it still accounted for 34 percent of the world total. In 1993 China, Russia, the United States, India, and North Korea were the only countries with armies of more than 1 million soldiers; these five together accounted for nearly 40 percent of the world's total military strength of 24,850,000 soldiers.

SOURCE: U.S. ACDA (1995), 4, 5.

in conflict and especially on how leaders perceive those circumstances. Such judgments are subjective, as power ratios are not strictly products of measured capabilities. Perceptions also matter.

In addition, power is not a tangible commodity that states can acquire. It has meaning only in terms of others. As we will explain more completely in Chapter 14, power is relational: A state can have power over some other actor only when it can prevail over that actor. Both actual and perceived strength determine who wins in a political contest. To make a difference, an adversary

TABLE 13.1 The Power Potential of the Great Powers: Rankings across Major Dimensions

Territorial Size (thousand square km)		Population, 1994 (millions)	
1. Russia	17,075	1. China	1190.4
2. Canada	9,976	2. India	919.4
3. China	9,561	3. United States	261.1
4. United States	9,363	4. Indonesia	200.4
5. Brazil	8,512	5. Brazil	158.7
6. Australia	7,686	6. Russia	149.6
7. India	3,288	7. Pakistan	128.9
8. Argentina	2,767	8. Japan	125.1
9. Kazakhstan	2,717	9. Bangladesh	125.1
10. Sudan	2,506	10. Nigeria	98.1
Gross Domestic Product, 1994 ($ billions)		**Scientists and Engineers in Research as Percent of World**	
1. United States	6,738	1. Russia	19.8
2. China	2,978	2. United States	18.2
3. Japan	2,519	3. Japan	12.2
4. Germany	1,344	4. Germany	5.6
5. France	1,078	5. India	2.3
6. United Kingdom	1,043	6. France	2.2
7. Italy	994	7. United Kingdom	2.0
8. Brazil	882	8. Italy	1.4
9. Russia	778	9. Czechoslovakia	1.3
10. Canada	640	10. Canada	1.2

SOURCE: Territory, *World Bank Atlas* (1995); population and GDP, Handbook of International Economic Statistics (1995), 32–33, 24–25; scientists, Hughes (1994), 82.

must know its enemy's capabilities and willingness to mobilize them for coercive purposes. For example, it must regard the opponent's threat to use military capabilities as credible. Intentions—and especially perceptions of them—are critically important in this respect. The mere possession of weapons does not increase a state's power if its adversaries do not believe it will use them.

Historically, those with the largest arsenals have not necessarily triumphed in political conflicts. Weaker states often successfully resist pressure from their military superiors. Although Vietnam was weak in the conventional military sense, it succeeded against a vastly stronger France and, later, the United States. Similarly, the United States' superior military power did not prevent either North Korea's seizure of the USS *Pueblo* in 1968 or Iran's taking of American diplomats as hostages a decade later. The Soviet Union's inability, prior to its disintegration, to control political events in Afghanistan, eastern Europe, or even its own constituent republics—despite an awesome weapons arsenal—shows that the impotence of military power is not peculiar to the United States.

Nonetheless, the quest for security through arms and the realist belief in military force remain widespread. Most policymakers assume that "while it could be a mistake to assume that political influence is proportional to military strength, it would be an even bigger mistake to deny any connection between the two" (Majeed 1991). Many believe that this is because military capability is a prerequisite to the successful exercise of "coercive diplomacy" (to be examined in Chapter 14), the employment of "threats or limited force to persuade an opponent to call off or undo an encroachment" (Craig and George 1990). The link between military power and foreign policy is intact even after Cold War hostility has ended; in fact, it may be "more pervasive and more comprehensive than in earlier periods of history when war was less dangerous" (Majeed 1991). Perhaps it was this conviction that inspired U.S. President Bill Clinton to assert to the West Point graduating class in May 1993 that "We have to ensure that the United States is ready, ready to win and superior to all other military forces in the world."

The Changing Nature of World Power

Military power is central in leaders' conceptualizations of national security. As noted in previous chapters, however, many analysts now argue that "the sources of power are, in general, moving away from the emphasis on military force and conquest that marked earlier eras. In assessing international power today, factors such as technology, education, and economic growth are becoming more important, whereas geography, population, and raw materials are becoming less important" (Nye 1990). In part this is because military force has often proven ineffectual, notably against belligerent revisionist states as well as politically mobilized nationalist and aggressive ethnic movements. Moreover, awareness of the importance of trade competitiveness to national standing has directed increasing attention to the nonmilitary dimensions of national security.

Political scientist Richard Rosecrance (1986) compares military-political and trade strategies as alternative methods for realizing national security, arguing that the latter increasingly has been more effective as a strategy toward political power and material advancement. "Since 1945 a few nations have borne the crushing weight of military expenditure," he observes, "while others have gained a relative advantage by becoming military free-riders who primarily rely on the security provided by others. While the United States spent nearly 50 percent of its research and development budget on arms, Japan devoted 99 percent to civilian production."

In addition to sacrificing other economic opportunities, Rosecrance continues, military spending has direct costs, because expensive equipment quickly becomes outdated in the face of rapid technological innovations. This creates the need for even more-sophisticated new weapons, whose costs are staggering. The anticipated costs for future weapons production in the 1995 U.S. military budget included $81 billion for the Trident II missile, $72 billion for the F-22 fighter, $45 billion for the C-17 transport plane, $57.6 billion for the DD-51 destroyer, and $44 billion for the B-2 Stealth bomber, among other weapons systems in a $402 billion weapons procurement allocation (*The Bulletin of Atomic Scientists* 51 [September/October 1995]: 38). Because "states can afford more 'butter' if they need fewer 'guns,'" Rosecrance (1997) notes, "the two objectives sometimes represent trade-offs: The achievement of one may diminish the realization of the other," and the substantial costs of defense can erode national welfare—what policymakers hope to defend with military might. Conversely, commercial clout and trade competitiveness for national exports may contribute more than military might to national power in a world in which trade bloc competition replaces the military and diplomatic struggles of the past. This thesis is a troublesome idea, to which we will return.

In addition to economic capability, other, less tangible sources of national power now figure more prominently in calculations regarding national defense, including the media empires' "power over opinion" and control of communications (Bell 1995). "Political leaders and philosophers have long understood that power comes from setting the agenda and determining the framework of a debate. The ability to establish preferences tends to be associated with intangible power resources such as culture, ideology, and institutions." These intangible resources constitute **soft power**, in contrast with the **hard power** "usually associated with tangible resources like military and economic strength" (Nye 1990). If soft power grows in relative importance, military force ratios will no longer translate into power potential in the way that they once did.

• • •

THE QUEST FOR MILITARY CAPABILITIES

How people spend their money reveals their values. Similarly, how governments allocate their revenues reveals their priorities. Examination of national budgets discloses an unmistakable pattern: Although the sources of world political power may be changing, nearly all states seek security by spending substantial portions of their national treasures on arms.

Trends in Military Spending

The commitment to purchase military protection is nearly universal. Globally, an estimated $868 billion was spent on military preparedness in 1993, reflecting an annual average decline of 7.2 percent since peaking in 1987, when spending reached $1.26 trillion (1993 dollars) (U.S. ACDA 1995, 1). The 1993 figure of $868 billion (after adjusting for inflation) is still 2.6 times that spent in 1960, 1.8 times that of the 1970 outlay, and 1.2 times the 1980 outlay (UNDP 1994, 48; Sivard 1993, 42).

Increases in military spending were especially evident during the 1980s, although on closer inspection they merely continued trends in place throughout the twentieth century. Military spending has increased fifteenfold since the mid-1930s, for example. Its rate of growth has exceeded the growth of world population, the global economy, and even prices since that time (Sivard 1991).

Historically the rich countries spent the most money on arms acquisitions.[1] The pattern continues today, with industrial countries spending an estimated $648 billion for defense in 1993, in contrast with the developing countries' $221 billion (U.S. ACDA 1995, 43; see also Chapter 5). Thus the developed countries'

---

[1]The United States, for example, spent nearly $3 trillion on defense in the 1980s, or $45,000 for each American household (Sivard 1991, 3). The end of the Cold War has not greatly reduced this level (declining by less than 20 percent in 1995 from its peak of $304 billion in 1991). Defense spending continues to grow even though the spiraling national debt, approaching $5 trillion in 1995, was an uncomfortable 4.1 percent of gross domestic product when Clinton became president. As former U.S. Assistant Secretary of Defense Lawrence J. Korb (1995a, 19) observed, U.S. defense spending, after adjusting for inflation, [was] actually $30 billion higher than it was in 1975, and both Clinton and the majority of Republicans [wanted] to make it higher [even though] the world's only military superpower [spent] about five times as much on defense as its closest competitor and almost as much as the rest of the world combined." In 1996, the Pentagon was spending about "$265 billion a year or $8,000 per second" (Lewis 1996, 8).

share of the world total is 75 percent. However, when measured as a proportion of gross national product, the levels now appear more equal. The developing countries in 1993 spent 3.1 percent on military preparedness, in contrast to the developed countries' 3.4 percent; in 1960 the percentages were 4.2 and 6.3 percent, respectively (U.S. ACDA 1995, 24). The changes in the developed and developing countries' military expenditures since 1961 are presented in Figure 13.2.

Although the leading military powers are among the largest and wealthiest countries, the drive to arm militarily is widespread. Developing countries have shown a historic tendency to mimic the past budgetary habits of the rich. The military expenditures of the countries in the Global South accounted for 6 percent of the world's total in 1955, but the proportion had climbed to more than 25 percent of the world total by 1993 (Ball 1994, 217; U.S. ACDA 1995, 2). Developing countries' military spending has increased sixfold since 1960 (in constant dollars). Significantly, the military expenditures of countries in the Global South in 1990 was 69 percent larger than their combined education and

F I G U R E   1 3 . 2

World Military Expenditures, 1961–1993

World military spending peaked in 1987 and then began to decline. Most of the cumulative reduction since 1987 (which amounts to over $1 trillion) has occurred in the developed countries. "This is not only because of their preeminence in such spending but also because their rate of decline was steeper, averaging over 9 percent annually since their aggregate spending peak in 1987" (U.S. ACDA 1995, 1). If these trends continue, as the United Nations (UNDP 1994) predicts, global spending will fall by the year 2000 to about $750 billion, with the developed countries' level at about $640 billion and the countries in the Global South at about $100 billion.

SOURCE: U.S. ACDA (1995), 1.

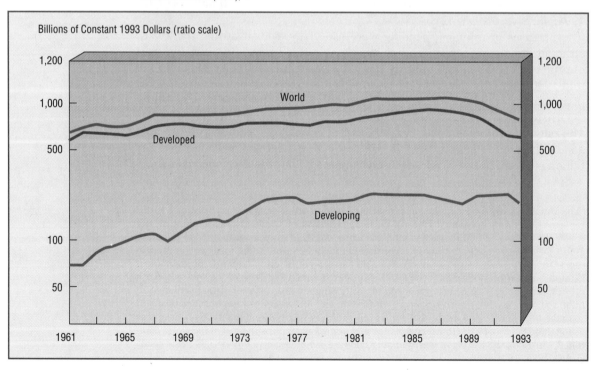

health expenditures (UNDP 1993, 205), even though by 1994 in those countries "the chances of dying from social neglect (from malnutrition and preventable disease) [was] 33 times greater than the chances of dying from external aggression" (UNDP 1994, 50).

The developing countries' military spending is extremely high given their poverty (see Chapter 5), resulting in large armies in the countries of the Global South that reflect their disproportionately large populations. Between 1960 and 1993, the armed forces of the developed world remained relatively constant at a little more than 10 million. However, the total in the developing world more than doubled, growing from 8.4 to 17.8 million—or to almost three-quarters of the world total (Sivard 1993, 42; U.S. ACDA 1995, 7).

Changes in Military Capabilities

The growing militarization of the Global South manifests itself in other ways. Military capabilities are now more widespread than ever. "The most striking geostrategic phenomenon of the past few decades," political scientist Michael Klare (1990a) posits, "is the extraordinary diffusion of war-making capabilities from the industrial North to the largely agrarian South. Nations which as recently as 1970 were equipped with a few obsolete tanks and subsonic aircraft, acquired as gifts from the major powers, [now have] large numbers of modern aircraft, tanks, and missiles." Parallel developments in the international arms trade and in the destructiveness of modern weapons underlie this diffusion.

The Transformation of the Arms Trade. The international trade in arms, spurred by developing countries' energetic search for armaments commensurate with those of the industrial countries, has fueled the dispersion of military capability throughout the globe. In 1993, eighty-four countries were recipients of at least $5 million worth of imported weapons (U.S. ACDA 1995, 100–38).

Growth in the value of arms sales attests to the present character of arms trafficking. In 1960 world weapons exports were valued at $2.4 billion (Sivard 1991, 50). They peaked in 1987 at $74 billion and then declined to $22 billion in 1993 (U.S. ACDA 1995, 9).[2]

The countries in the Global South have been the leading market for the traffic in arms, accounting since the late 1970s for three-fourths of all trade. They purchased an estimated $430.6 billion in armaments between 1980 and 1992 (U.S. ACDA 1992, 89; *The Defense Monitor* 22, no. 9 [1993]: 3). Since the Cold War ended, the developing countries' total purchases (between 1991 and 1994, $67.5 billion) accounted for 71 percent of arms delivered worldwide (Grimmett 1995, 35, 36). Today, in the face of fierce competition among an expanding number of suppliers, some of the world's most advanced weapons are being transferred to the Global South. Weapons delivered by major suppliers to developing countries between 1991 and 1994 included 3,577 tanks and self-propelled cannon, 3,520 artillery pieces, 660 supersonic combat aircraft,

---

[2]The 1980s witnessed a slight dip in the upward trend in arms sales, but the surge in new spending following the Persian Gulf War dispelled hopes that arms trafficking would plummet. The value of all arms *deliveries* worldwide between 1991 and 1994 ($106.1 billion) did decline 55 percent from the 1987–1990 level ($236.1 billion), but aggregate contract *agreements* worldwide for future sales between 1991 and 1994 of $152 billion assured that arms trafficking would continue apace (Grimmett 1995, 81–82).

4,281 surface-to-air missiles, and a large number of warships, submarines, antishipping missiles, and other weapon systems (Grimmett 1995, 75).

As noted, three-fourths of transnational arms shipments are imported by the less developed countries. However, the recipients are not spread evenly throughout the Global South. "Arms transfer agreements with the top ten developing world recipients, as a group, in 1994 alone totaled $20.8 billion or 81.9 percent of all arms transfer agreements with the developing world." In rank order of the value of their scheduled purchases, those countries were Saudi Arabia, China, Israel, Qatar, Pakistan, Egypt, Malaysia, Kuwait, Singapore, and Thailand (Grimmett 1995, 35, 59; for rankings between 1991 and 1994, see also Chapter 5).

The Middle East has been the locus of intense strife and chronic national security problems. It still includes many pairs of competitive states. In the wake of the Persian Gulf War and the 1993 Israeli-Palestine peace accord, enduring rivalries remained between Egypt and Libya, Iran and Iraq, Iran and Saudi Arabia, Iraq and Kuwait, Iraq and Syria, Iraq and Turkey, and Israel and Syria, and these states' high level of activity in the global arms market has continued. Middle Eastern countries in 1967 accounted for 11 percent of world arms imports. By 1993, when four of the world's top five arms-importing states were in the Middle East, the proportion had mushroomed to 43 percent (U.S. ACDA 1995, 9). Recently, Asia has joined the feverish rush to purchase arms, raising fears that an arms race similar to that of the Middle East will unfold there as well. "The risk, of course, is that there [are] no clearly defined boundaries between taking prudent defensive steps to prepare for future challengers, and taking actions that could be seen as threatening to other countries" (Richardson 1995a).

It is difficult to predict trends in the future purchases of arms. Shifts in procurement have regularly been rapid in response to war and threat perception. States' proportionate share of total weapons purchases is likely to change, depending on the location of the globe's hot spots and each state's involvement in them. Aggregate levels of world arms imports are similarly likely to be influenced by the climate of political tension and the international political economy generally, with activity fluctuating sharply from year to year.[3] To anticipate the future distribution of military power, it is important to observe not only the changing demands of arms importers, but also changes in the activities of arms suppliers.

During the Cold War the superpowers dominated the arms export market. Between 1975 and 1990 the U.S.-Soviet share of global arms exports varied between one-half and three-fourths. In that period the two superpowers together "supplied an estimated $325 billion worth of arms and ammunition to the Third World" (Klare 1994, 139). But with the demise of the Soviet Union, the United States has emerged as the "arms merchant of the world" (a phrase used by U.S. President Jimmy Carter to deplore what he sometimes regarded as an unsavory business). Between 1991 and 1994, the United States accounted for more than half of world arms transfer agreements, making it the uncontested leader in the sale of military supplies to the world. This contrasts sharply with the distribution exhibited among arms' suppliers in the closing years of the

---

[3]For example, "world arms sales agreements . . . declined generally over the [1982–1992] decade but reversed direction in 1993 to rise by 32 percent, suggesting a possible upturn in deliveries over the next few years" (U.S. ACDA 1995, 9). As the U.S. government observed, "the 1993 increase to $39 billion [was] attributable mainly to a $15 billion rise in United States sales agreements" (U.S. ACDA 1995, 9).

Cold War (1987–1990). Figure 13.3 reports the magnitude of the changes in the export of arms before and after the Cold War.

The future arms export market is likely to remain vigorous. The total arms that major suppliers actually delivered just to the developing countries in the Global South between 1987 and 1994 exceeded $218 billion (Grimmett 1995,

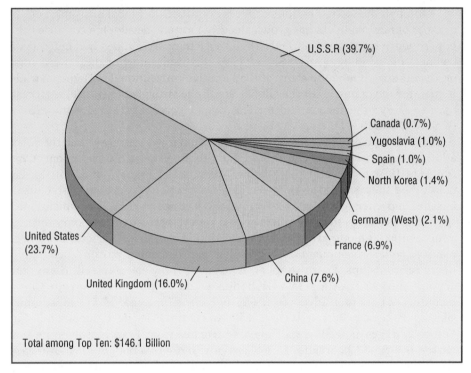

Total among Top Ten: $146.1 Billion

FIGURE 13.3

Arms Transfer Agreements by the Top Ten Suppliers, 1987–1990

The end of the Cold War produced a transformation in the structure of the export market for the supply of arms across borders. These figures trace the degree of change, showing the ascent of the United States as the dominant supplier of arms to the world since the end of the Cold War, as well as other changes in the suppliers' (exporters') share of the world market. "It should be noted that the United States share of the world rose even as its total arms sales declined, since world arms sales fell faster."

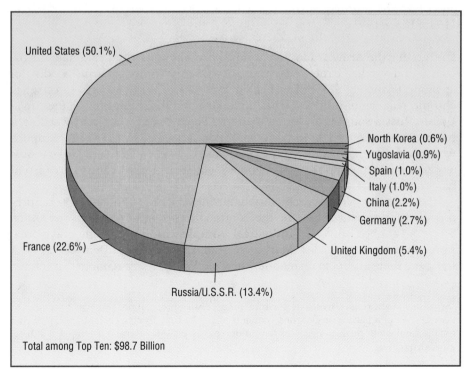

Total among Top Ten: $98.7 Billion

Arms Transfer Agreements by the Top Ten Suppliers, 1991–1994

SOURCE: Adapted from Grimmett (1995), 15.

387

60). The arms-sale agreements already under contract assure that the arms trade will remain sizable. The United States, with 63 percent of all contracted arms agreements in the world in 1993, is likely to remain the largest exporter (U.S. ACDA 1995, 16). However, a rising competitor is France, whose 1994 agreements with the developing countries were nearly twice the $6.1 billion the United States contracted to supply (Grimmett 1995, 56).

Although the top ten major suppliers dominate the global arms market, the number of new suppliers has grown steadily, as many developing countries also now produce arms for export. By 1990 more than sixty states had entered the business of "peddling arms" (Sivard 1991, 11). Still, most of these were small producers struggling for a share of the lucrative conventional armaments trade. In fact, for the countries in the Global South the struggle has not been successful, as in 1993 they accounted for less than 1 percent of world arms exports (U.S. ACDA 1995, 91).

A consequence of the increased competition for arms markets is the relaxation of export controls. The United Nations Register of Conventional Arms, begun in 1991 to monitor the weapons exports and imports of countries, has not curbed their sale. Moreover, the illegal export of Western nuclear, ballistic missile, and chemical weapons technology has not abated. Diversification of suppliers, as well as the coproduction and codevelopment of weaponry through joint ventures among arms manufacturers in different countries, have ended many supplier–consumer ties that earlier had cemented patron–client diplomatic relationships. Every supplier, it seems, is now eager to sell to any purchaser. In 1992 Russia sold $1.2 billion of its military hardware to China, including twenty-four advanced SU-27 fighters; China sold M-11 ballistic missiles to Pakistan; Taiwan bought 150 American F-16 jet fighters and sixty French Mirages as well as six Lafayette frigates from France; Singapore purchased five Type-62 corvettes from Germany; Indonesia bought most of the old East German navy; Thailand acquired six Jianhhu-class frigates from China; and China illegally acquired U.S. Patriot missiles reexported by Israel (Gordon 1993b; Klare 1993).

Motives for the Arms Trade. Economic gain is an important rationale for foreign military sales. Israel sells arms abroad to subsidize its arms production at home (Frankel 1987).[4] The United States uses arms exports to offset its chronic balance-of-trade deficits. Following the disintegration of the Soviet Union, Russia sought to raise desperately needed hard currency by selling at bargain-basement prices its one product mix still in demand: weapons, weapons technology, and weapons expertise. Cash is also the primary motive among other arms suppliers, for whom ideological considerations are virtually nonexistent.

Because the sale of weapons is big business, arms manufacturers comprise a powerful domestic lobby for the continuation of arms sales. In the United States a "gunbelt" **military-industrial complex** profits at home and abroad from continued arms sales (Markusen, Hall, Campbell, and Deitrick 1991). At the same time, efforts to dismantle "the Cold War military economy" by ending

---

[4]Arms manufacturing is, by its very nature, an expensive proposition. One way to reduce the per-unit cost of a particular weapons system is to produce for foreign consumption as well as for the immediate security needs of the producing state. Selling weapons abroad is thus an attractive option.

"welfare" for the defense industry have encountered broad-based, coordinated resistance (Cahn 1995). As Lawrence J. Korb (1995a), who served as U.S. Assistant Secretary of Defense for five years in the Reagan administration, explained, "The military has succeeded in inflating the threat of our foes and downplaying the contribution of our allies." Andrew Cockburn (1995) described what he saw as the unjustifiably high U.S. military budget by noting "The problem is that the apparent goal of military spending is to direct as much money as possible into corporate coffers." Russia's difficulties in "defense conversion" similarly are explainable in part by the resistance of Russia's military-industrial establishment, despite strong domestic support for conversion of the Russian defense economy (Cooper 1995; Shlykov 1995). In fact, many countries' civilian sectors are organized around preparations for militarization and arms manufacture and sales for the same reasons (Regan 1994).

The end of the Cold War ironically increased states' incentives to sell arms merely for profit. Nonetheless, many states continue to still sell arms (or make outright grants) for time-honored purposes: to support friendly governments, to honor allies' requests, and to earn political loyalty. This was illustrated by the U.S. agreements since the 1990 Persian Gulf War to transfer $44 billion worth of arms to seven Middle Eastern countries (Arms Control Association *Fact Sheet*, October 22, 1993). But the profit motive, fueled in part by the desire of defense contractors to maintain income in a less-hostile strategic environment, also continues to drive the spread of weapons worldwide. "The flourishing underground, or black market, trade supplying the wars in the former Yugoslavia and in Somalia" (Sivard 1993) reveals the greed behind suppliers' activities.

The Strategic Consequences of Arms Sales. Whether the arming of other countries has accomplished all of its intended goals is open to dispute. During the Cold War, for example, the United States and the Soviet Union thought they could maintain peace by spreading arms to politically pivotal recipients. Between 1983 and 1987 the United States provided arms to fifty-nine less developed countries while the Soviet Union supplied forty-two (Klare 1990b, 12). Yet many of the recipients engaged in war with their neighbors or experienced internal rebellion. Of the top twenty arms importers in 1988, more than half "had governments noted for the frequent use of violence" (Sivard 1991, 17). The toll in lives from the wars in the Global South since 1945 exceeds tens of millions of people. Undoubtedly, the import of such huge arsenals of weapons from abroad aided this level of destruction.

Also troubling is arms suppliers' questionable ability to control the uses to which their hardware is put. The United States armed both sides in several conflicts in the Global South since World War II, as did the Soviets. Moreover, loyalty is often a fragile commodity, and supplying weapons can backfire, as the United States discovered when the weapons it sold Iraq were used against it by Saddam Hussein in the Persian Gulf War (Timmerman 1991). Likewise, in 1982 Great Britain found itself shipping military equipment to Argentina just eight days before Argentina's attack on the British-controlled Falkland Islands (Sivard 1982).

Trends in Weapons Technology

The widespread quest for armaments has created a potentially explosive global environment. The description is especially apt when we consider not only trends in defense expenditures and the arms trade but also in the destructiveness of modern weapons.

Nuclear Weapons. Technological research and development has expanded radically the destructiveness of national arsenals. The largest "blockbuster" bombs of World War II delivered a power of ten tons of TNT. The atomic bomb that leveled Hiroshima had the power of over fifteen thousand tons of TNT. Less than twenty years later, the former Soviet Union built a nuclear bomb with the explosive force of fifty-seven megatons (million tons) of TNT. As 1995 ended, the world's nearly eighteen thousand nuclear warheads collectively had the explosive force of nine hundred thousand Hiroshima bombs.

The use of such weapons could destroy not only entire cities and countries but, conceivably, the world's entire population. Albert Einstein, the Nobel Prize-winning physicist whose ideas laid the basis for the development of nuclear weapons, was well aware of the threat they posed. He professed uncertainty about the weapons that would be used in a third world war, but was confident that in a fourth they would be "sticks and stones." He warned that inasmuch as "the unleashed power of the atom has changed everything save our modes of thinking . . . we thus drift toward unparalleled catastrophe."

The five principal nuclear-weapon states (the United States, the Soviet Union/Russia, Britain, France, and China) have continuously refined the deadliness of their weapons through testing. Between 1945 and 1996 they detonated a combined total of more than 2,000 nuclear explosions around the world (see Chapter 15). The United States, which alone had conducted 1,030 nuclear tests in the period, suspended its testing program in August 1995. However, France resumed its tests in September of that year in the South Pacific over the protests of its protectorate (Tahiti), New Zealand (which unsuccessfully attempted to block the resumption in the World Court), and world public opinion.

The nuclear arsenals of the United States and the former Soviet Union are particularly extensive and sophisticated. When World War II ended, the United States possessed the one atomic bomb still in existence. In 1967, at the height of the U.S. strategic stockpile, the United States had 32,500 warheads in its arsenal. In 1986, when the Soviet Union was at its peak, it had 45,000 (*Bulletin of Atomic Scientists* 49 [December 1993]: 57). In addition, during the Cold War the United States and the Soviet Union each deployed thousands of tactical nuclear weapons designed for the direct support of combat operations. Their combined arsenals ranged between 21,000 in 1961 to 46,000 in 1986 (Worldwatch data diskette 1995).

The 1987 Intermediate-range Nuclear Forces (INF) treaty began the elimination of short- and medium-range delivery vehicles from Europe. At the end of 1995, the deployed nuclear stockpiles of the five major powers were estimated to total about 17,400 strategic warheads. The U.S. arsenal had 7,700 nuclear warheads, and Russia had 8,700. In addition, France stockpiled an estimated 482 warheads; China had 284; and Britain retained 234. To this should be added the 2,670 strategic warheads of three former Soviet Republics (Ukraine, Kazakhstan, and Belarus), as well as the 100 to 200 nuclear warheads of the three "undeclared" nuclear countries (India, Israel, and Pakistan).

Technological Improvements and Weapon Delivery Capabilities. Advances in weapons technology have been rapid and extraordinary. Since the advent of the

Despite a worldwide surge in disarmament proposals since the end of the Cold War, some states continue to develop and refine their nuclear arsenal. On January 27, 1996, France tested its nuclear weapons in the Murura atoll of its South Pacific protectorate, Tahiti (an aerial photo of the shock waves during the test is shown here). Its decision to resume testing, justified by the proclaimed right to protect itself with weapons of mass destruction, provoked protests throughout the world. On January 29, 1996, France called a halt to its nuclear testing program and promised to sign the Comprehensive Nuclear Test Ban treaty.

atomic age, with the "gravity bombs of 1945 . . . a whole warehouse of varied weapons, each with its own special purpose" has been created. These include:

> clean bombs; dirty bombs; bombs that burrowed into the earth, seeking underground command posts; bombs that went off undersea, seeking submarines; bombs that went off high over earth, to fry the brains of electrical devices with a huge shower of electromagnetic pulses; bombs that killed tank crews with radiation but didn't flatten towns or cities; bombs delivered by guidance so precise that they could destroy anything with a known location on or near the surface of the earth. . . . The results of this tireless invention were weapons powerful enough to threaten human life on the planet. (Powers 1994, 123)

Particularly deadly have been the technological refinements that enable states to deliver weapons as far away as nine thousand miles within a few hundred feet of their targets in less than thirty minutes. In 1987, seven Western countries (Britain, Canada, France, Germany, Italy, Japan, and the United States) established the Missile Technology Control Regime (MTCR) to curtail the spread of missile technologies, especially those for the delivery of weapons of mass destruction. In 1993 the MTCR expanded its coverage to delivery systems for chemical and biological weapons. By December 1995 its formal membership included thirty-two states.

However, the MTCR is not a legally binding treaty, includes only a fraction of the missile-technology suppliers, and lacks an institution to monitor and enforce compliance with the voluntary agreement. Symptomatic of its weakness was the possession in 1993 of short- or medium-range surface-to-air missiles by twenty countries in the Global South, and the fact that seven of them have used missiles in warfare (Zimmerman 1994). Thus the highly threatening ballistic missile continues outside meaningful international restraints.

Other technological improvements have broadened the spectrum of available weapons. The United States and Russia, for example, equipped their ballistic missiles with MIRVs (multiple independently targetable reentry vehicles), which enable a single missile to launch multiple warheads toward different targets simultaneously and very accurately. One MIRVed U.S. MX (Peacekeeper) missile could carry ten nuclear warheads—enough to wipe out a city and everything else within a fifty-mile radius. The Minuteman III missile could carry three warheads with the equivalent of 300 kilotons explosive force; twenty-four missiles on each Trident submarine could carry eight warheads with an explosive force of one hundred kilotons. As a result of MIRVing, the number of deliverable nuclear warheads in the nuclear powers' arsenals increased far more rapidly than the number of delivery vehicles. Taking this capacity into account, before the superpowers agreed to the START II treaty to ban MIRVed intercontinental ballistic missiles, the world's combined nuclear inventory was nearly three times larger than the number of nuclear warheads in existence (in 1995, about 45,000).

Despite this effort to control missile capabilities, other kinds of technological improvements have led to steady increases in the speed, accuracy, range, and effectiveness of weapons. As Ruth Leger Sivard predicted,

> Now, with the improved yield-to-weight ratio, nuclear warheads can be incorporated in artillery shells with a weight of 95 pounds and a range of 18 miles. These have a yield of 2,000 tons of TNT equivalent. More powerful is the nuclear-headed cruise missile which weighs 2,650 pounds. Launched from a submarine at sea, it can travel 1,500 miles under its own power, and release up to 200,000 tons of explosives on the target. (Sivard 1991, 13)

New technologies also alter the character of weapons. Laser weapons, nuclear-armed tactical air-to-surface missiles (TASMs), Stealth air-launched cruise missiles (ACMs), and antisatellite weapons (ASAT) which can project force in and wage war from outer space, have become a part of the military landscape. In addition, a large number of innovative new weapons technologies are in use and in development—weapons so novel that they look like they belong in science fiction, although science and technology have now made them possible (see Focus 13.1).

Technological advances are likely to make obsolete orthodox ways of classifying weapons systems as well as prior equations for measuring power ratios. As an influential U.S. strategic report correctly predicted almost a decade ago:

> Dramatic developments in military technology appear feasible over the next twenty years. They will be driven primarily by the further exploitation of microelectronics, in particular for sensors and information processing, and the development of directed energy. The much greater precision,

The Next Generation of Weapons, Lethal and Nonlethal

A Revolution in Warfare

Technological breakthroughs have transformed the character of the battlefield of the twenty-first century. U.S. military planners speak loudly and hopefully of the "revolution in military affairs (RMA)," the "military-technical revolution (MTR)," and of "information age warfare." These concepts refer to the goal of seeking to increase military capabilities and effectiveness by seizing the opportunities created by microprocessors, instantaneous global communications, and precision-guided munitions technologies to confront and contain the armed conflicts of the future without relying on weapons of mass destruction. To advocates who seek a "kinder, gentler" type of warfare, the Revolution in Military Affairs promises to transform the ways wars will be fought and the way people think about them (E. Cohen 1996).

To alter the nature of warfare and the conduct of military operations, enthusiasts envision RMA and MTA developing in two stages:

> The first is based on stand-off platforms, stealth, precision, information dominance, improved communications, computers, global positioning systems, digitization, "smart" weapons systems, jointness, and use of ad hoc coalitions. The second may be based on robotics, nonlethality, psycho-technology, cyberdefense, nanotechnology, "brilliant" weapons systems, hyperflexible organizations, and "fire ant warfare." If this idea is correct, change that has occurred so far will soon be dwarfed by even more fundamental transformation. (Metz and Kievit 1995, vi)

Behind the technological revolution is the belief that nonlethal weapons are practical because they can obtain intelligence from computers and advanced technologies to enable precision strikes that can "blind, immobilize, and maintain the enemy at a distance while critical targets are identified, struck, and destroyed" (Tilford 1995; for an overview, see Kokoski 1994; also Schneider and Grinter 1995). The value of these weapons was illustrated dramatically during the Persian Gulf War by the United States' use of "smart" bombs that could

drop down chimneys, stealthy aircraft that could elude radar detection, and an airborne tracking system that could scout Iraqi military installations and movements. Their advantages also were illustrated during the 1994–1995 U.S. military intervention in Haiti, where American soldiers carried miniature video cameras on their rifles, enabling them to broadcast live images back to their headquarters and—by satellite—to the Pentagon.

Talk of stealth, precision, information dominance, and missile defense anticipates a day when robots will replace soldiers in combat and unmanned aircraft will replace pilots roaming the globe with laser weapons to destroy ground and air targets, and "cyberdefense" through the use of "smart" and "brilliant" weapons systems will be able to make sophisticated decisions about when and how to act (Metz and Kievit 1995). In this revolution, nonlethal weapons figure prominently. Among the devices already available are "guns that shoot rubber pellets, wooden batons and tiny beanbags to disperse a crowd; stinger grenades that fire rubber pellets; sticky foam that immobilizes people; and another foam system that creates a sudslike barrier two hundred feet long, twenty feet wide, and four feet high, laced with tear gas" (Graham 1995). Today's arsenal includes lasers that can blind people from a distance and a variety of biological and chemical weapons. Some advocate using the latter, arguing that a day of fever, coughing, vomiting, and internal bleeding is preferable to incineration. Still in design is a next-generation missile capable of being retargeted in flight based on intelligence from the battlefield (Graham 1995).

The revolution in technology may make for a new kind of warfare. Will operations on the new battlefield be more humane? Advocates believe that by reducing the exposure of pilots to enemy anti-aircraft devices, precision guided weapons can contain killing and deter adversaries while minimizing collateral casualties to civilians. However, critics question the effectiveness and ethics of remote and robotic killing with nonlethal arsenals.

range, and destructiveness of weapons could extend war across a much wider geographic area, make war much more rapid and intense, and require entirely new modes of operation. Application of new technologies to both offensive and defensive systems will pose complicated problems for designing forces and assessing enemy capabilities. (U.S. Commission on Integrated Long-Term Strategy 1988, 8)

For decades, a **firebreak** has separated conventional from nuclear wars. The term comes from the barriers of cleared land with which firefighters keep forest fires from racing out of control. In the context of modern weaponry, it is a psychological barrier whose purpose is to "prevent even the most intensive forms of conventional combat from escalating into nuclear war." As both nuclear and conventional weapons technologies advance, there is danger that the firebreak is being crossed from both directions—by a new generation of "near-nuclear" conventional weapons capable of "levels of violence approximating those of a limited nuclear conflict" and by a new generation of "near-conventional" nuclear weapons able "to inflict damage not much greater than that of the most powerful conventional weapons" (Klare 1985).[5]

Unconventional Weapons: Biological and Chemical. Biological and chemical weapons pose a special and growing threat. Each is sometimes regarded as a "poor man's atomic bomb," because they can be built at comparatively small cost and cause widespread injury and death. Despite the 1972 Biological Weapons Convention prohibiting the development, production, and stockpiling of biological weapons, "the United States, the United Kingdom, and Japan are known to have developed several types of biological weapons in the past (such stocks have since been destroyed), and Iraq and Syria are strongly suspected of stockpiling such weapons" (Fetter 1991) as is North Korea (Zimmerman 1994). Similarly, chemical weapons proliferation is a worldwide concern. In addition to Iran, Iraq, Russia, and the United States (the only states confirmed to possess chemical weapons), twenty-one other countries—mostly in the Global South—are suspected to have produced chemical weapons (Stock and De Geer 1995, 340).

International law prohibits the use of chemical weapons: The 1925 Geneva Protocol banned the use of chemical weapons in warfare, and the Chemical Weapons Convention (CWC) signed by 159 countries by September 1995 required the destruction of existing stocks. Nevertheless, legal restraints do not assure that states will forgo them. Iran's and Iraq's use of gas in warfare demonstrated this; Iraq even used chemical weapons against its own Kurdish people. Thus the firebreak has already been breached.

A number of factors limit the use of chemical weapons, including weather conditions and the ability to defend against them. They are nonetheless capable of causing widespread death and suffering. The use of chemical weapons (gas) used during World War I, for example, produced "about one hundred thousand battle fatalities and over one million total casualties" (Fetter 1991, 15). The proliferation of ballistic missiles among regional rivals in the Middle

---

[5]The precision and power of today's conventional weapons have expanded exponentially. Note also that while the nuclear powers retain the capacity to turn cities into glass, they increasingly rely on a variety of new cyberstrategies to deter and demobilize enemies. Examples include such futuristic weapons as the *electromagnetic-pulse* (EMP) bomb, which can be hand-delivered in a suitcase and can fry the enemy's computer and communications systems within an entire city; computer viruses of electronics-eating microbates that can eliminate a country's telephone system; and logic bombs that can confuse and redirect traffic on the target country's air and rail system. Also planned are *infowar* tactics that deploy information-age technics "to disrupt the enemy's economy and military preparedness, perhaps without firing a shot." One example of these is the U.S. Air Force's Commando Solo psychological operations plane, which can "jam signals from the government television station and insert in its place a 'morphed' TV program, in which the enemy leader appears on the screen and makes unpopular announcements, alienating him from his people" (Waller 1995).

East, Northeast Asia, and elsewhere, particularly raises the danger of their use because they enable chemical weapons to be readily delivered at great distances. The possibility that these weapons might be acquired and used by terrorists poses still another kind of threat.

The Proliferation Problem

Do arms acquisitions promote war? "Many amply supplied armed forces may incline governments to use force rather than to negotiate to resolve conflicts." Even so, "the possession of weapons does not guarantee their use" (Ball 1991). In fact, as we will discuss in Chapter 14, the primary purpose of arming is to *prevent* the use of force (*deterrence*), not to encourage it. Hence, as Michael Klare (1987) reasons, "it would be foolish to argue that increased arms transfers automatically increase the risk of war—the decision to wage war is determined by numerous factors."

Still, Klare continues, "There is no doubt that the widespread availability of modern arms has made it *easier* for potential belligerents to choose the military rather than the diplomatic option when seeking to resolve local disputes." Huge arms purchases by Iraq, for example, may have set the stage for its invasion of Kuwait and the subsequent Persian Gulf War. Iraq bought $75 billion in military equipment during the 1970s and 1980s, or nearly 10 percent of all arms transfers. "The weapons . . . may have encouraged Saddam Hussein to believe that his invasion of Kuwait would not be challenged" (Ball 1991, 20). Thus, even if the arms trade and arms races do not necessarily make the world more violent, they do make it less secure (Johansen 1995). Hence the proliferation of arms is a serious global concern.

Nuclear Weapons. The addition of new nuclear states is commonly referred to as the **Nth country problem.** The increase in the number of nuclear states is called **horizontal nuclear proliferation.** This is in contrast with increases in the capabilities of existing nuclear powers, known as **vertical nuclear proliferation.**

As Map 13.1 summarizes, in 1996 there were only five "official" members of the nuclear club—the United States, Russia, Great Britain, France, and China. However, three countries are *de facto* or undeclared nuclear weapon states (India, Israel, and Pakistan). Two others (North Korea, which agreed to freeze its nuclear program in October 1994; and Iraq, which is subject to UN monitoring) are classifiable as "states of immediate concern." In addition, Iran and Libya warrant long-term concern because they are widely suspected of having secret nuclear weapons development programs in operation.

Most countries dread the chain reaction that might lead to widespread horizontal proliferation. It increases the likelihood that one or more states will choose to use nuclear weapons or that an accident or miscalculation will lead to catastrophe. Although estimates vary, experts agree that perhaps as many as thirty other states now have the economic and technological potential to become nuclear powers. By the year 2000, the number could grow to forty (Albright 1993).

On the optimistic side of the ledger, seven states (Algeria, Argentina, Belarus, Brazil, Kazakhstan, South Africa, and Ukraine), once regarded as nuclear aspirants, have now reversed their former position and joined the nonproliferation regime. On the pessimistic side, "If we totally ignore the mounting

MAP 13.1

Nuclear States and the States Likely to Join the Nuclear Club

A number of countries are capable of producing nuclear weapons on short notice and are regarded as probable candidates for joining the "nuclear club" of declared nuclear weapon states. Others, such as Sweden, have long possessed the capability, but few experts consider them likely to seize the option. This map pictures the state of nuclear proliferation in June 1996.

SOURCE: Projections based on predictions provided by the Arms Control Association in June 1996.

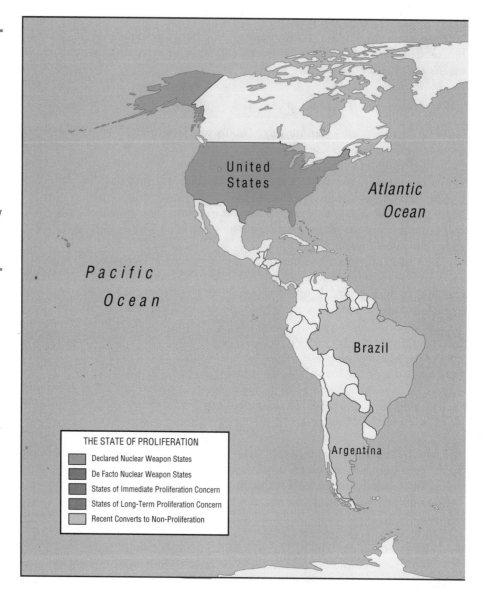

threats from nongovernmental groups and focus on nation-states alone, we can conclude that approximately twenty countries are either in or are knocking at the door of the nuclear club. . . . We may be looking at a world in which a third to a half of all countries have some hideous weapons of mass murder locked away in their arsenals" (Toffler and Toffler 1993; see also Spector and McDonough with Medeiros 1995).

The Nonproliferation Regime. The Nuclear Nonproliferation Treaty (NPT), first signed in 1968, seeks to prevent further proliferation by prohibiting the transfer of nuclear weapons technology from the now-nuclear states to the nonnuclear states. However, the nuclear states are obligated to provide others with nuclear information and technology for peaceful purposes.

Since the nonproliferation regime went into force on March 5, 1970, 181 states have become members. NPT membership is divided into two categories:

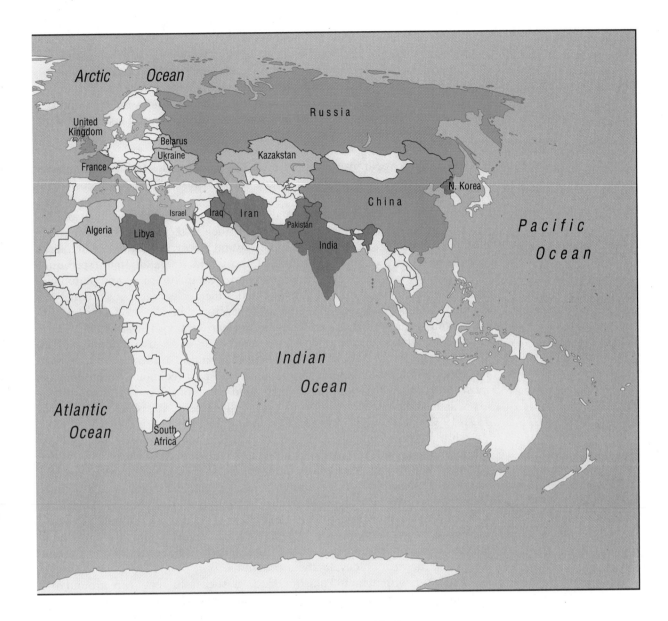

nuclear weapon states and non-nuclear weapon states. Nuclear states are defined as those which manufactured and exploded a nuclear weapon prior to January 1, 1967. This definition includes only China, France, Russia, the United Kingdom, and the United States—all of which are members of the NPT. All other parties to the agreement are non-nuclear weapon states.[6]

The NPT strikes a bargain between nuclear and non-nuclear weapon states. Under the treaty, the non-nuclear weapon states agree not to acquire nuclear weapons and to accept comprehensive International Atomic Energy Agency (IAEA) safeguards over all of their nuclear materi-

---

[6]Three states widely believed to possess nuclear weapons—India, Israel, and Pakistan—are not NPT members. In order to join the NPT, they would have to dismantle their nuclear weapons and place *all* of their nuclear facilities under IAEA safeguards.

als to ensure that they are used exclusively for peaceful purposes. In exchange, the nuclear weapon states agree to freely share the benefits of peaceful nuclear energy and technology and not to assist other states to acquire nuclear weapons. In addition, the nuclear weapon states pledged to pursue "good faith" negotiations toward an end to the arms race and toward general and complete disarmament. (Arms Control Association *Fact Sheet*, October 1, 1995, 1)

Despite the apparent success of the NPT, the obstacles to increased proliferation are fragile. The incentives to join the nuclear club are strong for several reasons.

First, the materials needed to make a nuclear weapon are widely available. This is partly due to the widespread use of nuclear technology for generating electricity. Today hundreds of nuclear power and research reactors are in operation in dozens of countries throughout the world. In addition to spreading nuclear know-how, states could choose to reprocess the uranium and plutonium that power plants produce as waste for clandestine nuclear weapons production. By the year 2000, commercial reprocessing reactors could be producing enough plutonium to make thirty-seven thousand nuclear weapons (Sivard 1993, 13).

Second, the scientific expertise necessary for weapons development has spread with the globalization of advanced scientific training. "In the near future it will be possible to duplicate almost all past technology in all but the most forlorn of Third World backwaters, and much of the present state-of-the-art will be both intellectually and practically accessible" (Clancy and Seitz 1991–1992).

Third, export controls designed to stop technology transfer for military purposes are weak. "A large and growing number of states can now export material, equipment, technology, and services needed to develop nuclear weapons" (Potter 1992). In addition, the leaks in nuclear export controls make "a mockery of the long-revered nuclear nonproliferation regime" (Leventhal 1992). Conversion of peacetime nuclear energy programs to military purposes can occur either overtly or, as in the case of India, covertly. The safeguards built into the nonproliferation regime are simply inadequate to detect and prevent secret nuclear weapon development programs.

The ease with which Pakistan made a successful end run around the technology-export controls of the United States and western European governments illustrates the problem of control. In 1979 Pakistan quietly bought all the basic parts—allegedly with funds supplied by the Libyan government—necessary for a uranium-enrichment plant. Similarly, UN inspectors discovered after the Persian Gulf War that Iraq was much closer to building an atomic weapon than previously suspected. Yet Iraq "remained a member [of the nonproliferation regime] in good standing for more than a decade. This was possible because the [NPT] treaty allows members legally to get much too close to weapons capability. . . . The Iraqi experience suggests that it is impossible to effectively safeguard weapons-grade materials" (Mathews 1991). No less than eight countries have constructed secret nuclear production plants, underscoring the difficulties of managing effective inspections and monitoring nuclear developments (Albright 1993).

Fourth, other states have strong incentives to develop nuclear weapons similar to those once cited by the members of the nuclear club. French President Charles de Gaulle argued that, without an independent nuclear capability,

France could not "command its own destiny." Similarly, in 1960 Britain's Labour Party leader Aneurin Bevan asserted that without the bomb Britain would go "naked into the council chambers of the world." And in 1993 North Korean President Kim Il Sung defiantly withdrew from the nonproliferation pact, refusing to allow even routine monitoring of his country's five declared nuclear sites at Yongbyon. The desire to act independently and to assert North Korea's power and independence were the primary motives. In response to President Clinton's June 1994 pledge that the United States "would not allow North Korea to develop a nuclear bomb," North Korea dug in its heels. Reluctantly, however, it agreed to freeze its nuclear development program in October 1994.

Many non-nuclear states want the same command of their own fate and the same diplomatic influence that the nuclear powers seem to enjoy. Why, non-nuclear states ask, should they heed a nonproliferation agreement that dooms them to others' domination and security guarantees? Consider Iran's sentiments: In January 1992 its spiritual leader, the Ayatollah Ali Khamenenei, declared that the United States had no business questioning the nuclear weapons program designed to make Iran the most powerful military force in the Persian Gulf. "Iran's revolutionary Muslim people recognize no false hegemony for America or any other power," he exclaimed. Similarly, in November 1993, Pakistan's Prime Minister, Benazir Bhutto, asserted that "It is degrading and humiliating to expect Pakistan to roll back its nuclear program." Pakistan developed a nuclear capability, she explained, to deter India, its archenemy, and "should be rewarded" for stopping short of building a weapon.

Fifth, the breakup of the Soviet Union has spread the number of nuclear weapon states. As of November 1995, 2,270 warheads remained on the soil of Belarus, Kazakhstan, and Ukraine (nearly 40 percent as many as in Russia). Uncertainty persists about when they will be dismantled. Each of the newly independent republics had incentives to assert continued control over the weapons (although all of them accepted joint command over them). For example, Ukrainian nationalist lawmaker Oles Shevchenko declared in late November 1993: "We've got to keep nuclear weapons to defend our territory against the eastern aggressor. [Russia's new military doctrine justifying intervention in the 'near abroad' makes it] a thousand times more dangerous for us to disarm."

Nuclear Disarmament? Some see the end of the Cold War as an opportunity to begin eliminating nuclear weapons. In 1992 Russia advocated complete nuclear disarmament. Moreover, the United States and Russia undertook a number of important steps toward meaningful disarmament (see Chapter 15). This set the stage for expanding the nonproliferation regime. In accordance with the provisions of the Non-Proliferation Treaty, 175 of its signatories met in the 1995 arms control conference in New York to decide, by majority vote, whether the NPT should remain in force indefinitely or be extended only for an additional fixed period or periods.

The New York NPT Review and Extension Conference resulted in a consensus decision "to negotiate in good faith an effective nuclear disarmament, and to convene an extensive conference in twenty-five years to determine the duration of the treaty" (Epstein 1995). Nonetheless, it is unlikely that the nuclear threat will cease. "There's not a snowball's chance in hell we'll eliminate all nuclear weapons from the face of the earth," explains Matthew Bunn, editor of *Arms Control Today*. "That genie is long since out of the bottle and there's no chance of ever getting him back in." Moreover, a world nearing nuclear disarmament would not end the threat. "The problem is, if you eliminate them all, then any country that built just a few nuclear weapons would have enormous blackmail potential" (Davidson 1991).

• • •

THE SOCIAL AND ECONOMIC CONSEQUENCES OF MILITARY PREPARATIONS FOR WAR

Global patterns of military spending and arms acquisitions testify to the prevalence of the realist belief that power can be purchased. However, liberal and neoliberal challengers to this world view ask: What are the effects of this belief about security on national well-being? Do military expenditures and armaments promote national prosperity and security? Or are the consequences destructive?

The Burden of Defense

The **relative burden of military spending,** the ratio of defense spending to gross national product (GNP), is one way to measure the sacrifices that military spending requires. In 1993 the relative defense burden for the world as a whole was 3.3 percent. The average among developed countries fell to 3.4 percent, a historic low since 1960. The average among developing countries also declined (after rising in 1990) to a new low of 3.1 percent (ACDA 1995, 24).

It is customary to show the wide range in states' willingness to pay a heavy burden for defense by grouping them according to the share of GNP they devote to the military and then juxtaposing this relative burden with their GNP per capita. Such studies reveal wide variations. As shown in Table 13.2, some comparatively wealthy states (e.g., Israel, Qatar, and Kuwait) bear a heavy burden. In contrast, other states providing a high average income for their citizens (e.g., Austria, Japan, and Switzerland) pay a low defense burden. Likewise, the citizens of some very poor countries (Bhutan, Somalia, and Nepal) are heavily burdened, whereas others (Sudan and Mozambique) are not. Thus it is difficult to generalize about the precise relationship between a country's defense burden and its citizens' standard of living or stage of development. Still, the available data do suggest two general patterns.

First, those most burdened by the costs of defense include a disproportionate share of poor countries experiencing civil or international war or security threats. Second, many of the countries least able to afford it bear a major share of the world's military burden. Because many of those countries least able to afford weapons make the greatest sacrifices to get them, it appears that the costs of arming for security pose "a formidable barrier" to the alleviation of poverty and suffering. The developing countries in the late 1980s "lost to the arms race in a single year the equivalent of 187 million human-years of income" (Sivard 1991, 11). This impact raises questions about the social costs of expenditures to prepare for war (see Focus 13.2).

"The problem in defense spending," as President Eisenhower observed in 1956, "is to figure how far you should go without destroying from within what you are trying to defend from without." Now the concern is how "downsizing" military establishments geared toward Cold War competition will affect employment levels and research, development, and production opportunities in

ME/GNP* (percent)	Under $200	$200–499	$500–999	$1,000–2,999	$3,000–9,999	$10,000 and Over
			GNP per Capita (1993 dollars)			
10% and over		Bosnia and Herzegovina[†] Angola[†]	North Korea[†] Iraq[†] Serbia and Montenegro[†]		Oman Saudi Arabia Russia	Qatar[†] Kuwait
5–9.99%	Sudan[†] Rwanda Mozambique Afghanistan[†]	Laos Pakistan Liberia[†] Zimbabwe Mauritania	Yemen[†] Congo[†]	Croatia[†] Jordan Syria[†] Djibouti Botswana Turkey Mongolia[†]	Bahrain Greece Lithuania Libya	Brunei[†] Israel
2–4.99%	Ethiopia Tanzania Kenya Sierra Leone Burundi[†]	Togo Cambodia India Guinea-Bissau[†] Equatorial Guinea[†] Chad[†] Nicaragua Vietnam[†] Central African Republic[†] Mali Burkina Faso	Sri Lanka Morocco Egypt Lesotho[†] Albania[†] Senegal Bolivia Swaziland Philippines Cameroon	Tajikistan[†] Azerbaijan[†] Iran Lebanon Tunisia Burma[†] Georgia[†] Algeria Thailand South Africa Colombia Romania Namibia China	Estonia Malaysia South Korea Cyprus Gabon[†] Bulgaria Portugal Czech Republic Slovakia Chile Poland	Singapore United Arab Emirates Taiwan United States United Kingdom France Norway Sweden Australia Netherlands Finland Germany Italy Denmark
1–1.99%	Bangladesh Nepal	Guyana[†] Zambia Zaire[†] Guinea[†] Niger Haiti[†] Uganda Benin[†] Madagascar Malawi	Ivory Coast[†] Macedonia[†] Indonesia Honduras Cape Verde[†]	Cuba Papua New Guinea Venezuela Peru Paraguay[†] Fiji Dominican Republic El Salvador Jamaica Belize Ecuador Guatemala	Uruguay Hungary Ukraine[†] Trinidad and Tobago Turkmenistan[†] Argentina Slovenia Brazil	Canada Belgium Spain Switzerland New Zealand Ireland Suriname
Under 1%	Bhutan[†] Somalia[†]	Gambia Nigeria Ghana[†]	São Tomé and Principe[†]	Armenia[†] Uzbekistan Kyrgyzstan Mauritius Costa Rica[†] Panama	Latvia Malta[†] Belarus[†] Barbados[†] Mexico Kazakhstan Moldova[†]	Japan Austria Luxembourg Iceland

Notes:
*Countries are listed within blocks in descending order of their military expenditures as a percentage of their gross national product.
[†]Ranking is based on a rough approximation of one or more variables, for which 1993 data or a reliable estimate is not available.

SOURCE: U.S. ACDA (1995), 25.

Military Spending and Social Priorities

The comparatively greater resources that military preparedness commands in relation to other problems has been a persistent concern to people seeking the best means to a just world order. Consider the following representative indicators:

- World military expenditures from 1960 to 1990 were $21 trillion in 1987 dollars, equivalent (in 1990) to the value of all goods and services produced by and for the globe's expanding population (Sivard 1991, 11).
- World military spending in 1992 equaled the combined income of 49 percent of the world's people (UNDP 1994, 48).
- Military expenditures worldwide exceed 1 million dollars a minute and more than three-fourths as much as public spending on health (Kidron and Segal 1995, 95).
- The developed countries spend as much on military power in a year as the poorest 2 billion people on earth earn in total income (Sivard 1993, 5).
- The price of one ballistic submarine ($1,453,000,000) would double the education budget of eighteen poor countries with 129,110,000 children to educate (Sivard 1991, 5).
- Between $15 and $20 of every $100 spent by central governments now goes to military purposes—triple their budgets for education, eight times their budgets for housing (Sivard 1991, 26).
- For military objectives, governments invest an average of $36,000 per year per member of the armed forces, thirty times more than they invest in the education of a school-child (Sivard 1991, 27).
- Developing countries have eight times as many soldiers as physicians (Sivard 1991, 5).

These statistics show that most countries are more concerned with defending their citizens from foreign attack than they are with protecting them from social, educational, and health insecurities. They also suggest that military spending reduces social welfare. The connection is not direct, but military spending and global deprivation are linked. Consider, for example, how the United States, first in military spending, ranked (in 1990) among 140 countries across various social indicators (Sivard 1993, 37, 39, 41):

Social Indicator	U.S. Rank Compared with 140 Other Countries
Literacy rate	4
Per-capita GNP	6
Per-capita public expenditure for education	9
Maternal mortality rate	13
Per-capita public expenditure for health	11
Life expectancy	10
School-age population per teacher	12
Average scores of students on science and math tests	13
Primary school-age population in school	15
Proportion of population protected by public health insurance	18
Infant mortality rate	21
Population per physician	22
Percent population with access to sanitation	25

These rankings suggest that high military spending reduces the quality of citizens' lives. Security in the broadest sense means security in the expectation that one will live a full life. Yet, do arms contribute to increased life expectancy or freedom from want? When expenditures for arms go up, so do disease, illiteracy, and suffering (Nincic 1982; Russett 1982; UNDP 1994). As U.S. President Dwight D. Eisenhower observed, "The world in arms is not spending money alone. It is spending the sweat of its laborers, the genius of its scientists, the hopes of its children."

defense-related industries. The goal of **defense conversion**—redirecting budgets from armaments to internal development—is "bedeviled by two conflicting objectives: how to shift firms out of defense and into civilian pursuits, and how to preserve a mobilization base to meet conceivable future defense needs" (Adelman and Augustine 1992). Even the absorption of large numbers of military personnel into the domestic economy has been a matter of concern on both sides of the one-time East–West divide.

Just as excessive military spending has its costs, conversion to a much smaller, "peace-maintaining" military posture may also exact a domestic economic toll. Perhaps this explains why the Clinton administration's fiscal 1994 defense budget did "not abolish a single new weapons system." "There is a tendency," observes Robert Reno (1993) "to build an inventory of possible wars to match present levels of defense spending and present levels of manpower, [which is why] defense conversion in Russia will [also] be a very difficult undertaking."

Military Spending and Economic Development

How are military expenditures and economic growth linked? Many politicians and experts argue that a tradeoff exists between "guns and butter"— between military spending and economic prosperity. Much evidence on the relationship points to "retarding effects through inflation, diversion of investment, use of scarce materials, misuse of human capital" (Sivard 1979). This is due to the tendency of defense expenditures to divert resources away from growth-promoting investments and inhibit research and development in export-generating industries. One study, for example, found that every additional dollar spent on arms in the Global South reduced domestic investment by 25 cents and agricultural output by 20 cents (Klare 1987, 1279–1280). Other studies agree, showing that in most developing countries when military spending rises the rate of economic growth declines (Deger and Smith 1983; also Lipow 1990; Payne and Sahu 1993; Väyrynen 1992) and debt increases (Snider 1991).

Despite this evidence, the guns-versus-growth issue remains controversial. "Previous research on the impact of military spending on the economy has pro-

Critics of excessive military spending cite the waste and fraud that often occurs in defense contracts, claiming that unneeded weapons systems are produced as a result of lobbying by what President Dwight D. Eisenhower termed "the military-industrial complex." In 1995, Congress proposed spending almost $36 billion for the new B-2 bombers, over the objections of Senator John McCain (R-Arizona.) McCain complained that "The prospect of utilizing the B-2 in a conventional role is akin to mosquito hunting with an elephant gun. It is neither practical nor cost effective."

duced disparate, inconsistent, and unstable results" (Chan 1987; cf. Sandler and Hartley 1995). A strong correlation does not hold for all countries. "The effects of military expenditure on the economy," conclude Ron P. Smith and George Georgiou (1983), "depend on the nature of the expenditure, the prevailing circumstances, and the concurrent government policies." In many advanced industrial economies, for instance, military spending stimulates economic growth, at least in the short run. This especially holds true during periods of unemployment, when the infusion of capital can provide jobs, training, and social infrastructure in the form of investments in highways, airports, communications, and the like.

The strain of military spending on economic growth, however, seems to be especially severe in many societies, particularly when it persists for many years (Väyrynen 1992; Ward, Davis, and Lofdahl 1995). Compare Japan with the United States and the former Soviet Union. The former country, relatively freed of the burden of funding militarization since the 1950s, expanded its economies greatly; the latter pair of countries, paying high costs for military power, fell behind economically. It appears that excessive military spending was a primary cause of the Soviet Union's demise. "No other industrialized state in the world [had] for so long spent so much of its national wealth on armaments and military forces. Soviet militarism, in harness with communism, destroyed the Soviet economy and thus hastened the self-destruction of the Soviet Empire" (Iklé 1991–1992, 28).

The end of the Cold War poses special problems for the United States, which now stands alone at the pinnacle of world power. What defense commitments and responsibilities should engage the United States now that the challenges of communist ideology and Soviet expansionism have disappeared? As we saw in Chapter 8, there are no easy answers to these questions.

Maintaining a balance between military preparedness and economic revitalization presents a serious challenge not just to the United States, but to the other major powers as well. A comparison of the great powers' new defense policies informs us about the ways states are thinking about national security as they prepare for the threats of the twenty-first century.

● ● ●

THE GREAT POWERS' NATIONAL SECURITY STRATEGIES

The threat of the Cold War turning hot may have disappeared. In response, the superpowers have retired their strategic nuclear arsenals more rapidly than they have replaced them, and the size of those arsenals is scheduled to decline to their lowest levels in fifty years (see Chapter 15). As a consequence, the geostrategic landscape now bears little resemblance to the terrain of the early 1990s.

The transformed security environment has deprived the strongest states of a clear vision of how to protect their country's national interests and prosperity. In Washington, Moscow, Beijing, Tokyo, and Berlin, defense planners are struggling to construct strategies and defense doctrines.

As we noted in Chapter 4, the choices range between the extremes of isolationist withdrawal from participation in world affairs to active international engagement. The options also require choices to be made between *unilateral* self-help actions on one end of the continuum to *multilateral* joint action with others on the other, and with *specialized bilateral alliances* and ad hoc partnerships in between.

Based on the strongest powers' recent actions and statements, they appear to agree on certain fundamental priorities in the emerging twenty-first century:

- Forestalling a new major war, because all other national security interests, such as prosperity, will be jeopardized if peace does not endure.

- Economic development will be of vital and growing importance to military security and to the position of each power in the globe's future hierarchy of power.

- The world pyramid of power is moving to a *multipolar* distribution, in which no hegemon will be dominant and three, four, or more great powers will share approximately equal military power.

Given the prevailing consensus about these probabilities, what sort of national security response is most likely? We will look briefly at the emerging security policies of the five major great powers.

The United States' New Security Policies

A key to understanding U.S. national security policy is America's economic decline relative to an ascending China, Japan, and Germany (see Chapter 8). To many observers, America is now more imperiled than imperial. It faces stiff trade competition, and its rivals' economies are growing at a faster pace, as "the American share of world GNP has declined . . . to about 22 percent, more or less the same level as in 1870" (Clarke 1995–1996, 44). In the long run these trends may reduce U.S. influence and its ability to lead in world affairs, forcing a commitment to make economic renewal and recovery at home a priority.

Yet this does not mean that military competition and threats will necessarily recede in importance. As UN Ambassador Madeleine Albright said in 1993, "Wherever we turn, someone is fighting or threatening to fight someone else." Former Secretary of State Lawrence Eagleburger explained at the same time, that "The dangers of the period into which we are going can be as unpleasant, if not as bloody, as most of the first fifty years of this century." We are returning to the raucous multipolarity more reminiscent of the nineteenth century than the past fifty years of the Cold War, he warned. Given this threat, military security will probably command as important a place in U.S. strategy as will trade, prosperity, and the promotion of free governments and markets throughout the world.

The tradeoffs between these economic and military objectives have divided Americans about the appropriate U.S. response. Three schools of thought about America's role in world affairs have emerged:

Neo-isolationists want the U.S. to deal only with threats to America's physical security, political independence, and domestic liberty. They find no such threats at present, and therefore argue that the U.S. should let other powers, and regional balances of power, take care of all the world's woes. Realists such as Henry Kissinger want the U.S. to continue to be the holder of the world balance of power, the arbiter of the main regional power groups, and the watchdog against all potential imperialistic trouble-makers. Internationalists want a greater role for multilateral institutions and more emphasis on human needs and rights, the environment and democracy. (Hoffmann 1992, 59)

The Clinton administration attempted to reconcile these divergent outlooks. Trying to strike a balance, Clinton argued in 1993 that "putting our economic house in order cannot mean that we shut our windows to the world." As he elaborated in December 1995, "problems that start beyond our borders can quickly become problems within them." This reality commends, as Clinton declared in his inaugural address, that "America must continue to lead the world. . . . When our vital interests are challenged, or the will and conscience of the international community is defied, we will act—with peaceful diplomacy whenever possible, with force when necessary."

But how to prepare militarily to act? To help define a post-Cold War strategy against unknown threats, the Clinton administration initiated a *Bottom Up Review*. Released in September 1993, it stressed the need for military preparedness, in order to:

- Deter the use of nuclear, biological, or chemical weapons against the United States, its forces, and its allies.

- Halt or at least slow the proliferation of such weapons.

- Deter and, if necessary, defeat major aggression in regions important to the United States.

- Be capable of fighting and winning two major regional conflicts nearly simultaneously, . . . while minimizing American casualties.

- Prepare U.S. forces to participate effectively in multilateral peace enforcement and unilateral intervention operations that could include peacekeeping, humanitarian assistance, counterdrug, and counterterrorism activities.

- Foster democratic values in other countries.

- Maintain technological superiority. (Collins 1994, 5–6)

Viewed in light of this *realpolitik* definition of its evolving defense doctrines, the United States has committed itself to rely heavily on military might while attempting to build liberal ideals into the definition of its goals. Labeling his policy "democratic realism," President Clinton in February 1993 explained that U.S. security is linked to helping prevent or to resolving conflicts throughout the world and to "enlarging" the community of liberal democracies. Colin Powell, Chairman of the Joint Chiefs of Staff, elaborated: "The central idea in the strategy is the change from a focus on global war-fighting to a focus on regional contingencies" through what Pentagon officials call "mid-intensity conflict" (MIC). Thus, the United States will continue to prepare to be able to intervene militarily around the world and will seek to promote democracy throughout the world, because peace-loving democracies would help to make for international security.

These strategic priorities preserve deterrence as the cornerstone of a revised post-Cold War U.S. strategy. The enemy changes, new threats are identified, powerful conventional weapons will meet and deter them, and the definition of national security is broadened. The purpose of U.S. military might remains the same, however: deterring the aggression of any other great power, militarized powers in the Global South, or terrorist threats to global security (which CIA Director John M. Deutch predicted in 1996 would grow "tremendously in the next 10 to 15 years").

Inherent in this strategy is a U.S. preference to share the burden of protecting international security with others where possible. Instead of striving to police the world alone, U.S. policy seeks to safeguard peace through "assertive multilateralism," by "bargaining out a common policy with its allies" (Rosenfeld 1995). Support of UN peacekeeping operation (see Chapter 16) is consistent with this strategy, as was the U.S. decision in November 1995 to send peacekeeping forces into Bosnia alongside the sixty thousand-strong military contingents of its NATO allies. But the limits to this approach are suggested by the U.S. insistence on a reduction of its financial assessment to support the United Nations. Limits on U.S. resources are likely to constrain America's capacity to take a unilateral approach to heavy international responsibilities in the new millennium.

Russian Strategy in the Coming Century

For Russia, the primary threat is not external. It is the threat of civil violence from within as well as from the former Soviet Republics on its periphery. At the same time, fears of encirclement and/or isolation from abroad have intensified as Russia's power has plummeted. Although assertive in its rhetoric, Russia finds itself "too weak to reestablish a military or economic presence much beyond its borders" (Hiatt and Shapiro 1995).

Russian strategic planning must confront several tasks. First, it must ensure control over its nuclear arsenal. This requires managing the military establishment; preventing internal differences within the officer corps and between it and enlisted soldiers; institutionalizing civilian authority over the armed forces; and preserving command of the nuclear warheads based in Belarus, Kazakhstan, and Ukraine until they are successfully dismantled. Second, Russia must assure that no foreign power will attack it. Third, Russia must seek to contain the escalation of ethnonational civil war in the neighbors on its borders, with China, India, and the Islamic countries to the south posing potential threats.

Several components in Russia's existing security policy now define its likely direction:

- Russian leaders, like those in the United States, have pledged to keep their arsenal formidable so that Russia "still remains a leading military power in Europe and the world" (Arbatov 1995). As former Soviet Foreign Minister Alexander Bessmertnykh underscored in January 1992, "Russia will remain a great power. It may not be a superpower, but it will be a great military power and part of the global strategic balance."

- Russian force reconstruction seeks, as strategist Sergei Karaganov defined the goal in February 1992, to produce "a more efficient military, but one that is less threatening to the world." In 1995, Russia's defense budget was only $15 billion, less than 10 percent of America's (Zakaria 1995, A15). However, the defense expenditure accounted for 22 percent of Russia's national budget (George et al. 1995, 404).

- "Instead of preparing to fight the West or keep control of eastern Europe, the new military is focusing on protecting Russian interests in the former Soviet Union. Instead of huge tank armies, the military's new plans feature rapidly deployable airborne troops and peacekeeping units" (Gordon 1993a).

- Russian strategy places special emphasis on preventing the proliferation of weapons of mass destruction.

- Russian military planners paid close attention "to the lessons of the Gulf War, particularly because of their persistent past shortcomings in both the strategic and tactical fields. They are applying these lessons, [seeking to rely on] advanced non-nuclear weapons [to accomplish] all of the missions previously reserved for strategic nuclear forces" (Nitze 1991).

Russia's new defense doctrine thus rests on two primary principles. The first is the desire to avoid military conflict with other powers. "There are no potential enemies," President Boris Yeltsin explained, adding that "Russia will engage in warfare only in self- or collective defense." But the need for protection persists. Therefore, the second principle of Russia's new defense doctrine is its continuing reliance on military might to, as Yeltsin put it, "defend itself and its people." The doctrine justifies using interventionary troops in what the Russians call "the near abroad" (i.e, the former Soviet republics and Eastern Europe, as distinct from the "far abroad"—countries outside the old Soviet empire).[7]

Especially instructive is the revision of nuclear strategy that Russia's new doctrine embraces. It drops the pledge of no first use of nuclear weapons in the event of an attack. While it rules out using nuclear weapons against non-nuclear states, "for those states that have nuclear weapons, the doctrine says nothing," General Pavel S. Grachev declared. Presumably, "with Russia's conventional forces in disarray . . . the country evidently [thinks it needs] to remind potential aggressors, especially China, that it is prepared to use nuclear weapons in its defense" (Schmemann 1993).

These departures from Cold War strategic doctrines exhibit an acute awareness that Russia's geostrategic position has declined. This sense of vulnerability explains Russia's professed desire to work cooperatively with others to preserve international security while it contends with security threats arising from ethnonational uprisings in Russia and along its borders. Russia seeks to forge a multilateral approach to its many security problems. This is evidenced by its 1996 military involvement of at least fifteen hundred troops in NATO peacekeeping operations in Bosnia—symbolically under the command of an American general—while at the same time seeking to prevent NATO from expanding eastward to build a new wall around an isolated Russia.

China's Global Presence and Security Posture

In U.S. and Russian conceptions of security, China figures prominently.

> The rise of China, if it continues, may be the most important trend in the world for the next century. When historians one hundred years hence write about our time, they may well conclude that the most significant development was the emergence of a vigorous market economy—and army—in the

---

[7]The professed aim is to enforce stability and protect the rights of the 25 million Russians living in the "near abroad," but critics fear that this peacekeeping role could be an excuse for restoring Russian imperial rule.

most populous country of the world. This is particularly likely if many of the globe's leading historians and pundits a century from now do not have names like Smith but rather ones like Wu.

China is the fastest growing economy in the world, with what may be the fastest growing military budget. It has nuclear weapons, border disputes with most of its neighbors, and a rapidly improving army that may—within a decade or so—be able to resolve old quarrels in its own favor. The United States has possessed the world's largest economy for more than a century, but at present trajectories China may displace it in the first half of the next century and become the number one economy in the world. (Kristof 1993, 59)

China is an economic giant and potential military colossus bent on modernizing its maritime and air capabilities. Therefore, its rise and growing assertiveness have understandably heightened concerns of the other great powers—especially Russia, Japan, and the United States. China has sought to reduce their fears by claiming it seeks peaceful relations with all. In 1994, for example, China signed an agreement with Russia aimed at preventing inadvertent or dangerous military confrontations between their forces. Moreover, China asserts that it does not crave military prowess. However "the officially disclosed military budget [of $52.4 billion in 1994 (George et al. 1995, 436)] is a bit of a joke, for it does not even include sums spent on weapons procurement or on research and development. . . . As a very crude benchmark, . . . total military spending in international prices is much higher, perhaps as much as $90 billion" (Kristof 1993, 65).

The direction of China's policies seem geared to ensuring its rise to prominence in the Pacific Rim, as shown by its military threats in 1996 against Taiwan. To this end, China has continued to arm, to test its nuclear weapons, and to equip the globe's largest standing army (3 million soldiers). At the same time, China seems committed to developing the strategic and military might that the Chinese believe its status as an economic giant justifies. This attitude is evidenced by China's resistance to its ASEAN neighbors' effort in 1995 to establish a nuclear-free zone in Southeast Asia.

However, despite its assertiveness toward its neighbors China can be expected to concentrate on its internal development and trade relations, while seeking to contain domestic instability which threatens to tear apart national unity (especially if ethnic tensions and regional economic differences within China increase). Preserving domestic tranquility and growth is a priority.

As its power and wealth have grown, China has steadfastly refused to take instructions from its great-power rivals, insisting on its right to chart a foreign policy guided by its own perceptions of national interests. As yet, this does not mean that China is necessarily preparing for or planning foreign military engagement, as China argues that defense is the purpose of its military buildup and that its sabre-rattling toward Taiwan and Hong Kong are permissible actions toward provinces that are a part of China. Still, if the vigorous rearmament and force-modernization program inspired by reawakened nationalist pride continue, China's arsenal will position it to play a dominant military role in Asia and the entire world. Napoleon Bonaparte counseled in the early nineteenth century that the world should "let China sleep"; now, as he predicted, when China awakens, "the world will tremble."

China is an ascendant military power with the capacity to intimidate its Asian neighbors (especially Taiwan, but also India, Vietnam, and Russia). Pictured here is the Beijing honor guard—a symbol of China's defiant defense posture and assertive effort to regain the status and suzerainty or right to exercise influence over its neighbors that most Chinese think China deserves to receive. "The Chinese believe, with much reason, that for most of the past 3000 years, their nation was the largest, most prosperous, best governed and militarily most proficient society on the planet. The loss of that status more than three centuries ago and China's eclipse by European powers has always been regarded as a temporary aberration" (Mufson 1995).

Japan's Search for a Strategy

Japan is now an economic superpower—the third richest country on earth, just behind the United States and China (see Table 13.1). On a per-person basis, its citizens enjoyed in 1993 an average income of $31,450—far exceeding that of the average American ($24,138) (Reid and Blustein 1995, 21). Yet, Japan's "dramatic postwar ascent . . . has not been accompanied by a comparable rise in its international political and strategic weight" (Brown 1993). Since its defeat in World War II, Japan has adhered to the guidelines of the **Yoshida Doctrine,** in which Prime Minister Shigeru Yoshida argued that Japanese security policy should be to avoid international disputes, keep a low profile on divisive global issues, and concentrate on economic pursuits.

That preference continues to underlie Japan's strategy today. But the new international setting has called into question the wisdom of this traditional posture—especially in light of the transformed distribution of power, with U.S. power declining, Russia's having fallen, and China's on the rise. A larger role and presence are imminent.

Prime Minister Kiichi Miyazawa's policy departures in 1992 signaled the new direction that Japan's security policies are likely to take. He won passage of the Peacekeeping Operations Bill, which enabled Japan to deploy a self-defense force to participate in UN peacekeeping operations in Cambodia—the first use of Japanese armed forces abroad since World War II. Japan's push for inclusion as a permanent member of the UN Security Council and its rise to the top of the world's foreign aid donors also suggest a rise in Japanese international activism.

Japan seeks to discard its isolation and become an involved player in world affairs. Its rising defense expenditures and efforts to cement cordial relations with its Asian neighbors also speak to this redirection. Japan in 1996 still adhered to its policy of spending no more than 1 percent of its gross national product on defense, and remained committed to its postwar constitution which forbid remilitarization (George et al. 1995). But its Self-Defense Force is impressive, with 237,000 soldiers in uniform and the Pacific's largest navy. Although Japan does not have advanced offensive weapons such as long-range bombers and aircraft carriers, Japan has seventeen of the most sophisticated submarines. "Most analysts say that although Japan's air force and navy are numerically inferior to China's, they are more potent and will remain so for at least the next ten or twenty years" (Richardson 1995b). This power worries Japan's neighbors, who remember well its violent past. Postwar Japanese pacifism could, with this military clout, give way to resurgent militarism aimed at its simmering territorial disputes with both Russia and China. Regardless of the future use of this military power, Japan faces a wide range of security concerns, which would intensify if the troubled situation in Northeast Asia (especially North Korea) worsens or the United States reduces its presence in Asia. These fears are likely to prompt continuing Japanese participation in the rapid Asian arms race (Mufson 1995).

Even more problematically, with its neighbors arming to the teeth, Japan has begun to have second thoughts about nuclear weapons. It balked at the Clinton administration's attempt to press for a Japanese commitment to support the "indefinite and unconditional extension of the nuclear nonproliferation treaty when it expires in 1995" (Harrison 1993). This symbolic reversal of Japanese doctrine signaled the possibility of a radical departure in Japan's posture toward its future military role in the world. Indeed, as neorealists argue, it is extremely unlikely that Japan will refuse to develop military capabilities commensurate with its economic power and political ambitions.

Germany's Strategic Vision

Now united, Germany is likely to show signs of a new assertiveness once the immense costs of reunification and rebuilding the former German Democratic Republic are digested. Given its size, economic strength, and geographic location, the challenge for Europeans will be to find a way to absorb Germany within a broad European power-sharing arrangement. According to some analysts, however, Germany is too powerful to disappear into a wider European framework. It already accounts for almost one-third of the European Union's gross national product. In addition, its share of the EU budget is "three times the contribution of Great Britain and twice the amount of Great Britain and France combined." Moreover, most European states have linked the value of their currencies to the mark, therein giving Germany enormous leverage over interest rates and economic growth. This extraordinary economic clout assures Germany's continued dominance within any emergent amalgamated European political entity, whether it is built around the federalist idea of a supranational government or some other, more modest pan-European institutional structure. In either case, there is no set of states in the European Union capable of balancing the power of a united Germany. "Too big for Europe, too small for the world" describes Germany's place in continental affairs.

If Germany's economic strength and diplomatic independence continue to grow, one consequence will be greater competition with the United States and other trade rivals. Yet this is not likely to result in a renewed push to flex German military muscle—even with "a standing army that is becoming the strongest in Europe" (Fitchett 1995). Despite the parliamentary amendment to Germany's constitution which permitted German troops to take part in international peacekeeping operations (e.g., the participation of four thousand Germans in the 1996 NATO-led Bosnian peacekeeping operations), an independent German military presence on the world stage is unlikely. Renewed militarism is even less so. Germany's armed forces are still deeply entrenched in and constrained by the joint command in NATO, the Western European Union, and its mutual Franco-German force structure. Because Germany remains a fervent advocate of the nuclear nonproliferation regime and shows no inclination to build its own nuclear-weapons capability, economic rivalry is unlikely to culminate in military activity in the foreseeable future.

Germany likely will continue its effort to push for collective security with the military divisions it has created to assist multinational peacemaking units, both within Europe and globally. The drive to become a permanent member of the UN Security Council speaks to Germany's emphasis on multilateral approaches to international security; its armed force of 398,000 soldiers addresses its abiding desire to be prepared for defense. Similarly, Germany's continuing preference to rely on the United States and NATO for a nuclear guarantee reveals a preference for cooperative partnership in international security, even as fears that the United States may not always respond has made Germany prepare to shoulder Europe's post-2000 military burden (Fitchett 1995). German leaders "have preferred to treat the cynical pleasures of *realpolitik* with suspicion and to believe that foreign policy could and should be grounded in defense of virtuous principles such as democracy, self-determination, free trade, and human rights" (*The Economist*, 333 [Sept. 20, 1993]). A strong German aversion to militarism persists, and is likely to shape Germany's security policies well into the next century. In this regard, German defense strategy differs from the posture the other great powers have assumed.

• • •

THE SEARCH FOR SECURITY IN AN INSECURE WORLD

Preparation for war continues to command support from defense planners as an approach to peace. Rationalized by realism, the quest is understandable in a world where states alone remain responsible for their own self-defense. As President Eisenhower once noted, "until war is eliminated from international relations, unpreparedness for it is well nigh as criminal as war itself."

The fears produced by visions of national vulnerability also explain why many defense planners base their plans on worst-case analyses of others' capabilities and intentions. The urge to arm is further stimulated by defense planners' influence in the policy-making process of most countries and the tendency of political leaders to adopt the vocabulary and concepts of their military advisers.

Redefining "Security" in the New World Order

Two authorities, Michael Klare and Daniel Thomas, call for new, broadened ways of thinking about national and international security and how they might be achieved.

> The concept of "security" must include protection against all major threats to human survival and well-being, not just military threats. Until now, "security"—usually addressed as "national security"—has meant the maintenance of strong military defenses against enemy invasion and attack. This approach may have served us well in the past, when such attack was seen as the only real threat to national survival; today, however, when airborne poisons released by nuclear and chemical accidents can produce widespread death and sickness (as occurred with the Bhopal and Chernobyl disasters), and when global epidemiological and environmental hazards such as AIDS and the "greenhouse effect" can jeopardize the well-being of the entire planet, this perspective appears increasingly obsolete. As individual economies become ever more enmeshed in the world economy, moreover, every society becomes more vulnerable to a global economic crisis. And, as modern telecommunications bring us all closer together, we are made acutely aware of the pain and suffering of those living under oppression, tyranny, and injustice.
>
> Given the fact that our individual security and well-being will depend to an ever-increasing extent on the world's success in mastering complex political, economic, environmental, and epidemiological problems, we must redefine "security" to embrace all of those efforts taken to enhance the long-term health and welfare of the human family. Defense against military aggression will obviously remain a vital component of security, but it must be joined by defenses against severe environmental degradation, worldwide economic crisis, and massive human suffering. Only by approaching the security dilemma from this multifaceted perspective can we develop the strategies and instruments that will be needed to promote global health and stability.
>
> Given the multiplicity of pressing world hazards, the concept of "national security" must be integrated with that of "world security." Until now, most people have tended to rely on the nation-state to provide protection against external threats, and have viewed their own nation's security as being adversely affected by the acquisition of power and wealth of other nations. Thus, in the interests of "national security," nation-states have often engaged in a competitive struggle to enhance their own economic and military strength at the expense of other nations' capabilities. This us-versus-them, zero-sum competition for security is naturally biased toward unilateral solutions to critical problems, frequently entailing military and/or economic coercion. In today's interdependent world, however, the quest for security is rapidly becoming a *positive-sum* process, whereby national well-being is achieved jointly by all countries—or not at all. (Klare and Thomas 1991, 3)

Approaches to the study of national security now frequently advocate putting these nonmilitary dimensions of the subject into the picture (for example, Shultz, Godson, and Quester 1997). At issue is whether this new way of organizing perceptions of national security is an idea whose time has come.

Asking whether military preparedness endangers, rather than ensures, national security raises an uncomfortable question which challenges the prevailing approach to national security throughout much of the world's history. Yet many experts believe that questioning is justified (e.g., Porter 1995; UNDP 1994). To their way of thinking, now that fears of great-power war have receded, the economic and ecological dimensions of national security have assumed relatively greater prominence, and in the twenty-first century "security" should be defined more broadly so as to include both military and nonmilitary threats to human survival (see Focus 13.3).

Because a wide spectrum of problems has risen on political agendas, the concerns of today's foreign policymakers arguably *are* different and more diverse than they were just a short time ago. Though the danger of nuclear weapons and inter- and intra-state warfare continues, it would be foolish to neglect the dangers posed by such emergent threats as trade-bloc competition, neomercantilism, trade protectionism, the continuing impoverishment of the least developed countries, acid rain, deforestation, global warming, soaring population growth, the AIDS epidemic, international narcotic trafficking, the depletion of the earth's finite resources, and destruction of its protective ozone layer. These nonmilitary threats must command attention, as human survival may depend on mastering them.

However, the critical questions in an age of vulnerability to annihilation persist: How can states escape the prospect of destruction? How can they meet these emergent nonmilitary threats when the threat of warfare in a nationalistic age remains as pervasive as ever?

The security situation of the twenty-first century is unlikely to provide much room for maneuver. The world has yet to accept *common security* and *nonoffensive defense*, strategies that would eliminate offensive capabilities (Møller 1992). As we will see in the next chapter, many states still build weapons of attack for deterrence, even though conventional deterrence has failed frequently in the past (Huth 1988; Mearsheimer 1983). Moreover, contemporary deterrence theory remains based on the almost illogical premise that successful defense requires the continuing vulnerability of all states. Nonetheless, most believe that the threat system must be preserved to counter the threat.

Thus, security may depend as much on the control of force as on its pursuit. In the next chapter, we will examine the ways in which national leaders put armaments and arsenals to use for purposes of coercive diplomacy. We will then evaluate the effectiveness of the bargaining strategies of coercive diplomacy on which states rely to defend themselves and to exercise influence over others.

● ● ●

KEY TERMS

national security
power potential
soft power
hard power
military-industrial complex
firebreak

Nth country problem
horizontal nuclear proliferation
vertical nuclear proliferation
relative burden of military spending
defense conversion
Yoshida Doctrine

CHAPTER 14

Coercive Diplomacy: The Use of Power for Defense, Deterrence, and Bargaining

All diplomacy is a continuation of war by other means.

—CHOU EN-LAI, *premier,*
   The People's Republic of China, 1954

We have grasped the mystery of the atom and rejected the Sermon on the Mount.

—OMAR N. BRADLEY,
   U.S. General, Armistice Day, 1945

As we documented in Chapter 12, one of the most disquieting long-term global trends is the exponential increase in the destructiveness of warfare and its human toll. The average time it took for one million people to die in war from the rise of Rome to the beginning of the twentieth century was fifty years, whereas the average time it has taken that many people to die in war throughout the twentieth century was one year. (WorldWatch 7 [March/April 1994], 39). Observing that "the rise in war deaths has far outstripped the rise in population," another study (Sivard 1991, 20) concludes that "wars now are shockingly more destructive and deadly. So far, in the ninety years of this century, there have been over four times as many war deaths as in the four hundred years preceding."

Preventing this kind of human devastation is a primary security problem of all states—powerful and weak. As we noted in Chapter 13, the traditional (realist) approach of most state defense planners to the danger of foreign aggression has been to build weapons systems and expand their country's military capabilities. However, arms in and of themselves will not assure peace, no matter how awesome the arsenal. To understand the predicaments that arming for war can create, we begin this chapter with a discussion of the security dilemma which states face. Then, having described the dangers that weapons and preparations for war pose, we will examine the strategies states construct to prevent others from using arsenals against them, as well as how they use their own weapons to exercise influence over other global actors. The subject, in short, is **coercive diplomacy**—how states use military power for deterrence, defense, and bargaining.

• • •

THE SECURITY DILEMMA

What breeds the competition that propels states to seek security by preparing for war? The eighteenth-century French political philosopher Jean-Jacques Rousseau argued that "the state . . . always feels itself weak if there is another that is stronger. Its security and preservation demand that it make itself more powerful than its neighbors. It can increase, nourish, and exercise its power only at their expense. . . . Because the grandeur of the state is purely relative, it is forced to compare itself to that of the others. . . . It becomes small or great, weak or strong, according to whether its neighbor expands or contracts, becomes stronger or declines."

Concern for relative power derives from states' desire for many of the same things: self-preservation, national identity, freedom from the control of others, status, and wealth. They seek these in anarchical conditions which provide little protection from the hostile designs of others. Believing that their own strength will make them secure, many states attempt to build as much military might as their resources allow, often competing with one another in military capabilities.

Although states ostensibly arm for defensive purposes, their military might is often perceived as threatening. Alarmed, their neighbors are provoked to arm in response. Thus, as Rousseau observed, security is a relative phenomenon. Such fear and its reciprocated behaviors create a predicament known as the *security dilemma* (Herz 1951), defined as the consequences that result as "each party's power increments are matched by the others, and all wind up with no more security than when the vicious cycle began, along with the costs incurred in having acquired and having to maintain their power" (Snyder 1984).

Some scholars also describe the dynamics of this arms competition as the **spiral model** (Jervis 1976). The imagery is apt, as it captures the tendency of defense-enhancing efforts to result in escalating arms races which diminish the security of all. Sir Edward Grey, British foreign secretary before the First World War, described this process well:

> The increase in armaments, that is intended in each nation to produce consciousness of strength and a sense of security, does not produce these effects. On the contrary, it produces a consciousness of the strength of other nations and a sense of fear. Fear begets suspicion and distrust and evil imaginings of all sorts, till each government feels it would be criminal and a betrayal of its own country not to take every precaution, while every government regards every precaution of every other government as evidence of hostile intent. (Grey 1925, 92)

Despite the security dilemma that affects all states, leaders still refuse to accept vulnerability. Searching for strength, they often proceed from the assumptions that: (1) security is a function of power; (2) power is a function of military capability; and (3) military might is a measure of national greatness. Each of these suppositions is, of course, consistent with *realpolitik*.

Reformers in the liberal tradition question the logic by which states engage in competitive behavior that creates and sustains the security dilemma. To them, "the central theme of international relations is not evil but tragedy. States often share a common interest, but the structure of the situation prevents them from bringing about the mutually desired situation" (Jervis 1976).

To escape this predicament, neoliberal reformers call for changes in customary approaches to the problem of national security. Seeing weapons as "indefensible" (Lifton and Falk 1982), they argue that unarmed or defenseless countries enjoy a flexibility in their foreign policies that their armed neighbors do not. They are freed from the responsibilities that military power imposes and do not have to incur the costs of acquiring it. Although these countries might have to live in the constant shadow of others' missiles, they can take comfort in knowing that they are not the targets of the missiles. Appropriate in this context is John F. Kennedy's sober warning in 1963 that, in the event of another total war, regardless of how it might begin, those most heavily armed would automatically become its primary targets and victims.

Not surprisingly, realists are less than convinced by the liberal-idealists' views. Even if leaders and defense planners recognize the threats that arming for security provokes in others, they argue that international anarchy makes these threats inevitable. Since, by definition, there is no escaping a dilemma, the security dilemma explains why states sharing a common interest in security nonetheless engage in individual actions that prevent them from realizing it.

To understand how most states confront their lack of national security, we next describe the kinds of strategies they have created. We will first examine the ways the two leading military powers, the United States and the former Soviet Union, sought during the Cold War to prevent a nuclear attack through their evolving strategic doctrines regarding **nuclear deterrence.** We will then look at the strategies that other less-militarily-powerful states have forged for purposes of **conventional deterrence** (i.e., prevention of an attack with conventional, non-nuclear weapons).[1]

• • •

NUCLEAR DETERRENCE AND DEFENSE

The dropping of the atomic bomb on Japan in August 1945 is the most important event distinguishing pre- from post-World War II international politics. In the blinding flash of a single weapon and the shadow of its mushroom cloud, the international arena was transformed from a balance-of-power to a balance-of-terror system.

In the decades that followed, policymakers in the nuclear states had to grapple with two central policy questions: (1) Whether they should use nuclear weapons, and (2) how to prevent others from using them. The search for answers has been critical, as the failure to deter a nuclear attack would create unimaginable destruction.

The impact of a "limited" war with today's nuclear arms would not be limited. Studies of the immediate and delayed effects of nuclear war project a post-nuclear environment too terrifying to contemplate (see Focus 14.1, p. 420). Life as we know it could cease. The danger, moreover, persists: "If all planned cuts in nuclear weapons are implemented, in the year 2003 the world will still have as many as twenty thousand nuclear weapons containing the explosive power of more than two hundred thousand Hiroshima bombs" (*Defense Monitor* 22, no. 1 [1993]: 1) or "more than nine hundred times the six million tons of TNT expended in World War II" (Sivard 1993, 11).

The threat of nuclear war was, and remains, particularly pertinent to the United States and Russia, former Cold War adversaries and today's two most heavily armed nuclear powers. Their decisions during the Cold War—the formative period that still casts its shadow on defense planning—shaped strategic thinking and doctrines both at home and elsewhere. In order to grasp the influ-

---

[1]Although nuclear and conventional deterrence are often seen as the same, most theories of the former are guided by historical investigation of cases in the latter category (Harknett 1994). It is important to keep in mind the difference

> between strategic *nuclear deterrence* (the level at which the majority of the theorizing has occurred, at which the use of intercontinental thermonuclear weapons has been threatened, and at which deterrence is usually thought to have held) and *conventional* deterrence (the level that has received considerably less attention, at which, by definition, threats to use unconventional weapons of mass destruction are excluded, and at which deterrence, arguably, has been prone to fail). . . . The range of likely cost-benefit calculations shifts dramatically when the deterrent calculus of strategic nuclear warfare is compared with regional conventional conflict. (Haffa 1992, 9)

In the first true test of the awful destructive capabilities of atomic weapons on cities, American forces dropped an atomic bomb on Hiroshima on August 6, 1945, in an attempt to bring World War II to a speedy close. In an instant, what later became known as "the nuclear age" was ushered in and the Japanese city lay in flaming ruins.

ence of past strategies on present ones, we need to first understand how the United States and the former Soviet Union used their most powerful weapons to deter each other. This will also allow us to understand the larger subject of which it is a part: how states conceive of deterrence as a method of coercive diplomacy to intimidate a potential enemy from using its weapons aggressively.

Superpower Deterrence and Defense Policies

Although weapons of mass destruction have existed since World War II, the superpowers' postures toward them have evolved as technologies, defense needs, capabilities, and global conditions have changed. For analytical convenience, we can treat those postures in terms of three periods. The first began at the end of World War II and lasted until the Cuban missile crisis. U.S. nuclear superiority was the dominant characteristic of this period. The second began in 1962 and lasted until the breakup of the Soviet Union in 1991. Growing Soviet military capability was the dominant characteristic of this period (which meant that the United States no longer stood alone in its ability to annihilate another country without fear of its own destruction). The third phase began in 1992, as the former Cold War antagonists and other rising great powers began to restructure their forces and revise their strategic doctrines. To better understand this new thinking, we will first examine the superpowers' strategic policies during the precedent-setting Cold War period.

Compellence, 1945–1962. Countries that enjoy military superiority over their principal adversaries often think of weapons as instruments for coercive bargaining—that is, as tools for the political purpose of changing others' behavior. The United States, the world's first and, for many years, unchallenged nuclear power, was no exception. **Compellence** (Schelling 1966) described U.S. strategic doctrine when it enjoyed a clear-cut superiority in the nuclear balance of

The Aftermath of a Nuclear Attack
The View of Atmospheric Scientists

What would happen if even a fraction of today's nuclear weapons were used? Summarizing scientific studies, world-renowned researchers Carl Sagan and Richard P. Turco conclude that the planet would become uninhabitable:

> As bad as the prompt and local effects of nuclear war would be—the delayed and global consequences might be much worse. . . . Forest fires ignited in such a war could generate enough smoke to obscure the sun and perturb the atmosphere over large areas. . . . That smoke from the burning of modern cities would provide a still more serious threat. . . . Provided cities were targeted, even a "small" nuclear war could have disastrous climatic consequences; a global war, . . . might lower average planetary temperatures by 15 to 20°C, darken the skies sufficiently to compromise green plant photosynthesis, produce a witches' brew of chemical and radioac-

tive poisons, and significantly deplete the protective ozone layer. These effects, which had been almost wholly overlooked by the world's military establishments, [are] described as "nuclear winter." (Sagan and Turco 1993, 369)

It has been estimated that "the missiles on board a single [U.S.] SLBM submarine may be enough to initiate nuclear winter" (Quester 1992)—enough to end human existence. To defense planners, this prospect makes utilizing nuclear weapons for military purposes unthinkable. To the extent that nuclear states appreciate this fact, it reduces the purpose of nuclear weapons to one objective—deterring external aggression. However, if enemies do not believe that a sane nuclear arms state would actually use its weapons in retaliation against aggression, do those weapons become useless as a deterrent?

power. Compellence makes nuclear weapons instruments of political influence, used not for fighting but to get others to do what they might not otherwise do. Thus it refers to the use of nuclear weapons as instruments for "forceful persuasion" (George 1992), even if some question the ethics of a policy instrument that uses terror to pursue worthy ends such as peace (see Focus 14.2, p. 422).

The United States sought to gain bargaining leverage after World War II by conveying the impression that it would actually use nuclear weapons. Its posture was especially evident during the Eisenhower administration in the 1950s. To win political victories, Secretary of State John Foster Dulles practiced **brinkmanship,** deliberately threatening U.S. adversaries with nuclear destruction so that, at the brink of war, they would concede to U.S. demands.

Others went even further, seeing the new weapons of mass destruction as instruments for bargaining that could be safely used. For instance, to prevent the Soviets from also developing a hydrogen bomb, U.S. General Curtis Lemay, who would soon head the U.S. Strategic Air Command, in 1949 recommended "a nuclear Sunday punch," a preemptive strike against the Soviets. Lemay wanted to send "an armada of planes, carrying the entire Los Alamos stockpile (numbering more than one hundred atom bombs) to destroy seventy Soviet cities" (Stengal 1995). With hydrogen weapons such damage would have been even more annihilating.

Brinkmanship was part of the overall U.S. strategic doctrine adopted by the Eisenhower administration. Known as **massive retaliation,** it advocated the use of nuclear weapons to contain communism and Soviet expansionism. Massive retaliation was a **countervalue targeting strategy** because it aimed U.S. weapons at objects that the Soviets presumably valued most—their industrial

When informed of the possibility of designing a hydrogen bomb, U.S. President Truman asked, "What the hell are we waiting for?" Politicians hailed the nuclear weapon as a defensive force. However, scientists such as Robert Oppenheimer—who headed the Manhattan Project, which produced the atomic bomb—maintained that the hydrogen bomb was inherently immoral because it was a weapon of genocide which, unlike the atomic bomb, was so destructive that its use could not be restricted to military purposes. Pictured here is a test of the hydrogen bomb in 1952, which created a three-mile fireball a thousand times more powerful than the bombs that fell on Hiroshima and Nagasaki.

and population centers. The alternative is a **counterforce targeting strategy,** which targets an enemy's military forces and weapons, thus sparing the general civilian population from immediate destruction.

Massive retaliation and brinkmanship heightened Soviet fears. By 1949 the Soviet Union had broken the U.S. atomic monopoly. Thereafter, faced with U.S. belligerence, it pursued a twofold response. Following Nikita Khrushchev's rise to power in the mid-1950s, the Soviets ceased speaking of the usefulness of military power and instead pursued **peaceful coexistence** as an alternative nonmilitary strategy for continuing, by nonviolent economic and political means, the communist struggle with capitalism. Nonetheless, fearing that a nuclear exchange would destroy the Soviet Union but permit U.S. survival, Soviet leaders also expanded their nuclear arsenals. In 1957 the Soviet Union successfully launched the world's first space satellite (*Sputnik*), demonstrating its potential ability to deliver nuclear weapons far beyond the Eurasian landmass. The superpowers' strategic competition thus took a new turn, as the United States for the first time began to face a credible military threat to its own geophysical security.

Mutual Deterrence, 1962–1983. As U.S. strategic superiority eroded, American policymakers began to question the usefulness of weapons of mass destruction for political bargaining. They recoiled in horror at the thought of the destruction that could result if compellence should provoke a nuclear exchange. The nearly suicidal Cuban missile crisis of 1962 dealt coercive diplomacy a serious blow. Thereafter, the objective of nuclear weapons shifted to preventing an attack. That is, strategic policy shifted from compellence to deterrence.

Does War Necessitate Tragic, Even Evil, Action?
The Controversial Ethics of Peacemaking

During the American Civil War, Union General William Tecumseh Sherman declared that "war is hell." To end the war, he sought to literally make it hell by pursuing a ruthless "march to the sea" in the American South, ravaging civilians and their communities to force surrender. To put an end to killing, Sherman believed that killing must be devastating. Only by making war terrifying, he felt, could surrender be hastened.

Many since have adopted Sherman's scorched-earth strategy to demoralize a hostile civilian population in order to subdue its army leaders. They believe that terrorism—the wanton destruction of property and people—is the most effective method of bringing an adversary to its knees.

But where does this practice to stop war end and barbarism begin? To some there are no moral limits: The ends justify the terrible means. The savagery, of course, can never be justified to its victims. Critics argue that such strategies, which overlook the traditional right of innocent noncombatants to protection from genocide, violate international law and are crimes against humanity. Classic Christian theologians also condemn the philosophy that condones evil methods, maintaining that a right intention does not automatically justify any means to achieve it.

The debate over the ethics of cruel destruction as a strategy arose again in the closing days of World War II. At the insistence of the head of the Allied Bomber Command, Sir Arthur "Bomber" Harris authorized the devastation of the demilitarized German city of Dresden, "roasting at least twenty-five thousand of its inhabitants in the notorious firestorm," under the conviction that "bombing German cities simply for the sake of increasing terror" and "gunning down people fleeing the burning city the morning after the British raid" would speed a German surrender. However, after the deliberate attack on "city-center churches and palaces packed with refugees," German resistance to the Allies intensified. The strategy of terrorism by flattening cities backfired: "A year of saturation bombing had not brought an uprising" against Hitler and the Nazi regime (Jenkins 1995).

Yet many defense planners feel strongly that mass destruction can produce surrender. For example, the necessity of shocking the Japanese into submission was foremost among President Harry S Truman's reasons for dropping the atomic bomb on Japan. (When informed about the plan to use the bomb to force Japan's leaders into an immediate unconditional surrender, General Dwight D. Eisenhower expressed "grave misgivings" about using this "horrible and destructive" weapon, which he saw as "completely unnecessary" [Ambrose 1995].)

Experts in both defense and moral ethics remain divided as to the just means of limiting the evil of war. International law, too, reflects this division of opinion regarding the criteria that should govern the determination of the boundaries of legal conduct to coerce an aggressor's surrender. The issue of the ethical means of ending a war has not been resolved.

Both superpowers also pursued **extended deterrence**, protecting not only their homelands but also targets outside their adversary's defense perimeter and alliance network, to prevent an attack on their own allies. Extended deterrence was especially critical to the United States, as its allies were far from its own shores and geographically close to the Soviet Union. The United States repeatedly declared that it would defend its allies. However, the credibility of its guarantee to the NATO countries in particular was often questioned. Former U.S. Secretary of State Henry Kissinger punctuated this doubt when he noted in 1979 that the U.S. promise to defend Europe with nuclear weapons involved "strategic assurances that we cannot possibly mean or if we do mean, we should not execute because if we should execute, we risk the destruction of civilization." The dubious credibility of the U.S. deterrent led some critics to advocate "decoupling" Europe from the U.S. strategic security umbrella and encouraging individual NATO countries to develop their own nuclear capability.

Ironically, the shift from compellence to deterrence stimulated rather than inhibited the U.S.–Soviet arms race. A deterrent strategy depends on the ability to deliver without question unacceptable damage on an opponent. It requires a **second-strike capability** which enables a country to withstand an adversary's first strike and still retain the ability to retaliate with a devastating counterattack. To ensure a second-strike capability and an adversary's awareness of it, deterrence rationalized an unrestrained search for sophisticated retaliatory capabilities. Any system that could be built was built, because, as President Kennedy explained in 1961, "only when arms are sufficient beyond doubt can we be certain without doubt that they will never be employed."

To characterize the strategic balance that emerged during the 1960s and early 1970s, policymakers coined the phrase **mutual assured destruction (MAD).** It described the superpowers' essential military stalemate as mutual deterrence (based on the principle of assured destruction) rested on the military potential for and psychological expectation of widespread death and destruction by both combatants in a nuclear exchange. Peace—or at least stability—was viewed as the product of mutual vulnerability, which was seen in turn as a precondition for successful deterrence. Each superpower sought to preserve the other's second-strike capability, trusting that neither would then dare to attack the other at the price of its own subsequent destruction.

As the United States and the Soviet Union competed with each other, the differences in their strategic capabilities narrowed. By the early 1970s a *parity*, or equality, developed in the two superpowers' capabilities which reinforced the strategic assumptions of MAD. Thereafter both armed, not to gain superiority but to preserve a rough equivalence in their strategic arsenals.

The balance in the superpowers' arsenals laid the basis for negotiations on limiting strategic arms during the 1970s détente phase of the U.S.–Soviet rivalry. Two Strategic Arms Limitation Talks (SALT) agreements, both attempting to guarantee each superpower's second-strike capacity, were concluded during the 1970s. Although the pursuit of this shared goal posed difficulties, a precarious peace resulted. However, despite the superpowers' sometimes tacit, sometimes formal acceptance of the principles on which assured destruction rested, differences in their interpretation and practical application inevitably led to disagreements. As the strategic arms race continued into the 1980s, the concepts governing the competition began to revert from the principle of deterrence to the previous principle of compellence, which contemplated the actual use of nuclear weapons. Indeed, with superpower confrontation replacing cooperation, in the early 1980s a new debate raged regarding the role and purpose of nuclear weapons. Should nuclear weapons still be used exclusively for purposes of defense and deterrence? Or, assuming that a first-strike capability could be achieved, should they be used for offensive purposes?

Neither adversary had reason to trust the other. Each assumed that, unless deterred, its opponent would be tempted to use its arsenal for attack. As a result, bad faith and worst-case analyses governed the reformulation of strategic doctrines.

U.S. statements about the practicability of preemptive strikes and the "winnability" of a nuclear exchange alarmed the world. The atmosphere chilled as U.S. leaders spoke boldly of *damage limitation*. This concept was predicated on the belief that one way to avoid the destructive effects of nuclear weapons was to be the first to use them, destroying a portion of the adversary's weapons before they could be used in a retaliatory strike.

As U.S.–Soviet relations worsened, debate in the United States concerning the best way to protect national security with strategic weapons broke into polar positions. Although MAD continued to dominate the thinking of some, others advocated **nuclear utilization theory (NUTs),** an approach whereby nuclear weapons would not simply play a deterrent role, but could also be used in war. Such a posture was necessary, some U.S. policy advisers argued, because the Soviet Union was preparing to fight—and win—a nuclear war (Pipes 1977; c.f. Holloway 1983: Kennan 1984b). Furthermore, advocates of NUTs argued that any use of nuclear weapons would not necessarily escalate to an unmanageable, all-out nuclear exchange. Instead, they reasoned that it was possible to fight a protracted "limited" nuclear war. By making nuclear weapons more usable, they argued, the United States could make nuclear threats more credible.

Proponents of MAD, on the other hand, held that deterrence remained the only sane purpose for nuclear weapons, and contended that any use of nuclear weapons—however limited initially—would surely escalate to an unrestrained exchange. "It is inconceivable to me," former U.S. Secretary of Defense Robert McNamara reflected, "that limited nuclear wars would remain limited—any decision to use nuclear weapons would imply a high probability of the same cataclysmic consequences as a total nuclear exchange." According to this view, the technical requirements necessary to wage a protracted limited nuclear war would surely exceed the human capacity to control it.

In addition, advocates of MAD felt that because the threatened use of even tactical nuclear weapons would lower the nuclear threshold, a nuclear strategy based on their utility in war made war more likely, thereby diminishing the weapons' deterrent capability. From this viewpoint, both superpowers were destined to live in a MAD world—even if, ironically, this meant remaining in the "mutual hostage relationship" in which their earlier weapons decisions had imprisoned them (Keeny and Panofsky 1981).

As the 1980s nuclear debate raged, U.S. and Soviet leaders both professed their commitment to avoid nuclear war, viewing it as "unthinkable." This meant expanding the capabilities of both defensive and offensive systems. Thus each superpower continued developing and deploying the kinds of weapons that NUTs required—so-called discriminating low-yield nuclear weapons, made possible by new technologies in guidance and precision. This weaponry prepared the contestants for warfare short of a massive, all-out nuclear attack and sought to provide them with effective deterrents against a conventional war.

This search for new weapons and new ideas to govern their use did little to calm fears, however. Instead, a vigorous peace movement swept Europe and North America, as mass publics on both sides of the Atlantic voiced their desire for an alternative to the threat posed by nuclear weapons. Accordingly, the purposes that NUTs strategists assigned nuclear arsenals fell into disfavor.

From Offense to Defense, 1983–1993. A new challenge to strategic thinking was launched in 1983, when U.S. President Reagan proposed building a space-based defensive shield against ballistic missiles. The **Strategic Defense Initiative (SDI),** as it was known officially, called for the development of a "Star Wars" **ballistic missile defense (BMD)** system using advanced space-based technologies to destroy from outer space offensive weapons launched in fear, anger, or by accident. The goal, as President Reagan defined it, was to make nuclear weapons "impotent and obsolete." Thus SDI sought to shift U.S. nuclear strategy away from reliance on offensive missiles to deter attack—that is, away from dependence on mutual assured destruction, which President Reagan deemed "morally unacceptable."

From the start, scientists questioned the feasibility of SDI's technological fix to the security dilemma posed by strategic weapons. There was simply no assurance that a reliable system was possible (Slater and Goldfischer 1988). Critics warned that the projected costs in excess of $140 billion for SDI were prohibitive and that SDI was dangerous, capable of inducing an unwarranted sense of safety, when in fact it "almost surely would not work in the event of an all-out attack." Critics also warned that SDI would stimulate development of a new generation of offensive weapons designed to overwhelm the defensive ones, and that, in addition, it violated the Anti-ballistic Missile (ABM) treaty of 1972 (Moore 1995).

Despite this uncertainty and questionable legality, the United States continued to support SDI even after the end of the Cold War and the demise of the Soviet Union. In the view of the Bush administration, SDI still had a mission in providing "protection from limited ballistic missile assaults, whatever their source," rather than relying on "some abstract theory of deterrence." The Pentagon disagreed, pointing out the inability of a space-based system to protect against the many other ways that an enemy can deliver tactical weapons, including "short-range missiles or intermediate-range ballistic missiles that fly slightly depressed trajectories" (Fetter 1991), or even in a hand-carried suitcase.

This argument notwithstanding, in late 1995 the Star Wars era continued. As Lawrence J. Korb, formerly a defense secretary in the Reagan administration, complained:

> Republicans seem determined to spend additional funds [on] revival of the Strategic Defense Initiative, now known as National Missile Defense. Support for strategic defense has become a litmus test of loyalty to the Reagan legacy. . . . Thus, almost in lockstep, Republicans in Congress are voting to double the amount currently spent [on missile defense, seeking] to throw some $40 billion or $50 billion at a multisite continental defense system, although there are serious doubts about necessity and cost-effectiveness and although such a system would violate the 1972 Antiballistic Missile Treaty, negotiated by a Republican president. (Korb 1995b, 29–30)

Thus, the search for security through defense continues.

The Shifting Strategic Situation

The Cold War, the third global conflict of the twentieth century, concluded without bloodshed. Some attributed this remarkable achievement to the effectiveness of the superpowers' deterrence strategies—the intimidating power of their weapons, which made aggression suicidal—and to the rationality of leaders, inspired by their awareness that survival was preferable to victory. To others, the superpowers averted apocalypse *despite* their awesome arsenals and deterrence doctrines rather than because of them.[2]

Regardless of its causes, the halt to the Cold War rivalry has ended the former adversaries' need to prepare for war against each other. In a radical change, they now perceive their interests served by *reducing* their armaments,

---

[2]Critics of strategic nuclear deterrence (e.g., Johansen 1991; Vasquez 1991) point out that "Although it can be argued that nuclear deterrence worked during the Cold War, we do not know that for sure. (The USSR may never have wished to invade Europe nor to attack the United States with nuclear weapons.) It is very difficult to prove deterrent successes because that would require showing why an event did *not* occur" (Haffa 1992). "As for the assertion that nuclear weapons prevent wars," Joseph Rotblat (1996) asks, "how many more wars are needed to refute this argument?"

not increasing them, thus signaling the start of a new age. Not long after Mikhail Gorbachev assumed power in the Soviet Union in 1985, and shortly after Reagan's Star Wars speech, the superpowers negotiated a series of dramatic new arms control agreements (see Chapter 15). Reduced fears of an attack in Europe stripped away the rationale for tactical nuclear weapons. As a result, the precedent-setting Intermediate-Range Nuclear Forces (INF) treaty, followed by the Conventional Armed Forces in Europe (CFE) agreement, and then the *Strategic Arms Reduction Treaty (START)* hastened the emergence of a strategic setting less menaced by the spectre of global warfare.

The consequences of the reductions since 1990 in the U.S. and Russian strategic nuclear arsenals by 1995 are depicted in Figure 14.1. As shown, their post-START disarmament initiatives will cut their diminished arsenals even further by the year 2003. If this "deep cut" occurs, the strategic situation in the twenty-first century will look radically different, requiring the rethinking of traditional assumptions underlying strategic doctrines.

Few expect a war between the great powers in the foreseeable future, although most expect wars to continue in the Global South. The great powers have sought to restructure their armed forces in order to cope with the kinds of threats and weapons with which adversaries will fight such wars. This invites additional reductions of nuclear (strategic) arsenals, U.S. help to the former Soviet republics to destroy their nuclear weapons, and collective great-power efforts to keep nuclear weapons out of the hands of aggressors. It also calls for increasing the capacity to wage conventional wars in emergent trouble spots.

FIGURE 14.1

The Changing Strategic Balance, 1990, 1995, and 2003

The United States and Russia have agreed to reduce substantially the size of the nuclear arsenals. They no longer perceive huge inventories of these weapons of mass destruction as necessary for survival. It remains to be seen whether nuclear deterrence will continue, and whether technological advances will allow other kinds of weapons systems to keep the peace.

SOURCE: Adapted from the Stockholm International Peace Research Institute (1995), 642.

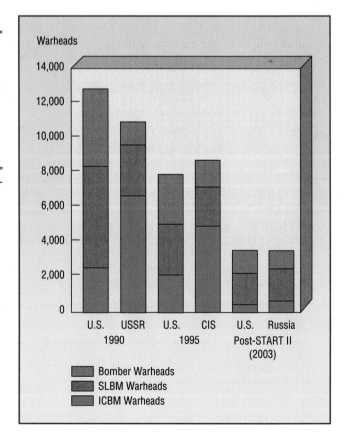

Military preparations have not ceased, but instead have been redirected toward short-term wars fought with increasingly sophisticated conventional weapons. The emerging strategies of the great powers now reflect their search for a new security architecture to contain regional conflicts and guard against the rising power of their rivals.

• • •

CONVENTIONAL FORCES AND THE FUTURE OF DETERRENCE

As we have seen, a number of states presently outside the circle of dominant military powers are striving to enter it. With ambitiously expanding armament programs, their quest for nuclear weapons and the potential collapse of the nonproliferation regime would radically transform the globe's security climate. Joseph Kruzel, a former U.S. defense expert who tragically lost his life in August 1995 while seeking to negotiate a peaceful solution to the warfare in the Balkans, wrote:

> Nuclear proliferation in other parts of the world must be reckoned as a high probability. The [U.S.] Central Intelligence Agency estimated that in the early 1990s over fifty countries were working on nuclear, chemical, or ballistic missile capabilities. By the end of the century, some number of these states will certainly develop operational weapons of mass destruction and the means to deliver them. Because nuclear forces could serve as an effective deterrent against retaliation by an outside state, more and more states may be inclined to see nuclear weapons as a serious military option. A nuclear-capable Azerbaijan, for example, could invade Armenia and present the world with a *fait accompli* backed by the threat of using its own nuclear weapons against any third party that would presume to meddle.
>
> Given these political and technological trends, it appears likely that before the end of the twentieth century, a nuclear weapon will be detonated in anger somewhere on the planet. That event, the first use of nuclear weapons since August 1945, could lead to a rapid expansion of the nuclear club as countries with the technical know-how hasten to cross the threshold. Several states are also likely to develop or acquire intermediate-range delivery capabilities. Even if there is no actual use of nuclear weapons, the proliferation of fingers on nuclear triggers will almost inevitably change . . . attitudes toward defense against such weapons. (Kruzel 1993, 4)

By most assessments, regional and ethnic violence is likely to be a stimulus to military action in the next century. The Global South is populated by many hypernationalist countries of growing military strength with an interest in controlling events in the areas where their primary security interests lie. This danger has increased the importance of conventional deterrence:

> The most important challenge for deterrence strategists may not be in dealing with the increased frequency of military conflict, but rather in dealing with an increased *variety* of sources of conflict. . . . The most important consequence of the end of the Cold War may be the recognition that the sources of conflict now emanate from less-clear and more-complex axes. Nationalist aspirations, religious cleavages, and resurgent authoritarian coups may all cut against established international political alignments. Now, and in the foreseeable future, the sources of war will have to be viewed across a variety of dimensions. (Harknett 1994, 102–3)

Many states are today highly agitated, and perceive military force below the threshold of nuclear weapons as an available means to achieve their political aims. Indeed, to the many states harboring historical grievances, armed coercion is a highly attractive option, as threats to initiate less-destructive and less-costly military actions with conventional weapons are far more likely to be believed than are threats to initiate a nuclear war. Conventional war gives the threatener an advantage in bargaining. The threat is more credible because the risks are lower. Moreover, the odds of a retaliation by the target are less effectual, because "from a challenging country's perspective, conventional deterrent costs are likely to be viewed as highly suspect. Regardless of formidability, conventional deterrence will be perceived as threatening costs that can be contested" (Harknett 1994).

Deterrence is a risky game, and the strategies on which most states today depend does not give them the reliable protection they seek. Conventional force can be used for coercive purposes, and frequently is. The activity is not just practiced by weak states in the Global South; the use of conventional armed conflict short of war is a component of the great powers' bargaining strategies, as the **low-intensity conflict (LIC)** programs of the United States and others illustrate (see Focus 14.3).

The methods through which coercive diplomacy is pursued are varied, for both the goals of deterrence and compellence. To bring about changes in other actors' behavior, states may rely on words and deeds, usually attempting to combine both. They talk tough by making threats and often act tough by using their military capabilities.

It is difficult to generalize about the effectiveness of these strategies, which have worked in some situations but not others. Bargaining strategies depend on the issue, the reputation of the actor pursuing a strategy of coercive diplomacy, and the commitment of the actor to its goals. The use of alternative strategies also varies with the purpose of the action. *Preventive diplomacy*— managing emergent threats by swiftly demonstrating intentions and capabilities—is one thing. The actual use of force in retaliation for acts deemed immoral, illegal, or threatening to national interests is another. Although those who initiate war often see it as a necessary instrument to pursue national interests, it takes the game to a high level. When push comes to shove, the escalation can either work or backfire. Consequently, the relationship between promises of rewards and military threats of destruction is complex. It works at times when the goal is war prevention as opposed to *peacekeeping* (stabilizing a threatening dispute) and *peace-enforcement* (deterring terminated military hostilities from reigniting), and it fails at other times.

Military Intervention

Making military threats to coerce others can come in many forms at many levels. However, the most frequent practice is **military intervention**—the sending of troops onto others' territory in order to influence developments and policies there. Coercive diplomacy sometimes moves from talking to bombing, and more frequently involves the sending of arms, armies, and aircraft to foreign territory. International military interventions provide evidence of the application of limited force in conflict situations, which occurred 690 times around the world between 1945 and 1991 (see Figure 14.2). These frequent interventions— averaging 14.7 each year—included seventy-one Cold War actions by the

Low-Intensity Conflicts
Coercive Bargaining Short of War?

The destructiveness of modern weapons reduces the incentives for great and small powers alike to resort to armed force and increases the propensity to substitute the threat of force for its actual use. Still, violence has not ended, as states increasingly rely on low-intensity conflict (LIC) to get their way with others.

> [Low-intensity conflict] is warfare that falls below the threshold of full-scale military combat between modern armies (of the sort that occurred in the Korean War and at the onset of the Iran-Iraq War). Under U.S. doctrine, low-intensity conflict encompasses four particular types of operations: (1) *counterinsurgency* [or] combat against revolutionary guerrillas...; (2) *pro-insurgency* [or] support for insurgents...; (3) *peacetime contingency operations* [or] police-type actions...; and (4) *military "shows of force"* [which threaten] military maneuvers. (Klare 1988, 12)

Low-intensity conflict is today a symbol of warfare between the haves and have-nots, referring primarily to methods for combating terrorism, insurgency, and guerrilla activities in the Global South to protect the interests of the powerful. This type of warfare below the level of overt military operations by a state's regular army includes proxy wars, wars fought with mercenaries, psychological operations to terrorize the populace, and death squads. "What is crucial to recognize," notes political scientist Michael T. Klare (1988), "is that low-intensity conflict is a form of warfare in which *your* side suffers very little death or destruction, while the other side suffers as much damage as possible without producing undue hardship for your own society."

Low-intensity conflict characterizes the great powers' methods of combating "revolutionary strife, random violence, nuclear terrorism, and drug-running. . . . The strategy for conducting low-intensity war strikes at the heart of the development process, and that is its purpose. Physical attacks on roads, dams, and so forth, with the inevitable collateral damage to houses, schools, and hospitals, is accompanied by a psychological attack on those aspects of a revolutionary government's program that establish its legitimacy" (Barnet 1990). Despite its name, low-intensity conflict does not necessarily mean low levels of death or destruction. "The low-intensity conflict in Guatemala, for instance, . . . claimed well over one hundred thousand lives" (Klare 1988, 12).

In an interdependent world that is fraught with ethnic and religious rivalries, armed conflicts short of full-scale war are likely to erupt often, and great powers are likely to influence the outcomes of the conflicts with low-intensity bargaining tactics.

United States and twenty-five by the Soviet Union between 1945 and 1988 (Pearson, Baumann, and Pickering 1991, Table 1). Excluded from this count are an unknown number of their covert or secret interventions. If these were tallied as well, the use of intervention would be even larger.

Conceptualizing foreign overt military intervention as a form of international behavior "most closely associated with international war," Herbert Tillema (1989) includes as instances "battles involving regular foreign military forces, at least on one side" that seldom result in more than one thousand fatalities. Interventions thus include "military operations undertaken openly by a state's regular military forces within a specific foreign land in such a manner as to risk immediate combat." They exclude "less-blatant forms of international interference such as covert operations; military alerts in place; shows of force; deployments of units not immediately prepared for combat; [and] incursions across international borders that do not involve occupation of territory . . ." (Tillema 1994). Conceived in this manner, intervention comprises a distinct category of militarized international behavior, which: (1) involves the use of force, (2) is intrinsically hostile in motive, (3) often results in the loss of soldiers' lives, and (4) is usually described by the target as an act of war.

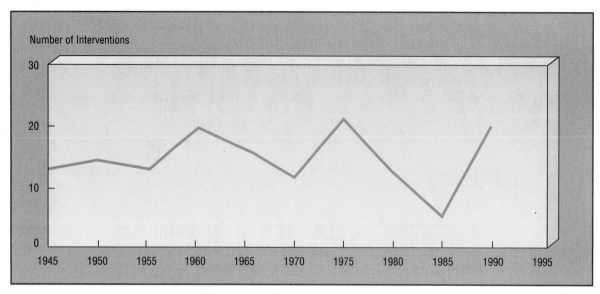

FIGURE 14.2

Military Interventions Initiated since 1945

States frequently have sent their troops into the sovereign territory of other states in order to influence the target, despite the fact that military intervention traditionally has been prohibited by international law. This figure shows fluctuations in the frequency of intervention since 1945.

Note: Trend line based on a five-year moving average.
SOURCE: Summary of data collected by Tillema (1989, 1996).

As a result of frequent overt and covert activity, military interventions often have heightened international tension and often have led to war.[3] The critical question about the use of military interventions for coercive diplomacy is their probable consequences. When states intervene, does this usually help peacekeeping, peacemaking, and preventive diplomacy by containing serious disputes from escalating to full-scale war? Or does their activity more often result in war than in pacification? To consider this question, we will look briefly at a sure consequence: Every war has begun by an act of military intervention; as a result military interventions produce crises.

International Crises

A **crisis** is a situation that (1) "threatens the high-priority goals of the decision-making unit, (2) restricts the amount of time available for response before the decision is transformed, and (3) surprises the members of the decision-making unit by its occurrence" (Hermann 1972). Most of the conspicuous military crises of our age, such as the Cuban missile crisis, the Berlin blockade, the Sino-Soviet border clash, and the Formosa Straits crisis, exhibited these attributes.[4] Each

---

[3]Thirty-five cases of third-party intervention occurred between 1816 and 1988, resulting in the internationalization of twenty-five civil wars (see Small and Singer 1982; Singer 1991, 60–75).
[4]Some situations popularly termed crises in fact do not meet these definitional criteria, however. The global energy crisis during the 1970s is an example. Surely the situation involved "threat," but neither "surprise" nor "time pressure" describes it appropriately. Our discussion here is confined to purely military crises.

430

contained the elements of surprise, threat, and time pressure, as well as the risk of war. In addition, each involved a sense of urgency provoked by others' unanticipated military maneuvers. None of these crises crossed the line into overt large-scale military hostilities, however; all were managed successfully.[5]

Crises result when one actor attempts to force an adversary to alter its behavior. "The strategy of coercive diplomacy . . . employs threats or limited force to persuade an opponent to call off or undo an encroachment—for example, to halt an invasion or give up territory that has been occupied" (Craig and George 1990). "Military power does not have to be used for it to be useful"; the threat of force may suffice by "coercing a country by demonstrating the quantity of force and highlighting the capability of, and intention to, use force" (Majeed 1991). "Coercive diplomacy offers the possibility of achieving one's objective economically, with little bloodshed, fewer political and psychological costs, and often with much less risk of escalation than does traditional military strategy" (Craig and George 1990).

The crises generated by coercive bargaining thus perform the function that war often traditionally played, namely, "to resolve without violence, or with only minimal violence, those conflicts that are too severe to be settled by ordinary diplomacy and that in earlier times would have been settled by war" (Snyder and Diesing 1977).

Figure 14.3 displays the distribution of 390 interstate crises between 1918 and 1988, revealing a continuous stream of changes "in the intensity of disruptive interactions between two or more states, with a heightened probability of military hostilities that destabilizes their relationships and challenges the structure of an international system" (Brecher 1993). Given this characteristic, it is understandable why the frequency of international crises is sometimes measured by the incidence of **militarized disputes**—"confrontations short of war characterized by the reciprocated threat, deployment, mobilization, or use of force" (Singer 1991; also Gochman and Maoz 1984).

Included in the category of militarized disputes is the practice of **gunboat diplomacy**—the high-profile sending of troops overseas to intimidate an enemy. Big-stick diplomacy—which relies on the threat of force to persuade and compel—is common, as many states believe that "actions speak louder than words" and that displaying one's military capabilities can convince the target to comply. The United States, for example, used shows of force 286 times between 1946 and 1984, an average of more than seven times a year (Blechman and Kaplan 1978, 547–53; Zelikow 1987, 34–36). Similarly, the former Soviet Union engaged in such behavior over 150 times between the mid-1940s and late 1970s (Kaplan 1981, 689–93). And in 1996 a bellicose China used this type of military intimidation when it conducted tests of its missiles by aiming them in a target area near a Taiwan port; in response and to send China a warning, the United States sent two Navy aircraft carriers to the Taiwan Straits.

---

[5]Many crises in the Global South were unsuccessfully managed, and escalated to war. Even with respect to crises between the great powers, the unbroken record of successful crisis management since 1945 should not necessarily instill confidence about the future. For crises to be managed successfully without escalating to war, policymakers, as rational actors, must be able to keep their quarrels within controllable bounds. Political scientist Ole R. Holsti questions the validity of this assumption: "There is scant evidence that along with more lethal weapons we have evolved leaders more capable of coping with stress." Crises can easily escalate to war because of the time pressures, inadequate information, fear and anxiety, and impulsive risk-taking that normally accompany decision-making procedures during threatening situations (see Holsti 1989).

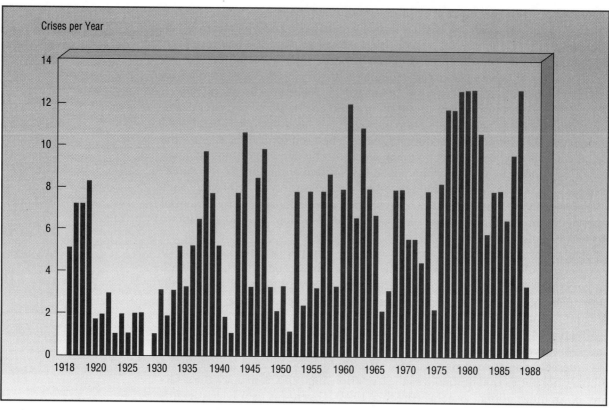

FIGURE 14.3

Seventy Years of International Crises

On 390 separate occasions, states confronted each other militarily between 1918 and 1988, in the hopes of forcing concessions. The frequency has varied over time, but its recurrence attests to states' compulsion to threaten each other with military force in the hope of getting their way.

SOURCE: Adapted from Brecher (1993), 69.

The evidence produced by behavioral research suggests a number of patterns. First, interstate crises have been ever present in the twentieth century; nearly four hundred such situations that threatened to escalate to war "occurred in all *regions* and in all of the seven *decades* since the end of World War I." Second, the frequency of crises varies annually, with many peaks and troughs. Third, many—in fact most—states either provoke or experience crises, as the 390 crises involved 826 individual states between 1918 and 1988. "Ninety-nine states triggered one or more crises, and no less than 123 states served as the target of crises." Fourth, some states are "more 'aggressive' in the crisis domain, that is, more prone to initiate crises." Finally, crises overall tend to be concentrated in the developing countries of the Global South; "Africa, Asia, and the Middle East accounted for two-thirds of the 390 international crises after World War I, compared to only 21 percent for Europe, the core of the dominant system" (Brecher 1993, 68–69, 171).

The use of military threat for bargaining purposes between states and the crises that result are important because crises are the circumstances that often trigger war. When crises are not successfully managed, violence results. Examples of violence that were preceded by crisis include World War I (1914), Kashmir (1948), Suez (1956), Tibet (1959), the Bay of Pigs (1961), Goa (1961), and Kuwait (1990). More than 30 percent of all crises escalate to violence, with a large proportion (95 percent) of the most intense crises involving the major powers (Brecher 1993, 333, 576). The lesson, in short, is that militarized disputes often lead to full-scale war rather than its deterrence, even if the latter was the threatener's original intention. Coercive diplomacy with conventional weapons is clearly a dangerous game.

If past experience is a model, then the threat of war for bargaining is likely to continue in the future, and we can predict that

> the post-Cold War subsystems will retain an abundance of conflicts within which international crises are likely to erupt. . . . The ethnic/nationalist virus has created a context for other crises in the future. . . . The conclusion is disquieting: Most anticipated international crises in the coming years are likely to erupt in violence, though its severity will vary from minor clashes to full-scale war. (Brecher 1993, 546, 548)

The Future of Conventional Military Coercion

The sobering conclusion that international crises are likely to increase in the future raises concerns about the use of coercive bargaining by military means as a method of dispute management. Is this kind of bargaining a solution, or part of the security-dilemma problem?

Policymakers today disagree about the appropriate place of coercive military bargaining in their strategic doctrines. Enthusiasts argue that the successful use of these strategies during the Cold War argues for applying the lessons of nuclear bargaining to situations requiring deterrence in the future. Skeptics disagree, maintaining that what may have worked in the realm of strategic deterrence is unlikely to work with respect to conventional deterrence, where in all probability most of the action will center. They feel that the kinds of armed conflicts and threats most in need of deterring will be most resistant to control through the strategies that help prevent nuclear attacks. Aggressors in the future—whether they are rough, outlaw states or criminal and terrorist organizations—very likely will employ advanced telecommunication networks to operate from dispersed locations, and this will make the threat of massive retaliatory strikes against specific geographic regions ineffective.

It will clearly be much more difficult to deter the kinds of aggression that will employ conventional weapons than to deter aggression using nuclear weapons. The key elements of deterrence require three ingredients: (1) *capabilities*, the possession of military resources that can make threats of military retaliation plausible; (2) *credibility*, the belief that the actor is willing to militarily defend its declared position; and (3) *communication*, the ability to send a potential aggressor the clear message that it is willing to carry out its threat. In today's world, it is very difficult to combine these ingredients to make conventional deterrence work. As Richard Harknett (1994) cautions, deterrence of conventional warfare only "will succeed if threatened costs can be communicated to the challenger, assessed by the challenger, and believed by the challenger." These requirements are difficult to satisfy in the world of diffuse conventional warfare raging throughout the world. "Unlike during the Cold War, interests deemed vital enough to fight for will be interests that probably will lead to actual fighting."

In September 1995, Operation Joint Endeavor sought to force the Bosnian Serbs to end their aggression in the Balkans. Shown here are British soldiers firing on Bosnian Serb artillery positions outside Sarajevo. This kind of coercive bargaining using conventional military force instead of ultimatums for deterrence and compellence is likely to be common in the future.

The prolonged difficulties that the United States and its NATO allies experienced trying to deter the Bosnian Serbs from pursuing their expansionist war in the Balkans provide a graphic example of the ineffectiveness of conventional deterrence. Talk and threat were not believed and did not work. In desperation, the frustrated NATO countries under the leadership of the Clinton administration responded to Serbian atrocities with force, initiating in September 1995 a series of air strikes, under the auspices of the United Nations and through NATO, to compel an end to Serbian defiance. Operation Joint Endeavor, the NATO assault on strategic targets of the Serbs, applied conventional force in order to relieve the cruel siege of Sarajevo and to persuade them through bombing to return to the bargaining table. As a U.S. State Department official explained, "Diplomacy was dead without the force" (Fedarko 1995). This episode could be an indication of how many future armed conflicts will be approached, through military coercion using conventional weapons.

However, bargaining by nonmilitary methods is also likely to be tried, and perhaps will be the method of choice, given the risks of military activities and the obstacles to their effective use. Among these alternative approaches to military methods, economic sanctions will figure prominently.

• • •

ECONOMIC SANCTIONS AS INSTRUMENTS OF COERCION

When the Arab members of OPEC placed an embargo on the shipment of oil to the United States and the Netherlands in 1973, their purpose was to alter these countries' policies toward the Arab-Israeli conflict. When the UN Security Council decided in August 1990 that the world organization should cease trade with Iraq, its purpose was to accomplish the immediate and unconditional withdrawal of Iraqi forces from Kuwait. Both are examples of the use of **economic sanctions**—"deliberate government actions to inflict economic deprivation on a target state or society, through the limitation or cessation of customary economic relations" (Leyton-Brown 1987).

Economic sanctions are an increasingly popular choice from the broad array of instruments of economic statecraft available to governments (see Baldwin 1985). An alternative to applying military force, sanctions are enacted to express outrage and to change the target's behavior. Since World War I, there have been 120 episodes of foreign policy sanctions observable, 104 of which were enacted since World War II (Hufbauer, Schott, and Elliott 1990).

Despite their frequent use, most efforts to apply economic sanctions have failed. This fact has led many policy analysts to question their cost-effectiveness (Knorr 1977). Why is failure so prevalent? And why, then, have economic sanctions "become the weapon of choice in diplomatic confrontation in the wake of the Cold War" (Hoagland 1993b)? We can address these questions by looking at several prominent sanctions cases.

Superpower Sanctions: Three U.S. Failures

Between 1945 and 1990, when more than sixty cases of sanctions were undertaken, "a rate averaging better than one new action per year, more than two-thirds were initiated and maintained by the United States" (Lopez and Cortright 1995, 5). Three conspicuous cases in which the United States applied economic sanctions illustrate their shortcomings: sanctions applied against Castro's Cuba beginning in 1960; against the Soviet Union following its intervention into Afghanistan in 1979; and against Poland and the Soviet Union between 1981 and 1982 after Poland's imposition of martial law in December 1981.

Cuba. The United States placed sanctions on the Castro regime shortly after it assumed power in 1960, beginning with a reduction in the amount of sugar permitted to enter the United States under its quota system. These sanctions later were extended to a full ban on all U.S. trade with Cuba, accompanied by pressure on other countries to follow suit. The U.S. goals were twofold: initially, to overthrow the Castro government; failing that, to contain the Castro revolution and Cuban interventionism in Central and South America and in Africa.

Through 1995 the United States remained unsuccessful in securing Castro's overthrow, and previously it had been only marginally successful in containing Cuba's promotion of revolution abroad. "The major accomplishment of the U.S. economic embargo . . . consisted of increasing the cost to Cuba of surviving and developing as a socialist country and of pursuing an international commitment" (Roca 1987). Several factors helped Cuba to withstand this pressure from the globe's foremost economic and military power for more than thirty-five years. Especially potent were the Soviet Union's prolonged subsidies of "as much as $2–3 billion annually" to Cuba (Elliott 1993, 35); U.S. inability to persuade its Western allies to curtail trade with and investment in Cuba; and Castro's charismatic leadership and popular support. Although the U.S. economic sanctions extracted a heavy burden on the target, they did not accomplish their political goals.

Not only did the United States fail to get its way, but it was snubbed by its key allies. In symbolic votes of defiance, in October 1994 they voted one-hundred-and-one to two in favor of a UN resolution condemning the U.S. embargo, asserting that the embargo infringed on their sovereignty, free trade, and navigation rights; in 1995, a similar resolution passed by a vote of one-hundred-and-seventeen to three. Without support and cooperation from others, the U.S. trade sanctions simply could not succeed. Latin America, once an obedient follower of the U.S. trade embargo against Cuba, now ignores the U.S. effort to isolate Cuba, "choosing to develop full economic and diplomatic relations with the Communist government. The United States is the only country in the Americas with a trade ban on Cuba and one of only five that do not have formal ties with it" (Brooke 1995), and Fidel Castro has survived the hostility of nine American presidents.

The Soviet Union and Afghanistan. After the Soviet Union's 1979 intervention in Afghanistan, the United States imposed a partial embargo on the sale of grain to the country and attempted to organize a boycott of the 1980 Moscow Summer Olympics. The sanctions also sought "to punish the Soviet Union while at the same time limiting the damage to the economic interests of important domestic groups" (Falkenheim 1987).

The grain embargo failed to stop the flow of agricultural produce to the Soviet Union, largely because other countries (principally Argentina) increased their exports to make up the shortfall in U.S. exports. Although the U.S. sanctions produced suffering for Soviet citizens, it did not force their leaders to reverse their foreign policy. There were two reasons for this. First, the Soviet economy was largely self-sufficient, which lessened the impact of trade compression on its economy. Second, because Soviet leaders were determined to resist external pressures, the U.S. sanctions increased their resolve (Falkenheim 1987).

The Soviet Union and Poland. Similar lessons apply to Poland. After the Polish government imposed martial law in 1981 to forestall continued labor unrest, the Reagan administration restricted U.S. government credits for Polish purchase of food and other commodities, banned high-technology exports to Poland, and suspended Poland's most-favored-nation trade status. To stiffen the sanctions' impact, the United States also targeted Poland's patron and primary trade partner, the Soviet Union. U.S. actions restricted the flow of Western goods and technology needed for the trans-Siberian gas pipeline to bring Soviet energy into Western European markets in the hope also of increasing the economic strains under which both Poland and the Soviet system would have to operate (Marantz 1987).

The strategy failed to achieve these objectives, however, as the Reagan administration was forced to seek a face-saving compromise with its European allies permitting continued construction of the pipeline. The absence of consensus among the NATO allies contributed to the sanctions' failure. Other factors included the Soviet Union's ability and willingness to support its client, Poland. While the sanctions may have had some liberalizing influence on Poland, in the end the Soviet Union did not budge.

These three examples suggest that a superpower's successful use of economic sanctions faces substantial obstacles. The initiator often pays a high price (lost markets to exporters, increased costs to consumers) and receives a low payoff. In general, the more ambitious the goal, the less successful have been the efforts. "Sanctions are seldom effective in impairing the military potential of an important power, or in bringing about major changes in the policies of the target country" (Hufbauer, Schott, and Elliott 1990), and "have been absolutely ineffective in bringing about a change of government leadership within a target country" (Cortright and Lopez 1995).

Yet, as inventories of the use of economic sanctions indicate, states are increasingly prone to rely on them. In fact as a high-profile, low-risk tactic of coercive diplomacy, regarded as an attractive alternative to military intervention sanctions may be the tool of choice for states seeking to make other states comply. The world may be entering "the sanctions era" (Cortright and Lopez 1995) in part because the growing volume of international commerce has made "trade-based diplomacy an increasingly prominent tool of statecraft." The advantages rationalizing the use of boycotts are suggested by cases that met with relatively greater success.

Relatively Successful Sanctions: Two Controversial Examples

The usefulness of economic sanctions as instruments of foreign policy enjoys at best a checkered history. The case of South Africa illustrates the ability of sanctions to produce policy dividends. The case of Iraq illustrates the constraints on their use.

South Africa and Apartheid. For many years, the white leadership in South Africa practiced a punitive policy of racial separation known as **apartheid**. To force an end to this morally unjustifiable practice, in 1963 the United Nations, at the behest of Third World countries, imposed a voluntary arms and oil embargo against South Africa, which became mandatory in 1977.

Because U.S. corporations held major investments in South Africa and the United States was a primary importer of the country's rich mineral reserves, the U.S. attitude toward South Africa was of special concern to opponents of apartheid. A frequent argument in the United States concerning an appropriate response to apartheid focused on who would be the victims of internationally applied sanctions: South African blacks, already suffering under a policy of systematic racial discrimination, or the white minority regime who perpetuated apartheid? In 1981, the Reagan administration adopted toward South Africa a policy it termed *constructive engagement*, whose broad purpose was a soft diplomatic approach to the Pretoria regime. In 1985, however, in an unusual domestic political development, the U.S. Congress legislated, over a presidential veto, harsh mandatory sanctions against South Africa, hoping to change Reagan's weak policies that Congress found objectionable.

In 1989, F. W. de Klerk, a reformer, came to power in South Africa and released Nelson Mandela, leader of the African National Congress (ANC), who had been a political prisoner for twenty-seven years. De Klerk also lifted the ban on the ANC and other anti-apartheid groups, opening the door to negotiations on political reforms between the South African government and the ANC. Thus the process of dismantling apartheid finally began and culminated in a historic agreement in 1993, which restored democracy for all South Africa's citizens and made possible black majority rule. As trade restrictions were lifted, investors rushed into the vacuum and South Africa rejoined the community of nations. It no longer was an international pariah.

Were the sanctions responsible for setting South Africa on a path toward reform and majority rule? While the sanctions were being applied, analysts' evaluations differed, but now that apartheid has been officially lifted, most believe that the sanctions eventually paid off. Apartheid has been ended through the concerted cooperation and economic sanctions of many states in combination with the human rights activities of international institutions and nongovernmental organizations throughout the world (Davis 1995).

Iraq and the Crisis over Kuwait. Restraints on the long-term use of economic sanctions for political purposes are illustrated by the 1990 conflict in the Middle East. The first response of the international community to Iraq's invasion of Kuwait was to impose sanctions, including the prohibition of all exports to and imports from Iraq except for humanitarian shipments of medicine and some food. The embargo sought to cause economic hardship in order to compel the Iraqi government to withdraw from Kuwait and to foment enough discontent within Iraq to cause the ouster of the Hussein regime. In the months that followed, a vigorous debate took place at the United Nations and in various national capitals over the utility of the sanctions. Would they force Saddam Hussein from Kuwait? How long should they be applied before resorting to military power?

Iraq was especially vulnerable to a total embargo because it imported nearly three-fourths of its food and depended almost completely on oil exports for its foreign exchange. In addition, its oil could pass through only two routes, by ship through the Persian Gulf—which was easily blockaded—or overland through pipelines across other countries. In December 1990, the director of the U.S. Central Intelligence Agency reported that "more than 90 percent of imports and 97 percent of exports have been shut off." He also reported, however, that "we see no indication that Saddam is concerned at this point that domestic discontent is growing to levels that may threaten his regime or that problems resulting from the sanctions are causing him to rethink his policy on Kuwait. . . . There is no assurance or guarantee that economic hardships will compel Saddam to change his policies or lead to internal unrest that would threaten his regime." Little more than a month later, military power replaced economic sanctions to force Iraq from Kuwait.

During the debate over force and sanctions, two former chairmen of the U.S. Joint Chiefs of Staff urged that sanctions be given a year or more to work. "If in fact the sanctions will work in twelve to eighteen months instead of six months, the trade-off of avoiding war with its attendant sacrifices and uncertainties would, in my view, be worth it," Admiral William J. Crowe testified before the U.S. Congress. Historically, however, sanctions applied over long periods have seldom produced success, with the exceptions of the South African and Rhodesian situations:

> Sanctions imposed slowly or incrementally may simply strengthen the target government at home as it marshals the forces of nationalism. Moreover, such measures are likely to be undercut over time either by the sender's own firms or by foreign competitors. Sanctions are generally regarded as a short-term policy, with the anticipation that normal relations will be reestablished after the resolution of the crisis. Thus, even though popular opinion in the sender country may welcome the introduction of sanctions, the longer an episode drags on, the public support for sanctions dissipates. (Hufbauer, Schott, and Elliott 1990, 100-101)

Largely for these reasons, and because of growing concern for how long the coalition against Iraq would hold together, economic sanctions were abandoned in favor of the use of overwhelming military force. Whether this was wise or foolish remains debatable. The use of military force in the Gulf War did (at an estimated cost of $57 billion) drive Iraq from Kuwait, and arguably helped prevent Saddam Hussein from carrying out his crash program to build a nuclear weapon, develop an arsenal of toxins for biological warfare, and contain his aggression (Hoaglund 1996). Nonetheless, the effort to topple the Iraqi dictator failed, and his ruthless moves to retain power in Iraq succeeded. "Iraq was bombed into the Stone Age" with eighty-nine thousand tons of explosives killing more than forty-six thousand children (Al-Samarrai 1995), but the sanctions targeted the wrong party in operations "analogous to blowing up an aircraft with all passengers aboard to kill the hijacker." This case thus demonstrates the limits of economic statecraft in crisis circumstances where many others believe there is a need for an immediate remedy.

Why Sanction?

The long and generally unsuccessful history of international economic sanctions has led many critics to conclude that sanctions are a weak tool in statecraft (Elliott 1993; Førland 1993). They argue that:

- A typical response to economic coercion in the sanctioned society is a heightened sense of nationalism, a *laager* mentality (circle the wagons to face oncoming enemies), which stimulates resistance in the target state.

- Sanctions sometimes hurt the disempowered people they seek to help—the country's average citizens. "Sanctions substitute for military action against rulers who have total disregard for the economic hardships faced by their subjects. The logic of the policy [unrealistically] seems to be to make unarmed citizens desperate enough to rise up and throw off brutal regimes that . . . other powers are not willing to use the world's best armies to topple" (Hoagland 1993b).

- Governments often act covertly to support the sanctioned state even as they publicly profess their support of sanctions.

- "Midsized countries can thwart sanctions, when local dictators are able to quell dissent with a powerful military and divert pain to citizens with no influence" (Hufbauer 1994).

- The credibility of the state(s) imposing sanctions is often low, given their transparent costs and the fact that "economic sanctions always involve something lost for both sides" (Howell 1995).[6]

- Widespread and sustained cooperation from the international community and international organizations seldom materializes, and unilateral sanctions seldom succeed in a globalized market with many competitive suppliers of embargoed goods.

The suitability of sanctions as instruments of persuasion is therefore customarily questioned whenever they are proposed or imposed. Recent examples include the OAS embargo of Haiti to force the military junta to step down (and subsequent military intervention to fulfill the objective); the embargo of North Korea to dissuade it from building a nuclear bomb; the economic sanctions

---

[6]Sanctions impose costs on the initiators as well as the targets. Poland, for example, reportedly lost $1 billion in arms sales and construction contracts with Iraq, its main economic partner in the Middle East, as a result of the Iraqi sanctions (Burgess and Auerbach 1990, 21). Earlier, in the case of the U.S. grain embargo against the Soviet Union, American farmers who depended on exports were especially hard hit by Washington's policies.

against the rebel army UNITA in Angola; and U.S.. threats of trade sanctions against China in 1996 in response to its shipment of cruise missiles to Iran and its missile tests near Taiwan. Critics invariably argue that

> Policymakers often have inflated expectations of what sanctions can and cannot accomplish. . . . At most there is a weak correlation between economic deprivation and political willingness to change. The *economic* impact of sanctions may be pronounced, both on the sender and the target country, but other factors in the situational context almost always overshadow the impact of sanctions in determining the *political* outcome. (Hufbauer, Schott, and Elliott 1990, 94)

If they usually encounter opposition and seldom prove effective, why have "sanctions become the main tool of coercive diplomacy" (Hoagland 1996) and now "the most favored tool of diplomats" (Pound and El-Tahri 1994)? The most convincing answer resides in the primary purposes underlying policymakers' preferences. Political scientist James M. Lindsay (1986) argues that sanctioning countries' goals fall into five basic categories:

- *Compliance* ("to force the target to alter its behavior to conform with the initiator's preferences"), as in the case of the 1982 U.S. embargo of Libya designed to force it to end its support of terrorism.

- *Subversion* ("to remove the target's leaders . . . or overthrow the regime"), as in the case of the 1993–1994 U.S. trade embargo on Haiti.

- *Deterrence* ("to dissuade the target from repeating the disputed action in the future"), as in the case of the Soviet grain embargo by the United States.

- *International symbolism* ("to send messages to other members of the world community"), as in the case of the British sanctions against Rhodesia after its unilateral declaration of independence in 1965.

- *Domestic symbolism* ("to increase its domestic support or thwart international criticism of its foreign policies by acting decisively"), as in the case of U.S. sanctions against Iran following its seizure of U.S. diplomats in 1979.

Past cases of sanctions suggest that *symbolism* is a primary motivation behind the impulse to use this tool. Sanctions enable a leader to show leadership without bearing the costs and dangers that other policy options, particularly military force, entail. "When military options are not feasible or desirable and the initiator wants to respond forcefully to the target's behavior, sanctions provide a means of 'doing something'" (Lindsay 1986).

It is disputable whether the "symbolic utility" of economic sanctions in the face of their otherwise "apparent disutility" is a cause for applause or concern. "Critics may deride the symbolic uses of trade sanctions as empty gestures, but symbols are important in politics. This is especially so when inaction can signal weakness and silence can mark complicity" (Lindsay 1986). Thus, economic sanctions often are used even though they sometimes fail to achieve the most visible aims for which they are implemented:

> Although sanctions were successful . . . in 34 percent of 115 cases [between 1914 and 1989] (the overall U.S. success rate was 32 percent), success has

become increasingly elusive in recent years. . . . The success rate among [forty-six] cases begun after 1973 was a little less than 26 percent. Even more striking is the decline in the effectiveness of sanctions imposed in pursuit of modest goals—mostly sought by the United States—which plummeted from 75 percent to 21 percent. (Elliott 1993, 34)

Nonetheless, sanctions serve important functions. They provide a policy alternative to the use of force to publicize and condemn unacceptable behavior and intolerable situations, thereby expressing outrage and making it appear that something is being done. In addition, under particular conditions, "sanctions work—if imposed by a major power against a much weaker, unstable, and economically dependent foe with no friends among the rival powers" (Elliott 1993). "Sanctions can be used to deter aggression, defend human rights, and discourage nuclear proliferation" (Lopez and Cortright 1993). For these reasons we can expect sanctions to remain popular.

In this chapter we have reviewed three basic approaches to controlling the behavior of others, especially their use of force. Whether for deterrence or compellence, we can predict that states will continue to rely on strategic weapons to prevent their own mass destruction. They will also continue to use conventional weapons and economic sanctions to defend themselves while bargaining to protect national interests. All three of these methods of coercive diplomacy place an emphasis on capabilities—both military and economic. In the next chapter we will evaluate how these approaches to the management of armed conflict are often complemented by other strategies advocated by realism.

● ● ●

KEY TERMS

coercive diplomacy

spiral model

nuclear deterrence

conventional deterrence

compellence

brinkmanship

massive retaliation

countervalue targeting strategy

counterforce targeting strategy

peaceful coexistence

extended deterrence

second-strike capability

mutual assured destruction (MAD)

nuclear utilization theory (NUTs)

Strategic Defense Initiative (SDI)

ballistic missile defense (BMD)

low-intensity conflict (LIC)

military intervention

crisis

militarized disputes

gunboat diplomacy

economic sanctions

apartheid

CHAPTER 15

The Realist Road to Security: Alliances, the Balance of Power, and Arms Control

OUTLINE

Aggression unopposed becomes a contagious disease.

—JIMMY CARTER,
  U.S. president, 1980

Bringing nuclear weaponry and the weapons of mass destruction under control and, I hope, achieving their total abolition [is one of the globe's greatest] interests.

—GEORGE F. KENNAN,
  U.S. diplomat and scholar, 1996

Many countries have the military power to inflict enormous destruction on their enemies. As a consequence, national security remains, as ever, elusive. Due to the escalating dangers of modern weapons, most states' sense of security has decreased, rather than increased, during this century.

To defend themselves, states have several options. They may (1) arm themselves; (2) form (or sever) alliances with other countries; or (3) negotiate arms control and disarmament agreements to reduce the threat of adversaries' weapons. Although most leaders usually pursue various combinations of these strategies, each nonetheless represents a distinct military approach to security.

In focusing on world conflict and its management, our discussion has followed a logical progression. We began in Chapter 12 by exploring why the frequency of war makes preparations for it so necessary. In Chapter 13 we examined the search for national security through the acquisition of military capabilities. We then assessed in Chapter 14 states' use of coercive diplomacy both to realize their national goals abroad and to deter their rivals from aggression. We now concentrate on the other two military approaches to national security—the use of alliances and arms control to maintain a favorable balance of power and thereby enhance security. These approaches draw their inspiration primarily from the assumptions that realist theory makes about the most prudent paths to peace (see Table 15.1).

• • •

ALLIANCES

Alliances are formal agreements among states to coordinate their behavior in the event of military emergencies. Alliances thus are coalitions that heed realism's first rule of statecraft: to increase military capabilities. States can do this either by acquiring arms or by acquiring allies. Although alliances are more economical because they permit the defense burden to be shared, throughout history states have vigorously pursued both methods. While alliances appear to be the preferred method for increasing military capabilities, this solution has significant disadvantages. Making alliance choices has seldom been easy, as it requires weighing the military strength, goals, and reliability of allies and adversaries alike.

Alliances in World Politics: Rival Realist Images

Three contending schools of thought exist within realism (see Kegley and Raymond 1994). The first holds that alliances are basically advantageous. The second maintains that the costs of alliances usually outweigh the benefits, and

TABLE 15.1 The Realist Road to Security: Assumptions and Policy Recommendations

The Realist Picture of the International Environment	
Primary global condition:	Anarchy
Probability of system change/reform:	Low
Prime actors:	States, and especially great powers
Principal actor goals:	Power over others, self-preservation, and physical security
Predominant pattern of actor interaction:	Competition and conflict
Pervasive concern:	National security
Prevalent state priorities:	Acquiring military capabilities
Popular state practice:	Use of armed force for coercive diplomacy
Realist Policy Prescriptions	
Preparations for war:	"If you want peace, prepare for war."
Perpetual vigilance:	"No state is to be trusted further than its national interest."
Persistent involvement and intervention:	"Isolationism is not an alternative to active global involvement."
Preparedness with arms:	"Strive to increase military capabilities, and fight rather than submit to subordination."
Preserve the balance of power:	"Do not let any state or coalition of states become predominant."
Prevent arms races from resulting in military inferiority with rivals:	"Negotiate agreements with competitors to maintain a favorable military balance."

therefore, states should avoid them except when absolutely necessary. The third holds alliances in contempt, arguing that they have proved so dangerous that prudent policymakers must bypass them altogether.

The Advantages of Alliance. Allies offer a means to counterbalance threats posed by potential aggressors in the anarchical international environment. Accordingly, "whenever in recorded history a system of multiple sovereignty has existed, some of the sovereign units when involved in conflicts with others have entered into alliances" (Wolfers 1968), "even in advance, against [a] probable aggressor" (Morgenthau 1959). Alliances are "typically against, and only derivatively for, someone or something" (Liska 1962).

Facing common dangers, states have several good reasons to ally. "The primary benefit of alliance is obviously security. . . . Security benefits in a mutual defense alliance include chiefly a reduced probability of being attacked (deterrence), greater strength in case of attack (defense), and prevention of the ally's alliance with one's adversary (preclusion)" (G. Snyder 1991).

Many alliances have not lasted long, however, and have often dissolved when the common threat disappeared. For this reason, realists primarily see alliance formation as a strategy that includes both the recruitment and abandonment of allies. Recognizing that "alignment and dealignment are the main short-term strategies for increasing security," there are three basic options. These options consist of seeking "changes in foreign policy commitments, adding or expanding relations with nations that can provide immediate increases in one's security, and eliminating or curtailing relations with nations that are a drain on security" (Scarborough and Bueno de Mesquita 1988). According to the logic of *realpolitik*, the only good alliance is one that can be dissolved easily when the threat to one's own security declines. As Britain's Lord Palmerston admonished in 1848, states "should have no eternal allies and no perpetual enemies." Their only duty, then, is to follow their interests, which may require abandoning an ally when it ceases to be useful.

The Disadvantages of Alliance. The greatest risk in forming alliances is that they bind one's state to a commitment that later may become disadvantageous. Throughout history, policymakers have been mindful of the risk of entanglement. Entrusting their security to the pledges of others reduces their future freedom of action. Consequently, leaders usually heed warnings about the costs of commitments to allies, such as the one advanced by the realist U.S. policymaker, George F. Kennan:

> The relations among nations, in this imperfect world, constitute a fluid substance, always in motion, changing subtly from day to day in ways that are difficult to detect from the myopia of the passing moment, and even difficult to discern from the perspective of the future one. The situation at one particular time is never quite the same as the situation of five years later—indeed it is sometimes very significantly different, even though the stages by which this change came about are seldom visible at the given moment. This is why wise and experienced statesmen usually shy away from commitments likely to constitute limitations on a government's behavior at unknown dates in the future in the face of unpredictable situations. (Kennan 1984a, 238)

Although alliances provide some measure of protection, they also reduce a state's capacity to make accommodative realignments when conditions change. In fact, the usefulness of any alliance is destined to lessen once the common external threat that brought it together declines, as inevitably it will (Wolfers 1962). Policymakers are therefore often advised not to take a fixed position on temporary convergences of national interests and to forge alliances only to deal with immediate threats.

States' alliance policies are usually shaped by an acute awareness of the many risks of sharing their fate with allies. While realists perceive alliances as a tool states can use for their own benefit, they caution that alliance formation tends to:

- Foreclose options.
- Reduce the states' capacity to adapt to changing circumstances.
- Weaken a state's capability to influence others by decreasing the number of additional partners with which it can align.
- Eliminate the advantages in bargaining that can be derived from deliberately fostering ambiguity about one's intentions.
- Provoke the fears of adversaries.

- Entangle states in disputes with their allies' enemies.
- Interfere with the negotiation of disputes involving an ally's enemy by precluding certain issues from being placed on the agenda for debate.
- Preserve existing rivalries.
- Stimulate envy and resentment on the part of friends who are outside the alliance and therefore are not eligible to recieve its advantages.

The Dangers of Alliance. Many realists recommend avoiding alliances altogether, citing five basic reasons. First, alliances enable aggressive states to combine military capabilities for aggression. This was the thinking of Adolf Hitler, who maintained that "Any alliance whose purpose is not the intention to wage war is senseless and useless." Alliances are to be feared because they allow expansionist states, counting on their allies' assistance, to act more aggressively than they otherwise would.

Second, alliances threaten enemies and provoke them to form counteralliances. This results in the reduction of security of *both* coalitions.

> Peacetime alliances may occur in order to reduce the insecurity of anarchy or reduce armament costs. If they do, they will tend to create relations of enmity as well as alignment. Even if the initial alliance is not directed at a specific opponent, other states will perceive it as a threat and begin to behave as enemies, perhaps by forming a counteralliance. Not only will alliances identify friends and foes, they will create interests consistent with such relations. (G. Snyder 1991, 88)

In a similar vein, "alliances both reveal any added support that a state may have, and the amount of support that a potential belligerent may need. . . . The reduction of uncertainty brought about by such information may be all that is

Policymakers' perceptions of alliances have varied, depending on their personal philosophy and the country's circumstances. In 1796 George Washington reflected a realist perspective when he counseled the United States to "steer clear of permanent alliances" because whereas a state "may safely trust to temporary alliances for extraordinary emergencies" it is an "illusion . . . to expect or calculate upon real favors from nation to nation."

needed to facilitate an aggressor's desire to attack another state" (Bueno de Mesquita 1981).

Third, alliance formation may draw otherwise neutral parties into opposed coalitions. As Thomas Jefferson warned, alliances can be dangerously "entangling." They require members to come to one another's aid, involving members in the wars of their partners.

Fourth, once states join forces, they must control the behavior of their own allies. Management of intra-alliance relations is necessary to discourage each member from reckless aggression against its enemies, threatening the security of the alliance's other members. In addition, allies must work to deter defection from the alliance and to ensure that allies' commitments to one another are faithfully honored.

Finally, the possibility always exists that today's ally might become tomorrow's enemy. Realists believe that all states are natural enemies, that there are no permanent friends or adversaries. The historical record is noteworthy in this respect. In the period between the Congress of Vienna in 1815 and the 1960s, wars between allies were commonplace: "More than 25 percent of coalition partners eventually [went] to war against each other" (Russett and Starr 1996, 91). Thus, when alliances form, they can increase the prospects for and the scope of war.

Alliances in the Realist Image and the Liberal Critique

In a 1917 address to the U.S. Senate, President Woodrow Wilson proposed that "all nations avoid entangling alliances which would draw them into . . . a net of intrigue and selfish rivalry." His advice reflected the liberal belief that alliances and secret diplomacy transform limited conflicts into global wars with many participants.

Realists also stress the dangers and disadvantages of alliances. However, realists qualify their criticism by holding that alliances can be beneficial if policymakers remain flexible and if prevailing international norms support an elastic interpretation of alliance commitments and the rights of neutrals. Most policymakers schooled in *realpolitik* contend that entanglements occur only when alliance structures become rigid, when commitments are interpreted as irrevocable pledges, and when states operate from the belief that their commitments oblige them to take sides in their allies' disputes. The accuracy of these arguments is best evaluated by exploring the possible contribution of alliance formation to maintaining the balance of power.

● ● ●

THE BALANCE OF POWER

International anarchy makes each state responsible for its own national security. The seventeenth-century English realist philosopher Thomas Hobbes observed that this condition encourages among states a perpetual "war of all against all." To realists and neorealists, reforming this system is unrealistic because international anarchy is permanent, as is the selfish drive for power over rivals. Survival and world order rest on the proper functioning of a system of shifting military alignments commonly referred to as the "balance of power."

Balance of power is an ambiguous concept used in a variety of ways (see Claude 1962; Haas 1953). At its core is the idea that peace will result when military power is distributed so that no one state is strong enough to dominate the others. If one state, or a combination of states, gains enough power to threaten others, compelling incentives will exist for those threatened to disregard their superficial differences and unite in a defensive alliance. The power resulting from such collaboration would, according to this conception, deter the would-be attacker from pursuing expansionism. Thus, from the laissez-faire competition of predatory and defensive rivals would emerge a balance of contending factions, which would maintain the status quo.

Balance-of-power theory is also founded on the realist premise that weakness invites attack and that countervailing power must be used to deter potential aggressors. Because realists assume that the drive for expanded power guides every state's actions, it follows that all countries are potential adversaries, and each must strengthen its military capability to protect itself. Invariably, this reasoning rationalizes the quest for military superiority because others pursue it as well.

On the surface, these realist assumptions appear dubious (especially to liberals). Self-fulfillingly, the arms races they justify can easily breed the very outcome most feared—a destructive, global war. However, the realist policymakers in Europe who formulated classical balance-of-power theory after the Peace of Westphalia in 1648 were not irrational (Gulick 1955). They reasoned that a system founded on suspicion and competition, in which all states were independent and free to act in their perceived national interests, would distribute power evenly through realignments. This, they believed, would curtail the temptation of any actor to seek to dominate others.

The Balance Process. In classic balance-of-power theory, fear of a third party would encourage *alignments*—shifts by neutrals to one coalition or the other—because those threatened would need help to offset the power of the mutual adversary. An alliance would add the ally's power to its own and deny the addition of that power to the enemy. As alliances combine power, the offsetting coalitions would give neither a clear advantage. Therefore, aggression would appear unattractive and would be averted.

To deter an aggressor, counteralliances were expected to form easily, because states sitting on the sidelines could not risk **nonalignment.** If they refused to ally, their own vulnerability would encourage the expansionist state to attack them at a later time. In theory, the result of these individual calculations would be the formation of coalitions approximately equal in power.[1]

To maintain an even distribution of power, realists recommended certain *rules* be followed to promote fluid and rapidly shifting alliances. They recognized that a balance would develop only if states practiced certain behaviors. One requirement was that a great power not immediately threatened by the rise

---

[1]According to the so-called *size principle*, rational actors tend to form coalitions sufficient in size to ensure victory and no larger; thus political coalitions tend to be roughly equal in size (see Riker 1962). Morgenthau (1985) and Gulick (1955) discuss the rationality of policies aimed at equalizing the power of competing coalitions, based on the willingness to recognize states' interest in stopping aggression.

of another power or coalition would perform the role of a **balancer** by offsetting the new challenger's power. Since the modern state system began in the seventeenth century, Great Britain has often played this role by consistently supporting the weaker coalition to prevent an expansionist state and its allies from achieving dominance.

In addition to needing a balancer, all states had to obey the following "essential rules": "(1) increase capabilities but negotiate rather than fight; (2) fight rather than fail to increase capabilities; (3) stop fighting rather than eliminate an essential actor; (4) oppose any coalition or single actor which tends to assume a position of predominance within the system; (5) constrain actors who subscribe to supranational organizational principles; and (6) permit defeated or constrained essential national actors to reenter the system as acceptable role partners" (Kaplan 1957).

According to these rules, competition is proper because it leads to the equalization of capabilities among the major competitors. The balance-of-power approach deals with the problem of war in a way that preserves the problem. War is a way to measure national power as well as a means for changing the distribution of power in order to preserve the essential features of the system itself.

The successful operation of a balance-of-power system also presupposes some important preconditions for its successful operation.[2] To maintain a balance, for example, the following conditions must exist:

- States must possess accurate information about others' capabilities and motives and react rationally to this information.

- There must be a sufficient number of independent states to make alliance formation and dissolution readily possible.[3]

- There must be a limited geographic area.

- National leaders must have freedom of action.

- States' capabilities must be relatively equal.

- States must share a common political culture in which the rules of the security regime are recognized and respected.

- States in the system must have similar types of government and ideologies.

- States must have a weapons technology that inhibits **preemption**—quick mobilizations for war, first-strike attacks that defeat the enemy before it can organize a retaliatory response—and wars of annihilation.

- There must be no supranational institutions capable of interfering with states' alignments and realignments.

These preconditions characterized the environment of international politics during most periods before World War II. But do they exist today? Are the assumptions underlying classic balance-of-power theory still warranted?

---

[2]The conditions believed necessary for the successful operation of the balance-of-power mechanism remain a topic of theoretical debate. Waltz (1979) provides a useful review and critique of the conventional reasoning associated with this issue, advancing the neorealist thesis that "balance-of-power politics prevail whenever two, and only two, requirements are met: that the order be anarchic and that it be populated by units wishing to survive."

[3]Kaplan (1957) theorizes that a stable balance-of-power system requires at least five great powers or blocs of states.

The Breakdown of Power Balances. Is international order truly a product of alliance formation and power balances, as many realists (Liska 1968; Osgood 1968) believe? Or, when arms races and alliance formation combine power into contending blocs, do the states aligned find that their security actually declines and that major wars then usually erupt?

If the assumptions of the balance-of-power theory are correct, historical periods in which the basic preconditions listed above were in evidence should also have been periods in which war was less frequent. What does the historical record suggest?

The Eurocentric system that existed from the mid-seventeenth century until World War I is generally regarded as the "golden age" of balance-of-power politics. But even then the balance of power was always precarious at best (Dehio 1962). Indeed, the regularity with which wars broke out in Europe between the mid-1600s and the early twentieth century (the period when the necessary conditions for the "invisible hand" of the balance of power most clearly existed) attests to the repeated failure of its mechanisms to preserve peace (see Focus 15.1). Although the classical systems may at times have prolonged the intervals of peace between conflicts and possibly limited wars' duration and damage when they occurred, a balancing of power never kept the peace.[4] To be sure, several "long peaces"—long-lasting periods of great-power peace—occurred in Europe during the balance of power (between the Congress of Vienna in 1815 and the outbreak of war across Europe in 1848, and after the Franco-Prussian War in 1871 until 1914).[5] But more striking was the destructiveness of the general wars that erupted each time these balance-of-power systems collapsed.

In light of the previous repetitious breakdown of the balance of power, it is noteworthy that the pattern of recurrent general wars ended when the nuclear era began, after World War II. Since then, war among great powers has been virtually nonexistent. Another "long peace" (Gaddis 1991) has taken root. Could it be that the **balance of terror** created by nuclear weapons deterred great-power belligerence since 1945 more than the balance of power? Arguably, alliance formation and balance-of-power politics could not have caused this long peace. The rigid alliance blocs during the Cold War halted the rapid realignments necessary for the equilibrium that balance-of-power theory envisions. If that is so, then it seems likely that the annihilating destructiveness of nuclear weapons since the 1950s kept the peace—not the alliances and power balances that the great powers constructed.

Equally debatable is the realist assumption underlying balance-of-power theory that countries with dominant strength will be secure. Contrary evidence suggests that rapidly arming countries may actually invite attack. In five of the nine great-power wars which occurred in the 150 years following the 1815 Congress of Vienna, the countries attacked were stronger militarily than those initiating the war (Singer and Small 1974; see also Chapter 13). This belies the premise

---

[4]Research shows that although during the nineteenth century alliance formation within the balance-of-power system was associated with the absence of war, throughout the first half of the twentieth century this linkage no longer held. As many states became members of alliances, the international system became relatively more war-prone (Singer and Small 1968).
[5]It could be argued that the relative peace during several prolonged periods in nineteenth-century Europe was *not* the product of an equilibrium resulting from balance-of-power politics but rather resulted from the extraordinary dominance of power possessed and used by Great Britain, the world's hegemonic leader, to keep peace among its European rivals (see Organski 1968).

The Balance of Power
A Precarious and Failed Security System?

Perhaps the foremost expert on the balance of power, the realist political scientist Inis L. Claude, came to this sobering conclusion:

> Balance-of-power theory is concerned mainly with the rivalries and clashes of great powers—above all—what we have come to describe as world wars, the massive military conflicts that engulf and threaten to destroy the entire multistate system. It is difficult to consider world wars as anything other than catastrophic failures, total collapses, of the balance-of-power system. They are hardly to be classed as stabilizing manoeuvres or equilibrating processes, and one cannot take seriously any claim of maintaining international stability that does not entail the prevention of such disasters as the Napoleonic wars or World War I. Mention of those and similar disasters, however, frequently evokes the reminder that the would-be universal emperor—be it Louis XIV or Napoleon or Hitler—was defeated; in accordance with balance of power principles, a coalition arose to put down the challenger and maintain or restore the independence of the various states. In short, the system worked. Or did it? Is the criterion of the effectiveness of the balance of power that Germany lose its bid for conquest, or that it be deterred from precipitating World War I? It is not easy to justify the contention that a system for the management of international relations that failed to prevent the events of 1914–1918 deserves high marks as a guardian of stability or order, or peace. If the balance of power system does not aim at the prevention of world war, then it aims too low; if it offers no hope of maintaining the general peace, then the quest for a better system is fully warranted. (Claude 1989, 78)

The question to be asked is whether the balance of power is a reliable mechanism to prevent global war or whether there is a better approach. If so, what is it? Is it collective security, as liberal idealists such as Woodrow Wilson believed, or some other approach?

that seeking military advantages over others deters aggression. Instead, as liberal idealists warn, the growth of a state's military power may so terrify its adversaries that they are motivated to initiate a preemptive strike in order to prevent their defeat.

Collective Security versus Power Balances

The outbreak of World War I, perhaps more than any other event, discredited balance-of-power politics and promoted the search for alternatives. The catastrophic proportions of that war led many, especially those attracted to the liberal theoretical interpretation of world politics, to view the balance-of-power mechanism as a *cause* of war instead of an instrument for its prevention. These critics cited the arms races, secret treaties, and cross-cutting alliances driving balance-of-power politics before the outbreak of the war as its immediate precipitants.

Assumptions Underlying Collective Security. President Woodrow Wilson voiced the most vehement opposition to balance-of-power politics. He and other liberal idealists hoped to replace the alliances and counteralliances within the balance of power with the principle of *collective security*, a system of world order in which aggression by any state would be met by a collective response.

The League of Nations embodied this belief, built on the assumption that peace-loving countries could collectively deter—and, if necessary, counteract—aggression. Instead of accepting war as a legitimate instrument of national policy, collective security advocates sought to inhibit war through the threat of collective action. The theory proposed: (1) to retaliate against *any* aggression or attempt to establish hegemony—not just those acts that threatened particular countries; (2) to involve the participation of *all* member states—not just a sufficient number to stop the aggressor; and (3) to create an international organization to identify acts of aggression and to organize a military response to them—not just to let individual states decide for themselves whether to undertake self-help measures. In essence, collective security may be defined as "collective self-regulation," occurring when "a group of states attempts to reduce security threats by agreeing to collectively punish any member state that violates the system's norms" (Downs 1994).[6]

To the disappointment of its advocates, collective security was not endorsed by the very powers that after World War I had most championed it, such as the United States. Japan's aggression against Manchuria in 1931 (and China proper in 1937) and Italy's invasion of Ethiopia in 1935 were widely condemned. However, collective resistance was not forthcoming. Furthermore, Germany's encroachment on Czechoslovakia and other European countries in the late 1930s elicited no collective response. When World War II broke out, collective security was discredited.

The Revival of Balance-of-Power Politics. Following World War II, realists maintained that national self-reliance was the only trustworthy safeguard of security, that peace must come through national rather than multilateral military might, and that it was necessary to confront a potential aggressor with an abundance of power to successfully deter its aggression. U.S. President Richard Nixon was one of many leaders who reaffirmed the balance-of-power approach when he opined, "We must remember the only time in the history of the world that we have had any extended period of peace is when there has been a balance of power. . . . It will be a safer world . . . if we have a strong, healthy United States, Europe, Soviet Union, China, Japan, each balancing the other." To place this realist proposition underlying balance-of-power theory into context, it is instructive to review the evolution of the international system's polarity structure in the post–World War II era, the world's longest period of great-power peace.

Post–World War II Models of the Balance of Power

Military power can be distributed in different ways. Historically, these have ranged from highly concentrated distributions on one end of the continuum to highly dispersed distributions on the other. The former have included regional

---

[6]As one (realist) authority impartially describes the concept:

> The rock bottom principle upon which collective security is founded provides that an attack on any one state will be regarded as an attack on all states. It finds its measure in the simple doctrine of one for all and all for one. War anywhere . . . is the concern of every state.
>
> Self-help and neutrality, it should be obvious, are the exact antithesis of such a theory. States under an order of neutrality are impartial when conflict breaks out, give their blessings to combatants to fight it out, and defer judgment regarding the justice or injustice of the cause involved. Self-help in the past was often "help yourself" so far as the great powers were concerned; they enforced their own rights and more besides. In the eighteenth and nineteenth centuries this system was fashionable, and wars, although not eliminated, were localized whenever possible. In a more integrated world environment, a conflict anywhere has some effect on conditions of peace everywhere. A disturbance at one point upsets the equilibrium at all other points, and the adjustment of a single conflict restores the foundations of harmony at other points throughout the world. (Thompson 1953, 755)

empires (e.g., the Roman Empire), while an example of the latter is the approximate equality of power held by the European powers at the conclusion of the Napoleonic Wars in 1815. Following the conventional periodizations of analysts (e.g., Kaplan 1957; Kegley and Raymond 1994; Thompson 1988), we can identify three major distributions of international power since 1945, with a fourth probably emergent in the post-Cold War period.

Unipolarity. Most countries were devastated by the global war that ended in 1945. The United States, however, was left in a clearly dominant position, its economy accounting for about half the world's combined gross national product. The United States was also the only country with an awesome new weapon, the atomic bomb, which it had already demonstrated its willingness to use. This underscored to others that it was without rival and incapable of being counterbalanced. The United States was not just stronger than anybody—it was stronger than *everybody*. This immediate postwar power configuration was unipolar, because power was concentrated in the hands of a single hegemon. This period, however, was short-lived.

Bipolarity. The recovery of the Soviet economy, the growth of its military capabilities, its maintenance of a large army, and growing Soviet–U.S. rivalry soon gave rise to a new distribution of world power. The Soviets broke the U.S. monopoly on atomic weapons in 1949 and exploded a thermonuclear device in 1953, less than a year after the United States. This achievement symbolized the creation of a *bipolar* distribution, as military capabilities became concentrated in the hands of two competitive "superpowers," whose capacity to massively destroy anyone made comparisons with the other great powers meaningless.

The concentration of power (what scholars term **polarity**) into two dominant actors encouraged polarization. Power combined through alliance formation to form two opposing *blocs* or coalitions.[7] The concept of **polarization,** the tendency of actors to cluster in alliances around the most powerful states, is especially apt in this context because a *pole* is a fit metaphor for a magnet—it both repels and attracts (Nogee 1975).

The formation of the **North Atlantic Treaty Organization (NATO),** linking the United States to the defense of Western Europe, and the Warsaw Pact, linking the former Soviet Union in a formal alliance with its Eastern European clients, were evidence of the polarization process. Through this process, states combined their military resources in countercoalitions to reinforce a bipolar structure. The opposing alliance systems, or blocs, formed in part because the superpowers competed for allies and in part because the less-powerful states looked to one superpower or the other for protection. Correspondingly, each superpower's allies gave it forward bases from which to carry on the competition. In addition, the involvement of most other states in

---

[7]Note that the concepts of *polarity* and *polarization* are sometimes incorrectly used interchangeably. They refer to two distinct dimensions of the primary ways military power is aggregated (or dispersed) at any point in time in the international system. When states independently build arms at home, their differential production rates change the system's *polarity,* or number of power centers (poles). In contrast, when states combine their arms through alliance formation, the aggregation of power through *polarization* changes the system's balance of power. A system with multiple power centers can be said to be moving toward a greater degree of polarization if its members form separate blocs whose external interactions are characterized by increasing levels of conflict while their internal interactions become more cooperative (Rapkin and Thompson with Christopherson 1989). Conversely, polarization decreases when the number of cross-cutting alignments expands.

the superpowers' struggle globalized the East–West conflict. Few states remained outside the superpowers' rival alliance networks as neutral or non-aligned countries.

By grouping the system's states into two blocs, each led by a superpower, the Cold War's bipolar structure bred insecurity among all. The balance was constantly at stake. Each bloc leader, fearing that its adversary would attain hegemony, viewed every move, however defensive, as the first step toward world conquest. *Zero-sum conflict* was endemic as both sides viewed what one side gained as a loss for the other. Both the United States and the former Soviet Union therefore attached great importance to recruiting new allies. Fear that an old ally might desert the fold was ever present. Bipolarity left little room for compromise or maneuver and worked against the normalization of super-power relations (Waltz 1993).

Bipolycentrism. The major Cold War coalitions associated with bipolarity began to disintegrate in the 1960s and early 1970s. As their internal cohesion eroded and new centers of power emerged, a bipolycentric system (Spanier 1975) came into being. **Bipolycentrism** described the continued military superiority of the two superpowers and their allies' continued reliance on their respective patrons for security. At the same time, the weaker alliance partners were afforded more room for maneuvering. Thus the term **polycentrism** was coined to describe the emergence of diverse relationships among the states subordinate to the superpowers at this second tier (e.g., the friendly relations between the United States and Romania, on the one hand, and those between France and the Soviet Union, on the other). The secondary powers also began to cultivate ties across alliance boundaries (e.g., between Poland and West Germany) to enhance their bargaining position within their own alliance. Although the superpowers remained dominant militarily, this less-rigid system allowed other states to perform new foreign policy roles, other than simply aligned or nonaligned.

Rapid technological innovation in the superpowers' major weapons systems was a principal catalyst to the crumbling of the blocs. **Intercontinental ballistic missiles (ICBMs),** capable of delivering nuclear weapons through space from one continent to another, eroded the necessity of forward-base areas for striking at the heart of the adversary. ICBMs also diminished the need to maintain tight, cohesive alliance systems composed of reliable partners.

In addition, the narrowed differences in the superpowers' arsenals loosened the ties that had previously bound allies to one another. The European members of NATO in particular began to question whether the United States would, as it had pledged, protect Paris or Bonn by sacrificing New York. Under what conditions might Washington or Moscow be willing to risk a nuclear holocaust? The uncertainty became pronounced as the pledge to protect allies through *extended deterrence* by retaliating against their attacker seemed increasingly insincere. As former CIA director Stansfield Turner acknowledged in 1986, "It's not conceivable that any president would risk the very existence of [the United States] in order to defend [our] European allies from a convention-al assault."

In partial response to the dilemma this posed, other states, particularly France, decided to protect themselves by developing their own nuclear capabilities. As a result, the diffusion of power already under way gathered momentum.

As these changes unfolded in the 1970s and 1980s, Cold-War categories used to classify "free world" and communist countries' foreign policy alignments lost much of their relevance, as bipolycentrism implies. The acceptance of capitalism by many communist states in the late 1980s. This eroded further the adhesive bonds of ideology that formerly had helped these countries face their security problems from a common posture. Fissures in both blocs widened, as disputes arose in the Western alliance over strategic doctrine, arms control, U.S. military bases on allies' territory, and especially "out-of-area conflicts" (those beyond the traditional geographical boundaries of NATO). Not only decomposing blocs, but also declining support in general for the sanctity of alliance commitments became evident (Kegley and Raymond 1990). As fears of a new world war steadily lessened and the Cold War began to fade, leaders questioned whether defense alliances were still needed.

The 1989 dismantling of the Berlin Wall tore apart the post-World War II architecture of competing blocs. With the end of this division, and without a Soviet threat, the consistency of outlook and singularity of purpose that once bound NATO members together disappeared. To many critics, NATO and the Warsaw Pact had institutionalized antagonisms and perpetuated the Cold War—and were no longer needed.

Central to the unfolding debate was "the German question." According to Lord Ismay, the first Secretary General of NATO, the original purpose of the Atlantic alliance was "to keep the Russians out, the Americans in, and the Germans down." In 1990, although fearing a "Fourth Reich" (i.e., a united, powerful, and potentially expansionist German state), the Soviet Union reversed its long-standing opposition to German unification and agreed to withdraw its military forces from Europe. It did not make that dramatic concession without conditions, however. It insisted that unification be orchestrated through the active management of *all* the major World War II allies, that Germany reduce its armed forces, and that the United States keep a military presence in NATO on German soil.

Germany met all of these preconditions. In September 1990 the Four Powers (the United States, the Soviet Union, Great Britain, and France) and the two Germanys (the "Two plus Four") negotiated a treaty in Moscow which terminated the Four Powers' rights over Germany. German leaders declared they had no territorial claims to make in Europe, including the territories in Poland that were annexed after World War II. Moreover, they pledged to never obtain nuclear weapons, and to reduce their 670,000-person armed forces to 370,000 troops (in exchange for the removal of 370,000 Soviet soldiers from Germany). Germany and the former Soviet Union also signed a bilateral treaty under which the two powers promised not to attack each other.

The West greeted these agreements (and Soviet concessions) with enthusiasm. The agreements symbolized at once the retreat of the Soviet Union from a region (east Europe) it had long regarded as central to its security. They also symbolized the geostrategic shift of NATO influence into the heartland of the Warsaw Pact, which formally dissolved early in 1991.

In the early 1990s many perceived the need to replace NATO and the defunct Warsaw Pact with a new security arrangement. However, most leaders maintained that some configuration of a European defense architecture was still necessary to cement relationships and stabilize the rush of cascading events. Presidents George Bush and Bill Clinton, for instance, were vocal advocates of the continuing need to anchor security in alliances, pledging to keep

Realists argue that common interests are the only glue capable of holding alliances together. Others see convergent ideologies as important forces that can bind states together in alliances. In 1996 only five countries (China, Cuba, Laos, North Korea, and Vietnam) remained members of the "communist bloc." In 1988, before the Cold War ended, that coalition consisted of fifteen countries. Pictured here is Cuba's Fidel Castro being assisted by Vietnam's General Secretary Do Muoi and a Vietnamese soldier at farewell ceremonies to a 1995 summit in Hanoi. The Cuban leader visited both China and Vietnam to observe how they had adapted Marxism to market economies. The meeting raises the question of whether communist ideology can still unify what remains of the communist bloc in a common coalition.

U.S. troops in Europe and promising that the United States would remain the backbone of NATO.

To others, a new *concert* system of conference diplomacy was needed, like the Concert of Europe which the great powers created in 1815 in the wake of the Napoleonic Wars to keep the peace. Leaders in Moscow and some Western analysts recommended redefining NATO's purpose from the containment of enemies to the control of allies. For that, *all* the countries in Europe would be required to coordinate their defense policies. This would incorporate the east European and former Soviet republics pursuing democratization into a European-wide framework. It might also shift peacekeeping responsibilities from NATO to the larger Organization for Security and Cooperation in Europe (OSCE).

An alternative scenario was the conversion of NATO from a military alliance designed for defense against a predetermined enemy to a larger collective security community. The 1991 Rome Summit moved in this direction by creating a new **North Atlantic Cooperation Council (NACC)** "to build genuine partnership among the North Atlantic Alliance and the countries of Central and Eastern Europe." The next meeting of defense ministers months later witnessed the members of NATO sitting at the same table with the former Warsaw Pact states and newly independent Baltic republics, facing a request from Russia to become a member.

The goal was to keep NATO alive even though the Cold War had died. The old NATO was built on the joint will to resist Soviet aggression. The new NATO sought to survive by preparing to contain ethnonational conflicts and foster disarmament and by remaining an instrument for preserving U.S. involvement in European security.

In January 1994 the historic dynamics of balance-of-power realignments again were exhibited when the four most advanced democracies in the former communist bloc (Poland, the Czech Republic, Slovakia, and Hungary) lobbied aggressively for full NATO membership. Rather than accept this effort to **bandwagon** by permitting states to abandon one alliance and join the stronger one, under U.S. advocacy NATO cut a compromise deal by offering them **Partnerships for Peace (PFP).** As Secretary of State Warren Christopher explained,

> The Alliance must embrace innovation or risk irrelevance. . . . The January (1994) summit [opens] the door to an evolutionary process of NATO expansion. This process should be nondiscriminatory and inclusive. It should . . . initiate practical military cooperation between NATO forces and those of the East. To that end, we have proposed a Partnership for Peace. The Partnership would be open to all members of the North Atlantic Cooperation Council as well as others. It excludes no nations and forms no blocs.

The PFP permits the "peace partners" to participate and train with NATO troops for peacekeeping and crisis-management operations. But it does not extend to the new peace partners the full members' security guarantee of aid in the event of attack. Instead, the peace partners were told that they must await the unspecified day when they could become full members of NATO, with the collective defense commitment that this membership would provide.

Still, by extending NATO to the east, a precedent was set for further enlarging and modifying the European security framework. And that was precisely what followed. Shortly thereafter, to dispel growing Russian distrust of exclusion, NATO did expand. Russia agreed to join twenty other neutrals and former-Warsaw Pact countries in the Partnership for Peace plan. With this territorial expansion, the balance of power again started to shift (see Map 15.1), and NATO began to restructure itself for a single common defense without specifying a single common enemy.

In December 1995, NATO traveled down the long, winding road toward acting on the enlarged mission that these transformations made feasible, notwithstanding growing fears among the eastern European countries that with the rise of communist hardliners in Russia the "window of opportunity" for their membership may be closing as a consequence (Buerke 1996). In the first joint session of its foreign and defense ministers since 1979, the sixteen-member alliance met in Brussels to approve the largest joint-military ground action in its history and the first outside NATO's territory. The action, Operation Joint Endeavor, dispatched sixty thousand troops (including fifteen hundred Russian soldiers and volunteers from seventeen other countries) to end the violence in Bosnia. To many observers, this bold mission of mercy opened a new chapter in the alliance's history, shoring up NATO and demonstrating its relevance.

MAP 15.1

The Enlarged NATO under the Partnership for Peace and the New European Balance of Power

The inclusion of Russia and the other former Warsaw Pact members under the NATO Partners for Peace regime transforms the European geostrategic landscape. NATO now casts its security concerns across the continent, consolidating all of Europe in a common collective security regime.

Indeed, revitalized with a redefined purpose, NATO found not only a new role but also a rationale for its survival.

This breakthrough creates a far different distribution of power than that which existed in the bipolycentric system of the 1970s and 1980s and the bipolar system that preceded it in the 1950s and 1960s. The waves of change that have unfolded foretell the beginning of a new multipolar system.

Multipolarity. U.S. Secretary of State Lawrence Eagleburger proclaimed in 1989 that "we are now moving into . . . a world in which power and influence [are] diffused among a multiplicity of states—[a] multipolar world." A *multipolar* system of relatively equal powers, similar to the classical European balance-of-power system, may indeed best describe the emerging distribution of power. Such a multipolar system is likely to consist of the United States, China, Germany, Japan, and Russia. To these might someday be added a consolidated European Union as a product of the treaty signed in February 1992 calling for the eventual political integration of the European Union and its pursuit of a common defense policy (see Chapter 16).

What will be the likely character of such a multipolar world? As we have seen, when power has been relatively evenly distributed in the past, each player has been assertive, independent, and competitive; diplomacy has displayed a nonideological, chesslike character; and conflict has been intense as each contender has nervously feared the power of its rivals.

If a truly multipolar world develops, it is difficult to foresee how each great power's relationship with the others will evolve. Realignments—sometimes rapid—are to be expected. With the probable expansion of the number of great powers to as many as five, realist theory predicts that new cleavages inevitably will develop. It also predicts that rivalry likely will intensify as each jockeys for privilege, position, and power.

A world consisting of five or more independent and approximately equal centers of power will create an enlarged global chessboard of multiple bilateral geostrategic relationships. Such a congested landscape will be fraught with great potential for conflict and much confusion about the identity of friends and foes. To make the setting even more confusing, the interplay is likely to take place simultaneously on two playing fields—the first economic and the second military (recall Table 4.2).

In a new multipolar system, we can expect the major powers to align together against others on particular issues, as interests dictate. Behind the diplomatic smiles and handshakes, one-time friends and allies are likely to grow apart, and formally "specialized" relationships are likely to dissolve. Consider the already heated U.S.–Japan–EU rivalry on the economic battlefield (Thurow 1992; see also Chapter 8).

Multipolarity also foretells the potential alignment of former adversaries. The United States and Russia, allied victors in World War II, are now both apprehensive about the powers they defeated: Japan and Germany. Therefore, as balance-of-power theory would predict and as Russian strategist Peter Gladkov prescribed in 1992, the United States and Russia may be "natural" allies. But other realignments are also likely, as suggested by Russia's determination to improve its "relations with China, its onetime ally and longtime rival," which the Russians regard "as an uneasy, prickly neighbor with superpower ambitions" (Erlanger 1996). Russia is also determined to avoid leaning too much to the West while deterring China's expansionism. Thus, as the fundamental trend toward the dispersion of global power continues, the prospects for peace undoubtedly will be affected (see Focus 15.2).

Contemplating a Multipolar Future

The emergence of a multipolar international system appears very likely, but the probable consequences are not clear, as the three schools of thought on the relationship between polarity and global stability suggest. Because there is no real consensus on whether systems with a certain number of poles are more war-prone than others (Russett and Starr 1996; see also Levy 1997), it would be imprudent to conclude that a new multipolar system will necessarily spell another period of warfare or of peace. Different types of multipolar systems can emerge involving variant armament ratios and levels of alliances. These combinations can produce very different outcomes. Alternate scenarios are both possible and plausible, and the presence or absence of a particular polarity balance by itself probably will not dictate whether war will result. Thus we have reasons both to celebrate and to mourn the passing of the Cold War's competitive bipolar world as well as the disappearance of the unipolar system after World War II in which the United States dominated as the world's hegemon.

The preservation of peace by states aggregating power in order to balance power has a rather checkered history. In the long run, the resulting alliances and distributions of power have failed to avert a breakdown of world order. The

Polarity and Peace?
Three Schools of Thought

In the wake of the Cold War and the disintegration of its bipolar structure, the long-standing debate has intensified about which type of polarity distribution—unipolar, bipolar, or multipolar—is the most stable.

One interpretation holds that "There were periods when an equal distribution of power between contenders actually existed . . . but these. . . were the exception rather than the rule. . . . Closer examination reveals that they were periods of war, not peace" (Organski 1968). If this view is accurate, then peace will occur when one hegemonic state acquires enough power to deter others' expansionist ambitions. If we think of the United States as the hegemonic power in the post-World War II system, this seemingly plausible conclusion about the stability of unipolar systems does not bode well for peace in the future. If present trends continue, the so-called "unipolar moment" of unchallenged U.S. hegemony (Krauthammer 1991) will pass and, without a dominant global leader, the twenty-first century will be increasingly disorderly.

In contrast, a second school of thought (e.g., Waltz 1964) maintains that bipolar systems are the most stable. According to this line of reasoning, stability, ironically, results from "the division of all nations into two camps [because it] raises the costs of war to such a high level that all but the most fundamental conflicts are resolved without resort to violence" (Bueno de Mesquita 1975). Under such stark simplicities and balanced symmetries, the two leading rivals have incentives to manage crises so that they do not escalate to war.

Those who believe that a bipolar world is inherently more stable than either its unipolar or multipolar counterparts draw support from the fact that in the bipolar environment of the 1950s, when the threat of war was endemic, major war did not occur. Extrapolating, these observers (e.g., Mearsheimer 1990) reason that because now a new multipolar distribution of global power makes it impossible to run the world from one or two centers, disorder will result:

> It is rather basic. So long as there were only two great powers, like two big battleships clumsily and cautiously circling each other, confrontations—or accidents—were easier to avoid. Now, with the global lake more crowded with ships of varying sizes, fueled by different ambitions and piloted with different degrees of navigational skill, the odds of collisions become far greater. (House 1989, A10)

A third school of thought argues that multipolar systems are the least war-prone. While the reasons differ, advocates share the belief that polarized systems that either concentrate power, as in a unipolar system, or that divide the world into two antagonistic blocs, as in a bipolar system, promote struggles for dominance (see Thompson 1988; Morgenthau 1985). The peace-through-multipolarity school perceives multipolar systems as stable because they encompass a larger number of autonomous actors, giving rise to more potential alliance partners. This is seen as pacifying because it is essential to counterbalancing a would-be aggressor, as shifting alliances can occur only when there are multiple power centers (Deutsch and Singer 1964).

Abstract deductions and historical analogies can lead to contradictory conclusions, as the logic underlying these three inconsistent interpretations illustrate. The future will determine which of these rival theories is the most accurate.

great powers have persistently been drawn into wars this century by the collapse of the balance of power in either Europe or East Asia or both at the same time. Yet history also suggests that the prospects for peace in multipolar systems depend on other factors as well. Negotiated arms agreements designed to change the existing balance of power are a critical component which could alter the tendency of multipolar systems to culminate in widespread warfare.

• • •

CONTROLLING MILITARY POWER THROUGH ARMS AGREEMENTS CONTROL

Liberal reformers have often attacked the theory that power can be balanced with power to preserve world order. They have advocated instead the biblical prescription that nations should beat their swords into plowshares. The destructiveness and dispersion of today's weapons have inspired many people once again to take this tenet of liberal theory seriously. But this approach is not solely a liberal preserve. Most realists also see arms control as a way of influencing the international distribution of military power in ways that promote peace and individual states' national security. In fact, the policymakers who have negotiated arms control agreements most often have been realists who perceived these kinds of treaties as a prudent tool to promote their countries' security. At times, they have been the leading advocates of arms control to adjust their states' military power relative to the rivals', and to help maintain the balance of power.

Controlling Weapons: Approaches

It will be useful to review the historical record of negotiators' efforts to preserve the global distribution of weapons and the uses to which they can be put. This will allow us to assess the implications of such negotiations for peace. However, two concepts must first be distinguished. Many people incorrectly assume that the terms "arms control" and "disarmament" are synonymous. **Arms control** refers to agreements designed to regulate arms levels either by limiting their growth or by restricting how they may be used. This is a far less-ambitious endeavor than **disarmament,** which seeks to reduce or eliminate weapons.

> In its most general conception, arms control is any type of restraint on the use of arms, any form of military cooperation between adversaries. Arms control can be implicit or explicit, formal or informal, and unilateral, bilateral, or multilateral. It is a process of jointly managing the weapons-acquisition processes of the participant states in the hope of reducing the risk of war. . . . Arms control [refers] to formal agreements imposing significant restrictions or limitations on the weapons or security policies of the signatories.
>
> Disarmament rests on a fundamentally different philosophical premise than arms control. It envisions the drastic reduction or elimination of all weapons, looking toward the eradication of war itself. Disarmament is based on the notion that if there were no more weapons there would be no more war. This is a compelling proposition, with enough truth to give it a very long life in the history of thought about war and peace. Arms control, on the other hand, accepts the existence of weapons and the possibility of conflict. Contrary to popular impression, it is not necessarily about reducing arms levels. Arms control attempts to stabilize the status quo and to manage conflict, to encourage peaceful resolution of disputes, and limit the resort to military force. Although many visceral opponents would be shocked at the thought, arms control is fundamentally a conservative enterprise. Disarmament, by contrast, is a radical one. Disarmament seeks to overturn the status quo; arms control works to perpetuate it. (Kruzel 1991, 249)

Bilateral agreements should also be differentiated from **multilateral agreements.** Because the former are agreements between only two countries, they are often easier to negotiate and to enforce than are the latter, which are agreements among three or more countries. Negotiating a multilateral agreement, simultaneously binding on many states, poses many obstacles because states' security interests are very different, as are the domestic processes by which governments approve international agreements. As a result, the record of bilateral agreements differs from that of multilateral agreements with respect to both arms control and disarmament.

Multilateral Diplomacy: The Disarmament and Arms Control Record

It is hardly a novel idea that it is possible to control war by reducing the world's military arsenals. Yet until very recently one of the few constants in the changing international system has been the repetition with which states have advocated disarmament but failed to implement it. Some countries have succeeded in reducing their armaments levels,[8] but these achievements are rare. Many more countries have raced to expand their arsenals than have tried to cut them. Most disarmament is involuntary, the product of reductions imposed by coercion of the vanquished by the victors in the immediate aftermath of a war, as when the Allied powers after World War I attempted (unsuccessfully) to disarm permanently a defeated Germany.

In contrast with disarmament, there are many historical examples of arms control efforts. As early as the eleventh century, the Second Lateran Council prohibited the use of crossbows in fighting. The 1868 St. Petersburg Declaration prohibited the use of explosive bullets. In 1899 and 1907, International Peace Conferences at the Hague restricted the use of some weapons and prohibited others. The leaders of the United States, Britain, Japan, France, and Italy signed treaties at the Washington Naval Conferences (1921–1922) agreeing to adjust the relative tonnage of their fleets.

The post-World War II period saw a variety of new arms control proposals. The **Baruch Plan** (1946) called for the creation of a United Nations Atomic Development Authority, which would have placed atomic energy under an international authority to ensure its use for only peaceful purposes. However, the great powers never approved the proposal. The **Rapacki Plan** (1957), which would have prevented the deployment of nuclear weapons in central Europe, also failed.

Nonetheless, leaders have made recurrent efforts to resolve differences so formal arms control agreements might be realized. Prominent among them were the arms control summit meetings of the great powers, of which those between the United States and former Soviet Union—the world's nuclear superpowers—were the most frequent. Summit talks between the Cold War antagonists began in July 1955, when U.S. President Eisenhower and Soviet leader Nikita Khrushchev met in Geneva. Among other things, these summits sought and often resulted in an improved atmosphere for serious arms control negotiations. In addition, they paved the way for the ambitious agreements that were reached as the Cold War ended to cement a new world order based on a reduced and stable military power balance.

Multilateral negotiations on particular issues have also taken on the character of institutionalized efforts to reach arms control agreements. Nine examples illustrate their range and breadth:

- The **Mutual and Balanced Force Reductions (MBFR)** talks were conducted from 1973 to 1988 in an effort to realize force reductions between the blocs dividing Europe. Although they did not produce a treaty, during

---

[8]The Chinese states in 600 B.C.E. formed a disarmament league which produced a peaceful century for the league's members, and in the Rush-Bagot Agreement of 1818 Canada and the United States disarmed the Great Lakes. Disarmament proposals have also figured prominently in the League of Nations' abortive World Disarmament Conference of 1932 and rather continuously in the United Nations since 1946, but especially in its many "special sessions" on disarmament.

Efforts to reduce tensions between adversaries have often centered on negotiations to reduce armament levels. Pictured here are U.S. President Dwight David Eisenhower and Soviet Premier Nitika Khrushchev meeting at the Geneva Summit. In the so-called "Open Skies" agreement, the leaders agreed to permit each superpower to monitor the other's activities from space.

the Cold War they sustained a "consensus that arms control negotiations are a necessary component of alliance defense strategy" and "were helpful in preparing for the negotiations on Conventional Armed Forces in Europe (CFE)" (Hallenbeck and Shaver 1991).

- The **Comprehensive Test Ban (CTB)** negotiations have been held periodically since the late 1950s in an effort to reach agreement on a treaty banning all nuclear explosions. The Reagan administration broke off negotiations in 1982, citing verification obstacles and the need to test nuclear weapons as long as deterrence rested on them. Nonetheless, negotiations on verification protocols resumed in November 1987, and new protocols were added to the existing Threshold Test Ban Treaty and the Peaceful Nuclear Explosions Treaty. Since then, negotiations have proceeded on further limits to nuclear testing. A new draft Comprehensive Test Ban Treaty (CTBT) emerged from the discussions in the 38-member Conference on Disarmament that began in 1994 and continued in 1996 which—if entered into force as scheduled at the end of 1997—would ban all nuclear explosions.

- The Conventional Force Reductions in Europe negotiations, which began in 1989, produced the **Conventional Armed Forces in Europe (CFE) treaty,** which entered into force in late 1992. The CFE set ceilings on five categories of conventional arms (battle tanks, armored combat vehicles, artillery pieces, combat aircraft, and attack helicopters) for the thirty countries in an area stretching from the Atlantic to the Urals (the ATTU zone). Inspections were conducted between November 1995 and January 1996 to ensure the agreed ceilings were not exceeded, and to prepare for the subsequent Review Conference to consider further conventional arms reductions in the pan-European context.

- The **Organization for Security and Cooperation in Europe (OSCE)** emerged from the Conference on Security and Cooperation in Europe

(CSCE), which began in Helsinki in 1973. Soon thereafter it became the leading multilateral institution for managing the transformation of Europe from a system of counterpoised alliances (NATO and the Warsaw Pact) to one based on common principles stretching across the entire continent and North America. Formalized in 1995, the OSCE has fifty-three members, including all NATO and former Warsaw Pact states (except Yugoslavia, which was suspended). The Paris Heads of State summit in 1990 established a permanent CSCE secretariat and Conflict Prevention Center. The 1992 Helsinki Summit discussed the paths by which this enlarged community could apply the military, economic, and human rights provisions of the 1975 Helsinki accords to the new European geopolitical environment. The December 1994 Budapest Summit transformed the conference into a permanent organization and reached agreement on a Code of Conduct on Politico-Military Aspects of Security. It also strengthened the OSCE for preventive diplomacy activities aimed at early warning, and it defined the prevention of a new division in Europe as a goal.

- The signatories of the **nuclear nonproliferation Treaty (NPT)** following the historic Treaty on Nonproliferation of Nuclear Weapons, signed by 138 non-nuclear weapons parties in 1968—have held Review Conferences at five-year intervals since 1975 to discuss compliance and enforcement programs. The 1995 twenty-five-year review conference faced the difficult task of renewing the NPT. With disagreements surfacing among the 175 participating parties, the conference reached a consensus decision to "indefinitely extend" the provisions of the existing NPT. Its "Twenty Principles" called for "the nuclear-weapon states to negotiate in good faith on effective nuclear disarmament, and to convene an extension conference in twenty-five years to determine the duration of the treaty." The 181 parties to the agreement identified objectives on seven issues (universality, nonproliferation, nuclear disarmament, nuclear-weapon-free zones, security assurances, safeguards, and peaceful uses of nuclear energy). They provided for continuation of review conferences every five years in the interim and also called upon states that have not yet joined the NPT (such as India, Iran, Iraq, Israel, Libya, North Korea and Pakistan) "to accede to the treaty at the earliest convenience" (Epstein 1995). Yet, doubts remain about the NPT's ability to contain the spread of nuclear weapons (see Chapter 13 and Map 13.1).

- The **Conference on Disarmament (CD)** emerged from the bilateral U.S.–Soviet negotiations that began in 1976 to ban the production, stockpiling, and use of chemical weapons. In 1981 those closed negotiations moved to the multilateral Conference on Disarmament forum in Geneva. These meetings produced the U.S.–Soviet Chemical Weapons Destruction Agreement in June 1990. At its August 1991 meeting, the thirty-eight-state Conference on Disarmament gave its Ad Hoc Committee on a Nuclear Test Ban a mandate to negotiate a Comprehensive Test Ban Treaty (CTBT), which was scheduled for ratification in 1996. At the same time, the CD pursued a comprehensive and worldwide multilateral chemical weapons disarmament convention. The Persian Gulf War intensified interest in reaching the accord, resulting in the 1993 multilateral treaty described below.

- The Review Conferences of the **Biological Weapons Convention (BWC)** have convened periodically since the 1972 Bacteriological (Biological) and Toxin Weapons Convention (TWC) was ratified in 1972. The TWC was the first multilateral arms control agreement aimed at prohibiting the development of an entire category of weapons of mass destruction. It banned the development, production, stockpiling, acquisition, or retention of biological and toxin weapons but did not specifically ban their use. That had already been done by the 1925 Geneva Protocol for the Prohibition of the Use in War of Asphyxiating, Poisonous, or Other Gases and of Bacteriological Methods of Warfare. The two instruments were seen as complementing each other. From these emanated the 1993 **Chemical Weapons Convention (CWC).** Signed by 159 countries as of September 1995, the CWC calls for the destruction of all chemical weapons by the year 2003. It is administered by the Organization for the Prevention of Chemical Weapons (OPCU) in the Hague.

- The **Missile Technology Control Regime (MTCR)** is an informal arrangement among the world's most advanced suppliers of missile-related equipment to control the export of ballistic and cruise missiles and missile-related technologies. Initially designed to deter the spread of nuclear-capable missiles, the MTCR was expanded in 1993 to prevent the diffusion of missile systems for delivering chemical and biological weapons. The regime, created by seven founding countries in 1987, has since expanded to include twenty-five additional states. Following U.S. President Bill Clinton's advocacy in 1993, the 1994 Stockholm MTCR plenary meeting sought to transform the export regime into a set of rules commanding universal adherence. However, the MTCR currently relies on voluntary compliance and is neither an international treaty nor a legally binding agreement. Its weaknesses were illustrated in 1993 when the United States determined that China, which had earlier pledged to abide by the terms of the MTCR Regime, transferred missile components to Pakistan in violation of its provisions.

- The **United Nations Register of Conventional Arms** is the first international effort to gather official information on the weapons trade since the League of Nations attempted to compile a similar list. Implemented in 1992, the register invites states to submit information voluntarily about their trade in various categories of major weapons. Each of the world's top suppliers has submitted reports. However, by early 1995 the UN had received replies from only eighty-eight countries—less than half its members.

Table 15.2 summarizes the major multilateral arms control agreements reached since World War II. These agreements limit the range of permissible actions and weapons systems available to states. They also have helped to slow the global arms race and paved the way for still more ambitious proposals. In addition, they contribute important confidence-building measures which reduce the political tensions underlying the urge to arm.

Bilateral Diplomacy and the Control of Nuclear Arms: Superpower Agreements

Throughout the Cold War, Soviet and U.S. arms control efforts understandably focused on ways to lessen the threat of nuclear war. These efforts intensified with the disintegration of the Soviet Union into separate, independent republics. Table 15.3 summarizes the results of these negotiations, listing the major bilateral arms control agreements between the two superpowers since 1960.

TABLE 15.2 Major Multilateral Arms Control Treaties since 1945

Date	Agreement	Number of Parties (1995)	Principal Objectives
1959	Antarctic Treaty	42	Prevents the military use of the Antarctic, including the testing of nuclear weapons
1963	Limited Test Ban Treaty	124	Prohibits nuclear weapons in the atmosphere, outer space, and under water
1967	Outer Space Treaty	94	Outlaws the use of outer space for testing or stationing any weapons, as well as for military maneuvers
1967	Treaty of Tlatelolco	29	Creates the Latin America Nuclear Free Zone by prohibiting the testing and possession of nuclear facilities for military purposes
1968	Nuclear Nonproliferation Treaty	181	Prevents the transfer of nuclear weapons and nuclear-weapons-production technologies to non-nuclear-weapon states
1971	Seabed Treaty	92	Prohibits the deployment of weapons of mass destruction and nuclear weapons on the seabed beyond a twelve-mile coastal limit
1972	Biological Weapons Convention	133	Prohibits the production and storage of biological toxins; calls for the destruction of biological weapons stocks
1977	Environmental Modifications Convention (Enmod Convention)	63	Bans the use of technologies that could alter the earth's weather patterns, ocean currents, ozone layer, or ecology
1981	Inhumane Weapons Convention	49	Prohibits the use of such weapons as fragmentation bombs, incendiary weapons, booby traps, and mines to which civilians could be exposed
1985	South Pacific Nuclear Free Zone (Roratonga) Treaty	11	Prohibits the testing, acquisition, or deployment of nuclear weapons in the South Pacific

To these we might add an indeterminate number of tacit understandings about the level and use of weapons to which the two powers agreed. These understandings did not achieve the status of formal agreements but were observed by the two superpowers nonetheless. They included occasional pledges to refrain from the offensive use of nuclear arsenals, as indicated by President Carter's and Soviet Foreign Minister Andrei Gromyko's promise that their states would never be the first to use nuclear weapons in any conflict. Such commitments were not legally binding. Indeed, NATO based its "flexible response" strategy on the right to retaliate with nuclear weapons against an attack. More recently, in 1993, Russia's new strategic doctrine reserved the right to use nuclear weapons in the event of an attack. Nonetheless, these understandings undeniably help enforce great-power respect for the "no-first-use doctrine" (as do China's vocal support for the same principle and the 1995 agreement between China and Russia to stop aiming nuclear weapons at each other). Such informal rules have paved the way to creating greater institutional controls over the use of strategic weapons.

TABLE 15.2 *Continued*

Date	Agreement	Number of Parties (1995)	Principal Objectives
1986	Confidence-Building and Security-Building Measures and Disarmament in Europe (CDE) Agreement (Stockholm Accord)	29	Requires prior notification and mandatory on-site inspection of conventional military exercises in Europe
1987	Missile Technology Control Regime (MTCR)	32	Restricts export of ballistic missiles and production facilities
1990, 1992	Conventional Armed Forces in Europe (CFE)	30	Places limits on five categories of weapons in Europe and lowers force levels
1990	Confidence- and Security-Building Measures (CSBM) Agreement	53	Improves measures for exchanging detailed information on weapons, forces, and military exercises
1991	UN Register of Conventional Arms	88	Calls on all states to submit information on seven categories of major weapons exported or imported during previous year
1992	Open Skies Treaty	27	Permits flights by unarmed surveillance aircraft over the territory of the signatory states
1993	Chemical Weapons Convention (CWC)	159	Requires all stockpiles of chemical weapons to be destroyed within ten years
1995	Protocol to the Inhumane Weapons Convention	135	Bans some types of laser weapons that cause permanent loss of eyesight
1996	ASEAN Nuclear Free Zone Treaty	10	Prevents signatories in Southeast Asia from making, possessing, storing, or testing nuclear weapons
1996	Comprehensive Test Ban Treaty (CTBT)	38	If ratified, will ban all testing of nuclear weapons

SOURCE: Stockholm International Peace Research Institute (1995), 841–71; Arms Control Association Fact files.

SALT. Of the superpowers' explicit, formal arms control agreements, the two so-called Strategic Arms Limitation Talks (SALT) agreements were precedent-setting. SALT I, signed in 1972, consisted of: (1) a treaty restricting the deployment of antiballistic missile defense systems to equal and very low levels, and (2) a five-year interim accord on strategic offensive arms which restricted intercontinental ballistic missile (ICBM) and submarine-launched ballistic missile (SLBM) launchers. The SALT I agreement was essentially a confidence-building, "stopgap" step toward a longer-term, more comprehensive treaty. The 1979 SALT II agreement, then the most extensive arms control agreement ever negotiated, sought to realize that aim. The agreement called for placing an eventual overall ceiling for each superpower of 2,250 on the number of ICBM launchers, SLBM launchers, heavy bombers, and air-to-surface ballistic missiles (ASBMs) with ranges over six hundred kilometers. These limitations reduced by as many as 8,500 the total number of strategic nuclear weapons that the United States and the Soviet Union would have possessed by 1985 without the agreement.

TABLE 15.3 **Major Bilateral Arms Control Agreements between the United States and the Soviet Union/Russia**

Date	Agreement	Principal Objectives
1963	Hot Line Agreement	Establishes a direct radio and telegraph communication system between the governments to be used in times of crisis
1971	Hot Line Modernization Agreement	Puts a hot line satellite communication system into operation
1971	Nuclear Accidents Agreement	Creates a process for notification of accidental or unauthorized detonation of a nuclear weapon; creates safeguards to prevent accidents
1972	Anti-ballistic Missile (ABM) Treaty (SALT I)	Restricts the deployment of antiballistic missile defense systems to one area and prohibits the development of a space-based ABM system
1972	SALT I Interim Agreement on Offensive Strategic Arms	Freezes the superpowers' total number of ballistic missile launchers for a five-year period
1972	Protocol to the Interim Agreement	Clarifies and strengthens prior limits on strategic arms
1973	Agreement on the Prevention of Nuclear War	Requires superpowers to consult if a threat of nuclear war emerges
1974	Threshold Test Ban Treaty with Protocol	Restricts the underground testing of nuclear weapons above a yield of 150 kilotons
1974	Protocol to the ABM Treaty	Reduces permitted ABMs to one site
1976	Treaty on the Limitation of Underground Explosions for Peaceful Purposes	Broadens the ban on underground nuclear testing stipulated in the 1974 Threshold Test Ban Treaty; requires on-site observers of tests with yields exceeding 150 kilotons
1977	Convention on the Prohibition of Military or Any Other Hostile Use of Environmental Modification Techniques	Bans weapons that threaten to modify the planetary ecology
1979	SALT II Treaty (never ratified)	Places ceilings on the number of strategic delivery vehicles, MIRVed missiles, long-range bombers, cruise missiles, ICBMs, and other weapons; restrains testing
1987	Nuclear Risk Reduction Centers Agreement	Creates facilities in each national capital to manage a nuclear crisis
1987	Intermediate-range Nuclear Force (INF) Treaty	Eliminates U.S. and USSR ground-level intermediate- and shorter-range nuclear weapons in Europe and permits on-site inspection to verify compliance
1990	Chemical Weapons Destruction Agreement	Ends production of chemical weapons; commits cutting inventories of chemical weapons in half by the end of 1999 and to five thousand metric tons by the end of 2002
1990	Nuclear Testing Talks	New protocol improves verification procedures of prior treaties
1991	START (Strategic Arms Reduction Treaty)	Reduces arsenals of strategic nuclear weapons by about 30 percent
1992	START I Protocol	Holds Russia, Belarus, Ukraine, and Kazakhstan to strategic weapons reductions agreed to in START by the former USSR
1993	START II	Cuts the deployed U.S. and Russian strategic nuclear warheads on each side to between 3,000 and 3,500 by the year 2003; bans multiple-warhead land-based missiles

The obstacles to arms control were illustrated by the problems that SALT II encountered. The U.S. Senate deferred ratification of the SALT II treaty indefinitely following the 1979 Soviet invasion of Afghanistan. Although both superpowers continued to abide by the basic terms of SALT II through the early 1980s, the "final result as embodied in SALT II was a clear disappointment to the hopes generated in the early 1970s. In essence, SALT II failed to achieve actual arms reductions. Its basic fault was that it would have permitted substantial growth in the strategic forces of both sides" (U.S. Department of State 1983).

START. Against the background of what U.S. leaders labeled "the failed promise of SALT," they set the agenda for new approaches to strategic arms control.[9] In June 1982 the Reagan administration initiated a new round of arms talks aimed at significantly reducing both superpowers' strategic arsenals. Termed the Strategic Arms Reduction Talks (START), the initiative resumed the SALT process but expanded its agenda by seeking to remove inequalities that had developed in the superpowers' weapons systems.

After nine years of bargaining, the negotiators overcame their differences and concluded the START treaty, committing each side to reduce its strategic forces by one-third. Signed in July 1991, the treaty was designed to provide a baseline for future reductions in the superpowers' capabilities (recall Figure 14.1).

The Post-Cold War Disarmament Race. In September 1991, responding to widespread complaints that the START treaty barely initiated the arms reductions possible now that the threat of a Soviet attack had vanished, President Bush declared that the United States must seize "the historic opportunity now before us." Describing the Soviet Union as "no longer a realistic threat," he called long-range bombers off twenty-four-hour alert, canceled plans to deploy the long-range MX on rail cars, and offered to negotiate with the Soviets sharp reductions in the most dangerous kinds of globe-spanning missiles. Bush also proposed removing short-range nuclear weapons from U.S. bases in Europe and Asia and from U.S. Navy vessels around the world. However, Bush warned that the proposed U.S. cuts might not be made if the Soviet Union did not respond in kind. This set the stage for a showdown on a new race to *dis*arm.

The fragmentation of the Soviet Union shortly thereafter and the improved political relationship between Russia and the United States removed the major barriers to disarmament. Instructively, the disarmament process began first

---

[9]At this time, the fear inspired by the relentless arms race and frustration with the lack of progress in the arms control process caused the idea of a "nuclear freeze" on the testing, production, and deployment of nuclear weapons to gain momentum on both sides of the Atlantic. Freeze advocates were motivated by the view, expressed by one realist U.S. policymaker, that it was a "delusion" to see "nuclear weapons as just one more weapon, like any other weapon, only more destructive" (Kennan 1982). To help dispel this delusion, the American Catholic bishops composed a widely read Pastoral Letter which called for an immediate end to the arms race. It also asserted that the deliberate initiation of nuclear warfare, on however restricted a scale, could not be morally justified. As a policy proposal, a total freeze envisioned a path to disarmament that would first stop production of new weapons systems before starting to reduce the existing ones. This vision was premised on the belief that both sides' deterrent capabilities were invulnerable and that a freeze would keep them that way. Once the arms race was curtailed, it was reasoned, arms reductions could then be considered. The "nuclear freeze" movement in the early 1980s helped set the stage for the progress that occurred in the early 1990s when the Cold War no longer constrained negotiations.

through unilateral proposals and gained momentum only later through incremental accords painstakingly negotiated at the bargaining table. But when disarmament agreements finally came, they came about rapidly.

On January 25, 1992, new Russian President Boris Yeltsin declared that his country "no longer consider[ed] the United States our potential adversary." He then announced the decision to stop targeting U.S. cities with nuclear missiles, clearing the way for another U.S. response. Four days later, in his State of the Union Address, President Bush announced a series of unilateral arms cuts. Among them were the decision to suspend production of the B-2 bomber, halt development of the Midgetman mobile nuclear missile, and cease purchases of advanced cruise missiles. In addition, Bush canceled production of warheads used aboard Trident submarine missiles.

Yeltsin did not wait for his scheduled summit meeting with Bush at Camp David to reply to this initiative. Within hours, he recommended that the two powers reduce their nuclear arsenals to only two thousand to twenty-five hundred warheads each—far below the cuts called for in the START agreement and almost 50 percent greater than the reductions Bush had earlier proposed. In other statements, Yeltsin announced his intention to reduce Russian military spending to less than one-seventh of the previous year's allocation and to trim the Russian army in half. To emphasize the new climate of Russian–American friendship, Yeltsin proposed creating a joint U.S.–Russian global defense system and a new international agency to oversee the orderly reduction of nuclear weapons. He also proposed eliminating strategic nuclear weapons entirely by the year 2000.

Even in this hopeful climate of reciprocated reductions, obstacles remained to dismantling the weapons with which each superpower had threatened the existence of the other. The differences centered on where the cuts should be made. Bush called for the elimination of all land-based strategic missiles with multiple warheads (MIRVs), the category in which Russia was strongest. But on submarine-launched missiles, where the United States had the advantage, Bush refused to accept reductions beyond one-third and fought the Russian quest for across-the-board cuts.

The uncertain future of Russia's government complicated the situation further and impeded progress. Even more problematic were the nuclear arsenals of other former Soviet republics. Although Ukraine, Kazakhstan, and Belarus signed the May 1992 Lisbon protocol to the START agreement, pledging their elimination of all nuclear weapons on their territory by 1999 and their willingness to join the NPT as non-nuclear states, that full cooperation remained much in doubt. In fact, it was not forthcoming until several years later when Ukraine, Kazakhstan, and Belarus began to dismantle their strategic weapons in compliance with the spirit and letter of START.

However, even while this progress was occurring, the superpowers continued their efforts to modernize their arsenals. The former Cold War enemies planned to be heavily armed after their cuts were complete. The lack of realistic targets and the technological breakthrough of miniaturization made most of the discarded weapons obsolete. The former adversaries continued their armament modernization programs and were still militarily preparing to project power in the global arena, even with the planned cuts and while the United States was assisting the Russians in destroying their strategic arsenals.

Yet, just when it appeared that the disarmament process might lose momentum, a new breakthrough was achieved. At the June 1992 Washington summit, Presidents Yeltsin and Bush made the surprise announcement that Russia and the United States would make additional deep cuts in their strategic arsenals. The formal Joint Understanding accord to the START agreement called for a 60 percent reduction of the two powers' combined total nuclear arsenals from about fifteen thousand warheads to sixty-five hundred by the year 2003 (see Figure 15.1). Even more dramatically, this so-called "Follow-on" treaty to START reshaped the strategic landscape. Signed in January 1993, START II not only cut by three-fifths the number of actual warheads in each side's strategic arsenal that

FIGURE 15.1

Countdown to Strategic Parity: The Negotiated End of the U.S.–Russian Arms Race

After years of rapid buildup of their nuclear weapons, the United States and (now) Russia have agreed to cut dramatically the size of their nuclear arsenals.

SOURCE: Based on data from Worldwatch data diskette and Arms Control Association Fact Files.

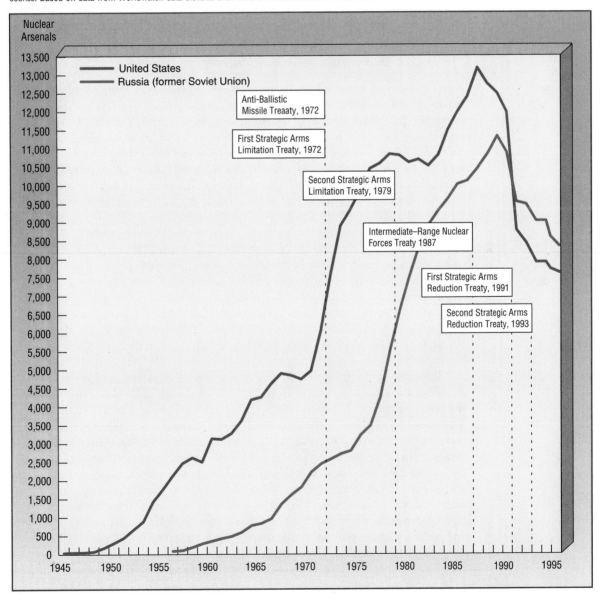

had been projected under START, but it also altered drastically the kinds of weapons in each country's arsenal. Under the agreement, Russia and the United States agreed to give up all the multiple warheads on their land-based ICBM missiles. Specifically, by banning all MIRVed ICBMs and reducing SLBM warheads to no more than 1,750, the new agreement "promised a significant enhancement of U.S.-Russian strategic stability since these missiles have long been seen as the most threatening because of their preemptive capabilities" (Keeny 1993).

If adhered to, the Follow-on START agreement could reduce the chances of a war of annihilation by banning the nuclear weapons that both powers would be most likely to use in a preemptive strike. The agreement would leave them with only those weapons they would be likely to use in a retaliatory strike. By reducing the probability of a nuclear war, the agreement thus signaled the potential dawning of a new era. As President Bush put it, "With this agreement the nuclear nightmare recedes more and more for ourselves, for our children, and for our grandchildren." President Yeltsin concurred, noting that, "we are departing from the ominous parity where each country was exerting every effort to keep up."

The Problematic Future of Arms Control

As promising as some of the great powers' recent arms control agreements might appear, the history of their past negotiations testifies to the many obstacles that exist to arms control agreements. It also attests to the extent to which they are dependent on prior improvement in adversaries' political relations. That history raises questions as to whether arms control agreements can restrain the arms race in the long run. After all, these obstacles could resurface in a new multipolar system characterized by rivalry among five or more great powers and a potentially large number of new nuclear-weapon states.

Until recently, it could be said that "the weapons prohibited had little, if any, military importance, and the outlawed activities [had] never been seriously contemplated as methods of war" (Goldblat 1982). The international agreements controlled only obsolete armaments or ones that the parties to the agreements had little incentive for developing in the first place. Do states purposely leave the most threatening problems outside negotiations and seek only to control the insignificant ones? Several indicators suggest that states rarely take arms control seriously when they perceive their survival to be at stake.

Consider first the disregard that some signatories to agreements demonstrate toward them. Twelve instances of chemical and biological warfare allegedly occurred between 1975 and 1981, violating the 1972 Biological Weapons Convention (Goldblat 1982, 100). Included among the allegations were Vietnam's use of poison gas against China (1979), U.S. use of chemical weapons in covert actions in Cuba (1978–1981), Iraq's use of "chemical bombs" in occupied Iranian territory (1980), and Soviet use of lethal chemical weapons in Laos and Afghanistan over prolonged periods in such quantities as to produce a toxic "yellow rain." Violations of the Chemical Weapons Convention (CWC) continue: In May 1993 the United States claimed that at least twenty-four states had developed a chemical-weapons capability (Stock and De Geer 1994, 315)—which suggests a broader lesson, that there "is no substitute for eternal vigilance and the will to deal with rule breakers" (*The Economist* 338 [February 10, 1996]: 37).

Second, the testing of nuclear weapons also speaks to the tendency of states to make improving their weaponry a priority over controlling it. The six known nuclear states conducted 2,046 nuclear explosions between 1945 and 1995 (*Bulletin of the Atomic Scientists*, 52 [May/June 1996]: 62), an average of one test almost every nine days. The pace did not slow as a result of the partial test ban treaty of 1963, which prohibited atmospheric and underwater testing but not underground explosions.[10] In fact, three-fourths of all nuclear tests took place after the ban went into effect in 1963. Disclosures by the U.S. government in December 1993 revealed 204 previously unannounced secret nuclear-weapons tests above the 1,030 officially reported tests between 1945 and 1994. Some of these resulted in accidental releases of radioactive gases into the atmosphere. Energy Secretary Hazel R. O'Leary described the arms race cult by lamenting that "We were shrouded and clouded in an atmosphere of secrecy that compromised safety and environmental considerations. . . . I would call it repression."

Third, recall that the Nuclear Nonproliferation Treaty (NPT) of 1968 obligates the non-nuclear countries to refrain from manufacturing or acquiring nuclear weapons. Adherence to the agreement has been widespread, with 181 states in 1996 members of the arms control regime. However, India, Israel and Pakistan broke the barriers the NPT sought to create by becoming *de facto* nuclear-weapon states capable of producing nuclear weapons on short notice, and Iraq, Iran, Libya and North Korea remain outside the treaty and are suspected of having ambitions to become nuclear-weapon states. In addition, even the existing nuclear states have sought to develop ever more imposing arsenals at the same time they were reducing the size of their arsenals, as indicated by the fact that while the United States began eliminating some of its warheads, since 1990 it increased the number of Trident II warheads by 960 (*Harper's*, 292 [March 1996]: 13). Given their historic appetite for expanded strategic inventories, it is understandable that the non-nuclear members of the NPT question why they should remain restrained while the existing nuclear states refuse to destroy their nuclear arsenals.

Finally, consider the sobering lessons suggested by the SALT agreements. SALT I did freeze the number of strategic launchers in operation or under construction but did not cover strategic bombers or prevent the kinds of qualitative improvements that would make quantitative thresholds meaningless. For instance, the superpowers deployed four times as many multiple independently targetable warheads (MIRVs) on missiles in 1977 as when the SALT talks began, even though SALT I froze the number of delivery vehicles at the superpowers' disposal. Perhaps this troublesome outcome led Herbert Scoville, a former deputy director of the U.S. Central Intelligence Agency, to note at the time of the signing of SALT I that "arms control negotiations [were] rapidly becoming the best excuse for escalating rather than toning down the arms race." The

---

[10]Testing continued even in the wake of the Cold War. This is evidenced by the United States having conducted seven nuclear tests in 1991 and six in 1992, and France, the United Kingdom, and China collectively having conducted another nineteen tests between 1991 and 1996. In August 1995, after the Pentagon proposed a resumption of underground nuclear tests in July, President Clinton announced the suspension of the U.S. nuclear testing program. In September 1995, however, France resumed its nuclear testing in the South Pacific—a step that was suspended (after six tests) in February 1996 after the tests were vocally criticized throughout the world. Declaring "a new chapter is opening," French President Jacques Chirac announced that hereafter France "would play an active and determined role for disarmament in the world." This set the stage for the 1996 negotiations among thirty-eight members of the Conference on Disarmament for the Comprehensive Test Ban Treaty (CTBT).

pattern revealed in this and other developments prompted one former U.S. policymaker to conclude that "three decades of U.S.–Soviet negotiations to limit arms competition have done little more than to codify the arms race" (Gelb 1979). This grim conclusion is validated by the existence in 1996 of eight nuclear powers whose combined strategic and tactical nuclear inventories numbered "at least 40,000 weapons" (Burroughs and Cabasso 1996, 41).

These Cold War experiences created doubt about the ability of agreements to control the size and dispersion of weapons, let alone bring rules to restrict use of the wide range of novel new weapons and non-lethal weapons now on the drawing board (see Focus 15.3). What is more, with "the case for cutting nuclear weapons as strong as ever," and with acceptance of the fact during the Cold War "that the nuclear balance would be firmer and cheaper to maintain with fewer weapons, not more," why is it that START II did not go further? Why couldn't the superpowers "finish what they STARTED"? (*The Economist* 338 [January 27, 1996]: 17). Why do states often take decisions to arm that apparently imprison them in the grip of perpetual insecurity? On the surface, the incentives for meaningful arms control seem numerous. Significant controls would save money, reduce tension and hence the dangers of war, symbolize leaders' desire for peace, lessen health hazards, reduce the environmental hazards of nuclear waste, diminish the potential destructiveness of war, dampen the incentive for one state to seek a power advantage over others, reduce the possibility of being the target of a preemptive attack, and achieve a propaganda advantage for those advocating peace. To these we can add moral satisfaction and the opportunity to live in a less-threatening global environment.

However, states did not—and perhaps still do not—control significantly the growth of arms. There are many reasons to rely on military preparedness as a path to peace; they stem from the fear that is endemic to international anarchy. Most countries are reluctant to engage in arms limitations in a self-help system that requires each state to protect itself. Thus states find themselves caught in a vicious circle of fear. This creates the *security dilemma*—a condition that is in no actor's interest but which permits no easy escape. Its influence on behavior is potent and helps explain why throughout the Cold War military establishments subscribed to two basic principles: "(1) 'Don't negotiate when you are behind. Why accept a permanent position of number two?' and (2) 'Don't negotiate when you are ahead. Why accept a freeze in an area of military competition when the other side has not kept up with you?'" (Barnet 1977). The result of this syndrome is clear: When fearful states abide by the axiom that they should never negotiate from a position of weakness, then they are left with no option but to refuse to negotiate.

Arms bargaining is a game of give and take, but all participants typically want to take much and give little. As a result, with the powerful restraining impact of domestic politics on the negotiation process (see Caldwell 1991),[11] it

---

[11]Many people benefit financially from the perpetuation of arms races and lobby against arms agreements because they can lose their jobs by an abatement of military spending. Military-industrial complexes (see Rosen 1973; Markusen and Yudken 1992; Paget 1995) exist in all societies whose influence is tied to high defense spending. The resistance of military planners and defense specialists to reductions in arsenals even in the wake of the Cold War attests to the continuing penchant of defense experts and arms manufacturers to insist that "prudence" dictates preparing for the worst contingency by retaining military preparedness at as high a level as possible. "The business of defense is defending business" is the way one analyst summarized the problem (Mulhollin 1994).

Can Arms Agreements Control the Next Generation of Weapons?

Although the 1991 Persian Gulf War involved six hundred thousand troops, with new high-tech weapons, the conflict ended with a victory that involved only 148 combat deaths. This has instilled confidence that future wars will involve "clean combat," which—like a video-arcade game—will convey the impression that war is not dirty. Nonetheless, General John Shalikashvili, Chairman of the U.S. Joint Chiefs of Staff, warned in 1995 that the hope of a new generation of new "nonlethal weapons" is an illusion: "It is that somehow you can make combat surgical and clean and pristine. And you cannot. Combat . . . is dirty and painful, and casualties are almost a natural by-product."

War might be made to appear more acceptable in the public eye as stealth technology, pilotless combat airplanes, and electronic warfare keep killing from view. The new robotic and laser weapons offer little protection to innocent noncombatants (e.g., civilians, clergy, children) who easily can become the targets. In 1995 the United States had plans to develop an antipersonnel weapon known as the Laser Countermeasure, based on a secret technology that was "cruel and inhumane even by the standards of war. It is a forty-pound portable gun that fires a beam powerful enough to burn out human retinas from up to three thousand feet away" (Arkin 1995). By blinding people—so the rationale for the construction of this and other equally awesome new weapons goes—war could be made safe for the attacker.

Is the rationale sound? Who will protect us all from ruthless aggressors using such weapons as these instruments of violence spread to terrorists and governments unrestrained by moral compassions (as they surely will on the covert arms market)? Concerns such as these reduce confidence in the ability of the world to control the armament innovations that advanced technology makes possible, despite the "surprising" 1996 agreement to ban the use (but not the production) of some types of blinding laser weapons (Wurst 1996).

is little wonder that meaningful agreements are so hard to achieve and that states develop weapons systems as bargaining chips for future negotiations.

Arms control still remains a murky policy area. Proposing to modify the 1972 Anti-ballistic Missile Treaty between the United States and the former Soviet Union, the Clinton administration in 1994 sought to further develop Thaad—a heat-seeking interceptor system capable of shooting down medium-range enemy missiles. While arms control groups criticized the proposal and accused it of undermining previous arms control agreements, administration officials argued that "the greater danger is not a superpower arms race but rather Third World governments with shorter-range and medium-range missiles" (Gordon, 1993b) and the efforts of some countries to develop "computer viruses to disrupt [an enemy's] command and control systems" (Cetron with Davies 1994). Thus future arms control may be undermined by a shifting playing field and the increasing military capabilities of developing countries in the Global South. This is especially true inasmuch as "the International Atomic Energy Agency (IAEA), the world's primary means of monitoring clandestine nuclear programs worldwide, remains chronically starved for funding at $60 million and has even been forced to cut inspections" (Sommer 1994, 23).

Clearly, then, we should not expect too much of arms control or exaggerate its potential. As one expert concludes,

> The history of the postwar era proves that arms control, if pursued wisely and properly, can reduce the threat; it can never eliminate the risk of war altogether. Arms control is not a substitute for weapons but a complement

to them. Arms and arms control, one by creating the means to inflict unacceptable damage on a potential enemy and the other by protecting that capability from enemy attack, are both necessary for national security. A defense policy that fails to pursue the two together, that emphasizes one approach to the exclusion of the other, is dangerous and incomplete. . . .

True international security depends not as much on arms or arms control as on reducing as much as possible the sources of conflict in international relations and on finding effective nonviolent means of resolving the conflicts that remain. (Kruzel 1991, 268)

• • •

MILITARY POWER AND THE SEARCH FOR PEACE

The obstacles to the control of arms are formidable. The idea that a disarmed world would be a more secure one does not have the force of history behind it, whereas the realist idea that military preparedness produces security does. As long as aggressive states exist, it would be imprudent to disarm. Arms control does not solve the basic problem of rivalry between states, because as long as states have and can use weapons, such agreements are little more than cooperative arrangements between adversaries. They define the competition and confine the potential destruction that war brings but do not remove the *source* of the conflict.

Alternatively, managing political conflicts without violence may be the key to arms control. Arms, after all, are less causes of war than symptoms of political tension: People "do not fight because they have arms. They have arms because [they are afraid and] they deem it necessary to fight" (Morgenthau 1985). From this perspective, controlling arms is contingent on removing the fears that underlie states' conflicts. The quest for national security in an anarchical world springs from states' fear of one another. Yet, because one country's security makes others insecure, nearly all states prepare for war to defend themselves. In this sense the realists' military paths to peace discussed in this chapter are intimately related to the widespread quest for armaments described in Chapter 13.

Still at issue, however, is whether world security is served by states' military search for their own national security. Perhaps the forces that propel the pursuit of peace and security through military might have sown the seeds of the world's destruction. Nothing makes the search for peace through political means more compelling. Hope may be inspired by the observations of former U.S. Secretary of Defense Robert McNamara: "We have reached the present dangerous and absurd confrontation by a long series of steps, many of which seemed rational in their time. Step by step we can undo much of the damage."

We turn in Chapter 16 to examine some proposals recommended especially by liberal theorists for preventing the damage that armed conflict causes.

KEY TERMS

alliances

balance of power

nonalignment

balancer

preemption

balance of terror

polarity

polarization

North Atlantic Treaty Organization
(NATO)

bipolycentrism

polycentrism

intercontinental ballistic missiles
(ICBMs)

North Atlantic Cooperation Council
(NACC)

bandwagon

Partnership for Peace (PFP)

arms control

disarmament

bilateral arms control agreements

multilateral arms control agreements

Baruch Plan

Rapacki Plan

Mutual and Balanced Force Reductions
(MBFR) Talks

Comprehensive Test Ban (CTB)

Conventional Armed Forces in Europe
(CFE) treaty

Organization for Security and
Cooperation in Europe (OSCE)

Nuclear nonproliferation Treaty (NPT)

Conference on Disarmament (CD)

Biological Weapons Convention (BWC)

Chemical Weapons Convention (CWC)

Missile Technology Control Regime
(MTCR)

UN Register of Conventional Arms

Liberal Paths to Peace: International Law, Organization, Integration, and Democratization

OUTLINE

We cannot "go it alone." In fact, no one can. International cooperation is needed to make this world a livable place.

—Willem Kok,
Prime Minister, The Netherlands, 1995

My first axiom: The quest for international security involves the unconditional surrender by every nation, in a certain measure, of its liberty of action, its sovereignty that is to say, and it is clear beyond all doubt that no other road can lead to such security.

—Albert Einstein,
German-born Swiss-American Scientist, 1932

Since antiquity, the world has pursued two primary paths to peace. The realist road emphasizes *military* solutions; the liberal road emphasizes *political* solutions. In this chapter we examine four principal approaches to the control of armed conflict from the liberal theoretical tradition: international law, organization, integration, and democratization (see Table 16.1). Because all four stress institutions, the new advocates of these liberal-idealist paths are sometimes referred to collectively as "neoliberal institutionalists" (Grieco 1995).

• • •

INTERNATIONAL LAW AND WORLD ORDER

In 1984, the United States announced that it would unilaterally withdraw from the World Court's jurisdiction. This followed disputes with several Central American countries after Nicaragua's accusation that the U.S. Central Intelligence Agency had illegally attempted to "overthrow and destabilize" the elected Sandinista government. Nicaragua charged that the United States had illegally mined its ports and supplied money, military assistance, and training to the rebel *contra* forces. The United States denied the tribunal's authority. In so doing, however, it was not acting without precedent; others had done so previously. Nonetheless, by thumbing its nose at the court and the rule of law it represents, had it, as some claimed, become an "international outlaw?"[1] Or, as others asserted, had it acted within its rights?

The World Court supported the former view. In 1984, the court ruled as follows:

> The right to sovereignty and to political independence possessed by the Republic of Nicaragua, like any other state of the region or of the world, should be fully respected and should not in any way be jeopardized by any

---

[1]The American Society of International Law voted overwhelmingly in 1984 to urge the United States to reverse its decision. Harvard law professor Abram Chayes (who earlier in his career provided the legal defense of the Kennedy administration's naval quarantine of Cuba during the 1962 missile crisis) represented Nicaragua in its suit against the United States. Believing that the Nicaraguan leaders were acting "to uphold the rule of law in international affairs," Chayes stated that he thought it appropriate for the United States, which "purports to be bound by the rule of law," to be judged under "appropriate international procedures." He asserted that "there is nothing wrong with holding the United States to its own best standards and best principles" (*New York Times*, April 11, 1983).

479

TABLE 16.1   Some Liberal Idealist Paths to International Security

Prescription	Premise
Provide states rules of international law to regulate competition.	"Interstate cooperation can be encouraged by creating rules for peaceful interaction."
Participate in the creation of international organizations.	"If you want peace, prepare global institutions to keep it."
Practice collaboration to bind independent states together in integrated security communities.	"Interdependence makes imperative the amalgamation of states, not their division."
Promote the spread of democratic governance.	"Countries that protect their own citizens' civil liberties do not wage war against other governments that also protect their citizens' human rights."
Prepare rules to facilitate free trade.	"Trade protectionism is counterproductive to prosperity and peace."
Produce agreements to reduce armaments to levels that discourage war.	"States get what they plan for—beat swords into plowshares."
Provide humanitarian assistance to the impoverished.	"Rich states can only help themselves by helping poor people also."
Principles are more important than power.	"Recognize the rewards of higher principles to one's self, such as *reciprocity*, or the Golden Rule to do unto others as you would have them do unto you."

military and paramilitary activities which are prohibited by the principles of international law, in particular the principle that states should refrain in their international relations from the threat or the use of force against the territorial integrity or the political independence of any state, and the principle concerning the duty not to intervene in matters within the domestic jurisdiction of a state. (*New York Times*, May 11, 1984, 8)

Yet this ruling had little effect, as neither the court nor Nicaragua had anyone to enforce it. Events such as this have led many critics to conclude that international law is "weak and defenseless" (Fried 1971). Indeed, many experts— whether they are realists or liberal idealists—skeptically ask whether international law is really law.

There are many reasons to answer this question affirmatively. Although international law is imperfect, actors regularly rely on it to redress grievances (see Joyner 1995; von Glahn 1996). Most of this activity falls within the realms of **private international law**—the regulation of routine transnational activities in such areas as commerce, communications, and travel. While largely invisible to the public, private international law is the locus for all but a small fraction of international legal activities. It is where the majority of transnational disputes are regularly settled and where the record of compliance compares favorably with that achieved in domestic legal systems (Brownlie 1990).

In contrast, **public international law** addresses government-to-government relations, and thus captures the headlines. It also captures most of the criticism; for here, failures—when they occur—are quite conspicuous. This is especially true with respect to the breakdown of peace and security. When states engage in armed conflict, criticism of its shortcomings also escalates. Consider Israeli Ambassador Abba Eban's lament that "international law is that law which the wicked do not obey and the righteous do not enforce."

Because this chapter examines the capacity of public international law to control war, our discussion will address only the laws and institutional machinery created to manage armed conflict between states. That is, it will explore that segment of public international law popularly regarded as the most deficient.

Law at the International Level: Core Principles

Public international law is usually defined as rules that govern the conduct of states in their relations with one another. The *corpus juris gentium* (the body of the law of nations) has grown considerably over the past three centuries, changing in response to transformations in international politics (Kaplan and Katzenbach 1961). An inventory of the basic legal principles relevant to the control of war clarifies the international system's character (for authoritative texts, see Higgins 1994: von Glahn 1996).

The Rules of International Law. No principle of international law is more critical than state sovereignty. *Sovereignty* means that no authority is legally above the state, except that which the state voluntarily confers on the international organizations it joins. In fact, international law "permits a complete freedom of action" (Parry 1968) of states to preserve their sovereign independence.

Enraged by the inhumane international conditions he witnessed during his lifetime, Dutch reformer Hugo Grotius (1583–1645) wrote *De Jure Belli et Pacis* (*On the Law of War and Peace*) in 1625. His treatise called on the great powers to resolve their conflicts by judicial procedures rather than on the battlefield, and specified the legal principles he felt could encourage cooperation, peace, and more humane treatment of people. Grotius consequently became known as the "founder of international law."

Nearly every legal doctrine supports and extends the cardinal principle that states are the primary subjects of international law. Although the Universal Declaration of Human Rights in 1948 expanded concern about states' treatment of individual people, states remain supreme. "Laws are made to protect the state from the individual and not the individual from the state" (Gottlieb 1982). Accordingly, the vast majority of rules address the rights and duties of states, not people. For instance, the principle of **sovereign equality** entitles each state to full respect by other states as well as equal protection by the system's legal rules. The right of independence also guarantees states' autonomy in their domestic affairs and external relations, under the logic that the independence of each presumes that of all. Similarly, the doctrine of **neutrality** permits states to avoid involvement in others' conflicts and coalitions.

Furthermore, the noninterference principle forms the basis for **nonintervention**—that is, states' duty to refrain from uninvited involvement in another's internal affairs. This sometimes abused classic rule gives governments the right to exercise jurisdiction over practically all things on, under, or above their bounded territory. (There are exceptions, however, such as **diplomatic immunity** for states' ambassadors from the domestic laws of the country where their embassies are located, and **extraterritoriality,** which allows control of embassies on other states' terrain. Nonetheless, the principle of territorial integrity remains sacrosanct.)

In practice, domestic jurisdiction permits a state to enact and enforce whatever laws it wishes for its own citizens, including the rules for citizenship.[2] A state can create whatever form of government it desires without regard to its acceptability to other states.[3] It also has freedom to regulate economic transactions within its boundaries and is empowered to draft those living on its soil into its armed forces to fight—and die, if necessary—to defend the state.

The Montevideo Convention of 1933 on the Rights and Duties of States summarizes the major components of **statehood.** A state must possess a permanent population, a well-defined territory, and a government capable of ruling its citizens and of managing formal diplomatic relations with other states. Other rules specify how and when these conditions are satisfied. Essentially, the acquisition of statehood depends on a political entity's recognition as such by other states. Whether a state exists thus rests in the hands of other states; that is, preexisting states are entitled to extend **diplomatic recognition** to another entity. **De facto recognition** is provisional and capable of being withdrawn in the event that the recognized government is superseded by another. It does not carry with it the exchange of diplomatic representatives or other legal benefits and responsibilities. The government that is recognized **de jure,** on the other hand, obtains full legal and diplomatic privileges from the granting state. This

---

[2]Prior to 1952 "there was no precedent in international law for a . . . . state to assume responsibility for the crimes it committed against a minority within its jurisdiction" (Wise 1993). A citizen was not protected against the state's abuse of human rights. Note that two basic principles govern the way nationality and citizenship are conferred. Under *jus soli*, citizenship is determined by the state on whose territory the birth took place. Under *jus sanguinis*, nationality is acquired by descent from a parent who is a national. Some states recognize a combination of these conventions.

[3]This principle dates from the earliest periods of modern international law. It was expressed in the Treaty of Augsburg (1515) and the Westphalian Treaties (1648), and was reaffirmed in the 1943 Atlantic Charter's pledge of "the right of all people to choose the form of government under which they will live." However, this rule has recently undergone an erosion, and the right of people to live under the liberties of democracy is increasingly being defined as an "entitlement" or a basic human right (Franck 1994; also von Glahn 1996).

distinction emphasizes that recognition is a political tool of international law, through which approval or disapproval of a government can be expressed.

Today, with the exception of Antarctica, which is administered jointly by several states and is outside the jurisdiction of any one of them, no significant land mass remains *terra nullius* (territory belonging legally to no one). Because nearly all of the earth's land surfaces are now within some state's sovereign control, the birth of a new state must necessarily be at the expense of an existing one. Thus, the recognition of a new state almost always means the recognition of a new government's control over a particular territory. Because recognition is a voluntary political act, **nonrecognition** is a legally institutionalized form of public insult to a government aspiring to be accepted as legitimate by other governments. It may be seen as a form of sanction against an unwanted political regime.

States are free to enter into treaty arrangements with other states. Rules specify how treaties are to be activated, interpreted, and abrogated. International law holds that treaties voluntarily entered into are binding (*pacta sunt servanda*). However, it also reserves for states the right unilaterally to terminate treaties previously agreed to, by reference to the escape clause known as *rebus sic stantibus*. This is the principle that a treaty is binding only as long as no fundamental change occurs in the circumstances that existed when it was concluded.

Procedures for Dispute Settlement. In addition to these general principles, international law provides a wide variety of legal methods for states to resolve their conflicts. The laws of negotiation do not obligate states to reach agreement or to settle their disputes peacefully. They do, however, provide rules for several conflict resolution procedures, including:

- **Mediation:** when a third party proposes a nonbinding solution to a controversy between two other states, as illustrated by U.S. President Carter's historic mediation at the 1978 Camp David meeting between Egypt and Israel.
- **Good offices:** when a third party offers a location for discussions among disputants but does not participate in the actual negotiations, as Switzerland often does.
- **Conciliation:** when a third party assists both sides but does not offer any solution.
- **Arbitration:** when a third party gives a binding decision through an ad hoc forum.
- **Adjudication:** when a third party offers a binding decision through an institutionalized tribunal, such as a court.

The Institutional Limitations of the International Legal System

Sovereignty and the legal principles derived from it shape and reinforce international anarchy. The nature of world politics is legally dependent on what governments choose to do with one another and the kinds of rules they voluntarily support. It is a legal system by and for states, which is often seen by liberal reformers as a serious flaw undermining the effectiveness of international law (see Focus 16.1).

Beyond the barriers to legal institutions that sovereignty poses, still other weaknesses reduce confidence in the capacity of international law to regulate relations between states and control armed conflict. Critics and reformers usually cite these alleged deficiencies:

The Institutional Deficiencies of International Law

Many theorists consider the international legal system institutionally defective due to its dependence on the attitudes and behaviors of those it governs. Because formal legal institutions (like those within states) are weak at the international level, critics make the following points.

First, in world politics no legislative body exists capable of making binding laws. Rules are made only when states willingly observe or embrace them in the treaties to which they voluntarily subscribe. There is no systematic method of amending or revoking them. Article 38 of the Statute of the International Court of Justice (or World Court) affirms this. Generally accepted as the authoritative definition of the "sources of international law," it states that international law derives from (1) custom, (2) international treaties and agreements, (3) national and international court decisions, (4) the writings of legal authorities and specialists, and (5) the "general principles" of law recognized since the Roman Empire as part of "natural law" and "right reason."

Second, in world politics no authoritative judicial body has power to identify the rules accepted by states, record the sub-stantive precepts reached, interpret when and how the rules apply, and identify violations. Instead, states are responsible for performing these tasks themselves. The World Court does not have the power to perform these functions without states' consent.

Finally, in world politics there is no executive body capable of enforcing the rules. Rule enforcement usually occurs through the self-help actions of the victims of a transgression or with the assistance of their allies or other interested parties. No centralized enforcement procedures exist, and compliance is voluntary. The whole system rests, therefore, on states' willingness to abide by the rules to which they consent and on the ability of each to enforce through retaliatory measures the norms of behavior they value.

Consequently, states themselves—not a higher authority—determine what the rules are, when they apply, and how they should be enforced. This raises the question: When everyone is above the law, is anyone ruled by it?

- *International law lacks universality.* An effective legal system must represent the norms shared by those it governs. According to the precept of Roman law, *ubi societas, ibi jus* (where there is society, there is law), shared community values are a minimal precondition for forming a legal system. Yet the contemporary international order is culturally and ideologically pluralistic and lacks consensus on common values. Although some claim the Western-based international legal order approximates universality, state practice and the simultaneous operation of often incompatible legal traditions throughout the world contradict this claim (Bozeman 1994).

- *International law justifies the competitive pursuit of national advantage without regard to morality or justice.* As in any legal system, in international politics the legal thing to do is not necessarily the moral thing to do (see Nardin 1983). In fact, international law legitimizes the drive for hegemony and contributes to conflict (Lissitzyn 1963). Self-help does not control power; it is a concession to power. By accepting the view that the unbridled autonomy of sovereign independence is sacrosanct, international law follows the realists' "iron law of politics"—that legal obligations must yield to the national interest (Morgenthau 1985).

- *International law is an instrument of the powerful to oppress the weak.* In a voluntary consent system, the rules to which the powerful willingly agree are those that serve their interests. These rules therefore preserve

484

the existing hierarchy (Friedheim 1965). For this reason, some liberal theorists claim that international law has traditionally bred the so-called **structural violence** resulting from the hierarchical organization of world politics in which the strong benefit at the expense of the weak (Galtung 1969). Enforcement is left "to the vicissitudes of the distribution of power between the violator of the law and the victim of the violation." Therefore, the political scientist Hans J. Morgenthau (1985) concedes, "it makes it easy for the strong both to violate the law and to enforce it, and consequently puts the rights of the weak in jeopardy. A great power can violate the rights of a small nation without having to fear effective sanctions on the latter's part."

- *International law is little more than a justification of existing practices*. When a particular behavior pattern becomes widespread, it becomes legally obligatory; rules *of* behavior become rules *for* behavior (Hoffmann 1971). International law is a codification of custom. The eminent legal scholar Hans Kelsen's contention that states ought to behave as they customarily have behaved (see Onuf 1982) and E. Adamson Hoebel's (1961) dictum that "what the most do, others should do" reflect the positivist legal theory that when a type of behavior occurs frequently it becomes legal.[4] The dependence of rules on *custom* means that the actions of states shape law, not vice versa.

- *International law's ambiguity reduces law to a policy tool for propaganda purposes*. The vague, elastic wording of international law makes it easy for states to define and interpret almost any action as legitimate. "The problem here," observes Samuel S. Kim (1991), "is the lack of clarity and coherence [that enables] international law [to be] easily stretched, . . . to be a flexible fig leaf or a propaganda instrument." This ambivalence makes it possible for states to exploit international law to get what they can and to justify what they have obtained (Wright 1953).

These deficiencies illustrate but do not exhaust the international legal order's alleged inadequacies. Critics conclude that international law is least developed in the state system's most critical realm: where national security is at stake when the threat of armed conflict arises.

The Relevance of International Law

International law is fraught with deficiencies. Still, we can question the proposition that it is irrelevant to contemporary international politics. States themselves do not deem public international law irrelevant. They attach considerable importance to it and expend considerable time and energy fighting over its interpretation while attempting to shape its evolution. If law were meaningless, we would not be able to point to the existence of a systematic code of rules repeatedly affirmed by states in multilateral agreements, resolutions, and

---

[4]Positivist legal theorists stress states' customs as the most important source from which laws derive. In the absence of formal machinery for creating international rules, for evidence of what the law is, positivists observe leaders' foreign policy pronouncements, repeated usage in conventions voluntarily accepted by states, general practices (by an overwhelmingly large number of states), the judicial decisions of national and international tribunals, and legal principles stated in the resolutions of multinational assemblies such as the UN General Assembly.

declarations (Jones 1991). These instrumentalities reflect state opinion and show that there *are* basic principles that states formally recognize and agree to respect.

"The reality as demonstrated through their behavior," legal scholar Christopher Joyner (1995) observes, "is that states do accept international law as law and, even more significant, in the vast majority of instances they . . . . obey it." The major reason states practice self-restraint is because even the most powerful states appreciate its benefits. International reputations are important. Those who play the game of international politics by recognized rules receive rewards, whereas states which ignore international law or who opportunistically break customary norms pay costs for doing as they please. For instance, other countries will be reluctant to cooperate with them. They also must fear reprisals and retaliation by those victimized, as well as the loss of prestige. For this reason only the most ambitious or reckless state is apt to disregard accepted standards of conduct flagrantly.

A primary reason why states value international law and affirm their commitment to it is that they need a common understanding of the "rules of the game." International law is an "institutional device for communicating to the policymakers of various states a consensus on the nature of the international system" (Coplin 1965). Law helps shape expectations, and rules reduce uncertainty and enhance predictability in international affairs. These communication functions serve every member of the international system. The benefits they confer explain why states usually support international law and voluntarily accommodate their actions and policies to it.

While the members of the state systems usually agree on certain general values, they often fail to recognize the responsibilities these values create for their own behavior (Coplin 1966). Thus it is tempting to agree with critics who assert that the lack of a centralized authority with supranational sanctioning powers makes international law useless for its most important function—the control of violence. This conclusion is questionable, however, as it stems from the misleading comparison critics often draw between the international legal order's primitive institutions and states' highly centralized domestic legal systems. Comparison invites the mistaken conclusion that a formal legal structure (a centralized, "vertical system of law") is automatically superior to a decentralized, self-help, "horizontal system of law." The organizational differences between domestic (municipal) and international legal systems hide similarities and obscure the key question: Which type of legal order is more effective?

Evidence shows that unorganized or primitive legal systems succeed in containing violence and ensuring compliance with rules (see Masters 1969). Even in systems without the kinds of institutionalized procedures typically found in municipal legal systems for punishing rule violation (such as tribal societies without formal governments), sanctions often operate effectively (Barkun 1968). Thus we should not be surprised to learn that "international law is not violated more often, or to a higher degree, than the law of other systems" (Joyner 1995). The historical record demonstrates that states regularly have resolved their differences through legal procedures. Of 97 interstate conflicts between 1919 and 1986, we observe no less than 168 attempts by the contending parties to negotiate, mediate, adjudicate, or otherwise settle their disputes through formal procedures of conflict resolution. More impressively, 68 of these attempts were successful (Holsti 1988, 420). In other words, since

World War I states have been able to resolve their differences 70 percent of the time by using one or more pacific settlement procedures.

It is also clear that formal institutions for rule enforcement do not guarantee rule compliance. No legal system can deter all of its members from breaking existing laws. Consequently it is a mistake to expect a legal system to prevent all criminal behavior or to assert that any violation of the law proves the inadequacy of the legal structure. Law is designed to deter crime, but it is unreasonable to expect it to prevent it.

Similarly, we should not view every breakdown of international law as confirming general lawlessness. Conditions of crisis strain all legal systems, and few, when tested severely, can contain all violence. Since 1500, more people have died from civil wars than from wars between sovereign states (Sivard 1991). Today, with street crime in cities worldwide at epidemic proportions and ethnonational warfare within countries exacting a deadly toll against hundreds of minority groups (Gurr 1995), states' domestic legal systems are patently failing to prevent killing. Thus, the allegedly "deficient" international legal system performs its primary job—inhibiting violence—more effectively than the supposedly more sophisticated domestic systems. Perhaps, then, the usual criteria by which critics assess legal systems are dubious. Should they be less concerned with structures and institutions, and more with performance?

Even the most skeptical of theorists who claim that leaders act without consideration of the rules must acknowledge that legal norms help to order the process of bargaining and the formation of **security regimes**—sets of rules to contain armed conflict (see Jervis 1982; Stein 1993). At the onset of militarized disputes, law "serves as a sort of signal to tell states which of these clashes are acceptable and which are deserving of retaliation" (D'Amato 1982). Once a crisis erupts, rules eliminate the need to decide on a procedure for deciding.

At another level, public international law makes possible the routine transactions otherwise governed by private international law in such activities as international trade, foreign travel, mail flows, currency exchange, environmental protection, and debt obligations. Parties to the *regimes*, or rules for cooperative exchanges, in these areas regard them as binding and abide by their provisions (Kim 1991; Soroos 1986). Arguably, by removing disputes from possible resolution by armed force, international law reduces the sources of aggression. This helps make an anarchical world an orderly world.

The Legal Control of Warfare

Liberal reformers often complain that law clearly fails in the realm of behavior most resistant to legal control—the management of conflict. If under international law, as fashioned by realist leaders, states are "legally bound to respect each other's independence and other rights, and yet free to attack each other at will" (Brierly 1944), international law may actually encourage war. The ethical and jurisprudential **just war doctrine** from which the laws of war stem shape discussions of contemporary public international law (see Focus 16.2).

Throughout history, international law has evolved in response to changing global conditions. We will illustrate this by reviewing changes in the rules for war's initiation and the means for waging it.

The Just War Doctrine
Ethical Perspectives on Violence

Many people are confused by international law because it both prohibits and justifies the use of force. The confusion derives from the just war tradition in "Christian realism," in which the rules of war are philosophically based. In the fourth century, St. Augustine questioned the strict view that those who take another's life to defend the state necessarily violate the commandment "Thou shalt not kill." He counseled that "it is the wrong-doing of the opposing party which compels the wise man to wage just wars." The Christian was obligated, he felt, to fight against evil and wickedness. To St. Augustine, the City of Man was sinful, in contrast to the City of God; in the secular world it was sometimes permissible to kill.

From this perspective evolved the modern just war doctrine as developed by such medieval secularists as Hugo Grotius, who challenged the warring Catholic and Protestant Christian powers to abide by humane standards of conduct. The just war doctrine consists of two categories of argumentation, *jus ad bellum* (the justice *of* a war) and *jus in bello* (justice *in* a war). The former sets the criteria by which a political leader may determine whether a war should be waged. The latter specifies restraints on the range of permissible tactics to be used in fighting a just war.

These distinctions have been hotly debated since their inception. Drawing the line between murder and just war is a controversial task. Yet just war theory seeks to define these boundaries. According to this legal tradition, some circumstances in which lethal force may be justifiable are recognized under international law, which also provides guidelines for sanctioned methods.

At the core of the just war tradition is the conviction that the taking of human life may be sanctioned as the "lesser evil" when necessary to prevent life-threatening aggression. St. Thomas More contended that the assassination of an evil leader responsible for starting a war was justified if it would prevent the taking of innocent lives. From this premise, a number of other principles follow:

1. *Last resort:* War is permissible only if all other means of resolution have been tried.
2. *Legitimate authority:* The decision to go to war can be made only by a duly constituted authority.
3. *Right intention:* War is justified only for the purpose of defense and not for revenge.
4. *Probability of success:* There must be a reasonable chance that the war will succeed at a reasonable cost of life.
5. *Appropriate goal:* A war can be initiated only to restore a peace that would be preferable to the conditions that were likely to materialize if the war had not been fought.
6. *Military purpose:* War is permitted to resist aggression but not to change an aggressor's type of government. (Henkin 1991)

These ethical criteria continue to color thinking about the rules for warfare and the circumstances under which the use of armed force is legally permissible.

The Use of Force. Especially since World War I, the international community's tolerance of war has declined. As Figure 16.1 shows, over time international law increasingly has rejected the traditional legal right of states to employ force to achieve their foreign policy objectives.[5]

---

[5]This is not to suggest that the right to use force to punish wrongdoers in just war theory has been repudiated. The "neo-just war doctrine . . . no longer seriously purports to accept the view that peace is unconditionally a higher view than justice. We have returned to the medieval view that it is permissible . . . to fight to promote justice, broadly conceived. Evil ought to be overturned, and good ought to be achieved, by force if necessary" (Claude 1988). Indeed, some interpret just war theory to condone savage behavior to end a war quickly and coerce surrender. As the Prussian military theorist Karl von Clausewitz (1976) argued in his 1832 treatise, *On War*, it is necessary to use "force unsparingly, without deference against the bloodshed involved. . . . To introduce into a philosophy of war a principle of moderation would be an absurdity. War is an act of violence pushed to its utmost bounds."

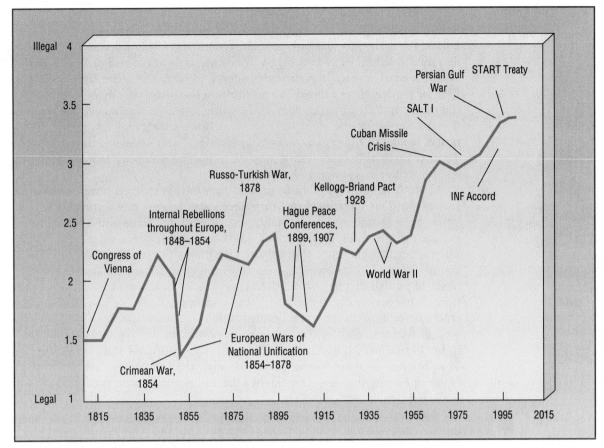

FIGURE 16.1

The Legal Prohibition of War of Aggression, 1815–1996

Legal restraints on the historic right of states to wage war have grown over time, but only steadily since World War I. The experience of past wars has impacted significantly the legal interpretation of prohibitions against wars of conquest. Transitions in the legal status of initiating war also have been influenced both by international crises and by international conventions.

SOURCE: Transnational Rules Indicators Project (TRIP), as described by Kegley and Raymond (1990).

The Hague conferences of 1899 and 1907 were early developments in shaping new attitudes toward war. World War I, however, revealed more than any other event the dangers inherent in the fact that "under general international law, as it stood up to 1914, any state could at any time and for any reason go to war without committing an international delinquency" (Kunz 1960).

In the aftermath of World War I, states began to reject the legal right to use force. The Covenant of the League of Nations, incorporated as Part I of the Treaty of Versailles in 1919, implemented a new regime. Articles 11 to 17 stipulated that in no case could a state resort to war until three months after a judicial determination by the League had elapsed. These articles also contained provisions subjecting any member "who committed an act of war against another member to sanctions."

Another important step was taken in 1928 in the Treaty Providing for the Renunciation of War as an Instrument of National Policy, known as the Kellogg-Briand Pact. The prohibition was reaffirmed in the 1933 Anti-War Treaty of Rio de Janeiro and in the Nuremberg war crimes trials at the end of World War II. Both spoke of war as "the supreme international crime." The United Nations Charter (Article 2) expanded the prohibition by unequivocally outlawing both the threat and initiation of war. At the same time, Article 39 gave the international community the right to determine "the existence of any threat to the peace, breach of the peace or act of aggression," and Article 42 authorized the Security Council "to take such action . . . as may be necessary to maintain or restore international peace and security."

Over time, legal injunctions increasingly have restricted states' right to resort to war. The doctrine of **military necessity** clarifies international law's position by restricting the justifiable use of military force only to occasions where it is absolutely necessary as a last recourse for defense (Claude 1988). The modern legal conception of just war thus still embraces the traditional *jus ad bellum*. Now, however, it confines the right to wage a war to the purposes of punishing aggression, deterring attack, protecting innocents' human rights, and generally defending "the system's rules" (Kelsen 1945). This change modifies the political culture in which states compete: "The willingness of nations to subscribe, even in principle, to the renunciation of their rights to use force (except in self-defense) is a significant step, an expression of willingness to move in one direction rather than the other, and a disclosure of consensus on the most important aspect of political order in world affairs" (Falk 1965).

Although acceptance of the use of force has declined, this has not reduced the incidence of war, much less (as some optimists had hoped) brought about its obsolescence. While the major powers have avoided direct combat with one another since World War II, they frequently have used force against other states, and war between states in the Global South has been especially frequent. Many of these actions were conducted in ways arguably prohibited by international law despite the attacking states' claims that international law sanctioned their behavior (Tillema and Van Wingen 1982).

Still, because war is no longer licensed, the intention to make war is a crime, and those who start a war are now criminals. That consensus may be an important psychological restraint on future policymakers' choices. (Some realists, however, would undoubtedly disagree, arguing that aggressive leaders will not be restrained by the mere delegitimization of violence.)

In addition to this prohibition, contemporary international law has sought to grapple with newer forms of armed conflict, though this has proven difficult. Consider three examples.

First, international law advances guidelines for states' permissible military response to the scourge of terrorism. It restricts that response to cases where another state's responsibility for the act of terrorism is beyond all doubt. Moreover, "this right does not allow retaliation for past attacks. The response in self-defense to an armed [terrorist] attack must be necessary and proportional . . . and the victim of an act of terrorism will have to pursue other remedies against states it believes responsible and against the states that encourage, promote, condone, or tolerate terrorism or provide a haven to terrorists" (Henkin 1991).

Second, consider the rise of military intervention and arms sales as policy instruments in world affairs alongside the decay since 1945 of the distinction between internal and international situations:

> International law does not forbid one state to sell arms to another state, and upon authentic invitation, a state may introduce military forces into the territory of another to assist the government for various purposes, including maintaining internal order. On the other hand, a state may not introduce arms or armed forces into a country without the consent of its government, surely not to support any groups hostile to the government. (Henkin 1991, 63)

Yet here we note that the traditional prohibition against external intervention in a sovereign state's territory has eroded since the mid-1970s. As Figure 16.2 shows, the nonintervention rule is increasingly challenged, and "the belief that governments have a right, even obligation, to intervene in the affairs of other states seems to have gained great currency in recent years" (Blechman 1995). Rising global interdependence has made the concepts of defined borders, external penetration, and sovereign territoriality less and less meaningful. In an age of instantaneous global communications, the unprecedented movement of people, goods, and money across national borders, and the heavy involvement of "foreigners" in the internal affairs of states everywhere, international law has broad-

FIGURE 16.2

The Changing Status of the Nonintervention Rule in International Law, 1815–1996

Over time, the illegality of intervening in sovereign states has changed. Recently, for a variety of purposes including humanitarian aid, preventing genocide, protecting civil liberties, and promoting democracy through "reform interventions," international law has adopted since 1960 an increasingly permissive posture toward this form of coercive diplomacy.

SOURCE: Transnational Rules Indicators Project (TRIP), as measured in Hermann, Kegley, and Raymond (1996).

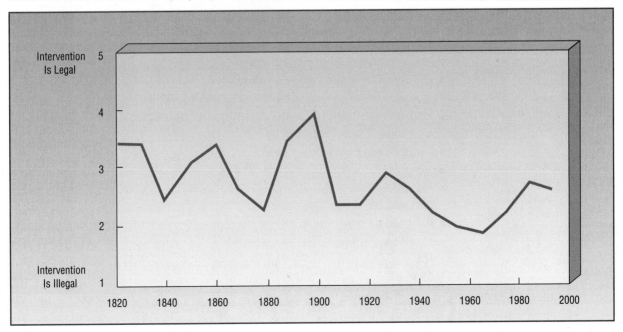

ened the definition of the conditions under which intervention is legally permissible, accepting the right of states to intervene for humanitarian purposes.

Third, international law has had great difficulty keeping pace with the rapid technological innovations in weapons systems. The recent creation of a whole category of "nonlethal weapons," for example, has raised serious questions about the ethics and legality of their use and the conditions under which they might be deployed. The slow pace of the movement to ban antipersonnel land mines, because about half the victims of the world's estimated 100 million land mines are civilians, not soldiers (Mintz 1996), illustrates the problems of legal reform. Today's technological advances in weapons are so fast-moving that international law has been unable to construct rules to regulate the types of military activities new technologies make possible. This problem prompts taking a closer look at the evolving legal rules for the conduct of armed conflict.

The Rules for War's Conduct. Laws regulating the methods that states may use in war have also grown. These restraints include the principles of **discrimination** and **noncombatant immunity,** which attempt to protect innocent civilians by restricting military targets to soldiers and supplies. The laws of retaliation specify conditions under which certain practices are legitimate. One category, **reprisals** (hostile and illegal acts permitted only if made in proportionate response to a prior hostile and illegal act), stipulates procedures for military occupations, blockades, shows of force, and bombardments. Another category, **retorsion** (hostile but legal retaliatory acts when made in response to similar legal acts initiated by other states), provides rules for embargoes, boycotts, import quotas, tariffs, and travel restrictions to redress grievances.

While the cynic may conclude that the laws of retaliation (particularly reprisals) are really instructions for killing, that conclusion is unwarranted. Restrictions on the weapons that can be used and the permissible methods of fighting, alongside the widening scope of acts regarded as war crimes (see Focus 16.3), may reduce killing in warfare. Consider the following examples from among more than thirty recognized rules (from von Glahn 1996):

- No attacking of unarmed enemies.
- No use of forbidden arms or munitions.
- No firing on undefended localities without military significance.
- No improper use or destruction of privileged (i.e., exempt, immune) buildings for military purposes.
- No poisoning streams or wells.
- No pillaging.
- No killing or wounding military personnel who have surrendered or are disabled by wounds or sickness.
- No assassinating and hiring of assassins.
- No ill-treating prisoners of war.
- No compelling the inhabitants of occupied enemy territory to furnish information about the armed forces of the enemy or its means of defense.
- No bombarding from the air to terrorize or attack civilian populations.
- No attacking enemy vessels that have indicated their surrender by lowering their flag.
- No destroying civilian cultural objects and places of worship.

Can the World Court Stop War Crimes?

When armed conflict erupts, international law requires the participants to refrain from activities that violate certain principles accepted by the international community. One of these rules is the protection of innocent noncombatants. But what can international judicial bodies do when violations occur? It can condemn the actions and the criminals who commit the crimes, but it cannot prevent the crime. This powerlessness was illustrated in Bosnia-Herzegovina on July 25, 1995, when Bosnian Serb rebels, seizing their second United Nations "safe area" in two weeks, marched into Zepa and began to methodically slaughter thousands of Muslims.

On the same day as the Serbs' latest conquest in their assault on the isolated Muslim enclaves, their leaders were called to appear before a UN court on charges of genocide and crimes against humanity for committing atrocities against civilians and captured soldiers. In the Hague, the Yugoslav War Crimes Tribunal indicted Bosnian Serb General Ratko Mladic and the nationalist rebels' political leader, Radovan Karadzic, as war criminals. Also indicted was Milan Martic, leader of rebel Serbs in Croatia, as well as twenty-one others. Mladic—a hero to his troops—personally oversaw the capture of the "safe area" Srebrenica, where UN officials said Muslims were then killed, raped, or taken captive. Up to seven thousand people remained missing. As the indictment was announced, Mladic was meeting with the UN commander for Bosnia, Lieutenant General Rupert Smith. Officials at UN headquarters in New York defended the decision to negotiate with the Serb nationalists despite the indictments.

The international community often finds itself facing ethical dilemmas of this sort. Although it sets standards for individuals and states to follow, those who flout these rules are the ones with which the community of nations must negotiate to settle the conflicts that have led to the illegal behavior. Although the criminals are outlaws (outside the law), they often are treated as respected leaders with whom bargaining must occur if the conflict is to be resolved. They are the only people who can make binding decisions for the groups they lead.

While many people and states still commit war crimes without facing punishment, the resumption of war crime tribunals in 1995 signaled to would-be perpetrators the global community's intolerance for these atrocities. The UN's International Criminal Tribunal, established in 1993, by February 1996 had indicted more than fifty people for crimes in Bosnia. Although there is little likelihood that all of the accused will face trial, the indicted "are not subject to any statute of limitations, and until the day they die, even if the tribunal has long since gone out of existence, they will be subject to prosecution and punishment anywhere in the world" (Neier 1995). Many Nazi war criminals even today face that haunting reality.

These illustrative objections to practices once condoned move warfare away from barbarism. This is underscored by the international community's impressive expansion of the legal human-rights protections it grants (see Table 16.2).

Law's Contribution to Peace. Cynics who contend that international law is irrelevant to the control of war overlook several dimensions of law's character. First, international law is not intended to prevent all warfare. Aggressive war is illegal, but defensive war is not. It is a mistake, therefore, to claim that international law has broken down whenever war breaks out.

Second, instead of doing away with war, international law preserves it as a sanction against the breaking of rules. Thus war is a device of last resort to punish aggressors and thereby maintain the system's legal framework.

Third, international law is an institutional substitute for war. Legal procedures exist to resolve conflicts before they erupt into open hostilities. Although they cannot prevent war, they sometimes make recourse to violence unnecessary by resolving disputes that otherwise might escalate to war.

493

TABLE 16.2 Legal Steps in the Development of Human Rights:
Some Major Conventions

Year	Convention
1948	Universal Declaration of Human Rights
1949	Convention on the Prevention and the Punishment of the Crime of Genocide
1950	European Convention for the Protection of Human Rights and Fundamental Freedoms
1951	Convention Relating to the Status of Refugees
1965	International Convention on the Elimination of All Forms of Racial Discrimination
1967	Convention on the Elimination of All Forms of Discrimination against Women
1967	Declaration on Territorial Asylum
1969	Inter-American Convention on Human Rights
1976	International Covenant on Civil and Political Rights
1976	International Covenant on Economic, Social, and Cultural Rights
1977	Convention on Humanitarian Law
1981	The International Bill of Rights: The Covenant of Civil and Political Rights
1981	Declaration on the Elimination of All Forms of Intolerance and of Discrimination Based on Religion or Belief
1983	Inhumane Weapons Convention
1984	Convention against Torture and Other Cruel, Inhuman, or Degrading Treatment or Punishment
1989	Convention on the Rights of the Child
1991	Convention on the Elimination of Political, Economic, Social, Cultural, and Civil Discrimination against Women
1992	Declaration of Principles of International Law on Compensation to Refugees

The demonstrable capacity of pacific methods to reduce the frequency of war does not mean that international adjudicative machinery is well developed or functionally effective. Nowhere is this more evident than with the World Court, created as the highest judicial body on earth. The World Court was until very recently an inactive judicial institution. Between 1946 and 1991 it heard only sixty-four contentious cases between states, rendered judgments on less than half of these, and handed down only nineteen advisory opinions (Riggs and Plano 1994, 138–39). Between 1993 and 1995, however, the court's caseload began to expand, as it heard nineteen cases (for an example, see Map 16.1). In 1996 the World Court's visibility increased further when it was asked by the United Nations to provide an advisory opinion on whether the use of nuclear weapons can be declared illegal.

The World Court's past impact has been marginal partly because most judicial conflict settlements take place in the domestic courts of one of the contestants or in other international tribunals, where there is stronger evidence of compliance with court decisions (Falk 1964; von Glahn 1996). Still other con-

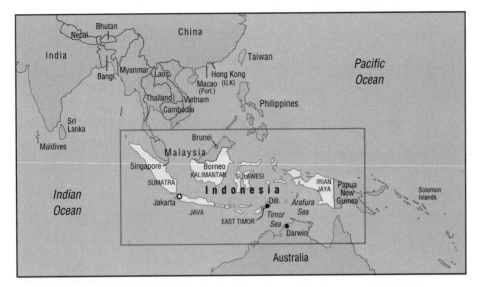

MAP 16.1

The Legal Battle over East Timor

Indonesia militarily took over East Timor after Portugal abandoned it as a colony in 1975. In 1995, Portugal took its case to the World Court in the Hague, challenging the Timor Gap Agreement between Indonesia and Australia which established a 38,125 square-mile zone in the sea, as shown in this map. Portugal is arguing before the World Court that Indonesia and Australia have granted oil concessions in territory that does not belong to them. This is the type of dispute that the World Court was created to resolve peacefully.

troversies are settled through ad hoc arbitration and mediation proceedings before they are referred to a court for resolution.

The most important reason, however, is that the World Court's jurisdiction is not compulsory. Although all UN members are members of the court, at the beginning of 1994 less than a third had affirmed their willingness to accept automatically the court's limited compulsory jurisdiction in conflicts involving them. All but a handful of these have stipulated reservations to their acceptance. The United States, for example, has undermined the drive to strengthen the World Court by adhering to the so-called Connally amendment, which reserves the U.S. right to determine the cases in which it will allow the court jurisdiction.

World order in the twenty-first century will depend to a considerable extent on the uses to which states put international law. Its alleged shortcomings lie not with the laws but with their creators—states and their addiction to sovereignty as a legal right. The intentions of states acting individually or in concert, and not the slow processes by which legal development grows, will be decisive. The international community could, in principle, strengthen international law's capacity to curtail aggression. Still, many barriers remain to creating, as John F. Kennedy expressed liberal theory's hope, "a new world of law, where the strong are just and the weak secure and the peace preserved." That conclusion leads naturally to a consideration of the role of international organizations in maintaining world peace.

• • •

INTERNATIONAL ORGANIZATION AND WORLD ORDER

Liberal theorists recommend as a second political path to peace the creation of international organizations. To understand this approach, we must also understand its theoretical underpinnings. The expectations about and performance of the United Nations exemplify those theoretical premises.

The United Nations and the Preservation of Peace

Like its predecessor, the League of Nations, the UN's primary mission—as its charter states—is the "maintenance of international peace and security." The stipulation that membership is open to all "peace-loving" countries reaffirms this purpose, as does the charter's requirements that members "settle their international disputes by peaceful means."

Collective Security. *Collective security* is often viewed as a liberal-idealist alternative to the competitive balanced alliances that realists recommend for preserving peace. In a balance-of-power system, it is assumed that each state acting in its own self-interest for its individual protection will form coalitions offsetting others and that the resulting equilibrium will prevent war. In contrast, collective security asks each state to share responsibility for every other states' security. It "assumes that every nation perceives every challenge to the international order in the same way, and is prepared to run the same risks to preserve it" (Kissinger 1992). All states are to take joint action against *any* transgressor, and *all* are to act in concert. This presumes that the superior power of the entire community will deter those contemplating aggression or, failing this, that collective action will defeat any violator of the peace.

In the aftermath of the League's inability to put collective security into practice, realist critics attacked what they regarded as the illusory expectations on which liberal proponents had built the model. Many of the preconditions necessary for an effective system of collective security were lacking. The League's failures stemmed from the U.S. refusal to join the organization; the other great powers' fear that the League's collective strength might be used against them; disagreement over objectively defining an instance of aggression in which all concurred; states' pervasive dread of inequities in sharing the risks and costs of mounting an organized response to aggression; and their tendency to voice approval of the value of general peace but unwillingness to organize resistance except when their own security was threatened. In the final analysis, the theory's central fallacy was that it expected a state to be as anxious to see others protected as it was to protect itself. That assumption was not upheld in the period between World War I and World War II. As a result, the League of Nations never became a true collective security system.

The architects of the United Nations were painfully aware of the League's disappointing experience. While they voiced support for collective security, their design restored the balance of power to maintain peace. The United Nations Charter, signed June 26, 1945, permitted any of the Security Council's five permanent members (the United States, the Soviet Union, Great Britain, France, and China) to veto and thereby block any proposed enforcement action that any of them disapproved. Because the Security Council could act in concert only when the permanent members fully agreed, the UN Charter was a concession to states' sovereign freedom:

> In the final analysis, the San Francisco Conference must be described as having repudiated the doctrine of collective security as the foundation for a general, universally applicable system for the management of power in international relations. The doctrine was given ideological lip service, and a scheme was contrived for making it effective in cases of relatively minor importance. But the new organization reflected the conviction that the concept of collective security had no realistic relevance to the problems posed by conflict among the major powers. (Claude 1962, 164–65)

To further enhance the great powers' authority relative to the United Nations, the charter severely restricted the capacity of the General Assembly to mount collective action. The charter authorized it only to initiate studies of conflict situations, bring perceived hostilities to the attention of the Security Council, and make recommendations for initiatives to keep the peace. Moreover, it restricted the role of the secretary general to that of chief administrative officer. Article 99 confined the secretary general, and the working staff of the Secretariat created to aid that person, to alerting the Security Council to peace-threatening situations and to providing administrative support for the operations that the Security Council authorized.

Although the UN's structure compromised the organization's security mission, it is still much more than a mere debating society. It is also more than an arena for the conduct of power politics. During the Cold War the United Nations fell short of many of the ideals its more ambitious founders envisioned, principally because its two most powerful members (the United States and the Soviet Union) in the Security Council did not cooperate (see Chapter 6). Nevertheless, like any adaptive institution, it found ways to overcome the compromising legal restrictions that inhibited its capacity to preserve world order.

From Collective Security to Peacekeeping. The Korean police action in 1950 provided a glimmer of hope that the United Nations might overcome its institutional barriers to preserving world order. However, that episode was an intervention sponsored and fought by the United States under UN auspices and did not set a precedent for equally ambitious initiatives in later conflicts. After the disillusioning Korean experience, the UN did not undertake another "enforcement" mission to defeat an aggressor for another forty years, when it mounted a collective response to Iraq's invasion of Kuwait.

During the long period between Korea and Kuwait, the UN adaptively sought to overcome the political obstacles posed by superpower discord. Its experiments with monitoring explosive situations began during its formative period. In 1948, for example, it created the United Nations Truce Supervision Organization (UNTSO) to monitor the ceasefire between Israel and neighboring countries. It also created the United Nations Military Observer Group in India and Pakistan (UNMOGIP) to protect a cease-fire zone in Kashmir. After the Korean War, these initiatives became precedents for a new approach, which now came to be called peacekeeping. In contrast to peace enforcement, as in Korea, peacekeeping means separating antagonists. Acting in response to the Suez crisis under the Uniting for Peace resolution, in 1956 the General Assembly created the United Nations Emergency Force (UNEF). It also charged the secretary general with primary responsibility for managing this, the UN's first peacekeeping operation, in the Sinai to prevent the combatants from resuming fighting.

The General Assembly designed UNEF to forestall the superpowers' competitive intrusion into a potentially explosive situation and to overcome the Security Council's inaction. This innovative approach went beyond prior UN fact-finding commissions and observer forces. It was largely improvisational, since the charter had not provided for peacekeeping activities authorized by the General Assembly and managed by the secretary general. The principles underlying UNEF were different from collective security. The latter emphasized checking aggression through collective enforcement. UNEF, by contrast, emphasized noncoercive activities aimed at placing the UN's neutral "thin blue line" between the clashing armies to permit time for negotiations to resolve the conflict.

Success can be infectious. Following UNEF, the UN sprang into action to authorize other operations designed to prevent conflicts from re-igniting. These missions have since become closely identified with the process of peacekeeping. For example, in 1958 the UN Observer Group helped to defuse the crisis in Lebanon. And in 1960 the largest UN peacekeeping force ever entered the Congo to stabilize that newly independent country. In 1964, the UN sent the UNFICYP peacekeeping force to Cyprus. Other increasingly diverse and ambitious UN peace missions followed from these precedents (see Ratner 1995 for descriptions of these operations). Map 16.2 displays the world-wide location throughout the globe of nearly forty of the UN's best-known operations.

Of these operations, nearly all have successfully fulfilled their goals. UN missions have usually succeeded in creating buffers between the warring disputants, providing time for negotiating cease-fires, and ensuring compliance with agreements. On many occasions they have also helped to contain conflicts that threatened to escalate to large-scale wars with additional participants. Over time, the roles associated with UN peacekeeping have moved from managing crises "during incipiency" to bolder security- and confidence-building measures, verification, legal assistance in civil wars, combating terrorism, humanitarian aid, drug interdiction, election monitoring, naval peacekeeping, and other operations beyond the activities originally envisioned.

The Changing Role of the Secretary General. Drawing on the UN's experience with UNEF, in 1960 Secretary General Dag Hammarskjöld of Sweden articulated in his annual report to the world organization his vision for a new UN role in managing peace and security, which he termed **preventive diplomacy.** Perceiving the need for the United Nations to take bolder conflict-avoidance measures, Hammarskjöld practiced preventive diplomacy to resolve conflicts before they reached the crisis stage (in contrast to ending wars once they erupted). His efforts were inspired greatly by his frustration with Security Council inaction.

More than his unobtrusive predecessor, Trygve Lie of Norway (who resigned under pressure in November 1952), Hammarskjöld saw the secretary general's role as that of an active crisis manager. He independently enlarged the defined responsibilities of the executive organ of the United Nations by using his "good offices" to mediate international disputes and by strengthening the UN's administrative support for peacekeeping operations.

After Hammarskjöld met an untimely tragic death in the line of duty in September 1961, his successor, U Thant of Burma, pursued a much less-activist program in his two terms of office, which ended in 1971. Constrained by in-

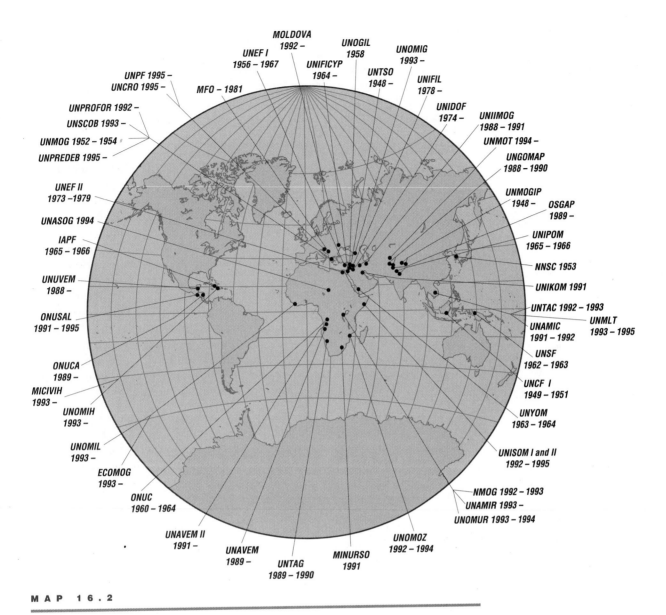

MAP 16.2

UN Peace Missions, 1948–1996

From its origin through 1996, the United Nations has undertaken nearly fifty peace missions worldwide. The UN's Blue Helmets have been dispatched to nearly eighty countries, with the UN personnel drawn from the armed forces of more than seventy-five UN members.

SOURCE: The United Nations.

creasing U.S. and Soviet pressure, U Thant concentrated on "quiet diplomacy" to manage crises that not he but the Security Council or the General Assembly identified. This approach was more akin to that which had prevailed in the early 1950s, stressing crisis response rather than crisis prevention.

The next secretary general, Kurt Waldheim of Austria, shared U Thant's preference to avoid offending the great powers. Waldheim did seek to resolve some interstate disputes; for example, he made efforts to obtain release of the U.S. hostages seized in Iran in 1979. His initiatives were restrained, however. In his first public statement as secretary general, Waldheim stressed that "in this position one has to know the limits." This passivity endeared Waldheim to the superpowers, who rewarded his submissiveness by supporting his reappointment in 1976 to a second five-year term and by promoting his reelection to a third in 1981. But by this time, China—insisting on the election of a candidate from the developing countries and vowing to use its veto to prevent Waldheim's reelection—paved the way for the election of a more-experienced diplomat with greater ambitions (Jakobson 1991).

Waldheim's successor, Javier Pérez de Cuéllar of Peru, also held "quiet diplomacy" in respect. Yet Pérez de Cuéllar was outspokenly critical of the "alarming succession of international crises" in which the United Nations was "unable to play as effective and decisive a role as the Charter certainly envisaged for it." To rectify its impotence, he called for renewed use of the Security Council that "too often [found] itself on the sidelines" because of alleged "partisanship, indecisiveness or incapacity arising from divisions among member states." He felt the Security Council should "keep an active watch on dangerous situations and, if necessary, initiate discussions with the parties" to defuse them "at an early stage before they degenerate into violence." Lamenting the fact that "the power of exposure" was the secretary general's only authorized power under the charter, in May 1989 Pérez de Cuéllar declared, "I cannot accept that, in each and every case, we need agreement by the two great powers before we can advance." Acting on this principle, he aggressively pursued both **peacemaking** and **peacekeeping** initiatives. He explained his approach in these terms:

> I have tried to simplify the procedures for finding peaceful solutions to international conflicts. The sequence of events is always the same. First you have to get a truce—end the hostilities. That is what we call "peacemaking" in diplomatic parlance. Once that is achieved and approved by the UN Security Council, we set up operations to keep the peace. That is what we call "peacekeeping."

Cold War Obstacles to Conflict Prevention. Pérez de Cuéllar's ambitious efforts strengthened the UN's capacity to preserve world peace (Skjelsbaek 1991). Still, until the closing days of the Cold War, the UN's record of preventing and settling conflicts attested to the barriers that then existed, for "only about two out of five" of the UN's attempts to mediate conflicts succeeded (Holsti 1988, 423). Similarly, of 319 international disputes in which some fighting occurred between 1945 and 1984, only 137, or 43 percent, were referred to the UN for management. Moreover, the United Nations failed to control nearly half of these disputes and failed to settle fully 75 percent of them (Haas 1986, 17). Hence, the UN's *peacemaking* achievements during the Cold War were, at best, modest.

Yet the achievements that were recorded demonstrate that the United Nations was, to some extent, able to transcend the substantial barriers symbolized by 264 vetoes in the Security Council, or on a third of its resolutions between 1945 and 1991 (Riggs and Plano 1994, 58). This mixed record, of success and impotence, suggests that the UN's usefulness as an instrument of conflict management in the Cold War's inauspicious climate was greatest when a conflict:

- Did not involve the superpowers.
- Was outside the context of the East–West rivalry.
- When Security Council wished to see it resolved.

- Was intense and in danger of spreading geographically.
- Entailed fighting (albeit at a limited level).
- Centered on a decolonization dispute.
- Involved middle-sized and small states, comparatively unprepared militarily.
- Was identified as a threat to peace by the secretary general, who led efforts to organize UN resistance to its continuation.

The record underscores the extent to which, as Trygve Lie noted in 1946, "the United Nations is no stronger than the collective will of the nations that support it. Of itself it can do nothing. It is a machinery through which nations can cooperate. It can be used and developed . . . or it can be discarded and broken."

Given this reality, it is understandable why, while the United Nations was a captive of Cold War competition, it directed its activities primarily toward addressing the deep-seated structural causes of war, where it could make a difference. This is seen in its "rear door" efforts to alleviate the conditions of poverty, inequality, frustration, and despair that provoke violence. Thus, for most of its existence, the United Nations has concentrated its efforts on "peacelessness." It does so in response to an awareness that poverty causes more death, suffering, and human incapacity than does war. The UN's greatest effort is geared toward **peacebuilding** (creating conditions that make war unlikely) rather than in peacemaking, to end fighting already under way.[6]

Despite its weaknesses, the United Nations in many respects is, as U.S. President John F. Kennedy (a realist who described himself as an "idealist without illusions") put it, "our last hope in an age where the instruments of war have far outpaced the instruments of peace." This fulfillment of promise gained new momentum when the end of the Cold War opened a new chapter on the UN's quest for world order.

The UN's Blue Helmets and Multilateral Peacekeeping. The United Nations was a victim of superpower rivalry for more than four decades. But the end of the Cold War removed impediments to the organization's ability to fulfill its security-preserving mission. That possibility was made clear in 1990, when Iraq invaded Kuwait. The Security Council promptly passed Resolution 678, authorizing member states "to use all necessary means" to coerce Iraq's withdrawal from Kuwait. Under the authority of this resolution, on January 16, 1991, U.S. President Bush ordered an air war against Iraq's military machine, the fourth largest in the world. Forty-three days later, Iraq agreed to a cease-fire and to a withdrawal from Kuwait.

Bolstered by this success at collective security, optimism about the UN's capacity to take the lead in peacemaking started to grow. This optimism was facilitated by the shift of power from the General Assembly back to the Security Council. Acting in concert, it authorized the United Nations to launch between 1988 and 1994 nearly twice the peacekeeping missions than it had in the previous forty-three years of its existence (see Table 16.3).

---

[6]These programs are inspired by the liberal idealist principle that improving the quality of people's lives can reduce the need for military arsenals. The conviction is expressed in the UN's work on human rights, technical assistance, refugees, decolonization, world trade, protection of children, world food, social discrimination, the equality of women, agricultural development, religious discrimination, disaster relief, environmental protection, and a host of other world problems that influence the quality of life and the prospects for conditions from which aggression springs.

TABLE 16.3   The UN's Expanded Peacekeeping Role, 1988 and 1994

	1988	1994
Security Council peacekeeping resolutions adopted	15	78
Disputes and conflicts in which the UN was actively involved in preventive diplomacy or peacemaking	11	28
Peacekeeping operations deployed	5	17
Military personnel deployed	9,570	73,393
Civilian police deployed	35	2,130
International civilian personnel deployed	1,516	2,206
Countries contributing military and police personnel	26	76
UN annual budget for peacekeeping operations	$230,000,000	$3,610,000,000
Countries in which the United Nations undertook electoral activities	0	21
Sanctions imposed by the Security Council	1	7

SOURCE: The United Nations.

In 1992, when Boutros Boutros-Ghali became Secretary General, the United Nations greatly expanded its profile and agenda. Under his lobbying, the UN peacekeepers—its so-called "Blue Helmets"—increased from four thousand to more than seventy thousand by 1995. Boutros-Ghali's bold "Agenda for Peace" proposed creation of a standing UN "peace enforcement force" to quickly "enforce a ceasefire by taking coercive action against either party, or both, if they violate it." Under this innovation, the UN rapid deployment units would be established by the voluntary contribution of member states, go into action when authorized by the Security Council, and serve under the command of the secretary general. Unlike traditional peacekeeping operations, however, their use could be ordered without the express consent of the disputants, and they would be trained and equipped to use force if necessary. This would enable UN forces, "by presenting a credible military threat, . . . to convince all con-flictual parties that violence will not succeed. . . . The military objective of the strategy, then, is to deter, dissuade, and deny (D^3)" (Ruggie 1993).

A number of barriers exist to the realization of these ambitious security goals. The first barrier is political—the expanded size of the United Nations, which complicates decision making. Between March 1992 and March 1995, 20 countries joined the United Nations. This swelled its number to 185 mem-bers, ranging in size from geographic giants such as Russia and China to mi-crostates such as tiny new members Andorra, Palau, and Eritrea. In addition, the proposals in 1996 to expand the permanent Security Council to eight or ten members (a move to make it more representative by bringing in Germany, Japan, and perhaps leading Global South countries) would make agreements about new peacekeeping ventures difficult, because great powers' interests are often incompatible and the prospects for reaching a consensus declines when the size of a group increases. Even if the post-Cold War environment is more hospitable to global security enforcement than in the past, implement-ing collective security through the United Nations will not be easy.

As in the past, there remains the temptation for members to support only those peacekeeping efforts that affect their own immediate security interests.

UN Secretary General Boutros Boutros-Ghali is a reformer in the liberal-idealist tradition. Lamenting the obstacles he and the United Nations face in providing moral authority for humanitarian causes, he observed in 1995 that "Everywhere we work, we are struggling against a culture of death." Yet he has persevered in his efforts to give the United Nations the means to carry out its security mission, confronting leaders with the challenge that "Your enemy is not each other but fear and cowardice. . . . You must assume your responsibility."

For example, the September 1993 U.S. Presidential Decision Directive 13 prohibited contributing U.S. military units to a permanent standby force such as that authorized by Article 43 of the UN Charter. This prohibition was despite more than fifteen other UN members having earlier agreed to provide fifty-four thousand troops to the secretary general's proposed rapid-response standing force. The decision by the United States thus increased the gap between the UN's aspirations for maintaining peace and its capabilities, since "Without U.S. leadership and power, the United Nations lacks muscle," but with it, ironically, "the United Nations loses its independent identity" (Gelb 1993).

The second constraint to realizing the UN's security goals is organizational. The United Nations remains poorly designed to carry out a full-fledged peace and security program. The goals have exceeded the institutional apparatus. UN troops no longer just patrol truce lines. Now they are asked to "monitor elections, protect human rights, train local police, guard humanitarian relief deliveries, and take up arms against those who get in their way. The growing operations have not been accompanied by any serious reassessment of the UN's capacity to manage them effectively." As a UN internal report concluded, "the United Nations lacks the technical, administrative and logistical tools required to implement effectively the peacekeeping agenda" (Michaels 1993).

The danger of becoming overwhelmed by the extraordinary tasks the UN has been asked to perform was illustrated by its UNPROFUR mission in Croatia and Bosnia-Herzegovina. The forty thousand Blue Helmets sent there in 1992 were not prepared (or fully authorized) to stop the carnage that threatened to take millions of lives. It was only after NATO's air strikes in September 1995 and the alliance's Operation Joint Endeavor got under way in early January 1996 that the prospects for peace brightened. UNPROFUR showed that UN peacemaking initiatives are destined to fail unless the great powers allow the United Nations "to do the job it is capable of doing," as Boutros Boutros-Ghali concluded. The lesson many drew was that the United Nations was managing too many crises with too few resources.

The third barrier is financial. The UN's peacekeeping budget is less than the amount it takes to run the New York City police and fire departments and prisons (Evans 1995, 8). This lack of funds works against a managerial security role for the United Nations. Indeed, the United Nations cannot pay for its expanded list of expensive peace missions, let alone assume responsibility for even further new initiatives. In 1987 peacekeeping cost UN members $240 million in assessments; by 1995 the bill had risen to $3.6 billion. A larger future UN peacekeeping agenda will require even more resources—a dim prospect given the fact that in October 1995, while it was spending $6 million a day in the former Yugoslavia, UN members were $3.7 billion in arrears. In fact, in January 1996 the United Nations was practically bankrupt, with the United States alone responsible for 45 percent of the total UN deficit (Goshko 1996, 6). Under severe criticism for financial mismanagement, the United Nations remains budgetarily crippled and unprepared to carry out its peacemaking goals.[7] "Money, money, money—that is the prerequisite for the United Nations playing the role it could play after the Cold War," Secretary General Boutros-Ghali lamented.

Together, the UN's political, organizational, and financial problems raise concerns about its future ability to police the many ethnic conflicts and potential civil and interstate wars on the horizon. The United Nations is not yet a true collective security organization. Its blueprint for global involvement is just that—a blueprint. It is a design without a realistic structure, and the United Nations is not yet empowered for the high purposes it has been asked to perform. Currently, its advocates' expectations exceed its capabilities.

Impeding the United Nations' success are the same forces that have eroded past collective security mechanisms. In the face of aggression, many states have sought to "free-ride" on the defense efforts of others, and have only supported collective efforts when their own immediate security was at stake. If countries do not act on the perception that violence and injustice anywhere are threats everywhere, the prospects for collective responses are poor. Still, it is likely that powerful members of the international community will, at times, respond to the threats and human suffering that aggression will cause. That collective response is likely, moreover, to be mobilized through the United Nations.

> In the great uncertainties and disorders that lie ahead, the United Nations, for all its shortcomings, will be called on again and again, because there is no other global institution, because there is a severe limit to what even the strongest powers wish to take on themselves. . . . Either the UN is vital to a more stable and equitable world and should be given the means to do its job, or peoples and governments should be encouraged to look elsewhere. But is there really an alternative? (Urquhart 1994, 33)

---

[7]These pressures have forced organizational reforms and policy innovations for the UN's thirty-three thousand employees in twenty-seven agencies worldwide. For example, in 1994 and 1995, as a cost-saving measure, the United Nations began to contract out through competitive bidding to private multinational corporations logistical support for its peace operations. These contractors provided services in Bosnia, Rwanda, Somalia, and Haiti at costs far less than the United Nations estimated it would incur. This success led the UN to consider privatizing some of its military operations, but it stopped short of hiring mercenaries managed by defense contractors to conduct its operations.

Actually, there *is* a conspicuous alternate. The great powers' reluctance to equip the United Nations to contain raging brush fires and civil wars lends credence to the 1995 prophecy of Karel Kovanda (the Czech Republic's UN ambassador), that "The important issues are going to be taken care of by regional organizations . . . with the United Nations giving its blessings."

Regional Security Organizations and Conflict Management

If the United Nations reflects the lack of shared values and a common purpose characteristic of a global community, perhaps geographically restricted regional organizations whose members already share some interests and cultural traditions offer better prospects. UN Secretary General Boutros Boutros-Ghali endorses that idea, calling on regional bodies to play a larger role in the security affairs of their regions.

During the Cold War, the North Atlantic Treaty Organization (NATO) and the Warsaw Pact were the best-known regional security organizations. Others included the ANZUS pact (Australia, New Zealand, and the United States) and the Southeast Asia Treaty Organization (SEATO). Regional organizations with somewhat broader political mandates beyond defense include the Organization of American States (OAS), the League of Arab States, the Organization of African Unity (OAU), the Nordic Council, the Association of Southeast Asian Nations (ASEAN), and the Gulf Cooperation Council.

Although Article 51 of the United Nations Charter encourages creation of regional organizations for collective self-defense, it would be misleading to describe NATO and the other Cold War regional organizations as a substitute collective security instrument for the United Nations. They were not. More accurately, they were and remain regional collective defense systems designed to deter a potential common external enemy (one typically identified in advance).

Many of today's regional security organizations are influenced by reductions in their members' perception of a common threat. A sign of the times was NATO's response to the virtual disappearance of the threat of a Soviet invasion which it was created to prevent. At the January 1994 summit in Brussels, NATO ministers formally opened the door to NATO's expansion to incorporate as participants the former Soviet satellites and Russia itself. By June 1994 nineteen non-NATO countries had joined the Partnership for Peace (PFP) program, including Russia, which agreed to work with the alliance under the terms of the partnership accord. Yet, as monumental as was this historic step, the expansion did not strengthen NATO's capacity to act as a regional alliance for collective security. The new "peace partners" were not offered the security guarantee that NATO's full members enjoy—that an attack on one would be considered an attack on all. Thus NATO's security-protecting capacity remains in doubt, and skeptics ask what the military alliance's purposes are without an agreed-upon external enemy.

The European setting after the Cold War is marked by numerous ethnonational conflicts and separatist revolts, as in Bosnia, and other areas of Europe, including parts of Russia itself. NATO was not designed to deal with this vague kind of threat. Its original charter envisioned only one purpose—mutual self-protection from external attack; it never defined policing internal rebellions as a goal. Consequently, it was not surprising that the sixteen full-member states and the now twenty-one "partners for peace" were reluctant to call upon NATO to intervene to contain ethnic warfare. However, they eventually overcame that reluctance in December 1995, when NATO took charge from the United Nations of all military operations in Bosnia-Herzegovina. The departure in mission adapted the alliance to a new purpose and gave it a new lease on life. Operation Joint Endeavor demonstrated that NATO had a positive role to play, as President Clinton described it in January 1996, in making "the difference between a war that starts again and peace that takes hold." Nonetheless, doubt remains as to whether NATO will be willing to undertake similar interventions to contain ethnic violence *within* other countries.

Likewise, in other regional mutual security systems controversies among the coalition partners about the identity of "the enemy" and the conditions warranting intervention raise doubts about their capacity to engineer collective defense projects. These doubts are fueled by the history of regional organizations in peacemaking efforts. Between 1945 and 1984, of 319 disputes, 86 (or only 27 percent) were referred to regional organizations for management. These regional organizations were unable to halt 44 percent and failed to settle 74 percent of these referrals (Haas 1986, 20, 17). This record suggests that although regional organizations were, to some extent, created to overcome the deficiencies of global institutions (e.g., those that paralyzed the United Nations during the Cold War), in many ways they are not realistic substitutes for global institutions.

The crisis in Bosnia again exemplifies the obstacles that regional organizations often face. Recall that when the civil war broke out in June 1991 and Croatia declared its independence, neither NATO nor the European Union was able to agree on action to preserve peace. Both initially relied on the United Nations to enforce a cease-fire and orchestrate a peace plan. Only reluctantly did they succumb in 1995 to UN pressure to participate militarily. This case and others suggest that regional organizations have the capacity to bring under

After years of empty ultimatums in the Balkans, NATO finally responded militarily to the atrocities committed in the Bosnian struggle. The action was precipitated by the September 1995 Serbian shelling of a marketplace in Sarajevo. The West announced its intentions with aerial attacks and artillery shellings by its rapid-reaction force. Soon thereafter progress commenced on a negotiated settlement, followed by Operation Joint Endeavor in December 1995 to enforce the agreement.

control armed conflict within their territory (or in close proximity) when their members are in agreement. However, it also indicates that they often lack the consensus and political will to control controversial conflicts, and require pressure from world public opinion mobilized in global organizations like the United Nations to take action.

In the long run, however, regional organizations may help build security communities in which the expectation of peace exceeds the expectation of war. The processes through which such metamorphoses might occur are addressed by the functional and neofunctional approaches to peace within the liberal idealist paradigm.

• • •

POLITICAL INTEGRATION: THE FUNCTIONAL AND NEOFUNCTIONAL PATHS TO PEACE

Political integration refers to either the process or the product of efforts to build new political communities and supranational institutions that transcend the state. Their purposes are to remove states' incentives for war and to engineer reform programs to transform international institutions from instruments *of* states to structures *over* them.

World Federalism

Functionalism in its various forms does not represent a frontal attack on the state by proposing to replace it with some central authority. That radical remedy is represented by **world federalism,** an approach to integration based on the merger of previously sovereign states into a single federal union. Federalists follow the liberal physicist Albert Einstein's conviction that "there is no salvation for civilization, or even the human race, other than the creation of a world government."

Federalists reason that if people value survival more highly than relative national advantage, they will willingly transfer their loyalty to a supranational authority to dismantle the system of competitive territorial states which produces war. "World government," they believe, "is not only possible, it is inevitable," because it appeals to the patriotism of people who "love their national heritages so deeply that they wish to preserve them in safety for the common good" (Ferencz and Keyes 1991).

It is not surprising that ardent nationalists have vehemently attacked the revolutionary federalist "top-down" peace plan. Because it seeks to subvert the system of sovereign states, the plan threatens many entrenched interests. More abstractly, other critics reject the world federalists' proposition that governments are bad but people are good, wise, and enlightened (see Claude 1971). Likewise, they challenge the assumption that the need for changes will automatically lead to global institutional innovation.

The United World Federalists (an international nongovernmental pressure group) still actively promotes a world government. Nevertheless, aversion to war and raised consciousness of its dangers have not mobilized widespread grass-roots enthusiasm for this radical step. Other approaches to reforming the world political system have attracted more adherents.

Classical functionalism is a rival but complementary reform movement associated with liberal idealism. In contrast to federalism, **functionalism** is not directed to creating a world federal structure with all its constitutional paraphernalia. Rather it seeks to build "peace by pieces" through transnational organizations that emphasize the "sharing of sovereignty" instead of its surrender. Functionalism advocates a "bottom-up," evolutionary strategy for building cooperative ties among states.

According to functionalists, technical experts, rather than professional diplomats, are the best agents for building collaborative links across national borders. They see diplomats as being overly protective of their country's national interests at the expense of collective human interests. Rather than addressing the immediate sources of national insecurity, the functionalists' peace plan calls for transnational cooperation in technical (primarily social and economic) areas as a first step. Habits of cooperation learned in one technical area (e.g., telecommunications or medicine), they assume, will "spill over" into others—especially if the experience is mutually beneficial and demonstrates the potential advantages of cooperative ventures in other related functional areas (e.g., transportation and communication).

To enhance the probability that cooperative endeavors will prove rewarding rather than frustrating, the functionalist plan recommends that less-difficult tasks be tackled first. It assumes that successful mastering of one problem will then encourage attacking other problems collaboratively. If the process continues unabated, the bonds among countries will multiply, because no government would oppose a web of functional organizations that provide such clearcut benefits to its citizens. Thus, "the mission of functionalism is to make peace possible by organizing particular layers of human social life in accordance with their particular requirements, breaking down the artificialities of the zoning arrangements associated with the principle of sovereignty" (Claude 1971). Its intellectual parent, David Mitrany (1966), argued in *A Working Peace System* (first published in 1943) that functionalism is based on self-interest.

> Functionalism proposes not to squelch but to utilize national selfishness; it asks governments not to give up sovereignty which belongs to their peoples but to acquire benefits for their peoples which were hitherto unavailable, not to reduce their power to defend their citizens but to expand their competence to serve them. It intimates that the basic requirement for peace is that states have the wit to cooperate in pursuit of national interests that coincide with those of other states rather than the will to compromise national interests that conflict with those of others. (Claude 1971, 386)

Persuaded by the logic of this argument, far-sighted liberals such as Jean Monnet applied functionalist theory to begin the process by which war-prone Europe began after World War II to form an integrated "security community" (Deutsch et al. 1997).

The permanent problem-solving organizations created in the 1800s, such as the Rhine River Commission (1804), the Danube River Commission (1857), the International Telegraphic Union (1865), and the Universal Post Union (1874), suggested a process by which states might cooperate to enjoy mutual benefits and hence to launch the more ambitious experiments that functionalists anticipated. Their lessons informed the early organizational ideology which also inspired the missions assigned to the UN's specialized agencies (such as the World Health Organization) and the growth of international intergovernmental (IGO) and nongovernmental (NGO) organizations generally.

Functionalism, as originally formulated, did not pertain to multinational corporations—to some, the "dominant governance institutions on the planet" (Korten 1995). However, it is tempting to speculate that multinational corporations may encourage the transformation of world politics in a manner consistent with functionalist logic. Individuals who manage global corporations often think and speak of themselves as a "revolutionary class," possessing a holistic, cosmopolitan, or supranational vision of the earth that challenges traditional nationalism (Barnet and Müller 1974). This ideology and the corresponding slogan "Down with borders" are based on the assumptions that the world can be managed as an integrated unit, that global corporations can serve as agents of social change, that governments interfere unnecessarily with the free flow of capital and technology, and that multinational corporations can promote cooperation and compromise between otherwise competitive states.

As a theory of peace and world order, though, critics charge that functionalism does not take into account some important political realities. First, they question its assumption about the causes of war. Do poverty and despair cause war, or does war cause poverty and despair? Indeed, may not material deprivation sometimes breed, not aggression, but rather apathy, hopelessness, and hostility without recourse to violence? Why should we assume that the functionalist theory of war is more accurate than the many other explanations of global violence?

Second, functionalism assumes that political differences among countries will be dissolved by the habits of cooperation learned by experts organized transnationally to cope with technical problems such as global warming, environmental deterioration, or infectious disease. To critics, the reality is that technical cooperation is often more strongly influenced by politics than the other way around. The U.S. withdrawal from the International Labor Organization (ILO) and the United Nations Educational, Scientific, and Cultural Organization (UNESCO) because of their politicized nature dramatizes the primacy of politics.

As skeptics conclude, functionalists are naive to argue that technical (functional) undertakings and political affairs can be separated, because they cannot. If technical cooperation becomes as important to state welfare as the functionalists argue that it will, states will not step aside. Welfare and power cannot be separated, because the solution of economic and social problems cannot be divorced from political considerations. The expansion of transnational institutions' authority and competency at the expense of national governments is, therefore, unlikely. Functionalism, in short, is an idea whose time has passed.

Neofunctionalism

A new, albeit derivative, theory arose in the 1950s to question the assumption that ever-expanding functional needs for joint action to address property rights, health, technological change, and other shared problems would force the resolution of political disputes. Termed **neofunctionalism,** the reconstructed liberal theory sought to address directly the political factors that dominate the process of merging formerly independent states.

Neofunctionalism holds that political institutions and policies should be crafted so that they lead to further integration through the process of . . . "the expansive logic of sector integration." For example, [the first] president of the ECSC [European Coal and Steel Community], [Jean] Monnet, sought to use the integration of the coal and steel markets of the six member countries as a lever to promote the integration of their social security and transport policies, arguing that such action was essential to eliminate distortions in coal and steel prices. [The] neofunctionalism of Monnet and others [had] as its ultimate goal . . . the creation of a federal state. (Jacobson 1984, 66)

Neofunctionalism thus proposes to accelerate the processes leading to new supranational communities by purposely pushing for cooperation in politically controversial areas, rather than by avoiding them. It advocates that the proponents of integration bring political pressure to bear at crucial decision points to persuade their opponents of the greater benefits of forming a larger community among its formerly independent national members.

The European Experience. Western Europe is the preeminent example of the application of neofunctionalist principles to the development of an integrated political community (see Deutsch et al. 1997). Within a single generation, cooperation across European borders advanced progress toward a single European economic market and toward the promise of a politically integrated Europe (see Chapter 6). The 1992 Maastricht Treaty on European Union set the stage for EU expansion. In 1995 Austria, Finland, and Sweden joined the European Union, swelling its membership to fifteen countries, and other states have since applied for membership (see Map 16.3).

Yet despite EU enlargement and the opportunities that this movement symbolizes for writing a new chapter of European history, obstacles remain. These were made evident in the wake of the Maastricht Treaty, which entered into force in November 1993 and created the European Union (EU) as the umbrella term for the European Community's diverse institutions. The treaty provided a timetable for completing a single-market Economic and Monetary Union (EMU) and aimed to create a single currency in 1999 to serve as the most potent symbol of Europe's new dynamism. In addition, the EU states pledged to cooperate not just in finance and economics but in defense and foreign policy as well, with endorsement of the Common Foreign and Security Policy (CFSP).

These ambitious goals notwithstanding, progress has proven difficult. As Jacques Delors, former President of the European Commission, lamented in December 1995, "Building Europe has never been a long, calm river. There are moments of stagnation, of crises. At the moment we are in a phase of stagnation." As new economic worries—especially rising joblessness—gripped the EU's leaders, profound doubts replaced the previous optimism about the EU's ability to stick to the Maastricht schedule for monetary union (Friedman 1996a). It is now unclear whether the dream of true European unity in a wider confederation will someday become a reality. Contributing to the doubts are chronic suspicion, selfishness, and tenacious national memories of the dark side of Europe's twentieth-century history. Furthermore, EU states are aware of the potential for interdependence to provoke competition and struggles for advantage amidst capsizing currencies. The 1993 resistance of voters in Denmark, Great Britain, and elsewhere to ratification of the treaty, and Norway's 1995 outright

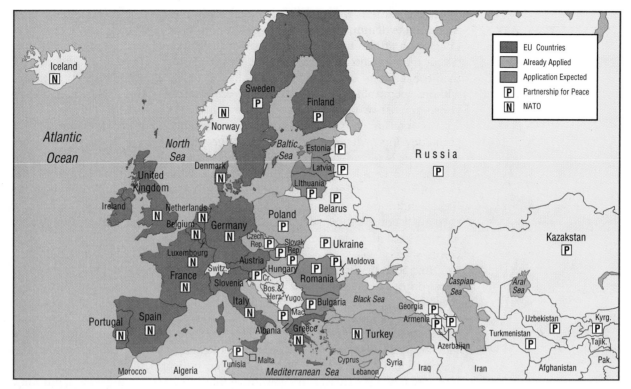

MAP 16.3

The Expanding European Union, 1996

The European Union is a premier example of a supranational regional organization. It has grown from the six countries that formed the European Economic Community in 1957 to fifteen in 1996, with further expansion on the horizon. Note the overlap in membership between the EU and NATO (which includes twenty-six countries in its Partnership for Peace); with their joint expansion, the two organizations have pushed into the geographic heart of the continent.

rejection, brought the problems into the open. So, too, did the conflicts among the fifteen existing members at the March 1996 reform conference in Florence, Italy, about the prospects for majority voting and for enlarging the EU to include eastern Europe and to encompass twenty-seven states by the year 2010. Thus, disagreement about the desirability of true European political unification remains.

Even if Europeans do not soon realize their aspiration of political union, Europe has already constructed a **security community** in which the expectation of war between states has vanished from one of the historically most violence-prone regions of the world (Deutsch et al. 1957; 1997). The onset of armed conflict between the EU's democracies is *very* unlikely. Still, the issue of how deep and geographically wide this integrative process will go is highly uncertain (see Chapter 6). In addition, the uncertain membership of this "common European home" is likely to prove consequential for European security because there is a danger that the "one Europe" proponents envisioned will in fact be two Europes, one rich and stable and the other poor and unstable. That could create future conflicts not unlike those of the past.

511

The Preconditions for Regional Integration. The record of previous integrative experiments demonstrates that the factors promoting (or inhibiting) successful integration efforts are many and their mixture complex. It is not enough that two or more countries choose to interact cooperatively. Research indicates that the probability of such cooperative behavior resulting in integration is remote without geographical proximity, steady economic growth, similar political systems, supportive public opinion led by enthusiastic leaders, cultural homogeneity, internal political stability, similar experiences in historical and internal social development, compatible forms of governmental and economic systems, similar levels of military preparedness and economic resources, a shared perception of a common external threat, bureaucratic compatibilities, and previous collaborative efforts (Cobb and Elder 1970; Deutsch 1953). While not all of these conditions must be present for integration to occur, the absence of more than a few considerably reduces the chances of success. The integration of two or more societies—let alone entire world regions—is, in short, not easily accomplished.

European institution building nonetheless has served as a model for the application of the neofunctionalist approach to integration and the pooling of sovereignty in other regions, including Africa, Asia, and Latin America. However, the evidence to date suggests that the integration of states into larger political communities may be peculiarly relevant to the Global North's advanced industrial democracies but of doubtful applicability to the developing countries of the Global South. The record, moreover, indicates that even where conditions are favorable there is no guarantee that integration will proceed automatically. As noted, even in Europe high hopes have alternated with periods of disillusionment. When momentum has occurred, **spillover**—involving either the deepening of ties in one functional area or their expansion to another to ensure the members' satisfaction with the integrative process—has led to further integration. But there is no inherent expansive momentum in integration schemes. Thus, **spillback** (when a regional integration scheme fails, as in the case of the East African Community) and **spillaround** (when a regional integration scheme stagnates or its activities in one area work against integration in another) are also possibilities.

Political Disintegration

The substantial difficulty that most regions have experienced in achieving a level of institution building similar to that of the European Union suggests the magnitude of existing barriers to creating new political communities out of previously divided ones. Furthermore, the paradox that the planet is falling apart precipitately *and* coming together reluctantly at the very same moment confounds predictions. We are witnessing "a convulsive ingathering of nations" (Gardels 1991), as hundreds of ethnic nationalities are currently seeking to separate themselves from the states that rule them. Consider Europe, where in 1991 hypernationalism led to the creation of fifteen newly independent countries. Since then four new states achieved independence at precisely the time when important steps toward economic and political integration were being undertaken.

The surge of ethnic and religious tensions tearing countries apart is not confined to the larger European continent. Equally sobering is the possibility that "the world could fracture into five hundred states from the current two hundred" (Davis 1994). Between 1989 and 1991, fifty regions worldwide declared themselves autonomous (*Harper's* [December 1991]: 17). And in a world in which "few modern states—probably fewer than twenty—are ethnically homogenous" (Gurr 1990, 85), the prospects are high that **political disintegration** will continue. This hypernationalist quest for independence by minorities and nationalist grievance groups under the banner of self-determination threatens to dismember formerly integrated sovereign states, including such widely dissimilar states as Canada, Russia, Spain, South Africa, and the United Kingdom. Such developments are not new, of course, as witnessed by the U.S. Civil War in 1861 and the thirty-year civil war in Ethiopia which enabled Eritrea to gain independence in 1991. These counterintegrative tendencies remind us that states may either merge or fragment. There is little reason to expect integrative processes, once under way, to continue by the force of their own momentum.

• • •

A DEMOCRATIC PEACE

The liberal path to peace historically has focused on the global or structural characteristics of international society, such as anarchy, as most in need of institutional reform. For this reason liberalism is closely associated with international law, organization, and integration. But a fourth institutional approach is also central to the liberal idealist tradition: that the types of governments in the world are relevant to the probability of armed conflict. It matters—and matters greatly—whether states are ruled democratically, because if so, the world will become peaceful. (This liberal thesis, of course, runs directly counter to the realist and especially the neorealist assumption that states' forms of government do not influence very much their foreign relations. They believe that governments—whether democratic or autocratic—respond similarly to similar security threats.)

The liberal ideas underlying expectations about "a democratic peace" spring from convictions that first were popularized in the late eighteenth century, the age of democratic revolution against absolute monarchy. Then—when only the fledgling United States, Switzerland, and Republican France could reasonably be counted as democratic—liberal enthusiasts voiced their belief about the impact that the spread of democratic institutions might have on international security. German philosopher Immanuel Kant predicted in 1795 that republican governments ruled by the consent of the governed would likely maintain friendly relations with one another, and would resolve any disputes at the bargaining table instead of the battlefield. This core idea had been advanced three years earlier, when a future American President, James Madison, argued that "in the advent of republican governments [would be found] not only the prospect of a radical decline in the role played by war but the prospect as well of a virtual revolution in the conduct of diplomacy" (Tucker and Hendrickson 1990).

Liberal and now neoliberal theorists have found much reason to rely heavily on these prophecies. They have put faith in the discovery that "wars between democracies are extremely rare events" (Russett 1995), as "stable democracies sharing common concepts of democratic legitimacy have . . . a remarkable record in not fighting one another" (Fukuyama 1994). There is much evidence to suggest that liberal expectations are not wishful thinking. "Well-established democracies have never made war on one another [and] republics and only republics have tended to form durable, peaceful leagues" (Weart 1994). Democracies not only routinely refrain from using armed conflict to settle disputes with one another, but they also are far less likely to be attacked by other governments, whether democratic or dictatorial (Kegley and Hermann 1996). Democratization *does*, as Woodrow Wilson and other post-World War I idealists hoped, demonstrably help to make democratic states secure. Thus the spread of democracy portends that a world made up exclusively of democracies *would* be a much safer world.

This lesson has not been lost on leaders in democratic states seeking to find a principle on which to ground their twenty-first-century national security strategies. The United States under President Clinton embraced the thesis of democratic-peace advocates enthusiastically. In his 1994 State of the Union Address, Clinton declared, "Democracies don't attack each other," and argued that because of this empirical law, "ultimately the best strategy to insure our security and to build a durable peace is to support the advance of democracy elsewhere." The 1994 *U.S. National Strategy of Engagement and Enlargement* defined the promotion of democracy throughout the world as a pillar of America's post-Cold War foreign policy. Clinton's goal is to enlarge the existing community of liberal democracies beyond its present confines (refer again to Chapters 3 and 12).

As the United States has pushed its democratization agenda to the forefront, many other democracies and international organizations have also embraced the aspiration. For example, the Group of Seven (G-7) has gravitated around the promotion of democracy. So, too, have the World Bank, the International Monetary Fund, and the OECD—all of which have designated democratic reform as a condition for loans and development assistance. The Organization of American States (OAS) similarly has accepted the principle that it is permissible to export democracy. Its June 1991 *Santiago Commitment to Democracy and Renewal of the Inter-American System* established an OAS intervention policy to guarantee hemispheric democracy. Following suit, the United Nations has affirmed democratization in many of its recent resolutions. Thus, the United States and the democratic majority have the numbers to seek revision of international law. They are exercising their influence multilaterally to permit intervention on behalf of democratic reforms (von Glahn 1996).

The existing liberal democracies' efforts to enlarge their community could, potentially, usher in a major transformation of world politics—providing that they continue to abide by their past record of dealing with conflicts by compromise through negotiation, mediation, arbitration, and adjudication. If so, liberalism will be vindicated; the future will witness less bloodshed, and the hopes Pope John Paul II expressed in the United States in October 1995 could make an ancient dream a reality: "No more war, war never again."

However, promise dictates neither performance nor destiny. As Prime Minister Ingvar Caalsson of Sweden warned in 1995, "If we fail to nurture democracy—the most fundamental political project of this century—we will never be able to realize our goals and the responsibilities which the future will call for."

• • •

INSTITUTIONS AND WORLD ORDER

Liberal and neoliberal theories that focus on international law, organization, integration, and democratization see armed conflict as deriving from prevailing and deeply rooted institutional deficiencies. Neoliberal reformers believe that the current anarchical system is the problem, not the solution, because weak institutions make security dear and global welfare subservient to national welfare. To change this, they advocate legal and institutional methods to pool sovereignty and reform the character of nondemocratic governments. Seeing the international system as underdeveloped and unstructured, advocates of these reforms believe that a rebuilt state system can best eliminate the roots from which war so often has grown. As one liberal scholar argues, global change requires innovation because "During the coming decades global challenges will continue and may increase. . . . There is more and more of an overlap between national interests and global responsibilities. The task of multilateral diplomacy is to cope with new issues, new demands and new situations [through] 'shared responsibilities' and 'strengthened partnership'" (Kinnas 1992).

To liberal advocates, the big problems on the global agenda are ones that simultaneously affect many states. They cannot be meaningfully managed unilaterally; they are transnational and cannot be met effectively with a national response. In such areas as trade, the environment, the control of AIDS, or even armed conflict, arguably a multilateral cooperative approach is required under conditions of interdependence. In this context, Bill Clinton claimed that "multilateral action holds promise as never before" and pledged that his administration would therefore seek "collective stands against aggression," providing that multilateral institutions such as the United Nations "reinvent" the way they operate.

The contributions of international institutions to this grand purpose have, until recently, been rather modest. Despite some promising developments, armed conflict has been frequent. This is not surprising in a system in which states allocate less than $2 for every man, woman, and child to the United Nations for humanitarian and security emergencies, while at the same time their combined annual defense expenditures exceed $960 billion (Laurenti 1995, 11; Evans 1995, 8). However, the impact of multilateral management of strife-torn areas should not be minimized. As Inis L. Claude maintains,

> Particular *organizations* may be nothing more than playthings of power politics and handmaidens of national ambitions. But international *organization*, considered as an historical process, represents a secular trend toward the systematic development of an enterprising quest for political means of making the world safe for human habitation. It may fail, and peter out ignominiously. But if it maintains the momentum that it has built up in the twentieth century, it may yet effect a transformation of human relationships on this planet which will at some indeterminate point justify the assertion that the world has come to be governed—that mankind has become a community capable of sustaining order, promoting justice, and establishing the conditions of that good life which Aristotle took to be the supreme aim of politics. (Claude 1971, 447–48, emphasis added)

• • •

KEY TERMS

private international law

public international law

sovereign equality

neutrality

nonintervention

diplomatic immunity

extraterritoriality

statehood

diplomatic recognition

de facto recognition

de jure recognition

nonrecognition

mediation

good offices

conciliation

arbitration

adjudication

structural violence

security regime

just war doctrine

military necessity

discrimination

noncombatant immunity

reprisal

retorsion

preventive diplomacy

peacemaking

peacekeeping

peacebuilding

political integration

world federalism

functionalism

neofunctionalism

security community

spillover

spillback

spillaround

political disintegration

CHAPTER 17

The Global Predicament: Ten Questions on the Cusp of a New Century

OUTLINE

Trend is not destiny.

—René Dubos,
French author, 1975

We stand on the brink of shaping a new world of extraordinary hope and opportunity.... The new world we seek will not emerge on its own. We must shape the transformation that is underway in a time of great fluidity.

—Warren Christopher,
U.S. secretary of state, 1993

The opposing global trends toward globalization and fragmentation in the twilight of the twentieth century point toward a new international system—one whose character has yet to develop definition and coloration. Uncertainty and unpredictability thus define the current mood toward this approaching historic juncture of past and future.

Despite confusion as to the directions that will characterize the next century, one thing is certain: The seismic shifts under way will challenge the wisdom of old beliefs and orthodox visions. Because turmoil and turbulence govern contemporary international affairs, they require our asking unconventional questions about conventional ideas.

In Chapter 1 we suggested that the investigative challenge to interpreting the future of world affairs would require the consideration of five controversial questions:

1. Are states becoming obsolete and losing their power and sovereign control?

2. Is interdependence a cure or a curse?

3. Is technological innovation a blessing or a burden?

4. Will geo-economics replace geopolitics as transnational economic forces become more important relative to interstate armed conflict over territory?

5. What constitutes human well-being in an ecologically fragile planet?

Answers to these questions are elusive. The conclusions being asserted boldly by would-be prophets are not likely to prove definitive, because "those caught up in revolutionary change rarely understand its ultimate significance" (Boutros-Ghali 1996). As a result, it is important to weigh plausible answers critically as we contemplate twenty-first-century world politics.

In addition to the five questions we confronted at the outset of our inquiry, in this final chapter we pose additional questions about the future, based on our preceding discussion of the major trends currently unfolding in world politics.

• • •

TOWARD THE FUTURE: MORE CRITICAL QUESTIONS AT THE DAWN OF THE NEW MILLENNIUM

Leaders and policy analysts worldwide are debating a number of controversial issues that require policy choices. Although the coverage in this chapter is not exhaustive, we select ten such critical questions to evaluate. How these questions are answered will significantly shape world politics in the next century.

What goals should states pursue? In earlier times, the answer was easy: The state should promote the internal welfare of its citizens, provide for defense against external aggression, and preserve the state's values and way of life.

Leaders pursue the same goals today, but increasingly their domestic and foreign policy options are limited. In an age of tradeoffs, many problems can be resolved only at the risk of worsening others. Under such conditions, the quest for narrow self-advantage often carries prohibitively high costs. The historic tendency to define the national interest chauvinistically (my country, right or wrong) can be counterproductive domestically as well as internationally. No country can long afford to pursue its own welfare in ways that reduce the security and welfare of its competitors.

Those who questioned orthodox definitions of the national interest in the past seldom found support, but this is changing. As the eminent anthropologist Margaret Mead mused, "Substantially we all share the same atmosphere today, and we can only save ourselves by saving other people also. There is no longer a contradiction between patriotism and concern for the world." Former U.S. Secretary of State Cyrus Vance voiced a similar idea when he observed that "more than ever cooperative endeavors among nations are a matter not only of idealism but of direct self-interest."

E. H. Carr (1939), a pioneering realist, was convinced of the realism of idealism, maintaining that opposing the general interests of humankind does not serve one's self-interest. Failing to recognize the plight of others can ultimately threaten one's own well-being—a view underscored by Martin Luther King Jr., who urged that "injustice anywhere is a threat to justice everywhere." If these ideas, largely rooted in the legacy of liberal idealism, gain a large following, will the collective concerns of all humanity begin to compete for attention with states' traditional preoccupation with their own narrow national interests?

2. Of What Value Is Military Power?

In the past, military might enabled states to project power, exercise influence, and dominate others. Today the destructiveness of nuclear weapons and sophisticated conventional and unconventional biological and chemical weapons makes their use risky. Continuing arms proliferation raises new questions alongside old ones. Does the acquisition of more weapons increase security, which is a psychological phenomenon? Or are preparations for war and defense responsible for the security dilemma that all countries face?

To be sure, most leaders agree with the ancient Greek philosopher Aristotle, who argued that "a people without walls is a people without choice." Thus most assume that preparing for war against other states is necessary for peace. Yet, the capacity to destroy does not always make for a convincing threat, even against countries without the capacity to retaliate. Today, the threat of force often lacks credibility. Military power has become impotent by its very strength. And when military might no longer compels others' compliance, then weapons will have lost their primary role as a basis, or substitute, for diplomacy.

No level of military might can guarantee a state's invulnerability. And states' primary security problem today is internal, not external, aggression (K. Holsti 1995). Therefore, preparations for war can be assessed only in terms of other consequences. Thresholds may exist beyond which the addition of

In 1995, UN personnel discovered and destroyed bombs designed for germ-warfare by Iraq—a country which, after its defeat in the Persian Gulf War of 1991, came under multilateral supervision. Events like this have led many to speculate that international institutions are destined to play a larger role in managing the globe's problems.

greater destructive power is meaningless. Furthermore, excessive preparations for war may leave a country heavily fortified with little left to defend, as U.S. President Eisenhower warned in 1961.

Although the end of the Cold War has further eroded justifications for the pursuit of military power, states' traditional quest for military superiority has not entirely lost its appeal. Nonetheless, its allure in many national capitals has declined. Perhaps this is because policymakers have begun to recognize that over the long run, high military spending reduces a state's industrial growth, weakens its economic competitiveness, and ultimately undermines its ability to pursue and preserve dominance (Kennedy 1987).

Many leaders will not take this lesson seriously, though, as the one predicament that nearly every state finds worse than being preeminent is being subject to another's dictates. Consequently, the pursuit of military preeminence is likely to continue, and the relative costs and benefits of preparations for war are likely to be weighed against the kinds of threats to national security that are most likely to arise.

3. Is War between States Obsolete?

Prevalent practices tend to wither away when they cease to serve their intended purpose, as the examples of slavery, dueling, and colonialism illustrate. Is war between states subject to these same forces? Since World War II, legal prohibitions against military aggression have expanded, and war has occurred almost exclusively among and within the developing countries of the Global South. The period since 1945 has been the longest span of great-power peace since the seventeenth century, raising expectations that the major powers have "retreated from doomsday" (Mueller 1989) and that large-scale wars between states will continue to decline and perhaps cease altogether. (This hope exists even as internal or civil wars are increasing, threatening to draw others into them.) "For modern states the anticipated costs [of waging war], political and economic as well as human, generally exceed the benefits" (Mack 1996).

It is, of course, debatable whether the disincentives and dangers of using today's destructive weapons are truly making war between states obsolete. Instead, this kind of war may eventually disappear in another, far more frightening way—because resort to weapons of mass destruction will obliterate humankind. The puzzle, then, is when and by what means war will become obsolete. As Martin Luther King Jr. put it, "The choice is either nonviolence or nonexistence."

4. Can Cultural Conflict Be Controlled?

Throughout the world's history, when distinct cultures have come into contact, either the collisions have sparked communication and a healthy respect for diversity or familiarity has bred contempt. When followers have embraced the ethnocentric view that their own group's values are inherently superior, animosity and disrespect for differences have been especially characteristic, and warfare has often followed.

The fading of the ideological contest between communism and capitalism that divided the world during the Cold War has witnessed the reappearance of another major kind of divisive conflict—cultural cleavages and hatreds. Tribalism, religious fanaticism, and hypernational ethnicity are again on the move and are breeding large-scale violence and repression. With conflicts between "cultures"—ethnic groups who share a language, religion or history that bind them together and make them feel different from others—have come "ethnic cleansing," genocidal efforts to destroy unprotected members of other ethnic groups. Hypernationalistic movements respect neither liberty nor life.

Hundreds of minority groups are at risk throughout the globe. They have been denied basic human rights, and prejudice has made them the victims of aggression, persecution, and human rights abuses. Minorities consistently have become refugees, fleeing across borders in order to survive. According to the UN High Commissioner on Refugees, in 1995 some 27 million people were forced from their homes, causing them to seek sanctuary elsewhere.

National armies are neither well prepared nor well trained to defend these victims. (Indeed, in many cases the armies perpetrate violence against their own people.) Likewise, few international organizations are empowered through widespread multilateral cooperation to stop the carnage. The fact that the weak, the poor, and the exploited have no power simply contributes to their victimization.

Most states are multiethnic societies, and many people give primary loyalty to their ethnic group rather than their country. Therefore, the predictable consequence of ethnonationalism is the disintegration into smaller and smaller units of "failed" states, incapable of preserving their sovereign statehood. Cultures pitted against cultures and the retribalization of cultural groupings threaten to balkanize states into divided units (Barber 1995). If this happens, the twenty-first century will see the creation of many new states beyond the nearly 200 that presently exist. What is more, there will be reason to worry that a "clash of civilizations" will occur between groups of people belonging to "cultural areas" who share similar religious or philosophical beliefs and a common historical experience (Huntington 1993). Such competition between world cultures or civilizations that refuse to surrender their separate identities will prevent people coming together in unity in a globalized system; it will tear them apart and could spark a new era of mass violence.

Of great concern, therefore, is whether the moral outrage of the world's states is sufficient to end, through concerted action, the ethnic and cultural conflicts that now rage out of control. Will a humanitarian concern for the victims of ethnic conflicts and cultural clashes crystallize in collaborative responses? Or will the victims perish in a sea of indifference?

5. Has the Quest for Empire Ended?

Much of world history is written in terms of dreams of world conquest, the quest of rulers for world domination, and the efforts of others to prevent it. Some leaders continue to think and act as though they believe others still actively plan territorial conquest. However, the past five decades have witnessed the great powers' race to relinquish their overseas empires, not expand them. Even the Soviet Union, the last world empire of any size, has now disintegrated—by choice, not by coercion from abroad.

Why has the quest for empire seemingly ended? A plausible explanation is that empire did not benefit the imperial powers materially (Boulding 1978). Political scientist William Langer, writing in the early 1960s, the height of the decolonization period, argued similarly:

> It is highly unlikely that the modern world will revert to the imperialism of the past. History has shown that the nameless fears which in the late nineteenth century led to the most violent outburst of expansionism were largely unwarranted. The Scandinavian states and Germany since Versailles have demonstrated that economic prosperity and social well-being are not

Although its quest for empire has ostensibly ended, Russia engaged in a brutal on-going internal conflict against the secessionist movement in Chechnya in the mid-1990s. No less than its survival as a single country was at stake, as a successful bid for independence by the Chechen rebels could have encouraged similar secessionist movements in other dissatisfied governments in the Russian Federation. Pictured here, Chechnya's national colors are waved from the roof of the destroyed presidential palace in the capital city of Grozny.

dependent on the exploitation of other peoples, while better distribution of wealth in the advanced countries has reduced if not obviated whatever need there may have been to seek abroad a safety-valve for the pressures building up at home. Even in the field of defense, the old need for overseas bases or for the control of adjacent territories is rapidly being outrun. (Langer 1962, 129)

If imperialism, empire building, and territorial acquisition are no longer in a state's self-interest, why should anyone continue to prepare for military defense against the expansionist aims of others?

6. Who Will Cope with Globalization?

In 1517 Martin Luther nailed his ninety-five theses to the door of a church in Wittenberg, Germany, and ignited the Protestant Reformation. To his surprise, his effort at religious reform undermined the authority of the Catholic church over states. Ever since then, sovereign states have assumed primary responsibility for controlling affairs within their territorial borders and managing foreign relations with other similarly empowered secular state actors.

This system put sovereign states in charge of world affairs, without serious challenge. "People did what they were told to do because that is what one did. As a result, authority structures remained in place for decades, even centuries, as people tended to yield unquestionably to the dictates of governments" (Rosenau 1995).

That has begun to change. The power of sovereign states to control their internal affairs and external relations has eroded precipitously. "Today's wars," U.S. Secretary General Boutros Boutros-Ghali warned in 1996, "occur mainly within, not across, state borders," and "the forces of fragmentation" are causing states "to fail, leaving its people without a government to protect them from chaos." As anarchy within states has risen (K. Holsti 1995), doubt has climbed about the capacity of states to exercise control over behavior within their territory. The very concept of governmental authority is being challenged by public opinion, which no longer automatically accepts leaders' decisions as legitimate. And in the realm of foreign relations, the political underpinnings of the past legal and political system of independent states are being undermined by the forces of globalization. The lightning speed with which information, capital, and trade move across borders, alongside the accelerating spread of technological innovation internationally and the growing interdependence of states' markets and economies, are creating pressures with which states are not very well organized to address. The globalization process "has noticeably tamed the state's old feelings of confident independence. . . . These basic units have all, big and small, become less dominant, less independent, and, in a way, less separate than they were in their prime" (*The Economist* 337 [January 5, 1996]). They are less and less capable of coping with the "increasingly interconnected" international system, and "globalization is the world's long-term problem" (Boutros-Ghali 1996).

Moreover, there are serious questions about whence the power to address domestic and international problems will come. These questions are prompted by the challenge of minority groups' quest for autonomy from within, and the challenge of nongovernmental organizations (e.g., Doctors without Borders and multinational corporations such as McDonald's) from outside the direct control of governments. Many observers have blamed the end of the Cold War and the absence of identifiable enemies for world leaders' confusion as to how to react. But the crisis of understanding may be deeper. It may be embedded in the problem of determining whether any actor is, or can be, in charge.

However, although internal fragmentation and globalization are undermining the state as it has existed for nearly two centuries, "the emasculated state is a myth" (*The Economist* 337 [October 7, 1995]). Despite the state's loss of control, it remains the most powerful instrument for managing global change. If states fail to respond to the challenge, can the world count on supranational global institutions to take charge? This may be the most important issue facing the world in the twenty-first century. For if states will not take the lead, or take charge, can the global community count on other actors to assume responsibility?

7. Is "Realism" Still Realistic?

Since the eve of the Second World War, realism has been by far the most prevalent theoretical perspective for viewing world affairs. Leaders and scholars alike have organized their thoughts and images almost exclusively within its outlook. Their reliance on realism to explain and predict international developments was understandable. Finding a fertile ground in which to flourish during the conflict-ridden fifty-year period between 1939 and 1989, realism accounted for the prevailing lust for power, the appetite for imperial expansion and struggle for hegemony, the all-consuming arms race, and the obsession with military security better than did any other theoretical perspective.

Now, however, in the aftermath of the Cold War conflict, a window has opened to expose quite different dimensions of world politics heretofore largely neglected. The global agenda has shifted as new issues and problems have risen to prominence. Joseph S. Nye Jr. (1992), a U.S. political scientist and policymaker, writes, "The problem . . . today is not new challengers for hegemony; it is the new challenge of transnational interdependence." Others agree: predicting that "Welfare, not warfare, will shape the rules [and] global threats like ozone holes and pollution will dictate the agenda" (Joffe 1990).

To a number of theorists, the broadened and transformed post-Cold War global agenda goes beyond what realism can be expected to address accurately. To their mind, "realist preoccupations operate as a gigantic distraction from the deeper challenges associated with [the] political, economic, and social restructuring" that has occurred in international affairs (Falk 1992), and "international relations have parts which realist theory cannot reach" (Scholte 1993). "The approach of classical realism," political scientist Robert Jervis (1992) predicts, "will not be an adequate guide for the future of international politics."

Other critics are disturbed by the inability of realism to anticipate the democratic revolutions that accompanied the Cold War's end, the voluntary retreat of the Soviet Union, and global change and cooperation generally. "The wisdom [that] calls itself 'realism'," scolds Harvard political scientist Stanley Hoffmann (in Friedman 1993), "is utter nonsense today." Realism *was* predictively weak. Moreover, critics charge that realism is scientifically inaccurate and fails to provide

> an adequate understanding of the dynamics of peace and war [which are]
> at the heart of the paradigm (on the topics that realism claims to pro-

vide the best answers). . . . An entirely new theoretical approach may be needed, that will put both existing findings and unresolved questions into a perspective that makes sense of both. (Vasquez 1993, 3–4, 10)

If these critics of realism's receding accuracy and relevance are correct, then the question, "Is realism finished?" (Zakaria 1992–1993), will be asked increasingly in the future. Pressure will mount for a new theoretical approach to replace orthodox realism and its more recent neorealist variant.

What a new theory will or should look like is not presently obvious, as challengers to realism differ in their prescriptions. Yet many agree with the general view that "It is time for a new, more rigorous idealist alternative to realism" (Kober 1990) and that "there are good reasons for examining aspects of the liberal international legacy once again" (Fukuyama 1992a) by giving Woodrow Wilson's liberal vision "the fair test it has never received" (Gaddis 1990). Will a reconstructed theory that fuses the best properties of realism and emerging (neo)liberal theories provide the intellectual framework needed to understand world politics in the twenty-first century?

8. Is the World Preparing for the Wrong War?

To preserve peace, one must prepare for war. That remains the classical realist formula for national security. But would states not be wiser to prepare to conquer the conditions that undermine prosperity, freedom, and welfare? "War for survival is the destiny of all species," observes philosopher Martin J. Siegel (1983). "In our case, we are courting suicide [by waging war against one another]. The world powers should declare war against their common enemy—the catastrophic and survival-of-the-fittest forces that destroyed most of the species of life that came before us."

Not all world leaders succumb to the single-mindedness of preparing to compete with other states. Increasingly, voices that challenge the prevailing penchant are heard. President François Mitterrand of France warned in 1983 that "together we must urgently find the solutions to the real problems at hand—especially unemployment and underdevelopment. This is the battlefield where the outlines of the year 2000 will be drawn." India's Prime Minister Indira Gandhi predicted that "either nuclear war will annihilate the human race and destroy the earth, thus disposing of any future, or men and women all over must raise their voices for peace and for an urgent attempt to combine the insights of different civilizations with contemporary knowledge. We can survive in peace and goodwill only by viewing the human race as one, and by looking at global problems in their totality." These prescriptions adhere to a fundamental premise, as expressed in 1995 by Martti Ahtisaari, President of Finland: "To deal with the great security challenges of our time, including population growth, the spread of weapons of mass destruction, crime, environmental degradation and ethnic conflicts, we must resolutely adopt new methods of managing change and building global security."

Mitterrand's and Gandhi's rhetorical positions doubtless reflected the problems and self-interests the leaders faced at home and abroad. Nonetheless, they reveal a minority view. The war of people against people goes on. Humankind may consequently self-destruct, not because it lacks opportunities, but because of its collective inability to see and to seize them. "Perhaps we will destroy ourselves. Perhaps the common enemy within us will be too strong for us to recognize and overcome," the eminent astronomer Carl Sagan (1988) lamented. "But," he continued, "I have hope. . . . Is it possible that we humans are at last coming to our senses and beginning to work together on behalf of the species and the planet?"

9. Is This the "End of History"?

To many observers, the history of world affairs is the struggle between tyranny and liberty. The contest has taken various forms since antiquity: between kings and mass publics; authoritarianism and republicanism; despotism and democracy; ideological principle and pragmatic politics. Labels are misleading and sometimes dangerous. However, they form the vocabulary of diplomacy and inform theoretical discourse about governance and statecraft. History, in this image, is a battle for the hearts and minds of civilizations. It is an ideological contest for the allegiance of humankind to a particular form of political, social, and economic organization.

Since the Bolshevik revolution in 1917 brought socialism to power in Russia and made Marxism a force in international affairs, the fight for allegiance in the twentieth century has been dominated by the contests between communism, fascism, and democratic capitalism. With the defeat of fascism in World War II and the collapse of the international communist movement a generation later, it has become fashionable to argue that we have witnessed the end of a historic contest of epic proportions—and thus the triumph of liberalism and the "end of history":

> The twentieth century saw the developed world descend into a paroxysm of ideological violence, as liberalism contended first with the remnants of absolutism, then bolshevism and fascism, and finally an updated Marxism that threatened to lead to the ultimate apocalypse of nuclear war. But the century that began full of self-confidence in the ultimate triumph of Western liberal democracy seems at its close to be returning full circle to where it started: not to an "end of ideology" of a convergence between capitalism and socialism, as earlier predicted, but to the unabashed victory of economic and political liberalism. (Fukuyama 1989, 3)

The abrupt repudiation of communism in Moscow and eastern Europe and China's embrace of a free market economy have raised expectations that history has indeed "ended," in the sense that liberal democratic capitalism has triumphed throughout much of the world. Believers of the liberal faith are heartened by the doubling since the mid-1980s of the number of countries practicing multiparty elections and capitalism at home and in foreign trade. World order, they believe, can be created best by free governments practicing free trade. As Woodrow Wilson argued, making the world "safe for democracy" would make the world itself safe. From this liberal perspective, the diffusion of democratic capitalism bodes well for the future of world politics in the next millennium.

A less-reassuring possibility is that history has not "ended" and that the battle between totalitarian and democratic governance is not truly over. Instead, with the end of the ideological dimension to the Cold War, we may be witnessing not history's end but a watershed. Like previous turning points in history, today's trends may signal history's resumption: the return to the ageless search for barriers against the resurgence of tyranny, nationalism, and war. Especially to followers of *realpolitik*, the most salient feature of world politics—

the relentless competitive struggle for power under international anarchy—is permanent. The end of the Cold War does not assure us that the international community has moved beyond tyranny or interstate competition and war. As former Soviet President Mikhail Gorbachev noted in 1992, "In the major centers of world politics, the choice, it would seem, has today been made in favor of peace, cooperation, interaction, and overall security." However, he warned, "A major international effort will be needed to render irreversible the shift in favor of a democratic world—and democratic for the whole of humanity, not just half of it."

10. Is There a Reordered Global Agenda?

The paradox of contemporary world politics is that a world liberated from the paralyzing grip of the Cold War must now face a series of challenges every bit as threatening and as potentially unmanageable. Globalization, the integration and interdependence of the world's peoples, simultaneously has enlarged the responsibilities and expanded the issues to be confronted. As Bill Clinton observed in 1993, "Profound and powerful forces are shaking and remaking our world. And the urgent question of our time is whether we can make change our friend and not our enemy."

The changes in recent years have spawned threats to world order, other than the resurgence of nationalism, ethnic conflict, and separatist revolts. These include acid rain, AIDS, drug trafficking, international organized crime, ozone depletion, climate change, energy and food insecurity, desertification and deforestation, chronic debt, and neomercantilism and trade protectionism.

The potential impact of these additional threats is formidable, as emerging trends suggest that nonmilitary dangers will multiply alongside the continuing threat of arms and ethnic and regional conflict. Accordingly, the distinction between *high politics* (war and peace) and *low politics* (economic and other issues of human welfare) may disappear. "In the post-Cold War world low politics is becoming high politics" (Moran 1991).

● ● ●

A NEW WORLD ORDER?

From our vantage point on the eve of the twenty-first century, the world appears to have undergone a fundamental transformation. Previously established patterns and relationships have been obliterated. Something revolutionary, not simply new, has unfolded.

Juxtaposed against the revolutionary is the persistent—the durability of accepted rituals, existing rules, established institutions, and entrenched customs. These resist the pull of the momentous recent changes in world politics. Change and persistence coexist uneasily, and it is this mixture that makes the future so uncertain.

Two races govern the path between the world that is and the world that will be. The first is the race between knowledge and oblivion. Ignorance stands in the way of global progress and justice. Advances in science and technology far outpace resolution of the social and political problems they generate. Building the knowledge to confront these problems may therefore present the ultimate challenge. "The splitting of the atom," Albert Einstein warned, "has changed everything save our modes of thinking, and thus we drift toward unparalleled catastrophe. Unless there is a fundamental change in [our] attitudes toward one another as well as [our] concept of the future, the world will face unprecedented disaster."

"Knowledge is our destiny," philosopher Jacob Bronowski declared. If the world is to forge a promising future, it must develop more-sophisticated knowledge. Sophistication demands that we see the world as a whole as well as in terms of its individual parts. We most overcome the temptation to picture others according to our images of ourselves and to project onto them our own aims and values. We must discard the belief in a simple formula for a better tomorrow and resist single-issue approaches to reform. Toleration of ambiguity, even the pursuit of it, is essential.

The future of world politics also rests on a race between states' ability to cooperatively act in concert and their historic tendency to compete and fight. As U.S. Secretary of State James A. Baker urged in 1990, the international community must "use the end of the Cold War to get beyond the whole pattern of settling conflicts by force." Only concerted international cooperation can avert slipping "back into ever more savage regional conflicts in which might alone makes right." The world's political will to implement the reforms necessary to meet global challenges is being tested.

The world's future is uncertain, but it is our future. The moving words of President Kennedy thus describe a posture we might well assume: "However close we sometimes seem to that dark and final abyss, let no man of peace and freedom despair. For he does not stand alone. . . . Together we shall save our planet or together we shall perish in its flames. Save it we can, and save it we must, and then shall we earn the eternal thanks of mankind."

Glossary

acid rain: precipitation that has been made acidic through contact with sulfur dioxide and nitrogen oxides.

actor: a state or nonstate entity engaged in international activities.

adjudication: a conflict resolution procedure whereby a third party makes a binding decision through an institutionalized tribunal.

Algiers Summit Conference (1973): the international meeting that resulted in the Group of 77 joining forces with the nonaligned movement.

alliances: formal agreements among states for the purpose of coordinating their behavior in the event of certain specified military contingencies.

anarchy: an absence of governmental authority.

apartheid: the South African policy of racial separation.

appeasement: a policy that attempts to buy off a potential aggressor with concessions that may conflict with the country's principles.

arbitration: a conflict resolution procedure where a third party makes a binding decision through an ad hoc forum.

arms control: agreements designed to regulate arms levels.

Asian Tigers: the four Asian Newly Industrialized Economies (NIEs), (Hong Kong, South Korea, Singapore, and Taiwan) that experienced rates of economic growth during the 1980s far greater than the more advanced industrial societies of the Global North.

Atlantic Charter: a declaration issued in 1941 by U.S. President Franklin D. Roosevelt and British Prime Minister Winston Churchill outlining the principles that would guide the construction of a postwar general security system.

autocratic rule: a system of government where unlimited power is concentrated in the hands of a single person.

balance of payments: a summary statement of a state's financial transactions with the rest of the world, including such items as foreign aid transfers and the income of citizens employed abroad who send their paychecks home.

balance of power: a distribution of military capabilities where no one state can dominate the others.

balance of terror: a concept used to describe situations of mutual nuclear deterrence.

balance of trade: a state's net trade surplus or deficit, based on the difference in the value of its imports and exports.

balancer: a role played in the balance of power by a state that gives its support to one or another side of a dispute to ensure that no one achieves preponderance.

ballistic missile defense (BMD): a system to defend against an attack by incoming ballistic missiles.

Bandung Conference (1955): a meeting of twenty-nine Asian and African nations that was held in Bandung, Indonesia, to devise a strategy to combat colonialism.

bandwagon: the alignment of states with the most militarily powerful state.

Baruch Plan (1946): a call for the creation of a UN Atomic Development Authority that would place atomic energy under international authority.

beggar-thy-neighbor policies: efforts to increase domestic welfare by promoting trade surpluses that can be realized only at other countries' expense.

behavioralism: an approach to the study of international relations that emphasizes the application of scientific methods.

bilateral arms control agreements: arms control agreements negotiated between two states.

billiard ball model: a metaphor that compares world politics to a game in which billiard balls (states) continuously clash and collide with one another. The actions of each are determined by its interactions with the others, not by what occurs within it.

biodiversity: the degree of variety in living systems, including genetic, species, and ecosystem diversity.

Biological Weapons Convention (BWC): a 1972 agreement prohibiting the development, production, and stockpiling of biological weapons.

bipolarity, bipolar distribution of power: an international system containing two dominant power centers.

bipolarization: the clustering of smaller states in alliances around the two dominant power centers.

bipolycentrism: the existence during the Cold War of military bipolarity between the United States and Soviet Union coupled with multiple political centers of independent foreign policy decision making.

bloc: a rigid, highly cohesive alliance among a group of states.

Bretton Woods system: the rules, institutions, and decision-making procedures devised during World War II to govern international economic relations in the postwar era.

Brezhnev Doctrine: the assertion by Leonid Brezhnev following the 1968 Soviet invasion of Czechoslovakia that the USSR had the right to intervene to preserve Communist party rule in any state within the Soviet bloc.

brinkmanship: the threat of nuclear escalation in a confrontation to compel submission.

Brundtland Commission: the 1987 World Commission on Environment and Development which called for sustainable development.

bureaucratic politics model: an interpretation of policy making that stresses the bargaining and compromises among the contending governmental organizations that exert influence on the foreign policy choices of political leaders.

capital mobility hypothesis: the claim that increases in the volume of international financial transactions influence states' policy choices on economic matters.

carrying capacity: earth's ability to support human and other life forms.

cartel: an organization of the producers of a commodity that seeks to regulate the pricing and production of the commodity.

Carter Doctrine: a statement by President Jimmy Carter declaring U.S. willingness to use military force to protect its interests in the Persian Gulf.

Chemical Weapons Convention (CWC): an international agreement requiring the destruction of existing stocks of chemical weapons.

civil war: war between political factions within the same country.

classical imperialism: the first wave of European empire building that began during the fifteenth century, as the English, French, Dutch, Portuguese, and Spanish used their military power to achieve commercial advantages overseas.

classical liberal economic theory: a body of thought based on Adam Smith's ideas about the forces of supply and demand in the marketplace, emphasizing the benefits of minimal governmental regulation of the economy and trade.

Club of Rome: a private group that popularized a neo-Malthusian interpretation of the consequences of unrestrained growth.

coercive diplomacy: the use of threats or limited force to persuade an adversary to call off or undo an encroachment.

collective goods: goods that are jointly supplied and from which it is not possible to exclude beneficiaries.

collective security: a system of world order in which aggression by any state will be met by a collective response from all.

colonialism: the rule of a region by an external sovereign power.

Cominform (Communist Information Bureau): a Soviet organization created during the Cold War to coordinate the activities of Communist parties throughout the world.

common market: a form of economic integration where restrictions on the free movement of commodities, capital, and labor among member states are abolished and a common external tariff is established.

Commonwealth of Independent States (CIS): the political entity that replaced the Soviet Union on January 1, 1992.

comparative advantage: the principle that any two states will benefit if each specializes in those goods it produces comparatively cheaply and acquires, through trade, goods that it can only produce at a higher cost.

compellence: the use of nuclear weapons as instruments of coercive diplomacy.

complex interdependence: an approach to the study of international relations that challenges the realist assumptions that states are the only important actors, that national security issues dominate decision-making agendas, and that military force is the only means of exercising influence in a global system of vanishing borders.

Comprehensive Test Ban (CTB): negotiations held periodically since the 1950s aimed at banning all nuclear testing.

concert: a cooperative agreement among great powers to manage jointly the international system.

Concert of Europe: a system of great-power conference diplomacy organized in Europe after the Napoleonic Wars.

conciliation: a conflict-resolution procedure whereby a third party assists both sides in resolving their disputes.

Conference on Disarmament (CD): a multilateral arms-reduction conference held in Geneva beginning in 1981 which produced the U.S.-Soviet Chemical Weapons Destruction Agreement of 1990.

conflict: discord, often arising in international relations over perceived incompatibilities of interest.

constitutional democracy: a political system in which political leaders' power is limited and leaders are accountable to the population through elections.

containment: a strategy adopted by the United States during the Cold War, aimed at preventing the expansion of Soviet influence by encircling the Soviet Union with military forces.

Conventional Armed Forces in Europe (CFE) Treaty: a treaty entered into force in 1992 which set ceilings on five categories of conventional arms for its thirty signatories.

conventional deterrence: dissuading an adversary from attacking by means of non-nuclear weapons.

Conventional Forces in Europe (CFE) Treaty: an agreement between the United States and the Soviet Union to reduce the Soviet military presence in Europe.

conventional (liberal) theory of economic development: a theory that emphasizes indigenous impediments to Third World development. Based on the assumption that growth meant increasing increments of per-capita GNP, the task was to identify and remove obstacles to growth and supply missing components, such as investment capital.

cornucopians: optimists who question limits-to-growth analyses and contend that markets effectively maintain a balance among population, resources, and the environment.

Council for Mutual Economic Assistance (CMEA): an international economic organization created in 1949 to contain the former Soviet Union and the countries of Eastern Europe.

counterforce targeting strategy: targeting an opponent's military forces and weapons.

countervalue targeting strategy: targeting an opponent's industrial and population centers.

crisis: a situation that threatens high-priority goals, restricts the time available for response, and surprises decision makers.

cultural imperialism: imposing one country's value system on another population which does not welcome such foreign influence.

current history: an approach to understanding international relations that focuses on the description of contemporary events, and their causes.

customs union: a form of economic integration where member states have eliminated duties on commodities exchanged among themselves while also levying a common external tariff on commodities from nonmember states.

cyberspace: metaphorical term used to describe the global, electronic web of people, ideas, and interactions on the Internet, which is unencumbered by the borders of a geopolitical world.

cycle: a succession of periodically recurring events or phenomena.

de facto recognition: provisional legal acceptance of another entity's status as a state.

de jure recognition: full legal recognition of another entity's official status as a state.

debt decade: a prolonged financial crisis that began in 1982 when it appeared that Third World debtor states might default on their loans.

Declaration on the Granting of Independence to Colonial Countries and Peoples (1960): a declaration passed by the UN General Assembly that proclaimed the subjection of any people to colonial domination to be a denial of human rights.

decolonization: the political process freeing colonial peoples from their dependent status.

defense conversion: the process of shifting resources from the production of military-related goods to civilian products.

deforestation: the destruction of forests.

demographic transition: an explanation of population changes over time that highlights the causes of declines in birth and death rates.

dependency theory: a theory that claims advanced capitalist societies exploit those at the periphery of the world economy.

détente: the relaxation of tensions between adversaries.

deterrence: a preventive strategy designed to dissuade an adversary from doing what it otherwise would do.

developed countries: a category used by the World Bank to designate those countries with a GNP per capita (in 1993) above $8,628 annually.

developing countries: a category used by the World Bank to designate those countries with a GNP per capita (in 1993) equal to or below $8,628 annually.

development: the ability of a country to advance economically as measured by increments in its GNP per capita.

diaspora: the scattering of a religious or ethnic group to countries outside of its homeland.

diplomatic immunity: the legal doctrine that gives ambassadors immunity from the domestic laws of the country where their embassies are located.

diplomatic recognition: the formal legal acceptance of a state's official status.

disarmament: agreements designed to reduce or eliminate weapons.

diversionary theory of war: the contention that leaders initiate conflict abroad as a way of increasing national cohesion at home.

domino theory: a metaphor popular during the Cold War predicting that the fall to communism in one country would cause the fall of its neighbors, and in turn still others.

dual use technology: technology that has both commercial and military uses.

dualism: the existence of a rural, impoverished, and neglected sector of society operating alongside an urban, developing, and modernizing sector, where there is little interaction between the two sectors.

Earth Summit: an international meeting held during 1992 in Rio de Janeiro, Brazil, aimed at creating a program of action to address a broad range of environmental and developmental issues.

economic sanctions: governmental actions aimed at inflicting deprivation on a target state through the limitation or termination of economic exchanges.

economies in transition: remnants of the former Second World involved in a shift from planned to market economies.

ecopolitics: a concept that pertains to how political actors influence perceptions of, and responses to, their environments.

elitism: a model of the policy-making process that ascribes disproportionate control over foreign policy making to a small ruling group.

emerging markets: a group of nearly thirty developing and transitional economies that are identified by the World Bank as particularly ripe for foreign investment.

entente: an agreement between states to consult if one side is attacked by another party.

environmental refugee: a person who abandons land no longer fit for human habitation due to environmental degradation.

ethnic cleansing: the use of a program of terror to force a rival nationality out of a geographic region.

ethnic group: a group of people from the same nationality who share a common culture, set of ancestors, or language.

ethnic nationalism: devotion to a cultural, ethnic, or linguistic community.

ethnocentrism: the belief that one's nationality or state is special and superior and that others are secondary and inferior.

ethnonational group: a body of people who give primary allegiance to their ethnic nationality rather than to the state and government that rule them.

European Community (EC)/European Union (EU): a regional organization created by the merger of the European Coal and Steel Community, the European Atomic Energy Community, and the European Economic Community; known as the European Union after November 1993.

European Free Trade Association (EFTA): an organization created in 1960 as a counterpoint to the European Economic Community.

European Political Cooperation (EPC): the ongoing effort by European Union members to devise a common position on foreign policy issues through regular meetings among EU foreign ministers.

export-led industrialization: a strategy that involves developing domestic export industries capable of competing in overseas markets.

export quotas: barriers to free trade imposed pursuant to negotiated agreements between producers and consumers.

extended deterrence: a strategy that seeks to deter an adversary from attacking one's allies.

externalities: the social costs of environmental exploitation excluded from market costs.

extraterritoriality: the legal doctrine that allows a state to maintain jurisdiction over its embassies on other states' territory.

fascism: a far-right ideology that promotes extreme nationalism and the establishment of an authoritarian society built around a single party with dictatorial leadership.

feminist theory: a body of scholarship that emphasizes gender and women's issues in the study of world politics.

fertility rate: the average number of children born to a woman (or group of women) during her (their) lifetime(s).

financial veto: withholding payment selectively from certain UN programs as a way to register resentment of the organization's activities and to change them.

firebreak: the psychological barrier between conventional and nuclear war.

First World: economically developed countries that share a commitment to varying forms of democratic political institutions and developed market economies.

fixed exchange rates: an international system under which states establish the parity of their currencies and commit themselves to keeping fluctuations in their exchange rates within narrow limits.

floating exchange rates: an international monetary system where market forces rather than government intervention determine currency values.

food security: access by all people to enough food for an active, healthy life.

foreign direct investment: ownership of assets in one country by residents of another for the purpose of controlling the use of those assets.

foreign policy: purposive actions undertaken by states toward actors outside their boundaries to achieve the states' goals on international issues.

Fourteen Points speech (1918): a speech delivered by U.S. President Woodrow Wilson that called for open diplomacy, self-determination, democracy, free trade, freedom of the seas, disarmament, and collective security.

Fourth World: indigenous people that often live in poverty and deprivation within a state that occupies the land from which they originate.

free riders: those who enjoy the benefits of collective goods but pay little or nothing for them.

functionalism: a bottom-up approach to fostering political integration through transnational organizations that emphasizes sharing sovereignty.

General Agreement on Tariffs and Trade (GATT): an international organization that sought to promote and protect the most-favored-nation principle as the basis for free trade. The World Trade Organization superseded GATT in 1995.

General Assembly: one of six principle organs established by the UN Charter. It is the only body representing all the member states. Decision making follows the principle of majority rule, with no state given a veto.

Generalized System of Preferences (GSP): a scheme that permits states to grant preferences to developed countries without violating GATT's nondiscrimination principle.

genocide: the deliberate extermination of an ethnic or minority group.

geo-economics: a term used to describe the emergence of economic issues and conflicts as a significant component of world politics.

geopolitics: a school of thought stressing the influence of geographic factors on state power and international conduct.

Global Environment Facility (GEF): a joint enterprise within the World Bank involving the United Nations Environment (UNEP) and Development (UNDP) programs, whose purpose is to facilitate adoption of environmentally sensitive policies in the Global South.

Global North: a term used to refer to the world's wealthy, industrialized countries.

Global South: a term now often used instead of "Third World" to refer to the world's less economically developed countries.

global warming: the gradual rise of global temperature attributed to greenhouse gases which trap heat remitted from earth that otherwise would escape into outer space.

globalization: the growth and intensification of political, economic, social, and cultural relations across borders.

globalization of finance: the growth of a single unified world financial market where geographic location does not play a significant role.

good offices: the third-party offering of a location for discussions among disputants.

greenhouse gases: carbon dioxide, methane, nitrous oxide, chloroflourocarbons, and other gas molecules that tend to trap heat remitted from earth that otherwise would escape into outer space.

gross national product (GNP): the total value of goods and services produced in a nation during a specified period, usually a year.

Group of Seven (G-7): the United States, Britain, France, Japan, Germany, Canada, and Italy. Leaders from these industrialized states meet in regular economic summit conferences.

Group of 77 (G-77): a coalition of the world's poor countries, formed during the 1964 United Nations Conference on Trade and Development (UNCTAD) in Geneva. Originally composed of 77 states, the coalition now numbers over 120 developing countries and continues to press for concessions from the wealthy states.

groupthink: the propensity of cohesive, insulated groups to suffer from a deterioration of mental efficiency, reality testing, and moral judgment.

gunboat diplomacy: a show of military force, historically naval force, for the purpose of coercing another state.

Hague Peace Conferences (1899, 1907): international meetings that restricted the use of certain weapons and sought to promote peaceful methods of dispute resolution.

hard power: the ability to exercise influence in world politics because of the user's possession of tangible military and economic resources.

hegemon: a dominant military and economic state that uses its unrivaled power to create and enforce rules aimed at preserving the existing world order and its own position in that order.

hegemonic stability theory: a theory that draws attention to the impact of a preeminent state (a hegemon) in maintaining international cooperation.

hegemony: the ability of one state to dominate the rules and arrangements governing international economics and politics.

Helsinki Accord (1975): an agreement signed by NATO, the Warsaw Pact, and thirteen neutral and nonaligned European countries, which sought to establish peace in Europe by calling for the implementation of confidence-building measures; economic, environmental, and scientific cooperation; the free flow of people, ideas, and information; and a democratization and respect for human rights.

hero-in-history model: an interpretation of foreign policy behavior that equates state action with the preferences and initiatives of the highest officials in national governments.

hidden veto: the ability of the United States during the formative period of the United Nations to persuade a sufficient majority of other UN Security Council members to vote negatively on an issue so as to avoid the stigma of having to cast the single blocking vote.

horizontal nuclear proliferation: an increase in the number of states that possess nuclear weapons.

human development index (HDI): a measure that uses life expectancy, literacy, educational attainment, and income to assess a country's human development performance.

idealism: an approach to international relations that assumes people are not by nature sinful or wicked, and that harmful behavior is the result of structural arrangements that motivate people to act selfishly.

imperial overstretch: a condition where commitments exceed a hegemon's ability to fulfill them.

imperialism: a relationship of dominance and subordination where one state controls the people and territory of another area.

import quotas: nontariff barriers to free trade that involve limits on the quantity of a particular product that can be imported from abroad.

import-substitution industrialization: a strategy that involves encouraging domestic entrepreneurs to manufacture products otherwise imported from abroad.

inadvertent war: a war that is not the result of anyone's master plan, but rather occurs due to uncertainty, confusion, and circumstances beyond the control of those involved.

indigenous peoples: people native to a specific geographic area.

individual levels of analysis: an analytical approach to the study of world politics that emphasizes the psychological and perceptual origins of states' foreign policy behavior, with special attention to leaders.

infant industry: a newly established industry that is not yet strong enough to compete effectively in the global marketplace.

instrumental rationality: a conceptualization of rationality asserting that individuals have preferences and, when faced with two or more alternatives, they will choose the one that yields the preferred outcome.

intercontinental ballistic missiles (ICBMs): rockets capable of carrying weapons from one continent to another.

interdependence: a situation of mutual dependence defined as mutual sensitivity and mutual vulnerability.

interethnic competition: a struggle for supremacy within a geographic area between two or more ethnic groups.

intergovernmental organizations (IGOs): an international organization whose members are states.

Intergovernmental Panel on Climate Change (IPCC): a team of scientists from around the world who are studying global climate change under the sponsorship of the United Nations.

Intermediate-Range Nuclear Force (INF) disarmament agreement (1987): a treaty between the United States and Soviet Union to remove intermediate-range nuclear forces from Europe.

International Court of Justice: the primary judicial organ of the United Nations; also known as the World Court.

International Labor Organization: a UN specialized agency responsible for improving working conditions in member countries.

international liquidity: reserve assets used to settle international accounts.

International Monetary Fund (IMF): a specialized agency of the United Nations that seeks to maintain monetary stability and assist member states in funding balance-of-payments deficits.

international political system: a pattern of interactions among world political actors who have sufficient regular contact to make the behavior of each a central part of the calculations of the others.

international regimes: sets of rules, norms, and decision-making procedures that coordinate state behavior within a given area of activity.

international terrorism: the use of terrorism against targets outside the boundaries of one's own country.

interspecific aggression: killing species other than one's own kind.

intraspecific aggression: killing species of one's own kind.

illegal doctrine: a doctrine that pertains to the moral considerations under which war may be undertaken and how it should be fought once it begins.

irredentism: the desire by one state to annex or reclaim territory held by another that was historically or ethnically connected to the first state.

Kellogg-Briand Pact (Pact of Paris, 1928): a treaty that sought to outlaw war as an instrument of national policy.

laissez-faire economies: economies based on the philosophic principle of free markets with little governmental regulation of the marketplace.

League of Nations: a global intergovernmental organization established after World War I.

League of Nations mandate system: the placement of colonies previously held by the Central Powers of World War I under the administration of certain Allied nations. Implicit in the system was the idea that colonies were a trust rather than a territory to be exploited.

least developed of the less-developed countries (LLDCs): the most impoverished members of the Global South.

levels of analysis: alternative perspectives on world politics that may focus on the personal characteristics of decision makers, the attributes of states, or the structure of the international system.

Liberal International Economic Order (LIEO): the set of regimes created after World War II designed to promote monetary stability and reduce barriers to the free flow of trade and capital.

linkage strategy: a set of assertions that claims leaders should take into account another country's overall behavior when deciding whether to reach agreement on any one specific issue.

long cycle theory: a theory that focuses on the rise and fall of the leading global power (hegemon) as the central political and economic process of the modern world system and that treats recurrent general wars as a cause and consequence of these dynamics.

long peace: the period of great-power relations extending from the end of World War II until the present. It represents the longest period of great-power peace in modern history.

low-intensity conflict: fighting that falls below the threshold of full-scale military combat between modern armies.

Maastricht summit (1991): a meeting of European Community members in The Netherlands that created a framework for achieving greater European unity.

machtpolitik: power politics.

Malthusian Projection: the prediction that population, when unchecked, increases in a geometric ratio, whereas subsistence increases in only an arithmetic ratio.

Marshall Plan: a program of grants and loans established by the United States to assist the recovery of Western Europe after World War II.

massive retaliation: the strategic weapons posture of the U.S. during the Eisenhower administration which threatened the Soviet Union with annihilation in the event of its aggression.

mechanical majority: a complaint voiced by the Soviet Union during the early history of the United Nations that the United States enjoyed a commanding position in the General Assembly due to the fact that its allies constituted a majority of the UN membership on whose support the United States could always depend.

mediation: a conflict-resolution procedure where a third party offers a nonbinding solution to the disputants.

mercantilism: the economic philosophy advocating government regulation of economic life to increase state power and security. Under this philosophy, state power was assumed to flow from the possession of national wealth measured in terms of gold and silver. Exporting more than is imported constitutes one way to accumulate the desired bullion.

migration: movement from one place of abode to another.

militarized disputes: confrontations short of war characterized by the reciprocated threat, deployment, mobilization, or use of force.

military-industrial complex: a concept that refers to the convergence of interests between the professional military and arms manufacturers in keeping defense spending high.

military intervention: an overt or covert use of force by one or more countries that crosses the border of another country in order to affect the government and policies of the target country.

military necessity: the legal doctrine asserting that violations of the rules of warfare may be excused during periods of extreme emergency.

mirror images: the propensity of each member of a conflict to see the other as the other sees it.

MIRV: multiple independently targetable-re-entry vehicle, a technological innovation permitting many weapons to be delivered from a single missile.

Missile Technology Control Regime (MTCR): an informal arrangement among the most advanced suppliers of missile-related equipment to control the export of ballistic and cruise missiles and associated technologies.

mortality rate: crude death-rate is the most common measure of mortality. The age-adjusted death rate is often used in its place because it is free of distortions due to differences in age composition.

most-favored-nation (MFN) principle: tariff preferences granted to one nation must be granted to all others exporting the same product.

muddling through: a model of the policy-making process that highlights incremental modifications of existing policy through trial and error.

multilateral arms control agreements: arms control agreements negotiated among more than two states.

multinational corporation (MNC): a business enterprise organized in one society with activities in another growing out of direct investment abroad.

multipolar: an international system containing more than two dominant power centers.

Munich Conference (1938): the conference at which Britain and France accepted Adolf Hitler's demand to annex the German-populated area of Sudetenland in Czechoslovakia.

Mutual and Balanced Force Reduction (MBFR): a series of discussions held between 1973 and 1988 which attempted to reduce the military forces possessed by the East and West blocs.

mutual assured destruction (MAD): a system of deterrence in which both sides possess the ability to survive a first strike and launch a devastating retaliatory attack.

mutual sensitivity: the liability of states to costs imposed by external events before policies are changed to deal with the situation.

mutual vulnerability: the liability of states to costs imposed by external events even after policies have been changed to deal with the situation.

nation: a collection of people who, on the basis of ethnic, linguistic, or cultural affinity, perceive themselves to be members of the same group.

national character: the collective characteristics ascribed to a nation-state.

national level of analysis: an analytical approach to the study of world politics that emphasizes how the internal attributes of states' explain their foreign policy behavior.

national security: a country's psychological freedom from fear of foreign attack.

nationalism: loyalty to a nation.

nation-state: a polity (system of government) controlled by members of some nationality recognizing no higher authority.

neocolonialism, neo-imperialism: unequal exchanges that permit the wealthy countries of the Global North to exploit others through the institutionalized processes of the contemporary world political economy.

neofunctionalism: a reconstitution of the functionalist theory of integration that directly addresses the political obstacles to the merger of two or more independent states.

neoliberalism: a perspective on world politics that concentrates on the ways in which international organizations and other nonstate actors promote international change.

neo-Malthusians: pessimists who warn of the global ecopolitical dangers of uncontrolled population growth and exploitation of finite resources.

neomercantilism: a trade policy whereby a state seeks to maintain a balance-of-trade surplus by reducing imports, stimulating domestic production, and promoting exports.

neonationalism: the expression of communal or ethnic aspirations of dissatisfied groups within a given state.

neorealism: a variant of realism that emphasizes the anarchic structure of world politics rather than human nature in its explanation of how and why states competitively interact.

neutrality: the legal doctrine that provides rights and duties for states who remain nonaligned with adversaries during wartime.

New Imperialism: the second wave of European empire building that began in the 1870s and extended until the outbreak of World War I. Extraordinary competition among the imperial powers marked the new imperialism as colonies became important symbols of national power and prestige.

New International Economic Order (NIEO): a demand by the Global South to replace the U.S.-sponsored Liberal International Economic Order (LIEO) with an international economic regime that is more favorable to the interests of developing countries.

New World Information and Communication Order (NWICO): a demand by the Third World for a new regime covering the flow of information between North and South due to dissatisfaction with the media coverage provided by news agencies from the developed countries.

newly industrialized economies (NIEs): the most prosperous members of the Global South, which have become important exporters of manufactured goods as well as important markets for the major industrialized countries that export capital goods.

nonaligned movement (NAM): an organization founded in Belgrade during 1961 to promote nonalignment and a reduction in East–West tension.

nonaligned states: those countries that did not participate in military alliances with either the East or West during the Cold War because of a fear that one form of domination might be replaced by another.

nonalignment: the refusal of a state to join an alliance.

noncombatant immunity: the legal principle that military force should not be used against innocent civilians.

nongovernmental organization (NGO): an international organization whose members are private individuals and groups.

nonintervention, noninterference principle: the duty of states to refrain from uninvited involvement in another's internal affairs.

Nuclear Nonproliferation Treaty (NPT) (1968): an international agreement that seeks to prevent horizontal proliferation.

nonrecognition: withholding official legal acceptance as a form of sanction against another established government recognized as an independent state by others.

nonstate actors: associations of individuals and/or groups that play significant roles in world politics but are not established by agreements among states.

nontariff barriers (NTBs): inhibitions against the free flow of goods and services across national boundaries that does not involve an import tax or duty.

North American Free Trade Agreement (NAFTA): a 1993 agreement bringing Mexico, Canada, and the United States together in a free-trade zone.

North Atlantic Cooperation Council (NACC): a NATO council proposed in 1991 to build a partnership between NATO and the countries of central and eastern Europe.

North Atlantic Treaty Organization (NATO): a military alliance created in 1949 in order to deter a Soviet attack on western Europe that continues to exist after the Cold War.

nth country problems: the addition of new states to the group of those who possess nuclear weapons.

nuclear deterrence: dissuading an adversary from attacking by threatening retaliation with nuclear weapons.

nuclear utilization theory (NUTs): a body of strategic thought that claims deterrent threats could be more credible if nuclear weapons were made more usable.

oil shocks: the rapid increases in oil prices in the aftermath of the Yom Kippur War, the revolution in Iran, and the invasion of Kuwait.

OPEC: Organization of Petroleum Exporting Countries.

open skies proposal (1955): a call for allowing aerial reconnaissance to monitor military maneuvers.

Orderly Market Arrangement (OMA): a voluntary export restriction that involves a government-to-government agreement and often specific rules of management.

Organization for the Prevention of Chemical Weapons (OPCW): an international organization headquartered in The Hague that is designed to control chemical weapons.

Organization for Security and Cooperation in Europe (OSCE): a multilateral institution that led in the transformation of Europe from a system of counterpoised military alliances to one based on common principles for maintaining security in the post-Cold War World.

ozone depletion: the thinning of the ozone layer in the upper atmosphere due to the release of chlorofluorocarbons (CFCs).

pacta sunt servanda: the legal doctrine that treaties are binding.

paradigm: a theoretical perspective that gives direction to research by indicating what problems in a field of inquiry are more important than others and what criteria and methods should govern their investigation.

parallel currency: the universal acceptance of the U.S. dollar in the immediate postwar period as the currency against which every other country sold or redeemed its own national currency in exchange markets.

Partnership for Peace (PFP): a plan proposed in 1993 by the United States that establishes limited military partnerships between NATO and former Warsaw Pact countries.

pax atomica: the belief that nuclear weapons preserved peace between the superpowers during the Cold War.

peacebuilding: creating conditions that make war unlikely.

peaceful coexistence: a policy adopted by the Soviet Union following Joseph Stalin's death, based on the assumption that war between communist and capitalist countries was not inevitable.

peacekeeping: the use of a United Nations military force to function as a buffer between disputants in order to prevent fighting.

peacemaking: efforts by the UN to obtain a truce between the belligerents in an ongoing military conflict.

pluralism: a model of the policy-making process that highlights the impact of competitive domestic groups in pressuring the government for policies responsive to their interests and needs.

polarity: the degree to which power is concentrated among the major powers in the state system.

polarization: the degree to which states cluster in alliances around the most powerful members of the state system.

political disintegration: the political fragmentation of a state.

political economy: a field of study that focuses on the intersection of politics and economics in international relations.

political efficacy: a person's self-image of his or her own ability to control events politically.

political integration: the process or the product of efforts to build new political communities and supranational institutions that transcend the state.

politics: the exercise of influence.

polycentrism: a concept used to describe the emergence of new centers of independent power within the polarized bloc structure of the Cold War.

pooled sovereignty: the sharing of decision-making responsibility among several governments and between them and international institutions.

population momentum: the concept that population growth will continue for several decades after replacement-level fertility is achieved.

positivism: a philosophical tradition underlying the scientific method that focuses on positive facts, to the exclusion of speculation about ultimate causes or origins.

postbehavioralism: an approach to the study of international relations that calls for increased attention to the policy relevance of research.

postmodernism: an approach to the study of international relations that emphasizes the study of texts, hidden meanings, and discourse in the writings and speeches of those policymakers and analysts who interpret world affairs.

power: the capacity to influence others to continue a course of action, change what is being done, or refrain from acting.

power potential: the relative amount of capabilities or resources that are presumed necessary for a state to achieve influence over others.

power transition theory: the contention that war is most likely when the differentials between the capabilities of rival states narrow.

preemption: a quick first-strike attack that seeks to defeat an adversary before it can organize a retaliatory response.

preventive diplomacy: active, conflict-avoidance measures, first advocated in 1960 by UN Secretary-General Dag Hammarskjöld.

private international law: law pertaining to routinized transnational intercourse between or among nongovernmental actors.

procedural rationality: a conceptualization of rationality that emphasizes perfect information and a careful weighing of all possible courses of action when decisions are made.

prospect theory: a body of thought contending that policymakers are more risk acceptant with respect to gains than they are risk averse with respect to potential losses.

protectionism: the use of tariff and nontariff barriers to restrict imports.

public international law: law pertaining to government-to-government relations.

Rapacki Plan (1957): a call for the denuclearization of Central Europe.

rationality, rational choice: an idealized portrayal of decision making according to which the individual uses the best information available to choose from the set of possible responses that alternative most likely to maximize his or her goals.

Reagan Doctrine: a pledge of U.S. support for anticommunist insurgents who sought to overthrow Soviet-supported governments.

realism: an approach to international relations that assumes people by nature are sinful or wicked, and that the purpose of statecraft is to acquire the power needed to survive in a competitive, anarchical environment.

realpolitik: policies that seek to maximize power in an anarchical state system.

rebus sic stantibus: the legal doctrine that reserves the right of states to terminate treaties unilaterally if conditions present at the time of the signing have since changed.

refugees: people who flee for safety to another country because of a well-founded fear of persecution.

relative burden of military spending: the ratio of defense spending to gross national product.

relative deprivation: the belief that one is unfairly deprived, in comparison to others, of the wealth and status that one deserves.

reparations: compensation paid by a defeated state for damages or expenditures sustained by the victor during hostilities.

replacement-level fertility: the average number of children born to a woman in her lifetime required to stabilize the population of a given geographic area.

reprisal: hostile and illegal retaliatory acts.

retorsion: hostile but legal retaliatory acts.

reversible conservation measures: nonpermanent conservation measures that often derive from behavioral changes.

satisficing behavior: the propensity of decision makers to select the first choice identified that meets minimally acceptable standards.

schematic reasoning: the processing of new information according to an established set of memories that structure thinking about choices.

secession, separative revolts: the attempt by an ethnic, religious minority, or political independence movement to break away from an internationally recognized state.

second-strike capability: the capacity of a state to retaliate after absorbing a first-strike military attack.

Second World: Countries with centrally planned economies, principally the Soviet Union and its allies in Eastern Europe during the Cold War.

Secretary-General: the chief administrative officer of the United Nations and the head of the Secretariat, one of the six principal organs established by the UN Charter.

security community: a group of states whose high level of noninstitutionalized collaboration results in the settlement of disputes by compromise rather than by force.

Security Council: one of six principle organs established by the UN Charter. Its primary responsibility is the maintenance of international peace and security.

security dilemma: the propensity of armaments undertaken by one state for ostensibly defensive purposes to be perceived by others as threatening, provoking arms races that undermine the security of all.

security regime: rules, norms, and decision-making procedures designed for the peaceful management of disputes.

self-determination: the doctrine asserting that nationalities have the right to determine what political authority will represent and rule them.

self-fulfilling prophecy: the tendency for one's expectations to evoke behavior that confirms the expectation.

self-help: the dependence of the state on its own resources to promote its interests and protect itself from external attack.

SLBM: submarine-launched ballistic missile.

socialization: the processes by which one learns the beliefs, values, and behaviors that are acceptable in a given society.

soft power: the ability to exercise influence in world politics due to such intangible resources as a nation's culture and ideas.

sovereign equality: the principle that states, as legally equal, are entitled to equal protection under international law.

sovereignty: the principle that no authority is above the state.

special drawing rights (SDRs): reserves created and held by the International Monetary Fund (IMF) that member states can draw upon to help manage the values of their currencies.

sphere of influence: a region dominated by a powerful foreign state.

spillaround: the stagnation of regional integration, when cooperative ventures in one area of activity interferes with cooperative ventures in other areas.

spillback: the loss of forward momentum in regional integration.

spillover: within the process of international integration, the deepening of ties among states in one sector or expansion of ties to another sector.

spiral model: a metaphor used to describe the tendency of

efforts to enhance defense to result in escalating arms races.

standard operating procedures (SOPs): established methods to be followed for the performance of designated tasks by bureaucracies which implement leaders' foreign policy decisions.

state: a legal entity that possesses a permanent population, a well-defined territory, and a government capable of managing public affairs.

state system: a pattern of interaction among sovereign states that are in regular contact with one another.

state terrorism: the support of terrorist groups by governmental authorities.

statehood: as outlined in the Montevideo Convention of 1933, a state must possess a permanent population, a well-defined territory, and a government capable of ruling its citizens and managing diplomatic relations with other states.

states' attributes: characteristics of states (such as military capability, level of economic development, and type of government) that may influence foreign policy behavior.

Strategic Arms Limitations Talks (SALT): two sets of agreements reached during the 1970s between the United States and the Soviet Union that established limits on strategic nuclear delivery systems.

Strategic Arms Reduction Talks (START): a series of negotiations that led to a 1991 treaty to reduce U.S. and Soviet strategic forces.

Strategic Defense Initiative (SDI): a ballistic missile defense system which, if created, would use space-based laser technology.

strategic trade policy: an industrial policy that targets government subsidies toward particular industries so as to gain a competitive advantage over foreign producers.

structural realism: a neorealistic approach to international relations that emphasizes the global system's structure as a determinant of the behavior of those units that constitute the system.

structural violence: oppression resulting from the hierarchical structure of world politics, which makes it difficult for weak states to impose effective sanctions on the powerful.

supranational entities: international institutions with the power to make decisions binding on their national members without being subject to members' individual approval.

sustainable development: economic growth that does not deplete the resources needed to maintain growth. This concept urges that the present generation meets its needs without comprising the ability of future generations to meet theirs.

system level of analysis: an analytical approach to world politics that emphasizes the impact of global conditions on foreign policy behavior.

terms of trade: the ratio of export prices to import prices.

terrorists: those who use or threaten violence for a political goal, who deliberately use indiscriminate means and violate the principle of noncombatant immunity.

theory: a set of interrelated propositions that purports to explain or predict.

Third World: a term commonly used during the Cold War to refer to the world's poorer, economically less-developed countries in the Global South.

tied aid: the existence of conditions or "strings" attached to foreign aid.

Tokyo Round of GATT: multilateral trade negotiations held between 1973 and 1979.

trade integration: the difference between growth rates in trade and gross domestic product.

tragedy of the commons: a metaphor widely used to explain the impact of human behavior on ecological systems. Rational self-interested behavior by individuals often produces destruction for the collectivity.

transfer-pricing mechanism: the trading of commodities among a parent company's subsidiaries in different countries in order to record profits in jurisdictions where taxes are low.

Treaty of Rome (1957): the agreement that created the European Economic Community, popularly known for many years as the European Common Market.

Truman Doctrine: the declaration by U.S. President Harry S Truman that the U.S. policy must be to support "free peoples who are resisting attempted subjugation by armed minorities or by outside pressures."

unipolarity: an international system containing a single dominant power center.

unitary actor: a conceptualization based on the assumption that all states and individuals responsible for their foreign policies confront the problem of national survival in similar ways, and, accordingly, that states can be conceived of as monolithic actors.

United Nations: a global, multipurpose international, intergovernmental organization established in 1945, consisting of six major organs and numerous specialized agencies, conferences, and commissions.

United Nations Conference on Trade and Development (UNCTAD): a special trade conference held in Geneva during 1964 which has become a regular forum for developing world trade policies.

United Nations Educational, Scientific and Cultural Organization (UNESCO): the UN specialized agency responsible for promoting cooperation in the fields of education, science, and culture.

United Nations Emergency Force (UNEF): authorized by the General Assembly in 1956 under the Uniting for Peace resolution to attempt to restore peace in the Middle East following the outbreak of war between Egypt and a coalition of Israel, Britain, and France.

United Nations Register of Conventional Arms: an effort begun in 1992 to have states submit information on their trade in various categories of weapons.

Uniting for Peace Resolution: a U.S. sponsored device designed to enable the United Nations General Assembly to meet in emergency sessions to deal with threats to peace and acts of aggression.

Uruguay Round: the eighth in a series of multinational trade negotiations conducted since the end of World War II under the sponsorship of GATT, culminating in the creation of the World Trade Organization (WTO).

vertical nuclear proliferation: an increase in the capabilities of existing nuclear powers.

voluntary export restrictions (VERs): a generic term for all bilaterally agreed restraints on trade.

war contagion: a metaphor that likens the diffusion of war to the spread of disease.

war weariness hypothesis: the contention that a nation at war will become exhausted and lose its enthusiasm for another war, but only for a time.

Warsaw Pact: a military alliance created by the Soviet Union in 1955 which included communist regimes in Eastern Europe; disbanded in 1991.

Washington Naval Conferences (1921–1922): arms control meetings that resulted in agreements among the U.S., Britain, France, Japan, and Italy to adjust the relative tonnage of their fleets.

weighted voting: a system in which votes are distributed among states in proportion to their financial contribution to an organization.

Western European Union (WEU): a military pact composed of ten European countries.

world federalism: an approach to integration based on the merger of previously sovereign states into a single federal union.

world-system theory: a theory claiming that there is an international division of labor in which core states specialize in the capital-intensive production of sophisticated manufactured goods and peripheral states concentrate on the labor-intensive production of raw materials and agricultural commodities.

World Trade Organization (WTO): a multilateral organization that monitors the implementation of trade agreements and settles disputes among trade partners.

Yalta Conference (1945): a meeting of Winston Churchill, Franklin Roosevelt, and Joseph Stalin in the Russian Crimea to design a new, post-World War II order.

Yoshida Doctrine: a security policy proposing that Japan should avoid international disputes, keep a low profile on divisive global issues, and concentrate on economic pursuits.

zeitgeist: spirit of the times.

zero-sum: the perception that gains for one side in a rivalry are losses for the other side.

References

Abernethy, Virginia. (1994) "Optimism and Overpopulation," *Atlantic Monthly* 274 (December): 84–91.

Adelman, Kenneth L., and Norman R. Augustine. (1992) "Defense Conversion," *Foreign Affairs* 71 (Spring): 26–47.

Albright, David. (1993) "A Proliferation Primer," *Bulletin of the Atomic Scientists* 49 (June): 14–23.

Allison, Graham T. (1971) *Essence of Decision: Explaining the Cuban Missile Crisis.* Boston: Little, Brown.

Al-Sammarrai, Bashir. (1995) "Economic Sanctions against Iraq," pp. 133–39 in David Cortright and George A. Lopez (eds.), *Economic Sanctions.* Boulder, Colo.: Westview.

Ambrose, Stephen E. (1995) "The Bomb: It Was More than Death," *New York Times* (August 5): 15.

Amin, Samir. (1974) *Accumulation on a World Scale: A Critique of the Theory of Underdevelopment.* New York: Monthly Review Press.

Amuzegar, Jahangir. (1987) "Dealing with Debt," *Foreign Policy* 68 (Fall): 140–58.

Andrews, David M. (1994) "Capital Mobility and State Autonomy: Toward a Structural Theory of International Monetary Relations," *International Studies Quarterly* 38 (June): 193–218.

Angell, Norman. (1910) *The Great Illusion: A Study of the Relationship of Military Power in Nations to Their Economic and Social Advantage.* London: Weidenfeld and Nicholson.

Apter, David E., and Louis W. Goodman (eds.). (1976) *The Multinational Corporation and Social Change.* New York: Praeger.

Arat, Zehra F. (1995) "Women under Layers of Oppression: The (Un)Changing Political Economy of Gender," pp. 265–93 in Manochehr Dorraj (ed.), *The Changing Political Economy of the Third World.* Boulder, Colo.: Lynne Rienner.

Arbatov, Alexei. (1995) "NATO and Russia," *Security Dialogue* 26 (June): 135–46.

Arkin, William M. (1995) "The Pentagon's Blind Ambition," *New York Times* (May 10): A19.

Ashford, Lori S. (1995) "New Perspectives on Population: Lessons from Cairo," *Population Bulletin* 50 (March): 1–44.

Ashley, Richard K., and R. B. J. Walker (eds.). (1990) "Speaking the Language of Exile: Dissident Thought in International Studies," Special issue, *International Studies Quarterly* 34 (September): 259–417.

Åslund, Anders. (1994) "Russia's Success Story," *Foreign Affairs* 73 (September/October): 58–70.

Avery, Dennis. (1995) "Saving the Planet with Pesticides," pp. 49–82 in Ronald Bailey (ed.), *The True State of the Planet.* New York: Free Press.

Ayoob, Mohammed. (1995) *The Third World Security Predicament.* Boulder, Colo.: Lynne Rienner.

Babai, Don. (1993) "General Agreement on Tariffs and Trade," pp. 342–48 in Joel Krieger (ed.), *The Oxford Companion to Politics of the World.* New York: Oxford University Press.

Bagdikian, Ben H. (1992) *The Media Monopoly.* Boston: Beacon Press.

Bailey, Ronald (ed.). (1995) *The True State of the Planet.* New York: Free Press.

Balaam, David N., and Michael Veseth. (1996) *Introduction to International Political Economy.* Upper Saddle River, N.J.: Prentice Hall.

Baldwin, David A. (ed.). (1993) *Neorealism and Neoliberalism: The Contemporary Debate.* New York: Columbia University Press.

———. (1989) *Paradoxes of Power.* New York: Basil Blackwell.

———. (1985) *Economic Statecraft.* Princeton, N.J.: Princeton University Press.

Ball, Nicole. (1994) "Demilitarizing the Third World," pp. 216–35 in Michael T. Klare and Daniel C. Thomas (eds.), *World Security.* New York: St. Martin's Press.

———. (1991) *Briefing Book on Conventional Arms Transfers.* Boston: Council for a Livable World Education Fund.

Baran, Paul. (1968) *The Political Economy of Growth.* New York: Monthly Review Press.

Barber, Benjamin R. (1995) *Jihad vs. McWorld.* New York: Random House.

———. (1992) "Jihad vs. McWorld," *Atlantic Monthly* 269 (March): 53–63.

Barkun, Michael. (1968) *Law without Sanctions: Order in Primitive Societies and the World Community.* New Haven, Conn.: Yale University Press.

Barnet, Richard J. (1980) *The Lean Years.* New York: Simon & Schuster.

———. (1977) *The Giants: Russia and America.* New York: Simon & Schuster.

Barnet, Richard J., and John Cavanagh. (1994) *Global Dreams: Imperial Corporations and the New World Order.* New York: Simon & Schuster.

Barnet, Richard J., and Ronald E. Müller. (1974) *Global Reach: The Power of the Multinational Corporations.* New York: Simon & Schuster.

Baron, Samuel H., and Carl Pletsch (eds.). (1985) *Introspection in Biography: The Biographer's Quest for Self-Awareness.* Hillsdale, N.J.: Analytic Press.

Bayard, Thomas O., and Kimberly Ann Elliott. (1994) *Reciprocity and Retaliation in U.S. Trade Policy.* Washington, D.C.: Institute for International Economics.

Beckman, Peter R., and Francine D'Amico (eds.). (1994) *Women, Gender, and World Politics.* Westport, Conn.: Bergin & Garvey.

Beer, Francis A. (1981) *Peace against War: The Ecology of International Violence.* San Francisco: Freeman.

Bell, Coral. (1995) "The Future of Power in World Affairs," *Quadrant* 39 (September): 49–56.

Bendor, Jonathan. (1995) "A Model of Muddling Through," *American Political Science Review* 89 (December): 819–840.

Bendor, Jonathan, and Thomas H. Hammond. (1992) "Rethinking Allison's Models," *American Political Science Review* 86 (June): 301–22.

Benedick, Richard Elliot. (1991) "Protecting the Ozone Layer: New Directions in Diplomacy," pp. 112–53 in Jessica Tuchman Mathews (ed.), *Preserving the Global Environment*. New York: Norton.

Bennett, A. Leroy. (1988) *International Organizations*, 4th ed. Englewood Cliffs, N.J.: Prentice–Hall.

Berger, Mark T. (1994) "The End of the Third World?" *Third World Quarterly* 15 (June): 257–75.

Bergesen, Albert, and Ronald Schoenberg. (1980) "Long Waves of Colonial Expansion and Contraction, 1415–1969," pp. 231–77 in Albert Bergesen (ed.), *Studies of the Modern World-System*. New York: Academic Press.

Berghahn, Volker R. (1995) *Imperial Germany, 1871–1914*. Providence, R.I.: Berghahn Books.

Bergsten, C. Fred. (1994a) "APEC and World Trade," *Foreign Affairs* 73 (May/June): 20–26.

———. (1994b) "Managing the World Economy of the Future," pp. 341–74 in Peter B. Kenen (ed.), *Managing the World Economy: Fifty Years after Bretton Woods*. Washington, D.C.: Institute for International Economics.

———. (1992a) "The Primacy of Economics," *Foreign Policy* 87 (Summer): 3–24.

———. (1992b) "The World Economy after the Cold War," *California Management Review* 34 (Winter): 51–65.

———. (1988) *America in the World Economy: A Strategy for the 1990s*. Washington, D.C.: Institute for International Economics.

Bergsten, C. Fred, and Marcus Noland. (1993) *Reconcilable Differences? United States–Japan Economic Conflict*. Washington, D.C.: Institute for International Economics.

Bernhardi, Frederich von. (1912) *Germany and the Next War*. Berlin: J. G. Cotta.

Berry, John M. (1994) "Dollar's Continuing Slide Really Reflects Japan's Problems, Analysts Say," *Washington Post* (June 30): A25.

Bertelsen, Judy S. (ed.). (1977) *Nonstate Nations in International Politics*. New York: Praeger.

Bhagwati, Jagdish. (1993) "The Case for Free Trade," *Scientific American* 269 (November): 41–49.

Bienefeld, Manfred. (1994) "The New World Order: Echoes of a New Imperialism," *Third World Quarterly* 15 (March): 31–48.

Biers, Dan, and Craig Forman. (1994) "Asia-Pacific Forum Finds Focus," *Wall Street Journal* (November 14): A6.

Blainey, Geoffrey. (1988) *The Causes of War*, 3rd ed. New York: Free Press.

Blechman, Barry M. (1995) "The Intervention Dilemma," *Washington Quarterly* 18 (Summer): 63–73.

Blechman, Barry M., and Stephen S. Kaplan, with David K. Hall, William B. Quandt, Jerome N. Slater, Robert M. Slusser, and Philip Windsor. (1978) *Force without War*. Washington, D.C.: Brookings Institution.

Block, Fred L. (1977) *The Origins of International Economic Disorder*. Berkeley: University of California Press.

Blumenthal, W. Michael. (1988) "The World Economy and Technological Change," *Foreign Affairs* 66 (no. 3): 529–50.

Boonekamp, Clemens F. J. (1987) "Voluntary Export Restraints," *Finance & Development* 24 (December): 2–5.

Borrus, Michael, Steve Weber, John Zysman, and Joseph Willihnganz. (1992) "Mercantilism and Global Security," *The National Interest* 29 (Fall): 21–29.

Bostdorff, Denise M. (1993) *The Presidency and the Rhetoric of Foreign Crisis*. Columbia: University of South Carolina Press.

Boswell, Terry. (1989) "Colonial Empires and the Capitalist World-Economy: A Time Series Analysis of Colonization, 1640–1960," *American Sociological Review* 54 (April): 180–96.

Boulding, Kenneth E. (1978) *Stable Peace*. Austin: University of Texas Press.

Boutros-Ghali, Boutros. (1996) "Global Leadership after the Cold War," *Foreign Affairs* 75 (March/April): 86–98.

———. (1995) "Ways to Improve the United Nations," *International Herald Tribune* (August 17): 8.

———. (1992–1993) "Empowering the United Nations," *Foreign Affairs* 72 (Winter): 89–102.

Bozeman, Adda B. (1994) *Politics and Culture in International History*. New Brunswick, N.J.: Transaction.

BP Statistical Review of World Energy. (1995). London: British Petroleum Company.

Brecher, Jeremy. (1993) "Global Village or Global Pillage?" *The Nation* 257 (December 6): 685–88.

Brecher, Michael. (1993) *Crises in World Politics: Theory and Reality*. Oxford, Eng.: Pergamon.

Brenner, Michael J. (1993) "EC: Confidence Lost," *Foreign Policy* 91 (Summer): 24–43.

Brierly, James L. (1944) *The Outlook for International Law*. Oxford, Eng.: Clarendon Press.

Broad, Robin, and John Cavanagh. (1988) "No More NICs," *Foreign Policy* 72 (Fall): 81–103.

Bronfenbrenner, Urie. (1971) "The Mirror Image in Soviet–American Relations," *Journal of Social Issues* 27 (no. 1): 46–51.

Brooke, James. (1995) "Latin America Now Ignores U.S. Lead in Isolating Cuba," *New York Times* (July 8): 1, 5.

Brown, Harold. (1983) *Thinking about National Security: Defense and Foreign Policy in a Dangerous World*. Boulder, Colo.: Westview.

Brown, Lester R. (1995) *Who Will Feed China? Wake-Up Call for a Small Planet*. New York: Norton.

———. (1994) "The Cairo Plan," *World Watch* 7 (November/December): 2.

———. (1979) *Resource Trends and Population Policy: A Time for Reassessment*. Washington, D.C.: Worldwatch Institute.

———. (1972) *World without Borders*. New York: Vintage Books.

Brown, Lester R., et al. (1996) *State of the World 1996*. New York: Norton.

———. (1995) *State of the World 1995*. New York: Norton.

———. (1987) *State of the World 1987*. New York: Norton.

Brown, Lester R., and Hal Kane. (1994) *Full House: Reassessing the Earth's Population Carrying Capacity*. New York: Norton.

Brown, Lester, R., Nicholas Lenssen, and Hal Kane. (1995) *Vital Signs 1995*. New York: Norton.

Brown, Seyom. (1994) "World Interests and the Changing Dimensions of Security," pp. 10–26 in Michael T. Klare and Daniel C. Thomas (eds.), *World Security*. New York: St. Martin's Press.

Brownlie, Ian. (1990) *Principles of Public International Law*, 4th ed. New York: Oxford University Press.

Bueno de Mesquita, Bruce. (1981) *The War Trap*. New Haven, Conn.: Yale University Press.

Bueno de Mesquita, Bruce, and David Lalman. (1992) *War and Reason: Domestic and International Imperatives*. New Haven, Conn.: Yale University Press.

———. (1975) "Measuring Systemic Polarity," *Journal of Conflict Resolution* 22 (June): 187–216.

Buerke, Tom. (1996) "East Europeans Fear Losing Their Shot at Joining NATO," *International Herald Journal* (February 1): 1, 7.

Bull, Hedley. (1977) *The Anarchical Society: A Study of Order in World Politics*. New York: Columbia University Press.

Bundy, McGeorge. (1990) "From Cold War to Trusting Peace," *Foreign Affairs* 69 (no. 1): 197–212.

Burgess, John, and Stuart Auerbach. (1990) "Many Losers but Some Winners in the Gulf Crisis," *Washington Post National Weekly Edition* 7 (August 20–26): 21.

Burkhart, Ross E., and Michael S. Lewis-Beck. (1994) "Comparative Democracy: The Economic Development Thesis," *American Political Science Review* 88 (December): 903–10.

Burki, Shahid Javed. (1983) "UNCTAD VI: For Better or for Worse?" *Finance & Development* 20 (December): 16–19.

Burroughs, John, and Jacqueline Cabasso. (1996) "Nukes on Trial," *The Bulletin of the Atomic Scientists* 52 (March/April): 41–45.

Burton, Daniel F., Jr. (1994) "Competitiveness: Here to Stay," *Washington Quarterly* 17 (Autumn): 99–109.

Cahn, Anne H. (1995) "Does Defense Industry Really Need Welfare?" *Christian Science Monitor* 87 (May 15): 19.

Cairncross, Frances. (1994) "Environmental Pragmatism," *Foreign Policy* 95 (Summer): 35–52.

Caldwell, Dan. (1991) *The Dynamics of Domestic Politics and Arms Control*. Columbia: University of South Carolina Press.

———. (1977) "Bureaucratic Foreign Policy Making," *American Behavioral Scientist* 21 (September–October): 87–110.

Calvocoressi, Peter, Guy Wint, and John Pritchard. (1989) *Total War: The Causes and Courses of the Second World War*, 2nd ed. New York: Pantheon.

Caporaso, James A. (1992) "International Relations Theory and Multilateralism: The Search for Foundations," *International Organization* 46 (Summer): 599–631.

———. (1980) "Dependency Theory: Continuities and Discontinuities in Development Studies," *International Organization* 34 (Autumn): 605–28.

———. (ed.) (1978) "Dependence and Dependency in the Global System," Special issue, *International Organization* 32 (Winter): 1–300.

Carment, David. (1993) "The International Dimensions of Ethnic Conflict," *Journal of Peace Research* 30 (May): 137–50.

Carpenter, Ted Galen. (1991) "The New World Disorder," *Foreign Policy* 84 (Fall): 24–39.

Carr, E. H. (1939) *The Twenty-Years' Crisis, 1919–1939*. London: Macmillan.

Carter, Ashton B. (1990–1991) "Chairman's Note," *International Security* 15 (Winter): 3–4.

Cashman, Greg. (1993) *What Causes War? An Introduction to Theories of International Conflict*. New York: Lexington Books.

Caspary, William R. (1993) "New Psychoanalytic Perspectives on the Causes of War," *Political Psychology* 14 (September): 417–46.

Centre on Transnational Corporations. (1991) *World Investment Report 1991: The Triad in Foreign Direct Investment*. New York: United Nations.

Cerny, Philip G. (1995) "Globalization and the Changing Logic of Collective Action," *International Organization* 49 (Autumn): 595–625.

———. (1994) "The Dynamics of Financial Globalization: Technology, Market Structure, and Policy Response," *Policy Sciences* 287 (no. 4): 319–42.

———. (1993) "The Deregulation and Re-regulation of Financial Markets in a More Open World," pp. 51–85 in Philip G. Cerny

(ed.), *Finance and World Politics: Markets, Regimes, and States in the Post-Hegemonic Era*. Aldershot, Eng.: Edward Elgar.

Cetron, Marvin J., with Owen Davies. (1994) "The Future Faces of Terrorism," *Futurist* 28 (November–December): 10–15.

Chaliand, Gérald, and Jean-Pierre Rageau. (1993) *Strategic Atlas*, 3rd ed. New York: Harper Perennial.

Chan, Steve. (1987) "Military Expenditures and Economic Performance," pp. 29–37 in U.S. Arms Control and Disarmament Agency, *World Military Expenditures and Arms Transfers 1986*. Washington, D.C.: U.S. Government Printing Office.

———. (1984) "Mirror, Mirror on the Wall . . .: Are the Free Countries More Pacific?" *Journal of Conflict Resolution* 28 (December): 617–48.

Chatterjee, Partha. (1993) *The Nation and Its Fragments*. Princeton, N.J.: Princeton University Press.

Chen, Lincoln C., Winifred M. Fitzgerald, and Lisa Bates. (1995) "Women, Politics, and Global Management," *Environment* 37 (January/February): 5–9, 31–33.

Chubin, Shahram. (1993) "The South and the New World Order," *Washington Quarterly* 16 (Autumn): 87–107.

Clad, James C. (1994) "Slowing the Wave," *Foreign Policy* 95 (Summer): 139–50.

Clancy, Tom, and Russell Seitz. (1991–1992) "Five Minutes Past Midnight—and Welcome to the New Age of Proliferation," *The National Interest* 26 (Winter): 3–17.

Clarke, Jonathan. (1995–1996) "Leaders and Followers," *Foreign Policy* 101 (Winter): 37–51.

Claude, Inis L., Jr. (1989) "The Balance of Power Revisited," *Review of International Studies* 15 (January): 77–85.

———. (1988) *States and the Global System: Politics, Law, and Organization*. New York: St. Martin's Press.

———. (1971) *Swords into Plowshares*, 4th ed. New York: Random House.

———. (1967) *The Changing United Nations*. New York: Random House.

———. (1962) *Power and International Relations*. New York: Random House.

Clausewitz, Karl von. (1976 [1832]) *On War*. Princeton, N.J.: Princeton University Press.

Cline, William. (1995) "Managing International Debt: How the Big Battle Was Won," *The Economist* 334 (February 18): 17–19.

Cobb, Roger, and Charles Elder. (1970) *International Community*. New York: Harcourt, Brace & World.

Cockburn, Andrew. (1995) "A U.S. Military Porkfest Fattens Contractors," *International Herald Tribune* (October 5): 9.

Cohen, Benjamin J. (1996) "Phoenix Risen: The Resurrection of Global Finance," *World Politics* 48 (January): 268–96.

———. (1983) "Trade and Unemployment: Global Bread-and-Butter Issues," *Worldview* 26 (January): 9–11.

———. (1973) *The Question of Imperialism*. New York: Basic Books.

Cohen, Eliot A. (1996) "A Revolution in Warfare," *Foreign Affairs* 75 (March/April): 37–54.

———. (1995) "The Future of Military Power: The Continuing Utility of Force," pp. 35–43 in Charles W. Kegley Jr. and Eugene R. Wittkopf (eds.), *The Global Agenda*, 4th ed. New York: McGraw-Hill.

Cohen, Joel E. (1995) *How Many People Can the Earth Support?* New York: Norton.

Collins, John M. (1994) *Military Preparedness: Principles Compared with U.S. Practices*. Washington, D.C.: Congressional Research Service.

Commager, Henry Steele. (1983) "Misconceptions Governing American Foreign Policy," pp. 510–17 in Charles W. Kegley Jr. and Eugene R. Wittkopf (eds.), *Perspectives on American Foreign Policy*. New York: St. Martin's Press.

Commission on Transnational Corporations. (1991) "Recent Developments Related to Transnational Corporations and International Economic Relations," U.N. Doc. E/E.10/1991/2, United Nations Economic and Social Council.

Connelly, Matthew, and Paul Kennedy. (1994) "Must It Be the Rest against the West?" *Atlantic Monthly* 274 (December): 61–84.

Cooper, Julian. (1995) "Demilitarizing the Russian Defense Economy," *Security Dialogue* 26 (March): 35–39.

Cooper, Richard. (1968) *The Economics of Interdependence*. New York: McGraw-Hill.

Coplin, William D. (1971) *Introduction to International Politics*. Chicago: Markham.

———. (1966) *The Functions of International Law*. Chicago: Rand McNally.

———. (1965) "International Law and Assumptions about the State System," *World Politics* 17 (July): 615–34.

Cortwright, David, and George A. Lopez. (1995) "The Sanctions Era: An Alternative to Military Intervention," *The Fletcher Forum of World Affairs* 19 (May): 65–85.

Coser, Lewis. (1956) *The Functions of Social Conflict*. London: Routledge & Kegan Paul.

Costanza, Robert, et al. (1995) "Sustainable Trade: A New Paradigm for World Welfare," *Environment* 37 (June): 16–20, 39–44.

Craig, Gordon A., and Alexander L. George. (1990) *Force and Statecraft*, 2nd ed. New York: Oxford University Press.

Crenshaw, Martha. (1990) "Is International Terrorism Primarily State-Sponsored?" pp. 163–69 in Charles W. Kegley Jr. (ed.), *International Terrorism: Characteristics, Causes, Controls*. New York: St. Martin's Press.

Crossette, Barbara. (1995) "The Second Sex in the Third World," *New York Times* (September 10): E1, E3.

D'Amato, Anthony. (1982) "What 'Counts' as Law?" pp. 83–107 in Nicholas Greenwood Onuf (ed.), *Law-Making in the Global Community*. Durham, N.C.: Carolina Academic Press.

Dabelko, Geoffrey D., and David D. Dabelko. (1995) "Environmental Security: Issues of Conflict and Redefinition," *Environmental Change and Security Project Report* 1 (Spring): 3–13.

Dadush, Uri, and Dong He. (1995) "China: A New Power in World Trade," *Finance & Development* 32 (June): 36–38.

Dahl, Robert. (1989) *Democracy and Its Critics*. New Haven, Conn.: Yale University Press.

Daly, Herman E. (1993) "The Perils of Free Trade," *Scientific American* 269 (November): 50–57.

———. (1973) "Introduction," pp. 1–29 in Herman E. Daly (ed.), *Toward a Steady-State Economy*. San Francisco: Freeman.

Daly, Herman E., and John B. Cobb Jr. (1989) *For the Common Good*. Boston: Beacon Press.

Davidson, Keay. (1991) "Slashing U.S. Nuclear Arsenal Now Thinkable," *Sunday Advocate* (Baton Rouge, La.) (November 10): E1.

Davis, Bob. (1994) "Global Paradox: Growth of Trade Binds Nations but It Can Also Spur Separatism," *Wall Street Journal* (June 20): A1, A10.

Davis, Jennifer. (1995) "Sanctions and Apartheid," pp. 173–84 in David Cortright and George A. Lopez (eds.), *Economic Sanctions*. Boulder, Colo.: Westview.

Deger, Saadet, and Ron Smith. (1983) "Military Expansion and Growth in Less Developed Countries," *Journal of Conflict Resolution* 27 (June): 335–53.

Dehio, Ludwig. (1962) *The Precarious Balance*. New York: Knopf.

Demko, George J., and William B. Wood. (1994) *Reordering the World: Geopolitical Perspectives on the 21st Century*. Boulder, Colo.: Westview.

Dentzer, Susan. (1993) "Meet the New Economic Bogymen," *U.S. News and World Report* (October 18): 67.

Der Derian, James. (ed.) (1995) *International Theory: Critical Investigations*. New York: New York University Press.

DeRivera, Joseph H. (1968) *The Psychological Dimension of Foreign Policy*. Columbus, Ohio: Merrill.

Destler, I. M. (1995) *American Trade Politics*, 3rd ed. Washington, D.C.: Institute for International Economics.

de Tocqueville, Alexis. (1969 [1835]) *Democracy in America*. New York: Doubleday.

Deudney, Daniel. (1995) "Environment and Security, Muddled Thinking," pp. 446–545 in Charles W. Kegley Jr. and Eugene R. Wittkopf (eds.), *The Global Agenda: Issues and Perspectives*, 4th ed. New York: McGraw-Hill.

Deutsch, Karl W. (1974) *Politics and Government*. Boston: Houghton Mifflin.

———. (1953) "The Growth of Nations: Some Recurrent Patterns in Political and Social Integration," *World Politics* 5 (October): 168–95.

Deutsch, Karl W., et al. (1997) *Backgrounds to Community*. Columbia: University of South Carolina Press.

———. (1957) *Political Community and the North Atlantic Area*. Princeton, N.J.: Princeton University Press.

Deutsch, Karl W., and J. David Singer. (1964) "Multipolar Power Systems and International Stability," *World Politics* 16 (April): 390–406.

Development Cooperation: 1995 Report. (1995) Paris: Organisation for Economic Co-operation and Development.

Dietrich, William S. (1992) *In the Shadow of the Rising Sun: The Political Roots of American Economic Decline*. University Park: Penn State Press.

Direction of Trade Statistics Yearbook 1995. (1995) Washington, D.C.: International Monetary Fund

DiRenzo, Gordon J. (ed.). (1974) *Personality and Politics*. Garden City, N.Y.: Doubleday-Anchor.

Diwan, Ishac, and Ana Revenga. (1995) "Wages, Inequality, and International Integration," *Finance & Development* 32 (September): 7–9.

Dixon, William J. (1994) "Democracy and the Peaceful Settlement of International Conflict," *American Political Science Review* 88 (March): 14–32.

Dobbs, Michael. (1991) "Disaster, Nuclear and Bureaucratic," *Washington Post National Weekly Edition* 8 (May 6–12): 10–11.

Dorraj, Manochehr. (1995) "Introduction: The Changing Context of Third World Political Economy," pp. 1–13 in Manochehr Dorraj (ed.), *The Changing Political Economy of the Third World*. Boulder, Colo.: Lynne Rienner.

Dos Santos, Theotonio. (1970) "The Structure of Dependence," *American Economic Review* 60 (May): 231–36.

Downs, George W. (ed.). (1994) *Collective Security beyond the Cold War*. Ann Arbor: University of Michigan Press.

Doyle, Michael W. (1995) "Liberalism and World Politics Revisited," pp. 83–106 in Charles W. Kegley Jr. (ed.), *Controversies in International Relations Theory: Realism and the Neoliberal Challenge*. New York: St. Martin's Press.

Drucker, Peter F. (1994) "Trade Lessons from the World Economy," *Foreign Affairs* 73 (January/February): 99–108.

Dulles, John Foster. (1939) *War, Peace, and Change.* New York: Harper.

Durbin, Andrea C. (1995) "Trade and the Environment," *Environment* 37 (September): 16–20, 37–41.

Durning, Alan Thein. (1993) "Supporting Indigenous Peoples," pp. 80–100 in Lester R. Brown et al., *State of the World 1993.* New York: Norton.

———. (1991) "Asking How Much Is Enough," pp. 153–69 in Lester R. Brown et al., *State of the World 1991.* New York: Norton.

———. (1990) "Ending Poverty," pp. 135–53 in Lester R. Brown et al., *State of the World 1990.* New York: Norton.

Easton, David. (1969) "The New Revolution in Political Science," *American Political Science Review* 63 (December): 1051–1061.

Easton, Stewart C. (1964) *The Rise and Fall of Western Colonialism.* New York: Praeger.

Eberstadt, Nicholas. (1995) "Population, Food, and Income: Global Trends in the Twentieth Century," pp. 7–47 in Ronald Bailey (ed.), *The True State of the Planet.* New York: Free Press.

———. (1991) "Population Change and National Security," *Foreign Affairs* 70 (Summer): 115–31.

Economic Report of the President. (1994). Washington, D.C.: Government Printing Office.

Edwards, Stephen R. (1995) "Conserving Biodiversity: Resources for Our Future," pp. 212–65 in Ronald Bailey (ed.), *The True State of the Planet.* New York: Free Press.

Ehrlich, Paul. (1968) *The Population Bomb.* New York: Ballantine.

Eichengreen, Barry, and Peter B. Kenen. (1994) "Managing the World Economy under the Bretton Woods System: An Overview," pp. 3–57 in Peter B. Kenen (ed.), *Managing the World Economy: Fifty Years after Bretton Woods.* Washington, D.C.: Institute for International Economics.

Elliott, Kimberly Ann. (1993) "Sanctions: A Look at the Record," *Bulletin of the Atomic Scientists* 49 (November): 32–35.

Emmanuel, Arghiri. (1972) *Unequal Exchange: An Essay on the Imperialism of Trade.* New York: Monthly Review Press.

Emmott, Bill. (1994) *Japanophobia: The Myth of the Invincible Japanese.* New York: Times Books.

Enloe, Cynthia. (1993) *The Morning After: Sexual Politics at the End of the Cold War.* Berkeley: University of California Press.

"Environmental Intelligence." (1994) *World Watch* 7 (November/December): 6–8.

Epstein, William. (1995) "NPT Wrap-Up: Indefinite Extension—With Increased Accountability," *Bulletin of Atomic Scientists* 51 (July/August): 27–30.

Erikson, Kai. (1994) "Out of Sight, Out of Our Minds," *New York Times Magazine* (March 6): 36–49, 63.

Erlanger, Steven. (1996) "Russia and China Getting Together Again," *International Herald Tribune* (January 1): 1, 5.

Etzioni, Amital. (1968) "Toward a Sociological Theory of Peace," pp. 403–28 in Leon Bramson and George W. Goethals (eds.), *War.* New York: Basic Books.

European Commission Delegation to the United States. (1994) *The European Union: A Guide.* Washington, D.C.: The European Commission Delegation to the United States.

Evans, Gareth. (1995) "A Struggling UN Must Now Appreciate the Art of the Possible," *International Herald Tribune* (October 7–8): 8.

Falk, Richard A. (1993) "Sovereignty," pp. 851–54 in Joel Krieger (ed.), *The Oxford Companion to Politics of the World.* New York: Oxford University Press.

———. (1992) *Explorations at the Edge of Time: The Prospects for World Order.* Philadelphia: Temple University Press.

———. (1970) *The Status of Law in International Society.* Princeton, N.J.: Princeton University Press.

———. (1965) "World Law and Human Conflict," pp. 227–49 in Elton B. McNeil (ed.), *The Nature of Human Conflict.* Englewood Cliffs, N.J.: Prentice-Hall.

———. (1964) *The Role of Domestic Courts in the International Legal Order.* Syracuse, N.Y.: Syracuse University Press.

Falkenheim, Peggy L. (1987) "Post-Afghanistan Sanctions," pp. 105–30 in David Leyton-Brown (ed.), *The Utility of International Economic Sanctions.* New York: St. Martin's Press.

Fallows, James. (1994) *Looking at the Sun: The Rise of the New East Asian Economic and Political System.* New York: Pantheon.

FAO Yearbook: Production 1994. (1995). Rome: Food and Agriculture Organization of the United Nations.

FAO Yearbook: Production 1990. (1991). Rome: Food and Agriculture Organization of the United Nations.

Fedarko, Kevin. (1995) "Louder than Words," *Time* (September 11): 49–59.

Federal Reserve System. (1981) *Annual Statistical Digest, 1970–1979.* Washington, D.C.: Federal Reserve System.

Feinberg, Richard E., and Delia M. Boylan. (1991) *Modular Multilateralism: North–South Economic Relations in the 1990s.* Washington, D.C.: Overseas Development Council.

Ferencz, Benjamin B., and Ken Keyes Jr. (1991) *PlanetHood.* Coos Bay, Ore.: Love Line Books.

Festinger, Leon. (1957) *A Theory of Cognitive Dissonance.* Evanston, Ill.: Row, Peterson.

Fetter, Steve. (1991) "Ballistic Missiles and Weapons of Mass Destruction: What Is the Threat? What Should Be Done?" *International Security* 16 (Summer): 5–42.

Fieldhouse, D. K. (1973) *Economics and Empire, 1830–1914.* Ithaca, N.Y.: Cornell University Press.

"Financing the United Nations." (n.d.) UNA–USA Fact Sheet. United Nations Association of the United States of America.

Fitchett, Joseph. (1995) "Germany Moves to Shoulder Europe's Post-2000 Military Burden," *International Herald Tribune* (December 7): 1, 8.

Flavin, Christopher. (1996) "Facing Up to the Risks of Climate Change," pp. 21–39 in Lester R. Brown et al. *State of the World 1996.* New York: Norton.

———. (1992) "Building a Bridge to Sustainable Energy," pp. 27–45 in Lester R. Brown et al. *State of the World 1992.* New York: Norton.

Flavin, Christopher, and Odil Tunali. (1995) "Getting Warmer: Looking for a Way Out of the Climate Impasse," *World Watch* 18 (March/April): 10–19.

Foley, Michael W. (1995) "Debt, Democracy, and Neoliberalism in Latin America: Losses and Gains of the 'Lost Decade,'" pp. 17–43 in Manochehr Dorraj (ed.), *The Changing Political Economy of the Third World.* Boulder, Colo.: Lynne Rienner.

Førland, Tor Egil. (1993) "The History of Economic Warfare: International Law, Effectiveness, Strategies," *Journal of Peace Research* 30 (May): 151–62.

Francis, Emerich K. (1976) *Interethnic Relations.* New York: Elsevier.

Franck, Thomas M. (1994) "The Emerging Democratic Entitlement," pp. 367–73 in Anthony D'Amato (ed.), *International Law Anthology.* Cincinnati, Ohio: Anderson.

Frank, Andre Gunder. (1969) *Latin America: Underdevelopment or Revolution*. New York: Monthly Review Press.

Frankel, Glenn. (1987) "Weapons: The Global Commodity," *Washington Post National Weekly Edition* 4 (January 12): 6–7.

Freeman, Orville L. (1990) "Meeting the Needs of the Coming Decade: Agriculture vs. the Environment," *Futurist* 24 (November–December): 15–20.

French, Hilary F. (1994) "Can the Environment Survive Industrial Demands," *USA Today* 122 (January): 66–69.

Freud, Sigmund. (1968) "Why War," pp. 71–80 in Leon Bramson and George W. Goethals (eds.), *War*. New York: Basic Books.

Fried, John H. E. (1971) "International Law—Neither Orphan nor Harlot, Neither Jailer nor Never-Never Land," pp. 124–76 in Karl W. Deutsch and Stanley Hoffmann (eds.), *The Relevance of International Law*. Garden City, N.Y.: Doubleday-Anchor.

Frieden, Jeffry A. (1991) "Invested Interests: The Politics of National Economic Policies in a World of Global Finance," *International Organization* 45 (Autumn): 425–452.

Friedheim, Robert L. (1965) "The 'Satisfied' and 'Dissatisfied' States Negotiate International Law," *World Politics* 18 (October): 20–41.

Friedman, Alan. (1996) "New Economic Worry Grips EU's Leaders," *International Herald Journal* (January 11): 1, 8.

Friedman, Thomas L. (1996) "Answers Needed to Globalization Dissent," *Houston Chronicle* (February 8): 30.

———. (1993) "Friends like Russia Make Diplomacy a Mess," *New York Times* (March 28): E5.

Frown, Warren, and Frank Swoboda. (1994) "Ford's Vision: A Company without Borders," *Washington Post National Weekly Edition* 11 (October 24–30): 18.

Fry, Earl H., Stan A. Taylor, and Robert S. Wood. (1994) *America the Vincible*. Englewood Cliffs, N.J.: Prentice-Hall.

Fukuyama, Francis. (1994) "The Ambiguity of National Interest," pp. 10–23 in Stephen Sestanovich (ed.), *Rethinking Russia's National Interests*. Washington, D.C.: Center for Strategic and International Studies.

———. (1992a) "The Beginning of Foreign Policy," *The New Republic* 207 (August 17 and 24): 24–32.

———. (1992b) *The End of History and the Last Man*. New York: Free Press.

———. (1989) "The End of History?" *The National Interest* 16 (Summer): 3–16.

Fuller, Graham E. (1995) "The Next Ideology," *Foreign Policy* 98 (Spring): 145–58.

———. (1991–1992) "The Breaking of Nations--and the Threat to Ours," *The National Interest* 26 (Winter): 14–21.

Gaddis, John Lewis. (1991) "Great Illusions, the Long Peace, and the Future of the International System," pp. 25–55 in Charles W. Kegley Jr. (ed.), *The Long Postwar Peace*. New York: HarperCollins.

———. (1990) "Coping with Victory," *Atlantic Monthly* 265 (May): 49–60.

———. (1983) "Containment: Its Past and Future," pp. 16–31 in Charles W. Kegley Jr. and Eugene R. Wittkopf (eds.), *Perspectives on American Foreign Policy*. New York: St. Martin's Press.

———. (1972) *The United States and the Origins of the Cold War*. New York: Columbia University Press.

Galtung, Johan. (1969) "Violence, Peace, and Peace Research," *Journal of Peace Research* 6 (no. 3): 167–91.

Gardels, Nathan. (1991) "Two Concepts of Nationalism," *New York Review of Books* 38 (November 21): 19–23.

Gardner, Gary. (1995) "Third World Debt Is Still Growing," *World Watch* 8 (January/February): 27–28.

Gardner, Lloyd C. (1970) *Architects of Illusion*. Chicago: Quadrangle.

Garrett, Lauri. (1994) *The Coming Plague: Newly Emerging Diseases in a World Out of Balance*. New York: Farrar, Straus, & Giroux.

Gelb, Leslie H. (1993) "Tailoring a U.S. Role at the U.N.," *International Herald Tribune* (January 2–3): 4.

———. (1979) "The Future of Arms Control: A Glass Half Full," *Foreign Policy* 36 (Fall): 21–32.

Gelb, Leslie H., and Morton H. Halperin. (1973) "The Ten Commandments of the Foreign Affairs Bureaucracy," pp. 250–59 in Steven L. Spiegel (ed.), *At Issue*. New York: St. Martin's Press.

Gelbspan, Ross. (1995) "The Heat Is On," *Harper's* 291 (December): 31–37.

George, Alexander L. (1992) *Forceful Persuasion: Coercive Diplomacy as an Alternative to War*. Washington, D.C.: United States Institute of Peace.

———. (1986) "U.S.–Soviet Global Rivalry: Norms of Competition," *Journal of Peace Research* 23 (September): 247–62.

———. (1972) "The Case for Multiple Advocacy in Making Foreign Policy," *American Political Science Review* 66 (September): 751–85.

George, Paul, et al. (1995) "World Military Expenditure," pp. 389–454 in Stockholm International Peace Research Institute, *SIPRI Yearbook 1995*. New York: Oxford University Press.

German, F. Clifford. (1960) "A Tentative Evaluation of World Power," *Journal of Conflict Resolution* 4 (March): 138–44.

Gill, Stephen. (1993a) "Group of 7," pp. 369–70 in Joel Krieger (ed.), *The Oxford Companion to Politics of the World*. New York: Oxford University Press.

———. (1993b) "Hegemony," pp. 384–86 in Joel Krieger (ed.), *The Oxford Companion to Politics of the World*. New York: Oxford University Press.

Gill, Stephen, and David Law. (1988) *The Global Political Economy: Perspectives, Problems, and Policies*. Baltimore: Johns Hopkins University Press.

Gilpin, Robert. (1987) *The Political Economy of International Relations*. Princeton, N.J.: Princeton University Press.

———. (1985) "The Politics of Transnational Economic Relations," pp. 171–94 in Ray Maghroori and Bennett Ramberg (eds.), *Globalism versus Realism: International Relations' Third Debate*. Boulder, Colo.: Westview.

———. (1984) "The Richness of the Tradition of Political Realism," *International Organization* 38 (Spring): 287–304.

———. (1981) *War and Change in World Politics*. Cambridge, Eng.: Cambridge University Press.

———. (1975) *U.S. Power and the Multinational Corporation*. New York: Basic Books.

Glahn, Gerhard von. (1996) *Law among Nations*, 7th ed. Boston: Allyn & Bacon.

Gleditsch, Nils Petter. (1995) "35 Major Wars?" *Journal of Conflict Resolution* 39 (September): 584–587.

Gleick, Peter H. (1993) "Water and Conflict: Fresh Water Resources and International Security," *International Security* 18 (Summer): 79–112.

Global 2000 Report of the President (1980) Washington, D.C.: Government Printing Office.

Gochman, Charles S., and Zeev Maoz. (1984) "Militarized Interstate Disputes, 1816–1976: Procedures, Patterns, and Insights," *Journal of Conflict Resolution* 28 (December): 585–616.

Goldblat, Jozef. (1982) *Agreements for Arms Control: A Critical Survey*. London: Taylor & Francis.

Goldgeier, James M., and Michael McFaul. (1992) "A Tale of Two Worlds: Core and Periphery in the Post-Cold War Era," *International Organization* 46 (Spring): 467–91.

Goldsmith, James. (1994) *The Trap*. New York: Carroll & Graf.

Goldstein, Joshua S. (1988) *Long Cycles: Prosperity and War in the Modern Age*. New Haven, Conn.: Yale University Press.

Goldstein, Morris. (1995) *The Exchange Rate System and the IMF: A Modest Agenda*. Washington, D.C.: Institute for International Economics.

Gordon, Michael R. (1993a) "As Its World View Narrows, Russia Seeks a New Mission," *New York Times* (November 29): A1, A7.

———. (1993b). "U.S. Seeking to Ease 1972 Treaty Limits on Missile Defenses," *New York Times* (December 3): A7.

Gore, Al. (1993) *Earth in the Balance: Ecology and the Human Spirit*. New York: Plume.

Goshko, John M. (1996) "UN Leader Dangles a Carrot to U.S. over Dues," *International Herald Tribune* (February 8): 6.

Gottlieb, Gidon. (1982) "Global Bargaining: The Legal and Diplomatic Framework," pp. 109–30 in Nicholas Greenwood Onuf (ed.), *Law-Making in the Global Community*. Durham, N.C.: Carolina Academic Press.

Graham, Bradley. (1995) "Revolutionary Warfare: New Technologies Are Transforming the U.S. Military," *Washington Post National Weekly Edition* 12 (March 6–12): 6–7.

Graham, Edward M., and Paul R. Krugman. (1995) *Foreign Direct Investment in the United States*. Washington, D.C.: Institute for International Economics.

Graham, Thomas R. (1979) "Revolution in Trade Politics," *Foreign Policy* 26 (Fall): 49–63.

Grant, Rebecca, and Kathleen Newland (eds.). (1991) *Gender and International Relations*. Bloomington: Indiana University Press.

Greenfield, Meg. (1995) "When the Budget Is Colonized: Cutting a Program Is like Bombing a Settlement," *Newsweek* (May 22): 78.

Greenstein, Fred I. (1987) *Personality and Politics*. Princeton, N.J.: Princeton University Press.

Gregg, Robert W. (1977) "The Apportioning of Political Power," pp. 69–80 in David A. Kay (ed.), *The Changing United Nations*. New York: Academy of Political Science.

Grey, Edward. (1925) *Twenty-Five Years, 1892–1916*. New York: Frederick Stokes.

Grieco, Joseph M. (1995) "Anarchy and the Limits of Cooperation: A Realist Critique of the Newest Liberal Institutionalism," pp. 151–71 in Charles W. Kegley Jr. (ed.), *Controversies in International Relations Theory: Realism and the Neoliberal Challenge*. New York: St. Martin's Press.

Grieve, Malcolm J. (1993) "Debt and Imperialism: Perspectives on the Debt Crisis," pp. 51–68 in Stephen P. Riley (ed.), *The Politics of Global Debt*. New York: St. Martin's.

Grimmett, Richard F. (1995) *Conventional Arms Transfers to Developing Nations 1987–1994*. Washington, D.C.: Congressional Research Service, U.S. Library of Congress.

Guéhenno, Jean-Marie. (1995) *The End of the Nation-State*. Minneapolis, Minn.: University of Minnesota Press.

Gulick, Edward Vose. (1955) *Europe's Classical Balance of Power*. Ithaca, N.Y.: Cornell University Press.

Gurney, Kevin Robert. (1996) "Saving the Ozone Layer Faster," *Technology Review* 99 (January): 58–59.

Gurr, Ted Robert. (1995) "Communal Conflicts and Global Security," *Current History* 94 (May): 212–17.

———. (1994) "Peoples against States: Ethnopolitical Conflict and the Changing World System," *International Studies Quarterly* 38 (September): 347–77.

———. (1990) "Ethnic Warfare and the Changing Priorities of Global Security," *Mediterranean Quarterly* 1 (Winter): 82–98.

———. (1970) *Why Men Rebel*. Princeton, N.J.: Princeton University Press.

Haas, Ernst B. (1986) *Why We Still Need the United Nations: The Collective Management of International Conflict, 1945–1984*. Berkeley: Institute of International Studies, University of California.

———. (1953) "The Balance of Power: Prescription, Concept, or Propaganda?" *World Politics* 5 (July): 442–77.

Haas, Ernst B., and Allen S. Whiting. (1956) *Dynamics of International Relations*. New York: McGraw-Hill.

Haas, Peter M., Robert O. Keohane, and Marc A. Levy (eds.). (1993) *Institutions for the Earth: Sources of Effective International Environmental Protection*. Cambridge, Mass.: The MIT Press.

Haffa, Robert P., Jr. (1992) "The Future of Conventional Deterrence," pp. 5–30 in Gary L. Guertner, Robert Haffa Jr., and George Quester, *Conventional Forces and the Future of Deterrence*. Carlisle Barracks, Penn.: U.S. Army War College.

Hagan, Joe D. (1993) *Political Opposition and Foreign Policy in Comparative Perspective*. Boulder, Colo.: Lynne Rienner.

Haggard, Stephan, and Sylvia Maxfield. (1996) "The Political Economy of Financial Internationalization in the Developing World," *International Organization* 50 (Winter): 35–68.

Haggard, Stephan, and Beth A. Simmons. (1987) "Theories of International Regimes," *International Organization* 41 (Summer): 491–517.

Hall, John A. (1993) "Liberalism," pp. 538–42 in Joel Krieger (ed.), *The Oxford Companion to Politics of the World*. Oxford, Eng.: Oxford University Press.

Hamilton, Kimberly A. (1994) "The HIV and AIDS Pandemic as a Foreign Policy Concern," *Washington Quarterly* 17 (Winter): 201–15.

Handbook of International Economic Statistics 1995. (1995). Washington, D.C.: Central Intelligence Agency.

Handelman, Stephen. (1994) "The Russian 'Mafiya,'" *Foreign Affairs* 73 (March/April): 83–96.

Hardin, Garrett. (1993) *Living within Limits*. New York: Oxford University Press.

———. (1968) "The Tragedy of the Commons," *Science* 162 (December): 1243–48.

Harknett, Richard J. (1994) "The Logic of Conventional Deterrence and the End of the Cold War," *Security Studies* 4 (Autumn): 86–114.

Harries, Owen. (1995) "Realism in a New Era," *Quadrant* 39 (April): 11–18.

Harrison, Selig S. (1993) "Japan's Second Thoughts about Nuclear Weapons: With Its Neighbors Armed to the Teeth, Will Tokyo Join the Club?" *Washington Post National Weekly Edition* 11 (November 8–14): 23–24.

Hassner, Pierre. (1968) "The Nation–State in the Nuclear Age," *Survey* 67 (April): 3–27.

Heilbroner, Robert L. (1991) *An Inquiry into the Human Prospect: Looked at Again for the 1990s*. New York: Norton.

Heilig, Gerhard, Thomas Büttner, and Wolfgang Lutz. (1990) "Germany's Population: Turbulent Past, Uncertain Future," *Population Bulletin* 45 (no. 4). Washington, D.C: Population Reference Bureau.

Helman, Udi. (1995) "Sustainable Development: Strategies for Reconciling Environment and Economy in the Developing World," *Washington Quarterly* 18 (Autumn): 189–207.

Henkin, Louis. (1991) "The Use of Force: Law and U.S. Policy," pp. 37–69 in Stanley Hoffmann et al. (eds.), *Right vs. Might: International Law and the Use of Force,* 2nd ed. New York: Council on Foreign Relations.

Hermann, Charles F. (1988) "New Foreign Policy Problems and Old Bureaucratic Organizations," pp. 248–265 in Charles W. Kegley Jr. and Eugene R. Wittkopf (eds.), *The Domestic Sources of American Foreign Policy.* New York: St. Martin's Press.

———. (1972) "Some Issues in the Study of International Crisis," pp. 3–17 in Charles F. Hermann (ed.), *International Crises.* New York: Free Press.

Hermann, Charles F., Charles W. Kegley Jr. and James N. Rosenau (eds.). (1987) *New Directions in the Study of Foreign Policy.* Boston: Allen & Unwin.

Hermann, Margaret G. (1988) "The Role of Leaders and Leadership in the Making of American Foreign Policy," pp. 266–84 in Charles W. Kegley Jr. and Eugene R. Wittkopf (eds.), *The Domestic Sources of American Foreign Policy.* New York: St. Martin's Press.

———. (1976) "When Leader Personality Will Affect Foreign Policy: Some Propositions," pp. 326–33 in James N. Rosenau (ed.), *In Search of Global Patterns.* New York: Free Press.

Hermann, Margaret G., Charles W. Kegley Jr., and Gregory A. Raymond. (1996) "The Decay of the Nonintervention Principle." Paper presented at the Joint Conference of the Japan Association of International Relations (JAIR) and the International Studies Association (ISA), Tokyo, September 20–22.

Herz, John H. (1951) *Political Realism and Political Idealism.* Chicago: University of Chicago Press.

Hiatt, Fred, and Margaret Shapiro. (1995) "Russia Recovers from a Nervous Breakdown," *Washington Post National Weekly Edition* 12 (July 31–August 6): 23–24.

Higgins, Benjamin, and Jean Downing Higgins. (1979) *Economic Development of a Small Planet.* New York: Norton.

Higgins, Rosalyn. (1994) *Problems and Process: International Law and How We Use It.* Oxford, Eng.: Oxford University Press.

Hilsman, Roger. (1967) *To Move a Nation.* New York: Doubleday.

Hoagland, Jim. (1996) "Yes, Sanctions Can Be Effective, But You Have to Work at It," *International Herald Tribune* (February 8): 8.

———. (1993a) "A Breakthrough for Clinton Too," *Washington Post National Weekly Edition* 10 (September 20–26): 29.

———. (1993b) "Economic Sanctions Sometimes Do More Harm Than Good," *The State* (Columbia, S.C.) (November 11): A12.

Hoebel, E. Adamson. (1961) *The Law of Primitive Man.* Cambridge, Mass.: Harvard University Press.

Hoffmann, Stanley. (1993) "The Passion of Modernity," *Atlantic Monthly* 272 (August): 101–9.

———. (1992) "To the Editors," *The New York Review of Books* 40 (June 24): 59.

———. (1971) "International Law and the Control of Force," pp. 34–66 in Karl W. Deutsch and Stanley Hoffmann (eds.), *The Relevance of International Law.* Garden City, N.Y.: Doubleday–Anchor.

———. (1961) "International Systems and International Law," pp. 205–37 in Klaus Knorr and Sidney Verba (eds.), *The International System.* Princeton, N.J.: Princeton University Press.

Holloway, David. (1983) *The Soviet Union and the Arms Race.* New Haven, Conn.: Yale University Press.

Holm, Hans-Henrik, and Georg Sørensen. (1995a) "International Relations Theory in a World of Variation," pp. 187–206 in Hans-Henrik Holm and Georg Sørensen (eds.), *Whose World Order? Uneven Globalization and the End of the Cold War.* Boulder, Colo.: Westview.

———. (1995b) "Introduction: What Has Changed?" pp. 1–17 in Hans-Henrik Holm and Georg Sørensen (eds.), *Whose World Order? Uneven Globalization and the End of the Cold War.* Boulder, Colo.: Westview.

———. (eds.). (1995c) *Whose World Order? Uneven Globalization and the End of the Cold War.* Boulder, Colo.: Westview.

Holsti, Kalevi J. (1995) "War, Peace, and the State of the State," *International Political Science Review* 16 (October): 319–39.

———. (1992) *International Politics: A Framework for Analysis.* 6th ed. Englewood Cliffs, N.J. Prentice Hall.

———. (1991) *Peace and War: Armed Conflicts and International Order, 1648–1989.* Cambridge, Eng.: Cambridge University Press.

———. (1988) *International Politics: A Framework for Analysis,* 5th ed. Englewood Cliffs, N.J.: Prentice–Hall.

Holsti, Ole R. (1995) "Theories of International Relations and Foreign Policy: Realism and Its Challengers," pp. 35–65 in Charles W. Kegley, Jr. (ed.), *Controversies in International Relations Theory: Realism and the Neoliberal Challenge.* New York: St. Martin's.

———. (1989) "Crisis Decision Making," pp. 8–84 in Philip E. Tetlock et al. (eds.), *Behavior, Society, and Nuclear War.* N.Y.: Oxford University Press.

———. (1972) *Crisis Escalation War.* Montreal: McGill–Queen's University Press.

Homer–Dixon, Thomas F. (1994) "Environmental Scarcities and Violent Conflict: Evidence from Cases," *International Security* 19 (Summer): 5–40.

———. (1991) "On the Threshold: Environmental Changes as Causes of Acute Conflict," *International Security* 16 (Fall): 76–116.

Homer-Dixon, Thomas F., Jeffrey H. Boutwell, and George W. Rathjens. (1993) "Environmental Change and Violent Conflict," *Scientific American* 268 (February): 38–45.

Hormats, Robert D. (1994) "Making Regionalism Safe," *Foreign Affairs* 73 (March/April): 97–108.

Horton, Richard. (1995) "Infection: The Global Threat," *New York Review of Books* 42 (April 6): 24–28.

House, Karen Elliot. (1989) "As Power Is Dispersed among Nations, Need for Leadership Grows," *Wall Street Journal* (February 21): A1, A10.

Howard, Michael E. (1983) *The Causes of War.* Cambridge, Mass.: Harvard University Press.

———. (1978) *War and the Liberal Conscience.* New York: Oxford University Press.

Howell, Llewellyn D. (1995) "Economic Sanctions as Weapons," *USA Today* 124 (July): 37.

Hufbauer, Gary Clyde. (1994) "The Futility of Sanctions," *Wall Street Journal* (June 1): A14.

Hufbauer, Gary Clyde, Jeffrey J. Schott, and Kimberly Ann Elliott. (1990) *Economic Sanctions Reconsidered: History and Current Policy,* 2nd ed. Washington, D.C.: Institute for International Economics.

548

Hughes, Barry B. (1994) *Continuity and Change in World Politics: The Clash of Perspectives,* 2nd ed. Englewood Cliffs, N.J.: Prentice-Hall.

Hunter, Robert E. (1996) "For a Renewed NATO, the Obituaries Were Premature," *International Herald Tribune* (January 4): 6.

Huntington, Samuel P. (1993) "The Clash of Civilizations?" *Foreign Affairs* 72 (Summer): 22–49.

———. (1991a) "America's Changing Strategic Interests," *Survival* 33 (January/February): 3–17.

———. (1991b) *The Third Wave: Democratization in the Late Twentieth Century.* Norman: University of Oklahoma Press.

———. (1989) "No Exit: The Errors of Declinism," *The National Interest* 17 (Fall): 3–10.

Hurwitz, Jon, and Mark Peffley. (1987) "How Are Foreign Policy Attitudes Structured? A Hierarchical Model," *American Political Science Review* 81 (December): 1099–1120.

Huth, Paul. (1988) *Extended Deterrence and the Prevention of War.* New Haven, Conn.: Yale University Press.

Ikenberry, G. John. (1993) "Salvaging the G-7," *Foreign Affairs* 72 (Spring): 132–39.

Iklé, Fred Charles. (1991–1992) "Comrades in Arms," *The National Interest* 26 (Winter): 22–32.

Isaak, Robert A. (1995) *Managing World Economic Change: International Political Economy,* 2nd ed. Englewood Cliffs, N.J.: Prentice Hall.

———. (1975) *Individuals and World Politics.* North Scituate, Mass.: Duxbury.

Jackson, John H. (1994) "Managing the Trading System: The World Trade Organization and the Post–Uruguay Round GATT Agenda," pp. 131–51 in Peter B. Kenen (ed.), *Managing the World Economy: Fifty Years after Bretton Woods.* Washington, D.C.: Institute for International Economics.

Jacobson, Harold K. (1984) *Networks of Interdependence: International Organizations and the Global Political System.* New York: Knopf.

Jaggers, Keith, and Ted Robert Gurr. (1995) "Transitions to Democracy: Tracking Democracy's Third Wave," *Journal of Peace Research* 32 (November): 469–82.

Jakobson, Max. (1991) "Filling the World's Most Impossible Job," *World Monitor* 4 (August): 25–33.

James, Barry. (1995) "Religious Fanaticism Fuels Terrorism," *International Herald Tribune* (October 31): 6.

James, Patrick. (1993) "Neorealism as a Research Enterprise: Toward Elaborated Structural Realism," *International Political Science Review* 14 (no. 2): 123–48.

Janis, Irving. (1982) *Groupthink: Psychological Studies of Policy Decisions and Fiascoes,* 2nd ed. Boston: Houghton Mifflin.

Jenkins, Simon. (1995) "Dresden: Time to Say We're Sorry," *The Wall Street Journal* (February 14): A22.

Jensen, Lloyd. (1982) *Explaining Foreign Policy.* Englewood Cliffs, N.J.: Prentice-Hall.

Jervis, Robert. (1992) "A Usable Past for the Future," pp. 257–68 in Michael J. Hogan (ed.), *The End of the Cold War.* New York: Cambridge University Press.

———. (1991–1992) "The Future of World Politics: Will It Resemble the Past?" *International Security* 16 (Winter): 39–73.

———. (1991) "Will the New World Be Better?" pp. 7–19 in Robert Jervis and Seweryn Bialer (eds.), *Soviet-American Relations after the Cold War.* Durham, N.C.: Duke University Press.

———. (1982) "Security Regimes," *International Organization* 16 (Spring): 357–78.

———. (1976) *Perception and Misperception in World Politics.* Princeton, N.J.: Princeton University Press.

Joffe, Josef. (1990) "Entangled Forever," *The National Interest* 21 (Fall): 35–40.

———. (1985) "The Foreign Policy of the Federal Republic of Germany," pp. 72–113 in Roy C. Macridis (ed.), *Foreign Policy in World Politics,* 6th ed. Englewood Cliffs, N.J.: Prentice-Hall.

Johansen, Robert C. (1995) "Swords into Plowshares: Can Fewer Arms Yield More Security?" pp. 253–79 in Charles W. Kegley Jr. (ed.), *Controversies in International Relations Theory: Realism and the Neoliberal Challenge.* New York: St. Martin's.

———. (1991) "Do Preparations for War Increase or Decrease International Security?" pp. 224–44 in Charles W. Kegley Jr. (ed.), *The Long Postwar Peace.* New York: HarperCollins.

Jonah, James O. C. (1993) "Differing States' Perspectives on the United Nations in the Post-Cold War World," *ACUNS Reports and Papers,* no. 4. Providence, R.I.: Academic Council on the United Nations, Brown University.

———. (1991) "Critical Commentary: A Third World View of the Implications of Superpower Collaboration," pp. 161–73 in Thomas G. Weiss and Meryl A. Kessler (eds.), *Third World Security in the Post-Cold War Era.* Boulder, Colo.: Lynne Rienner.

Jones, Dorothy V. (1991) *Code of Peace: Ethics and Security in the World of the Warlord States.* Chicago: University of Chicago Press.

Joyner, Christopher. (1995) "The Reality and Relevance of International Law in the Post-Cold War Era," pp. 211–24 in Charles W. Kegley Jr. and Eugene R. Wittkopf (eds.), *The Global Agenda,* 4th ed. New York: McGraw-Hill.

Juergensmeyer, Mark. (1993) *The New Cold Cold? Religious Nationalism Confronts the Secular State.* Berkeley: University of California Press.

Kagan, Donald. (1995) *On the Origins of War and the Preservation of Peace.* New York: Doubleday.

Kahler, Miles. (1995) "A World of Blocs: Facts and Factoids," *World Policy Journal* 12 (Spring): 19–27.

Kaiser, David. (1990) *Politics and War: European Conflict from Philip II to Hitler.* Cambridge, Mass.: Harvard University Press.

Kane, Hal. (1995a) *The Hour of Departure: Forces that Create Refugees and Migrants.* Washington, D.C.: Worldwatch Institute.

———. (1995b) "Wars Reach a Plateau," pp. 110–11, 165 in Linda Starke (ed.), *Vital Signs 1995.* New York: Norton.

Kaplan, Morton A. (ed.). (1968) *New Approaches to International Relations.* New York: St. Martin's Press.

———. (1957) *System and Process in International Politics.* New York: Wiley.

Kaplan, Morton A., and Nicholas DeB. Katzenbach. (1961) *The Political Foundations of International Law.* New York: Wiley.

Kaplan, Robert. (1994) "The Coming Anarchy," *Atlantic Monthly* 273 (February): 44–76.

Kaplan, Stephen S. (1981) *Diplomacy of Power.* Washington, D.C.: Brookings Institution.

Kapstein, Ethan Barnaby. (1994) *Governing the Global Economy: International Finance and the States.* Cambridge, Mass.: Harvard University Press.

———. (1991–1992) "We Are Us: The Myth of the Multinational," *The National Interest* 26 (Winter): 55–62.

Keegan, John. (1994) *A History of Warfare.* New York: Knopf.

Keeny, Spurgeon M., Jr. (1993) "Arms Control during the Transition to the Post-Soviet World," pp. 175–97 in Joseph Kruzel (ed.), *American Defense Annual*, 8th ed. New York: Lexington Books.

Keeny, Spurgeon M., Jr., and Wolfgang K. H. Panofsky. (1981) "MAD vs. NUTS: Can Doctrine or Weaponry Remedy the Mutual Hostage Relationship of the Superpowers?" *Foreign Affairs* 60 (Winter): 287–304.

Kegley, Charles W., Jr. (ed.). (1995) *Controversies in International Relations Theory: Realism and the Neoliberal Challenge*. New York: St. Martin's Press.

———. (1993) "The Neoidealist Moment in International Studies? Realist Myths and the New International Realities," *International Studies Quarterly* 37 (June): 131–46.

Kegley, Charles W., Jr., and Margaret G. Hermann. (1996) "How Democracies Use Intervention: A Neglected Dimension in Studies of the Democratic Peace," *Journal of Peace Research* 33 (August): forthcoming.

———. (1995) "Military Intervention and the Democratic Peace," *International Interactions* 2 (no. 1): 1–21.

Kegley, Charles W., Jr., and Gregory A. Raymond. (1994) *A Multipolar Peace? Great-Power Politics in the Twenty-First Century.* New York: St. Martin's Press.

———. (1990) *When Trust Breaks Down: Alliance Norms and World Politics.* Columbia: University of South Carolina Press.

Kegley, Charles W., Jr., and Eugene R. Wittkopf. (1996) *American Foreign Policy: Pattern and Process*, 5th ed. New York: St. Martin's Press.

Kelman, Herbert C. (1965) *International Behavior: A Social-Psychological Analysis.* New York: Holt, Rinehart & Winston.

Kelsen, Hans. (1945) *General Theory of Law and State.* Cambridge, Mass.: Harvard University Press.

Kennan, George F. (1984a) *The Fateful Alliance: France, Russia, and the Coming of the First World War.* New York: Pantheon.

———. (1984b) "Soviet-American Relations: The Politics of Discord and Collaboration," pp. 107–20 in Charles W. Kegley Jr. and Eugene R. Wittkopf (eds.), *The Global Agenda.* New York: Random House.

———. (1982) *The Nuclear Delusion.* New York: Pantheon.

———. (1976) "The United States and the Soviet Union, 1917–1976," *Foreign Affairs* 54 (July): 670–90.

———. (1967) *Memoirs.* Boston: Little, Brown.

———. (1954) *Realities of American Foreign Policy.* Princeton, N.J.: Princeton University Press.

———. (1951) *American Diplomacy, 1900–1950.* New York: New American Library.

——— ["X"]. (1947) "The Sources of Soviet Conduct," *Foreign Affairs* 25 (July): 566–82.

Kennedy, Paul. (1994) "Overpopulation Tilts the Planet," *New Perspectives Quarterly* 11 (Fall): 4–6.

———. (1993) *Preparing for the Twenty-First Century.* New York: Random House.

———. (1992) "A Declining Empire Goes to War," pp. 344–46 in Charles W. Kegley Jr. and Eugene R. Wittkopf (eds.), *The Future of American Foreign Policy.* New York: St. Martin's Press.

———. (1987) *The Rise and Fall of the Great Powers.* New York: Random House.

Keohane, Robert O. (1989) "International Relations Theory: Contributions from a Feminist Standpoint," *Millennium* 18 (Summer): 245–53.

——— (ed.). (1986a) *Neorealism and Its Critics.* New York: Columbia University Press.

———. (1986b) "Realism, Neorealism and the Study of World Politics," pp. 1–26 in Robert O. Keohane (ed.), *Neorealism and Its Critics.* New York: Columbia University Press.

———. (1984) *After Hegemony: Cooperation and Discord in the World Political Economy.* Princeton, N.J.: Princeton University Press.

———. (1983) "Theory of World Politics: Structural Realism and Beyond," pp. 503–40 in Ada Finifter (ed.), *Political Science: The State of the Discipline.* Washington, D.C.: American Political Science Association.

Keohane, Robert O., and Stanley Hoffmann. (1991) "Institutional Change in Europe in the 1980s," pp. 1–39 in Robert O. Keohane and Stanley Hoffmann (eds.), *The New European Community: Decisionmaking and Institutional Change.* Boulder, Colo.: Westview.

Keohane, Robert O., and Lisa L. Martin. (1995) "The Promise of Institutionalist Theory," *International Security* 20 (Summer): 39–51.

Keohane, Robert O., and Joseph S. Nye Jr. (1989) *Power and Interdependence*, 2nd ed. Glenview, Ill.: Scott, Foresman/Little Brown.

———. (1988) "Complex Interdependence, Transnational Relations, and Realism: Alternative Perspectives on World Politics," pp. 257–71 in Charles W. Kegley Jr. and Eugene R. Wittkopf (eds.), *The Global Agenda*, 2nd ed. New York: Random House.

———. (1977) *Power and Interdependence.* Boston: Little, Brown.

Kidder, Rushworth, M. (1990) "Why Modern Terrorism?" pp. 135–38 in Charles W. Kegley Jr. (ed.), *International Terrorism: Characteristics, Causes, Controls.* New York: St. Martin's Press.

Kidron, Michael, and Ronald Segal. (1995) *The State of the World Atlas*, new rev. 5th ed. London: Penguin Reference.

Kim, Samuel S. (1991) "The United Nations, Lawmaking and World Order," pp. 109–24 in Richard A. Falk, Samuel S. Kim, and Saul H. Mendlovitz (eds.), *The United Nations and a Just World Order.* Boulder, Colo.: Westview.

Kindleberger, Charles P. (1973) *The World in Depression, 1929–1939.* Berkeley: University of California Press.

Kinnas, J. N. (1992) "Global Challenges and Multilateral Diplomacy," pp. 23–48 in Ludwik Dembinski (ed.), *International Geneva Yearbook.* Berne, Switzerland: Peter Lang.

Kinsella, Kevin G. (1994) "An Aging World Population," *World Health* 47 (July–August): 6.

Kirschten, Dick. (1994) "No Refuge," *National Journal* (September 10): 2068–73.

Kissinger, Henry A. (1994) *Diplomacy.* New York: Simon & Schuster.

———. (1992) "Balance of Power Sustained," pp. 238–48 in Graham Allison and Gregory F. Treverton (eds.), *Rethinking America's Security: Beyond Cold War to New World Order.* New York: Norton.

———. (1979) *White House Years.* Boston: Little, Brown.

———. (1969) "Domestic Structure and Foreign Policy," pp. 261–75 in James N. Rosenau (ed.), *International Politics and Foreign Policy.* New York: Free Press.

———. (1964) *A World Restored.* New York: Grosset & Dunlap.

Klare, Michael T. (1994) "Adding Fuel to the Fires: The Conventional Arms Trade in the 1990s," pp. 134–54 in Michael T. Klare and Daniel C. Thomas (eds.), *World Security.* New York: St. Martin's Press.

———. (1993) "The Next Great Arms Race," *Foreign Affairs* 72 (Summer): 136–52.

———. (1990a) "An Arms Control Agenda for the Third World," *Arms Control Today* 20 (April 1990): 8–12.

———. (1990b) "Wars in the 1990s: Growing Firepower in the Third World," *Bulletin of Atomic Scientists* 46 (May): 9–13.

———. (1988) "Low-Intensity Conflict," *Christianity and Crisis* 48 (February 1): 11–14.

———. (1987) "The Arms Trade: Changing Patterns in the 1980s," *Third World Quarterly* 9 (October): 1257–81.

———. (1985) "Leaping the Firebreak," pp. 168–73 in Charles W. Kegley Jr. and Eugene R. Wittkopf (eds.), *The Nuclear Reader: Strategy, Weapons, War.* New York: St. Martin's Press.

Klare, Michael T., and Daniel C. Thomas (eds.). (1991) *World Security: Trends and Challenges at Century's End.* New York: St. Martin's Press.

Kluckhohn, Clyde. (1944) "Anthropological Research and World Peace," pp. 143–52 in L. Bryson, Laurence Finkelstein, and Robert MacIver (eds.), *Approaches to World Peace.* New York: Conference on Science, Philosophy, and Religion.

Knickerbocker, Brad. (1994) "Report on Environment Paints Sober Picture of World's Future," *The Christian Science Monitor* 87 (March 23): 7.

Knorr, Klaus. (1977) "International Economic Leverage and Its Uses," pp. 99–126 in Klaus Knorr and Frank N. Trager (eds.), *Economic Issues and National Security.* Lawrence: Regents Press of Kansas.

———. (1975) *The Power of Nations.* New York: Basic Books.

Knorr, Klaus, and James N. Rosenau. (eds.). (1969) *Contending Approaches to International Politics.* Princeton, N.J.: Princeton University Press.

Knorr, Klaus, and Sidney Verba (eds.). (1961) *The International System.* Princeton, N.J.: Princeton University Press.

Kober, Stanley. (1990) "Idealpolitik," *Foreign Policy* 79 (Summer): 3–24.

Kohn, Hans. (1944) *The Meaning of Nationalism.* New York: Macmillan.

Kokoski, Richard. (1994) "Non-Lethal Weapons: A Case Study of New Technology Developments," pp. 367–88 in the Stockholm International Peace Research Institute, *SIPRI Yearbook 1994.* New York: Oxford University Press.

Korany, Bahgat. (1994) "End of History, or Its Continuation? The Global South and the 'New Transformation' Literature," *Third World Quarterly* 15 (March): 7–15.

———. (1986) *How Foreign Policy Decisions Are Made in the Third World.* Boulder, Colo.: Westview.

Korb, Lawrence J. (1995a) "The Indefensible Defense Budget," *Washington Post National Weekly Edition* 12 (July 17–23): 19.

———. (1995b) "Our Overstuffed Armed Forces," *Foreign Affairs* 74 (November/December): 23–34.

Korten, David. (1995) *When Corporations Rule the World.* West Hartford, Conn.: Berrett–Koehler.

Krasner, Stephen D. (1993) "International Political Economy," pp. 453–55 in Joel Krieger (ed.), *The Oxford Companion to Politics of the World.* New York: Oxford University Press.

———. (1991) "Global Communications and National Power: Life on the Pareto Frontier," *World Politics* 43 (April): 336–66.

———. (1985) *Structural Conflict: The Third World against Global Liberalism.* Berkeley: University of California Press.

———. (1982) "Structural Causes and Regime Consequences," *International Organization* 36 (Spring): 185–206.

———. (1979) "The Tokyo Round: Particularistic Interests and Prospects for Stability in the Global Trading System," *International Studies Quarterly* 23 (December): 491–531.

———. (1976) "State Power and the Structure of International Trade," *World Politics* 28 (April): 317–47.

Krauthammer, Charles. (1991) "The Unipolar Moment," *Foreign Affairs* 70 (no. 1): 23–33.

Kristof, Nicholas D. (1993) "The Rise of China," *Foreign Affairs* 72 (November/December): 59–74.

Krugman, Paul. (1994) "Competitiveness: A Dangerous Obsession," *Foreign Affairs* 73 (March/April): 28–44.

———. (1990) *The Age of Diminished Expectations: U.S. Economic Policy in the 1990s.* Cambridge, Mass.: MIT Press.

Kruzel, Joseph. (1993) "American Security Policy in a New World Order," pp. 1–23 in Joseph Kruzel (ed.), *American Defense Annual,* 8th ed. New York: Lexington Books.

———. (1991) "Arms Control, Disarmament, and the Stability of the Postwar Era," pp. 247–69 in Charles W. Kegley Jr. (ed.), *The Long Postwar Peace.* New York: HarperCollins.

Kugler, Jacek. (1993) "War," pp. 962–66 in Joel Krieger (ed.), *The Oxford Companion to Politics of the World.* New York: Oxford University Press.

Kunz, Josef L. (1960) "Sanctions in International Law," *American Journal of International Law* 54 (April): 324–47.

Kurzer, Paulette. (1993) *Business and Banking: Political Change and Economic Integration in Western Europe.* Ithaca, N.Y.: Cornell University Press.

Lake, David A. (1992) "Powerful Pacifists: Democratic States and War," *American Political Science Review* 86 (March): 24–37.

Langer, William L. (1962) "Farewell to Empire," *Foreign Affairs* 41 (October): 115–30.

Laqueur, Walter. (1986) "Reflections on Terrorism," *Foreign Affairs* 65 (Fall): 86–100.

Laurenti, Jeffrey. (1995) *National Taxpayers, International Organizations.* New York: United Nations Association of the United States.

Lebow, Richard Ned. (1981) *Between Peace and War: The Nature of International Crisis.* Baltimore: Johns Hopkins University Press.

Lebow, Richard Ned, and Janice Gross Stein. (1994) *We All Lost the Cold War.* Princeton, N.J.: Princeton University Press.

Lee, Rensselaer W., III. (1995) "Global Reach: The Threat of International Drug Trafficking," *Current History* 94 (May): 207–11.

Leventhal, Paul L. (1992) "Plugging the Leaks in Nuclear Export Controls: Why Bother?" *Orbis* 36 (Spring): 167–80.

Levi, Isaac. (1990) *Hard Choices: Decision Making under Unresolved Conflict.* New York: Cambridge University Press.

Levy, Jack S. (1997) *Power, Politics, and Perception: Essays on the Causes of War.* Columbia: University of South Carolina Press.

———. (1995) "War in the Post–Cold War Era: Structural Perspectives on the Causes of War," pp. 64–74 in Charles W. Kegley Jr. and Eugene R. Wittkopf (eds.), *The Global Agenda,* 4th ed. New York: McGraw-Hill.

———. (1992) "An Introduction to Prospect Theory," *Political Psychology* 13 (June): 171–86.

———. (1991) "Long Cycles, Hegemonic Transitions, and the Long Peace," pp. 147–76 in Charles W. Kegley Jr. (ed.), *The Long Postwar Peace.* New York: HarperCollins.

———. (1990–1991) "Preferences, Constraints, and Choices in July 1914," *International Security* 15 (Winter): 151–86.

———. (1989a) "The Causes of War: A Review of Theories and Evidence," pp. 209–333 in Philip E. Tetlock, Jo L. Husbands, Robert Jervis, Paul C. Stern, and Charles Tilly (eds.), *Behavior, Society, and Nuclear War.* New York: Oxford University Press.

———. (1989b) "The Diversionary Theory of War: A Critique," pp. 259–88 in Manus I. Midlarsky (ed.), *Handbook of War Studies*. Boston: Unwin Hyman.

Levy, Marc A. (1995) "Is the Environment a National Security Issue?" *International Security* 20 (Fall): 35–62.

Lewis, Anthony. (1996) "Wanted, a Leader to Rein in Military Spending," *International Herald Tribune* (January 23): 8.

Lewontin, R. C., Steven Rose, and Leon J. Kamin. (1984) *Not in Our Genes: Biology, Ideology, and Human Nature*. New York: Pantheon.

Leyton-Brown, David. (1987) "Introduction," pp. 1–4 in David Leyton-Brown (ed.), *The Utility of International Economic Sanctions*. New York: St. Martin's Press.

Licklider, Roy. (1995) "The Consequences of Negotiated Settlements in Civil Wars, 1945–1993," *American Political Science Review* 89 (September): 681–90.

Lifton, Robert Jay, and Richard Falk. (1982) *Indefensible Weapons: The Political and Psychological Case against Nuclearism*. New York: Basic Books.

Lind, Michael. (1993) "Of Arms and the Woman," *The New Republic* 209 (November 15): 36–38.

Lindblom, Charles E. (1979) "Still Muddling, Not Yet Through," *Public Administration Review* 39 (November/December): 517–26.

Linden, Eugene. (1996) "The Exploding Cities of the Developing World," *Foreign Affairs* 75 (January/February): 52–65.

Lindsay, James M. (1986) "Trade Sanctions as Policy Instruments: A Re–examination," *International Studies Quarterly* 30 (June): 153–73.

Lipow, Jonathan. (1990) "Defense, Growth, and Disarmament: A Further Look," *Jerusalem Journal of International Relations* 12 (June): 49–59.

Lipset, Seymour M. (1959) "Some Social Requisites of Democracy," *American Political Science Review* 53 (March): 69–105.

Liska, George. (1968) *Alliances and the Third World*. Baltimore: Johns Hopkins University Press.

———. (1962) *Nations in Alliance: The Limits of Interdependence*. Baltimore: Johns Hopkins University Press.

Lissitzyn, Oliver J. (1963) "International Law in a Divided World," *International Conciliation* 542 (March): 3–69.

Little, David. (1993) "The Recovery of Liberalism," *Ethics and International Affairs* 7: 171–201.

Lopez, George A., and David Cortright. (1995) "Economic Sanctions in Contemporary Global Relations," pp. 3–16 in David Cortright and George A. Lopez (eds.), *Economic Sanctions*. Boulder, Colo.: Westview.

———. (1993) "Sanctions: Do They Work?" *Bulletin of the Atomic Scientists* 49 (November): 14–15.

Lopez, George A., Jackie G. Smith, and Ron Pagnucco. (1995) "The Global Tide," *Bulletin of the Atomic Scientists* 51 (July/August): 33–39.

Lorenz, Konrad. (1963) *On Aggression*. New York: Harcourt, Brace & World.

Low, Patrick. (1993) *Trading Free: The GATT and U.S. Trade Policy*. New York: Twentieth Century Fund Press.

Lundestad, Geir. (1994) *The Fall of the Great Powers*. Oslo: Scandinavian University Press.

Luttwak, Edward N. (1993) *The Endangered American Dream: How to Stop the United States from Becoming a Third World Country and How to Win the Geo-Economic Struggle for Economic Supremacy*. New York: Simon & Schuster.

Lutz, Wolfgang. (1994) "The Future of World Population," *Population Bulletin* 49 (June): 1–47.

MacFarquhar, Emily. (1994) "The War against Women," *U.S. News & World Report* (March 28): 42–48.

Mack, Andrew. (1996) "Allow the Idea of Nuclear Disarmament a Hearing," *International Herald Tribune* (January 26): 8.

Mackinder, Sir Halford. (1919) *Democratic Ideals and Reality*. New York: Henry A. Holt.

Mahan, Alfred Thayer. (1890) *The Influence of Sea Power in History*. Boston: Little, Brown.

Majeed, Akhtar. (1991) "Has the War System Really Become Obsolete?" *Bulletin of Peace Proposals* 22 (December): 419–25.

Malkin, Lawrence. (1995) "Two New York Banks Join to Become Largest in U.S.," *International Herald Tribune* (August 19): 1, 8.

Mann, Jonathan M., and Daniel J. M. Tarantola. (1995) "Preventive Medicine: A Broader Approach to the AIDS Crisis," *Harvard International Review* 17 (Fall): 46–49, 87.

Mansfield, Edward D., and Jack Snyder. (1995) "Democratization and the Danger of War," *International Security* 20 (Summer): 5–38.

Marantz, Paul. (1987) "Economic Sanctions in the Polish Crisis," pp. 131–46 in David Leyton-Brown (ed.), *The Utility of International Economic Sanctions*. New York: St. Martin's Press.

Markusen, Ann, Peter Hall, Scott Campbell, and Sabina Dietrick. (1991) *The Rise of the Gunbelt: The Military Remapping of America*. New York: Oxford University Press.

Markusen, Ann, and Joel Yudken. (1992) *Dismantling the Cold War Economy*. New York: Basic Books.

Marshall, Ray. (1995) "The Global Jobs Crisis," *Foreign Policy* 100 (Fall): 50–68.

Martin, Linda G. (1989) "The Graying of Japan," *Population Bulletin* 44 (no. 2). Washington, D.C.: Population Reference Bureau.

Mastanduno, Michael. (1991) "Do Relative Gains Matter? America's Response to Japanese Industrial Policy," *International Security* 16 (Summer): 73–113.

Masters, Roger D. (1969) "World Politics as a Primitive Political System," pp. 104–18 in James N. Rosenau (ed.), *International Politics and Foreign Policy*. New York: Free Press.

Mathews, Jessica T. (1996) "Global Warming: No Longer in Doubt," *Washington Post National Weekly Edition* 13 (January 1–7): 29.

———. (1991) "Iraq's Nuclear Warning," *Washington Post National Weekly Edition* 9 (July 22–28): 19.

———. (1989) "Redefining Security," *Foreign Affairs* 68 (Spring): 162–77.

McGowan, Patrick J., with the assistance of Bohdan Kordan. (1981) "Imperialism in World–System Perspective," *International Studies Quarterly* 25 (March): 43–68.

McGranahan, Donald. (1995) "Measurement of Development," *International Social Science Journal* 143 (March): 39–59.

McKibben, Bill. (1995) "An Explosion of Green," *Atlantic Monthly* 275 (April): 61–83.

Mead, Margaret. (1968) "Warfare Is Only an Invention—Not a Biological Necessity," pp. 270–74 in Leon Bramson and George W. Goethals (eds.), *War*. New York: Basic Books.

Mead, Walter Russell. (1995) "Forward to the Past," *New York Times Magazine* (June 4): 48–49.

———. (1990) "On the Road to Ruin: Winning the Cold War, Losing Economic Peace," *Harper's* 280 (March): 59–64.

Meadows, Donella H. (1993) "Seeing the Population Issue Whole," *The World & I* 8 (June): 396–409.

Meadows, Donella H., Dennis L. Meadows, Jørgen Randers, and William W. Behrens III. (1974) *The Limits to Growth*. New York: New American Library.

Mearsheimer, John J. (1994–1995) "The False Promise of International Institutions," *International Security* 19 (Winter): 5–49.

———. (1990) "Back to the Future: Instability in Europe after the Cold War," *International Security* 15 (Summer): 5–56.

———. (1983) *Conventional Deterrence*. Ithaca, N.Y.: Cornell University Press.

Melanson, Richard A. (1983) *Writing History and Making Policy: The Cold War, Vietnam, and Revisionism*. Lanham, Md.: University Press of America.

Metz, Steven, and James Kievit. (1995) *Strategy and the Revolution in Military Affairs*. Carlisle Barracks, Penn.: U.S. Army War College.

Michaels, Marguerite. (1993) "Blue–Helmet Blues," *Time* (November 15): 66–67.

Midlarsky, Manus I. (1988) *The Onset of World War*. Boston: Unwin Hyman.

Miller, Marian A. L. (1995) *The Third World in Global Environmental Politics*. Boulder, Colo.: Lynne Rienner.

Mills, C. Wright. (1956) *The Power Elite*. New York: Oxford University Press.

Minton–Beddoes, Zanny. (1995) "Why the IMF Needs Reform," *Foreign Affairs* 74 (May/June): 123–33.

Mintz, John. (1996) "The Weapon That Knows No Borders: A Worldwide Ban on Mines Is Sought," *Washington Post National Weekly Edition* 13 (February 12–18): 16–18.

Mitchell, George H., Jr. (1993) "Economics and Development," pp. 145–69 in John Tessitore and Susan Woolfson (eds.), *A Global Agenda: Issues before the 48th General Assembly of the United Nations*. Lanham, Md.: University Press of America.

Mitrany, David. (1966) *A Working Peace System*. Chicago: Quadrangle.

Modelski, George (ed.). (1987a) *Exploring Long Cycles*. Boulder, Colo.: Lynne Rienner.

———. (1987b) "The Study of Long Cycles," pp. 1–15 in George Modelski (ed.), *Exploring Long Cycles*. Boulder, Colo.: Lynne Rienner.

———. (1978) "The Long Cycle of Global Politics and the Nation-State," *Comparative Studies in Society and History* 20 (April): 214–35.

———. (1964) "The International Relations of Internal War," pp. 14–44 in James N. Rosenau (ed.), *International Aspects of Civil Strife*. Princeton, N.J.: Princeton University Press.

Modelski, George, and William R. Thompson. (1996) *Leading Sectors and World Powers*. Columbia: University of South Carolina Press.

———. (1989) "Long Cycles and Global War," pp. 23–54 in Manus I. Midlarsky (ed.), *Handbook of War Studies*. Boston: Unwin Hyman.

Moffett, George D. (1994) *Critical Masses: The Global Population Challenge*. New York: Viking.

Møller, Bjørn. (1992) *Common Security and Nonoffensive Defense: A Neorealist Perspective*. Boulder, Colo.: Lynne Rienner.

Moon, Bruce E., and William J. Dixon. (1992) "Basic Needs and Growth-Welfare Trade-offs," *International Studies Quarterly* 36 (June): 191–212.

———. (1985) "Politics, the State, and Basic Human Needs: A Cross-National Study," *American Journal of Political Science* 29 (November): 661–94.

Moore, Mike. (1995) "Midnight Never Came," *Bulletin of the Atomic Scientists* 51 (November/December): 16–27.

Moran, Theodore H. (1991) "International Economics and U.S. Security," *Foreign Affairs* 69 (Winter): 74–90.

Morgan, T. Clifton, and Kenneth N. Bickers. (1992) "Domestic Discontent and the External Use of Force," *Journal of Conflict Resolution* 36 (March): 25–52.

Morgan, T. Clifton, and Sally Howard Campbell. (1991) "Domestic Structure, Decisional Constraints and War," *Journal of Conflict Resolution* 35 (June): 187–211.

Morgan, T. Clifton, and Valerie L. Schwebach. (1992) "Take Two Democracies and Call Me in the Morning: A Prescription for Peace?" *International Interactions* 17 (no. 4): 305–20.

Morgenthau, Hans J. (1985) *Politics among Nations*, 6th ed. Revised by Kenneth W. Thompson. New York: Knopf.

———. (1983) "Defining the National Interest—Again," pp. 32–39 in Charles W. Kegley Jr. and Eugene R. Wittkopf (eds.), *Perspectives on American Foreign Policy*. New York: St. Martin's Press.

———. (1959) "Alliances in Theory and Practice," pp. 184–212 in Arnold Wolfers (ed.), *Alliance Policy in the Cold War*. Baltimore: Johns Hopkins University Press.

———. (1948) *Politics among Nations*. New York: Knopf.

Morley, Samuel A. (1994) *Poverty and Inequality in Latin America: Past Evidence, Future Prospects*. Washington, D.C.: Overseas Development Council.

Morris, Desmond. (1969) *The Human Zoo*. New York: Dell.

Morse, Stephen S. (1995) "Controlling Infectious Diseases," *Technology Reviewed* 98 (October): 54–61.

Mowlana, Hamid. (1995) "The Communications Paradox," *Bulletin of the Atomic Scientists* 51 (July): 40.

———. (1983) "Needed: A New World Information Order," *USA Today* 112 (September): 42–44.

Mueller, John. (1989) *Retreat from Doomsday: The Obsolescence of Major War*. New York: Basic Books.

Mufson, Steven. (1995) "Measuring the Muscle in China's Military Future," *Washington Post National Weekly Edition* 12 (July 31–August 6): 16–17.

Mulhollin, Gary. (1994) "The Business of Defense Is Defending Business," *Washington Post National Weekly Edition* 11 (February 14–20): 23.

Myers, Norman. (1993) *Ultimate Security: The Environmental Basis of Political Stability*. New York: Norton.

———. (1989) "Environment and Security," *Foreign Policy* 74 (Spring): 23–41.

Nardin, Terry. (1983) *Law, Morality, and the Relations of States*. Princeton, N.J.: Princeton University Press.

Nardin, Terry, and David R. Mapel. (eds.). (1992) *Traditions of International Ethics*. New York: Cambridge University Press.

Nathan, James A. (ed.). (1992) *The Cuban Missile Crisis Revisited*. New York: St. Martin's Press.

Nau, Henry R. (1990) *The Myth of America's Decline: Leading the World Economy in the 1990s*. New York: Oxford University Press.

Neier, Aryeh. (1995) "War Crime Doesn't Pay," *Washington Post* (July 30): C2.

Nelson, Stephan D. (1974) "Nature/Nurture Revisited: A Review of the Biological Bases of Conflict," *Journal of Conflict Resolution* 18 (June): 285–335.

Neuman, Johanna. (1995–1996) "The Media's Impact on International Affairs, Then and Now," *The National Interest* 16 (Winter): 109–23.

Newark, John W. (1995) "Foreign Aid in the 1990s: The New Realities," pp. 223–44 in Manochehr Dorraj (ed.), *The Changing Political Economy of the Third World*. Boulder, Colo.: Lynne Rienner.

Newland, Kathleen. (1994) "Refugees: The Rising Flood," *World Watch* 7 (May/June): 10–20.

Nicholson, Michael. (1992) *Rationality and the Analysis of International Conflict*. Cambridge, Eng.: Cambridge University Press.

Niebuhr, Reinhold. (1947) *Moral Man and Immoral Society*. New York: Scribner's.

Nietschmann, Bernard. (1991) "Third World War: The Global Conflict over the Rights of Indigenous Nations," pp. 172–76 in Robert M. Jackson (ed.), *Global Issues 91/92*. Guilford, Conn.: Dushkin.

Nincic, Miroslav. (1992) *Democracy and Foreign Policy: The Fallacy of Political Realism*. New York: Columbia University Press.

———. (1982) *The Arms Race: The Political Economy of Military Growth*. New York: Praeger.

Nitze, Paul. (1991) "After Iraq, Nukes Can Be Junked," *Wall Street Journal* (December 24): A6.

Nnoli, Okwudiba. (1993) "Ethnicity," pp. 280–84 in Joel Krieger (ed.), *The Oxford Companion to Politics of the World*. New York: Oxford University Press.

Nogee, Joseph L. (1975) "Polarity: An Ambiguous Concept," *Orbis* 28 (Winter): 1193–1224.

Nowzad, Bahram. (1990) "Lessons of the Debt Decade," *Finance and Development* 27 (March): 9–13.

Nunn, Sam, and Pete Domenici. (1992) *The CIS Strengthening of America Commission*. Washington, D.C.: Center for Strategic and International Studies.

Nye, Joseph S., Jr. (1992) "The Changing Nature of World Power," pp. 117–29 in Charles W. Kegley Jr. and Eugene R. Wittkopf (eds.), *The Global Agenda* 3rd ed. New York: McGraw-Hill.

———. (1990) *Bound to Lead: The Changing Nature of American Power*. New York: Basic Books.

———. (1988) "Neorealism and Neoliberalism," *World Politics* 40 (January): 235–51.

———. (1987) "Nuclear Learning and U.S.–Soviet Security Regimes," *International Organization* 41 (Summer): 371–402.

Nye, Joseph S., and William A. Owens. (1996) "America's Information Edge," *Foreign Affairs* 75 (March/April): 20–36.

Oberdorfer, Don. (1991) *The Turn: From the Cold War to a New Era*. New York: Poseidon.

O'Brien, Conor Cruise. (1993) "The Wrath of Ages," *Foreign Affairs* 72 (November/December): 142–49.

———. (1977) "Liberty and Terrorism, *International Security* 2 (Fall): 56–67.

O'Brien, Richard. (1992) *Global Financial Integration: The End of Geography*. New York: Council on Foreign Relations Press.

Olson, Mancur. (1971) "Rapid Growth as a Destabilizing Force," pp. 215–227 in James C. Davies (ed.), *When Men Revolt and Why*. New York: Free Press.

Onuf, Nicholas Greenwood. (1989) *World of Our Making: Rules and Rule in Social Theory and International Relations*. Columbia: University of South Carolina Press.

———. (1982) "Global Law–Making and Legal Thought," pp. 1–82 in Nicholas Greenwood Onuf (ed.), *Law-Making in the Global Community*. Durham, N.C.: Carolina Academic Press.

Onuf, Nicholas, and Thomas Johnson. (1995) "Republicanism and International Thought," pp. 179–97 in Charles W. Kegley Jr. (ed.), *Controversies in International Relations Theory: Realism and the Neoliberal Challenge*. New York: St. Martin's Press.

Ophuls, William, and A. Stephen Boyan. (1992) *Ecology and the Politics of Scarcity Revisited*. San Francisco: Freeman.

Organski, A. F. K. (1968) *World Politics*. New York: Knopf.

Organski, A. F. K., and Jacek Kugler. (1980) *The War Ledger*. Chicago: University of Chicago Press.

Osgood, Robert E. (1968) *Alliances and American Foreign Policy*. Baltimore: Johns Hopkins University Press.

Ostrom, Charles W., and Brian L. Job. (1986) "The President and the Use of Force," *American Political Science Review* 80 (June): 554–66.

Paarlberg, Robert L. (1994) "The Politics of Agricultural Resource Abuse," *Environment* 36 (October): 7–9, 33–42.

Packenham, Robert. (1992) *The Dependency Movement: Scholarship and Politics in Dependency Studies*. Cambridge, Mass.: Harvard University Press.

Paddock, William, and Paul Paddock. (1967) *Famine—1975!* Boston: Little, Brown.

Paget, Karen M. (1995) "Can't Touch This? The Pentagon's Budget Fortress," *The American Prospect* 23 (Fall): 37–43.

Painter, David S. (1995) "Explaining U.S. Relations with the Third World," *Diplomatic History* 19 (Summer):525–48.

Parry, Clive. (1968) "The Function of Law in the International Community," pp. 1–54 in Max Sorensen (ed.), *Manual of Public International Law*. New York: St. Martin's Press.

Passel, Jeffrey S., and Michael Fix. (1994) "Myths about Immigrants," *Foreign Policy* 95 (Summer): 151–60.

Payne, James E., and Anandi P. Sahu (eds.). (1993) *Defense Spending and Economic Growth*. Boulder, Colo.: Westview.

Pearson, Frederic S., Robert A. Baumann, and Jeffrey J. Pickering. (1991) "International Military Intervention: Global and Regional Redefinitions of Realpolitik." Paper presented at the Annual Meeting of the American Political Science Association, Washington, D.C., August 29–September 1.

Peterson, Erik. (1994) "Looming Collision of Capitalisms," *Washington Quarterly* 17 (Spring): 65–75.

Peterson, V. Spike, and Anne Sisson Runyan. (1993) *Global Gender Issues*. Boulder, Colo.: Westview.

Philips, Rosemarie, and Stuart K. Tucker. (1991) *U.S. Foreign Policy and Developing Countries: Discourse and Data 1991*. Washington, D.C.: Overseas Development Council.

Phillips, David. (1993) "Dolphins and GATT," pp. 133–138 in Ralph Nader (ed.), *The Case Against Free Trade*. San Francisco: Earth Island Press.

Pierre, Andrew J. (1984) "The Politics of International Terrorism," pp. 84–92 in Charles W. Kegley Jr. and Eugene R. Wittkopf (eds.), *The Global Agenda*. New York: Random House.

Pipes, Richard. (1977) "Why the Soviet Union Thinks It Could Fight and Win a Nuclear War," *Commentary* 26 (July): 21–34.

Pirages, Dennis. (1995) "Microsecurity: Disease Organisms and Human Well–Being," *Washington Quarterly* 18 (Autumn): 5–12.

———. (1986) "World Energy Crisis 1995," *Futures Research Quarterly* 2 (Fall): 31–47.

Population Reference Bureau. (1995) *1995 World Population Data Sheet*. Washington, D.C.: Population Reference Bureau.

Population Reference Bureau. (1981) *World Population: Toward the Next Century*. Washington, D.C.: Population Reference Bureau.

Porter, Bruce D. (1994) *War and the Rise of the State*. New York: Free Press.

Porter, Gareth. (1995) "Environmental Security as a National Security Issue," *Current History* 94 (May): 218–22.

Porter, Gareth, and Janet Welsh Brown. (1996) *Global Environmental Politics*, 2nd ed. Boulder, Co.: Westview.

Postel, Sandra. (1994) "Carrying Capacity: Earth's Bottom Line," pp. 39–55 in Lester R. Brown et al., *State of the World 1994*. New York: Norton.

———. (1993) "The Politics of Water," *World Watch* 6 (July–August): 10–18.

Potter, William C. (1992) "The New Nuclear Suppliers," *Orbis* 46 (Spring): 199–210.

Pound, Edward T., and Jihan El-Tahri. (1994) "Sanctions: The Pluses and Minus," *U.S. News & World Report* (October 31): 58–71.

Pourgerami, Abbas. (1991) *Development and Democracy in the Third World*. Boulder, Colo.: Westview.

Powers, Thomas. (1994) "Downwinders: Some Casualties of The Nuclear Age," *Atlantic Monthly* 273 (March): 119–24.

Preeg, Ernest H. (1994) "Krugmanian Competitiveness: A Dangerous Obfuscation," *Washington Quarterly* 17 (Autumn): 111–22.

Preston, Richard. (1994) *The Hot Zone*. New York: Random House.

Prestowitz, Clyde V., Jr. (1995) "The Gunfight at the OK Corral Turns Out the Be 'Rashomon,'" *Washington Post National Weekly Edition* 12 (July 10–16): 24.

Princen, Thomas, and Matthias Finger. (1994) *Environmental NGOs in World Politics: Linking the Local and the Global*. London: Routledge.

Puchala, Donald J. (1994) "Some World Order Options for Our Time," *Peace Forum* 11 (November): 17–30.

Quandt, William B. (1991) "The Middle East in 1990," *Foreign Affairs* 70 (No. 1): 49–69.

Quester, George. (1992) "Conventional Deterrence: The Past as Prologue," pp. 31–51 in Gary L. Guertner, Robert Haffa, Jr., and George Quester, *Conventional Forces and the Future of Deterrence*. Carlisle Barracks, Penn.: U.S. Army War College.

Rabkin, Jeremy. (1994) "Trading In Our Sovereignty?" *National Review* 46 (June 13): 34–36, 73.

Rapkin, David, and William Thompson, with Jon A. Christopherson. (1989) "Bipolarity and Bipolarization in the Cold War Era," *Journal of Conflict Resolution* 23 (June): 261–95.

Raspberry, William. (1992) "Seeing Past the Children," *Washington Post* (January 1): A31.

Ratner, Steven R. (1995) *The New UN Peacekeeping*. New York: St. Martin's Press.

Ray, James Lee. (1995) *Democracy and International Conflict: An Evaluation of the Democratic Peace Proposition*. Columbia: University of South Carolina Press.

Raymond, Gregory A. (1994) "Democracies, Disputes, and Third Party Intermediaries," *Journal of Conflict Resolution* 38 (March): 24–42.

Reardon, Betty. (1985) *Sexism and the War System*. New York: Teachers College Press.

Regan, Patrick M. (1994) *Organizing Societies for War: The Process and Consequences of Societal Militarization*. Westport, Conn.: Praeger.

Reich, Robert. (1990) "Who Is Us?" *Harvard Business Review* 68 (January–February): 53–64.

Reid, T. R., and Paul Blustein. (1995) "What a Difference a Half Century Makes," *Washington Post National Weekly Edition* 12 (August 21–27): 21.

Renner, Michael. (1989) *National Security: The Economic and Environmental Dimensions*. Washington, D.C.: Worldwatch Institute.

Reno, Robert. (1993) "Defense Conversion Bombs Out," *The State* (Columbia, S.C.) (April 2): A15.

Reutlinger, Shlomo. (1985) "Food Security and Poverty in LDCs," *Finance & Development* 22 (December): 7–11.

Richardson, Lewis F. (1960a) *Arms and Insecurity*. Pittsburgh: Boxwood Press.

———. (1960b) *Statistics of Deadly Quarrels*. Chicago: Quadrangle.

Richardson, Michael. (1995) "Fears of a Militarily Resurgent Japan," *International Herald Journal Tribune* (August 15): 1, 7.

Riddell-Dixon, Elizabeth. (1995) "Social Movements and the United Nations," *International Social Science Journal* 144 (June): 289–303.

Riggs, Fred W. (1994) "Ethnonationalism, Industrialism, and the Modern State," *Third World Quarterly* 15 (no. 4): 583–611.

Riggs, Robert E., and Jack C. Plano. (1994) *The United Nations: International Organization and World Politics*, 2nd ed. Belmont, Calif.: Wadsworth.

Riker, William H. (1962) *The Theory of Political Coalitions*. New Haven, Conn.: Yale University Press.

Riley, Stephen P. (ed.). (1993) *The Politics of Global Debt*. New York: St. Martin's Press.

Rittberger, Volker (ed.). (1993) *Regime Theory and International Relations*. Cambridge, Eng.: Clarendon Press.

Robey, Bryant, Shea O. Rutstein, and Leo Morris. (1993) "The Fertility Decline in Developing Countries," *Scientific American* 269 (December): 60–67.

Roca, Sergio. (1987) "Economic Sanctions against Cuba," pp. 87–104 in David Leyton-Brown (ed.), *The Utility of International Economic Sanctions*. New York: St. Martin's Press.

Rosati, Jerel A., Joe D. Hagan, and Martin W. Sampson III (eds.). (1994) *Foreign Policy Restructuring: How Governments Respond to Global Change*. Columbia: University of South Carolina Press.

Rosecrance, Richard. (1997) "Economics and National Security: The Evolutionary Process," forthcoming in Richard Shultz, Roy Godson, and George Quester (eds.), *Security Studies for the Twenty-First Century*. New York: Brassey's.

———. (1992) "A New Concert of Powers," *Foreign Affairs* 71 (Spring): 64–82.

———. (1986) *The Rise of the Trading State: Commerce and Conquest in the Modern World*. New York: Basic Books.

Rosen, David. (1987) *The Basics of Foreign Trade and Exchange*. New York: Federal Reserve Board of New York.

Rosen, Steven J. (ed.). (1973) *Testing the Theory of the Military-Industrial Complex*. Lexington, Mass.: Heath.

Rosenau, James N. (1995) "Security in a Turbulent World," *Current History* 94 (May): 193–200.

———. (1990) *Turbulence in World Politics: A Theory of Change and Continuity*. Princeton, N.J.: Princeton University Press.

———. (1980) *The Scientific Study of Foreign Policy*. New York: Nichols.

Rosenau, Pauline Marie. (1992) *Post-Modernism and the Social Sciences*. Princeton, N.J.: Princeton University Press.

Rosenberg, Shawn W. (1988) *Reason, Ideology and Politics*. Princeton: Princeton University Press.

Rosenfeld, Stephen S. (1995) "For American Foreign Policy, Multilateralism Is the Only Option," *International Herald Tribune* (December 11): 8.

Rosenthal, Joel H. (1991) *Righteous Realists.* Baton Rouge: Louisiana State University Press.

Rostow, W. W. (1960) *The Stages of Economic Growth.* Cambridge, Eng.: Cambridge University Press.

Rotblat, Joseph C. (1996) "Remember Your Humanity," *The Bulletin of the Atomic Scientists* 52 (March/April): 26–28.

Rothgeb, John M., Jr. (1993) *Defining Power: Influence and Force in the Contemporary International System.* New York: St. Martin's Press.

Ruggie, John Gerard. (1995) "The False Promise of Realism," *International Security* 20 (Summer): 62–70.

———. (1993) "Wandering in the Void: Charting the U.N.'s New Strategic Role," *Foreign Affairs* 72 (November/December): 27–31.

———. (1983) "Continuity and Transformation in the World Polity: Toward a Neorealist Syfsthesis," *World Politics* 35 (January): 261–85.

Rummel, Rudolph J. (1994) *Death by Government.* New Brunswick, N.J.: Transaction Books.

———. (1983) "Libertarianism and International Violence," *Journal of Conflict Resolution* 27 (March): 27–71.

Rupert, James. (1995) "The Cloud over Chernobyl," *Washington Post National Weekly Edition* 12 (June 26–July 2): 6–7.

Russett, Bruce. (1995) "The Democratic Peace: 'And Yet It Moves'," *International Security* 19 (Spring): 164–75.

———. (1993) *Grasping the Democratic Peace: Principles for a Post–Cold War World.* Princeton, N.J.: Princeton University Press.

———. (1982) "Defense Expenditures and National Well–Being," *American Political Science Review* 76 (December): 767–77.

Russett, Bruce, and Harvey Starr. (1996) *World Politics: The Menu for Choice,* 5th ed. New York: W. H. Freeman.

Russett, Bruce, and James S. Sutterlin. (1991) "The U.N. in a New World Order," *Foreign Affairs* 70 (Spring): 69–83.

Ryser, Rudolph C. (1985) "Fourth World Wars: Indigenous Nationalism and the Emerging New International Political Order," pp. 304–15 in Menno Boldt and J. Anthony Long in association with Leroy Little Bear (eds.), *The Quest for Justice.* Toronto: University of Toronto Press.

Sachs, Aaron. (1996) "Upholding Human Rights and Environmental Justice," pp. 133–51 in Lester R. Brown et al. (eds.), *State of the World 1996.* New York: Norton.

Sachs, Jeffrey. (1989) "Making the Brady Plan Work," *Foreign Affairs* 68 (Summer): 87–104.

Sagan, Carl. (1988) "The Common Enemy," *Parade* (February 7): 4–7.

Sagan, Carl, and Richard Turco. (1993) "Nuclear Winter in the Post–Cold War Era," *Journal of Peace Research* 30 (November): 369–73.

Sagan, Scott D. (1993) *The Limits of Safety: Organizations, Accidents, and Nuclear Weapons.* Princeton, N.J.: Princeton University Press.

Sandel, Michael J. (1996) "America's Search for a New Public Philosophy," *Atlantic Monthly* 277 (March): 57–74.

Sandholtz, Wayne, Michael Borrus, John Zysman, Jay Stowsky, Ken Conca, Steven Vogel, and Steve Weber. (1992) *The Highest Stakes: The Economic Foundations of the Next Security System.* New York: Oxford University Press.

Sandler, Todd, and Keith Hartley. (1995) *The Economics of Defense.* New York: Cambridge University Press.

Scarborough, Grace E. Iusi, and Bruce Bueno de Mesquita. (1988) "Threat and Alignment," *International Interactions* 14 (no. 1): 85–93.

Schelling, Thomas C. (1978) *Micromotives and Macrobehavior.* New York: Norton.

———. (1966) *Arms and Influence.* New Haven, Conn.: Yale University Press.

Schlesinger, Arthur, Jr. (1986) *The Cycles of American History.* Boston: Houghton Mifflin.

———. (1983) "Pretension in the Presidential Pulpit," *Wall Street Journal* (March 17): 26.

Schmemann, Serge. (1993) "Russia Drops Pledge of No First Use of Atom Arms," *New York Times* (November 4): A5.

Schneider, Barry R., and Lawrence E. Grinter. (eds.). (1995) *Battlefield of the Future: 21st Century Warfare Issues.* Maxwell Air Force Base, Ala.: Air War College.

Scholte, Jan Aart. (1993) "From Power Politics to Social Change: An Alternative Focus for International Studies," *Review of International Studies* 19 (January): 3–21.

Schott, Jeffrey J. (1994) *The Uruguay Round: An Assessment.* Washington, D.C.: Institute for International Economics.

Schwab, Klaus, and Claude Smadja. (1996) "Start Taking the Backlash Against Globalization Seriously," *International Herald Tribune* (February 1): 1, 8.

Schweller, Randall L. (1992) "Domestic Structure and Preventive War," *World Politics* 44 (January): 235–69.

Seager, Joni. (1995) *The New State of the Earth Atlas.* New York: Touchstone.

Sebenius, James K. (1991) "Designing Negotiations toward a New Regime: The Case of Global Warming," *International Security* 15 (Spring): 110–48.

Sedjo, Robert A. (1995) "Forests: Conflicting Signals," pp. 177–209 in Ronald Bailey (ed.), *The True State of the Planet.* New York: Free Press.

Sen, Amartya. (1994) "Population: Delusion and Reality," *New York Review of Books* 41 (September 22): 62–71.

Sen, Gita. (1995) "The World Programme of Action: A New Paradigm for Population Policy," *Environment* 37 (January/February): 10–15, 34–37.

Shannon, Thomas Richard. (1989) *An Introduction to the World-System Perspective.* Boulder, Colo.: Westview.

Shaw, Timothy M. (1994) "Beyond Any New World Order: The South in the 21st Century," *Third World Quarterly* 15 (March): 139–46.

Shenon, Philip. (1996) "AIDS Epidemic, Late to Arrive, Now Explodes in Populous Asia," *New York Times* (January 21): 1, 8.

Shlykov, Vitaly V. (1995) "Economic Readjustment within the Russian Defense–Industrial Complex," *Security Dialogue* 26 (March): 19–34.

Shultz, Richard, Roy Godson, and George Quester (eds.). (1997) *Security Studies for the 21st Century.* New York: Brassey's.

Shultz, Richard H., Jr., and William J. Olson. (1994) *Ethnic and Religious Conflict: Emerging Threat to U.S. Security.* Washington, D.C.: National Strategy Information Center.

Siegel, Martin J. (1983) "Survival," *USA Today* 112 (August): 1–2.

Simmel, Georg. (1956) *Conflict.* Glencoe, Ill.: Free Press.

Simon, Herbert A. (1982) *Models of Bounded Rationality.* Cambridge, Mass.: MIT Press.

———. (1957) *Models of Man.* New York: Wiley.

Simon, Julian L. (1981) *The Ultimate Resource.* Princeton, N.J.: Princeton University Press.

Simon, Julian L., and Herman Kahn (eds.). (1984) *The Resourceful Earth: A Response to Global 2000.* Oxford, Eng.: Blackwell.

Simon, Julian L., and Aaron Wildavsky. (1984) "On Species Loss, the Absence of Data, and Risks to Humanity," in Julian L.

556

Simon and Herman Kahn (eds.), *The Resourceful Earth: A Response to Global 2000*. Oxford, Eng.: Basil Blackwell.

Singer, Hans W., and Javed A. Ansari. (1988) *Rich and Poor Countries*, 4th ed. London: Unwin Hyman.

Singer, J. David. (1991) "Peace in the Global System: Displacement, Interregnum, or Transformation?" pp. 56–84 in Charles W. Kegley Jr. (ed.), *The Long Postwar Peace*. New York: HarperCollins.

———. (1981) "Accounting for International War: The State of the Discipline," *Journal of Peace Research* 18 (no. 1): 1–18.

——— (ed.). (1968) *Quantitative International Politics*. New York: Free Press.

———. (1961) "The Level-of-Analysis Problem in International Relations," pp. 77–92 in Klaus Knorr and Sidney Verba (eds.), *The International System*. Princeton, N.J.: Princeton University Press.

———. (1960) "Theorizing about Theory in International Politics," *Journal of Conflict Resolution* 4 (December): 431–42.

Singer, J. David, and Melvin Small. (1968) "Alliance Aggregation and the Onset of War, 1815–1945," pp. 247–85 in J. David Singer (ed.), *Quantitative International Politics*. New York: Free Press.

Singer, Max, and Aaron Wildavsky. (1993) *The Real World Order: Zones of Peace/Zones of Turmoil*. Chatham, N.J.: Chatham House.

Sivard, Ruth Leger. (1993) *World Military and Social Expenditures 1993*. Washington, D.C.: World Priorities.

———. (1991) *World Military and Social Expenditures 1991*. Washington, D.C.: World Priorities.

———. (1982) *World Military and Social Expenditures 1982*. Leesburg, Va.: World Priorities.

Siverson, Randolph M., and Julian Emmons. (1991) "Democratic Political Systems and Alliance Choices," *Journal of Conflict Resolution* 35 (June): 285–306.

Sjolander, Claire Turenne, and Wayne S. Cox (eds.). (1994) *Beyond Positivism: Critical Reflections on International Relations*. Boulder, Colo.: Lynne Rienner.

Sklair, Leslie. (1991) *Sociology of the Global System*. Baltimore: Johns Hopkins University Press.

Slater, Jerome, and David Goldfischer. (1988) "Can SDI Provide a Defense?" pp. 74–86 in Charles W. Kegley Jr. and Eugene R. Wittkopf (eds.), *The Global Agenda*, 2nd ed. New York: Random House.

Small, Melvin, and J. David Singer. (1982) *Resort to Arms: International and Civil Wars, 1816–1980*. Beverly Hills, Calif.: Sage.

———. (1976) "The War-Proneness of Democratic Regimes, 1816–1965," *Jerusalem Journal of International Relations* 1 (March): 50–69.

———. (1972) "Patterns in International Warfare, 1816–1965," pp. 121–31 in James F. Short Jr. and Marvin E. Wolfgang (eds.), *Collective Violence*. Chicago: Aldine–Atherton.

Smith, Michael Joseph. (1986) *Realist Thought from Weber to Kissinger*. Baton Rouge: Louisiana State University Press.

Smith, Roger K. (1987) "Explaining the Non-Proliferation Regime: Anomalies for Contemporary International Relations Theory," *International Organization* 41 (Spring): 251–81.

Smith, Ron P., and George Georgiou. (1983) "Assessing the Effect of Military Expenditures on OECD Economies: A Survey," *Arms Control* 4 (May): 3–15.

Smith, Steve, and Michael Clarke. (1985) *Foreign Policy Implementation*. London: Allen & Unwin.

Smith, Tony. (1981) "The Logic of Dependency Theory Revisited," *International Organization* 35 (Autumn): 755–76.

———. (1979) "The Underdevelopment of Development Literature: The Case of Dependency Theory," *World Politics* 31 (January): 247–288.

Smyser, W. R. (1993) "Goodbye, G–7," *Washington Quarterly* 16 (Winter): 15–28.

Snidal, Duncan. (1993) "Relative Gains and the Pattern of International Cooperation," pp. 181–207 in David A. Baldwin, ed., *Neorealism and Neoliberalism: The Contemporary Debate*. New York: Columbia University Press.

Snider, Lewis W. (1991) "Guns, Debt, and Politics: New Variations on an Old Theme," *Armed Forces and Society* 17 (Winter): 167–90.

Snyder, Glenn H. (1991) "Alliance Threats: A Neorealist First Cut," pp. 83–103 in Robert L. Rothstein (ed.), *The Evolution of Theory in International Relations*. Columbia: University of South Carolina Press.

———. (1984) "The Security Dilemma in Alliance Politics," *World Politics* 36 (July): 461–95.

Snyder, Glenn H., and Paul Diesing. (1977) *Conflict among Nations: Bargaining, Decision-Making, and System Structure in International Crisis*. Princeton, N.J.: Princeton University Press.

Snyder, Jack. (1993) "The New Nationalism: Realist Interpretations and Beyond," pp. 179–200 in Richard Rosecrance and Anthony A. Stein (eds.), *The Domestic Bases of Grand Strategy*. Ithaca, N.Y.: Cornell University Press.

———. (1991) *Myths of Empire: Domestic Politics and International Ambition*. Ithaca, N.Y.: Cornell University Press.

Sobel, Andrew C. (1994) *Domestic Choices, International Markets: Dismantling National Barriers and Liberalizing Securities Markets*. Ann Arbor, Mich.: University of Michigan Press.

Sollenberg, Margareta, and Peter Wallensteen. (1995) "Major Armed Conflicts," pp. 19–35 in Stockholm International Peace Research Institute, *SIPRI Yearbook 1995*. New York: Oxford University Press.

Somit, Albert. (1990) "Humans, Chimps, and Bonobos: The Biological Bases of Aggression, War, and Peacemaking," *Journal of Conflict Resolution* 34 (September): 553–82.

Sommer, Mark. (1994) "Can Military Strategies Ban the Bomb?" *Christian Science Monitor* (April 29): 23.

Sørensen, Georg. (1995) "Four Futures," *Bulletin of the Atomic Scientists* 51 (July/August): 69–72.

Sorensen, Theodore C. (1963) *Decision Making in the White House*. New York: Columbia University Press.

Sorokin, Pitirim A. (1937) *Social and Cultural Dynamics*. New York: American Book.

Soroos, Marvin S. (1995) "The Tragedy of the Commons in Global Perspective," pp. 422–35 in Charles W. Kegley Jr. and Eugene R. Wittkopf (eds.), *The Global Agenda: Issues and Perspectives*, 4th ed. New York: McGraw-Hill.

———. (1986) *Beyond Sovereignty: The Challenge of Global Policy*. Columbia: University of South Carolina Press.

Spanier, John. (1975) *Games Nations Play*, 2nd ed. New York: Praeger.

Specter, Michael. (1994) "Climb in Russia's Death Rate Sets Off Population Implosion," *New York Times* (March 6): 1, 4.

Spector, Leonard S., and Mark G. McDonough with Evan S. Medeiros. (1995) *Tracking Nuclear Proliferation*. Washington, D.C.: Carnegie Endowment for International Peace.

Spero, Joan Edelman. (1990) *The Politics of International Economic Relations*, 4th ed. New York: St. Martin's Press.

Spykman, Nicholas. (1944) *Geography of Peace*. New York: Harcourt Brace.

Stanislaw, Joseph, and Daniel Yergin. (1993) "Oil: Reopening the Door," *Foreign Affairs* 72 (September/October): 81–93.

Stanley Foundation. (1993) *The UN Role in Intervention.* Muscatine, Iowa: The Stanley Foundation.

The State of the World's Children 1995. (1995). New York: Oxford University Press.

The State of the World Population 1995. (1995). New York: United Nations Population Fund.

The State of the World Population 1994. (1994). New York: United Nations Population Fund.

The State of the World Population 1993. (1993). New York: United Nations Population Fund.

Stein, Janice Gross. (1993) "Reassurance in International Conflict Management," pp. 77–97 in Demetrios Caraly and Cerentha Harris (eds.), *New World Politics.* New York: Academy of Political Science.

Stein, Janice Gross, and Louis W. Pauly. (1993) *Choosing to Cooperate: How States Avoid Loss.* Baltimore: Johns Hopkins University Press.

Steinbruner, John D. (1995) "Reluctant Strategic Realignment: The Need for a New View of National Security," *Brookings Review* 13 (Winter): 4–9.

Stengal, Richard. (1995) "Brink of Armageddon," *Time* (August 21): 44–46.

Sterling, Claire. (1994) *Thieves' World: The Threat of the New Global Network of Organized Crime.* New York: Simon & Schuster.

Stock, Thomas, and Anna De Geer. (1995) "Chemical and Biological Weapons: Development and Destruction," pp. 337–57 in the Stockholm International Peace Research Institute, *SIPRI Yearbook 1995.* New York: Oxford.

Stockholm International Peace Research Institute (SIPRI). (1995) *SIPRI Yearbook 1995.* New York Oxford University Press.

Strang, David. (1991) "Global Patterns of Decolonization, 1500–1987," *International Studies Quarterly* 35 (December): 429–545.

———. (1990) "From Dependence to Sovereignty: An Event History Analysis of Decolonization 1870–1987," *American Sociological Review* 55 (December): 846–60.

Strange, Susan. (1982) "Cave! Hic Dragones: A Critique of Regime Analysis," *International Organization* 36 (Spring): 479–96.

Sumner, William Graham. (1968) "War," pp. 205–28 in Leon Bramson and George W. Goethals (eds.), *War.* New York: Basic Books.

Talbott, Strobe. (1990) "Rethinking the Red Menace," *Time* (January 1): 66–72.

Taylor, Peter J. (ed.). (1990) *World Government.* New York: Oxford University Press.

Tefft, Sheila. (1995) "Rush to Burn Coal Turns China into Asia's Polluter," *Christian Science Monitor* (September 30): 1, 8.

Thompson, Kenneth W. (1960) *Political Realism and the Crisis of World Politics.* Princeton, N.J.: Princeton University Press.

———. (1953) "Collective Security Reexamined," *American Political Science Review* 47 (September): 753–72.

Thompson, William R. (1988) *On Global War: Historical-Structural Approaches to World Politics.* Columbia: University of South Carolina Press.

Thurow, Lester C. (1992) *Head to Head: Coming Economic Battles among Japan, Europe, and America.* New York: William Morrow.

Thygesen, Niels. (1994) "Comment on 'Managing the Monetary System,'" pp. 120–29 in Peter B. Kenen (ed.), *Managing the World Economy: Fifty Years after Bretton Woods.* Washington, D.C.: Institute for International Economics.

Tickner, J. Ann. (1992) *Gender in International Relations: Feminist Perspectives on Achieving Global Security.* New York: Columbia University Press.

Tilford, Earl H., Jr. (1995) *The Revolution in Military Affairs: Prospects and Cautions.* Carlisle Barracks, Penn.: U.S. Army War College.

Tillema, Herbert K. (1996) *Overt Military Intervention in the Cold War Era.* Columbia, S.C.: University of South Carolina Press.

———. (1994) "Cold War Alliance and Overt Military Intervention, 1945–1991," *International Interactions* 20 (no. 3): 249–278.

———. (1989) "Foreign Overt Military Intervention in the Nuclear Age," *Journal of Peace Research* 26 (May): 179–95.

Tillema, Herbert K., and John R. Van Wingen. (1982) "Law and Power in Military Intervention: Major States after World War II," *International Studies Quarterly* 26 (June): 220–50.

Timmerman, Kenneth. (1991) *The Death Lobby: How the West Armed Iraq.* Boston: Houghton Mifflin.

Todaro, Michael P. (1994) *Economic Development in the Third World,* 5th ed. New York: Longman.

Toffler, Alvin, and Heidi Toffler. (1993) *War and Anti-War: Survival at the Dawn of the Twenty-First Century.* New York: Little, Brown.

Toynbee, Arnold J. (1954) *A Study of History.* London: Oxford University Press.

Trachtenberg, Marc. (1990–1991) "The Meaning of Mobilization in 1914," *International Security* 15 (Winter): 120–50.

Triffin, Robert. (1978–1979) "The International Role and Fate of the Dollar," *Foreign Affairs* 57 (Winter): 269–86.

Tuchman, Barbara. (1962) *The Guns of August.* New York: Dell.

Tucker, Robert C., and David C. Hendrickson. (1990) *Empire of Liberty.* New York: Oxford University Press.

Tucker, Robert W. (1990) "1989 and All That," *Foreign Affairs* 69 (Fall): 93–114.

Ullman, Richard. (1983) "Refining Security," *International Security* 8 (Summer): 129–53.

UNCTAD. (1993) *World Investment Report 1993.* New York: United Nations.

United Nations. (1995) *World Population Prospects: The 1994 Revision.* New York: United Nations.

———. (1994a) *The Sex and Age Distribution of the World Populations: The 1994 Revision.* New York: United Nations.

———. (1994b) *World Social Situation in the 1990s.* New York: United Nations.

———. (1991) *World Economic Survey 1991.* (1991) New York: United Nations.

United Nations Development Programme (UNDP). (1995) *Human Development Report 1995.* New York: Oxford University Press.

———. (1994) *Human Development Report 1994.* New York: Oxford University Press.

———. (1993) *Human Development Report 1993.* New York: Oxford University Press.

———. (1991) *Human Development Report 1991.* New York: Oxford University Press.

United Nations Programme on Transnational Corporations. (1993) "World Investment Report 1993," *Transnational Corporations* 2 (August): 99–123.

U.S. ACDA [Arms Control and Disarmament Agency]. (1995) *World Military Expenditures and Arms Transfers 1993–1994.* Washington, D.C.: U.S. Government Printing Office.

———. (1992) *World Military Expenditures and Arms Transfers 1990*. Washington, D.C.: U.S. Government Printing Office.

U.S. Central Intelligence Agency. (1994) *The World Factbook 1994–95*. Washington, D.C.: Brassey's.

U.S. Commission on Integrated Long-Term Strategy. (1988) *Discriminate Deterrence*. Washington, D.C.: U.S. Government Printing Office.

———. (1981) *Technology and Soviet Energy Availability*. Washington, D.C.: U.S. Government Printing Office.

U.S. Department of State. (1996) *Patterns of Global Terrorism 1995*. Washington, D.C.: U.S. Department of State.

———. (1995) *Patterns of Global Terrorism 1994*. Washington, D.C.: U.S. Department of State.

———. (1993) *State 2000: A New Model for Managing Foreign Affairs*. Washington, D.C.: Office of Management Task Force, U.S. Department of State.

———. (1991) *Patterns of Global Terrorism 1990*. Washington, D.C.: U.S. Department of State.

———. (1983) *Security and Arms Control: The Search for a More Stable Peace*. Washington, D.C.: U.S. Government Printing Office.

———. (1978) "World Population: The Silent Explosion—Part 1," *Department of State Bulletin* 78 (October): 45–54.

Urquhart, Brian. (1994) "Who Can Police the World?" *New York Review of Books* 41 (May 12): 29–33.

van de Kaa, Dirk J. (1987) "Europe's Second Demographic Transition," *Population Bulletin* 42 (no. 1). Washington, D.C.: Population Reference Bureau.

Van Evera, Stephen. (1994) "Hypotheses on Nationalism and War," *International Security* 18 (Spring): 5–39.

———. (1990–1991) "Primed for Peace: Europe after the Cold War," *International Security* 15 (Winter): 7–57.

Vasquez, John. (1993) *The War Puzzle*. Cambridge, Eng.: Cambridge University Press.

———. (1991) "The Deterrence Myth: Nuclear Weapons and the Prevention of Nuclear War," pp. 205–23 in Charles W. Kegley Jr. (ed.), *The Long Postwar Peace*. New York: HarperCollins.

Väyrynen, Raimo. (1992) *Military Industrialization and Economic Development*. Aldershot, Eng.: Dartmouth.

Verba, Sidney. (1969) "Assumptions of Rationality and Non-Rationality in Models of the International System," pp. 217–31 in James N. Rosenau (ed.), *International Politics and Foreign Policy*. New York: Free Press.

Walker, Martin. (1995a) "The Next American Internationalism," *World Policy Journal* 12 (Summer): 52–54.

———. (1995b) "Overstretching Teutonia: Making the Best of the Fourth Reich," *World Policy Journal* 12 (Spring): 1–18.

Walker, R. B. J. (1993) *Inside/Outside: International Relations as Political Theory*. Cambridge, Eng.: Cambridge University Press.

Walker, William O. (1991) "Decision-Making Theory and Narcotic Foreign Policy: Implications for Historical Analysis," *Diplomatic History* 15 (Winter): 31–45.

Wallensteen, Peter, and Karin Axell. (1993) "Armed Conflict at the End of the Cold War, 1989–1992," *Journal of Peace Research* 30 (August): 331–346.

Wallensteen, Peter, and Margareta Sollenberg. (1995) "After the Cold War: Emerging Patterns of Armed Conflict 1989–94," *Journal of Peace Research* 32 (August): 345–360.

Waller, Douglas. (1995) "Onward Cyber Soldiers," *Time* (August 21): 40–46.

Wallerstein, Immanuel. (1988) *The Modern World-System III: The Second Era of Great Expansion of the Capitalist World-System, 1730–1840*. San Diego: Academic Press.

———. (1980) *The Modern World-System II*. New York: Academic Press.

———. (1974a) *The Modern World-System: Capitalist Agriculture and the Origins of the European World-Economy in the Sixteenth Century*. New York: Academic Press.

———. (1974b) "The Rise and Future Demise of the World Capitalist System: Concepts for Comparative Analysis," *Comparative Studies in Society and History* 16 (September): 387–415.

Walters, Robert S., and David H. Blake. (1992) *The Politics of Global Economic Relations*, 4th ed. Englewood Cliffs, N.J.: Prentice-Hall.

Waltz, Kenneth N. (1995) "Realist Thought and Neorealist Theory," pp. 67–83 in Charles W. Kegley Jr. (ed.), *Controversies in International Relations Theory: Realism and the Neoliberal Challenge*. New York: St. Martin's Press.

———. (1993) "The Emerging Structure of International Politics," *International Security* 18 (Fall): 44–79.

———. (1979) *Theory of International Politics*. Reading, Mass.: Addison-Wesley.

———. (1964) "The Stability of a Bipolar World," *Daedalus* 93 (Summer): 881–909.

———. (1954) *Man, the State, and War*. New York: Columbia University Press.

Ward, Michael D., David R. Davis, and Corey L. Lofdahl. (1995) "A Century of Tradeoffs: Defense and Growth in Japan and the United States," *International Studies Quarterly* 39 (March): 27–50.

Wayman, Frank, and Paul F. Diehl (eds.). (1995) *Reconstructing Realpolitik*. Ann Arbor: University of Michigan Press.

Weart, Spencer R. (1994) "Peace among Democratic and Oligarchic Republics," *Journal of Peace Research* 31 (August): 299–316.

Webb, Michael C. (1991) "International Economic Structures, Government Interests, and International Coordination of Macroeconomic Adjustment Policies," *International Organization* 45 (Summer): 309–42.

Weinberg, Gerhard L. (1994) *A World at Arms: A Global History of World War II*. Cambridge, Eng.: Cambridge University Press.

Weiner, Myron. (1995) *The Global Migration Crisis: Challenge to States and to Human Rights*. New York: HarperCollins.

Wendzel, Robert L. (1980) *International Relations: A Policymaker Focus*. New York: Wiley.

White, Ralph K. (1990) "Why Aggressors Lose," *Political Psychology* 11 (June): 227–42.

Whiting, Allen S. (1985) "Foreign Policy of China," pp. 246–90 in Roy C. Macridis (ed.), *Foreign Policy in World Politics*, 6th ed. Englewood Cliffs, N.J.: Prentice-Hall.

Whyman, William E. (1995) "We Can't Go On Meeting like This: Revitalizing the G–7 Process," *Washington Quarterly* 18 (Summer): 139–65.

Williamson, John, and C. Randall Henning. (1994) "Managing the Monetary System," pp. 83–111 in Peter B. Kenen (ed.), *Managing the World Economy: Fifty Years after Bretton Woods*. Washington, D.C.: Institute for International Economics.

Wilmer, Franke. (1993) *The Indigenous Voice in World Politics: Since Time Immemorial*. Newbury Park, Calif.: Sage.

Wilson, James Q. (1993) *The Moral Sense*. New York: Free Press.

Winiecki, Jan. (1989) "CPEs' Structural Change and World Market Performance: A Permanently Developing Country (PDC) Status," *Soviet Studies* 41 (July): 365–81.

"Wireless Phones Ring Off the Hook." (1995). *Christian Science Monitor* (May 31): 1, 7.

Wise, Michael Z. (1993) "Reparations," *Atlantic Monthly* 272 (October): 32–35.

Wittkopf, Eugene R. (1990) *Faces of Internationalism: Public Opinion and American Foreign Policy.* Durham, N.C.: Duke University Press.

Wolfers, Arnold. (1968) "Alliances," pp. 268–71 in David L. Sills (ed.), *International Encyclopedia of the Social Sciences.* New York: Macmillan.

———. (1962) *Discord and Collaboration.* Baltimore: Johns Hopkins University Press.

Wolf-Phillips, Leslie. (1987) "Why 'Third World'?: Origin, Definitions and Usage," *Third World Quarterly* 9 (October): 1311–27.

Women in a Changing Global Economy: 1994 World Survey on the Role of Women in Development. (1995). New York: United Nations.

Woods, Alan. (1989) *Development and the National Interest: U.S. Economic Assistance into the 21st Century.* Washington, D.C.: Agency for International Development.

Woodward, Bob. (1991) *The Commanders.* New York: Simon & Schuster.

Woodward, Bob, and Rick Atkinson. (1990) "Launching Operation Desert Shield," *Washington Post National Weekly Edition* 7 (September 3–9): 8–9.

The World Bank Atlas 1996. (1995). Washington, D.C.: World Bank.

World Bank. (1995a) *Global Economic Prospects and the Developing Countries 1995.* Washington, D.C.: World Bank.

———. (1995b) *Monitoring Environmental Progress.* Washington, D.C.: World Bank.

———. (1993a) *Global Economic Prospects and the Developing Countries 1993.* Washington, D.C.: World Bank.

———. (1993b) *World Debt Tables 1993–94.* Vol. 1, *Analysis and Summary Tables.* Washington, D.C.: World Bank.

World Commission on Environment and Development. (1987) *Our Common Future.* New York: Oxford University Press.

World Development Report 1995. (1995). New York: Oxford University Press.

World Development Report 1992. (1992) New York: Oxford University Press.

World Development Report 1991. (1991) New York: Oxford University Press.

World Disasters Report 1995. (1995). Geneva: International Federation of Red Cross and Red Crescent Societies.

World Economic and Social Survey 1995. (1995). New York: United Nations.

World Health Report 1995. (1995). Geneva: World Health Organization.

World Investment Report 1995. (1995). New York: United Nations.

World Investment Report 1994. (1994). New York: United Nations.

World Refugee Survey 1995. (1995). Washington, D.C.: U.S. Committee for Refugees.

World Resources Institute. (1994) *World Resources 1994–95.* New York: Oxford University Press.

———. (1990) *World Resources 1990–91.* New York: Oxford University Press.

Wright, Quincy. (1953) "The Outlawry of War and the Law of War," *American Journal of International Law* 47 (July): 365–76.

———. (1942) *A Study of War.* Chicago: University of Chicago Press.

Wurst, Jim. (1996) "Inching Toward a Ban," *Bulletin of the Atomic Scientists* 52 (March/April): 10–12.

Yearbook of International Organizations, 1993/94. (1993) Vol. 1. Munich: K. G. Sauer.

Yearbook of International Organizations, 1991/92. (1991) Vol. 2. Munich: K. G. Sauer.

Yoder, Edwin M., Jr. (1991) "Isolationists Would Put America on a Dangerous Course," *The State* (Columbia, S.C.) (December 14): A10.

Young, John E. (1991) "Reducing Waste, Saving Materials," pp. 39–55 in Lester R. Brown et al., *State of the World 1991.* New York: Norton.

Young, Oran R. (1995) "System and Society in World Affairs: Implications for International Organizations," *International Social Science Journal* 144 (June): 197–212.

———. (1986) "International Regimes: Toward a New Theory of Institutions," *World Politics* 39 (October): 104–22.

Zacher, Mark W. (1991) "Toward a Theory of International Regimes," pp. 119–37 in Robert L. Rothstein (ed.), *The Evolution of Theory in International Relations.* Columbia: University of South Carolina Press.

———. (1987) "Trade Gaps, Analytical Gaps: Regime Analysis and International Commodity Regulation," *International Organization* 41 (Spring): 173–202.

Zacher, Mark W., and Richard A. Matthew. (1995) "Liberal International Theory: Common Threads, Divergent Strands," pp. 107–49 in Charles W. Kegley Jr. (ed.), *Controversies in International Relations Theory: Realism and the Neoliberal Challenge.* New York: St. Martin's Press.

Zagare, Frank C. (1990) "Rationality and Deterrence," *World Politics* 42 (January): 238–60.

Zakaria, Fareed. (1995) "Offer Russia a Peace of Vienna," *New York Times* (May 9): A15.

———. (1992–1993) "Is Realism Finished?" *The National Interest* 30 (Winter): 21–32.

Zanoyan, Vahan. (1995) "After the Oil Boom," *Foreign Affairs* 74 (November/December): 2–7.

Zelikow, Philip. (1987) "The United States and the Use of Force: A Historical Summary," pp. 31–81 in George K. Osburn, et al. (eds.), *Democracy, Strategy, and Vietnam.* Lexington, Mass.: Lexington Books.

Ziegler, David. (1995) Review of *World Politics and the Evolution of War* by John Weltman, *American Political Science Review* 89 (September): 813–814.

Zimmerman, Tim. (1994) "Arms Merchant to the World," *U.S. News & World Report* (April 4): 37.

Zinnes, Dina A., and Jonathan Wilkenfeld. (1971) "An Analysis of Foreign Conflict Behavior of Nations," pp. 167–213 in Wolfram F. Handieder (ed.), *Comparative Foreign Policy.* New York: McKay.

Acknowledgments *(continued from copyright page)*

Map 1.4: World View Time. Source: Copyright © World View Time, Inc., 1989. Reprinted by permission of World View Time, Inc., P.O. Box 266, Brockville, Ontario, Canada K6V5V5.

Map 2.1: Regimes and the Transnational Management of Global Problems: Acid Rain. Source: Adapted from Seager (1995), *The New State of the Earth Atlas* (New York: Touchstone), 48–49.

Focus 3.1: Democracies in Foreign Affairs: A U.S. Policymaker's Characterization. Source: Excerpt from George F. Kennan, *American Diplomacy 1900–1950* (1951: New American Library), p. 59. Reprinted by permission of the University of Chicago Press.

Map 3.2: The Diffusion of Democracy. Source: Polity III data set (Jaggers and Gurr, 1995). Design: Michael D. Ward and John O'Loughlin; Cartography: Michael Shin. Reprinted by permission.

Map 4.1: Territorial Changes in Europe following World War I. Source: *Strategic Atlas, Comparative Geopolitics of the World's Powers*, third edition by Gérard Chaliand and Jean-Pierre Rageau. Copyright © 1993 by Gérard Chaliand and Jean-Pierre Rageau. Reprinted by permission of HarperCollins Publishers, Inc.

Map 4.2: Territorial Changes in Europe following World War II. Source: Europe 1938 is based on Map 5.3 from Charles W. Kegley, Jr. and Gregory A. Raymond (1944a: 118); Europe 1945 is from *Strategic Atlas, Comparative Geopolitics of the World's Powers*, third edition by Gérard Chaliand and Jean-Pierre Rageau. Copyright © 1993 by Gérard Chaliand and Jean-Pierre Rageau. Reprinted by permission of HarperCollins Publishers, Inc.

Figure 4.1: U.S.–Soviet Relations during the Cold War, 1948–1991. Source: Adapted from Edward E. Azar's Conflict and Peace Data Bank (COPDAB), with data based on Edward E. Azar and Thomas J. Sloan (1973). Data for 1966–1991 are derived from the World Interaction Survey (WEIS), as compiled and scaled by Professor Rodney G. Tomlinson.

Map 4.3: Emerging Centers of Power in a New International Hierarchy. Source: United States Central Intelligence Agency (1994:22).

Figure 5.1: Differences in the Global North and South. Source: Population Reference Bureau, McEvedy and Jones. Data presented in *World Bank Atlas, 1995*.

Map 5.2: Uneven Spread: Global Connections to the Internet. Source: Adapted from *Time* (1995), 81.

Map 5.3: Groups of Economies: The Geographic Distribution of GNP per Capita 1993. Source: *World Development Report 1995*, pp. 158–159. World Bank, Washington, D.C.

Figure 5.2: The Geographic Spread of International Conflict, 1990–1995. Source: *World Disasters Report, 1995*, p. 112. International Federation of Red Cross and Red Crescent Societies, 1995.

Figure 5.3: Arms Transfer Agreements by Top Ten Recipients, 1987–1990 and 1991–1994. Source: Adapted from Richard F. Grimmett, "Conventional Arms Transfers to Developing Nations, 1987–1994." *CRS Report for Congress*. Washington, Congressional Research Service.

Figure 5.4: Regional Distribution of Bilateral and Multilateral Aid, 1990–1993. Source: Adapted from the Organization for Economic Cooperation and Development 1995 Report. Copyright © OECD 1995. Reproduced by permission of the OECD.

Focus 5.1: Measuring Living Standards: GNP per Capita versus Purchasing Power Parity. Source: *1995 World Population Data Sheet*. Population Reference Bureau.

Focus 5.2: Measuring Development: GNP per Capita versus Human Development. Source: United Nations Development Programme (UNDP), *Human Development Report 1995*. Reprinted by permission of the United Nations Bureau of External Relations.

Focus 5.3: A Balance Sheet on Human Development in the Global South. Source: Extracted and adapted from the United Nations Development Programme, *Human Development Report 1995*. Reprinted by permission of the United Nations Bureau of External Relations.

Table 5.6: Level of Human Development and Related Economic Attributes (selected countries). Source: Adapted from the United Nations Development Programme, *Human Development Report 1995*. Reprinted by permission of the United Nations Bureau of External Relations.

Table 5.7: The Foreign Policy and Economic Goals of Foreign Aid Donors. Source: K.J. Holsti, *International Politics: A Framework for Analysis* (Englewood Cliffs, N.J.: Prentice Hall, 1995), p. 186.

Focus 6.1: The Politics of UN Membership: The Case of Taiwan. Source: *The Economist* (December 10, 1994: 16). Copyright © 1994 The Economist Newspaper Group, Inc. Reprinted with permission. Further reproduction prohibited.

Figure 6.1: The Number of States, IGOs, and NGOs since 1990. Note: Figures for states are based on the Correlates of War (COW) project at the University of Michigan under the direction of J. David Singer. Source: States, Polity III data (Jaggers and Gurr, 1995); IGOs and Ngos, *Yearbook of International Organizations, 1993/1994* (1993: 1699), and moving averages from selected prior volumes. Reprinted with permission of the Union of International Associations, Belgium.

Figure 6.2: The Changing Membership of the United Nations, 1946–1996. Source: United Nations, using classifications of regions of the U.S. Department of State (1985: 18).

Figure 6.3: The Structure of the United Nations. Source: Based on representation suggested by Peter J. Taylor in *World Government* (1990: 49).

Figure 6.4: The United Nations System. Source: *The UN Chronicle*, as reprinted in U.S. CIA (1993: 386).

Figure 6.5: The UN at Fifty: A Look at Its First Half-Century. Source: *New York Times* (October 22, 1995: 8). Copyright © 1995 by The New York Times Company. Reprinted by permission.

Figure 6.6: The Structure of the European Union. Source: Adapted from the European Commission to the United States, 1995.

Figure 6.7: The Co-Decision Procedure. Source: The European Commission Delegation to the United States (1994:10 11).

Map 6.1: Members of the European Union, 1996. Source: Adapted from *New York Times* (November 11, 1994). Copyright © 1994 by The New York Times Company. Reprinted by permission.

Figure 6.8: The Cross-Crossing Memberships of Europe's Primary International Institutions. Source: *NATO Review* 43 (November 1995).

Table 7.1: States and Indigenous Nations at War. Source: Rudolph C. Ryser. "Fourth World Wars: Indigenous Nationalism and the Emerging New International Political Order," pp.

304–315 in *The Quest for Justice* by Menno Boldt and J. Anthony Long, in association with Leroy Little Bear, eds. (Toronto: University of Toronto Press). Reprinted by permission.

Focus 7.2: Where the Creed Is Greed: The Threat of the Global Network of Organized Crime. Source: Richard H. Schultz, National Strategy Information Agency. Reprinted by permission.

Table 7.2: The World's Top Twenty Banks, 1995 (ranked by assets). Source: *International Herald Tribune* (August 19, 1995: 1, 8).

Table 7.3: Countries and Corporations: A Ranking by Size of Economy and Sales, 1994. Source: *World Military Expenditures and Arms Transfers 1993–1994*. U.S. Arms Control and Disarment Agency.

Page 200: Excerpt from *Global Dreams: Imperial Corporations and the New World Order* by Richard J. Barnet and John J. Cavanagh. Copyright © 1994 by Richard J. Barnet and John J. Cavanagh. Simon & Schuster, Inc.

Page 201: Excerpt from The Commission on Transnational Corporations, 1991. Source: The Commission on Transnational Corporations, 1991: 33.

Map 7.1: The World's Great Cultural Domains. Source: *Strategic Atlas, Comparative Geopolitics of the World's Powers*, third edition by Gérard Chaliand and Jean-Pierre Rageau. Copyright © 1993 by Gérard Chaliand and Jean-Pierre Rageau. Reprinted by permission of HarperCollins Publishers, Inc.

Map 7.2: The Geographic Concentration of the World's Principal Religions. Source: *Concise Earth Atlas* (1994: 11). Bo Gramfors and Siu Eklund, Maps International AB. Reprinted by permission.

Figure 7.1: Ethnopolitical Groups Involved in Serious Conflicts, 1945–1994. Source: *Minorities at Risk: A Global View of Ethnopolitical Conflicts*. Ted Robert Gurr (1993). United States Institute of Peace: Washington, D.C.

Map 7.3: Caesar and God: State Support for Particular Religions in a Pluralistic World Community. Source: Adapted from *State of the World Atlas*, New Edition, by Michael Kidron and Ronald Segal. Copyright © 1995 by Michael Kidron and Ronald Segal, text. Copyright © 1995 by Myriad Editions Limited, maps and graphics. Used by permission of Viking Penguin, a division of Penguin Books USA Inc., and Myriad Editions Limited: London, England.

Figure 7.2: Automobile Operations of Toyota in Four ASEAN Countries. Source: *World Investment Report 1991: The Triad in Foreign Direct Investment*. Centre on Transnational Corporations (1991: 62).

Focus 8.1: Comparative Advantage and the Gains from Trade. Source: Adapted from Daniel Rosen, "The Basics of Foreign Trade and Exchange" (New York: Federal Reserve Bank of New York, 1987).

Figure 8.3: The Decline of Tariffs in the Industrialized Countries, 1940 Projected to 2000. Source: Office of the U.S. Trade Representative and the Center for International Economics as upgraded by *Time* (December 27, 1993: 16).

Figure 8.4: Share of World Exports within and between Trading Areas, 1990. Source: United Nations (1991a: 6). Data presented in *Directory of Trade Statistics Yearbook, 1995*. International Monetary Fund, Washington, D.C.

Focus 9.1: The Internet: Cyberspace Pros and Cons. Source: Excerpt from "The Internet Elite" pp. 44–45 in *Bulletin of the Atomic Scientists* 51 (July/August 1995). Copyright © 1995 by

the Educational Foundation for Nuclear Science, 6042 South Kimbark Avenue, Chicago, Illinois, 60637, USA. A one-year subscription is $36.00 Reprinted by permission.

Focus 9.2: Servicing Long Distance. Source: The World Bank, Washington, D.C. (1995a, 52).

Focus 9.3: Ford's Concept of a World Car. Source: *World Economic and Social Survey 1995:* 250. Copyright © United Nations. All United Nations rights reserved.

Focus 9.4: Inappropriate Products in a Homogenizing World. Source: Lopez, George A., Jackie G. Smith, and Ron Pagnucco, "The Global Tide" *Bulletin of the Atomic Scientists* 51 (July/August 1995): 33–39.

Figure 9.1: Growth of World Output and Trade, 1981–1996. Source: *World Economic and Social Survey 1995:* 35. Copyright © United Nations. All United Nations rights reserved.

Figure 9.2: The Global South in World Trade, Past and Projected. Source: *Global Economic Prospects and the Developing Countries, 1995* (Washington: D.C. The World Bank, 1995: 58).

Figure 9.3: Non-Oil Commodity Prices, 1948 Projected to 2004. Source: *Global Economic Prospects and the Developing Countries, 1995* (Washington, D.C.: The World Bank, 1995): 19.

Figure 9.4: Same Work, Different Pay. Source: Ishac Diwan and Ana Revenga, "Wages, Inequality, and International Integration" *Finance & Development* 32 (September 1995), p. 8.

Map 9.1: The Vulnerable: Commodity-Dependent Economies Source: *Handbook of International Economic Statistics 1995* (Washington, D.C.: Central Intelligence Agency, 1995), pp. 130-131.

Table 10.1: Population, Fertility, Growth Rates, and Doubling Times for the World's Twenty Largest Countries, 1995. Source: *World Population Data Sheet 1995* (Washington, D.C.: Population Reference Bureau, 1995).

Focus 10.1: The "Graying" of Nations. Source: Kevin G. Kinsella, "An Aging World Population." from *World Health* (July-August 1994), the magazine of the World Health Organization. Reprinted with permission.

Figure 10.3: AIDS' Global Spread: Estimates of Total Adult HIV Infections, 1994. Source: *The State of the World Population Report 1995*, p. 51. United Nations Population Fund. Reprinted with permission.

Figure 10.6: The Demographic Transition: Birth and Death Rates in Mauritius, 1871–1991. Source: Wolfgang Lutz, "The Future of World Population," *Population Bulletin* 49 (June 1994): 9. (Washington, D.C.: Population Reference Bureau, Inc., 1994.)

Focus 11.1: National Security and Environmental Security: Competing or Complementary? Source: Excerpt from pp. 218–220 from *Current History*. Reprinted by permission.

Focus 11.2: The Making of an Ecological Disaster: The Aral Sea. Source: Excerpt from p. 38 in *World Development Report 1992*.

Pages 329–330: Excerpt from "Heading for Apocalypse" *Time* October 2, 1995: 55. Copyright © 1995 Time, Inc. Reprinted by permission.

Focus 11.3: Free Trade and Sustainable Development: An Oxymoron? Source: excerpt from p. 67 in *World Development Report 1992*.

Figure 11.1: World Oil Demand, 1994 and 2010. Source: Adapted from *World Economic and Social Survey 1995* (New York: United Nations, 1995: 168).

Figure 11.2: Crude Oil Prices since 1891. Source: *BP Statistical Review of World Energy* (1995): 12.

Figure 11.3: Ratio of Fossil-Fuel Reserves to Production, 1994. Source: *BP Statistical Review of World Energy* (1995): 36.

Figure 11.4: Carbon Emissions from Burning Fossil Fuels, 1950–1994. Source: Worldwatch database diskette, 1996. Copyright © 1996. Reprinted with permission. (Washington, D.C.: Worldwatch Institute.)

Map 11.1: Forests and Rainforests. Source: Pulp and Paper International, 600 Harrison Street, San Francisco, CA. 94107.

Figure 12.1: Armed Conflicts throughout the World, 1945–1994. Source: Adapted from *World Watch*. Reprinted with permission. (Washington, D.C: Worldwatch Institute.)

Figure 12.2: The Percentage of the World's Governments That Are Democratic, 1920–1993. Source: Herman, Kegley, and Raymond (1995), based on Polity III data (Jaggers and Gurr, 1995).

Figure 12.3: The Long Cycle of Global Leadership and Global War, 1492–2000. Source: Adapted from George Modelski (1987a: 6).

Figure 12.4: International Terrorist Incidents, 1968–1995. Source: Office of the Coordination of Counterterrorism, U.S. Department of State.

Map 12.1: International Terrorist Incidents, 1994. Source: Office of the Coordinator for Counterterrorism. U.S. Department of State (1996: 69).

Figure 13.1: Leading Military Powers, 1993. Source: U.S. Arms Control and Disarmament Agency (1995: 4).

Figure 13.2: World Military Expenditures, 1961–1993. Source: U.S. Arms Control and Disarmament Agency (1995: 1).

Figure 13.3: Arms Transfer Agreements by the Top Ten Suppliers, 1987–1990 and 1991–1994. Source: Adapted from Richard F. Grimmett, "Conventional Arms Transfers to Developing Nations, 1987–1994" *CRS Report for Congress* (Washington, D.C.: Congressional Research Service), p. 55.

Map 13.1: Nuclear Nations and the States Likely to Join the Nuclear Club. Source: Projections based on predictions provided by the Arms Control Association, March 1996.

Table 13.1: The Power Potential of the Great Powers: Rankings Across Major Dimensions. Source: Territory, *World Bank Atlas* (1995); population and GDP, U.S. CIA (1995: 32–33, 24–25); scientists, Hughes (1994: 82).

Table 13.2: The Relative Burden of Countries' Military Expenditures, 1993. Source: U.S. ACDA (1995: 25).

Focus 13.3: Redefining "Security" in the New World Order. Source: Excerpt from *World Security* by Michael T. Klare and Daniel C. Thomas, editors. Copyright © 1991 by Michael T. Klare and Daniel C. Thomas. Reprinted with permission of St. Martin's Press, Inc.

Page 427: Excerpts from pp. 247–269 in *The Long Postwar Peace* by Charles W. Kegley, Jr. Copyright © 1990 by Charles W. Kegley, Jr. Reprinted by permission of HarperCollins Publishers, Inc.

Figure 14.1: The Changing Strategic Balance, 1990, 1995, and 2003. Source: Adapted from the Stockholm International Peace Research Institute (SIPRI): *SIPRI Yearbook 1995*.

Figure 14.2: Military Interventions Initiated since 1945. Source: Data collected by Herbert Tillema (1989, 1996).

Figure 14.3: Seventy Years of International Crises. Source: *Crises in World Politics: Theory and Reality* by Michael Brecher. Copyright © 1993 by Michael Brecher. (Oxford, England: Pergamon).

Focus 15.1: The Balance of Power: A Precarious and Failed Security System? Source: Excerpt from *Review of International Studies* 15 (January 1989): 77–85. Reprinted with permission.

Page 461: Excerpt from "Arms Control, Disarmament, and the Stability of the Postwar Era," in *The Long Postwar Peace*, pp. 247–269, Charles W, Kegley, Jr. (ed.) Copyright © 1991 by Charles W. Kegley, Jr. HarperCollins Publishers, Inc.

Table 15.2: Major Multilateral Arms Control Treaties since 1945. Source: Adapted from R. Ferm, "Arms Control and Disarmament Agreements." Stockholm International Peace Research Institute, SIPRI Yearbook 1995: Armaments, Disarmament, and International Security (Oxford University Press: Oxford, 1995), Annexe A, pp. 839–871. Reprinted by permission.

Map 15.1: The Enlarged NATO under the Partnership for Peace and the New European Balance of Power. Source: Adapted from "NATO/Partnership for Peace Members" map by Dave Herring. *Christian Science Monitor* (December 18, 1995). Copyright © The Christian Science Monitor. Reprinted with permission.

Figure 15.1: Countdown to Strategic Parity: The Negotiated End of the U.S.–Russian Arms Race. Source: Robert S. Norris and William M. Arkin, "Estimated U.S. and Soviet/Russian Nuclear Stockpiles, 1945–1994" *Bulletin of Atomic Scientists* (November/December 1994). See Worldwatch publication *Vital Signs 1995* for further information. Reprinted by permission.

Figure 16.1: The Legal Prohibition of War of Aggression, 1815–1996. Source: Transnational Rulies Indicators Project (TRIP) from *When Trust Breaks Down: Alliance Norms and World Politics* by Charles W. Kegley, Jr. and Gregory A. Raymond. Copyright © 1990 by Charles W. Kegley, Jr. and Gregory A. Raymond. The University of South Carolina Press. Reprinted by permission.

Figure 16.2: The Changing Status of the Nonintervention Rule in International Law, 1815–1996. Source: As measured in "The Decay of the Nonintervention Principle" paper presented at the Joint Conference of the Japan Association of International Relations (JAIR) and the International Studies Association (ISA), Tokyo (September 20, 1995). Margaret G. Hermann and Charles W. Kegley Jr., and Gregory A. Raymond. Reprinted by permission.

Map 16.1: The Battle over East Timor. Source: Adapted from "East Timor" map by Dave Herring. *Christian Science Monitor* (February 1, 1995), p. 7. Copyright © The Christian Science Monitor. Reprinted by permission.

Map 16.2: UN Peace Missions, 1948–1996. Source: United Nations.

Photo Credits

Chapter 1: Page 3: Eric Bouvet/Gamma Liaison; 10: AP/Wide World; 14: NASA.

Chapter 2: Page 20: The Granger Collection, N.Y.; The Bettmann Archive; 23: Scala/Art Resource, N.Y.; Bridgeman/Art Resource, N.Y.

Chapter 3: Page 44: Orban/Sygma; 57: UPI/Bettmann; 65: AP/Wide World.

Chapter 4: Page 70: UPI/Bettmann; 78: Culver Pictures; 89: Biber/Sipa.

Chapter 5: Page 106: The Bettmann Archive; 117: J.P. Laffont/Sygma; 128: Louise Gubb/JB Pictures.

Index

Key terms and the pages on which they are defined appear in boldface type.